GEORGE BERNARD SHAW was born in Dublin, Ireland, on July 26, 1856. He attended four different schools but his real education came from a thorough grounding in music and painting, which he obtained at home. In 1871, he was apprenticed to a Dublin estate agent, and later he worked as a cashier. In 1876, Shaw joined his mother and sister in London, where he spent the next nine years in unrecognized struggle and genteel poverty.

From 1885 to 1898, he wrote for newspapers and magazines as critic of art, literature, music, and drama. But his main interest at this time was political propaganda, and, in 1884, he joined the Fabian Society. From 1893 to 1939, the most active period of his career, Shaw wrote 47 plays. By 1915, his international fame was firmly established and productions of *Candida, Man and Superman, Arms and the Man, The Devil's Disciple,* were being played in many countries of the world, from Britain to Japan. In 1925, the playwright was awarded the Nobel Prize for Literature. Between the ages of fifty-seven and sixty-seven, Shaw wrote such dramas as *Heartbreak House, Back to Methusclah, Androcles and the Lion, St. Joan.* During his lifetime he was besieged by offers to film his plays, but he accepted only a few, the most notable being *Pygmalion,* which was adapted (after his death) as the basis for the musical *My Fair Lady*. He died at the age of ninety-four at Ayot St. Lawrence, England, on November 2, 1950.

PLAYS BY

GEORGE BERNARD

SHAW

MRS. WARREN'S PROFESSION

ARMS AND THE MAN

CANDIDA

MAN AND SUPERMAN

With a Foreword by ERIC BENTLEY

A SIGNET CLASSIC

SIGNET CLASSIC
Published by the Penguin Group
Penguin Books USA Inc., 375 Hudson Street,
New York, New York 10014, U.S.A.
Penguin Books Ltd, 27 Wrights Lane,
London W8 5TZ, England
Penguin Books Australia Ltd, Ringwood,
Victoria, Australia
Penguin Books Canada Ltd, 10 Alcorn Avenue,
Toronto, Ontario, Canada M4V 3B2
Penguin Books (N.Z.) Ltd, 182–190 Wairau Road,
Auckland 10, New Zealand

Penguin Books Ltd, Registered Offices:
Harmondsworth, Middlesex, England

Published by Signet Classic, an imprint of New American Library,
a division of Penguin Books USA Inc.

27 26 25 24 23 22 21 20

Foreword © 1960 by New American Library, a division of
Penguin Books USA Inc.

Acknowledgment is made to the Public Trustee and the Society of Authors (London).

CONTENTS

FOREWORD

The Making of a Dramatist (1892–1903)

It was clear from the start that Bernard Shaw was a man of ideas. Later it turned out that he was a fabulous entertainer. But few have granted that the two Shaws were one. The old tendency was to grant that he was a publicist, a critic, an essayist, even a philosopher, but to add: "not, of course, a dramatist." The later tendency was to concede that he was a great showman but to discount his thoughtful side. As Egon Friedell said, you could suck the theatrical sugar from the pill of propaganda, and put the pill itself back on the plate.

Neither in the old days, then, nor in the later ones was Shaw considered a dramatist, for even the later generations have only thought him a master of the theatrical occasion, a man with a theatrical line of talk and a theatrical bag of tricks, a highly histrionic jokester—a comedian, certainly, but hardly a writer of serious comedy. The fact is that the shock of that long career in the theater has still not been absorbed. Shaw has not yet been seen in perspective.

In these circumstances, it is interesting to go back and look at what happened in the eighteen nineties. In 1891, Bernard Shaw had still not written a play, though he was thirty-five years old. A dozen years later, though he could describe himself as "an unperformed playwright in London," he had written *Widowers' Houses* (1892), *The Philanderer* (1893), *Mrs. Warren's Profession* (1893–94), *Arms and the Man* (1894), *Candida* (1894–95), *The Man of Destiny* (1895), *You Never Can Tell* (1895–96), *The Devil's Disciple* (1896–97), *Caesar and Cleopatra* (1898), *Captain Brassbound's Conversion* (1899), *The Admirable Bashville* (1901), and *Man and Superman* (1901–03).

Let us take for granted that these plays are full of ideas and jokes, and ask if they do not also meet the demands of dramatic criticism as such. The drama, everyone agrees, presents character in action. Human actions become "an action" in the drama when they are arranged effectively—when, that is, they are given what we can recognize as a proper and praiseworthy structure. Of character dramatic critics have required many different things. One of them is emotional substance.

Let us ask, then, how Shaw, when he set about playwriting, tackled the problem of structure; and let us ask if he gave his characters' existence the requisite emotional substance.

Structure

How did Shaw put a play together? To think of questions about Shaw is to think also of the answers he invariably provided to them. In this case, he said: "I avoid plots like the plague. . . . My procedure is to imagine characters and let them rip. . . ." The quotation is from his *Table-talk* but (again, as usual) he said the same thing on many other occasions. One always has to ask not what he means (which may be clear) but what he is getting at. All Shaw's critical prose is polemical, as he freely admitted, and his writing on the theater is devoted to the destruction of some kinds of drama and their replacement by some others (or one other). Here the enemy is the kind of play which had been dominant throughout the latter half of the nineteenth century—"the well-made play," as perfected by Eugène Scribe. In this dramaturgy, the Aristotelian doctrine of the primacy of plot had been driven to an improper extreme. The plot was now not *primus inter pares,* but all that mattered. It lost its originally organic relation to character and theme. So it became anathema to the apostles of the New Drama at the century's close. As late as 1946, when Allardyce Nicoll declared that Shaw was himself influenced by the well-made play, the old playwright went into print to deny it.

If the well-made play is defined as having no serious content, if it is defined by the relation (or lack of relation) of its plot to character and theme, then obviously Shaw did not write well-made plays. Yet, Professor Nicoll had a point, and a strong one, which was that, for all the disclaimers, Shaw's plays did have plots and, furthermore, that these plots tended to be old acquaintances for those who knew

their well-made play. Actually, the playwright had no need
to be scandalized, for no dramatist had been more influenced
by the well-made play than his own idol of those days,
Henrik Ibsen. The Norwegian had begun his theatrical career by directing a large number of these plays; he made an
exact imitation of them in his own *Lady Inger of Östrät;*
and he had continued to the end to use many of their characteristic devices. Hence, it would have been quite possible
for a writer in 1890 to denounce Scribe and Sardou and
simultaneously to steal their bag of tricks—from Ibsen. It
is doubtful, though, if Bernard Shaw needed to deceive himself in this way. It seems more likely that he took the
main stituation in *Arms and the Man* from one of Scribe's
most successful plays, *Bataille de Dames.*

A situation is not, of course, a plot, and the plot of
Arms and the Man is not simply lifted from Scribe, even
though parts of it may have been. Plagiarism is not the
point. The point is that even when Shaw's story diverges
from Scribe, it remains Scribean. The play *Arms and the
Man* is hung, as it were, on the cunningly told tale of the
lost coat with the photograph in its pocket. The reader need
only go through the text and mark the hints, incidents, accidents, and contretemps of this tale and he will be finding
the layout, the plan—yes, the plot—of this play. Or at any
rate, the plot of what could have been a first draft of the
play. Shaw, one gathers, did not write such first drafts but,
supposing he had, what would be the difference between the
first draft and the final one? In the answer to this question
lies the secret of Shavian dramaturgy.

A corollary of the view that "plot is all" is this proposition: the cause of any incident is another incident. It is
known that Scribe used to chart out a configuration of incidents and then write his play. This is to go far beyond
Aristotle. It is to set no store at all by human initiative
and assign to events themselves a kind of fatality: they are
a network in which mankind is caught. Granted that the
conception might in certain hands have its awesomeness; in
Scribe's hands it had only triviality, because he manipulated
the events till the issue was a pleasant one. It is curious how
often that manipulation had to be arbitrary and drastic. Do
events, when given their head, rush downward to disaster?
To guarantee a happy ending, the well-making playwrights
often needed their emergency weapon: sheer accident. Hence

the Shavian complaint that well-made plays were badly made, after all.

Hence also Bernard Shaw's first drama, which is an adaptation of an adaptation of a well-made play. The subject is one that Scribe and the younger Dumas brought to the nineteenth-century theater: marrying, or refusing to marry, money. The immediate source is an unfinished play of William Archer's, *Rhinegold*. Archer's source is *La Ceinture Dorée*, by Emile Augier. When a young man discovers that his young lady's inherited money was acquired by her father in an immoral way, what does he do? William Archer's answer was: he pitches it into the Rhine. One presumes that Archer's action would have been set on a convenient balcony beside that river. Augier's hero is not so privileged. To preserve his honor, he would simply have to forgo the pleasure of marrying the lady, if the author did not provide him and the play with a convenient accident (or money *ex machina*). The whole French economy has to meet with a crisis (war breaks out) so that our heroine's father may be reduced to poverty; it is now honorable for our hero to propose to our heroine. In the well-made play, one incident leads to another with a logic that is inescapable—except when the author decides to escape it. Perhaps Shaw's objection was less to the inescapability than to the egregious, last-minute escapes.

His first play, *Widowers' Houses*, may not be great art but it is a great reversal of custom. Shaw's key decision was to refuse to accept Augier's ending, to refuse to have accident (masquerading as fate or otherwise) intervene. Such a refusal leads a man—leads a born playwright, at least—back and back into the earlier stages of a story and he ends up writing an utterly different play—an utterly different *kind* of play.

Not one but two conceptions of Augier's were being rejected: not just the solution-by-sheer-accident (which condemns a play to meaninglessness) but also the autonomy-of-incidents—something, by the way, which was no part of Augier's conscious philosophy but was imposed on him by the Scribean design. Dramatists are committed to the doctrine of free will. They can say they don't believe in it, but they have to write their plays as if they did. (In this they resemble human beings in general, for your most ardent determinist acts on the assumption that determinism is false.) People in plays have got to be able to make decisions, and these decisions have got to be both real and influential: they have to affect events. I see no reason to object to Aristotle's declaration that plot is the soul of the drama, but Aristotle would have objected to Scribe's attempt to cut the soul off from the body—that is, from character.

What *does* a young man do when he finds that his bride's dowry comes from a tainted source? There are two ways for a writer to arrive at an answer. He can say: "I can think of several answers—on the basis of several different possibilities of 'theater.' Answer A will give you Big Scene X; Answer B will give you Ending Y; and so on." Or he can say: "I cannot give you any answer at all until the terms of the proposition are defined, including the term 'tainted.' Above all, I need to know who these people are: what bride? what young man?" The first way to arrive at an answer would commonly be thought the playwright's way: the reasoning is "craftsmanlike" and "of the theater," and would earn a man commendation on Broadway in 1960. The second way is only the human way. That makes it the way of the real dramatist and so of Bernard Shaw.

It could be said that we have this perfectly functioning machine of the well-made play and that a Bernard Shaw is throwing a monkey wrench into it—the monkey wrench of character. That is how it must seem from the Scribean viewpoint. From the viewpoint of dramatic art, however, one would say that this particular engine had been revolving all too fast and uselessly; only when a Shaw slips in the clutch can the gear engage and the vehicle prove itself a vehicle by moving.

"My procedure is to imagine characters and let them rip. . . ." The pertinence of this remark may by now be clearer: if the young man has been "imagined," the dramatist can find the decision he would make as to the young lady's money. But at this point, we realize that Shaw's words leave out of account the fact that the situation confronting the young man had been established in advance of the imagining of his character. It had been established by Augier and Archer and by Shaw's own decision to use their work. Hence, Shaw's own interpretation is both helpful and misleading—or, perhaps, is helpful only if those who are helped do a lot of work on their own.

Shaw put *Widowers' Houses* together—how? He took from certain predecessors not only a situation but a story, and not only a story but that clever, orderly, and theatrical ar-

rangement of a story which we call a plot. Then he changed
the plot—or as he would have said, let the characters change
it for him. Now, had he retained Augier's characters, they
could only have caused him to break off the action one
scene earlier than Augier did: instead of the happy ending
created by a national emergency, we would get the unhappy
ending which the emergency reversed.

Characters in a well-made play are "conventional"—that
is, they behave, not according to laws of psychology but according to the expectations of an audience in a theater. A
type of drama in which the plot is given a free hand cannot
afford any less passive or more obtrusive *personae*. Con-
versely, if a playwright abandons the plot-determined play,
he will have to be more inventive as to character. To assume
the initiative, his characters will have to be capable of it.
So Shaw's first contribution to the drama was: more active
characters. They were more active, first of all, in the most
obvious fashion: they were violent. More important, they
made decisions which affected the course of events, and they
made them on the basis of their own nature, not of the
spectator's. And so these characters were surprising. For a
number of years, they were too surprising to be acceptable.
Like all surprising art, Shaw's dramaturgy was damned as
non-art. The critics' formula was: Not a Play.

Augier's hero could not consider being the husband of a
woman with a tainted dowry. Shaw creates a hero who has
the effrontery to ask the heroine to throw up her dowry for
his sake. But the Shavian joke—the Shavian reversal—is already what it would characteristically be in the future: a
double one. To this demanding hero he adds an even more
demanding heroine: she simply refuses to be poor to preserve
her innocence. That is the nub of the first Shaw comedy.
Then Shaw works his way out of the apparent deadlock, not
by having the heroine weaken (that is, "improve"), but by
having the hero renew his strength (that is, "deteriorate").
This the latter does by way of recovering from a shock.
The shock comes from without and might be called an accident (like Augier's outbreak of war), except that it belongs
to the logic of the situation. It turns out that the source of
the hero's own unearned income is the same as that of his
girl's father. End of Act Two. In the third and last act, our
hero comes around and gets the girl by accepting the nature
of capitalism. Socialist propaganda? Precisely. Shaw boasted

of it. But he boasted with equal reason that he was writing
comedy in the most traditional sense.

"Take what would be done by Scribe, Sardou, Dumas *fils*,
or Augier and do the opposite." Is that the Shavian formula?
It is certain that Shavian comedy is parodistic in a way, or
to an extent, that Plautus, Jonson, and Molière were not.
These others, one would judge, took a convention they respected and brought it to the realization of its best possibilities. Shaw took conventions in which he saw no possibilities—except insofar as he would expose their bank-
ruptcy. The injunction "Do the opposite" was not whimsical.
Shaw decided to "do the opposite" of Scribe in much the
way Marx decided to do the opposite of Hegel—not to stand
everything on its head (Hegel, he held, had done this) but
to set everything back on its feet again. That was revolutionary thinking, and Shaw's art, for all the polite and
charming trappings, was revolutionary art. The usual relations were reversed.

Such reversals as we see in the ending of *Widowers'
Houses* are relatively simple. Shaw's weakest plays are those
in which he has done little more than turn the ending
around: the price you pay for the brilliant ending of *The
Devil's Disciple* is that of a rather dull, and decidedly conventional, first act. His best plays are those in which the
principle of reversal has pervaded the whole. Such a play is
Arms and the Man.

The idea of taking two couples and causing them to exchange partners is hardly novel and, as I have said, the
little tale of the coat and the portrait is Scribean in pattern.
But Shaw can justifiably plead that this is no well-made play
because the artifices of the plot are not what ultimately
achieve the result. Here is one of the decisive turns in the
action:

BLUNTSCHLI. When you get into that noble attitude and
speak in that thrilling voice, I admire you; but I find it impossible to believe a single word you say.

RAINA. Captain Bluntschli!

BLUNTSCHLI. Yes?

RAINA. Do you mean what you said just now? Do you
know what you said just now?

BLUNTSCHLI. I do.

RAINA. I! I!!! How did you find me out?

With this last query, Raina passes over forever from
Sergius's world to Bluntschli's: as a result of nothing in
the Scribean arrangement of incidents, but of words, words,
words. It is here that, to many, the Shavian drama seems
vulnerable. In drama, actions are supposed to speak louder
than words. Writers on the subject invariably know their
etymology—"drama" derives from a Greek verb meaning
"to do"—and use it as a cudgel. Their error is a vulgar
one: action need not be external. It can often be carried by
words alone. Shaw used to remark that his plays were all
words just as Raphael's paintings were all paint.

There is a degree of legerdemain in that remark, for
Scribe, too, put down his plays in words. What was con-
fusing to Shaw's readers and spectators half a century ago
was that after indicating unmistakably that he was playing
Scribe's game, Shaw proceeded to break the rules. The fact
that Bluntschli conquers by words gains its peculiar force
from a context in which the opposite was to be expected. To
look over *Arms and the Man* with an eye to technique
would be to conclude that what we have here is Scribe
most subtly interwoven with Shaw. Yet this formulation is
inadequate, for who did the interweaving? There was a
Scribe in Shaw, and there was a counter-Scribe in Shaw;
what makes his works dramatic is the interaction of the
two.

The passion and preoccupation of Scribe was the idea of
climax: to the Big Scene at the end—or, rather, a little before the end—all his arts are dedicated. In Bernard Shaw
there was almost as great a predilection for anticlimax. It
is the Shavian "effect" par excellence; no other playwright
has come near finding so many possibilities in it. The bit I
have quoted from Bluntschli and Raina is an apt example.
Arms and the Man contains a corresponding scene between
Sergius and Louka. Where, in a well-made play, Bluntschli
and Louka would have to soar to the heights of Raina and
Sergius, in the Shaw play Raina and Sergius drop with a
bump to the level of Bluntschli and Louka. Such is resolution by anticlimax. It is dramaturgically effective, and it enforces the author's theme. But this is not all of Shaw: it is
only the counter-Scribe.

The dual anticlimaxes do not round off *Arms and the Man*.
What does? Not the disenchantment of Raina and Sergius but
the discovery that Bluntschli the realist is actually an enchanted
soul whom nothing will disenchant. He has destroyed their

romanticism but is himself "incurably romantic." This is
another point that is made in "mere words"—"mere words
stuck on at the end," if you wish—and yet stuck on very well,
for they are firmly attached to that little tale of the coat and the
photograph which gives the work its continuity and shape:

> BLUNTSCHLI. Yes: that's the coat I mean. . . . Do you
> suppose I am the sort of fellow a young girl falls in love
> with? Why, look at our ages! I'm thirty-four: I don't
> suppose the young lady is much over seventeen. All that
> adventure which was life or death to me was only a school-
> girl's game to her . . . would a woman who took the affair
> seriously have sent me this and written on it: "Raina, to her
> chocolate cream soldier—a souvenir"?
>
> PETKOFF. That's what I was looking for. How the deuce
> did it get there?
>
> BLUNTSCHLI. I have put everything right, I hope, gracious
> young lady.
>
> RAINA. I quite agree with your account of yourself. You
> are a romantic idiot. Next time I hope you will know the
> difference between a schoolgirl of seventeen and a woman
> of twenty-three.

In this scene, plot and theme reach completion together,
and the play of thesis and antithesis ends in synthesis.

The supreme triumph of Shaw's dramaturgical dialectics
is to be found in *Man and Superman,* and, for all the
blarney in the preface about the medieval *Everyman* and
the eighteenth-century *Don Giovanni,* the method is the conversion of old materials into nineteenth-century terms, both
thematic and technical. Shaw's claim to be returning to a
pristine Don Juan is valid to the extent that the theme had
originally been less of psychological than of philosophical,
indeed theological, interest. It is also true that Don Juan
had run away from his women. However, he had run away
from them only after possessing them. In Shaw's play, he
runs away to prevent *them* from possessing *him.* It is a
comic parody of the old motif, embodying Shaw's standard
new motif: the courting of the man by the woman. And
where the old dramatists and librettists had used the old,
"open" type of plot (or nonplot), Shaw substitutes an utterly
Scribean "closed" structure.

This very "modern" and "twentieth-century" play is made
up of narrative materials familiar to every Victorian

theatergoer. We have a hero who spends the entire evening hotly pursued by his foes; a clandestine marriage celebrated in defiance of a hostile father; a lovelorn hero who sacrifices himself so that the girl will go to his rival; a villain whose function is to constitute for a while the barrier to denouement and happy ending. The subplot about the Malone family rests upon two separate uses of the "secret skillfully withheld," then skillfully released. Traditional farcical coincidence binds together Straker and Mendoza. The play bears every sign of careful workmanship—all of it School of Scribe.

But as with *Arms and the Man*, as soon as we examine particulars, we find, interwoven with the Scribean elements, those typically Shavian verbal exchanges which constitute further action. Violet's marriage could have been made a secret of in any Scribe play, and Scribe could have been relied on to choose an effective moment for the release of the secret. In Shaw, what creates both the fun and the point of the news release is not the organization of the incidents but their relation to theme:

> TANNER. I know, and the whole world really knows, though it dare not say so, that you were right to follow your instinct; that vitality and bravery are the greatest qualities a woman can have, and motherhood her solemn initiation into womanhood; and that the fact of your not being legally married matters not one scrap either to your own worth or to our real regard for you.
>
> VIOLET. Oh! You think me a wicked woman, like the rest. . . . I won't bear such a horrible insult as to be complimented by Jack on being one of the wretches of whom he approves. I have kept my marriage a secret for my husband's sake.

An incident which Tanner wishes to use to illustrate his "modern" philosophy thus comes to illustrate a contrasting thesis: that Violet lives by a nonmodern philosophy.

Simple? Yes, but closely linked to a point that is unsimple enough to have generally been missed: Tanner is a windbag. Indeed, the mere fact of the woman courting the man would probably not yield comedy at all were it not for a further and more dynamic reversal: the woman, who makes no great claims for herself, has all the shrewdness, the real *Lebensweisheit*, while the man, who knows everything and can discourse like Bernard Shaw, is—a fool. Tanner is, in fact, like Molière's Alceste, the traditional fool of comedy in highly sophisticated intellectual disguise. Ann Whitefield, into whose trap Tanner falls, is the knave—in skirts.

While Don Juan Tenorio is Superman—or is on the road to him—John Tanner, M.I.R.C., is merely Man, and as such belongs to The World As It Is. Of dramaturgical interest is that the kind of plot Shaw evidently considers capable of giving an image of The World as It Is should be the kind that is generally considered (by himself, for instance) artificial, unreal, arbitrary, inane. Shaw the critic championed the new Naturalism, and among French dramatists especially favored Brieux, who produced dully literal theatrical documentaries. Yet, when Shaw wrote an essay entitled "A Dramatic Realist to His Critics," the example of "realism" he gave from his own work was *Arms and the Man*—on the grounds that the characters respond naturally even if the situations aren't natural. We are entitled, then, to insist on his choice of "unnatural" situations. He must intuitively have understood something which, as a critic, he failed to grasp: that plot does not merely reproduce external reality. The violence and intrigue in Shakespeare, which Shaw the critic declared extraneous, provides the objective correlative of Shakespeare's feelings about life, and the "idiocies" of the plot of *Man and Superman* provide an objective correlative for Shaw's sense of modern life. The very fact that Shaw despised Scribe helps to explain the particular use he made of him.

The Don Juan episode in Act Three is neither a well-made play nor a portion of a well-made play. It stands apart as something appropriately more austere and august. It is not a traditional work of any kind, not even a Platonic dialogue, the relation between Socrates and his interlocutors being quite different. It is not even a debate, for two of the speakers, the Commander and Ana, hardly present arguments at all: they simply represent a point of view. Do even the Devil and Don Juan *discuss* anything? A devil is scarcely a being one can convert to a Cause, and if the Don is busy convincing anyone it is himself. Certainly it is the philosophy of Bernard Shaw that he is given to speak, but is persuasion exercised—even on the audience? Rather, the contributions of the four presences come together as a vision of life—and an intimation of superlife.

Man—and Superman. The comedy of John Tanner—and

the vision of Don Juan Tenorio. Shaw—and counter-Shaw, Thesis and antithesis are, to be sure, of separate interest, and yet, as usual, the great Shavian achievement is to have related one to the other. Tanner seems a wise man and proves a fool. Don Juan passes for a philanderer but proves an explorer and a missionary of the truth. In our trivial, tawdry, clever, Scribean world, intellect is futile and ever at the mercy of instinct. Take away the episode in hell, and Shaw has written an anti-intellectual comedy. The episode assigns to intellect the highest role. No longer, therefore, is Ann the center and source of things—only a possible mother for Superman. Here Don Juan dominates. Here (or rather, in heaven) intellect is at home, and the Don is cured of that occupational disease of Shavian heroes—homelessness. He "comes to a good end"—only it is not an end, it is an episode, and from these celestial-infernal heights we must descend to earth with the shock of Shavian anticlimax, to earth and to Tanner, from Superman back to Man. One section of the play gets an electric charge from the other.

Of Shaw's "playmaking" one must conclude that he knew how to put together a Scribean plot; that he knew how to subordinate such a plot to his own purposes; and that, in *Man and Superman*, he knew how to take the resultant Shavian comedy and combine it dynamically with a disquisition on (and by) Don Juan.

Emotional Substance

If Shaw's plays are, or begin by being, a parody of the more conventional drama of his time, that parody is by no means confined to the form. We have already seen that the themes, too, tend to get turned around: these compositions not only do the opposite, as it were, but say the opposite.

What of the emotions? Whatever the ultimate purpose of drama, its immediate impact is a strongly emotional one, and one cannot conceive of a story having an emotional effect upon an audience unless it is an emotional story and has a certain emotional structure. I may be forgiven for stating so rudimentary a principle because the Shavian drama presents us with a paradox: it has flooded a thousand theaters with emotion and yet has often been held to be emotionless.

Of course, this common opinion is absurd, bolstered

hough it can be with remarks of Shaw's own about being a
mere "work machine" and the like. What we confront here
is originality. Shaw may not have been an original thinker;
he tried, rather, to make a synthesis of what certain others
had thought. But he was an original person. What fitted
him so well for the role of the enemy of convention was
that his natural responses were not those of other people
but all his own. His emotional constitution was a peculiar
one, and that peculiarity is reflected in his plays.

Sex is, without doubt, the crucial issue. Comedy remains
fertility worship, however sublimated, and it is fair enough
to ask what Bernard Shaw made of the old sexual rigmarole
—courtship and the barriers thereto. It is even fair to use any
facts about Shaw himself that are a matter of public record.

On the other hand, one is not honor-bound to side with
"modern" opinion against "Victorian" as to what is good and
bad. The very "modern" Dr. Kinsey implied that human vitality could be measured in statistics on orgasms. Our subject
Bernard Shaw will not pass into any Kinseyite paradise.
Though he lived to be ninety-four, he seems to have experienced sexual intercourse only between the ages of twenty-
nine and forty-three. "I lived a continent virgin . . . until
I was 29. . . . During the fourteen years before my marriage
at 43 there was always some lady in the case. . . . As man
and wife we found a new relation in which sex had no
part. It ended the old gallantries, flirtations, and philander-
ings for both of us." This quotation is from a letter to Frank
Harris, who, as a Kinseyite before Kinsey, wrote: "Compare
his [Shaw's] private life with Shakespeare's. While Mary
Fitton was banished from London Shakespeare could write
nothing but tragedies. That went on for five years. When the
Queen died and Shakespeare's Dark Lady returned, he wrote
Antony and Cleopatra, his greatest love story. As nothing
like that happened in Shaw's life we can only get a textbooky,
sexless type of play." A remarkable blend of ignorance, invention, and arbitrary assumption! For, actually, Shaw concealed from Harris most of his private life; nothing whatever is known about Shakespeare's feelings for any woman;
and no critic or psychologist of repute has even argued that a
man's writing has to be "textbooky" and "sexless" unless he
is carrying on an adulterous romance; a more familiar argument would be that precisely the abstinent man's imagination might well be crammed with sex. But there is no settling
the question a priori.

William Archer declared that Shaw's plays reeked wit
sex. It is a more suggestive declaration than Harris's. It re
minds us that Shaw was able to re-create the sexual charr
of both men and women to a degree unequaled by any Eng
lish dramatist except Shakespeare. To be sure, he doesn
need bedroom scenes to do this. Morell only has to tal
and we understand "Prossy's complaint." Undershaft onl
has to talk and we understand why he is a problem to hi
daughter. To say nothing of the long line of sirens from
Candida to Orinthia! Few of the "sexy" ladies of Restoration
comedy, by contrast, have any sex appeal at all. One thing
Archer is sure to have had in mind is that the women in
Shaw pursue a sexual purpose in a way absolutely unknown
to Victorian literature. Of all the reversals in Shavian drama
this is inevitably the most famous: the reversal in the roles
of the sexes. Shaw once committed himself to the view tha
all superior women are masculine and all superior men are
feminine. In his comedies, most often, the woman is active
the man passive. Perhaps by 1960 the theme has been re
stated *ad nauseam;* to Archer it was startling—as was Shaw's
determination to rub the sore places of the sexual morality
of his time. *Mrs. Warren's Profession* was for many years
too "raw" a play for production in London, and it created
a memorable scandal when it was produced in New Haven
and New York in 1905. Like most of the major modern
dramatists and novelists, Shaw mentioned the unmentionable.
He even claimed to have "put the physical act of sexual intercourse on the stage" (in *Overruled*). Archer evidently
felt that Shaw could not give the subject of sex a rest: he
may not always have been at the center of it but he was forever touching its fringes.

Here Frank Harris would have interjected: "He was always *avoiding* the center of it." And the interjection is called
for. The impression that a man is unemotional in general
and sexless in particular does not come from nowhere. Nor
are the kinds of sex I have been noting what the average
spectator is looking for if he demands a "sexy" show. *Overruled* does not really "put the physical act of sexual intercourse on the stage," and, even if it did, it would do so
comically—depriving the act of precisely that element which
people miss in Shaw, which is not sex in general but the tor-
ridity of sexual romance. At that, if this element were simply
absent, Shaw might very well have got away with the omission. But it is explicitly rejected. It is not that a Shavian

couple cannot consider intercourse but that they are likely
to consider it and decide not to. If the characteristic act of
the French drama of the period was the plunge into bed, that
of the Shavian drama is the precipitate retreat from the bedroom door.

Harris would be right in reminding us that such was Bernard Shaw's emotional constitution. What other writer has
ever created all the normal expectations in a scene between
a king and his mistress (*The Apple Cart*), only to reveal later
that their relationship is purely platonic? *Captain Brassbound's Conversion* shows the Shavian pattern to perfection.
Is there sexual feeling in the play? There is. The process by
which Brassbound and Lady Cicely are brought closer and
closer is positively titillating. After which, what happens?
They are parted. The play has a superb final curtain. "How
glorious!" says Lady Cicely, "how glorious!" Then with one
of those quick changes of tone that mark the Shavian dialogue: "And what an escape!" Is this unemotional? No. But
the emotion is not erotic—rather, it is relief at a release
from the erotic. Such is the emotional content of this particular Shavian anticlimax.

As far as conscious intention goes, all Shaw's plays might
bear the title he gave to three of them—Plays for Puritans—
for that intention is to show romance transcended by a
higher-than-erotic purpose. It is a classic intention—an application, really, of the traditional conflict of love and honor,
with honor winning hands down, as it did in Corneille and
even in one masterpiece of Racine's, *Bérénice*. We are concerned here not with philosophic intention but psychological
substance. Where the philosopher insists that Shaw does not
cross the threshold of the bedroom, the psychologist asks:
why does he hover at the bedroom door?

We know from the correspondence with Mrs. Pat Camp-
bell that Shaw liked to play with fire. Even the correspondence with Ellen Terry entailed a playfulness not quite devoid
of "danger." The boy Shaw had been witness to an odd household arrangement whereby his mother's music teacher con-
trived to be (it would seem) almost but not quite her lover.
A slightly older Shaw has recently been portrayed as the in-
truder into a friend's marriage, like his own Eugene Marchbanks: this is speculation. Let us look at the play *Candida*,
which is a fact.

It has a notable Big Scene at the end, which is characterized by an equally notable improbability. A comfortable, sen-

sible parson's wife doesn't let herself get jockeyed into
"choosing" between her husband and an almost total
stranger. People—such people at least—don't do such things.
A respectable woman's choice was made before the banns
were read.

Perhaps Candida is not really respectable? That is the
line of interpretation taken by Beatrice Webb, who declared
her a prostitute. Will the play, taken as a play, bear this interpretation out? A dramatist's license to have the truth turn
out different from the impression given to the audience is
very limited, for it is to a large extent by giving impressions
that he creates characters. Shaw has given the impression
that Candida is *not* a prostitute.

Against this it can be urged that Shaw himself took Beatrice Webb's side and attacked Candida—in remarks he
made about her in letters to James Huneker, Richard Burton,
and others. True, but was that legitimate? He himself admitted that he had no more right to say what his plays meant
than any other critic. One might add that he may have had
less, for when an author intervenes to correct our impressions of his work, he is often intervening to change or mis-
interpret that work.

Outside the play, Shaw is against Candida. Inside it, he is
both for and against her, but he is for her effectually, and
against her ineffectually, because the direct impression is
favorable, while it is only by throwing logic back into the
story when it is over that you can reach an unfavorable
judgment. This means, I should think, that though Shaw's
intellect is against Candida, his emotions are for her.

What is it that this play has always projected in the theater, and can always be counted on to project again? The
charm of Candida. This is a reality so immediate and all-
pervasive that it is hard for any other element in the play to
make headway against it. Leading actresses know this, and
hearing their director speak of Candida's essential badness,
can afford to smile a Candida smile, strong in the knowledge
that there is nothing a director can do about this badness,
once that smile has been displayed on stage as well as off.

I would say that it is a confused play but that the confusion goes unnoticed because of Candida's charm and may
even be the cause of a degree of emotional tension unusual
in a Shaw play. Candida is made out of a Shavian ambivalence: he would like to reject this kind of woman, but actually he dotes on her. One quickly senses that he *is* March-

banks. One also finds he protests (too much) that he is *not*
Marchbanks. "I had in mind De Quincey's account of his
adolescence in his Confessions," he wrote. "I certainly never
thought of myself as a model." From the empty pretence of
being De Quincey, no doubt, comes the prodigious unreality
of many of the lines. As a character, Marchbanks must be
reckoned a failure. Shaw was hiding. What better image to
hide behind than that of the kind of writer he himself was
not—a romantic poet? Especially if De Quincey would do the
job for him?

It didn't work, of course, except as pure histrionics.
(Marchbanks, though a poorly drawn character, is always an
effective stage role, and still seems to correspond to the
actors' idea of a poet.) But if no one in the play can reject
Candida, there is a noteworthy niche in it for the man whom
she will reject. This niche Marchbanks can fill nobly, and
has his dramatic moment as he marches into it: his final
exit is a magnificent piece of action. Possibly everything before that (in this role) is just an improvisation. Shaw could
not make us believe in the poet's poetry, but he does make us
believe in his pain and his nobility, for at these points he
could identify himself with Eugene completely without having to "think of himself as a model."

Dramatists usually speak of their characters individually,
and that could be regarded as strange, because the drama,
all through the centuries, has done much less with separate
persons than with relationships. The traditional characters
are, if you will, simplified to the point of crudity. What is
not crude, as treated by the old dramatists, is the interaction
of these characters: the dynamics of human relations are
fully rendered. If what you do not get is the detailed psychological biography, what you do get is the essence of such
relations as parent and child, boy and girl, man and wife.

Now, modern playwrights, happily, have not departed
from the classic patterns as much as they are supposed to
have, and what rings true, emotionally, in *Candida* corre-
sponds to Shaw's ability to find and re-create some of these
elemental relationships. An inner obstacle, one would judge,
hampered him when he tried to "do" the Marchbanks-
Candida relationship, but the Morell-Candida relation is
both clear and challenging. It is, as Shaw himself said, the
relationship of Nora and Torvald Helmer turned around: in
Shaw's play the man is the doll. But where Ibsen tells the
story of a doll who finally comes to life, Shaw tells the story

of a seemingly living person who turns out to have been a doll all along. (In other words, the relation of Shaw to Ibsen, instead of being as direct as it might seem, is an inverse one, exactly like the relation of Shaw to other nineteenth-century drama.) Into Morell Shaw can put that part of himself (a child) which finds Candida irresistible, just as into Candida he can put that part of Woman which he finds irresistible—the mother in her. One would have to be as naïve a psychologist as Frank Harris to consider the mother-and-child relation less emotional than that of lovers.

Or less dramatic. Relationships become dramatic not in the degree of their eroticism but to the extent that they contain conflict. Pure love would not be a dramatic subject at all. Love becomes dramatic when it is impure—when the loving element is submerged in a struggle for power. The axis about which *Candida* revolves is that of strength and weakness, not love and hate. And if one knows Shaw's views on the topic of the "weaker sex" in general, the conclusion of *Candida* follows naturally: instead of the little woman reaching up toward the arms of the strong man, we have the strong woman reaching down to pick up her child. It is remarkable how far Shaw's thought is from the standard "advanced thinking" of his generation, with its prattle of equality and comradeship. He is closer to Nietzsche.

Of the ending of *A Doll's House* it has been said: perhaps Nora has walked out in a mere tantrum and will be back in the morning. How much more savage is the ending of *Candida!* Only Strindberg could have written a sequel to it. The cruelty of the heroine—merely implicit in the present play—would have to come to the surface in any continuation of the story. Candida has chosen to let her husband discover his shame: she, as well as he, will have to take the consequences. Let the stage manager hold razors and strait jackets in readiness!

One reason why Shaw got so little credit for his treatment of the emotions is that the emotions he treats are not the ones people expect. The very fact that his favorite device is anticlimax should tell us that what he most insistently feels is "letdown." It may be retorted that on the contrary, Bernard Shaw was the most buoyant and vivacious of men. That is also true. The axis "strength-weakness" is not more important to Shaw's content than the axis "elation-depression" is to his form. The dialogue ripples gaily along; then comes the sudden letdown. The circus has familiarized us with the pattern: it is the light of heart who take the pratfall. Even as the fool pops up in Shavian comedy in the highly intellectualized shape of a Jack Tanner, so the pratfall is transmuted into an anticlimax that has a positively climactic force. It has been customary to take these anticlimaxes as expressions of an idea—the idea of disenchantment. It is *the* idea of modern literature, and it is inseparable from an emotion far commoner and far more influential than romantic excitement. There seems to be no name for this emotion—and that, too, is significant. Let us call it desolation.

You cannot be disenchanted without having been enchanted. One is sometimes tempted to believe that our human desolation might have been avoided if only we had not started out so undesolate. It is not the fact that we don't have things that worries us, but that we have lost them—or rather, been deprived of them. Desolation is the feeling of having been driven from paradise.

A friend of Bernard Shaw's said that when he saw *The Wild Duck*, the bottom dropped out of the universe. One difference between Ibsen and Shaw is that the former produced this effect on the audience, whereas the latter produced it on the characters in a play. Just as a character in a melodrama loses a fortune, so a character in a Shaw play loses a universe. The experience may be given a playful treatment, as with Raina and Sergius. In the case of Morell, the treatment is only partly playful. It gets more serious as the play *Candida* proceeds. Morell finally loses his image of his wife and of himself. The curtain has to be rung down to save us from the Strindberg play that would have to follow.

What of *Mrs. Warren's Profession?* The starting point was a treatment by Maupassant of the theme of a girl finding out that her mother is a courtesan. In an early version of the tale, Maupassant had the girl kill herself. In the later and better-known text (*Yvette*), he saves her life to engineer for himself an ironic-poignant ending: she becomes a kept woman like her mother before her. Curtain! That is the kind of inversion of a suicidal ending which Shaw did *not* go in for. Or not any more. If Shaw had shown a "surrender to the system" (in comical fashion) in the ending to *Widowers' Houses*, he was now intent on showing a rejection of the system. In the first instance, Vivie Warren's revolt represents Shaw's rational rejection of capitalism, but the play culminates in a scene that has no necessary connection with economics—

a scene of family crisis, a scene in which a daughter rejects her mother. Which, after all, is archetypal Shaw: instead of the emotions of lover and mistress, he renders the emotions of parents and children, and particularly the emotion of the child rejecting the parent. *Major Barbara* is perhaps the grandest example of this archetype. The great last act of *Pygmalion* is the same thing in disguise, for Henry Higgins is the progenitor of the new Eliza, and that is why she must break free of him. Shaw's Joan has a father, too—in heaven—and she comes at times almost to the point of breaking with Him. That she does not quite do so is the upshot of a play which, while it shows Joan's isolation from men, ends with a stretching of arms toward the heavenly Father. Vivie Warren is already a Saint Joan in that the experience Shaw gives her is that of being desolated. It is the experience he felt most deeply—presumably because it was the experience he had most deeply experienced. In any event, the two long scenes between Vivie and Mrs. Warren are emotional playwriting such as England had not seen for a couple of centuries.

The background, however, is blurred. A Scribean climax is arranged to provide *élan* for the announcement that Vivie's romance is incestuous:

CROFTS. Allow me, Mister Frank, to introduce you to your half-sister, the eldest daughter of the Reverend Samuel Gardner. Miss Vivie: your half-brother. Good morning.

FRANK [. . . *raising the rifle*]. You'll testify before the coroner that it's an accident, Viv. [*He takes aim at the retreating figure of Crofts. Vivie seizes the muzzle and pulls it round against her breast.*]

VIVIE. Fire now. You may.

Direct climax (as against anticlimax) was not really in Shaw's line, and in failing to parody Scribe here, Shaw has himself tumbled into the ridiculous. Perhaps the following act was bound to be an anticlimax in a way not intended—a mere disappointment. Yet, it is hard to believe that the particular disappointments it brings are simply the result of a technical ineptitude. Rather, they involve hesitations about the subject. After so strongly creating the impression of incest, Shaw shuffles the notion off in the next act in a surprisingly ambiguous way. It would be easy enough, from a technical viewpoint, to make clear that no incest had been committed. Why did Shaw leave the situation doubtful? So that Vivie could dismiss the issue as irrelevant? In that case, what is relevant? Why is she giving Frank up? One can think of possible reasons, but what reason is one *supposed* to think of?

Unclarity in the work of so careful a craftsman, a writer, moreover, who has more than once been accused of excessive clarity, surely bears witness to inner uncertainty and conflict. To think of *Mrs. Warren's Profession* in this personal way is to realize what powerful aggressions it embodies. Shaw combined the themes of prostitution and incest in order to make quite a rational point: our mad society draws back in horror from incest, which is certainly not a pressing menace and perhaps not even a bad thing, while it encourages prostitution, which is a virulent social pestilence. But both themes have a resonance far beyond the bounds of intellect. It is as if they proved more than Shaw had bargained for. The incest theme is sounded—all too boldly. Then the young dramatist has no idea what to do with it. He takes it back. Only, it is too late. So he half takes it back. After all, what is troubling Vivie does go beyond the rationally established causes. Deep water! And Shaw flounders in it. Which has some interest for the student of the emotions. Even where Shaw's plays are faulty, they are not unemotional. On the contrary, it is because of a certain emotional involvement in the material, not because of incapacity for such involvement, that Shaw was not able to resolve certain problems and truly finish certain plays. *Candida* and *Mrs. Warren's Profession* could be cited in evidence. There is material in both which was not successfully "worked through."

Is there similar material in Shaw's collected plays which *was* worked through? To my mind, a good answer would be: yes, *Pygmalion*. This play might well have proved just as ambiguous as the others, for it might have seemed that Eliza must love Higgins, and therefore that her leaving him is but an overrational afterthought of the author's, like his afterthoughts on Candida. Some people, including the author of *My Fair Lady*, think that is just what the Shavian ending is. I, on the other hand, feel—and it is feeling that is in question —that Eliza's rebellion grows organically out of what preceded. She is Higgins' creation: she cannot *be* at all unless she become independent of her creator. If he has "sex appeal," that makes the break more difficult but not less necessary. A girl's father quite normally has sex appeal for her.

That is not to justify incest. Here Shaw does cope with incest, and in the best way—by avoiding it.

The ending of *Pygmalion* is the classic Shavian situation: someone is clamorously refusing to enter the bedroom. The friends of Frank Harris are thereby disgusted. That is their right. But there is a point to be made about Shaw's rendering of emotion. Refusal is emotional. There is more turbulence in conflict between Eliza and Higgins as conceived by Shaw than in romance between them as in *My Fair Lady*.

Man and Superman, on the other hand, might seem to be without emotional substance. The attempt made at a straightforward emotional climax is certainly rather unsuccessful:

TANNER. I love you. The Life Force enchants me. I have the whole world in my arms when I clasp you. But I am fighting for my freedom, for my honor, for my self, one and undivisible.

ANN. Your happiness will be worth them all.

TANNER. You would sell freedom and honor and self for happiness?

ANN. It would not be all happiness for me. Perhaps death.

TANNER [*groaning*]. Oh, that clutch holds and hurts. What have you grasped in me? Is there a father's heart as well as a mother's?

If there is capital here, it is the kind that yields no dramatic return, and indeed a criticism of this false climax would lead us to complain of the introduction of the "Life Force" in the first place. There seems no such organic relation between Tanner and Ann as there is between Vivie and her mother, Eliza and Higgins, Candida and Morell. The pair are sometimes compared to Benedick and Beatrice. The comparison is not apt. Shakespeare shows the erotically "dangerous" element in the hostility of his couple. But Tanner and Ann draw no sparks from each other. A cynic might say: here there can be no love since there is no hate. There is really no relationship at all, except that she insists on having him and he cannot evade her successfully because the author won't let him. In this case, we have either to conclude that Frank Harris's kind of criticism applies—or that this is "drama of ideas" and we must not ask it to be otherwise.

Emotional substance? The farce of Tanner and Ann, taken

in isolation, has very little, but oddly enough, the episode in hell has a good deal, and this spreads itself over the work as a whole. Even here, though, there is a discrepancy between intention and achievement. The final effect of the Don Juan scene is not that we find the positive message inspiring. We find it at best important, at worst gallant—a brave effort to make sense of things that cannot be made sense of. It is all rather like a speech made in wartime, saying that our side is bound to win because we are right. Perhaps. Perhaps. But the words that burn with irrefutability are all words expressing not aspiration toward a better future, but recognition of a bad present. Don Juan himself is at his best when denouncing people. The speech that steals the show ("And is Man any the less destroying himself . . .") is made by the Devil. Which is because it is not only a very reasonable speech but a very emotional one, a speech that springs from that very desolation which Shaw's best people experience.

This note of personal poignancy is not heard very often after *Saint Joan* (1923). So much the worse, perhaps, for the later plays. They have considerable merit, yet they often lack urgency even when the author makes Urgent Statements in them. And it is interesting that they lack not only dynamic and turbulent personal relationships but also close structure. There had been a connection between the emotional and the dramaturgic construction of the earlier plays; and when one went, so did the other.

I am not proposing a complete theory of the Shavian drama. Nor am I asking my reader to assume that all is dominated by the emotional conflicts of its author, much less that it ought to be. For that matter, I have had to remark that unresolved conflict sometimes resulted in unresolved art. What I am affirming is, first, that some Shaw plays communicate personal feeling of great intensity and, second, that even some Shaw plays which are less overtly emotional do embody powerful feelings, though not of the kind that is usually expected.

ERIC BENTLEY

A Bibliographical Note

A selective bibliography was included in my *Bernard Shaw: a Reconsideration* (New Directions, 1947) and revised for the paperback reprint of the book ten years later. The following items are of special interest in relation to the plays in the

present volume. Several of these items appeared too late
for mention in my book:

ARCHER, WILLIAM. *Study & Stage*: A Year-book of Criticism.
  London: G. Richards, 1899.

HANLEY, TULLAH I. *The Strange Triangle of G.B.S.* Boston:
  Bruce Humphries, 1957.

HARRIS, FRANK. *Bernard Shaw*. New York: Simon and
  Schuster, 1931.

HENDERSON, ARCHIBALD. *Table-talk of G.B.S.* New York:
  Harper, 1925.

MCKEE, IRVING. "Bernard Shaw's Beginnings on the London
  Stage," *Publications of the Modern Language Association
  of America*, September, 1959.

SHATTUCK, CHARLES H. "Bernard Shaw's 'Bad Quarto,'"
  The Journal of English and Germanic Philology, October,
  1955.

SHAW, BERNARD. *Sixteen Self Sketches*. New York: Dodd,
  Mead, 1949.

            Shaw on Theatre. Edited by E. J. West.
  New York: Hill and Wang, 1958.

STANTON, STEPHEN S., (ed.). *Camille and Other Plays*. New
  York: Hill and Wang, 1957.

            "English Drama and the French
  Well-Made Play." Unpublished doctoral dissertation, Columbia University, 1955.

WEISSMAN, PHILIP. "Shaw's Childhood and *Pygmalion*," *The
  Psychoanalytic Study of the Child*, 1958.

WELLWARTH, GEORGE E. "Mrs. Warren Comes to America:
  or the Blue-Noses, the Politicians, and the Procurers,"
  The Shaw Review, May, 1959.

                                                    E. B.

Mrs. Warren's Profession

The harlot's cry from street to street
Shall weave old England's winding sheet.
William Blake

THE AUTHOR'S APOLOGY

Mrs. Warren's Profession has been performed at last, after
a delay of only eight years; and I have once more shared
with Ibsen the triumphant amusement of startling all but the
strongest-headed of the London theatre critics clean out of
the practice of their profession. No author who has ever
known the exultation of sending the press into an hysterical
tumult of protest, of moral panic, of involuntary and frantic
confession of sin, of a horror of conscience in which the
power of distinguishing between the work of art on the stage
and the real life of the spectator is confused and overwhelmed, will ever care for the stereotyped compliments
which every successful farce or melodrama elicits from the
newspapers. Give me that critic who rushed from my play to
declare furiously that Sir George Crofts ought to be kicked.
What a triumph for the actor, thus to reduce a jaded London
journalist to the condition of the simple sailor in the Wapping
gallery, who shouts execrations at Iago and warnings to
Othello not to believe him! But dearer still than such simplicity is that sense of the sudden earthquake shock to the
foundations of morality which sends a pallid crowd of
critics into the street shrieking that the pillars of society are
cracking and the ruin of the state at hand. Even the Ibsen
champions of ten years ago remonstrate with me just as the
veterans of those brave days remonstrated with them. Mr.
Grein, the hardy iconoclast who first launched my plays on
the stage alongside *Ghosts* and *The Wild Duck*, exclaims
that I have shattered his ideals. Actually his ideals! What
would Dr. Relling say? And Mr. William Archer himself dis-
owns me because I "cannot touch pitch without wallowing
in it." Truly my play must be more needed than I knew;
and yet I thought I knew how little the others know.

Do not suppose, however, that the consternation of the

press reflects any consternation among the general public. Anybody can upset the theatre critics, in a turn of the wrist, by substituting for the romantic commonplaces of the stage the moral commonplaces of the pulpit, the platform, or the library. Play *Mrs. Warren's Profession* to an audience of clerical members of the Christian Social Union and of women well experienced in Rescue, Temperance, and Girls' Club work,[1] and no moral panic will arise: every man and woman present will know that as long as poverty makes virtue hideous and the spare pocket-money of rich bachelordom makes vice dazzling, their daily hand-to-hand fight against prostitution with prayer and persuasion, shelters and scanty alms, will be a losing one. There was a time when they were able to urge that though "the white-lead factory where Anne Jane was poisoned" may be a far more terrible place than Mrs. Warren's house, yet hell is still more dreadful. Nowadays they no longer believe in hell; and the girls among whom they are working know that they do not believe in it, and would laugh at them if they did. So well have the rescuers learnt that Mrs. Warren's defence of herself and indictment of society is the thing that most needs saying, that those who know me personally reproach me, not for writing this play, but for wasting my energies on "pleasant plays" for the amusement of frivolous people, when I can build up such excellent stage sermons on their own work. *Mrs. Warren's Profession* is the one play of mine which I could submit to a censorship without doubt of the result; only, it must not be the censorship of the minor theatre critic, nor of an innocent court official like the King's Reader of Plays, much less of people who consciously profit by Mrs. Warren's profession, or who personally make use of it, or who hold the widely whispered view that it is an indispensable safety-valve for the protection of domestic virtue, or, above all, who are smitten with a sentimental affection for our fallen sister, and would "take her up tenderly, lift her with care, fashioned so slenderly, young, and *so* fair." Nor am I prepared to accept the verdict of the medical gentlemen who would compulsorily examine and register Mrs. Warren, whilst leaving Mrs. Warren's patrons, especially her military pa-

---

[1] Many a specialist of the stalls will shudder at his own dreary conception of such an audience: but I can assure him that he would hardly know where he was on such an occasion, so much more vital would the atmosphere be, and so much jollier and better looking the people.

trons, free to destroy her health and anybody else's without fear of reprisals. But I should be quite content to have my play judged by, say, a joint committee of the Central Vigilance Society and the Salvation Army. And the sterner moralists the members of the committee were, the better.

Some of the journalists I have shocked reason so unripely that they will gather nothing from this but a confused notion that I am accusing the National Vigilance Association and the Salvation Army of complicity in my own scandalous immorality. It will seem to them that people who would stand this play would stand anything. They are quite mistaken. Such an audience as I have described would be revolted by many of our fashionable plays. They would leave the theatre convinced that the Plymouth Brother who still regards the playhouse as one of the gates of hell is perhaps the safest adviser on the subject of which he knows so little. If I do not draw the same conclusion, it is not because I am one of those who claim that art is exempt from moral obligations, and not that the writing or performance of a play is a moral act, to be treated on exactly the same footing as theft or murder if it produces equally mischievous consequences. I am convinced that fine art is the subtlest, the most seductive, the most effective instrument of moral propagandism in the world, excepting only the example of personal conduct; and I waive even this exception in favor of the art of the stage, because it works by exhibiting examples of personal conduct made intelligible and moving to crowds of unobservant unreflecting people to whom real life means nothing. I have pointed out again and again that the influence of the theatre in England is growing so great that whilst private conduct, religion, law, science, politics, and morals are becoming more and more theatrical, the theatre itself remains impervious to common sense, religion, science, politics, and morals. That is why I fight the theatre, not with pamphlets and sermons and treatises, but with plays; and so effective do I find the dramatic method that I have no doubt I shall at last persuade even London to take its conscience and its brains with it when it goes to the theatre, instead of leaving them at home with its prayer book as it does at present. Consequently, I am the last man to deny that if the net effect of performing *Mrs. Warren's Profession* were an increase in the number of persons entering that profession, its performance should be dealt with accordingly. Now let us consider how such recruiting can be encouraged by the theatre. Nothing is easier. Let the King's Reader of Plays, backed by the press, make an unwritten but perfectly well understood regulation that members of Mrs. Warren's profession shall be tolerated on the stage only when they are beautiful, exquisitely dressed, and sumptuously lodged and fed; also that they shall, at the end of the play, die of consumption to the sympathetic tears of the whole audience, or step into the next room to commit suicide, or at least be turned out by their protectors and passed on to be "redeemed" by old and faithful lovers who have adored them in spite of all their levities. Naturally the poorer girls in the gallery will believe in the beauty, in the exquisite dresses, and the luxurious living, and will see that there is no real necessity for the consumption, the suicide, or the ejectment: mere pious forms, all of them, to save the Censor's face. Even if these purely official catastrophes carried any conviction, the majority of English girls remain so poor, so dependent, so well aware that the drudgeries of such honest work as is within their reach are likely enough to lead them eventually to lung disease, premature death, and domestic desertion or brutality, that they would still see reason to prefer the primrose path to the strait path of virtue, since both, vice at worst and virtue at best, lead to the same end in poverty and overwork. It is true that the Board School mistress will tell you that only girls of a certain kind will reason in this way. But alas! that certain kind turns out on inquiry to be simply the pretty, dainty kind: that is, the only kind that gets the chance of acting on such reasoning. Read the first report of the Commission on the Housing of the Working Classes [Bluebook C 4402, 1889]; read the Report on Home Industries (sacred word, Home!) issued by the Women's Industrial Council [Home Industries of Women in London, 1897]; and ask yourself whether, if the lot in life therein described were your lot in life, you would prefer the lot of Cleopatra, of Theodora, of the Lady of the Camellias, of Mrs. Tanqueray, of Zaza, or Iris. If you can go deep enough into things to be able to say no, how many ignorant half-starved girls will believe you are speaking sincerely? To them the lot of Iris is heavenly in comparison with their own. Yet our King, like his predecessors, says to the dramatist "Thus, and thus only, shall you present Mrs. Warren's profession on the stage, or you shall starve. Witness Shaw, who told the untempting truth about it, and whom We, by the Grace of God, accordingly disallow and suppress, and do what in Us lies to silence." Fortunately, Shaw cannot be silenced. "The harlot's cry from street to street" is louder than the voices of all the kings. I am not dependent on the theatre, and cannot be starved into making my play a standing advertisement of the attractive side of Mrs. Warren's business.

Here I must guard myself against a misunderstanding. It is not the fault of their authors that the long string of wantons' tragedies, from *Antony and Cleopatra* to *Iris*, are snares to poor girls, and are objected to on that account by many earnest men and women who consider *Mrs. Warren's Profession* an excellent sermon. Mr. Pinero is in no way bound to suppress the fact that his Iris is a person to be envied by millions of better women. If he made his play false to life by inventing fictitious disadvantages for her, he would be acting as unscrupulously as any tract writer. If society chooses to provide for its Irises better than for its working women, it must not expect honest playwrights to manufacture spurious evidence to save its credit. The mischief lies in the deliberate suppression of the other side of the case: the refusal to allow Mrs. Warren to expose the drudgery and repulsiveness of plying for hire among coarse, tedious drunkards; the determination not to let the Parisian girl in Brieux's *Les Avariés* come on the stage and drive into people's minds what her diseases mean for her and for themselves. All that, says the King's Reader in effect, is horrifying, loathsome. Precisely: what does he expect it to be? would he have us represent it as beautiful and gratifying? The answer to this question, I fear, must be a blunt Yes; for it seems impossible to root out of an Englishman's mind the notion that vice is delightful, and that abstention from it is privation. At all events, as long as the tempting side of it is kept towards the public, and softened by plenty of sentiment and sympathy, it is welcomed by our Censor, whereas the slightest attempt to place it in the light of the policeman's lantern or the Salvation Army shelter is checkmated at once as not merely disgusting, but, if you please, unnecessary.

Everybody will, I hope, admit that this state of things is intolerable; that the subject of Mrs. Warren's profession must be either tapu altogether, or else exhibited with the warning side as freely displayed as the tempting side. But many persons will vote for a complete tapu, and an impartial clean sweep from the boards of Mrs. Warren and Gretchen and the rest: in short, for banishing the sexual instincts from the stage altogether. Those who think this impossible can hardly have considered the number and importance of the subjects which are actually banished from the stage. Many plays, among them *Lear, Hamlet, Macbeth, Coriolanus, Julius Cæsar,* have no sex complications: the thread of their action can be followed by children who could not understand a single scene of *Mrs. Warren's Profession* or *Iris.* None of our plays rouse the sympathy of the audience by an exhibition of the pains of maternity, as Chinese plays constantly do. Each nation has its particular set of tapus in addition to the common human stock; and though each of these tapus limits the scope of the dramatist, it does not make drama impossible. If Redford were to refuse to license plays with female characters in them, he would only be doing to the stage what our tribal customs already do to the pulpit and the bar. I have myself written a rather entertaining play with only one woman in it, and she quite heartwhole; and I could just as easily write a play without a woman in it at all. I will even go as far as to promise Redford my support if he will introduce this limitation for part of the year, say during Lent, so as to make a chosen season for that dullest of stock dramatic subjects, adultery, and force our managers and authors to find out what all great dramatists find out spontaneously: to wit, that people who sacrifice every other consideration to love are as hopelessly unheroic on the stage as lunatics or dipsomaniacs. Hector is the world's hero; not Paris nor Antony.

But though I do not question the possibility of a drama in which love should be as effectively ignored as cholera is at present, there is not the slightest chance of that way out of the difficulty being taken by Redford. If he attempted it there would be a revolt in which he would be swept away, in spite of my single-handed efforts to defend him. A complete tapu is politically impossible. A complete toleration is equally impossible to Redford, because his occupation would be gone if there were no tapu to enforce. He is therefore compelled to maintain the present compromise of a partial tapu, applied, to the best of his judgment, with a careful respect to persons and to public opinion. And a very sensible English solution of the difficulty, too, most readers will say. I should not dispute it if dramatic poets really were what English public opinion generally assumes them to be during their lifetime: that is, a licentiously irregular

group to be kept in order in a rough and ready way by a
magistrate who will stand no nonsense from them. But I
cannot admit that the class represented by Aeschylus,
Sophocles, Aristophanes, Euripides, Shakespeare, Goethe,
Ibsen, and Tolstoy, not to mention our own contemporary
playwrights, is as much in place in Mr. Redford's office as a
pickpocket is in Bow Street. Further, it is not true that the
Censorship, though it certainly suppresses Ibsen and Tolstoy,
and would suppress Shakespeare but for the absurd rule that
a play once licensed is always licensed (so that Wycherly is
permitted and Shelley prohibited), also suppresses unscrupulous playwrights. I challenge Mr. Redford to mention any
extremity of sexual misconduct which any manager in his
senses would risk presenting on the London stage that has
not been presented under his license and that of his predeces-
sor. The compromise, in fact, works out in practice in favor
of loose plays as against earnest ones.

To carry conviction on this point, I will take the extreme
course of narrating the plots of two plays witnessed within
the last ten years by myself at London West End theatres,
one licensed by the late Queen Victoria's Reader of Plays, the
other by the present Reader to the King. Both plots conform
to the strictest rules of the period when *La Dame aux
Camellias* was still a forbidden play, and when *The Second
Mrs. Tanqueray* would have been tolerated only on condition
that she carefully explained to the audience that when she
met Captain Ardale she sinned "but in intention."

Play number one. A prince is compelled by his parents to
marry the daughter of a neighboring king, but loves another
maiden. The scene represents a hall in the king's palace at
night. The wedding has taken place that day; and the closed
door of the nuptial chamber is in view of the audience. Inside, the princess awaits her bridegroom. A duenna is in at-
tendance. The bridegroom enters. His sole desire is to escape
from a marriage which is hateful to him. An idea strikes
him. He will assault the duenna, and get ignominiously
expelled from the palace by his indignant father-in-law. To
his horror, when he proceeds to carry out this stratagem, the
duenna, far from raising an alarm, is flattered, delighted,
and compliant. The assaulter becomes the assaulted. He
flings her angrily to the ground, where she remains placidly.
He flies. The father enters; dismisses the duenna; and listens
at the keyhole of his daughter's nuptial chamber, uttering
various pleasantries, and declaring, with a shiver, that a

sound of kissing, which he supposes to proceed from within, makes him feel young again.

In deprecation of the scandalized astonishment with which such a story as this will be read, I can only say that it was not presented on the stage until its propriety had been certified.

Story number two. A German officer finds himself in an inn with a French lady who has wounded his national vanity. He resolves to humble her by committing a rape upon her. He announces his purpose. She remonstrates, implores, flies to the doors and finds them locked, calls for help and finds none at hand, runs screaming from side to side, and, after a harrowing scene, is overpowered and faints. Nothing further being possible on the stage without actual felony, the officer then relents and leaves her. When she recovers, she believes that he has carried out his threat; and during the rest of the play she is represented as vainly vowing vengeance upon him, whilst she is really falling in love with him under the influence of his imaginary crime against her. Finally she consents to marry him; and the curtain falls on their happiness.

This story was certified by the present King's Reader, acting for the Lord Chamberlain, as void in its general tendency of "anything immoral or otherwise improper for the stage." But let nobody conclude therefore that Mr. Redford is a monster, whose policy it is to deprave the theatre. As a matter of fact, both the above stories are strictly in order from the official point of view. The incidents of sex which they contain, though carried in both to the extreme point at which another step would be dealt with, not by the King's Reader, but by the police, do not involve adultery, nor any allusion to Mrs. Warren's profession, nor to the fact that the children of any polyandrous group will, when they grow up, inevitably be confronted, as those of Mrs. Warren's group are in my play, with the insoluble problem of their own possible consanguinity. In short, by depending wholly on the coarse humors and the physical fascination of sex, they comply with all the formulable requirements of the Censorship, whereas plays in which these humors and fascinations are discarded, and the social problems created by sex seriously faced and dealt with, inevitably ignore the official formula and are suppressed. If the old rule against the exhibition of illicit sex relations on the stage were revived, and the subject absolutely barred, the only result would be that *Antony and Cleopatra, Othello* (because of the Bianca episode), *Troilus and Cressida, Henry IV, Measure for Measure, Timon of Athens, La Dame aux Camellias, The Profligate, The Second Mrs. Tanqueray, The Notorious Mrs. Ebbsmith, The Gay Lord Quex, Mrs. Dane's Defence,* and *Iris* would be swept from the stage, and placed under the same ban as Tolstoy's *Dominion of Darkness* and *Mrs. Warren's Profession,* whilst such plays as the two described above would have a monopoly of the theatre as far as sexual interest is concerned.

What is more, the repulsiveness of the worst of the certified plays would protect Censorship against effective exposure and criticism. Not long ago an American Review of high standing asked me for an article on the Censorship of the English Stage. I replied that such an article would involve passages too disagreeable for publication in a magazine for general family reading. The editor persisted nevertheless; but not until he had declared his readiness to face this, and had pledged himself to insert the article unaltered (the particularity of the pledge extending even to a specification of the exact number of words in the article) did I consent to the proposal. What was the result? The editor, confronted with the two stories given above, threw his pledge to the winds, and, instead of returning the article, printed it with the illustrative examples omitted, and nothing left but the argument from political principle against the Censorship. In doing this he fired my broadside after withdrawing the cannon balls; for neither the Censor nor any other Englishman, except perhaps Mr. Leslie Stephen and a few other veterans of the dwindling old guard of Benthamism, cares a dump about political principle. The ordinary Briton thinks that if every other Briton is not under some form of tutelage, the more childish the better, he will abuse his freedom viciously. As far as its principle is concerned, the Censorship is the most popular institution in England; and the playwright who criticizes it is slighted as a blackguard agitating for impunity. Consequently nothing can really shake the confidence of the public in the Lord Chamberlain's department except a remorseless and unbowdlerized narration of the licentious fictions which slip through its net, and are hallmarked by it with the approval of the throne. But as such stories cannot be made public without great difficulty, owing to the obligation an editor is under not to deal unexpectedly with matters that are not *virginibus puerisque,* the chances are heavily in favor of the Censor escaping all remonstrance. With the exception of such comments as I was able to make in my own

critical articles in the *World* and the *Saturday Review* when
the pieces I have described were first produced, and a few
ignorant protests by churchmen against much better plays
which they confessed they had not seen nor read, nothing
has been said in the press that could seriously disturb the
easy-going notion that the stage would be much worse than
it admittedly is but for the vigilance of the King's Reader.
The truth is, that no manager would dare produce on his
own responsibility the pieces he can now get royal certificates for at two guineas per piece.

I hasten to add that I believe these evils to be inherent in
the nature of all censorship, and not merely a consequence
of the form the institution takes in London. No doubt there
is a staggering absurdity in appointing an ordinary clerk to
see that the leaders of European literature do not corrupt
the morals of the nation, and to restrain Sir Henry Irving,
as a rogue and a vagabond, from presuming to impersonate
Samson or David on the stage, though any other sort of
artist may daub these scriptural figures on a signboard or
carve them on a tombstone without hindrance. If the General Medical Council, the Royal College of Physicians, the
Royal Academy of Arts, the Incorporated Law Society,
and Convocation were abolished, and their functions handed
over to Mr. Redford, the Concert of Europe would presumably declare England mad and treat her accordingly. Yet,
though neither medicine nor painting nor law nor the Church
moulds the character of the nation as potently as the theatre
does, nothing can come on the stage unless its dimensions
admit of its first passing through Mr. Redford's mind! Pray
do not think that I question Mr. Redford's honesty. I am
quite sure that he sincerely thinks me a blackguard, and my
play a grossly improper one, because, like Tolstoy's *Dominion of Darkness*, it produces, as they are both meant to produce, a very strong and very painful impression of evil. I do
not doubt for a moment that the rapine play which I have
described, and which he licensed, was quite incapable in
manuscript of producing any particular effect on his mind at
all, and that when he was once satisfied that the ill-con-
ducted hero was a German and not an English officer, he
passed the play without studying its moral tendencies. Even
if he had undertaken that study, there is no more reason to
suppose that he is a competent moralist than there is to
suppose that I am a competent mathematician. But truly it
does not matter whether he is a moralist or not. Let nobody

dream for a moment that what is wrong with the Censorship
is the shortcoming of the gentleman who happens at any
moment to be acting as Censor. Replace him tomorrow by an
Academy of Letters and an Academy of Dramatic Poetry,
and the new filter will still exclude original and epoch-making
work, whilst passing conventional, old-fashioned, and vulgar
work without question. The conclave which compiles the
Index of the Roman Catholic Church is the most august,
ancient, learned, famous, and authoritative censorship in Europe. Is it more enlightened, more liberal, more tolerant than
the comparatively infinitesimal office of the Lord Chamberlain? On the contrary, it has reduced itself to a degree of
absurdity which makes a Catholic university a contradiction
in terms. All censorships exist to prevent anyone from challenging current conceptions and existing institutions. All
progress is initiated by challenging current conceptions, and
executed by supplanting existing institutions. Consequently
the first condition of progress is the removal of censorships.
There is the whole case against censorships in a nutshell.

It will be asked whether theatrical managers are to be allowed to produce what they like, without regard to the public
interest. But that is not the alternative. The managers of our
London music halls are not subject to any censorship. They
produce their entertainments on their own responsibility,
and have no two-guinea certificates to plead if their houses
are conducted viciously. They know that if they lose their
character, the County Council will simply refuse to renew
their license at the end of the year; and nothing in the
history of popular art is more amazing than the improvement
in music halls that this simple arrangement has produced
within a few years. Place the theatres on the same footing,
and we shall promptly have a similar revolution: a whole
class of frankly blackguardly plays, in which unscrupulous
low comedians attract crowds to gaze at bevies of girls who
have nothing to exhibit but their prettiness, will vanish like
the obscene songs which were supposed to enliven the squalid
dulness, incredible to the younger generation, of the music
halls fifteen years ago. On the other hand, plays which treat
sex questions as problems for thought instead of as aphrodisiacs will be freely performed. Gentlemen of Mr. Redford's
way of thinking will have plenty of opportunity of protesting against them in Council; but the result will be that Mr.
Redford will find his natural level; Ibsen and Tolstoy theirs;
so no harm will be done.

This question of the Censorship reminds me that I have to apologize to those who went to the recent performance of *Mrs. Warren's Profession* expecting to find it what I have just called an aphrodisiac. That was not my fault: it was Mr. Redford's. After the specimens I have given of the tolerance of his department, it was natural enough for thoughtless people to infer that a play which overstepped his indulgence must be a very exciting play indeed. Accordingly, I find one critic so explicit as to the nature of his disappointment as to say candidly that "such airy talk as there is upon the matter is utterly unworthy of acceptance as being a representation of what people with blood in them think or do on such occasions." Thus am I crushed between the upper millstone of Mr. Redford, who thinks me a libertine, and the nether popular critic, who thinks me a prude. Critics of all grades and ages, middle-aged fathers of families no less than ardent young enthusiasts, are equally indignant with me. They revile me as lacking in passion, in feeling, in manhood. Some of them even sum the matter up by denying me any dramatic power: a melancholy betrayal of what dramatic power has come to mean on our stage under the Censorship! Can I be expected to refrain from laughing at the spectacle of a number of respectable gentlemen lamenting because a playwright lures them to the theatre by a promise to excite their senses in a very special and sensational manner, and then, having successfully trapped them in exceptional numbers, proceeds to ignore their senses and ruthlessly improve their minds? But I protest again that the lure was not mine. The play had been in print for four years; and I have spared no pains to make known that my plays are built to induce, not voluptuous reverie but intellectual interest, not romantic rhapsody but humane concern. Accordingly, I do not find those critics who are gifted with intellectual appetite and political conscience complaining of want of dramatic power. Rather do they protest, not altogether unjustly, against a few relapses into staginess and caricature which betray the young playwright and the old playgoer in this early work of mine. As to the voluptuaries, I can assure them that the playwright, whether he be myself or another, will always disappoint them. The drama can do little to delight the senses: all the apparent instances to the contrary are instances of the personal fascination of the performers. The drama of pure feeling is no longer in the hands of the playwright: it has been conquered by the musician, after whose enchantments all the verbal arts seem cold and tame. *Romeo and Juliet* with the loveliest Juliet is dry, tedious, and rhetorical in comparison with Wagner's *Tristan*, even though Isolde be both fourteen stone and forty, as she often is in Germany. Indeed, it needed no Wagner to convince the public of this. The voluptuous sentimentality of Gounod's *Faust* and Bizet's *Carmen* has captured the common playgoer; and there is, flatly, no future now for any drama without music except the drama of thought. The attempt to produce a genus of opera without music—and this absurdity is what our fashionable theatres have been driving at for a long time past without knowing it—is far less hopeful than my own determination to accept problem as the normal material of the drama.

That this determination will throw me into a long conflict with our theatre critics, and with the few playgoers who go to the theater as often as the critics, I well know; but I am too well equipped for the strife to be deterred by it, or to bear malice towards the losing side. In trying to produce the sensuous effects of opera, the fashionable drama has become so flaccid in its sentimentality, and the intellect of its frequenters so atrophied by disuse, that the reintroduction of problem, with its remorseless logic and iron framework of fact, inevitably produces at first an overwhelming impression of coldness and inhuman rationalism. But this will soon pass away. When the intellectual muscle and moral nerve of the critics has been developed in the struggle with modern problem plays, the pettish luxuriousness of the clever ones, and the sulky sense of disadvantaged weakness in the sentimental ones, will clear away; and it will be seen that only in the problem play is there any real drama, because drama is no mere setting up of the camera to nature: it is the presentation in parable of the conflict between Man's will and his environment: in a word, of problem. The vapidness of such drama as the pseudo-operatic plays contain lies in the fact that in them animal passion, sentimentally diluted, is shown in conflict, not with real circumstances, but with a set of conventions and assumptions half of which do not exist off the stage, whilst the other half can either be evaded by a pretence of compliance or defied with complete impunity by any reasonably strong-minded person. Nobody can feel that such conventions are really compulsory; and consequently nobody can believe in the stage pathos that accepts them as an inexorable fate, or in the reality of the figures who indulge in such pathos. Sitting at such plays we do not believe: we make believe. And the habit of make believe becomes at last so rooted, that criticism of the theatre insensibly ceases to be criticism at all, and becomes more and more a chronicle of the fashionable enterprises of the only realities left on the stage: that is, the performers in their own persons. In this phase the playwright who attempts to revive genuine drama produces the disagreeable impression of the pedant who attempts to start a serious discussion at a fashionable at-home. Later on, when he has driven the tea services out and made the people who had come to use the theatre as a drawing-room understand that it is they and not the dramatists who are the intruders, he has to face the accusation that his plays ignore human feeling, an illusion produced by that very resistance of fact and law to human feeling which creates drama. It is the *deus ex machina* who, by suspending that resistance, makes the fall of the curtain an immediate necessity, since drama ends exactly where resistance ends. Yet the introduction of this resistance produces so strong an impression of heartlessness nowadays that a distinguished critic has summed up the impression made on him by *Mrs. Warren's Profession*, by declaring that "the difference between the spirit of Tolstoy and the spirit of Mr. Shaw is the difference between the spirit of Christ and the spirit of Euclid." But the epigram would be as good if Tolstoy's name were put in place of mine and D'Annunzio's in place of Tolstoy's. At the same time I accept the enormous compliment to my reasoning powers with sincere complacency; and I promise my flatterer that when he is sufficiently accustomed to and therefore undazzled by problem on the stage to be able to attend to the familiar factor of humanity in it as well as to the unfamiliar one of a real environment, he will both see and feel that *Mrs. Warren's Profession* is no mere theorem, but a play of instincts and temperaments in conflict with each other and with a flinty social problem that never yields an inch to mere sentiment.

I go further than this. I declare that the real secret of the cynicism and inhumanity of which shallower critics accuse me is the unexpectedness with which my characters behave like human beings, instead of conforming to the romantic logic of the stage. The axioms and postulates of that dreary mimanthropometry are so well known that it is almost impossible for its slaves to write tolerable last acts to their plays, so conventionally do their conclusions follow from their premises. Because I have thrown this logic ruthlessly overboard, I am accused of ignoring, not state logic, but, of all things, human feeling. People with completely theatrified imaginations tell me that no girl would treat her mother as Vivie Warren does, meaning that no stage heroine would in a popular sentimental play. They say this just as they might say that no two straight lines would inclose a space. They do not see how completely inverted their vision has become even when I throw its preposterousness in their faces, as I repeatedly do in this very play. Praed, the sentimental artist (fool that I was not to make him a playwright instead of an architect!), burlesques them by expecting all through the piece that the feelings of the others will be logically deducible from their family relationships and from his "conventionally unconventional" social code. The sarcasm is lost on the critics: they, saturated with the same logic, only think him the sole sensible person on the stage. Thus it comes about that the more completely the dramatist is emancipated from the illusion that men and women are primarily reasonable beings, and the more powerfully he insists on the ruthless indifference of their great dramatic antagonist, the external world, to their whims and emotions, the surer he is to be denounced as blind to the very distinction on which his whole work is built. Far from ignoring idiosyncrasy, will, passion, impulse, whim, as factors in human action, I have placed them so nakedly on the stage that the elderly citizen, accustomed to see them clothed with the veil of manufactured logic about duty, and to disguise even his own impulses from himself in this way, finds the picture as unnatural as Carlyle's suggested painting of parliament sitting without its clothes.

I now come to those critics who, intellectually baffled by the problem in *Mrs. Warren's Profession*, have made a virtue of running away from it. I will illustrate their method by a quotation from Dickens, taken from the fifth chapter of *Our Mutual Friend*:

"Hem!" began Wegg. "This, Mr. Boffin and Lady, is the first chapter of the first wollume of the Decline and Fall off——" here he looked hard at the book, and stopped.

"What's the matter, Wegg?"

"Why it comes into my mind, do you know, sir," said Wegg with an air of insinuating frankness (having first again looked hard at the book), "that you made a little mistake this morning

which I had meant to set you right in; only something put it out
of my head. I think you said Rooshan Empire, sir?"

"It is Rooshan; ain't it Wegg?"

"No, sir. Roman. Roman."

"What's the difference, Wegg?"

"The difference, sir?" Mr. Wegg was faltering and in danger
of breaking down, when a bright thought flashed upon him. "The
difference, sir? There you place me in a difficulty, Mr. Boffin.
Suffice it to observe that the difference is best postponed to some
other occasion when Mrs. Boffin does not honor us with her
company. In Mrs. Boffin's presence, sir, we had better drop it."

Mr. Wegg thus came out of his disadvantage with quite a
chivalrous air, and not only that, but by dint of repeating with
a manly delicacy, "In Mrs. Boffin's presence, sir, we had better
drop it!" turned the disadvantage on Boffin, who felt that he had
committed himself in a very painful manner.

I am willing to let Mr. Wegg drop it on these terms, provided that I am allowed to mention here that *Mrs. Warren's
Profession* is a play for women; that it was written for
women; that it has been performed and produced mainly
through the determination of women that it should be performed and produced; that the enthusiasm of women made
its first performance excitingly successful; and that not one
of these women had any inducement to support their belief
their belief in the timeliness and the power of the lesson the
play teaches. Those who were "surprised to see ladies present" were men; and when they proceeded to explain that the
journals they represented could not possibly demoralize the
public by describing such a play, their editors cruelly devoted the space saved by their delicacy to an elaborate and
respectful account of the progress of a young lord's attempt
to break the bank at Monte Carlo. A few days sooner Mrs.
Warren would have been crowded out of their papers by an
exceptionally abominable police case. I do not suggest that
the police case should have been suppressed; but neither do
I believe that regard for public morality had anything to do
with their failure to grapple with the performance of the
Stage Society. And, after all, there was no need to fall back
on Silas Wegg's subterfuge. Several critics saved the faces of
their papers easily enough by the simple expedient of saying
all they had to say in the tone of a shocked governess lecturing a naughty child. To them, I might plead, in Mrs.
Warren's words, "Well, it's only good manners to be
ashamed, dearie;" but it surprises me, recollecting as I do

Fanny Brough's delivery of that line, that gentlemen who shivered like violets in a zephyr as it swept through them, should so completely miss the full width of its application as to go home and straightway make a public exhibition of mock modesty.

My old Independent Theatre manager, Mr. Grein, besides that reproach to me for shattering his ideals, complains that Mrs. Warren is not wicked enough, and names several romancers who would have clothed her black soul with all the terrors of tragedy. I have no doubt they would; but that is just what I did not want to do. Nothing would please our sanctimonious British public more than to throw the whole guilt of Mrs. Warren's profession on Mrs. Warren herself. Now, the whole aim of my play is to throw that guilt on the British public itself. You may remember that when you produced my first play, *Widowers' Houses,* exactly the same misunderstanding arose. When the virtuous young gentleman rose up in wrath against the slum landlord, the slum landlord very effectually shewed him that slums are the product, not of individual Harpagons, but of the indifference of virtuous young gentlemen to the condition of the city they live in, provided they live at the west end of it on money earned by somebody else's labor. The notion that prostitution is created by the wickedness of Mrs. Warren is as silly as the notion—prevalent, nevertheless, to some extent in Temperance circles—that drunkenness is created by the wickedness of the publican. Mrs. Warren is not a whit a worse woman than the reputable daughter who cannot endure her. Her indifference to the ultimate social consequences of her means of making money, and her discovery of that means by the ordinary method of taking the line of least resistance to getting it, are too common in English society to call for any special remark. Her vitality, her thrift, her energy, her outspokenness, her wise care of her daughter, and the managing capacity which has enabled her and her sister to climb from the fried fish shop down by the mint to the establishments of which she boasts, are all high English social virtues. Her defence of herself is so overwhelming that it provokes the *St. James's Gazette* to declare that "the tendency of the play is wholly evil" because "it contains one of the boldest and most specious defences of an immoral life for poor women that has ever been penned." Happily the *St. James's Gazette* here speaks in its haste. Mrs. Warren's defence of herself is not only bold and specious, but valid

and unanswerable. But it is no defence at all of the vice
which she organizes. It is no defence of an immoral life
to say that the alternative offered by society collectively to
poor women is a miserable life, starved, overworked, fetid,
ailing, ugly. Though it is quite natural and *right* for Mrs.
Warren to choose what is, according to her lights, the least
immoral alternative, it is none the less infamous of society
to offer such alternatives. For the alternatives offered are
not morality and immorality, but two sorts of immorality.
The man who cannot see that starvation, overwork, dirt, and
disease are as immoral as prostitution—that they are the
vices and crimes of a nation, and not merely its misfor-
tunes—is (to put it as politely as possible) a hopelessly Private
Person.

The notion that Mrs. Warren must be a fiend is only an
example of the violence and passion which the slightest
reference to sex rouses in undisciplined minds, and which
makes it seem natural to our lawgivers to punish silly and
negligible indecencies with a ferocity unknown in dealing
with, for example, ruinous financial swindling. Had my
play been entitled *Mr. Warren's Profession*, and Mr. Warren
been a bookmaker, nobody would have expected me to make
him a villain as well. Yet gambling is a vice, and bookmaking an institution, for which there is absolutely nothing to be said. The moral and economic evil done by trying
to get other people's money without working for it (and this
is the essence of gambling) is not only enormous but un-
compensated. There are no two sides to the question of
gambling, no circumstances which force us to tolerate it
lest its suppression lead to worse things, no consensus of
opinion among responsible classes, such as magistrates and
military commanders, that it is a necessity, no Athenian
records of gambling made splendid by the talents of its professors, no contention that instead of violating morals it only
violates a legal institution which is in many respects oppressive and unnatural, no possible plea that the instinct
on which it is founded is a vital one. Prostitution can confuse the issue with all these excuses: gambling has none of
them. Consequently, if Mrs. Warren must needs be a demon,
a bookmaker must be a cacodemon. Well, does anybody who
knows the sporting world really believe that bookmakers are
worse than their neighbors? On the contrary, they have to
be a good deal better; for in that world nearly everybody
whose social rank does not exclude such an occupation would

be a bookmaker if he could; but the strength of character required for handling large sums of money and for strict settlements and unflinching payment of losses is so rare that successful bookmakers are rare too. It may seem that at least public spirit cannot be one of a bookmaker's virtues; but I can testify from personal experience that excellent public work is done with money subscribed by bookmakers. It is true that there are abysses in bookmaking: for example, welshing. Mr. Grein hints that there are abysses in Mrs. Warren's profession also. So there are in every profession: the error lies in supposing that every member of them sounds these depths. I sit on a public body which prosecutes Mrs. Warren zealously; and I can assure Mr. Grein that she is often leniently dealt with because she has conducted her business "respectably" and held herself above its vilest branches. The degrees in infamy are as numerous and as scrupulously observed as the degrees in the peerage: the moralist's notion that there are depths at which the moral atmosphere ceases is as delusive as the rich man's notion that there are no social jealousies or snobberies among the very poor. No: had I drawn Mrs. Warren as a fiend in human form, the very people who now rebuke me for flattering her would probably be the first to deride me for deducing character logically from occupation instead of observing it accurately in society.

One critic is so enslaved by this sort of logic that he calls my portraiture of the Rev. Samuel Gardner an attack on religion. According to this view Subaltern Iago is an attack on the army, Sir John Falstaff an attack on knighthood, and King Claudius an attack on royalty. Here again the clamor for naturalness and human feeling, raised by so many critics when they are confronted by the real thing on the stage, is really a clamor for the most mechanical and superficial sort of logic. The dramatic reason for making the clergyman what Mrs. Warren calls "an old stick-in-the-mud," whose son, in spite of much capacity and charm, is a cynically worthless member of society, is to set up a mordant contrast between him and the woman of infamous profession, with her well-brought-up, straightforward, hardworking daughter. The critics who have missed the contrast have doubtless observed often enough that many clergymen are in the church through no genuine calling, but simply because, in circles which can command preferment, it is the refuge of "the fool of the family"; and that clergymen's sons are often conspicuous reactionists against the restraints imposed on them in

childhood by their father's profession. These critics must
know, too, from history if not from experience, that women
as unscrupulous as Mrs. Warren have distinguished themselves as administrators and rulers, both commercially and
politically. But both observation and knowledge are left behind when journalists go to the theatre. Once in their stalls,
they assume that it is "natural" for clergymen to be saintly,
for soldiers to be heroic, for lawyers to be hard-hearted, for
sailors to be simple and generous, for doctors to perform
miracles with little bottles, and for Mrs. Warren to be a beast
and a demon. All this is not only not natural, but not
dramatic. A man's profession only enters into the drama of
his life when it comes into conflict with his nature. The result
of this conflict is tragic in Mrs. Warren's case, and comic in
the clergyman's case (at least we are savage enough to laugh
at it); but in both cases it is illogical, and in both cases natural. I repeat, the critics who accuse me of sacrificing nature
to logic are so sophisticated by their profession that to them
logic is nature, and nature absurdity.

Many friendly critics are too little skilled in social questions
and moral discussions to be able to conceive that respectable gentlemen like themselves, who would instantly call the
police to remove Mrs. Warren if she ventured to canvass
them personally, could possibly be in any way responsible
for her proceedings. They remonstrate sincerely, asking me
what good such painful exposures can possibly do. They
might as well ask what good Lord Shaftesbury did by devoting his life to the exposure of evils (by no means yet reme-
died) compared to which the worst things brought into view
or even into surmise in this play are trifles. The good of mentioning them is that you make people so extremely uncomfortable about them that they finally stop blaming "human
nature" for them, and begin to support measures for their
reform. Can anything be more absurd than the copy of *The
Echo* which contains a notice of the performance of my play?
It is edited by a gentleman who, having devoted his life to
work of the Shaftesbury type, exposes social evils and clamors
for their reform in every column except one; and that one is
occupied by the declaration of the paper's kindly theatre
critic, that the performance left him "wondering what useful
purpose the play was intended to serve." The balance has to
be redressed by the more fashionable papers, which usually
combine capable art criticism with West-End solecism on
politics and sociology. It is very noteworthy, however, on

comparing the press explosion produced by *Mrs. Warren's Profession* in 1902 with that produced by *Widowers' Houses* about ten years earlier, that whereas in 1892 the facts were frantically denied and the persons of the drama flouted as monsters of wickedness, in 1902 the facts are admitted, and the characters recognized, though it is suggested that this is exactly why no gentleman should mention them in public. Only one writer has ventured to imply this time that the poverty mentioned by Mrs. Warren has since been quietly relieved, and need not have been dragged back to the footlights. I compliment him on his splendid mendacity, in which he is unsupported, save by a little plea in a theatrical paper which is innocent enough to think that ten guineas a year with board and lodging is an impossibly low wage for a barmaid. It goes on to cite Mr. Charles Booth as having testified that there are many laborers' wives who are happy and contented on eighteen shillings a week. But I can go further than that myself. I have seen an Oxford agricultural laborer's wife looking cheerful on eight shillings a week; but that does not console me for the fact that agriculture in England is a ruined industry. If poverty does not matter as long as it is contented, then crime does not matter as long as it is unscrupulous. The truth is that it is only then that it does matter most desperately. Many persons are more comfortable when they are dirty than when they are clean; but that does not recommend dirt as a national policy.

Here I must for the present break off my arduous work of educating the press. We shall resume our studies later on; but just now I am tired of playing the preceptor; and the eager thirst of my pupils for improvement does not console me for the slowness of their progress. Besides I must reserve space to gratify my own vanity and do justice to the six artists who acted my play, by placing on record the hitherto unchronicled success of the first representation. It is not often that an author, after a couple of hours of those rare alternations of excitement and intensely attentive silence which only occur in the theatre when actors and audience are reacting on one another to the utmost, is able to step on the stage and apply the strong word genius to the representation with the certainty of eliciting an instant and overwhelming assent from the audience. That was my good fortune on the afternoon of Sunday, the fifth of January last. I was certainly extremely fortunate in my interpretors in the enterprise, and that not alone in respect of their artistic talent; for had it not been for their superhuman patience, their imperturbable good humor and good fellowship, there could have been no performance. The terror of the Censor's power gave us trouble enough to break up any ordinary commercial enterprise. Managers promised and even engaged their theatres to us after the most explicit warnings that the play was unlicensed, and at the last moment suddenly realized that Mr. Redford had their livelihoods in the hollow of his hand, and backed out. Over and over again the date and place were fixed and the tickets printed, only to be canceled, until at last the desperate and overworked manager of the Stage Society could only laugh, as criminals broken on the wheel used to laugh at the second stroke. We rehearsed under great difficulties. Christmas pieces and plays for the new year were being prepared in all directions; and my six actor colleagues were busy people, with engagements in these pieces in addition to their current professional work every night. On several raw winter days stages for rehearsal were unattainable even by the most distinguished applicants; and we shared corridors and saloons with them whilst the stage was given over to children in training for Boxing night. At last we had to rehearse at an hour at which no actor or actress has been out of bed within the memory of man; and we sardonically congratulated one another every morning on our rosy matutinal looks and the improvement wrought by early rising in our healths and characters. And all this, please observe, for a society without treasury or commercial prestige, for a play which was being denounced in advance as unmentionable, for an author without influence at the fashionable theatres! I victoriously challenge the West End managers to get as much done for interested motives, if they can.

Three causes made the production the most notable that has fallen to my lot. First, the veto of the Censor, which put the supporters of the play on their mettle. Second, the chivalry of the Stage Society, which, in spite of my urgent advice to the contrary, and my demonstration of the difficulties, dangers, and expenses the enterprise would cost, put my discouragements to shame and resolved to give battle at all costs to the attempt of the Censorship to suppress the play. Third, the artistic spirit of the actors, who made the play their own and carried it through triumphantly in spite of a

series of disappointments and annoyances much more trying
to the dramatic temperament than mere difficulties.

The acting, too, required courage and character as well
as skill and intelligence. The veto of the Censor introduced
a quite novel element of moral responsibility into the undertaking. And the characters were very unusual in the English
stage. The young heroine is, like her mother, an Englishwoman to the backbone, and not, like the heroines of our
fashionable drama, a prima donna of Italian origin. Consequently she was sure to be denounced as unnatural and un-
dramatic by the critics. The most vicious man in the play
is not in the least a stage villain: indeed, he regards his own
moral character with the sincere complacency of a hero of
melodrama. The amiable devotee of romance and beauty is
shown at an age which brings out the futilization which
these worships are apt to produce if they are made the staple
of life instead of the sauce. The attitude of the clever young
people to their elders is faithfully presented as one of piti-
less ridicule and unsympathetic criticism, and forms a spectacle incredible to those who, when young, were not cleverer
than their nearest elders, and painful to those sentimental
parents who shrink from the cruelty of youth, which pardons
nothing because it knows nothing. In short, the characters
and their relations are of a kind that the routineer critic
has not learned to place; so that their misunderstanding was a
foregone conclusion. Nevertheless, there was no hesitation
behind the curtain. When it went up at last, a stage much
too small for the company was revealed to an audience
much too small for the audience. But the players, though
it was impossible for them to forget their own discomfort,
at once made the spectators forget theirs. It certainly was a
model audience, responsible from the first line to the last;
and it got no less than it deserved in return.

I grieve to have to add that the second performance,
given for the edification of the London press and of those
members of the Stage Society who cannot attend the Sunday performances, was a less inspiriting one than the first.
A solid phalanx of theatre-weary journalists in an afternoon
humor, most of them committed to irreconcilable disparagement of problem plays, and all of them bound by etiquette
to be as undemonstrative as possible, is not exactly the sort
of audience that rises at the performers and cures them of
the inevitable reaction after an excitingly successful first
night. The artist nature is a sensitive and therefore a vindic-

tive one; and masterful players have a way with recalcitrant
audiences of rubbing a play into them instead of delighting
them with it. I should describe the second performance of
Mrs. Warren's Profession, especially as to its earlier stages,
as decidedly a rubbed-in one. The rubbing was no doubt
salutary; but it must have hurt some of the thinner skins.
The charm of the lighter passages fled; and the strong
scenes, though they again carried everything before them,
yet discharged that duty in a grim fashion, doing execution
on the enemy rather than moving them to repentance and
confession. Still, to those who had not seen the first performance, the effect was sufficiently impressive; and they
had the advantage of a fresh development in Mrs. Warren,
who, artistically jealous, as I took it, of the overwhelming
effect of the end of the second act on the previous day,
threw herself into the fourth act in quite a new way, and
achieved the apparently impossible feat of surpassing herself. The compliments paid to Miss Fanny Brough by the
critics, eulogistic as they are, are the compliments of men
three-fourths duped as Partridge was duped by Garrick. By
much of her acting they were so completely taken in that
they did not recognize it as acting at all. Indeed, none of
the six players quite escaped this consequence of their own
thoroughness. There was a distinct tendency among the less
experienced critics to complain of their sentiments and behavior. Naturally, the author does not share that grievance.

Pigcard's Cottage, January, 1902.

ACT ONE

*Summer afternoon in a cottage garden on the eastern
slope of a hill a little south of Haslemere in Surrey.
Looking up the hill, the cottage is seen in the left hand
corner of the garden, with its thatched roof and porch, and
a large latticed window to the left of the porch. Farther back
a little wing is built out, making an angle with the right side
wall. From the end of this wing a paling curves across and
forward, completely shutting in the garden, except for a gate
on the right. The common rises uphill beyond the paling to
the sky line. Some folded canvas garden chairs are leaning
against the side bench in the porch. A lady's bicycle is*

propped against the wall, under the window. A little to the right of the porch a hammock is slung from two posts. A big canvas umbrella, stuck in the ground, keeps the sun off the hammock, in which a young lady lies reading and making notes, her head towards the cottage and her feet towards the gate. In front of the hammock, and within reach of her hand, is a common kitchen chair, with a pile of serious-looking books and a supply of writing paper upon it.

A gentleman walking on the common comes into sight from behind the cottage. He is hardly past middle age, with something of the artist about him, unconventionally but carefully dressed, and clean-shaven except for a moustache, with an eager, susceptible face and very amiable and considerate manners. He has silky black hair, with waves of grey and white in it. His eyebrows are white, his moustache black. He seems not certain of his way. He looks over the paling; takes stock of the place; and sees the young lady.

THE GENTLEMAN [*taking off his hat*]. I beg your pardon. Can you direct me to Hindhead View—Mrs. Alison's?

THE YOUNG LADY [*glancing up from her book*]. This is Mrs. Alison's. [*She resumes her work.*]

THE GENTLEMAN. Indeed! Perhaps—may I ask are you Miss Vivie Warren?

THE YOUNG LADY [*sharply, as she turns on her elbow to get a good look at him*]. Yes.

THE GENTLEMAN [*daunted and conciliatory*]. I'm afraid I appear intrusive. My name is Praed. [*Vivie at once throws her books upon the chair, and gets out of the hammock.*] Oh, pray don't let me disturb you.

VIVIE [*striding to the gate and opening it for him*]. Come in, Mr. Praed. [*He comes in.*] Glad to see you. [*She proffers her hand and takes his with a resolute and hearty grip. She is an attractive specimen of the sensible, able, highly-educated young middle-class Englishwoman. Age 22. Prompt, strong, confident, self-possessed. Plain, business-like dress, but not dowdy. She wears a chatelaine at her belt, with a fountain pen and a paper knife among its pendants.*]

PRAED. Very kind of you indeed, Miss Warren. [*She shuts the gate with a vigorous slam: he passes in to the middle of the garden, exercising his fingers, which are slightly numbed by her greeting.*] Has your mother arrived?

VIVIE [*quickly, evidently scenting aggression*]. Is she coming?

PRAED [*surprised*]. Didn't you expect us?

VIVIE. No.

PRAED. Now, goodness me, I hope I've not mistaken the day. That would be just like me, you know. Your mother arranged that she was to come down from London and that I was to come over from Horsham to be introduced to you.

VIVIE [*not at all pleased*]. Did she? H'm! My mother has rather a trick of taking me by surprise—to see how I behave myself when she's away, I suppose. I fancy I shall take my mother very much by surprise one of these days, if she makes arrangements that concern me without consulting me beforehand. She hasn't come.

PRAED [*embarrassed*]. I'm really very sorry.

VIVIE [*throwing off her displeasure*]. It's not your fault, Mr. Praed, is it? And I'm very glad you've come, believe me. You are the only one of my mother's friends I have asked her to bring to see me.

PRAED [*relieved and delighted*]. Oh, now this is really very good of you, Miss Warren!

VIVIE. Will you come indoors; or would you rather sit out here whilst we talk?

PRAED. It will be nicer out here, don't you think?

VIVIE. Then I'll go and get you a chair. [*She goes to the porch for a garden chair.*]

PRAED [*following her*]. Oh, pray, pray! Allow me. [*He lays hands on the chair.*]

VIVIE [*letting him take it*]. Take care of your fingers: they're rather dodgy things, those chairs. [*She goes across to the chair with the books on it; pitches them into the hammock; and brings the chair forward with one swing.*]

PRAED [*who has just unfolded his chair*]. Oh, now do let me take that hard chair! I like hard chairs.

VIVIE. So do I. [*She sits down.*] Sit down, Mr. Praed. [*This invitation is given with genial peremptoriness, his anxiety to please her clearly striking her as a sign of weakness of character on her part.*]

PRAED. By the way, though, hadn't we better go to the station to meet your mother?

VIVIE [*coolly*]. Why? She knows the way. [*Praed hesitates, and then sits down in the garden chair, rather disconcerted*]. Do you know, you are just like what I expected. I hope you are disposed to be friends with me?

PRAED [*again beaming*]. Thank you, my dear Miss Warren; thank you. Dear me! I'm so glad your mother hasn't spoilt you!

VIVIE. How?

PRAED. Well, in making you too conventional. You know, my dear Miss Warren, I am a born anarchist. I hate authority. It spoils the relations between parent and child—even between mother and daughter. Now I was always afraid that your mother would strain her authority to make you very conventional. It's such a relief to find that she hasn't.

VIVIE. Oh! have I been behaving unconventionally?

PRAED. Oh, no: oh, dear no. At least not conventionally unconventionally, you understand. [*She nods. He goes on, with a cordial outburst.*] But it was so charming of you to say that you were disposed to be friends with me! You modern young ladies are splendid—perfectly splendid!

VIVIE [*dubiously*]. Eh? [*watching him with dawning disappointment as to the quality of his brains and character.*]

PRAED. When I was your age, young men and women were afraid of each other: there was no good fellowship—nothing real—only gallantry copied out of novels, and as vulgar and affected as it could be. Maidenly reserve!—gentlemanly chivalry!—always saying no when you meant yes!—simple purgatory for shy and sincere souls!

VIVIE. Yes, I imagine there must have been a frightful waste of time—especially women's time.

PRAED. Oh, waste of life, waste of everything. But things are improving. Do you know, I have been in a positive state of excitement about meeting you ever since your magnificent achievements at Cambridge—a thing unheard of in my day. It was perfectly splendid, your tieing with the third wrangler. Just the right place, you know. The first wrangler is always a dreamy, morbid fellow, in whom the thing is pushed to the length of a disease.

VIVIE. It doesn't pay. I wouldn't do it again for the same money.

PRAED [*aghast*]. The same money!

VIVIE. I did it for £50. Perhaps you don't know how it was. Mrs. Latham, my tutor at Newnham, told my mother that I could distinguish myself in the mathematical tripos if I went for it in earnest. The papers were full just then of Phillipa Summers beating the senior wrangler—you remember about it; and nothing would please my mother but that I should do the same thing. I said flatly that it was not worth my while to face the grind since I was not going in for teaching; but I offered to try for fourth wrangler or thereabouts for £50. She closed with me at that, after a little grumbling; and I was better than my bargain. But I wouldn't do it again for that. £200 would have been nearer the mark.

PRAED [*much damped*]. Lord bless me! That's a very practical way of looking at it.

VIVIE. Did you expect to find me an unpractical person?

PRAED. No, no. But surely it's practical to consider not only the work these honors cost, but also the culture they bring.

VIVIE. Culture! My dear Mr. Praed: do you know what the mathematical tripos means? It means grind, grind, grind, for six to eight hours a day at mathematics, and nothing but mathematics. I'm supposed to know something about science; but I know nothing except the mathematics it involves. I can make calculations for engineers, electricians, insurance companies, and so on; but I know next to nothing about engineering or electricity or insurance. I don't even know arithmetic well. Outside mathematics, lawn-tennis, eating, sleeping, cycling, and walking, I'm a more ignorant barbarian than any woman could possibly be who hadn't gone in for the tripos.

PRAED [*revolted*]. What a monstrous, wicked, rascally system! I knew it! I felt at once that it meant destroying all that makes womanhood beautiful.

VIVIE. I don't object to it on that score in the least. I shall turn it to very good account, I assure you.

PRAED. Pooh! In what way?

VIVIE. I shall set up in chambers in the city and work at actuarial calculations and conveyancing. Under cover of that I shall do some law, with one eye on the Stock Exchange all the time. I've come down here by myself to read law—not for a holiday, as my mother imagines. I hate holidays.

PRAED. You make my blood run cold. Are you to have no romance, no beauty in your life?

VIVIE. I don't care for either, I assure you.

PRAED. You can't mean that.

VIVIE. Oh yes I do. I like working and getting paid for it. When I'm tired of working, I like a comfortable chair, a cigar, a little whisky, and a novel with a good detective story in it.

PRAED [*in a frenzy of repudiation*]. I don't believe it. I

am an artist; and I can't believe it: I refuse to believe it. [*Enthusiastically.*] Ah, my dear Miss Warren, you haven't discovered yet, I see, what a wonderful world art can open up to you.

VIVIE. Yes, I have. Last May I spent six weeks in London with Honoria Fraser. Mamma thought we were doing a round of sight-seeing together; but I was really at Honoria's chambers in Chancery Lane every day, working away at actuarial calculations for her, and helping her as well as a greenhorn could. In the evenings we smoked and talked, and never dreamt of going out except for exercise. And I never enjoyed myself more in my life. I cleared all my expenses and got initiated into the business without a fee into the bargain.

PRAED. But bless my heart and soul, Miss Warren, do you call that trying art?

VIVIE. Wait a bit. That wasn't the beginning. I went up to town on an invitation from some artistic people in Fitzjohn's Avenue: one of the girls was a Newnham chum. They took me to the National Gallery, to the Opera, and to a concert where the band played all the evening—Beethoven and Wagner and so on. I wouldn't go through that experience again for anything you could offer me. I held out for civility's sake until the third day; and then I said, plump out, that I couldn't stand any more of it, and went off to Chancery Lane. Now you know the sort of perfectly splendid modern young lady I am. How do you think I shall get on with my mother?

PRAED [*startled*]. Well, I hope—er—

VIVIE. It's not so much what you hope as what you believe, that I want to know.

PRAED. Well, frankly, I am afraid your mother will be a little disappointed. Not from any shortcoming on your part— I don't mean that. But you are so different from her ideal.

VIVIE. What is her ideal like?

PRAED. Well, you must have observed, Miss Warren, that people who are dissatisfied with their own bringing up generally think that the world would be all right if everybody were to be brought up quite differently. Now your mother's life has been—er—I suppose you know—

VIVIE. I know nothing. [*Praed is appalled. His consternation grows as she continues.*] That's exactly my difficulty. You forget, Mr. Praed, that I hardly know my mother. Since I was a child I have lived in England, at school or

college, or with people paid to take charge of me. I have
been boarded out all my life; and my mother has lived in
Brussels or Vienna and never let me go to her. I only see
her when she visits England for a few days. I don't complain; it's been very pleasant; for people have been very
good to me; and there has always been plenty of money to
make things smooth. But don't imagine I know anything
about my mother. I know far less than you do.

PRAED [*very ill at ease*]. In that case—[*He stops, quite at
a loss. Then, with a forced attempt at gaiety.*] But what nonsense we are talking! Of course you and your mother will
get on capitally. [*He rises, and looks abroad at the view.*]
What a charming little place you have here!

VIVIE [*unmoved*]. If you think you are doing anything
but confirming my worst suspicions by changing the subject
like that, you must take me for a much greater fool than I
hope I am.

PRAED. Your worst suspicions! Oh, pray don't say that.
Now don't.

VIVIE. Why won't my mother's life bear being talked
about?

PRAED. Pray think, Miss Vivie. It is natural that I should
have a certain delicacy in talking to my old friend's daughter
about her behind her back. You will have plenty of opportunity of talking to her about it when she comes. [*Anxiously.*]
I wonder what is keeping her.

VIVIE. No: She won't talk about it either. [*Rising.*] However, I won't press you. Only mind this, Mr. Praed. I strongly suspect there will be a battle royal when my mother
hears of my Chancery Lane project.

PRAED [*ruefully*]. I'm afraid there will.

VIVIE. I shall win the battle, because I want nothing but
my fare to London to start there to-morrow earning my own
living by devilling for Honoria. Besides, I have no mysteries
to keep up; and it seems she has. I shall use that advantage
over her if necessary.

PRAED [*greatly shocked*]. Oh, no. No, pray. You'd not
do such a thing.

VIVIE. Then tell me why not.

PRAED. I really cannot. I appeal to your good feeling.
[*She smiles at his sentimentality.*] Besides, you may be too
bold. Your mother is not to be trifled with when she's
angry.

VIVIE. You can't frighten me, Mr. Praed. In that month

at Chancery Lane I had opportunities of taking the measure
of one or two women very like my mother who came to
consult Honoria. You may back me to win. But if I hit
harder in my ignorance than I need, remember that it is you
who refuse to enlighten me. Now let us drop the subject.
[*She takes her chair and replaces it near the hammock with
the same vigorous swing as before.*]

PRAED [*taking a desperate resolution*]. One word, Miss
Warren. I had better tell you. It's very difficult; but—

[*Mrs. Warren and Sir George Crofts arrive at the gate.
Mrs. Warren is a woman between 40 and 50, good-looking,
showily dressed in a brilliant hat and a gay blouse fitting
tightly over her bust and flanked by fashionable sleeves.
Rather spoiled and domineering, but, on the whole, a genial
and fairly presentable old blackguard of a woman.*

*Crofts is a tall, powerfully-built man of about 50, fash-
ionably dressed in the style of a young man. Nasal voice,
reedier than might be expected from his strong frame. Clean-
shaven, bull-dog jaws, large flat ears, and thick neck, gentlemanly combination of the most brutal types of city man,
sporting man, and man about town.*]

VIVIE. Here they are. [*Coming to them as they enter the
garden.*] How do, mater. Mr. Praed's been here this half
hour, waiting for you.

MRS. WARREN. Well, if you've been waiting, Praddy, it's
your own fault: I thought you'd have had the gumption to know
I was coming by the 3:10 train. Vivie, put your hat on, dear:
you'll get sunburnt. Oh, forgot to introduce you. Sir George
Crofts, my little Vivie.

[*Crofts advances to Vivie with his most courtly manner.
She nods, but makes no motion to shake hands.*]

CROFTS. May I shake hands with a young lady whom I
have known by reputation very long as the daughter of one
of my oldest friends?

VIVIE [*who has been looking him up and down sharply*].
If you like. [*She takes his tenderly proffered hand and gives
it a squeeze that makes him open his eyes; then turns away
and says to her mother*] Will you come in, or shall I get a
couple more chairs? [*She goes into the porch for the chairs.*]

MRS. WARREN. Well, George, what do you think of her?

CROFTS [*ruefully*]. She has a powerful fist. Did you shake
hands with her, Praed?

PRAED. Yes: it will pass off presently.

CROFTS. I hope so. [*Vivie reappears with two more chairs. He hurries to her assistance.*] Allow me.

MRS. WARREN [*patronizingly*]. Let Sir George help you with the chairs, dear.

VIVIE [*almost pitching two into his arms*]. Here you are. [*She dusts her hands and turns to Mrs. Warren.*] You'd like some tea, wouldn't you?

MRS. WARREN [*sitting in Praed's chair and fanning herself*]. I'm dying for a drop to drink.

VIVIE. I'll see about it. [*She goes into the cottage. Sir George has by this time managed to unfold a chair and plant it beside Mrs. Warren, on her left. He throws the other on the grass and sits down, looking dejected and rather foolish, with the handle of his stick in his mouth. Praed, still very uneasy, fidgets about the garden on their right.*]

MRS. WARREN [*to Praed, looking at Crofts*]. Just look at him, Praddy: he looks cheerful, don't he? He's been worrying my life out these three years to have that little girl of mine shewn to him; and now that I've done it, he's quite out of countenance. [*Briskly.*] Come! sit up, George; and take your stick out of your mouth. [*Crofts sulkily obeys.*]

PRAED. I think, you know—if you don't mind my saying so—that we had better get out of the habit of thinking of her as a little girl. You see she has really distinguished herself; and I'm not sure, from what I have seen of her, that she is not older than any of us.

MRS. WARREN [*greatly amused*]. Only listen to him, George! Older than any of us! Well, she has been stuffing you nicely with her importance.

PRAED. But young people are particularly sensitive about being treated in that way.

MRS. WARREN. Yes; and young people have to get all that nonsense taken out of them, and a good deal more besides. Don't you interfere, Praddy. I know how to treat my own child as well as you do. [*Praed, with a grave shake of his head, walks up the garden with his hands behind his back. Mrs. Warren pretends to laugh, but looks after him with perceptible concern. Then she whispers to Crofts.*] What's the matter with him? What does he take it like that for?

CROFTS [*morosely*]. You're afraid of Praed.

MRS. WARREN. What! Me! Afraid of dear old Praddy! Why, a fly wouldn't be afraid of him.

CROFTS. You're afraid of him.

MRS. WARREN [*angry*]. I'll trouble you to mind your own business, and not try any of your sulks on me. I'm not afraid of you, anyhow. If you can't make yourself agreeable, you'd better go home. [*She gets up, and, turning her back on him, finds herself face to face with Praed.*] Come, Praddy, I know it was only your tender-heartedness. You're afraid I'll bully her.

PRAED. My dear Kitty: you think I'm offended. Don't imagine that: pray don't. But you know I often notice things that escape you; and though you never take my advice, you sometimes admit afterwards that you ought to have taken it.

MRS. WARREN. Well, what do you notice now?

PRAED. Only that Vivie is a grown woman. Pray, Kitty, treat her with every respect.

MRS. WARREN [*with genuine amazement*]. Respect! Treat my own daughter with respect! What next, pray!

VIVIE [*appearing at the cottage door and calling to Mrs. Warren*]. Mother: will you come up to my room and take your bonnet off before tea?

MRS. WARREN. Yes, dearie. [*She laughs indulgently at Praed and pats him on the cheek as she passes him on her way to the porch. She follows Vivie into the cottage.*]

CROFTS [*furtively*]. I say, Praed.

PRAED. Yes.

CROFTS. I want to ask you a rather particular question.

PRAED. Certainly. [*He takes Mrs. Warren's chair and sits close to Crofts.*]

CROFTS. That's right: they might hear us from the window. Look here: did Kitty ever tell you who that girl's father is?

PRAED. Never.

CROFTS. Have you any suspicion of who it might be?

PRAED. None.

CROFTS [*not believing him*]. I know, of course, that you perhaps might feel bound not to tell if she had said anything to you. But it's very awkward to be uncertain about it now that we shall be meeting the girl every day. We don't exactly know how we ought to feel towards her.

PRAED. What difference can that make? We take her on her own merits. What does it matter who her father was?

CROFTS [*suspiciously*]. Then you know who he was?

PRAED [*with a touch of temper*]. I said no just now. Did you not hear me?

CROFTS. Look here, Praed. I ask you as a particular favor. If you do know [*movement of protest from Praed*]— I only say, i f you know, you might at least set my mind at rest about her. The fact is I feel attracted towards her. Oh, don't be alarmed: it's quite an innocent feeling. That's what puzzles me about it. Why, for all I know, *I* might be her father.

PRAED. You! Impossible! Oh, no, nonsense!

CROFTS [*catching him up cunningly*]. You know for certain that I'm not?

PRAED. I know nothing about it, I tell you, any more than you. But really, Crofts—oh, no, it's out of the question. There's not the least resemblance.

CROFTS. As to that, there's no resemblance between her and her mother that I can see. I suppose she's not y o u r daughter, is she?

PRAED [*He meets the question with an indignant stare; then recovers himself with an effort and answers gently and gravely*]. Now listen to me, my dear Crofts. I have nothing to do with that side of Mrs. Warren's life, and never had. She has never spoken to me about it; and of course I have never spoken to her about it. Your delicacy will tell you that a handsome woman needs s o m e friends who are not— well, not on that footing with her. The effect of her own beauty would become a torment to her if she could not escape from it occasionally. You are probably on much more confidential terms with Kitty than I am. Surely you can ask her the question yourself.

CROFTS [*rising impatiently*]. I h a v e asked her often enough. But she's so determined to keep the child all to herself that she would deny that it ever had a father if she could. No: there's nothing to be got out of her—nothing that one can believe, anyhow. I'm thoroughly uncomfortable about it, Praed.

PRAED [*rising also*]. Well, as you are, at all events, old enough to be her father, I don't mind agreeing that we both regard Miss Vivie in a parental way, as a young girl whom we are bound to protect and help. All the more, as the real father, whoever he was, was probably a blackguard. What do you say?

CROFTS [*aggressively*]. I'm no older than you, if you come to that.

PRAED. Yes, you are, my dear fellow: you were born

old. I was born a boy: I've never been able to feel the assurance of a grown-up man in my life.

MRS. WARREN [*calling from within the cottage*]. Prad-dee!
George! Tea-ea-ea-ea!

CROFTS [*hastily*]. She's calling us. [*He hurries in. Praed
shakes his head bodingly, and is following slowly when he is
hailed by a young gentleman who has just appeared on the
common, and is making for the gate. He is a pleasant, pretty,
smartly dressed, and entirely good-for-nothing young fellow,
not long turned 20, with a charming voice and agreeably
disrespectful manner. He carries a very light sporting magazine rifle.*]

THE YOUNG GENTLEMAN. Hallo! Praed!

PRAED. Why, Frank Gardner! [*Frank comes in and
shakes hands cordially.*] What on earth are you doing here?

FRANK. Staying with my father.

PRAED. The Roman father?

FRANK. He's rector here. I'm living with my people this
autumn for the sake of economy. Things came to a crisis in
July: the Roman father had to pay my debts. He's stony
broke in consequence; and so am I. What are you up to in
these parts? Do you know the people here?

PRAED. Yes: I'm spending the day with a Miss Warren.

FRANK [*enthusiastically*].What! Do you know Vivie? Isn't
she a jolly girl! I'm teaching her to shoot—you see [*shewing
the rifle.*]! I'm so glad she knows you: you're just the sort
of fellow she ought to know. [*He smiles, and raises the
charming voice almost to a singing tone as he exclaims*] It's
ever so jolly to find you here, Praed. Ain't it, now?

PRAED. I'm an old friend of her mother's. Mrs. Warren
brought me over to make her daughter's acquaintance.

FRANK. The mother! Is she here?

PRAED. Yes—inside at tea.

MRS. WARREN [*calling from within*]. Prad-dee-ee-ee-eee!
The tea-cake'll be cold.

PRAED [*calling*]. Yes, Mrs. Warren. In a moment. I've
just met a friend here.

MRS. WARREN. A what?

PRAED [*louder*]. A friend.

MRS. WARREN. Bring him up.

PRAED. All right. [*To Frank.*] Will you accept the
invitation?

FRANK [*incredulous, but immensely amused*]. Is that
Vivie's mother?

PRAED. Yes.

FRANK. By Jove! What a lark! Do you think she'll like me?

PRAED. I've no doubt you'll make yourself popular, as usual. Come in and try [*moving towards the house*].

FRANK. Stop a bit. [*Seriously.*] I want to take you into my confidence.

PRAED. Pray don't. It's only some fresh folly, like the barmaid at Redhill.

FRANK. It's ever so much more serious than that. You say you've only just met Vivie for the first time?

PRAED. Yes.

FRANK [*rhapsodically*]. Then you can have no idea what a girl she is. Such character! Such sense! And her cleverness! Oh, my eye, Praed, but I can tell you she is clever! And the most loving little heart that—

CROFTS [*putting his head out of the window*]. I say, Praed: what are you about? Do come along. [*He disappears.*]

FRANK. Hallo! Sort of chap that would take a prize at a dog show, ain't he? Who's he?

PRAED. Sir George Crofts, an old friend of Mrs. Warren's. I think we had better come in.

[*On their way to the porch they are interrupted by a call from the gate. Turning, they see an elderly clergyman looking over it.*]

THE CLERGYMAN [*calling*]. Frank!

FRANK. Hallo! [*To Praed.*] The Roman father. [*To the clergyman.*] Yes, gov'nor: all right: presently. [*To Praed.*] Look here, Praed: you'd better go in to tea. I'll join you directly.

PRAED. Very good. [*He raises his hat to the clergyman, who acknowledges the salute distantly. Praed goes into the cottage. The clergyman remains stiffly outside the gate, with his hands on the top of it. The Rev. Samuel Gardner, a beneficed clergyman of the Established Church, is over 50. He is a pretentious, booming, noisy person, hopelessly asserting himself as a father and a clergyman without being able to command respect in either capacity.*]

REV. S. Well, sir. Who are your friends here, if I may ask?

FRANK. Oh, it's all right, gov'nor! Come in.

REV. S. No, sir; not until I know whose garden I am entering.

FRANK. It's all right. It's Miss Warren's.

REV. S. I have not seen her at church since she came.

FRANK. Of course not: she's a third wrangler—ever so intellectual!—took a higher degree than you did; so why should she go to hear you preach?

REV. S. Don't be disrespectful, sir.

FRANK. Oh, it don't matter: nobody hears us. Come in. [*He opens the gate, unceremoniously pulling his father with it into the garden.*] I want to introduce you to her. She and I get on rattling well together: she's charming. Do you remember the advice you gave me last July, gov'nor?

REV. S. [*severely*]. Yes. I advised you to conquer your idleness and flippancy, and to work your way into an honorable profession and live on it and not upon me.

FRANK. No: that's what you thought of afterwards. What you actually said was that since I had neither brains nor money, I'd better turn my good looks to account by marrying somebody with both. Well, look here. Miss Warren has brains: you can't deny that.

REV. S. Brains are not everything.

FRANK. No, of course not: there's the money—

REV. S. [*interrupting him austerely*]. I was not thinking of money, sir. I was speaking of higher things—social position, for instance.

FRANK. I don't care a rap about that.

REV. S. But I do, sir.

FRANK. Well, nobody wants you to marry her. Anyhow, she has what amounts to a high Cambridge degree; and she seems to have as much money as she wants.

REV. S. [*sinking into a feeble vein of humor*]. I greatly doubt whether she has as much money as you will want.

FRANK. Oh, come: I haven't been so very extravagant. I live ever so quietly; I don't drink; I don't bet much; and I never go regularly on the razzle-dazzle as you did when you were my age.

REV. S. [*booming hollowly*]. Silence, sir.

FRANK. Well, you told me yourself, when I was making ever such an ass of myself about the barmaid at Redhill, that you once offered a woman £50 for the letters you wrote to her when—

REV. S. [*terrified*]. Sh-sh-sh, Frank, for Heaven's sake! [*He looks round apprehensively. Seeing no one within earshot he plucks up courage to boom again, but more subduedly.*] You are taking an ungentlemanly advantage of what I confided to you for your own good, to save you from an error you would have repented all your life long. Take warning by your father's follies, sir; and don't make them an excuse for your own.

FRANK. Did you ever hear the story of the Duke of Wellington and his letters?

REV. S. No, sir; and I don't want to hear it.

FRANK. The old Iron Duke didn't throw away £50—not he. He just wrote: "My dear Jenny: Publish and be damned! Yours affectionately, Wellington." That's what you should have done.

REV. S. [*piteously*]. Frank, my boy: when I wrote those letters I put myself into that woman's power. When I told you about her I put myself, to some extent, I am sorry to say, in your power. She refused my money with these words, which I shall never forget: "Knowledge is power," she said; "and I never sell power." That's more than twenty years ago; and she has never made use of her power or caused me a moment's uneasiness. You are behaving worse to me than she did, Frank.

FRANK. Oh, yes, I dare say! Did you ever preach at her the way you preach at me every day?

REV. S. [*wounded almost to tears*]. I leave you, sir. You are incorrigible. [*He turns towards the gate.*]

FRANK [*utterly unmoved*]. Tell them I shan't be home to tea, will you, gov'nor, like a good fellow? [*He goes towards the cottage door and is met by Vivie coming out, followed by Praed, Crofts, and Mrs. Warren.*]

VIVIE [*to Frank*]. Is that your father, Frank? I do so want to meet him.

FRANK. Certainly. [*Calling after his father.*] Gov'nor [*The Rev. S. turns at the gate, fumbling nervously at his hat. Praed comes down the garden on the opposite side, beaming in anticipation of civilities. Crofts prowls about near the hammock, poking it with his stick to make it swing. Mrs. Warren halts on the threshold, staring hard at the clergyman.*] Let me introduce—my father: Miss Warren.

VIVIE [*going to the clergyman and shaking his hand*]. Very glad to see you here, Mr. Gardner. Let me introduce everybody. Mr. Gardner—Mr. Frank Gardner—Mr. Praed—Sir George Crofts, and—[*As the men are raising their hats to one another, Vivie is interrupted by an exclamation from her mother, who swoops down on the Reverend Samuel*].

MRS. WARREN. Why, it's Sam Gardner, gone into the church! Don't you know us, Sam? This is George Crofts, as large as life and twice as natural. Don't you remember me?

REV. S. [*very red*]. I really—er—

MRS. WARREN. Of course you do. Why, I have a whole album of your letters still: I came across them only the other day.

REV. S. [*miserably confused*]. Miss Vavasour, I believe.

MRS. WARREN [*correcting him quickly in a loud whisper*]. Tch! Nonsense—Mrs. Warren: don't you see my daughter there?

ACT TWO

Inside the cottage after nightfall. Looking eastward from within instead of westward from without, the latticed window, with its curtains drawn, is now seen in the middle of the front wall of the cottage, with the porch door to the left of it. In the left-hand side wall is the door leading to the wing. Farther back against the same wall is a dresser with a candle and matches on it, and Frank's rifle standing beside them, with the barrel resting in the plate-rack. In the centre a table stands with a lighted lamp on it. Vivie's books and writing materials are on a table to the right of the window, against the wall. The fireplace is on the right, with a settle: there is no fire. Two of the chairs are set right and left of the table.

The cottage door opens, shewing a fine starlit night without; and Mrs. Warren, her shoulders wrapped in a shawl borrowed from Vivie, enters, followed by Frank. She has had enough of walking, and gives a gasp of relief as she unpins her hat; takes it off; sticks the pin through the crown; and puts it on the table.

MRS. WARREN. O Lord! I don't know which is the worst of the country, the walking or the sitting at home with nothing to do: I could do a whisky and soda now very well, if only they had such a thing in this place.

FRANK [*helping her to take off her shawl, and giving her shoulders the most delicate possible little caress with his fingers as he does so*]. Perhaps Vivie's got some.

MRS. WARREN [*glancing back at him for an instant from the corner of her eye as she detects the pressure*]. Nonsense! What would a young girl like her be doing with such things!

Never mind: it don't matter. [*She throws herself wearily into a chair at the table.*] I wonder how she passes her time here! I'd a good deal rather be in Vienna.

FRANK. Let me take you there. [*He folds the shawl neatly; hangs it on the back of the other chair; and sits down opposite Mrs. Warren.*]

MRS. WARREN. Get out! I'm beginning to think you're a chip of the old block.

FRANK. Like the gov'nor, eh?

MRS. WARREN. Never you mind. What do you know about such things? You're only a boy.

FRANK. Do come to Vienna with me? It'd be ever such larks.

MRS. WARREN. No, thank you. Vienna is no place for you—at least not until you're a little older. [*She nods at him to emphasize this piece of advice. He makes a mock-piteous face, belied by his laughing eyes. She looks at him; then rises and goes to him.*] Now, look here, little boy [*taking his face in her hands and turning it up to her*]: I know you through and through by your likeness to your father, better than you know yourself. Don't you go taking any silly ideas into your head about me. Do you hear?

FRANK [*gallantly wooing her with his voice*]. Can't help it, my dear Mrs. Warren: it runs in the family. [*She pretends to box his ears; then looks at the pretty, laughing, upturned face for a moment, tempted. At last she kisses him and immediately turns away, out of patience with herself.*]

MRS. WARREN. There! I shouldn't have done that. I am wicked. Never you mind, my dear: it's only a motherly kiss. Go and make love to Vivie.

FRANK. So I have.

MRS. WARREN [*turning on him with a sharp note of alarm in her voice*]. What!

FRANK. Vivie and I are ever such chums.

MRS. WARREN. What do you mean? Now, see here: I won't have any young scamp tampering with my little girl. Do you hear? I won't have it.

FRANK [*quite unabashed*]. My dear Mrs. Warren: don't you be alarmed. My intentions are honorable—ever so honorable; and your little girl is jolly well able to take care of herself. She don't need looking after half so much as her mother. She ain't so handsome, you know.

MRS. WARREN [*taken aback by his assurance*]. Well, you have got a nice, healthy two inches thick of cheek all over you. I don't know where you got it—not from your father, anyhow. [*Voices and footsteps in the porch*]. Sh! I hear the others coming in. [*She sits down hastily.*] Remember: you've got your warning. [*The Rev. Samuel comes in, followed by Crofts.*] Well, what became of you two? And where's Praddy and Vivie?

CROFTS [*putting his hat on the settle and his stick in the chimney corner*]. They went up the hill. We went to the village. I wanted a drink. [*He sits down on the settle, putting his legs up along the seat.*]

MRS. WARREN. Well, she oughtn't to go off like that without telling me. [*To Frank.*] Get your father a chair, Frank: where are your manners? [*Frank springs up and gracefully offers his father his chair; then takes another from the wall and sits down at the table, in the middle, with his father on his right and Mrs. Warren on his left.*] George: where are you going to stay to-night? You can't stay here. And what's Praddy going to do?

CROFTS. Gardner'll put me up.

MRS. WARREN. Oh, no doubt you've taken care of yourself! But what about Praddy?

CROFTS. Don't know. I suppose he can sleep at the inn.

MRS. WARREN. Haven't you room for him, Sam?

REV. S. Well, er—you see, as rector here, I am not free to do as I like exactly. Er—what is Mr. Praed's social position?

MRS. WARREN. Oh, he's all right: he's an architect. What an old-stick-in-the-mud you are, Sam!

FRANK. Yes, it's all right, gov'nor. He built that place down in Monmouthshire for the Duke of Beaufort—Tintern Abbey they call it. You must have heard of it. [*He winks with lightning smartness at Mrs. Warren, and regards his father blandly.*]

REV. S. Oh, in that case, of course we shall only be too happy. I suppose he knows the Duke of Beaufort personally.

FRANK. Oh, ever so intimately! We can stick him in Georgina's old room.

MRS. WARREN. Well, that's settled. Now, if those two would only come in and let us have supper. They've no right to stay out after dark like this.

CROFTS [*aggressively*]. What harm are they doing you?

MRS. WARREN. Well, harm or not, I don't like it.

FRANK. Better not wait for them, Mrs. Warren. Praed will stay out as long as possible. He has never known before what it is to stray over the heath on a summer night with my Vivie.

CROFTS [*sitting up in some consternation*]. I say, you know. Come!

REV. S. [*startled out of his professional manner into real force and sincerity*]. Frank, once for all, it's out of the question. Mrs. Warren will tell you that it's not to be thought of.

CROFTS. Of course not.

FRANK [*with enchanting placidity*]. Is that so, Mrs. Warren?

MRS. WARREN [*reflectively*]. Well, Sam, I don't know. If the girl wants to get married, no good can come of keeping her unmarried.

REV. S. [*astounded*]. But married to him!—your daughter to my son! Only think: it's impossible.

CROFTS. Of course it's impossible. Don't be a fool, Kitty.

MRS. WARREN [*nettled*]. Why not? Isn't my daughter good enough for your son?

REV. S. But surely, my dear Mrs. Warren, you know the reason—

MRS. WARREN [*defiantly*]. I know no reasons. If you know any, you can tell them to the lad, or to the girl, or to your congregation, if you like.

REV. S. [*helplessly*]. You know very well that I couldn't tell anyone the reasons. But my boy will believe me when I tell him there are reasons.

FRANK. Quite right, Dad: he will. But has your boy's conduct ever been influenced by your reasons?

CROFTS. You can't marry her; and that's all about it. [*He gets up and stands on the hearth, with his back to the fireplace, frowning determinedly.*]

MRS. WARREN [*turning on him sharply*]. What have you got to do with it, pray?

FRANK [*with his prettiest lyrical cadence*]. Precisely what I was going to ask, myself, in my own graceful fashion.

CROFTS [*to Mrs. Warren*]. I suppose you don't want to marry the girl to a man younger than herself and without either a profession or twopence to keep her on. Ask Sam, if you don't believe me. [*To the Rev. S.*] How much more money are you going to give him?

REV. S. Not another penny. He has had his patrimony; and he spent the last of it in July. [*Mrs. Warren's face falls.*]

CROFTS [*watching her*]. There! I told you. [*He resumes

*his place on the settle and puts up his legs on the seat again,
as if the matter were finally disposed of.*]

FRANK [*plaintively*]. This is ever so mercenary. Do
you suppose Miss Warren's going to marry for money? If we
love one another—

MRS. WARREN. Thank you. Your love's a pretty cheap
commodity, my lad. If you have no means of keeping a wife,
that settles it: you can't have Vivie.

FRANK [*much amused*]. What do you say, gov'nor, eh?

REV. S. I agree with Mrs. Warren.

FRANK. And good old Crofts has already expressed his
opinion.

CROFTS [*turning angrily on his elbow*]. Look here: I
want none of your cheek.

FRANK [*pointedly*]. I'm ever so sorry to surprise you,
Crofts; but you allowed yourself the liberty of speaking to
me like a father a moment ago. One father is enough, thank
you.

CROFTS [*contemptuously*]. Yah! [*He turns away again.*]

FRANK [*rising*]. Mrs. Warren: I cannot give my Vivie
up even for your sake.

MRS. WARREN [*muttering*]. Young scamp!

FRANK [*continuing*]. And as you no doubt intend to hold
out other prospects to her, I shall lose no time in placing my
case before her. [*They stare at him; and he begins to declaim
gracefully*]

> He either fears his fate too much,
>   Or his deserts are small,
> That dares not put it to the touch
>   To gain or lose it all.

[*The cottage door opens whilst he is reciting; and Vivie
and Praed come in. He breaks off. Praed puts his hat on the
dresser. There is an immediate improvement in the company's behaviour. Crofts takes down his legs from the settle
and pulls himself together as Praed joins him at the fireplace. Mrs. Warren loses her ease of manner, and takes
refuge in querulousness.*]

MRS. WARREN. Wherever have you been, Vivie?

VIVIE [*taking off her hat and throwing it carelessly on
the table*]. On the hill.

MRS. WARREN. Well, you shouldn't go off like that without letting me know. How could I tell what had become of
you—and night coming on, too!

VIVIE [*going to the door of the inner room and opening it, ignoring her mother*]. Now, about supper? We shall be rather crowded in here, I'm afraid.

MRS. WARREN. Did you hear what I said, Vivie?

VIVIE [*quietly*]. Yes, mother. [*Reverting to the supper difficulty.*] How many are we? [*Counting.*] One, two, three, four, five, six. Well, two will have to wait until the rest are done: Mrs. Alison has only plates and knives for four.

PRAED. Oh, it doesn't matter about me. I—

VIVIE. You have had a long walk and are hungry, Mr. Praed: you shall have your supper at once. I can wait myself. I want one person to wait with me. Frank: are you hungry?

FRANK. Not the least in the world—completely off my peck, in fact.

MRS. WARREN [*to Crofts*]. Neither are you, George. You can wait.

CROFTS. Oh, hang it, I've eaten nothing since tea-time. Can't Sam do it?

FRANK. Would you starve my poor father?

REV. S. [*testily*]. Allow me to speak for myself, sir. I am perfectly willing to wait.

VIVIE [*decisively*]. There's no need. Only two are wanted. [*She opens the door of the inner room.*] Will you take my mother in, Mr. Gardner. [*The Rev. S. takes Mrs. Warren; and they pass into the next room. Praed and Crofts follow. All except Praed clearly disapprove of the arrangement, but do not know how to resist it. Vivie stands at the door looking in at them.*] Can you squeeze past to that corner, Mr. Praed: it's rather a tight fit. Take care of your coat against the white-wash—that's right. Now, are you all comfortable?

PRAED [*within*]. Quite, thank you.

MRS. WARREN [*within*]. Leave the door open, dearie. [*Frank looks at Vivie; then steals to the cottage door and softly sets it wide open.*] Oh, Lor', what a draught! You'd better shut it, dear. [*Vivie shuts it promptly. Frank noiselessly shuts the cottage door.*]

FRANK [*exulting*]. Aha! Got rid of 'em. Well, Vivvums: what do you think of my governor!

VIVIE [*preoccupied and serious*]. I've hardly spoken to him. He doesn't strike me as being a particularly able person.

FRANK. Well, you know, the old man is not altogether such a fool as he looks. You see, he's rector here; and in trying to live up to it he makes a much bigger ass of himself than he really is. No, the gov'nor ain't so bad, poor old chap;

and I don't dislike him as much as you might expect. He means well. How do you think you'll get on with him?

VIVIE [*rather grimly*]. I don't think my future life will be much concerned with him, or with any of that old circle of my mother's, except perhaps Praed. What do you think of my mother?

FRANK. Really and truly?

VIVIE. Yes, really and truly.

FRANK. Well, she's ever so jolly. But she's rather a caution, isn't she? And Crofts! Oh, my eye, Crofts!

VIVIE. What a lot, Frank!

FRANK. What a crew!

VIVIE [*with intense contempt for them*]. If I thought that *I* was like that—that I was going to be a waster, shifting along from one meal to another with no purpose, and no character, and no grit in me, I'd open an artery and bleed to death without one moment's hesitation.

FRANK. Oh, no, you wouldn't. Why should they take any grind when they can afford not to? I wish I had their luck. No: what I object to is their form. It isn't the thing: it's slovenly, ever so slovenly.

VIVIE. Do you think your form will be any better when you're as old as Crofts, if you don't work?

FRANK. Of course I do—ever so much better. Vivvums mustn't lecture: her little boy's incorrigible. [*He attempts to take her face caressingly in his hands.*]

VIVIE [*striking his hands down sharply*]. Off with you: Vivvums is not in a humor for petting her little boy this evening.

FRANK. How unkind!

VIVIE [*stamping at him*]. Be serious. I'm serious.

FRANK. Good. Let us talk learnedly. Miss Warren: do you know that all the most advanced thinkers are agreed that half the diseases of modern civilization are due to starvation of the affections in the young. Now, I—

VIVIE [*cutting him short*]. You are getting tiresome. [*She opens the inner door.*] Have you room for Frank there? He's complaining of starvation.

MRS. WARREN [*within*]. Of course there is [*clatter of knives and glasses as she moves the things on the table*]. Here: there's room now beside me. Come along, Mr. Frank.

FRANK [*aside to Vivie, as he goes*]. Her little boy will be ever so even with his Vivvums for this. [*He goes into the other room.*]

MRS. WARREN [*within*]. Here, Vivie: come on, you too, child. You must be famished. [*She enters, followed by Crofts, who holds the door open for Vivie with marked deference. She goes out without looking at him; and he shuts the door after her.*] Why, George, you can't be done: you've eaten nothing.

CROFTS. Oh, all I wanted was a drink. [*He thrusts his hands in his pockets and begins prowling about the room, restless and sulky.*]

MRS. WARREN. Well, I like enough to eat. But a little of that cold beef and cheese and lettuce goes a long way. [*With a sigh of only half repletion she sits down lazily at the table.*]

CROFTS. What do you go encouraging that young pup for?

MRS. WARREN [*on the alert at once*]. Now see here, George: what are you up to about that girl? I've been watching your way of looking at her. Remember: I know you and what your looks mean.

CROFTS. There's no harm in looking at her, is there?

MRS. WARREN. I'd put you out and pack you back to London pretty soon if I saw any of your nonsense. My girl's little finger is more to me than your whole body and soul. [*Crofts receives this with a sneering grin. Mrs. Warren, flushing a little at her failure to impose on him in the character of a theatrically devoted mother, adds in a lower key.*] Make your mind easy: the young pup has no more chance than you have.

CROFTS. Mayn't a man take an interest in a girl?

MRS. WARREN. Not a man like you.

CROFTS. How old is she?

MRS. WARREN. Never you mind how old she is.

CROFTS. Why do you make such a secret of it?

MRS. WARREN. Because I choose.

CROFTS. Well, I'm not fifty yet; and my property is as good as it ever was—

MRS. WARREN [*interrupting him*]. Yes; because you're as stingy as you're vicious.

CROFTS [*continuing*]. And a baronet isn't to be picked up every day. No other man in my position would put up with you for a mother-in-law. Why shouldn't she marry me?

MRS. WARREN. You!

CROFTS. We three could live together quite comfortably. I'd die before her and leave her a bouncing widow with plenty of money. Why not? It's been growing in my mind all the time I've been walking with that fool inside there.

MRS. WARREN [*revolted*]. Yes; it's the sort of thing that would grow in your mind. [*He halts in his prowling; and the two look at one another, she steadfastly, with a sort of awe behind her contemptuous disgust: he stealthily, with a carnal gleam in his eye and a loose grin, tempting her.*]

CROFTS [*suddenly becoming anxious and urgent as he sees no sign of sympathy in her*]. Look here, Kitty: you're a sensible woman: you needn't put on any moral airs. I'll ask no more questions; and you need answer none. I'll settle the whole property on her; and if you want a cheque for yourself on the wedding day, you can name any figure you like—in reason.

MRS. WARREN. Faugh! So it's come to that with you, George, like all the other worn out old creatures.

CROFTS [*savagely*]. Damn you! [*She rises and turns fiercely on him; but the door of the inner room is opened just then; and the voices of the others are heard returning. Crofts, unable to recover his presence of mind, hurries out of the cottage. The clergyman comes back.*]

REV. S. [*looking round*]. Where is Sir George?

MRS. WARREN. Gone out to have a pipe. [*She goes to the fireplace, turning her back on him to compose herself. The clergyman goes to the table for his hat. Meanwhile Vivie comes in, followed by Frank, who collapses into the nearest chair with an air of extreme exhaustion. Mrs. Warren looks round at Vivie and says, with her affectation of maternal patronage even more forced than usual.*] Well, dearie: have you had a good supper?

VIVIE. You know what Mrs. Alison's suppers are. [*She turns to Frank and pets him.*] Poor Frank! was all the beef gone? did it get nothing but bread and cheese and ginger beer? [*Seriously, as if she had done quite enough trifling for one evening.*] Her butter is really awful. I must get some down from the stores.

FRANK. Do, in Heaven's name!

[*Vivie goes to the writing-table and makes a memorandum to order the butter. Praed comes in from the inner room, putting up his handkerchief, which he has been using as a napkin.*]

REV. S. Frank, my boy: it is time for us to be thinking of home. Your mother does not know yet that we have visitors.

PRAED. I'm afraid we're giving trouble.

FRANK. Not the least in the world, Praed: my mother will be delighted to see you. She's a genuinely intellectual, artistic woman; and she sees nobody here from one year's end to another except the gov'nor; so you can imagine how jolly dull it pans out for her. [*To the Rev. S.*] You're not intellectual or artistic, are you, pater? So take Praed home at once; and I'll stay here and entertain Mrs. Warren. You'll pick up Crofts in the garden. He'll be excellent company for the bull-pup.

PRAED [*taking his hat from the dresser, and coming close to Frank*]. Come with us, Frank. Mrs. Warren has not seen Miss Vivie for a long time; and we have prevented them from having a moment together yet.

FRANK [*quite softened, and looking at Praed with romantic admiration*]. Of course: I forgot. Ever so thanks for reminding me. Perfect gentleman, Praddy. Always were—my ideal through life. [*He rises to go, but pauses a moment between the two older men, and puts his hand on Praed's shoulder.*] Ah, if you had only been my father instead of this unworthy old man! [*He puts his other hand on his father's shoulder*].

REV. S. [*blustering*]. Silence, sir, silence: you are profane.

MRS. WARREN [*laughing heartily*]. You should keep him in better order, Sam. Good-night. Here: take George his hat and stick with my compliments.

REV. S. [*taking them*]. Good-night. [*They shake hands. As he passes Vivie he shakes hands with her also and bids her good-night. Then, in booming command, to Frank.*] Come along, sir, at once. [*He goes out. Meanwhile Frank has taken his cap from the dresser and his rifle from the rack. Praed shakes hands with Mrs. Warren and Vivie and goes out, Mrs. Warren accompanying him idly to the door, and looking out after him as he goes across the garden. Frank silently begs a kiss from Vivie; but she, dismissing him with a stern glance, takes a couple of books and some paper from the writing-table, and sits down with them at the middle table, so as to have the benefit of the lamp.*]

FRANK [*at the door, taking Mrs. Warren's hand*]. Good night, dear Mrs. Warren. [*He squeezes her hand. She snatches it away, her lips tightening, and looks more than half disposed to box his ears. He laughs mischievously and runs off, clapping-to the door behind him.*]

MRS. WARREN [*coming back to her place at the table,*

opposite Vivie, resigning herself to an evening of boredom now that the men are gone]. Did you ever in your life hear anyone rattle on so? Isn't he a tease? [*She sits down.*] Now that I think of it, dearie, don't you go encouraging him. I'm sure he's a regular good-for-nothing.

VIVIE. Yes: I'm afraid poor Frank is a thorough good-for-nothing. I shall have to get rid of him; but I shall feel sorry for him, though he's not worth it, poor lad. That man Crofts does not seem to me to be good for much either, is he?

MRS. WARREN [*galled by Vivie's cool tone*]. What do you know of men, child, to talk that way about them? You'll have to make up your mind to see a good deal of Sir George Crofts, as he's a friend of mine.

VIVIE [*quite unmoved*]. Why? Do you expect that we shall be much together—you and I, I mean?

MRS. WARREN [*staring at her*]. Of course—until you're married. You're not going back to college again.

VIVIE. Do you think my way of life would suit you? I doubt it.

MRS. WARREN. Your way of life! What do you mean?

VIVIE [*cutting a page of her book with the paper knife on her chatelaine*]. Has it really never occurred to you, mother, that I have a way of life like other people?

MRS. WARREN. What nonsense is this you're trying to talk? Do you want to shew your independence, now that you're a great little person at school? Don't be a fool, child.

VIVIE [*indulgently*]. That's all you have to say on the subject, is it, mother?

MRS. WARREN [*puzzled, then angry*]. Don't you keep on asking me questions like that. [*Violently.*] Hold your tongue. [*Vivie works on, losing no time, and saying nothing.*] You and your way of life, indeed! What next? [*She looks at Vivie again. No reply.*] Your way of life will be what I please, so it will. [*Another pause.*] I've been noticing these airs in you ever since you got that tripos or whatever you call it. If you think I'm going to put up with them you're mistaken; and the sooner you find it out, the better. [*Muttering.*] All I have to say on the subject, indeed! [*Again raising her voice angrily.*] Do you know who you're speaking to, Miss?

VIVIE [*looking across at her without raising her head from her book*]. No. Who are you? What are you?

MRS. WARREN [*rising breathless*]. You young imp!

VIVIE. Everybody knows my reputation, my social standing, and the profession I intend to pursue. I know nothing about you. What is that way of life which you invite me to share with you and Sir George Crofts, pray?

MRS. WARREN. Take care. I shall do something I'll be sorry for after, and you, too.

VIVIE [*putting aside her books with cool decision*]. Well, let us drop the subject until you are better able to face it. [*Looking critically at her mother.*] You want some good walks and a little lawn tennis to set you up. You are shockingly out of condition: you were not able to manage twenty yards uphill to-day without stopping to pant; and your wrists are mere rolls of fat. Look at mine. [*She holds out her wrists.*]

MRS. WARREN [*after looking at her helplessly, begins to whimper*]. Vivie—

VIVIE [*springing up sharply*]. Now pray don't begin to cry. Anything but that. I really cannot stand whimpering. I will go out of the room if you do.

MRS. WARREN [*piteously*]. Oh, my darling, how can you be so hard on me? Have I no rights over you as your mother?

VIVIE. Are you my mother?

MRS. WARREN [*appalled*]. Am I your mother! Oh, Vivie!

VIVIE. Then where are our relatives—my father—our family friends? You claim the rights of a mother: the right to call me fool and child; to speak to me as no woman in authority over me at college dare speak to me; to dictate my way of life; and to force on me the acquaintance of a brute whom anyone can see to be the most vicious sort of London man about town. Before I give myself the trouble to resist such claims, I may as well find out whether they have any real existence.

MRS. WARREN [*distracted, throwing herself on her knees*]. Oh, no, no. Stop, stop. I am your mother: I swear it. Oh, you can't mean to turn on me—my own child: it's not natural. You believe me, don't you? Say you believe me.

VIVIE. Who was my father?

MRS. WARREN. You don't know what you're asking. I can't tell you.

VIVIE [*determinedly*]. Oh, yes, you can, if you like. I have a right to know; and you know very well that I have that right. You can refuse to tell me, if you please; but if you do, you will see the last of me to-morrow morning.

MRS. WARREN. Oh, it's too horrible to hear you talk like that. You wouldn't—you couldn't leave me.

VIVIE [*ruthlessly*]. Yes, without a moment's hesitation, if you trifle with me about this. [*Shivering with disgust.*] How can I feel sure that I may not have the contaminated blood of that brutal waster in my veins?

MRS. WARREN. No, no. On my oath it's not he, nor any of the rest that you have ever met. I'm certain of that, at least. [*Vivie's eyes fasten sternly on her mother as the significance of this flashes on her.*]

VIVIE [*slowly*]. You are certain of that, at least. Ah! You mean that that is all you are certain of. [*Thoughtfully.*] I see. [*Mrs. Warren buries her face in her hands.*] Don't do that, mother: you know you don't feel it a bit. [*Mrs. Warren takes down her hands and looks up deplorably at Vivie, who takes out her watch and says*] Well, that is enough for to-night. At what hour would you like breakfast? Is half-past eight too early for you?

MRS. WARREN [*wildly*]. My God, what sort of woman are you?

VIVIE [*coolly*]. The sort the world is mostly made of, I should hope. Otherwise I don't understand how it gets its business done. Come [*taking her mother by the wrist, and pulling her up pretty resolutely*]: pull yourself together. That's right.

MRS. WARREN [*querulously*]. You're very rough with me, Vivie.

VIVIE. Nonsense. What about bed? It's past ten.

MRS. WARREN [*passionately*]. What's the use of my going to bed? Do you think I could sleep?

VIVIE. Why not? I shall.

MRS. WARREN. You! you've no heart. [*She suddenly breaks out vehemently in her natural tongue—the dialect of a woman of the people—with all her affectations of maternal authority and conventional manners gone, and an overwhelming inspiration of true conviction and scorn in her.*] Oh, I won't bear it: I won't put up with the injustice of it. What right have you to set yourself up above me like this? You boast of what you are to me—to me, who gave you the chance of being what you are. What chance had I? Shame on you for a bad daughter and a stuck-up prude!

VIVIE [*cool and determined, but no longer confident; for her replies, which have sounded convincingly sensible and strong to her so far, now begin to ring rather woodenly and*] *even priggishly against the new tone of her mother*]. Don't think for a moment I set myself above you in any way. You attacked me with the conventional authority of a mother: I defended myself with the conventional superiority of a respectable woman. Frankly, I am not going to stand any of your nonsense; and when you drop it I shall not expect you to stand any of mine. I shall always respect your right to your own opinions and your own way of life.

MRS. WARREN. My own opinions and my own way of life! Listen to her talking! Do you think I was brought up like you—able to pick and choose my own way of life? Do you think I did what I did because I liked it, or thought it right, or wouldn't rather have gone to college and been a lady if I'd had the chance?

VIVIE. Everybody has some choice, mother. The poorest girl alive may not be able to choose between being Queen of England or Principal of Newnham; but she can choose between ragpicking and flowerselling, according to her taste. People are always blaming their circumstances for what they are. I don't believe in circumstances. The people who get on in this world are the people who get up and look for the circumstances they want, and, if they can't find them, make them.

MRS. WARREN. Oh, it's easy to talk, very easy, isn't it? Here!—would you like to know what my circumstances were?

VIVIE. Yes: you had better tell me. Won't you sit down?

MRS. WARREN. Oh, I'll sit down: don't you be afraid. [*She plants her chair farther forward with brazen energy, and sits down. Vivie is impressed in spite of herself.*] D'you know what your gran'mother was?

VIVIE. No.

MRS. WARREN. No, you don't. I do. She called herself a widow and had a fried-fish shop down by the Mint, and kept herself and four daughters out of it. Two of us were sisters: that was me and Liz; and we were both good-looking and well made. I suppose our father was a well-fed man: mother pretended he was a gentleman; but I don't know. The other two were only half sisters—undersized, ugly, starved looking, hard working, honest poor creatures: Liz and I would have half-murdered them if mother hadn't half-murdered us to keep our hands off them. They were the respectable ones. Well, what did they get by their respectability? I'll tell you. One of them worked in a whitelead factory twelve hours a day for nine shillings a week until she died of lead poisoning. She only expected to get her hands a little paralyzed; but she died. The other was always held up to us as a model because she married a Government laborer in the Deptford victualling yard, and kept his room and the three children neat and tidy on eighteen shillings a week—until he took to drink. That was worth being respectable for, wasn't it?

VIVIE [*now thoughtfully attentive*]. Did you and your sister think so?

MRS. WARREN. Liz didn't, I can tell you: she had more spirit. We both went to a church school—that was part of the ladylike airs we gave ourselves to be superior to the children that knew nothing and went nowhere—and we stayed there until Liz went out one night and never came back. I know the schoolmistress thought I'd soon follow her example; for the clergyman was always warning me that Lizzie'd end by jumping off Waterloo Bridge. Poor fool: that was all he knew about it! But I was more afraid of the whitelead factory than I was of the river; and so would you have been in my place. That clergyman got me a situation as scullery maid in a temperance restaurant where they sent out for anything you liked. Then I was waitress; and then I went to the bar at Waterloo station—fourteen hours a day serving drinks and washing glasses for four shillings a week and my board. That was considered a great promotion for me. Well, one cold, wretched night, when I was so tired I could hardly keep myself awake, who should come up for a half of Scotch but Lizzie, in a long fur cloak, elegant and comfortable, with a lot of sovereigns in her purse.

VIVIE [*grimly*]. My aunt Lizzie!

MRS. WARREN. Yes: and a very good aunt to have, too. She's living down at Winchester now, close to the cathedral, one of the most respectable ladies there—chaperones girls at the county ball, if you please. No river for Liz, thank you! You remind me of Liz a little: she was a first-rate business woman—saved money from the beginning—never let herself look too like what she was—never lost her head or threw away a chance. When she saw I'd grown up good-looking she said to me across the bar: "What are you doing there, you little fool? wearing out your health and your appearance for other people's profit!" Liz was saving money then to take a house for herself in Brussels: and she thought we two could save faster than one. So she lent me some money and gave me a start; and I saved steadily and first paid her back, and then went into business with her as her partner. Why shouldn't I have done it? The house in Brussels was real high class—a much better place for a woman to be in than the factory where Anne Jane got poisoned. None of our girls were ever treated as I was treated in the scullery of that temperance place, or at the Waterloo bar, or at home. Would you have had me stay in them and become a worn out old drudge before I was forty?

VIVIE [*intensely interested by this time*]. No; but why did you choose that business? Saving money and good management will succeed in any business.

MRS. WARREN. Yes, saving money. But where can a woman get the money to save in any other business? Could you save out of four shillings a week and keep yourself dressed as well? Not you. Of course, if you're a plain woman and can't earn anything more; or if you have a turn for music, or the stage, or newspaper-writing: that's different. But neither Liz nor I had any turn for such things: all we had was our appearance and our turn for pleasing men. Do you think we were such fools as to let other people trade in our good looks by employing us as shopgirls, or barmaids, or waitresses, when we could trade in them ourselves and get all the profits instead of starvation wages? Not likely.

VIVIE. You were certainly quite justified—from the business point of view.

MRS. WARREN. Yes; or any other point of view. What is any respectable girl brought up to do but to catch some rich man's fancy and get the benefit of his money by marrying him?—as if a marriage ceremony could make any difference in the right or wrong of the thing! Oh, the hypocrisy of the world makes me sick! Liz and I had to work and save and calculate just like other people; elseways we should be as poor as any good-for-nothing, drunken waster of a woman that thinks her luck will last for ever. [*With great energy.*] I despise such people: they've no character; and if there's a thing I hate in a woman, it's want of character.

VIVIE. Come, now, mother: frankly! Isn't it part of what you call character in a woman that she should greatly dislike such a way of making money?

MRS. WARREN. Why, of course. Everybody dislikes having to work and make money; but they have to do it all the same. I'm sure I've often pitied a poor girl, tired out and in low spirits, having to try to please some man that she doesn't care two straws for—some half-drunken fool that thinks he's making himself agreeable when he's teasing and worrying and disgusting a woman so that hardly any money could pay her for putting up with it. But she has to bear with disagreeables and take the rough with the smooth, just like a nurse in a hospital or anyone else. It's not work that any woman would do for pleasure, goodness knows; though to hear the pious people talk you would suppose it was a bed of roses.

VIVIE. Still you consider it worth while. It pays.

MRS. WARREN. Of course it's worth while to a poor girl, if she can resist temptation and is good-looking and well conducted and sensible. It's far better than any other employment open to her. I always thought that oughtn't to be. It can't be right, Vivie, that there shouldn't be better opportunities for women. I stick to that: it's wrong. But it's so, right or wrong; and a girl must make the best of it. But, of course, it's not worth while for a lady. If you took to it you'd be a fool; but I should have been a fool if I'd taken to anything else.

VIVIE [more and more deeply moved]. Mother: suppose we were both as poor as you were in those wretched old days, are you quite sure that you wouldn't advise me to try the Waterloo bar, or marry a labourer, or even go into the factory?

MRS. WARREN [indignantly]. Of course not. What sort of mother do you take me for! How could you keep your self-respect in such starvation and slavery? And what's a woman worth? what's life worth? without self-respect! Why am I independent and able to give my daughter a first-rate education, when other women that had just as good opportunities are in the gutter? Because I always knew how to respect myself and control myself. Why is Liz looked up to in a cathedral town? The same reason. Where would we be now if we'd minded the clergyman's foolishness? Scrubbing floors for one and sixpence a day and nothing to look forward to but the workhouse infirmary. Don't you be led astray by people who don't know the world, my girl. The only way for a woman to provide for herself decently is for her to be good to some man that can afford to be good to her. If she's in his own station of life, let her make him marry her; but if she's far beneath him she can't expect it—why should she? It wouldn't be for her own happiness. Ask any lady in London society that has daughters; and she'll tell you the same, except that I tell you straight and she'll tell you crooked. That's all the difference.

VIVIE [*fascinated, gazing at her*]. My dear mother: you are a wonderful woman—you are stronger than all England. And are you really and truly not one wee bit doubtful—or —or—ashamed?

MRS. WARREN. Well, of course, dearie, it's only good manners to be ashamed of it, it's expected from a woman. Women have to pretend to feel a great deal that they don't feel. Liz used to be angry with me for plumping out the truth about it. She used to say that when every woman could learn enough from what was going on in the world before her eyes, there was no need to talk about it to her. But then Liz was such a perfect lady! She had the true instinct of it; while I was always a bit of a vulgarian. I used to be so pleased when you sent me your photographs to see that you were growing up like Liz: you've just her ladylike, determined way. But I can't stand saying one thing when everyone knows I mean another. What's the use in such hypocrisy? If people arrange the world that way for women, there's no good pretending that it's arranged the other way. I never was a bit ashamed really. I consider that I had a right to be proud that we managed everything so respectably, and never had a word against us, and that the girls were so well taken care of. Some of them did very well: one of them married an ambassador. But of course now I daren't talk about such things: whatever would they think of us! [*She yawns.*] Oh, dear! I do believe I'm getting sleepy after all. [*She stretches herself lazily, thoroughly relieved by her explosion, and placidly ready for her night's rest.*]

VIVIE. I believe it is I who will not be able to sleep now. [*She goes to the dresser and lights the candle. Then she extinguishes the lamp, darkening the room a good deal.*] Better let in some fresh air before locking up. [*She opens the cottage door, and finds that it is broad moonlight.*] What a beautiful night! Look! [*She draws aside the curtains of the window. The landscape is seen bathed in the radiance of the harvest moon rising over Blackdown.*]

MRS. WARREN [*with a perfunctory glance at the scene*]. Yes, dear: but take care you don't catch your death of cold from the night air.

VIVIE [*contemptuously*]. Nonsense.

MRS. WARREN [*querulously*]. Oh, yes: everything I say is nonsense, according to you.

VIVIE [*turning to her quickly*]. No: really that is not so, mother. You have got completely the better of me to-night, though I intended it to be the other way. Let us be good friends now.

MRS. WARREN [*shaking her head a little ruefully*]. So it has been the other way. But I suppose I must give in to it. I always got the worst of it from Liz; and now I suppose it'll be the same with you.

VIVIE. Well, never mind. Come; good-night, dear old mother. [*She takes her mother in her arms.*]

MRS. WARREN [*fondly*]. I brought you up well, didn't I, dearie?

VIVIE. You did.

MRS. WARREN. And you'll be good to your poor old mother for it, won't you?

VIVIE. I will, dear. [*Kissing her.*] Good-night.

MRS. WARREN [*with unction*]. Blessings on my own dearie darling—a mother's blessing! [*She embraces her daughter protectingly, instinctively looking upward as if to call down a blessing.*]

ACT THREE

In the Rectory garden next morning, with the sun shining and the birds in full song. The garden wall has a five-barred wooden gate, wide enough to admit a carriage, in the middle. Beside the gate hangs a bell on a coiled spring, communicating with a pull outside. The carriage drive comes down the middle of the garden and then swerves to its left, where it ends in a little gravelled circus opposite the rectory porch. Beyond the gate is seen the dusty high road, parallel with the wall, bounded on the farther side by a strip of turf and an unfenced pine wood. On the lawn, between the house and the drive, is a clipped yew tree, with a garden bench in its shade. On the opposite side the garden is shut in by a box hedge; and there is a sundial on the turf, with an iron chair near it. A little path leads off through the box hedge, behind the sundial.

Frank, seated on the chair near the sundial, on which he has placed the morning papers, is reading the Standard. *His father comes from the house, red-eyed and shivery, and meets Frank's eyes with misgiving.*

FRANK [*looking at his watch*]. Half-past eleven. Nice hour for a rector to come down to breakfast!

REV. S. Don't mock, Frank: don't mock. I'm a little— er—[*Shivering.*]————

FRANK. Off colour?

REV. S. [*repudiating the expression*]. No, sir: unwell this morning. Where's your mother?

FRANK. Don't be alarmed: she's not here. Gone to town by the 11:13 with Bessie. She left several messages for you. Do you feel equal to receiving them now, or shall I wait till you've breakfasted?

REV. S. I have breakfasted, sir. I am surprised at your mother going to town when we have people staying with us. They'll think it very strange.

FRANK. Possibly she has considered that. At all events, if Crofts is going to stay here, and you are going to sit up every night with him until four, recalling the incidents of your fiery youth, it is clearly my mother's duty, as a prudent housekeeper, to go up to the stores and order a barrel of whisky and a few hundred siphons.

REV. S. I did not observe that Sir George drank excessively.

FRANK. You were not in a condition to, gov'nor.

REV. S. Do you mean to say that I—

FRANK [*calmly*]. I never saw a beneficed clergyman less sober. The anecdotes you told about your past career were so awful that I really don't think Praed would have passed the night under your roof if it hadn't been for the way my mother and he took to one another.

REV. S. Nonsense, sir. I am Sir George Crofts' host. I must talk to him about something; and he has only one subject. Where is Mr. Praed now?

FRANK. He is driving my mother and Bessie to the station.

REV. S. Is Crofts up yet?

FRANK. Oh, long ago. He hasn't turned a hair: he's in much better practice than you—has kept it up ever since, probably. He's taken himself off somewhere to smoke. [*Frank resumes his paper. The Rev. S. turns disconsolately towards the gate; then comes back irresolutely.*]

REV. S. Er—Frank.

FRANK. Yes.

REV. S. Do you think the Warrens will expect to be asked here after yesterday afternoon?

FRANK. They've been asked already. Crofts informed us at breakfast that you told him to bring Mrs. Warren and Vivie over here to-day, and to invite them to make this house their home. It was after that communication that my mother found she must go to town by the 11:13 train.

REV. S. [*with despairing vehemence*]. I never gave any such invitation. I never thought of such a thing.

FRANK [*compassionately*]. How do you know, gov'nor, what you said and thought last night? Hallo! here's Praed back again.

PRAED [*coming in through the gate*]. Good morning.

REV. S. Good morning. I must apologize for not having met you at breakfast. I have a touch of—of—

FRANK. Clergyman's sore throat, Praed. Fortunately not chronic.

PRAED [*changing the subject*]. Well, I must say your house is in a charming spot here. Really most charming.

REV. S. Yes: it is indeed. Frank will take you for a walk, Mr. Praed, if you like. I'll ask you to excuse me: I must take the opportunity to write my sermon while Mrs. Gardner is away and you are all amusing yourselves. You won't mind, will you?

PRAED. Certainly not. Don't stand on the slightest ceremony with me.

REV. S. Thank you. I'll—er—er— [*He stammers his way to the porch and vanishes into the house*].

PRAED [*sitting down on the turf near Frank, and hugging his ankles*]. Curious thing it must be writing a sermon every week.

FRANK. Ever so curious, if he did it. He buys 'em. He's gone for some soda water.

PRAED. My dear boy: I wish you would be more respectful to your father. You know you can be so nice when you like.

FRANK. My dear Praddy: you forget that I have to live with the governor. When two people live together—it don't matter whether they're father and son, husband and wife, brother and sister—they can't keep up the polite humbug which comes so easy for ten minutes on an afternoon call. Now the governor, who unites to many admirable domestic qualities the irresoluteness of a sheep and the pompousness and aggressiveness of a jackass—

PRAED. No, pray, pray, my dear Frank, remember! He is your father.

FRANK. I give him due credit for that. But just imagine his telling Crofts to bring the Warrens over here! He must have been ever so drunk. You know, my dear Praddy, my mother wouldn't stand Mrs. Warren for a moment. Vivie mustn't come here until she's gone back to town.

PRAED. But your mother doesn't know anything about Mrs. Warren, does she?

FRANK. I don't know. Her journey to town looks as if she did. Not that my mother would mind in the ordinary way: she has stuck like a brick to lots of women who had got into trouble. But they were all nice women. That's what makes the real difference. Mrs. Warren, no doubt, has her merits; but she's ever so rowdy; and my mother simply wouldn't put up with her. So—hallo! [*This exclamation is provoked by the reappearance of the clergyman, who comes out of the house in haste and dismay.*]

REV. S. Frank: Mrs. Warren and her daughter are coming across the heath with Crofts: I saw them from the study windows. What am I to say about your mother?

FRANK [*jumping up energetically*]. Stick on your hat and go out and say how delighted you are to see them; and that Frank's in the garden; and that mother and Bessie have been called to the bedside of a sick relative, and were ever so sorry they couldn't stop; and that you hope Mrs. Warren slept well; and—and—say any blessed thing except the truth, and leave the rest to Providence.

REV. S. But how are we to get rid of them afterwards?

FRANK. There's no time to think of that now. Here! [*He bounds into the porch and returns immediately with a clerical felt hat, which he claps on his father's head.*] Now: off with you. Praed and I'll wait here, to give the thing an unpremeditated air. [*The clergyman, dazed, but obedient, hurries off through the gate. Praed gets up from the turf, and dusts himself.*]

FRANK. We must get that old lady back to town somehow, Praed. Come! honestly, dear Praddy, do you like seeing them together—Vivie and the old lady?

PRAED. Oh, why not?

FRANK [*his teeth on edge*]. Don't it make your flesh creep ever so little?—that wicked old devil, up to every villainy under the sun, I'll swear, and Vivie—ugh!

PRAED. Hush, pray. They're coming. [*The clergyman and Crofts are seen coming along the road, followed by Mrs. Warren and Vivie walking affectionately together.*]

FRANK. Look: she actually has her arm round the old woman's waist. It's her right arm: she began it. She's gone sentimental, by God! Ugh! ugh! Now do you feel the creeps? [*The clergyman opens the gate; and Mrs. Warren and Vivie pass him and stand in the middle of the garden looking at the house. Frank, in an ecstasy of dissimulation, turns gaily to Mrs. Warren, exclaiming*] Ever so delighted to see you, Mrs. Warren. This quiet old rectory garden becomes you perfectly.

MRS. WARREN. Well, I never! Did you hear that, George? He says I look well in a quiet old rectory garden.

REV. S. [*still holding the gate for Crofts, who loafs through it, heavily bored*]. You look well everywhere, Mrs. Warren.

FRANK. Bravo, gov'nor! Now look here: let's have an awful jolly time of it before lunch. First let's see the church. Everyone has to do that. It's a regular old thirteenth century church, you know: the gov'nor's ever so fond of it, because he got up a restoration fund and had it completely rebuilt six years ago. Praed will be able to show its points.

REV. S. [*mooning hospitably at them*]. I shall be pleased, I'm sure, if Sir George and Mrs. Warren really care about it.

MRS. WARREN. Oh, come along and get it over. It'll do George good: I'll lay he doesn't trouble church much.

CROFTS [*turning back towards the gate*]. I've no objection.

REV. S. Not that way. We go through the fields, if you don't mind. Round here. [*He leads the way by the little path through the box hedge.*]

CROFTS. Oh, all right. [*He goes with the parson. Praed follows with Mrs. Warren. Vivie does not stir, but watches them until they have gone, with all the lines of purpose in her face marking it strongly.*]

FRANK. Ain't you coming.

VIVIE. No. I want to give you a warning, Frank. You were making fun of my mother just now when you said that about the rectory garden. That is barred in future. Please treat my mother with as much respect as you treat your own.

FRANK. My dear Viv: she wouldn't appreciate it. She's not like my mother: the same treatment wouldn't do for both cases. But what on earth has happened to you? Last night we were perfectly agreed as to your mother and her set. This morning I find you attitudinizing sentimentally with your arm round your parent's waist.

VIVIE [*flushing*]. Attitudinizing!

FRANK. That was how it struck me. First time I ever saw you do a second-rate thing.

VIVIE [*controlling herself*]. Yes, Frank: there has been a change; but I don't think it a change for the worse. Yesterday I was a little prig.

FRANK. And to-day?

VIVIE [*wincing; then looking at him steadily*]. To-day I know my mother better than you do.

FRANK. Heaven forbid!

VIVIE. What do you mean?

FRANK. Viv; there's a freemasonry among thoroughly immoral people that you know nothing of. You've too much character. That's the bond between your mother and me: that's why I know her better than you'll ever know her.

VIVIE. You are wrong: you know nothing about her. If you knew the circumstances against which my mother had to struggle—

FRANK [*adroitly finishing the sentence for her*]. I should know why she is what she is, shouldn't I? What difference would that make? Circumstances or no circumstances, Viv, you won't be able to stand your mother.

VIVIE [*very angry*]. Why not?

FRANK. Because she's an old wretch, Viv. If you ever put your arm round her waist in my presence again, I'll shoot myself there and then as a protest against an exhibition which revolts me.

VIVIE. Must I choose between dropping your acquaintance and dropping my mother's?

FRANK [*gracefully*]. That would put the old lady at ever such a disadvantage. No, Viv: your infatuated little boy will have to stick to you in any case. But he's all the more anxious that you shouldn't make mistakes. It's no use, Viv: your mother's impossible. She may be a good sort; but she's a bad lot, a very bad lot.

VIVIE [*hotly*]. Frank—! [*He stands his ground. She turns away and sits down on the bench under the yew tree, struggling to recover her self-command. Then she says*] Is she to be deserted by all the world because she's what you call a bad lot? Has she no right to live?

FRANK. No fear of that, Viv: she won't ever be deserted. [*He sits on the bench beside her.*]

VIVIE. But I am to desert her, I suppose.

FRANK [*babyishly, lulling her and making love to her with*] *his voice*]. Mustn't go live with her. Little family group of mother and daughter wouldn't be a success. Spoil our little group.

VIVIE [*falling under the spell*]. What little group?

FRANK. The babes in the wood: Vivie and little Frank. [*He slips his arm round her waist and nestles against her like a weary child.*] Let's go and get covered up with leaves.

VIVIE [*rhythmically, rocking him like a nurse*]. Fast asleep, hand in hand, under the trees.

FRANK. The wise little girl with her silly little boy.

VIVIE. The dear little boy with his dowdy little girl.

FRANK. Ever so peaceful, and relieved from the imbecility of the little boy's father and the questionableness of the little girl's—

VIVIE [*smothering the word against her breast*]. Sh-sh-sh-sh! little girl wants to forget all about her mother. [*They are silent for some moments, rocking one another. Then Vivie wakes up with a shock, exclaiming*] What a pair of fools we are! Come: sit up. Gracious! your hair. [*She smooths it.*] I wonder do all grown up people play in that childish way when nobody is looking. I never did it when I was a child.

FRANK. Neither did I. You are my first playmate. [*He catches her hand to kiss it, but checks himself to look round first. Very unexpectedly he sees Crofts emerging from the box hedge.*] Oh, damn!

VIVIE. Why damn, dear?

FRANK [*whispering*]. Sh! Here's this brute Crofts. [*He sits farther away from her with an unconcerned air.*]

VIVIE. Don't be rude to him, Frank. I particularly wish to be polite to him. It will please my mother. [*Frank makes a wry face.*]

CROFTS. Could I have a few words with you, Miss Vivie?

VIVIE. Certainly.

CROFTS [*to Frank*]. You'll excuse me, Gardner. They're waiting for you in the church, if you don't mind.

FRANK [*rising*]. Anything to oblige you, Crofts—except church. If you want anything, Vivie, ring the gate bell, and a domestic will appear. [*He goes into the house with unruffled suavity.*]

CROFTS [*watching him with a crafty air as he disappears, and speaking to Vivie with an assumption of being on privileged terms with her*]. Pleasant young fellow that, Miss Vivie. Pity he has no money, isn't it?

VIVIE. Do you think so?

CROFTS. Well, what's he to do? No profession, no property. What's he good for?

VIVIE. I realize his disadvantages, Sir George.

CROFTS [*a little taken aback at being so precisely interpreted*]. Oh, it's not that. But while we're in this world we're in it; and money's money. [*Vivie does not answer.*] Nice day, isn't it?

VIVIE [*with scarcely veiled contempt for this effort at conversation*]. Very.

CROFTS [*with brutal good humor, as if he liked her pluck*]. Well, that's not what I came to say. [*Affecting frankness.*] Now listen, Miss Vivie. I'm quite aware that I'm not a young lady's man.

VIVIE. Indeed, Sir George?

CROFTS. No; and to tell you the honest truth, I don't want to be either. But when I say a thing I mean it; when I feel sentiment I feel it in earnest; and what I value I pay hard money for. That's the sort of man I am.

VIVIE. It does you great credit, I'm sure.

CROFTS. Oh, I don't mean to praise myself. I have my faults, Heaven knows: no man is more sensible of that than I am. I know I'm not perfect: that's one of the advantages of being a middle-aged man; for I'm not a young man, and I know it. But my code is a simple one, and, I think, a good one. Honor between man and man; fidelity between man and woman; and no cant about this religion, or that religion, but an honest belief that things are making for good on the whole.

VIVIE [*with biting irony*]. "A power, not ourselves, that makes for righteousness," eh?

CROFTS [*taking her seriously*]. Oh, certainly, not ourselves, of course. You understand what I mean. [*He sits down beside her, as one who has found a kindred spirit.*] Well, now as to practical matters. You may have an idea that I've flung my money about; but I haven't: I'm richer today than when I first came into the property. I've used my knowledge of the world to invest my money in ways that other men have overlooked; and whatever else I may be, I'm a safe man from the money point of view.

VIVIE. It's very kind of you to tell me all this.

CROFTS. Oh, well, come, Miss Vivie: you needn't pretend you don't see what I'm driving at. I want to settle down with a Lady Crofts. I suppose you think me very blunt, eh?

VIVIE. Not at all: I am much obliged to you for being so definite and business-like. I quite appreciate the offer: the money, the position, Lady Crofts, and so on. But I think I will say no, if you don't mind. I'd rather not. [*She rises, and strolls across to the sundial to get out of his immediate neighborhood.*]

CROFTS [*not at all discouraged, and taking advantage of the additional room left him on the seat to spread himself comfortably, as if a few preliminary refusals were part of the inevitable routine of courtship*]. I'm in no hurry. It was only just to let you know in case young Gardner should try to trap you. Leave the question open.

VIVIE [*sharply*]. My no is final. I won't go back from it. [*She looks authoritatively at him. He grins; leans forward with his elbows on his knees to prod with his stick at some unfortunate insect in the grass; and looks cunningly at her. She turns away impatiently.*]

CROFTS. I'm a good deal older than you—twenty-five years—quarter of a century. I shan't live for ever; and I'll take care that you shall be well off when I'm gone.

VIVIE. I am proof against even that inducement, Sir George. Don't you think you'd better take your answer? There is not the slightest chance of my altering it.

CROFTS [*rising, after a final slash at a daisy, and beginning to walk to and fro*]. Well, no matter. I could tell you some things that would change your mind fast enough; but I won't, because I'd rather win you by honest affection. I was a good friend to your mother: ask her whether I wasn't. She'd never have made the money that paid for your education if it hadn't been for my advice and help, not to mention the money I advanced her. There are not many men would have stood by her as I have. I put not less than £40,000 into it, from first to last.

VIVIE [*staring at him*]. Do you mean to say you were my mother's business partner?

CROFTS. Yes. Now just think of all the trouble and the explanations it would save if we were to keep the whole thing in the family, so to speak. Ask your mother whether she'd like to have to explain all her affairs to a perfect stranger.

VIVIE. I see no difficulty, since I understand that the business is wound up, and the money invested.

CROFTS [*stopping short, amazed*]. Wound up! Wind up a business that's paying 35 per cent in the worst years! Not likely. Who told you that?

VIVIE [*her colour quite gone*]. Do you mean that it is still—? [*She stops abruptly, and puts her hand on the sundial to support herself. Then she gets quickly to the iron chair and sits down.*] What business are you talking about?

CROFTS. Well, the fact is, it's not what would be considered exactly a high-class business in my set—the county set, you know—our set it will be if you think better of my offer. Not that there's any mystery about it: don't think that. Of course you know by your mother's being in it that it's perfectly straight and honest. I've known her for many years; and I can say of her that she'd cut off her hands sooner than touch anything that was not what it ought to be. I'll tell you all about it if you like. I don't know whether you've found in travelling how hard it is to find a really comfortable private hotel.

VIVIE [*sickened, averting her face*]. Yes: go on.

CROFTS. Well, that's all it is. Your mother has a genius for managing such things. We've got two in Brussels, one in Berlin, one in Vienna, and two in Buda-Pesth. Of course there are others besides ourselves in it; but we hold most of the capital; and your mother's indispensable as managing director. You've noticed, I daresay, that she travels a good deal. But you see you can't mention such things in society. Once let out the word hotel and everybody says you keep a public-house. You wouldn't like people to say that of your mother, would you? That's why we're so reserved about it. By the bye, you'll keep it to yourself, won't you? Since it's been a secret so long, it had better remain so.

VIVIE. And this is the business you invite me to join you in?

CROFTS. Oh, no. My wife shan't be troubled with business. You'll not be in it more than you've always been.

VIVIE. *I* always been! What do you mean?

CROFTS. Only that you've always lived on it. It paid for your education and the dress you have on your back. Don't turn up your nose at business, Miss Vivie: where would your Newnhams and Girtons be without it?

VIVIE [*rising, almost beside herself*]. Take care. I know what this business is.

CROFTS [*starting, with a suppressed oath*]. Who told you?

VIVIE. Your partner—my mother.

CROFTS [*black with rage*]. The old—[*Vivie looks quickly at him. He swallows the epithet and stands swearing and raging foully to himself. But he knows that his cue is to be sympathetic. He takes refuge in generous indignation.*] She ought to have had more consideration for you. I'd never have told you.

VIVIE. I think you would probably have told me when we were married: it would have been a convenient weapon to break me in with.

CROFTS [quite sincerely]. I never intended that. On my word as a gentleman I didn't.

[Vivie wonders at him. Her sense of the irony of his protest cools and braces her. She replies with contemptuous self-possession].

VIVIE. It does not matter. I suppose you understand that when we leave here to-day our acquaintance ceases.

CROFTS. Why? Is it for helping your mother?

VIVIE. My mother was a very poor woman who had no reasonable choice but to do as she did. You were a rich gentleman; and you did the same for the sake of 35 per cent. You are a pretty common sort of scoundrel, I think. That is my opinion of you.

CROFTS [after a stare—not at all displeased, and much more at his ease on these frank terms than on their former ceremonious ones]. Ha, ha, ha, ha! Go it, little missie, go it: it doesn't hurt me and it amuses you. Why the devil shouldn't I invest my money that way? I take the interest on my capital like other people: I hope you don't think I dirty my own hands with the work. Come: you wouldn't refuse the acquaintance of my mother's cousin, the Duke of Belgravia, because some of the rents he gets are earned in queer ways. You wouldn't cut the Archbishop of Canterbury, I suppose, because the Ecclesiastical Commissioners have a few publicans and sinners among their tenants? Do you remember your Crofts scholarship at Newnham? Well, that was founded by my brother the M.P. He gets his 22 per cent out of a factory with 600 girls in it, and not one of them getting wages enough to live on. How d'ye suppose most of them manage? Ask your mother. And do you expect me to turn my back on 35 per cent when all the rest are pocketing what they can, like sensible men? No such fool! If you're going to pick and choose your acquaintances on moral principles, you'd better clear out of this country, unless you want to cut yourself out of all decent society.

VIVIE [conscience stricken]. You might go on to point out that I myself never asked where the money I spent came from. I believe I am just as bad as you.

CROFTS [greatly reassured]. Of course you are; and a very

good thing, too! What harm does it do after all? [*Rallying her jocularly.*] So you don't think me such a scoundrel now you come to think it over. Eh?

VIVIE. I have shared profits with you; and I admitted you just now to the familiarity of knowing what I think of you.

CROFTS [*with serious friendliness*]. To be sure you did. You won't find me a bad sort: I don't go in for being super-fine intellectually; but I've plenty of honest human feeling; and the old Crofts breed comes out in a sort of instinctive hatred of anything low, in which I'm sure you'll sympathize with me. Believe me, Miss Vivie, the world isn't such a bad place as the croakers make out. So long as you don't fly openly in the face of society, society doesn't ask any inconvenient questions; and it makes precious short work of the cads who do. There are no secrets better kept than the secrets that everybody guesses. In the society I can introduce you to, no lady or gentleman would so far forget themselves as to discuss my business affairs or your mother's. No man can offer you a safer position.

VIVIE [*studying him curiously*]. I suppose you really think you're getting on famously with me.

CROFTS. Well, I hope I may flatter myself that you think better of me than you did at first.

VIVIE [*quietly*]. I hardly find you worth thinking about at all now. [*She rises and turns towards the gate, pausing on her way to contemplate him and say almost gently, but with intense conviction.*] When I think of the society that tolerates you, and the laws that protect you—when I think of how helpless nine out of ten young girls would be in the hands of you and my mother—the unmentionable woman and her capitalist bully—

CROFTS [*livid*]. Damn you!

VIVIE. You need not. I feel among the damned already.

[*She raises the latch of the gate to open it and go out. He follows her and puts his hand heavily on the top bar to prevent its opening.*]

CROFTS [*panting with fury*]. Do you think I'll put up with this from you, you young devil, you?

VIVIE [*unmoved*]. Be quiet. Some one will answer the bell. [*Without flinching a step she strikes the bell with the back of her hand. It clangs harshly; and he starts back involuntarily. Almost immediately Frank appears at the porch with his rifle.*]

FRANK [*with cheerful politeness*]. Will you have the rifle, Viv; or shall I operate?

VIVIE. Frank: have you been listening?

FRANK. Only for the bell, I assure you; so that you shouldn't have to wait. I think I showed great insight into your character, Crofts.

CROFTS. For two pins I'd take that gun from you and break it across your head.

FRANK [*stalking him cautiously*]. Pray don't. I'm ever so careless in handling firearms. Sure to be a fatal accident, with a reprimand from the coroner's jury for my negligence.

VIVIE. Put the rifle away, Frank: it's quite unnecessary.

FRANK. Quite right, Viv. Much more sportsmanlike to catch him in a trap. [*Crofts, understanding the insult, makes a threatening movement.*] Crofts: there are fifteen cartridges in the magazine here; and I am a dead shot at the present distance at an object of your size.

CROFTS. Oh, you needn't be afraid. I'm not going to touch you.

FRANK. Ever so magnanimous of you under the circumstances! Thank you.

CROFTS. I'll just tell you this before I go. It may interest you, since you're so fond of one another. Allow me, Mister Frank, to introduce you to your half-sister, the eldest daughter of the Reverend Samuel Gardner. Miss Vivie: your half-brother. Good morning. [*He goes out through the gate and along the road.*]

FRANK [*after a pause of stupefaction, raising the rifle*]. You'll testify before the coroner that it's an accident, Viv. [*He takes aim at the retreating figure of Crofts. Vivie seizes the muzzle and pulls it round against her breast.*]

VIVIE. Fire now. You may.

FRANK [*dropping his end of the rifle hastily*]. Stop! take care. [*She lets it go. It falls on the turf.*] Oh, you've given your little boy such a turn. Suppose it had gone off—ugh! [*He sinks on the garden seat, overcome.*]

VIVIE. Suppose it had: do you think it would not have been a relief to have some sharp physical pain tearing through me?

FRANK [*coaxingly*]. Take it ever so easy, dear Viv. Remember: even if the rifle scared that fellow into telling the truth for the first time in his life, that only makes us the babes in the wood in earnest. [*He holds out his arms to her.*] Come and be covered up with leaves again.

VIVIE [*with a cry of disgust*]. Ah, not that, not that. You make all my flesh creep.

FRANK. Why, what's the matter?

VIVIE. Good-bye. [*She makes for the gate.*]

FRANK [*jumping up*]. Hallo! Stop! Viv! Viv! [*She turns in the gateway.*] Where are you going to? Where shall we find you?

VIVIE. At Honoria Fraser's chambers, 67 Chancery Lane, for the rest of my life. [*She goes off quickly in the opposite direction to that taken by Crofts.*]

FRANK. But I say—wait—dash it! [*He runs after her*].

ACT FOUR

Honoria Fraser's chambers in Chancery Lane. An office at the top of New Stone Buildings, with a plate-glass window, distempered walls, electric light, and a patent stove. Saturday afternoon. The chimneys of Lincoln's Inn and the western sky beyond are seen through the window. There is a double writing table in the middle of the room, with a cigar box, ash pans, and a portable electric reading lamp almost snowed up in heaps of papers and books. This table has knee holes and chairs right and left and is very untidy. The clerk's desk, closed and tidy, with its high stool, is against the wall, near a door communicating with the inner rooms. In the opposite wall is the door leading to the public corridor. Its upper panel is of opaque glass, lettered in black on the outside, "Fraser and Warren." A baize screen hides the corner between this door and the window.

Frank, in a fashionable light-colored coaching suit, with his stick, gloves, and white hat in his hands, is pacing up and down the office. Somebody tries the door with a key.

FRANK [*calling*]. Come in. It's not locked.

[*Vivie comes in, in her hat and jacket. She stops and stares at him.*]

VIVIE [*sternly*]. What are you doing here?

FRANK. Waiting to see you. I've been here for hours. Is this the way you attend to your business? [*He puts his hat and stick on the table, and perches himself with a vault on the clerk's stool, looking at her with every appearance of being in a specially restless, teasing, flippant mood.*]

VIVIE. I've been away exactly twenty minutes for a cup of tea. [*She takes off her hat and jacket and hangs them up behind the screen.*] How did you get in?

FRANK. The staff had not left when I arrived. He's gone to play football on Primrose Hill. Why don't you employ a woman, and give your sex a chance?

VIVIE. What have you come for?

FRANK [*springing off the stool and coming close to her*]. Viv: let's go and enjoy the Saturday half-holiday somewhere, like the staff. What do you say to Richmond, and then a music hall, and a jolly supper?

VIVIE. Can't afford it. I shall put in another six hours' work before I go to bed.

FRANK. Can't afford it, can't we? Aha! Look here. [*He takes out a handful of sovereigns and makes them chink.*] Gold, Viv, gold!

VIVIE. Where did you get it?

FRANK. Gambling, Viv, gambling. Poker.

VIVIE. Pah! It's meaner than stealing it. No: I'm not coming. [*She sits down to work at the table, with her back to the glass door, and begins turning over the papers.*]

FRANK [*remonstrating piteously*]. But, my dear Viv, I want to talk to you ever so seriously.

VIVIE. Very well: sit down in Honoria's chair and talk here. I like ten minutes' chat after tea. [*He murmurs.*] No use groaning: I'm inexorable. [*He takes the opposite seat disconsolately.*] Pass that cigar box, will you?

FRANK [*pushing the cigar box across*]. Nasty womanly habit. Nice men don't do it any longer.

VIVIE. Yes: they object to the smell in the office; and we've had to take to cigarets. See! [*She opens the box and takes out a cigaret, which she lights. She offers him one; but he shakes his head with a wry face. She settles herself comfortably in her chair, smoking.*] Go ahead.

FRANK. Well, I want to know what you've done—what arrangements you've made.

VIVIE. Everything was settled twenty minutes after I arrived here. Honoria has found the business too much for her this year; and she was on the point of sending for me and proposing a partnership when I walked in and told her I hadn't a farthing in the world. So I installed myself and packed her off for a fortnight's holiday. What happened at Haslemere when I left?

FRANK. Nothing at all. I said you'd gone to town on particular business.

VIVIE. Well?

FRANK. Well, either they were too flabbergasted to say anything, or else Crofts had prepared your mother. Anyhow, she didn't say anything; and Crofts didn't say anything; and Praddy only stared. After tea they got up and went; and I've not seen them since.

VIVIE [nodding placidly with one eye on a wreath of smoke]. That's all right.

FRANK [looking round disparagingly.] Do you intend to stick in this confounded place?

VIVIE [blowing the wreath decisively away and sitting straight up]. Yes. These two days have given me back all my strength and self-possession. I will never take a holiday again as long as I live.

FRANK [with a very wry face]. Mps! You look quite happy—and as hard as nails.

VIVIE [grimly]. Well for me that I am!

FRANK [rising]. Look here, Viv: we must have an explanation. We parted the other day under a complete misunderstanding.

VIVIE [putting away the cigaret]. Well: clear it up.

FRANK. You remember what Crofts said?

VIVIE. Yes.

FRANK. That revelation was supposed to bring about a complete change in the nature of our feeling for one another. It placed us on the footing of brother and sister.

VIVIE. Yes.

FRANK. Have you ever had a brother?

VIVIE. No.

FRANK. Then you don't know what being brother and sister feels like? Now I have lots of sisters: Jessie and Georgina and the rest. The fraternal feeling is quite familiar to me; and I assure you my feeling for you is not the least in the world like it. The girls will go their way; I will go mine; and we shan't care if we never see one another again. That's brother and sister. But as to you, I can't be easy if I have to pass a week without seeing you. That's not brother and sister. It's exactly what I felt an hour before Crofts made his revelation. In short, dear Viv, it's love's young dream.

VIVIE [*bitingly*]. The same feeling, Frank, that brought your father to my mother's feet. Is that it?

FRANK [*revolted*]. I very strongly object, Viv, to have my feelings compared to any which the Reverend Samuel is capable of harboring; and I object still more to a comparison of you to your mother. Besides, I don't believe the story. I have taxed my father with it, and obtained from him what I consider tantamount to a denial.

VIVIE. What did he say?

FRANK. He said he was sure there must be some mistake.

VIVIE. Do you believe him?

FRANK. I am prepared to take his word as against Crofts'.

VIVIE. Does it make any difference? I mean in your imagination or conscience; for of course it makes no real difference.

FRANK [*shaking his head*]. None whatever to me.

VIVIE. Nor to me.

FRANK [*staring*]. But this is ever so surprising! I thought our whole relations were altered in your imagination and conscience, as you put it, the moment those words were out of that brute's muzzle.

VIVIE. No: it was not that. I didn't believe him. I only wish I could.

FRANK. Eh?

VIVIE. I think brother and sister would be a very suitable relation for us.

FRANK. You really mean that?

VIVIE. Yes. It's the only relation I care for, even if we could afford any other. I mean that.

FRANK [*raising his eyebrows like one on whom a new light has dawned, and speaking with quite an effusion of chivalrous sentiment*]. My dear Viv: why didn't you say so before? I am ever so sorry for persecuting you. I understand, of course.

VIVIE [*puzzled*]. Understand what?

FRANK. Oh, I'm not a fool in the ordinary sense—only in the Scriptural sense of doing all the things the wise man declared to be folly, after trying them himself on the most extensive scale. I see I am no longer Vivvums' little boy. Don't be alarmed: I shall never call you Vivvums again— at least unless you get tired of your new little boy, whoever he may be.

VIVIE. My new little boy!

FRANK [*with conviction*]. Must be a new little boy. Always happens that way. No other way, in fact.

VIVIE. None that you know of, fortunately for you. [*Someone knocks at the door.*]

FRANK. My curse upon yon caller, whoe'er he be!

VIVIE. It's Praed. He's going to Italy and wants to say good-bye. I asked him to call this afternoon. Go and let him in.

FRANK. We can continue our conversation after his departure for Italy. I'll stay him out. [*He goes to the door and opens it.*] How are you, Praddy? Delighted to see you. Come in. [*Praed, dressed for travelling, comes in, in high spirits, excited by the beginning of his journey.*]

PRAED. How do you do, Miss Warren. [*She presses his hand cordially, though a certain sentimentality in his high spirits jars on her.*] I start in an hour from Holborn Viaduct. I wish I could persuade you to try Italy.

VIVIE. What for?

PRAED. Why, to saturate yourself with beauty and romance, of course. [*Vivie, with a shudder, turns her chair to the table, as if the work waiting for her there were a consolation and support to her. Praed sits opposite to her. Frank places a chair just behind Vivie, and drops lazily and carelessly into it, talking at her over his shoulder.*]

FRANK. No use, Praddy. Viv is a little Philistine. She is indifferent to my romance, and insensible to my beauty.

VIVIE. Mr. Praed: once for all, there is no beauty and no romance in life for me. Life is what it is; and I am prepared to take it as it is.

PRAED [*enthusiastically*]. You will not say that if you come to Verona and on to Venice. You will cry with delight at living in such a beautiful world.

FRANK. This is most eloquent, Praddy. Keep it up.

PRAED. Oh, I assure you *I* have cried—I shall cry again, I hope—at fifty! At your age, Miss Warren, you would not need to go so far as Verona. Your spirits would absolutely fly up at the mere sight of Ostend. You would be charmed with the gaiety, the vivacity, the happy air of Brussels. [*Vivie recoils.*] What's the matter?

FRANK. Hallo, Viv!

VIVIE [*to Praed with deep reproach*]. Can you find no better example of your beauty and romance than Brussels to talk to me about?

PRAED [*puzzled*]. Of course it's very different from Verona. I don't suggest for a moment that—

VIVIE [*bitterly*]. Probably the beauty and romance come to much the same in both places.

PRAED [*completely sobered and much concerned*]. My dear Miss Warren: I—[*looking enquiringly at Frank*] Is anything the matter?

FRANK. She thinks your enthusiasm frivolous, Praddy. She's had ever such a serious call.

VIVIE [*sharply*]. Hold your tongue, Frank. Don't be silly.

FRANK [*calmly*]. Do you call this good manners, Praed?

PRAED [*anxious and considerate*]. Shall I take him away, Miss Warren? I feel sure we have disturbed you at your work. [*He is about to rise.*]

VIVIE. Sit down: I'm not ready to go back to work yet. You both think I have an attack of nerves. Not a bit of it. But there are two subjects I want dropped, if you don't mind. One of them [*to Frank*] is love's young dream in any shape or form: the other [*to Praed*] is the romance and beauty of life, especially as exemplified by the gaiety of Brussels. You are welcome to any illusions you may have left on these subjects: I have none. If we three are to remain friends, I must be treated as a woman of business, permanently single [*to Frank*] and permanently unromantic [*to Praed*].

FRANK. I also shall remain permanently single until you change your mind. Praddy: change the subject. Be eloquent about something else.

PRAED [*diffidently*]. I'm afraid there's nothing else in the world that I can talk about. The Gospel of Art is the only one I can preach. I know Miss Warren is a great devotee of the Gospel of Getting On; but we can't discuss that without hurting your feelings, Frank, since you are determined not to get on.

FRANK. Oh, don't mind my feelings. Give me some improving advice by all means; it does me ever so much good. Have another try to make a successful man of me, Viv. Come: let's have it all: energy, thrift, foresight, self-respect, character. Don't you hate people who have no character, Viv?

VIVIE [*wincing*]. Oh, stop: stop: let us have no more of that horrible cant. Mr. Praed: if there are really only those two gospels in the world, we had better all kill ourselves; for the same taint is in both, through and through.

FRANK [*looking critically at her*]. There is a touch of

poetry about you to-day, Viv, which has hitherto been lacking.

PRAED [*remonstrating*]. My dear Frank: aren't you a little unsympathetic?

VIVIE [*merciless to herself*]. No: it's good for me. It keeps me from being sentimental.

FRANK [*bantering her*]. Checks your strong natural propensity that way, don't it?

VIVIE [*almost hysterically*]. Oh, yes: go on: don't spare me. I was sentimental for a moment in my life—beautifully sentimental—by moonlight; and now—

FRANK [*quickly*]. I say, Viv: take care. Don't give yourself away.

VIVIE. Oh, do you think Mr. Praed does not know all about my mother? [*Turning on Praed.*] You had better have told me that morning, Mr. Praed. You are very old-fashioned in your delicacies, after all.

PRAED. Surely it is you who are a little old-fashioned in your prejudices, Miss Warren. I feel bound to tell you, speaking as an artist, and believing that the most intimate human relationships are far beyond and above the scope of the law, that though I know that your mother is an unmarried woman, I do not respect her the less on that account. I respect her more.

FRANK [*airily*]. Hear, hear!

VIVIE [*staring at him*]. Is that all you know?

PRAED. Certainly that is all.

VIVIE. Then you neither of you know anything. Your guesses are innocence itself compared to the truth.

PRAED [*startled and indignant, preserving his politeness with an effort*]. I hope not. [*More emphatically.*] I hope not, Miss Warren. [*Frank's face shows that he does not share Praed's incredulity. Vivie utters an exclamation of impatience. Praed's chivalry droops before their conviction. He adds, slowly*] If there is anything worse—that is, anything else—are you sure you are right to tell us, Miss Warren?

VIVIE. I am sure that if I had the courage I should spend the rest of my life in telling it to everybody—in stamping and branding it into them until they felt their share in its shame and horror as I feel mine. There is nothing I despise more than the wicked convention that protects these things by forbidding a woman to mention them. And yet I can't tell you. The two infamous words that describe what my mother is are ringing in my ears and struggling on my tongue; but

I can't utter them: my instinct is too strong for me. [*She buries her face in her hands. The two men, astonished, stare at one another and then at her. She raises her head again desperately and takes a sheet of paper and a pen.*] Here: let me draft you a prospectus.

FRANK. Oh, she's mad. Do you hear, Viv, mad. Come: pull yourself together.

VIVIE. You shall see. [*She writes.*] "Paid up capital: not less than £40,000 standing in the name of Sir George Crofts, Baronet, the chief shareholder." What comes next?—I forget. Oh, yes: "Premises at Brussels, Berlin, Vienna and Buda-Pesth. Managing director: Mrs. Warren;" and now don't let us forget her qualifications: the two words. There! [*She pushes the paper to them.*] Oh, no: don't read it: don't! [*She snatches it back and tears it to pieces; then seizes her head in her hands and hides her face on the table. Frank, who has watched the writing carefully over her shoulder, and opened his eyes very widely at it, takes a card from his pocket; scribbles a couple of words; and silently hands it to Praed, who looks at it with amazement. Frank then remorsefully stoops over Vivie.*]

FRANK [*whispering tenderly*]. Viv, dear: that's all right. I read what you wrote: so did Praddy. We understand. And we remain, as this leaves us at present, yours ever so devotedly. [*Vivie slowly raises her head.*]

PRAED. We do, indeed, Miss Warren. I declare you are the most splendidly courageous woman I ever met. [*This sentimental compliment braces Vivie. She throws it away from her with an impatient shake, and forces herself to stand up, though not without some support from the table.*]

FRANK. Don't stir, Viv, if you don't want to. Take it easy.

VIVIE. Thank you. You can always depend on me for two things, not to cry and not to faint. [*She moves a few steps towards the door of the inner rooms, and stops close to Praed to say*] I shall need much more courage than that when I tell my mother that we have come to the parting of the ways. Now I must go into the next room for a moment to make myself neat again, if you don't mind.

PRAED. Shall we go away?

VIVIE. No: I'll be back presently. Only for a moment. [*She goes into the other room, Praed opening the door for her.*]

PRAED. What an amazing revelation! I'm extremely disappointed in Crofts: I am indeed.

FRANK. I'm not in the least. I feel he's perfectly accounted for at last. But what a facer for me, Praddy! I can't marry her now.

PRAED [*sternly*]. Frank! [*The two look at one another, Frank unruffled, Praed deeply indignant.*] Let me tell you, Gardner, that if you desert her now you will behave very despicably.

FRANK. Good old Praddy! Ever chivalrous! But you mistake: it's not the moral aspect of the case: it's the money aspect. I really can't bring myself to touch the old woman's money now.

PRAED. And was that what you were going to marry on?

FRANK. What else? *I* haven't any money, nor the smallest turn for making it. If I married Viv now she would have to support me; and I should cost her more than I am worth.

PRAED. But surely a clever, bright fellow like you can make something by your own brains.

FRANK. Oh, yes, a little. [*He takes out his money again.*] I made all that yesterday—in an hour and a half. But I made it in a highly speculative business. No, dear Praddy: even if Jessie and Georgina marry millionaires and the governor dies after cutting them off with a shilling, I shall have only four hundred a year. And he won't die until he's three score and ten: he hasn't originality enough. I shall be on short allowance for the next twenty years. No short allowance for Viv, if I can help it. I withdraw gracefully and leave the field to the gilded youth of England. So that's settled. I shan't worry her about it: I'll just send her a little note after we're gone. She'll understand.

PRAED [*grasping his hand*]. Good fellow, Frank! I heartily beg your pardon. But must you never see her again?

FRANK. Never see her again! Hang it all, be reasonable. I shall come along as often as possible, and be her brother. I cannot understand the absurd consequences you romantic people expect from the most ordinary transactions. [*A knock at the door.*] I wonder who this is. Would you mind opening the door? If it's a client it will look more respectable than if I appeared.

PRAED. Certainly. [*He goes to the door and opens it. Frank sits down in Vivie's chair to scribble a note.*] My dear Kitty: come in, come in.

[*Mrs. Warren comes in, looking apprehensively round for*

Vivie. She has done her best to make herself matronly and dignified. The brilliant hat is replaced by a sober bonnet, and the gay blouse covered by a costly black silk mantle. She is pitiably anxious and ill at ease—evidently panic-stricken.]

MRS. WARREN [*to Frank*]. What! You're here, are you?

FRANK [*turning in his chair from his writing, but not rising.*] Here, and charmed to see you. You come like a breath of spring.

MRS. WARREN. Oh, get out with your nonsense. [*In a low voice.*] Where's Vivie?

[*Frank points expressively to the door of the inner room, but says nothing.*]

MRS. WARREN [*sitting down suddenly and almost beginning to cry*]. Praddy: won't she see me, don't you think?

PRAED. My dear Kitty: don't distress yourself. Why should she not?

MRS. WARREN. Oh, you never can see why not: you're too amiable. Mr. Frank: did she say anything to you?

FRANK [*folding his note*]. She must see you, if [*very expressively*] you wait until she comes in.

MRS. WARREN [*frightened*]. Why shouldn't I wait?

[*Frank looks quizzically at her; puts his note carefully on the ink-bottle, so that Vivie cannot fail to find it when next she dips her pen; then rises and devotes his attention entirely to her.*]

FRANK. My dear Mrs. Warren: suppose you were a sparrow—ever so tiny and pretty a sparrow hopping in the roadway—and you saw a steam roller coming in your direction, would you wait for it?

MRS. WARREN. Oh, don't bother me with your sparrows. What did she run away from Haslemere like that for?

FRANK. I'm afraid she'll tell you if you wait until she comes back.

MRS. WARREN. Do you want me to go away?

FRANK. No. I always want you to stay. But I advise you to go away.

MRS. WARREN. What! And never see her again!

FRANK. Precisely.

MRS. WARREN [*crying again*]. Praddy: don't let him be cruel to me. [*She hastily checks her tears and wipes her eyes.*] She'll be so angry if she sees I've been crying.

FRANK [*with a touch of real compassion in his airy tenderness*]. You know that Praddy is the soul of kindness, Mrs. Warren. Praddy: what do you say? Go or stay?

PRAED [to Mrs. Warren]. I really should be very sorry to cause you unnecessary pain; but I think perhaps you had better not wait. The fact is—[Vivie is heard at the inner door.]

FRANK. Sh! Too late. She's coming.

MRS. WARREN. Don't tell her I was crying. [Vivie comes in. She stops gravely on seeing Mrs. Warren, who greets her with hysterical cheerfulness.] Well, dearie. So here you are at last.

VIVIE. I am glad you have come: I want to speak to you. You said you were going, Frank, I think.

FRANK. Yes. Will you come with me, Mrs. Warren? What do you say to a trip to Richmond, and the theatre in the evening? There is safety in Richmond. No steam roller there.

VIVIE. Nonsense, Frank. My mother will stay here.

MRS. WARREN [scared]. I don't know: perhaps I'd better go. We're disturbing you at your work.

VIVIE [with quiet decision]. Mr. Praed: please take Frank away. Sit down, mother. [Mrs. Warren obeys helplessly.]

PRAED. Come, Frank. Good-bye, Miss Vivie.

VIVIE [shaking hands]. Good-bye. A pleasant trip.

PRAED. Thank you: thank you. I hope so.

FRANK [to Mrs. Warren]. Good-bye: you'd ever so much better have taken my advice. [He shakes hands with her. Then airily to Vivie] Bye-bye, Viv.

VIVIE. Good-bye. [He goes out gaily without shaking hands with her. Praed follows. Vivie, composed and extremely grave, sits down in Honoria's chair, and waits for her mother to speak. Mrs. Warren, dreading a pause, loses no time in beginning.]

MRS. WARREN. Well, Vivie, what did you go away like that for without saying a word to me? How could you do such a thing! And what have you done to poor George? I wanted him to come with me; but he shuffled out of it. I could see that he was quite afraid of you. Only fancy: he wanted me not to come. As if [trembling] I should be afraid of you, dearie. [Vivie's gravity deepens.] But of course I told him it was all settled and comfortable between us, and that we were on the best of terms. [She breaks down.] Vivie: what's the meaning of this? [She produces a paper from an envelope; comes to the table; and hands it across.] I got it from the bank this morning.

VIVIE. It is my month's allowance. They sent it to me as

usual the other day. I simply sent it back to be placed to
your credit, and asked them to send you the lodgment receipt.
In future I shall support myself.

MRS. WARREN [*not daring to understand*]. Wasn't it
enough? Why didn't you tell me? [*With a cunning gleam in
her eye.*] I'll double it: I was intending to double it. Only let
me know how much you want.

VIVIE. You know very well that that has nothing to do
with it. From this time I go my own way in my own business and among my own friends. And you will go yours.
[*She rises.*] Good-bye.

MRS. WARREN [*appalled*]. Good-bye?

VIVIE. Yes: good-bye. Come: don't let us make a useless
scene: you understand perfectly well. Sir George Crofts has
told me the whole business.

MRS. WARREN [*angrily*]. Silly old— [*She swallows an
epithet, and turns white at the narrowness of her escape from
uttering it.*] He ought to have his tongue cut out. But I explained it all to you; and you said you didn't mind.

VIVIE [*steadfastly*]. Excuse me: I do mind. You explained
how it came about. That does not alter it.

[*Mrs. Warren, silenced for a moment, looks forlornly at
Vivie, who waits like a statue, secretly hoping that the
combat is over. But the cunning expression comes back into
Mrs. Warren's face; and she bends across the table, sly
and urgent, half whispering.*]

MRS. WARREN. Vivie: do you know how rich I am?

VIVIE. I have no doubt you are very rich.

MRS. WARREN. But you don't know all that that means:
you're too young. It means a new dress every day; it means
theatres and balls every night; it means having the pick of
all the gentlemen in Europe at your feet; it means a lovely
house and plenty of servants; it means the choicest of eating
and drinking; it means everything you like, everything you
want, everything you can think of. And what are you here?
A mere drudge, toiling and moiling early and late for your
bare living and two cheap dresses a year. Think it over.
[*Soothingly.*] You're shocked, I know. I can enter into your
feelings; and I think they do you credit; but trust me, nobody
will blame you: you may take my word for that. I know
what young girls are; and I know you'll think better of it
when you've turned it over in your mind.

VIVIE. So that's how it's done, is it? You must have said
all that to many a woman, mother, to have it so pat.

MRS. WARREN [*passionately*]. What harm am I asking you to do? [*Vivie turns away contemptuously. Mrs. Warren follows her desperately.*] Vivie: listen to me: you don't understand: you've been taught wrong on purpose: you don't know what the world is really like.

VIVIE [*arrested*]. Taught wrong on purpose! What do you mean?

MRS. WARREN. I mean that you're throwing away all your chances for nothing. You think that people are what they pretend to be—that the way you were taught at school and college to think right and proper is the way things really are. But it's not: it's all only a pretence, to keep the cowardly, slavish, common run of people quiet. Do you want to find that out, like other women, at forty, when you've thrown yourself away and lost your chances; or won't you take it in good time now from your own mother, that loves you and swears to you that it's truth—gospel truth? [*Urgently.*] Vivie: the big people, the clever people, the managing people, all know it. They do as I do, and think what I think. I know plenty of them. I know them to speak to, to introduce you to, to make friends of for you. I don't mean anything wrong: that's what you don't understand: your head is full of ignorant ideas about me. What do the people that taught you know about life or about people like me? When did they ever meet me, or speak to me, or let anyone tell them about me? —the fools! Would they ever have done anything for you if you hadn't paid them? Haven't I told you that I want you to be respectable? Haven't I brought you up to be respectable? And how can you keep it up without my money and my influence and Lizzie's friends? Can't you see that you're cutting your own throat as well as breaking my heart in turning your back on me?

VIVIE. I recognise the Crofts philosophy of life, mother. I heard it all from him that day at the Gardners'.

MRS. WARREN. You think I want to force that played-out old sot on you! I don't, Vivie: on my oath I don't.

VIVIE. It would not matter if you did: you would not succeed. [*Mrs. Warren winces, deeply hurt by the implied indifference towards her affectionate intention. Vivie, neither understanding this nor concerning herself about it, goes on calmly*] Mother: you don't at all know the sort of person I am. I don't object to Crofts more than to any other coarsely built man of his class. To tell you the truth, I rather admire him for being strong-minded enough to enjoy himself in his own way and make plenty of money instead of living the usual shooting, hunting, dining-out, tailoring, loafing life of his set merely because all the rest do it. And I'm perfectly aware that if I'd been in the same circumstances as my aunt Liz, I'd have done exactly what she did. I don't think I'm more prejudiced or straitlaced than you: I think I'm less. I'm certain I'm less sentimental. I know very well that fashionable morality is all a pretence: and that if I took your money and devoted the rest of my life to spending it fashionably, I might be as worthless and vicious as the silliest woman could possibly want to be without having a word said to me about it. But I don't want to be worthless. I shouldn't enjoy trotting about the park to advertise my dressmaker and carriage builder, or being bored at the opera to show off a shop windowful of diamonds.

MRS. WARREN [bewildered]. But—

VIVIE. Wait a moment: I've not done. Tell me why you continue your business now that you are independent of it. Your sister, you told me, has left all that behind her. Why don't you do the same?

MRS. WARREN. Oh, it's all very easy for Liz: she likes good society, and has the air of being a lady. Imagine me in a cathedral town! Why, the very rooks in the trees would find me out even if I could stand the dulness of it. I must have work and excitement, or I should go melancholy mad. And what else is there for me to do? The life suits me: I'm fit for it and not for anything else. If I didn't do it somebody else would; so I don't do any real harm by it. And then it brings in money; and I like making money. No: it's no use: I can't give it up—not for anybody. But what need you know about it? I'll never mention it. I'll keep Crofts away. I'll not trouble you much: you see I have to be constantly running about from one place to another. You'll be quit of me altogether when I die.

VIVIE. No: I am my mother's daughter. I am like you: I must have work, and must make more money than I spend. But my work is not your work, and my way not your way. We must part. It will not make much difference to us: instead of meeting one another for perhaps a few months in twenty years, we shall never meet: that's all.

MRS. WARREN [her voice stifled in tears]. Vivie: I meant to have been more with you: I did indeed.

VIVIE. It's no use, mother: I am not to be changed by a

few cheap tears and entreaties any more than you are, I dare say.

MRS. WARREN [*wildly*]. Oh, you call a mother's tears cheap.

VIVIE. They cost you nothing; and you ask me to give you the peace and quietness of my whole life in exchange for them. What use would my company be to you if you could get it? What have we two in common that could make either of us happy together?

MRS. WARREN [*lapsing recklessly into her dialect*]. We're mother and daughter. I want my daughter. I've a right to you. Who is to care for me when I'm old? Plenty of girls have taken to me like daughters and cried at leaving me; but I let them all go because I had you to look forward to. I kept myself lonely for you. You've no right to turn on me now and refuse to do your duty as a daughter.

VIVIE [*jarred and antagonized by the echo of the slums in her mother's voice*]. My duty as a daughter! I thought we should come to that presently. Now once for all, mother, you want a daughter and Frank wants a wife. I don't want a mother; and I don't want a husband. I have spared neither Frank nor myself in sending him about his business. Do you think I will spare you?

MRS. WARREN [*violently*]. Oh, I know the sort you are—no mercy for yourself or anyone else. *I* know. My experience has done that for me anyhow: I can tell the pious, canting, hard, selfish woman when I meet her. Well, keep yourself to yourself: *I* don't want you. But listen to this. Do you know what I would do with you if you were a baby again—aye, as sure as there's a Heaven above us?

VIVIE. Strangle me, perhaps.

MRS. WARREN. No: I'd bring you up to be a real daughter to me, and not what you are now, with your pride and your prejudices and the college education you stole from me —yes, stole: deny it if you can: what was it but stealing? I'd bring you up in my own house, so I would.

VIVIE [*quietly*]. In one of your own houses.

MRS. WARREN [*screaming*]. Listen to her! listen to how she spits on her mother's grey hairs! Oh, may you live to have your own daughter tear and trample on you as you have trampled on me. And you will: you will. No woman ever had luck with a mother's curse on her.

VIVIE. I wish you wouldn't rant, mother. It only hardens me. Come: I suppose I am the only young woman you ever had in your power that you did good to. Don't spoil it all now.

MRS. WARREN. Yes. Heaven forgive me, it's true; and you are the only one that ever turned on me. Oh, the injustice of it, the injustice, the injustice! I always wanted to be a good woman. I tried honest work; and I was slave-driven until I cursed the day I ever heard of honest work. I was a good mother; and because I made my daughter a good woman she turns me out as if I was a leper. Oh, if I only had my life to live over again! I'd talk to that lying clergyman in the school. From this time forth, so help me Heaven in my last hour, I'll do wrong and nothing but wrong. And I'll prosper on it.

VIVIE. Yes: it's better to choose your line and go through with it. If I had been you, mother, I might have done as you did; but I should not have lived one life and believed in another. You are a conventional woman at heart. That is why I am bidding you good-bye now. I am right, am I not?

MRS. WARREN [taken aback]. Right to throw away all my money!

VIVIE. No: right to get rid of you? I should be a fool not to? Isn't that so?

MRS. WARREN [sulkily]. Oh, well, yes, if you come to that, I suppose you are. But Lord help the world if everybody took to doing the right thing! And now I'd better go than stay where I'm not wanted. [She turns to the door.]

VIVIE [kindly]. Won't you shake hands?

MRS. WARREN [after looking at her fiercely for a moment with a savage impulse to strike her]. No, thank you. Good-bye.

VIVIE [matter-of-factly]. Good-bye. [Mrs. Warren goes out, slamming the door behind her. The strain on Vivie's face relaxes; her grave expression breaks up into one of joyous content; her breath goes out in a half sob, half laugh of intense relief. She goes buoyantly to her place at the writing table; pushes the electric lamp out of the way; pulls over a great sheaf of papers; and is in the act of dipping her pen in the ink when she finds Frank's note. She opens it unconcernedly and reads it quickly, giving a little laugh at some quaint turn of expression in it.] And good-bye, Frank. [She tears the note up and tosses the pieces into the wastepaper basket without a second thought. Then she goes at her work with a plunge, and soon becomes absorbed in her figures.]

Arms and the Man

ACT ONE

Night. A lady's bedchamber in Bulgaria, in a small town near the Dragoman Pass. It is late in November in the year 1885, and through an open window with a little balcony on the left can be seen a peak of the Balkans, wonderfully white and beautiful in the starlit snow. The interior of the room is not like anything to be seen in the east of Europe. It is half rich Bulgarian, half cheap Viennese. The counterpane and hangings of the bed, the window curtains, the little carpet, and all the ornamental textile fabrics in the room are oriental and gorgeous: the paper on the walls is occidental and paltry. Above the head of the bed, which stands against a little wall cutting off the right hand corner of the room diagonally, is a painted wooden shrine, blue and gold, with an ivory image of Christ, and a light hanging before it in a pierced metal ball suspended by three chains. On the left, further forward, is an ottoman. The washstand, against the wall on the left, consists of an enamelled iron basin with a pail beneath it in a painted metal frame, and a single towel on the rail at the side. A chair near it is Austrian bent wood, with cane seat. The dressing table, between the bed and the window, is an ordinary pine table, covered with a cloth of many colors, but with an expensive toilet mirror on it. The door is on the right; and there is a chest of drawers between the door and the bed. This chest of drawers is also covered by a variegated native cloth, and on it there is a pile of paper backed novels, a box of chocolate creams, and a miniature easel, on which is a large photograph of an extremely handsome officer, whose lofty bearing and magnetic glance can be felt even from the portrait. The room is lighted by a candle on the chest of drawers, and another on the dressing table, with a box of matches beside it.

The window is hinged doorwise and stands wide open,

116

*folding back to the left. Outside a pair of wooden shutters,
opening outwards, also stand open. On the balcony, a young
lady, intensely conscious of the romantic beauty of the night,
and of the fact that her own youth and beauty is a part of it,
is on the balcony, gazing at the snowy Balkans. She is covered
by a long mantle of furs, worth, on a moderate estimate,
about three times the furniture of her room.*

*Her reverie is interrupted by her mother, Catherine Petkoff,
a woman over forty, imperiously energetic, with magnificent
black hair and eyes, who might be a very splendid specimen
of the wife of a mountain farmer, but is determined to be a
Viennese lady, and to that end wears a fashionable tea gown
on all occasions.*

CATHERINE [*entering hastily, full of good news*]. Raina—
[*she pronounces it Rah-eena, with the stress on the ee*] Raina
—[*she goes to the bed, expecting to find Raina there.*] Why,
where—[*Raina looks into the room.*] Heavens! child, are you
out in the night air instead of in your bed? You'll catch your
death. Louka told me you were asleep.

RAINA [*coming in*]. I sent her away. I wanted to be alone.
The stars are so beautiful! What is the matter?

CATHERINE. Such news. There has been a battle!

RAINA [*her eyes dilating*]. Ah! [*She throws the cloak on
the ottoman, and comes eagerly to Catherine in her nightgown, a pretty garment, but evidently the only one she has
on.*]

CATHERINE. A great battle at Slivnitza! A victory! And
it was won by Sergius.

RAINA [*with a cry of delight*]. Ah! [*Rapturously.*] Oh,
mother! [*Then, with sudden anxiety*] Is father safe?

CATHERINE. Of course: he sent me the news. Sergius is
the hero of the hour, the idol of the regiment.

RAINA. Tell me, tell me. How was it! [*Ecstatically*] Oh,
mother, mother, mother! [*Raina pulls her mother down on
the ottoman; and they kiss one another frantically.*]

CATHERINE [*with surging enthusiasm*]. You can't guess
how splendid it is. A cavalry charge—think of that! He defied our Russian commanders—acted without orders—led a
charge on his own responsibility—headed it himself—was the
first man to sweep through their guns. Can't you see it, Raina;
our gallant splendid Bulgarians with their swords and eyes
flashing, thundering down like an avalanche and scattering
the wretched Servian dandies like chaff. And you—you kept

Sergius waiting a year before you would be betrothed to him. Oh, if you have a drop of Bulgarian blood in your veins, you will worship him when he comes back.

RAINA. What will he care for my poor little worship after the acclamations of a whole army of heroes? But no matter: I am so happy—so proud! [*She rises and walks about excitedly.*] It proves that all our ideas were real after all.

CATHERINE [*indignantly*]. Our ideas real! What do you mean?

RAINA. Our ideas of what Sergius would do—our patriotism—our heroic ideals. Oh, what faithless little creatures girls are!— I sometimes used to doubt whether they were anything but dreams. When I buckled on Sergius's sword he looked so noble: it was treason to think of disillusion or humiliation or failure. And yet—and yet— [*Quickly.*] Promise me you'll never tell him.

CATHERINE. Don't ask me for promises until I know what I am promising.

RAINA. Well, it came into my head just as he was holding me in his arms and looking into my eyes, that perhaps we only had our heroic ideas because we are so fond of reading Byron and Pushkin, and because we were so delighted with the opera that season at Bucharest. Real life is so seldom like that—indeed never, as far as I knew it then. [*Remorsefully.*] Only think, mother, I doubted him: I wondered whether all his heroic qualities and his soldiership might not prove mere imagination when he went into a real battle. I had an uneasy fear that he might cut a poor figure there beside all those clever Russian officers.

CATHERINE. A poor figure! Shame on you! The Servians have Austrian officers who are just as clever as our Russians; but we have beaten them in every battle for all that.

RAINA [*laughing and sitting down again*]. Yes, I was only a prosaic little coward. Oh, to think that it was all true— that Sergius is just as splendid and noble as he looks—that the world is really a glorious world for women who can see its glory and men who can act its romance! What happiness! what unspeakable fulfilment! Ah! [*She throws herself on her knees beside her mother and flings her arms passionately round her. They are interrupted by the entry of Louka, a handsome, proud girl in a pretty Bulgarian peasant's dress with double apron, so defiant that her servility to Raina is almost insolent. She is afraid of Catherine, but even with her goes as far as she dares. She is just now excited like the others; but she has no sympathy for Raina's raptures and looks contemptuously at the ecstasies of the two before she addresses them.*]

LOUKA. If you please, madam, all the windows are to be closed and the shutters made fast. They say there may be shooting in the streets. [*Raina and Catherine rise together, alarmed.*] The Servians are being chased right back through the pass; and they say they may run into the town. Our cavalry will be after them; and our people will be ready for them you may be sure, now that they are running away. [*She goes out on the balcony and pulls the outside shutters to; then steps back into the room.*]

RAINA. I wish our people were not so cruel. What glory is there in killing wretched fugitives?

CATHERINE [*business-like, her housekeeping instincts aroused*]. I must see that everything is made safe downstairs.

RAINA [*to Louka*]. Leave the shutters so that I can just close them if I hear any noise.

CATHERINE [*authoritatively, turning on her way to the door*]. Oh, no, dear, you must keep them fastened. You would be sure to drop off to sleep and leave them open. Make them fast, Louka.

LOUKA. Yes, madam. [*She fastens them.*]

RAINA. Don't be anxious about me. The moment I hear a shot, I shall blow out the candles and roll myself up in bed with my ears well covered.

CATHERINE. Quite the wisest thing you can do, my love. Good-night.

RAINA. Good-night. [*They kiss one another, and Raina's emotion comes back for a moment.*] Wish me joy of the happiest night of my life—if only there are no fugitives.

CATHERINE. Go to bed, dear, and don't think of them. [*She goes out.*]

LOUKA [*secretly, to Raina*]. If you would like the shutters open, just give them a push like this. [*She pushes them: they open: she pulls them to again.*] One of them ought to be bolted at the bottom; but the bolt's gone.

RAINA [*with dignity, reproving her*]. Thanks, Louka; but we must do what we are told. [*Louka makes a grimace.*] Good-night.

LOUKA [*carelessly*]. Good-night. [*She goes out, swaggering.*]

[*Raina, left alone, goes to the chest of drawers, and adores the portrait there with feelings that are beyond all expression.*

She does not kiss it or press it to her breast, or shew it any mark of bodily affection; but she takes it in her hands and elevates it like a priestess.]

RAINA [*looking up at the picture with worship*]. Oh, I shall never be unworthy of you any more, my hero—never, never, never. [*She replaces it reverently, and selects a novel from the little pile of books. She turns over the leaves dreamily; finds her page; turns the book inside out at it; and then, with a happy sigh, gets into bed and prepares to read herself to sleep. But before abandoning herself to fiction, she raises her eyes once more, thinking of the blessed reality and murmurs*] My hero! my hero! [*A distant shot breaks the quiet of the night outside. She starts, listening; and two more shots, much nearer, follow, startling her so that she scrambles out of bed, and hastily blows out the candle on the chest of drawers. Then, putting her fingers in her ears, she runs to the dressing-table and blows out the light there, and hurries back to bed. The room is now in darkness: nothing is visible but the glimmer of the light in the pierced ball before the image, and the starlight seen through the slits at the top of the shutters. The firing breaks out again: there is a startling fusillade quite close at hand. Whilst it is still echoing, the shutters disappear, pulled open from without, and for an instant the rectangle of snowy starlight flashes out with the figure of a man in black upon it. The shutters close immediately and the room is dark again. But the silence is now broken by the sound of panting. Then there is a scrape; and the flame of a match is seen in the middle of the room.*]

RAINA [*crouching on the bed*]. Who's there? [*The match is out instantly.*] Who's there? Who is that?

A MAN'S VOICE [*in the darkness, subduedly, but threateningly*]. Sh—sh! Don't call out or you'll be shot. Be good; and no harm will happen to you. [*She is heard leaving her bed, and making for the door.*] Take care, there's no use in trying to run away. Remember, if you raise your voice my pistol will go off. [*Commandingly.*] Strike a light and let me see you. Do you hear? [*Another moment of silence and darkness. Then she is heard retreating to the dressing-table. She lights a candle, and the mystery is at an end. A man of about 35, in a deplorable plight, bespattered with mud and blood and snow, his belt and the strap of his revolver case keeping together the torn ruins of the blue coat of a Servian artillery officer. As far as the candlelight and his unwashed, unkempt condition make it possible to judge, he is a man of middling*

*stature and undistinguished appearance, with strong neck
and shoulders, a roundish, obstinate looking head covered
with short crisp bronze curls, clear quick blue eyes and good
brows and mouth, a hopelessly prosaic nose like that of a
strong-minded baby, trim soldierlike carriage and energetic
manner, and with all his wits about him in spite of his
desperate predicament—even with a sense of humor of it,
without, however, the least intention of trifling with it or
throwing away a chance. He reckons up what he can guess
about Raina—her age, her social position, her character, the
extent to which she is frightened—at a glance, and continues,
more politely but still most determinedly]* Excuse my disturbing you; but you recognise my uniform—Servian. If I'm
caught I shall be killed. *[Determinedly.]* Do you understand
that?

RAINA. Yes.

MAN. Well, I don't intend to get killed if I can help it.
[Still more determinedly.] Do you understand that? *[He locks
the door with a snap.]*

RAINA *[disdainfully]*. I suppose not. *[She draws herself
up superbly, and looks him straight in the face, saying with
emphasis]* Some soldiers, I know, are afraid of death.

MAN *[with grim goodhumor]*. All of them, dear lady, all
of them, believe me. It is our duty to live as long as we can,
and kill as many of the enemy as we can. Now if you raise an
alarm—

RAINA *[cutting him short]*. You will shoot me. How do
you know that I am afraid to die?

MAN *[cunningly]*. Ah; but suppose I don't shoot you,
what will happen then? Why, a lot of your cavalry—the
greatest blackguards in your army—will burst into this
pretty room of yours and slaughter me here like a pig; for
I'll fight like a demon: they shan't get me into the street to
amuse themselves with: I know what they are. Are you prepared to receive that sort of company in your present un-
dress? *[Raina, suddenly conscious of her nightgown, instinctively shrinks and gathers it more closely about her. He
watches her, and adds, pitilessly]* It's rather scanty, eh? *[She
turns to the ottoman. He raises his pistol instantly, and cries]*
Stop! *[She stops.]* Where are you going?

RAINA *[with dignified patience]*. Only to get my cloak.

MAN *[darting to the ottoman and snatching the cloak]*.
A good idea. No: I'll keep the cloak: and you will take care
that nobody comes in and sees you without it. This is a better

weapon than the pistol. [*He throws the pistol down on the ottoman.*]

RAINA [*revolted*]. It is not the weapon of a gentleman!

MAN. It's good enough for a man with only you to stand between him and death. [*As they look at one another for a moment, Raina hardly able to believe that even a Servian officer can be so cynically and selfishly unchivalrous, they are startled by a sharp fusillade in the street. The chill of imminent death hushes the man's voice as he adds*] Do you hear? If you are going to bring those scoundrels in on me you shall receive them as you are. [*Raina meets his eye with unflinching scorn. Suddenly he starts, listening. There is a step outside. Someone tries the door, and then knocks hurriedly and urgently at it. Raina looks at the man, breathless. He throws up his head with the gesture of a man who sees that it is all over with him, and, dropping the manner which he has been assuming to intimidate her, flings the cloak to her, exclaiming, sincerely and kindly*] No use: I'm done for. Quick! wrap yourself up: they're coming!

RAINA [*catching the cloak eagerly*]. Oh, thank you. [*She wraps herself up with great relief. He draws his sabre and turns to the door, waiting.*]

LOUKA [*outside, knocking*]. My lady, my lady! Get up, quick, and open the door.

RAINA [*anxiously*]. What will you do?

MAN [*grimly*]. Never mind. Keep out of the way. It will not last long.

RAINA [*impulsively*]. I'll help you. Hide yourself, oh, hide yourself, quick, behind the curtain. [*She seizes him by a torn strip of his sleeve, and pulls him towards the window.*]

MAN [*yielding to her*]. There is just half a chance, if you keep your head. Remember: nine soldiers out of ten are born fools. [*He hides behind the curtain, looking out for a moment to say, finally*] If they find me, I promise you a fight—a devil of a fight! [*He disappears. Raina takes off the cloak and throws it across the foot of the bed. Then with a sleepy, disturbed air, she opens the door. Louka enters excitedly.*]

LOUKA. A man has been seen climbing up the water-pipe to your balcony—a Servian. The soldiers want to search for him; and they are so wild and drunk and furious. My lady says you are to dress at once.

RAINA [*as if annoyed at being disturbed*]. They shall not search here. Why have they been let in?

CATHERINE [*coming in hastily*]. Raina, darling, are you safe? Have you seen anyone or heard anything?

RAINA. I heard the shooting. Surely the soldiers will not dare come in here?

CATHERINE. I have found a Russian officer, thank Heaven: he knows Sergius. [*Speaking through the door to someone outside.*] Sir, will you come in now! My daughter is ready.

[*A young Russian officer, in Bulgarian uniform, enters, sword in hand.*]

THE OFFICER [*with soft, feline politeness and stiff military carriage*]. Good evening, gracious lady; I am sorry to intrude, but there is a fugitive hiding on the balcony. Will you and the gracious lady your mother please to withdraw whilst we search?

RAINA [*petulantly*]. Nonsense, sir, you can see that there is no one on the balcony. [*She throws the shutters wide open and stands with her back to the curtain where the man is hidden, pointing to the moonlit balcony. A couple of shots are fired right under the window, and a bullet shatters the glass opposite Raina, who winks and gasps, but stands her ground, whilst Catherine screams, and the officer rushes to the balcony.*]

THE OFFICER [*on the balcony, shouting savagely down to the street*]. Cease firing there, you fools: do you hear? Cease firing, damn you. [*He glares down for a moment; then turns to Raina, trying to resume his polite manner.*] Could anyone have got in without your knowledge? Were you asleep?

RAINA. No, I have not been to bed.

THE OFFICER [*impatiently, coming back into the room*]. Your neighbours have their heads so full of runaway Servians that they see them everywhere. [*Politely.*] Gracious lady, a thousand pardons. Good-night. [*Military bow, which Raina returns coldly. Another to Catherine, who follows him out. Raina closes the shutters. She turns and sees Louka, who has been watching the scene curiously.*]

RAINA. Don't leave my mother, Louka, whilst the soldiers are here. [*Louka glances at Raina, at the ottoman, at the curtain; then purses her lips secretively, laughs to herself, and goes out. Raina follows her to the door, shuts it behind her with a slam, and locks it violently. The man immediately steps out from behind the curtain, sheathing his sabre, and dismissing the danger from his mind in a businesslike way.*]

MAN. A narrow shave; but a miss is as good as a mile.

Dear young lady, your servant until death. I wish for your
sake I had joined the Bulgarian army instead of the Servian.
I am not a native Servian.

RAINA [*haughtily*]. No, you are one of the Austrians who
set the Servians on to rob us of our national liberty, and
who officer their army for them. We hate them!

MAN. Austrian! not I. Don't hate me, dear young lady.
I am only a Swiss, fighting merely as a professional soldier.
I joined Servia because it was nearest to me. Be generous:
you've beaten us hollow.

RAINA. Have I not been generous?

MAN. Noble!—heroic! But I'm not saved yet. This particular rush will soon pass through; but the pursuit will go
on all night by fits and starts. I must take my chance to get
off during a quiet interval. You don't mind my waiting just
a minute or two, do you?

RAINA. Oh, no: I am sorry you will have to go into
danger again. [*Motioning towards ottoman.*] Won't you sit—
[*She breaks off with an irrepressible cry of alarm as she
catches sight of the pistol. The man, all nerves, shies like a
frightened horse.*]

MAN [*irritably*]. Don't frighten me like that. What is it?

RAINA. Your pistol! It was staring that officer in the face
all the time. What an escape!

MAN [*vexed at being unnecessarily terrified*]. Oh, is that
all?

RAINA [*staring at him rather superciliously, conceiving a
poorer and poorer opinion of him, and feeling propor-
tionately more and more at her ease with him*]. I am sorry I
frightened you. [*She takes up the pistol and hands it to him.*]
Pray take it to protect yourself against me.

MAN [*grinning wearily at the sarcasm as he takes the
pistol*]. No use, dear young lady: there's nothing in it. It's
not loaded. [*He makes a grimace at it, and drops it disparagingly into his revolver case.*]

RAINA. Load it by all means.

MAN. I've no ammunition. What use are cartridges in
battle? I always carry chocolate instead; and I finished the
last cake of that yesterday.

RAINA [*outraged in her most cherished ideals of manhood*]. Chocolate! Do you stuff your pockets with sweets—
like a schoolboy—even in the field?

MAN. Yes. Isn't it contemptible?

[*Raina stares at him, unable to utter her feelings. Then*]

she sails away scornfully to the chest of drawers, and returns with the box of confectionery in her hand.]

RAINA. Allow me. I am sorry I have eaten them all except these. [*She offers him the box.*]

MAN [*ravenously*]. You're an angel! [*He gobbles the comfits.*] Creams! Delicious! [*He looks anxiously to see whether there are any more. There are none. He accepts the inevitable with pathetic goodhumor, and says, with grateful emotion*] Bless you, dear lady. You can always tell an old soldier by the inside of his holsters and cartridge boxes. The young ones carry pistols and cartridges; the old ones, grub. Thank you. [*He hands back the box. She snatches it contemptuously from him and throws it away. This impatient action is so sudden that he shies again.*] Ugh! Don't do things so suddenly, gracious lady. Don't revenge yourself because I frightened you just now.

RAINA [*superbly*]. Frighten me! Do you know, sir, that though I am only a woman, I think I am at heart as brave as you.

MAN. I should think so. You haven't been under fire for three days as I have. I can stand two days without shewing it much; but no man can stand three days: I'm as nervous as a mouse. [*He sits down on the ottoman, and takes his head in his hands.*] Would you like to see me cry?

RAINA [*quickly*]. No.

MAN. If you would, all you have to do is to scold me just as if I were a little boy and you my nurse. If I were in camp now they'd play all sorts of tricks on me.

RAINA [*a little moved*]. I'm sorry. I won't scold you. [*Touched by the sympathy in her tone, he raises his head and looks gratefully at her: she immediately draws back and says stiffly*] You must excuse me: our soldiers are not like that. [*She moves away from the ottoman*].

MAN. Oh, yes, they are. There are only two sorts of soldiers: old ones and young ones. I've served fourteen years: half of your fellows never smelt powder before. Why, how is it that you've just beaten us? Sheer ignorance of the art of war, nothing else. [*Indignantly.*] I never saw anything so unprofessional.

RAINA [*ironically*]. Oh, was it unprofessional to beat you?

MAN. Well, come, is it professional to throw a regiment of cavalry on a battery of machine guns, with the dead certainty that if the guns go off not a horse or man will ever get within fifty yards of the fire? I couldn't believe my eyes when I saw it.

RAINA [*eagerly turning to him, as all her enthusiasm and her dream of glory rush back on her*]. Did you see the great cavalry charge? Oh, tell me about it. Describe it to me.

MAN. You never saw a cavalry charge, did you?

RAINA. How could I?

MAN. Ah, perhaps not—of course. Well, it's a funny sight. It's like slinging a handful of peas against a window pane: first one comes; then two or three close behind him; and then all the rest in a lump.

RAINA [*her eyes dilating as she raises her clasped hands ecstatically*]. Yes, first One!—the bravest of the brave!

MAN [*prosaically*]. Hm! you should see the poor devil pulling at his horse.

RAINA. Why should he pull at his horse?

MAN [*impatient of so stupid a question*]. It's running away with him, of course: do you suppose the fellow wants to get there before the others and be killed? Then they all come. You can tell the young ones by their wildness and their slashing. The old ones come bunched up under the number one guard: they know that they are mere projectiles, and that it's no use trying to fight. The wounds are mostly broken knees, from the horses cannoning together.

RAINA. Ugh! But I don't believe the first man is a coward. I believe he is a hero!

MAN [*goodhumoredly*]. That's what you'd have said if you'd seen the first man in the charge to-day.

RAINA [*breathless*]. Ah, I knew it! Tell me—tell me about him.

MAN. He did it like an operatic tenor—a regular handsome fellow, with flashing eyes and lovely moustache, shouting a war-cry and charging like Don Quixote at the windmills. We nearly burst with laughter at him; but when the sergeant ran up as white as a sheet, and told us they'd sent us the wrong cartridges, and that we couldn't fire a shot for the next ten minutes, we laughed at the other side of our mouths. I never felt so sick in my life, though I've been in one or two very tight places. And I hadn't even a revolver cartridge—nothing but chocolate. We'd no bayonets—nothing. Of course, they just cut us to bits. And there was Don Quixote flourishing like a drum major, thinking he'd done the cleverest thing ever known, whereas he ought to be courtmartialled for it. Of all the fools ever let loose on a field of battle, that man must be the very maddest. He and his regiment simply committed suicide—only the pistol missed fire, that's all.

RAINA [*deeply wounded, but steadfastly loyal to her ideals*]. Indeed! Would you know him again if you saw him?

MAN. Shall I ever forget him. [*She again goes to the chest of drawers. He watches her with a vague hope that she may have something else for him to eat. She takes the portrait from its stand and brings it to him.*]

RAINA. That is a photograph of the gentleman—the patriot and hero—to whom I am betrothed.

MAN [*looking at it*]. I'm really very sorry. [*Looking at her.*] Was it fair to lead me on? [*He looks at the portrait again.*] Yes: that's him: not a doubt of it. [*He stifles a laugh.*]

RAINA [*quickly*]. Why do you laugh?

MAN [*shamefacedly, but still greatly tickled*]. I didn't laugh, I assure you. At least I didn't mean to. But when I think of him charging the windmills and thinking he was doing the finest thing—[*chokes with suppressed laughter*].

RAINA [*sternly*]. Give me back the portrait, sir.

MAN [*with sincere remorse*]. Of course. Certainly. I'm really very sorry. [*She deliberately kisses it, and looks him straight in the face, before returning to the chest of drawers to replace it. He follows her, apologizing.*] Perhaps I'm quite wrong, you know: no doubt I am. Most likely he had got wind of the cartridge business somehow, and knew it was a safe job.

RAINA. That is to say, he was a pretender and a coward! You did not dare say that before.

MAN [*with a comic gesture of despair*]. It's no use, dear lady: I can't make you see it from the professional point of view. [*As he turns away to get back to the ottoman, the firing begins again in the distance.*]

RAINA [*sternly, as she sees him listening to the shots*]. So much the better for you.

MAN [*turning*]. How?

RAINA. You are my enemy; and you are at my mercy. What would I do if I were a professional soldier?

MAN. Ah, true, dear young lady: you're always right. I know how good you have been to me: to my last hour I shall remember those three chocolate creams. It was unsoldierly; but it was angelic.

RAINA [*coldly*]. Thank you. And now I will do a soldierly thing. You cannot stay here after what you have just said about my future husband; but I will go out on the balcony and see whether it is safe for you to climb down into the street. [*She turns to the window.*]

MAN [*changing countenance*]. Down that waterpipe! Stop! Wait! I can't! I daren't! The very thought of it makes me giddy. I came up it fast enough with death behind me. But to face it now in cold blood!—[*He sinks on the ottoman.*] It's no use: I give up: I'm beaten. Give the alarm. [*He drops his head in his hands in the deepest dejection.*]

RAINA [*disarmed by pity*]. Come, don't be disheartened. [*She stoops over him almost maternally: he shakes his head.*] Oh, you are a very poor soldier—a chocolate cream soldier. Come, cheer up: it takes less courage to climb down than to face capture—remember that.

MAN [*dreamily, lulled by her voice*]. No, capture only means death; and death is sleep—oh, sleep, sleep, sleep, undisturbed sleep! Climbing down the pipe means doing something—exerting myself—thinking! Death ten times over first.

RAINA [*softly and wonderingly, catching the rhythm of his weariness*]. Are you so sleepy as that?

MAN. I've not had two hours undisturbed sleep since the war began. I'm on the staff: you don't know what that means. I haven't closed my eyes for thirty-six hours.

RAINA [*desperately*]. But what am I to do with you.

MAN [*staggering up*]. Of course I must do something. [*He shakes himself; pulls himself together; and speaks with rallied vigour and courage.*] You see, sleep or no sleep, hunger or no hunger, tired or not tired, you can always do a thing when you know it must be done. Well, that pipe must be got down—[*He hits himself on the chest, and adds*]—Do you hear that, you chocolate cream soldier? [*He turns to the window.*]

RAINA [*anxiously*]. But if you fall?

MAN. I shall sleep as if the stones were a feather bed. Good-bye. [*He makes boldly for the window, and his hand is on the shutter when there is a terrible burst of firing in the street beneath.*]

RAINA [*rushing to him*]. Stop! [*She catches him by the shoulder, and turns him quite round.*] They'll kill you.

MAN [*coolly, but attentively*]. Never mind: this sort of thing is all in my day's work. I'm bound to take my chance. [*Decisively.*] Now do what I tell you. Put out the candles, so that they shan't see the light when I open the shutters. And keep away from the window, whatever you do. If they see me, they're sure to have a shot at me.

RAINA [*clinging to him*]. They're sure to see you: it's bright moonlight. I'll save you—oh, how can you be so indifferent? You want me to save you, don't you?

MAN. I really don't want to be troublesome. [*She shakes him in her impatience.*] I am not indifferent, dear young lady, I assure you. But how is it to be done?

RAINA. Come away from the window—please. [*She coaxes him back to the middle of the room. He submits humbly. She releases him, and addresses him patronizingly.*] Now listen. You must trust to our hospitality. You do not yet know in whose house you are. I am a Petkoff.

MAN. What's that?

RAINA [*rather indignantly*]. I mean that I belong to the family of the Petkoffs, the richest and best known in our country.

MAN. Oh, yes, of course. I beg your pardon. The Petkoffs, to be sure. How stupid of me!

RAINA. You know you never heard of them until this minute. How can you stoop to pretend?

MAN. Forgive me: I'm too tired to think; and the change of subject was too much for me. Don't scold me.

RAINA. I forgot. It might make you cry. [*He nods, quite seriously. She pouts and then resumes her patronizing tone.*] I must tell you that my father holds the highest command of any Bulgarian in our army. He is [*proudly*] a Major.

MAN [*pretending to be deeply impressed*]. A Major! Bless me! Think of that!

RAINA. You shewed great ignorance in thinking that it was necessary to climb up to the balcony, because ours is the only private house that has two rows of windows. There is a flight of stairs inside to get up and down by.

MAN. Stairs! How grand! You live in great luxury indeed, dear young lady.

RAINA. Do you know what a library is?

MAN. A library? A roomful of books.

RAINA. Yes, we have one, the only one in Bulgaria.

MAN. Actually a real library! I should like to see that.

RAINA [*affectedly*]. I tell you these things to shew you that you are not in the house of ignorant country folk who would kill you the moment they saw your Servian uniform, but among civilized people. We go to Bucharest every year for the opera season; and I have spent a whole month in Vienna.

MAN. I saw that, dear young lady. I saw at once that you knew the world.

RAINA. Have you ever seen the opera of Ernani?

MAN. Is that the one with the devil in it in red velvet, and a soldier's chorus?

RAINA [*contemptuously*]. No!

MAN [*stifling a heavy sigh of weariness*]. Then I don't know it.

RAINA. I thought you might have remembered the great scene where Ernani, flying from his foes just as you are to-night, takes refuge in the castle of his bitterest enemy, an old Castilian noble. The noble refuses to give him up. His guest is sacred to him.

MAN [*quickly waking up a little*]. Have your people got that notion?

RAINA [*with dignity*]. My mother and I can understand that notion, as you call it. And if instead of threatening me with your pistol as you did, you had simply thrown yourself as a fugitive on our hospitality, you would have been as safe as in your father's house.

MAN. Quite sure?

RAINA [*turning her back on him in disgust.*] Oh, it is useless to try and make you understand.

MAN. Don't be angry: you see how awkward it would be for me if there was any mistake. My father is a very hospitable man: he keeps six hotels; but I couldn't trust him as far as that. What about your father?

RAINA. He is away at Slivnitza fighting for his country. I answer for your safety. There is my hand in pledge of it. Will that reassure you? [*She offers him her hand.*]

MAN [*looking dubiously at his own hand*]. Better not touch my hand, dear young lady. I must have a wash first.

RAINA [*touched*]. That is very nice of you. I see that you are a gentleman.

MAN [*puzzled*]. Eh?

RAINA. You must not think I am surprised. Bulgarians of really good standing—people in our position—wash their hands nearly every day. But I appreciate your delicacy. You may take my hand. [*She offers it again.*]

MAN [*kissing it with his hands behind his back*]. Thanks, gracious young lady: I feel safe at last. And now would you mind breaking the news to your mother? I had better not stay here secretly longer than is necessary.

RAINA. If you will be so good as to keep perfectly still whilst I am away.

MAN. Certainly. [*He sits down on the ottoman.*]

[*Raina goes to the bed and wraps herself in the fur cloak. His eyes close. She goes to the door, but on turning for a last look at him, sees that he is dropping off to sleep.*]

RAINA [*at the door*]. You are not going asleep, are you? [*He murmurs inarticulately: she runs to him and shakes him.*] Do you hear? Wake up: you are falling asleep.

MAN. Eh? Falling aslee—? Oh, no, not the least in the world: I was only thinking. It's all right: I'm wide awake.

RAINA [*severely*]. Will you please stand up while I am away. [*He rises reluctantly.*] All the time, mind.

MAN [*standing unsteadily*]. Certainly—certainly: you may depend on me.

[*Raina looks doubtfully at him. He smiles foolishly. She goes reluctantly, turning again at the door, and almost catching him in the act of yawning. She goes out.*]

MAN [*drowsily*]. Sleep, sleep, sleep, sleep, slee—[*The words trail off into a murmur. He wakes again with a shock on the point of falling.*] Where am I? That's what I want to know: where am I? Must keep awake. Nothing keeps me awake except danger—remember that—[*intently*] danger, danger, danger, dan— Where's danger? Must find it. [*He starts off vaguely around the room in search of it.*] What am I looking for? Sleep—danger—don't know. [*He stumbles against the bed.*] Ah, yes: now I know. All right now. I'm to go to bed, but not to sleep—be sure not to sleep—because of danger. Not to lie down, either, only sit down. [*He sits on the bed. A blissful expression comes into his face.*] Ah! [*With a happy sigh he sinks back at full length; lifts his boots into the bed with a final effort; and falls fast asleep instantly.*]

[*Catherine comes in, followed by Raina.*]

RAINA [*looking at the ottoman*]. He's gone! I left him here.

CATHERINE. Here! Then he must have climbed down from the—

RAINA [*seeing him*]. Oh! [*She points.*]

CATHERINE [*scandalized*]. Well! [*She strides to the left side of the bed, Raina following and standing opposite her on the right.*] He's fast asleep. The brute!

RAINA [*anxiously*]. Sh!

CATHERINE [*shaking him*]. Sir! [*Shaking him again, harder.*] Sir!! [*Vehemently shaking very hard.*] Sir!!!

RAINA [*catching her arm*]. Don't, mamma: the poor dear is worn out. Let him sleep.

CATHERINE [*letting him go and turning amazed to Raina*]. The poor dear! Raina!!! [*She looks sternly at her daughter. The man sleeps profoundly.*]

ACT TWO

The sixth of March, 1886. In the garden of Major Petkoff's house. It is a fine spring morning; and the garden looks fresh and pretty. Beyond the paling the tops of a couple of minarets can be seen, shewing that there is a valley there, with the little town in it. A few miles further the Balkan mountains rise and shut in the view. Within the garden the side of the house is seen on the right, with a garden door reached by a little flight of steps. On the left the stable yard, with its gateway, encroaches on the garden. There are fruit bushes along the paling and house, covered with washing hung out to dry. A path runs by the house, and rises by two steps at the corner where it turns out of the sight along the front. In the middle a small table, with two bent wood chairs at it, is laid for breakfast with Turkish coffee pot, cups, rolls, etc.; but the cups have been used and the bread broken. There is a wooden garden seat against the wall on the left.

Louka, smoking a cigaret, is standing between the table and the house, turning her back with angry disdain on a manservant who is lecturing her. He is a middle-aged man of cool temperament and low but clear and keen intelligence, with the complacency of the servant who values himself on his rank in servility, and the imperturbability of the accurate calculator who has no illusions. He wears a white Bulgarian costume jacket with decorated border, sash, wide knickerbockers, and decorated gaiters. His head is shaved up to the crown, giving him a high Japanese forehead. His name is Nicola.

NICOLA. Be warned in time, Louka: mend your manners. I know the mistress. She is so grand that she never dreams that any servant could dare to be disrespectful to her; but if she once suspects that you are defying her, out you go.

LOUKA. I do defy her. I will defy her. What do I care for her?

NICOLA. If you quarrel with the family, I never can marry you. It's the same as if you quarrelled with me!

LOUKA. You take her part against me, do you?

NICOLA [*sedately*]. I shall always be dependent on the good will of the family. When I leave their service and start a shop in Sofea, their custom will be half my capital: their bad word would ruin me.

LOUKA. You have no spirit. I should like to see them dare say a word against me!

NICOLA [*pityingly*]. I should have expected more sense from you, Louka. But you're young, you're young!

LOUKA. Yes; and you like me the better for it, don't you? But I know some family secrets they wouldn't care to have told, young as I am. Let them quarrel with me if they dare!

NICOLA [*with compassionate superiority*]. Do you know what they would do if they heard you talk like that?

LOUKA. What could they do?

NICOLA. Discharge you for untruthfulness. Who would believe any stories you told after that? Who would give you another situation? Who in this house would dare be seen speaking to you ever again? How long would your father be left on his little farm? [*She impatiently throws away the end of her cigaret, and stamps on it.*] Child, you don't know the power such high people have over the like of you and me when we try to rise out of our poverty against them. [*He goes close to her and lowers his voice.*] Look at me, ten years in their service. Do you think I know no secrets? I know things about the mistress that she wouldn't have the master know for a thousand levas. I know things about him that she wouldn't let him hear the last of for six months if I blabbed them to her. I know things about Raina that would break off her match with Sergius if——

LOUKA [*turning on him quickly*]. How do you know? I never told you!

NICOLA [*opening his eyes cunningly*]. So that's your little secret, is it? I thought it might be something like that. Well, you take my advice, and be respectful; and make the mistress feel that no matter what you know or don't know, they can depend on you to hold your tongue and serve the family faithfully. That's what they like; and that's how you'll make most out of them.

LOUKA [*with searching scorn*]. You have the soul of a servant, Nicola.

NICOLA [*complacently*]. Yes: that's the secret of success in service.

[*A loud knocking with a whip handle on a wooden door, outside on the left, is heard.*]

MALE VOICE OUTSIDE. Hollo! Hollo there! Nicola!

LOUKA. Master! back from the war!

NICOLA [*quickly*]. My word for it, Louka, the war's over. Off with you and get some fresh coffee. [*He runs out into the stable yard.*]

LOUKA [*as she puts the coffee pot and the cups upon the tray, and carries it into the house*]. You'll never put the soul of a servant into me.

[*Major Petkoff comes from the stable yard, followed by Nicola. He is a cheerful, excitable, insignificant, unpolished man of about 50, naturally unambitious except as to his income and his importance in local society, but just now greatly pleased with the military rank which the war has thrust on him as a man of consequence in his town. The fever of plucky patriotism which the Servian attack roused in all the Bulgarians has pulled him through the war; but he is obviously glad to be home again.*]

PETKOFF [*pointing to the table with his whip*]. Breakfast out here, eh?

NICOLA. Yes, sir. The mistress and Miss Raina have just gone in.

PETKOFF [*sitting down and taking a roll*]. Go in and say I've come; and get me some fresh coffee.

NICOLA. It's coming, sir. [*He goes to the house door. Louka, with fresh coffee, a clean cup, and a brandy bottle on her tray meets him.*] Have you told the mistress?

LOUKA. Yes: she's coming.

[*Nicola goes into the house. Louka brings the coffee to the table.*]

PETKOFF. Well, the Servians haven't run away with you, have they?

LOUKA. No, sir.

PETKOFF. That's right. Have you brought me some cognac?

LOUKA [*putting the bottle on the table*]. Here, sir.

PETKOFF. That's right. [*He pours some into his coffee.*]

[*Catherine who has at this early hour made only a very perfunctory toilet, and wears a Bulgarian apron over a once brilliant, but now half worn out red dressing gown, and a colored handkerchief tied over her thick black hair, with*

Turkish slippers on her bare feet, comes from the house, look-ing astonishingly handsome and stately under all the circum-stances. Louka goes into the house.]

CATHERINE. My dear Paul, what a surprise for us. [*She stoops over the back of his chair to kiss him.*] Have they brought you fresh coffee?

PETKOFF. Yes, Louka's been looking after me. The war's over. The treaty was signed three days ago at Bucharest; and the decree for our army to demobilize was issued yester-day.

CATHERINE [*springing erect, with flashing eyes*]. The war over! Paul: have you let the Austrians force you to make peace?

PETKOFF [*submissively*]. My dear: they didn't consult me. What could *I* do? [*She sits down and turns away from him.*] But of course we saw to it that the treaty was an honorable one. It declares peace—

CATHERINE [*outraged*]. Peace!

PETKOFF [*appeasing her*]. —but not friendly relations: remember that. They wanted to put that in; but I insisted on its being struck out. What more could I do?

CATHERINE. You could have annexed Servia and made Prince Alexander Emperor of the Balkans. That's what I would have done.

PETKOFF. I don't doubt it in the least, my dear. But I should have had to subdue the whole Austrian Empire first; and that would have kept me too long away from you. I missed you greatly.

CATHERINE [*relenting*]. Ah! [*Stretches her hand affection-ately across the table to squeeze his.*]

PETKOFF. And how have you been, my dear?

CATHERINE. Oh, my usual sore throats, that's all.

PETKOFF [*with conviction*]. That comes from washing your neck every day. I've often told you so.

CATHERINE. Nonsense, Paul!

PETKOFF [*over his coffee and cigaret*]. I don't believe in going too far with these modern customs. All this washing can't be good for the health: it's not natural. There was an Englishman at Phillipopolis who used to wet himself all over with cold water every morning when he got up. Disgusting! It all comes from the English: their climate makes them so dirty that they have to be perpetually washing themselves. Look at my father: he never had a bath in his life; and he lived to be ninety-eight, the healthiest man in Bulgaria. I don't mind a good wash once a week to keep up my position; but once a day is carrying the thing to a ridiculous extreme.

CATHERINE. You are a barbarian at heart still, Paul. I hope you behaved yourself before all those Russian officers.

PETKOFF. I did my best. I took care to let them know that we had a library.

CATHERINE. Ah; but you didn't tell them that we have an electric bell in it? I have had one put up.

PETKOFF. What's an electric bell?

CATHERINE. You touch a button; something tinkles in the kitchen; and then Nicola comes up.

PETKOFF. Why not shout for him?

CATHERINE. Civilized people never shout for their servants. I've learnt that while you were away.

PETKOFF. Well, I'll tell you something I've learnt, too. Civilized people don't hang out their washing to dry where visitors can see it; so you'd better have all that [indicating the clothes on the bushes] put somewhere else.

CATHERINE. Oh, that's absurd, Paul: I don't believe really refined people notice such things.

[Someone is heard knocking at the stable gates.]

PETKOFF. There's Sergius. [Shouting.] Hollo, Nicola!

CATHERINE. Oh, don't shout, Paul: it really isn't nice.

PETKOFF. Bosh! [He shouts louder than before.] Nicola!

NICOLA [appearing at the house door]. Yes, sir.

PETKOFF. If that is Major Saranoff, bring him round this way. [He pronounces the name with the stress on the second syllable—Sarah noff.]

NICOLA. Yes, sir. [He goes into the stable yard.]

PETKOFF. You must talk to him, my dear, until Raina takes him off our hands. He bores my life out about our not promoting him—over my head, mind you.

CATHERINE. He certainly ought to be promoted when he marries Raina. Besides, the country should insist on having at least one native general.

PETKOFF. Yes, so that he could throw away whole brigades instead of regiments. It's no use, my dear: he has not the slightest chance of promotion until we are quite sure that the peace will be a lasting one.

NICOLA [at the gate, announcing]. Major Sergius Saranoff! [He goes into the house and returns presently with a third chair, which he places at the table. He then withdraws.]

[Major Sergius Saranoff, the original of the portrait in Raina's room, is a tall, romantically handsome man, with the

*physical hardihood, the high spirit, and the susceptible imagina-
tion of an untamed mountaineer chieftain. But his remarkable
personal distinction is of a characteristically civilized type. The
ridges of his eyebrows, curving with a ram's-horn twist round
the marked projections at the outer corners, his jealously observant eye, his nose, thin, keen, and apprehensive in spite of
the pugnacious high bridge and large nostril, his assertive chin,
would not be out of place in a Paris salon. In short, the clever,
imaginative barbarian has an acute critical faculty which has
been thrown into intense activity by the arrival of western
civilization in the Balkans; and the result is precisely what the
advent of nineteenth century thought first produced in England: to-wit, Byronism. By his brooding on the perpetual failure, not only of others, but of himself, to live up to his imaginative ideals, his consequent cynical scorn for humanity,
the jejune credulity as to the absolute validity of his ideals and
the unworthiness of the world in disregarding them, his
wincings and mockeries under the sting of the petty disillu-
sions which every hour spent among men brings to his infallibly quick observation, he has acquired the half tragic,
half ironic air, the mysterious moodiness, the suggestion of a
strange and terrible history that has left him nothing but
undying remorse, by which Childe Harold fascinated the
grandmothers of his English contemporaries. Altogether it is
clear that here or nowhere is Raina's ideal hero. Catherine is
hardly less enthusiastic, and much less reserved in shewing
her enthusiasm. As he enters from the stable gate, she rises
effusively to greet him. Petkoff is distinctly less disposed to
make a fuss about him.]*

PETKOFF. Here already, Sergius. Glad to see you!

CATHERINE. My dear Sergius! [*She holds out both her
hands.*]

SERGIUS [*kissing them with scrupulous gallantry*]. My
dear mother, if I may call you so.

PETKOFF [*drily*]. Mother-in-law, Sergius; mother-in-law!
Sit down, and have some coffee.

SERGIUS. Thank you, none for me. [*He gets away from
the table with a certain distaste for Petkoff's enjoyment of it,
and posts himself with conscious grace against the rail of the
steps leading to the house.*]

CATHERINE. You look superb—splendid. The campaign
has improved you. Everybody here is mad about you. We
were all wild with enthusiasm about that magnificent cavalry
charge.

SERGIUS [*with grave irony*]. Madam: it was the cradle and the grave of my military reputation.

CATHERINE. How so?

SERGIUS. I won the battle the wrong way when our worthy Russian generals were losing it the right way. That upset their plans, and wounded their self-esteem. Two of their colonels got their regiments driven back on the correct principles of scientific warfare. Two major-generals got killed strictly according to military etiquette. Those two colonels are now major-generals; and I am still a simple major.

CATHERINE. You shall not remain so, Sergius. The women are on your side; and they will see that justice is done you.

SERGIUS. It is too late. I have only waited for the peace to send in my resignation.

PETKOFF [*dropping his cup in his amazement*]. Your resignation!

CATHERINE. Oh, you must withdraw it!

SERGIUS [*with resolute, measured emphasis, folding his arms*]. I never withdraw!

PETKOFF [*vexed*]. Now who could have supposed you were going to do such a thing?

SERGIUS [*with fire*]. Everyone that knew me. But enough of myself and my affairs. How is Raina; and where is Raina?

RAINA [*suddenly coming round the corner of the house and standing at the top of the steps in the path*]. Raina is here. [*She makes a charming picture as they all turn to look at her. She wears an underdress of pale green silk, draped with an overdress of thin ecru canvas embroidered with gold. On her head she wears a pretty Phrygian cap of gold tinsel. Sergius, with an exclamation of pleasure, goes impulsively to meet her. She stretches out her hand: he drops chivalrously on one knee and kisses it.*]

PETKOFF [*aside to Catherine, beaming with parental pride*]. Pretty, isn't it? She always appears at the right moment.

CATHERINE [*impatiently*]. Yes: she listens for it. It is an abominable habit.

[*Sergius leads Raina forward with splendid gallantry, as if she were a queen. When they come to the table, she turns to him with a bend of the head; he bows; and thus they separate, he coming to his place, and she going behind her father's chair.*]

RAINA [*stooping and kissing her father*]. Dear father! Welcome home!

PETKOFF [*patting her cheek*]. My little pet girl. [*He kisses her; she goes to the chair left by Nicola for Sergius, and sits down.*]

CATHERINE. And so you're no longer a soldier, Sergius.

SERGIUS. I am no longer a soldier. Soldiering, my dear madam, is the coward's art of attacking mercilessly when you are strong, and keeping out of harm's way when you are weak. That is the whole secret of successful fighting. Get your enemy at a disadvantage; and never, on any account, fight him on equal terms. Eh, Major!

PETKOFF. They wouldn't let us make a fair stand-up fight of it. However, I suppose soldiering has to be a trade like any other trade.

SERGIUS. Precisely. But I have no ambition to succeed as a tradesman; so I have taken the advice of that bagman of a captain that settled the exchange of prisoners with us at Peerot, and given it up.

PETKOFF. What, that Swiss fellow? Sergius: I've often thought of that exchange since. He over-reached us about those horses.

SERGIUS. Of course he over-reached us. His father was a hotel and livery stable keeper; and he owed his first step to his knowledge of horse-dealing. [*With mock enthusiasm.*] Ah, he was a soldier—every inch a soldier! If only I had bought the horses for my regiment instead of foolishly leading it into danger, I should have been a field-marshal now!

CATHERINE. A Swiss? What was he doing in the Servian army?

PETKOFF. A volunteer of course—keen on picking up his profession. [*Chuckling.*] We shouldn't have been able to begin fighting if these foreigners hadn't shewn us how to do it: we knew nothing about it; and neither did the Servians. Egad, there'd have been no war without them.

RAINA. Are there many Swiss officers in the Servian Army?

PETKOFF. No—all Austrians, just as our officers were all Russians. This was the only Swiss I came across. I'll never trust a Swiss again. He cheated us—humbugged us into giving him fifty able bodied men for two hundred confounded worn out chargers. They weren't even eatable!

SERGIUS. We were two children in the hands of that consummate soldier, Major: simply two innocent little children.

RAINA. What was he like?

CATHERINE. Oh, Raina, what a silly question!

SERGIUS. He was like a commercial traveller in uniform. Bourgeois to his boots.

PETKOFF [*grinning*]. Sergius: tell Catherine that queer story his friend told us about him—how he escaped after Slivnitza. You remember?—about his being hid by two women.

SERGIUS [*with bitter irony*]. Oh, yes, quite a romance. He was serving in the very battery I so unprofessionally charged. Being a thorough soldier, he ran away like the rest of them, with our cavalry at his heels. To escape their attentions, he had the good taste to take refuge in the chamber of some patriotic young Bulgarian lady. The young lady was enchanted by his persuasive commercial traveller's manners. She very modestly entertained him for an hour or so and then called in her mother lest her conduct should appear unmaidenly. The old lady was equally fascinated; and the fugitive was sent on his way in the morning, disguised in an old coat belonging to the master of the house, who was away at the war.

RAINA [*rising with marked stateliness*]. Your life in the camp has made you coarse, Sergius. I did not think you would have repeated such a story before me. [*She turns away coldly.*]

CATHERINE [*also rising*]. She is right, Sergius. If such women exist, we should be spared the knowledge of them.

PETKOFF. Pooh! nonsense! what does it matter?

SERGIUS [*ashamed*]. No, Petkoff: I was wrong. [*To Raina, with earnest humility.*] I beg your pardon. I have behaved abominably. Forgive me, Raina. [*She bows reservedly.*] And you, too, madam. [*Catherine bows graciously and sits down. He proceeds solemnly, again addressing Raina.*] The glimpses I have had of the seamy side of life during the last few months have made me cynical; but I should not have brought my cynicism here—least of all into your presence, Raina. I— [*Here, turning to the others, he is evidently about to begin a long speech when the Major interrupts him.*]

PETKOFF. Stuff and nonsense, Sergius. That's quite enough fuss about nothing: a soldier's daughter should be able to stand up without flinching to a little strong conversation. [*He rises.*] Come: it's time for us to get to business. We have to make up our minds how those three regiments are to get back to Phillipopolis:—there's no forage for them on the Sophia route. [*He goes towards the house.*] Come along. [*Sergius is about to follow him when Catherine rises and intervenes.*]

CATHERINE. Oh, Paul, can't you spare Sergius for a few moments? Raina has hardly seen him yet. Perhaps I can help you to settle about the regiments.

SERGIUS [*protesting*]. My dear madam, impossible: you—

CATHERINE [*stopping him playfully*]. You stay here, my dear Sergius: there's no hurry. I have a word or two to say to Paul. [*Sergius instantly bows and steps back.*] Now, dear [*taking Petkoff's arm*], come and see the electric bell.

PETKOFF. Oh, very well, very well. [*They go into the house together affectionately. Sergius, left alone with Raina, looks anxiously at her, fearing that she may be still offended. She smiles, and stretches out her arms to him.*]

SERGIUS [*hastening to her, but refraining from touching her without express permission*]. Am I forgiven?

RAINA [*placing her hands on his shoulder as she looks up at him with admiration and worship*]. My hero! My king.

SERGIUS. My queen! [*He kisses her on the forehead with holy awe.*]

RAINA. How I have envied you, Sergius! You have been out in the world, on the field of battle, able to prove yourself there worthy of any woman in the world; whilst I have had to sit at home inactive—dreaming—useless—doing nothing that could give me the right to call myself worthy of any man.

SERGIUS. Dearest, all my deeds have been yours. You inspired me. I have gone through the war like a knight in a tournament with his lady looking on at him!

RAINA. And you have never been absent from my thoughts for a moment. [*Very solemnly.*] Sergius: I think we two have found the higher love. When I think of you, I feel that I could never do a base deed, or think an ignoble thought.

SERGIUS. My lady, and my saint! [*Clasping her reverently.*]

RAINA [*returning his embrace*]. My lord and my g—

SERGIUS. Sh—sh! Let me be the worshipper, dear. You little know how unworthy even the best man is of a girl's pure passion!

RAINA. I trust you. I love you. You will never disappoint me, Sergius. [*Louka is heard singing within the house. They quickly release each other.*] Hush! I can't pretend to talk indifferently before her: my heart is too full. [*Louka comes from the house with her tray. She goes to the table, and begins to clear it, with her back turned to them.*] I will go and get my hat; and then we can go out until lunch time. Wouldn't you like that?

SERGIUS. Be quick. If you are away five minutes, it will seem five hours. [*Raina runs to the top of the steps and turns there to exchange a look with him and wave him a kiss with both hands. He looks after her with emotion for a moment, then turns slowly away, his face radiant with the exultation of the scene which has just passed. The movement shifts his field of vision, into the corner of which there now comes the tail of Louka's double apron. His eye gleams at once. He takes a stealthy look at her, and begins to twirl his moustache nervously, with his left hand akimbo on his hip. Finally, striking the ground with his heels in something of a cavalry swagger, he strolls over to the left of the table, opposite her, and says*] Louka: do you know what the higher love is?

LOUKA [*astonished*]. No, sir.

SERGIUS. Very fatiguing thing to keep up for any length of time, Louka. One feels the need of some relief after it.

LOUKA [*innocently*]. Perhaps you would like some coffee, sir? [*She stretches her hand across the table for the coffee pot.*]

SERGIUS [*taking her hand*]. Thank you, Louka.

LOUKA [*pretending to pull*]. Oh, sir, you know I didn't mean that. I'm surprised at you!

SERGIUS [*coming clear of the table and drawing her with him*]. I am surprised at myself, Louka. What would Sergius, the hero of Slivnitza, say if he saw me now? What would Sergius, the apostle of the higher love, say if he saw me now? What would the half dozen Sergiuses who keep popping in and out of this handsome figure of mine say if they caught us here? [*Letting go her hand and slipping his arm dexterously round her waist.*] Do you consider my figure handsome, Louka?

LOUKA. Let me go, sir. I shall be disgraced. [*She struggles: he holds her inexorably.*] Oh, will you let go?

SERGIUS [*looking straight into her eyes*]. No.

LOUKA. Then stand back where we can't be seen. Have you no common sense?

SERGIUS. Ah, that's reasonable. [*He takes her into the stableyard gateway, where they are hidden from the house.*]

LOUKA [*complaining*]. I may have been seen from the windows: Miss Raina is sure to be spying about after you.

SERGIUS [*stung—letting her go*]. Take care, Louka. I may

be worthless enough to betray the higher love; but do not you insult it.

LOUKA [*demurely*]. Not for the world, sir, I'm sure. May I go on with my work please, now?

SERGIUS [*again putting his arm round her*]. You are a provoking little witch, Louka. If you were in love with me, would you spy out of windows on me?

LOUKA. Well, you see, sir, since you say you are half a dozen different gentlemen all at once, I should have a great deal to look after.

SERGIUS [*charmed*]. Witty as well as pretty. [*He tries to kiss her.*]

LOUKA [*avoiding him*]. No, I don't want your kisses. Gentlefolk are all alike—you making love to me behind Miss Raina's back, and she doing the same behind yours.

SERGIUS [*recoiling a step*]. Louka!

LOUKA. It shews how little you really care!

SERGIUS [*dropping his familiarity and speaking with freezing politeness*]. If our conversation is to continue, Louka, you will please remember that a gentleman does not discuss the conduct of the lady he is engaged to with her maid.

LOUKA. It's so hard to know what a gentleman considers right. I thought from your trying to kiss me that you had given up being so particular.

SERGIUS [*turning from her and striking his forehead as he comes back into the garden from the gateway*]. Devil! devil!

LOUKA. Ha! ha! I expect one of the six of you is very like me, sir, though I am only Miss Raina's maid. [*She goes back to her work at the table, taking no further notice of him.*]

SERGIUS [*speaking to himself*]. Which of the six is the real man?—that's the question that torments me. One of them is a hero, another a buffoon, another a humbug, another perhaps a bit of a blackguard. [*He pauses and looks furtively at Louka, as he adds with deep bitterness*] And one, at least, is a coward—jealous, like all cowards. [*He goes to the table.*] Louka.

LOUKA. Yes?

SERGIUS. Who is my rival?

LOUKA. You shall never get that out of me, for love or money.

SERGIUS. Why?

LOUKA. Never mind why. Besides, you would tell that I told you; and I should lose my place.

SERGIUS [*holding out his right hand in affirmation*]. No;

on the honor of a—[*He checks himself, and his hand drops nerveless as he concludes, sardonically*] —of a man capable of behaving as I have been behaving for the last five minutes. Who is he?

LOUKA. I don't know. I never saw him. I only heard his voice through the door of her room.

SERGIUS. Damnation! How dare you?

LOUKA [*retreating*]. Oh, I mean no harm: you've no right to take up my words like that. The mistress knows all about it. And I tell you that if that gentleman ever comes here again, Miss Raina will marry him, whether he likes it or not. I know the difference between the sort of manner you and she put on before one another and the real manner. [*Sergius shivers as if she had stabbed him. Then, setting his face like iron, he strides grimly to her, and grips her above the elbows with both hands.*]

SERGIUS. Now listen you to me!

LOUKA [*wincing*]. Not so tight: you're hurting me!

SERGIUS. That doesn't matter. You have stained my honor by making me a party to your eavesdropping. And you have betrayed your mistress—

LOUKA [*writhing*]. Please—

SERGIUS. That shews that you are an abominable little clod of common clay, with the soul of a servant. [*He lets her go as if she were an unclean thing, and turns away, dusting his hands of her, to the bench by the wall, where he sits down with averted head, meditating gloomily.*]

LOUKA [*whimpering angrily with her hands up her sleeves, feeling her bruised arms*]. You know how to hurt with your tongue as well as with your hands. But I don't care, now I've found out that whatever clay I'm made of, you're made of the same. As for her, she's a liar; and her fine airs are a cheat; and I'm worth six of her. [*She shakes the pain off hardily; tosses her head; and sets to work to put the things on the tray. He looks doubtfully at her once or twice. She finishes packing the tray, and laps the cloth over the edges, so as to carry all out together. As she stoops to lift it, he rises.*]

SERGIUS. Louka! [*She stops and looks defiantly at him with the tray in her hands.*] A gentleman has no right to hurt a woman under any circumstances. [*With profound humility, uncovering his head.*] I beg your pardon.

LOUKA. That sort of apology may satisfy a lady. Of what use is it to a servant?

SERGIUS [*thus rudely crossed in his chivalry, throws it off with a bitter laugh and says slightingly*]. Oh, you wish to be paid for the hurt? [*He puts on his shako, and takes some money from his pocket.*]

LOUKA [*her eyes filling with tears in spite of herself*]. No, I want my hurt made well.

SERGIUS [*sobered by her tone*]. How?

[*She rolls up her left sleeve; clasps her arm with the thumb and fingers of her right hand; and looks down at the bruise. Then she raises her head and looks straight at him. Finally, with a superb gesture she presents her arm to be kissed. Amazed, he looks at her; at the arm; at her again; hesitates; and then, with shuddering intensity, exclaims*] Never! [*and gets away as far as possible from her.*]

[*Her arm drops. Without a word, and with unaffected dignity, she takes her tray, and is approaching the house when Raina returns wearing a hat and jacket in the height of the Vienna fashion of the previous year, 1885. Louka makes way proudly for her, and then goes into the house.*]

RAINA. I'm ready! What's the matter? [*Gaily.*] Have you been flirting with Louka?

SERGIUS [*hastily*]. No, no. How can you think such a thing?

RAINA [*ashamed of herself*]. Forgive me, dear: it was only a jest. I am so happy to-day.

[*He goes quickly to her, and kisses her hand remorsefully. Catherine comes out and calls to them from the top of the steps.*]

CATHERINE [*coming down to them*]. I am sorry to disturb you, children; but Paul is distracted over those three regiments. He does not know how to get them to Phillipopolis; and he objects to every suggestion of mine. You must go and help him, Sergius. He is in the library.

RAINA [*disappointed*]. But we are just going out for a walk.

SERGIUS. I shall not be long. Wait for me just five minutes. [*He runs up the steps to the door.*]

RAINA [*following him to the foot of the steps and looking up at him with timid coquetry*]. I shall go round and wait in full view of the library windows. Be sure you draw father's attention to me. If you are a moment longer than five minutes, I shall go in and fetch you, regiments or no regiments.

SERGIUS [*laughing*]. Very well. [*He goes in. Raina watches him until he is out of her sight. Then, with a perceptible relaxation of manner, she begins to pace up and down about the garden in a brown study.*]

CATHERINE. Imagine their meeting that Swiss and hearing the whole story! The very first thing your father asked for was the old coat we sent him off in. A nice mess you have got us into!

RAINA [*gazing thoughtfully at the gravel as she walks*]. The little beast!

CATHERINE. Little beast! What little beast?

RAINA. To go and tell! Oh, if I had him here, I'd stuff him with chocolate creams till he couldn't ever speak again!

CATHERINE. Don't talk nonsense. Tell me the truth, Raina. How long was he in your room before you came to me?

RAINA [*whisking round and recommencing her march in the opposite direction*]. Oh, I forget.

CATHERINE. You cannot forget! Did he really climb up after the soldiers were gone, or was he there when that officer searched the room?

RAINA. No. Yes, I think he must have been there then.

CATHERINE. You think! Oh, Raina, Raina! Will anything ever make you straightforward? If Sergius finds out, it is all over between you.

RAINA [*with cool impertinence*]. Oh, I know Sergius is your pet. I sometimes wish you could marry him instead of me. You would just suit him. You would pet him, and spoil him, and mother him to perfection.

CATHERINE [*opening her eyes very widely indeed*]. Well, upon my word!

RAINA [*capriciously—half to herself*]. I always feel a longing to do or say something dreadful to him—to shock his propriety—to scandalize the five senses out of him! [*To Catherine perversely.*] I don't care whether he finds out about the chocolate cream soldier or not. I half hope he may. [*She again turns flippantly away and strolls up the path to the corner of the house.*]

CATHERINE. And what should I be able to say to your father, pray?

RAINA [*over her shoulder, from the top of the two steps*]. Oh, poor father! As if he could help himself! [*She turns the corner and passes out of sight.*]

CATHERINE [*looking after her, her fingers itching*]. Oh, if you were only ten years younger! [*Louka comes from the house with a salver, which she carries hanging down by her side.*] Well?

LOUKA. There's a gentleman just called, madam—a Servian officer—

CATHERINE [*flaming*]. A Servian! How dare he—[*Checking herself bitterly.*] Oh, I forgot. We are at peace now. I suppose we shall have them calling every day to pay their compliments. Well, if he is an officer why don't you tell your master? He is in the library with Major Saranoff. Why do you come to me?

LOUKA. But he asks for you, madam. And I don't think he knows who you are: he said the lady of the house. He gave me this little ticket for you. [*She takes a card out of her bosom; puts it on the salver and offers it to Catherine.*]

CATHERINE [*reading*]. "Captain Bluntschli!" That's a German name.

LOUKA. Swiss, madam, I think.

CATHERINE [*with a bound that makes Louka jump back*]. Swiss! What is he like?

LOUKA [*timidly*]. He has a big carpet bag, madam.

CATHERINE. Oh, Heavens, he's come to return the coat! Send him away—say we're not at home—ask him to leave his address and I'll write to him—Oh, stop: that will never do. Wait! [*She throws herself into a chair to think it out. Louka waits.*] The master and Major Saranoff are busy in the library, aren't they?

LOUKA. Yes, madam.

CATHERINE [*decisively*]. Bring the gentleman out here at once. [*Imperatively.*] And be very polite to him. Don't delay. Here [*impatiently snatching the salver from her*]: leave that here; and go straight back to him.

LOUKA. Yes, madam. [*Going.*]

CATHERINE. Louka!

LOUKA [*stopping*]. Yes, madam.

CATHERINE. Is the library door shut?

LOUKA. I think so, madam.

CATHERINE. If not, shut it as you pass through.

LOUKA. Yes, madam. [*Going.*]

CATHERINE. Stop! [*Louka stops.*] He will have to go out that way [*indicating the gate of the stable yard.*] Tell Nicola to bring his bag here after him. Don't forget.

LOUKA [*surprised*]. His bag?

CATHERINE. Yes, here, as soon as possible. [*Vehemently.*] Be quick! [*Louka runs into the house. Catherine snatches her apron off and throws it behind a bush. She then takes up the salver and uses it as a mirror, with the result that the hand-*]

*kerchief tied round her head follows the apron. A touch to
her hair and a shake to her dressing gown makes her presentable.*] Oh, how—how—how can a man be such a fool!
Such a moment to select! [*Louka appears at the door of the
house, announcing "Captain Bluntschli;" and standing aside
at the top of the steps to let him pass before she goes in
again. He is the man of the adventure in Raina's room. He is
now clean, well brushed, smartly uniformed, and out of
trouble, but still unmistakably the same man. The moment
Louka's back is turned, Catherine swoops on him with hur-
ried, urgent, coaxing appeal.*] Captain Bluntschli, I am very
glad to see you; but you must leave this house at once. [*He
raises his eyebrows.*] My husband has just returned, with my
future son-in-law; and they know nothing. If they did, the
consequences would be terrible. You are a foreigner: you do
not feel our national animosities as we do. We still hate the
Servians: the only effect of the peace on my husband is to
make him feel like a lion baulked of his prey. If he discovered our secret, he would never forgive me; and my daughter's life would hardly be safe. Will you, like the chivalrous
gentleman and soldier you are, leave at once before he finds
you here?

BLUNTSCHLI [*disappointed, but philosophical*]. At once,
gracious lady. I only came to thank you and return the coat
you lent me. If you will allow me to take it out of my bag
and leave it with your servant as I pass out, I need detain
you no further. [*He turns to go into the house.*]

CATHERINE [*catching him by the sleeve*]. Oh, you must
not think of going back that way. [*Coaxing him across to the
stable gates.*] This is the shortest way out. Many thanks. So
glad to have been of service to you. Good-bye.

BLUNTSCHLI. But my bag?

CATHERINE. It will be sent on. You will leave me your
address.

BLUNTSCHLI. True. Allow me. [*He takes out his card-
case, and stops to write his address, keeping Catherine in an
agony of impatience. As he hands her the card, Petkoff, hat-
less, rushes from the house in a fluster of hospitality, followed
by Sergius.*]

PETKOFF [*as he hurries down the steps*]. My dear Captain Bluntschli—

CATHERINE. Oh Heavens! [*She sinks on the seat against
the wall.*]

PETKOFF [*too preoccupied to notice her as he shakes*

Bluntschli's hand heartily]. Those stupid people of mine thought I was out here, instead of in the—haw!—library. [*He cannot mention the library without betraying how proud he is of it.*] I saw you through the window. I was wondering why you didn't come in. Saranoff is with me: you remember him, don't you?

SERGIUS [*saluting humorously, and then offering his hand with great charm of manner*]. Welcome, our friend the enemy!

PETKOFF. No longer the enemy, happily. [*Rather anxiously.*] I hope you've come as a friend, and not on business.

CATHERINE. Oh, quite as a friend, Paul. I was just asking Captain Bluntschli to stay to lunch; but he declares he must go at once.

SERGIUS [*sardonically*]. Impossible, Bluntschli. We want you here badly. We have to send on three cavalry regiments to Phillipopolis; and we don't in the least know how to do it.

BLUNTSCHLI [*suddenly attentive and business-like*]. Phillipopolis! The forage is the trouble, eh?

PETKOFF [*eagerly*]. Yes, that's it. [*To Sergius.*] He sees the whole thing at once.

BLUNTSCHLI. I think I can shew you how to manage that.

SERGIUS. Invaluable man! Come along! [*Towering over Bluntschli, he puts his hand on his shoulder and takes him to the steps, Petkoff following. As Bluntschli puts his foot on the first step, Raina comes out of the house.*]

RAINA [*completely losing her presence of mind*]. Oh, the chocolate cream soldier!

[*Bluntschli stands rigid. Sergius, amazed, looks at Raina, then at Petkoff, who looks back at him and then at his wife.*]

CATHERINE [*with commanding presence of mind.*] My dear Raina, don't you see that we have a guest here—Captain Bluntschli, one of our new Servian friends?

[*Raina bows; Bluntschli bows.*]

RAINA. How silly of me! [*She comes down into the centre of the group, between Bluntschli and Petkoff.*] I made a beautiful ornament this morning for the ice pudding; and that stupid Nicola has just put down a pile of plates on it and spoiled it. [*To Bluntschli, winningly.*] I hope you didn't think that you were the chocolate cream soldier, Captain Bluntschli.

BLUNTSCHLI [*laughing*]. I assure you I did. [*Stealing a whimsical glance at her.*] Your explanation was a relief.

PETKOFF [*suspiciously, to Raina*]. And since when, pray, have you taken to cooking?

CATHERINE. Oh, whilst you were away. It is her latest fancy.

PETKOFF [*testily*]. And has Nicola taken to drinking? He used to be careful enough. First he shews Captain Bluntschli out here when he knew quite well I was in the—hum! —library; and then he goes downstairs and breaks Raina's chocolate soldier. He must— [*At this moment Nicola appears at the top of the steps R., with a carpet bag. He descends; places it respectfully before Bluntschli; and waits for further orders. General amazement. Nicola, unconscious of the effect he is producing, looks perfectly satisfied with himself. When Petkoff recovers his power of speech, he breaks out at him with*] Are you mad, Nicola?

NICOLA [*taken aback*]. Sir?

PETKOFF. What have you brought that for?

NICOLA. My lady's orders, sir. Louka told me that—

CATHERINE [*interrupting him*]. My orders! Why should I order you to bring Captain Bluntschli's luggage out here? What are you thinking of, Nicola?

NICOLA [*after a moment's bewilderment, picking up the bag as he addresses Bluntschli with the very perfection of servile discretion*]. I beg your pardon, sir, I am sure. [*To Catherine.*] My fault, madam! I hope you'll overlook it! [*He bows, and is going to the steps with the bag, when Petkoff addresses him angrily.*]

PETKOFF. You'd better go and slam that bag, too, down on Miss Raina's ice pudding! [*This is too much for Nicola. The bag drops from his hands on Petkoff's corns, eliciting a roar of anguish from him.*] Begone, you butter-fingered donkey.

NICOLA [*snatching up the bag, and escaping into the house*]. Yes, sir.

CATHERINE. Oh, never mind, Paul, don't be angry!

PETKOFF [*muttering*]. Scoundrel. He's got out of hand while I was away. I'll teach him. [*Recollecting his guest.*] Oh, well, never mind. Come, Bluntschli, let's have no more nonsense about you having to go away. You know very well you're not going back to Switzerland yet. Until you do go back you'll stay with us.

RAINA. Oh, do, Captain Bluntschli.

PETKOFF [*to Catherine*]. Now, Catherine, it's of you that he's afraid. Press him and he'll stay.

CATHERINE. Of course I shall be only too delighted if [*appealingly*] Captain Bluntschli really wishes to stay. He knows my wishes.

BLUNTSCHLI [*in his driest military manner*]. I am at madame's orders.

SERGIUS [*cordially*]. That settles it!

PETKOFF [*heartily*]. Of course!

RAINA. You see, you must stay!

BLUNTSCHLI [*smiling*]. Well, if I must, I must!

[*Gesture of despair from Catherine.*]

ACT THREE

In the library after lunch. It is not much of a library, its literary equipment consisting of a single fixed shelf stocked with old paper covered novels, broken backed, coffee stained, torn and thumbed, and a couple of little hanging shelves with a few gift books on them, the rest of the wall space being occupied by trophies of war and the chase. But it is a most comfortable sitting-room. A row of three large windows in the front of the house shew a mountain panorama, which is just now seen in one of its softest aspects in the mellowing afternoon light. In the left hand corner, a square earthenware stove, a perfect tower of colored pottery, rises nearly to the ceiling and guarantees plenty of warmth. The ottoman in the middle is a circular bank of decorated cushions, and the window seats are well upholstered divans. Little Turkish tables, one of them with an elaborate hookah on it, and a screen to match them, complete the handsome effect of the furnishing. There is one object, however, which is hopelessly out of keeping with its surroundings. This is a small kitchen table, much the worse for wear, fitted as a writing table with an old canister full of pens, an eggcup filled with ink, and a deplorable scrap of severely used pink blotting paper.

At the side of this table, which stands on the right, Bluntschli is hard at work, with a couple of maps before him, writing orders. At the head of it sits Sergius, who is also supposed to be at work, but who is actually gnawing the feather of a pen, and contemplating Bluntschli's quick, sure, businesslike progress with a mixture of envious irritation at his own incapacity, and awestruck wonder at an ability which seems to him almost miraculous, though its prosaic character for-

*bids him to esteem it. The major is comfortably established
on the ottoman, with a newspaper in his hand and the tube
of the hookah within his reach. Catherine sits at the stove,
with her back to them, embroidering. Raina, reclining on the
divan under the left hand window, is gazing in a daydream
out at the Balkan landscape, with a neglected novel in her
lap.*

*The door is on the left. The button of the electric bell is
between the door and the fireplace.*

PETKOFF [*looking up from his paper to watch how they
are getting on at the table*]. Are you sure I can't help you in
any way, Bluntschli?

BLUNTSCHLI [*without interrupting his writing or looking
up*]. Quite sure, thank you. Saranoff and I will manage it.

SERGIUS [*grimly*]. Yes: we'll manage it. He finds out
what to do; draws up the orders; and I sign 'em. Division of
labour, Major. [*Bluntschli passes him a paper.*] Another one?
Thank you. [*He plants the papers squarely before him; sets
his chair carefully parallel to them; and signs with the air
of a man resolutely performing a difficult and dangerous feat.*]
This hand is more accustomed to the sword than to the pen.

PETKOFF. It's very good of you, Bluntschli, it is indeed,
to let yourself be put upon in this way. Now are you quite
sure I can do nothing?

CATHERINE [*in a low, warning tone*]. You can stop interrupting, Paul.

PETKOFF [*starting and looking round at her*]. Eh? Oh!
Quite right, my love, quite right. [*He takes his newspaper up,
but lets it drop again.*] Ah, you haven't been campaigning,
Catherine: you don't know how pleasant it is for us to sit
here, after a good lunch, with nothing to do but enjoy ourselves. There's only one thing I want to make me thoroughly
comfortable.

CATHERINE. What is that?

PETKOFF. My old coat. I'm not at home in this one: I
feel as if I were on parade.

CATHERINE. My dear Paul, how absurd you are about
that old coat! It must be hanging in the blue closet where
you left it.

PETKOFF. My dear Catherine, I tell you I've looked
there. Am I to believe my own eyes or not? [*Catherine quietly
rises and presses the button of the electric bell by the fireplace*]. What are you shewing off that bell for? [*She looks at*

him majestically, and silently resumes her chair and her needlework.] My dear: if you think the obstinacy of your sex can make a coat out of two old dressing gowns of Raina's, your waterproof, and my mackintosh, you're mistaken. That's exactly what the blue closet contains at present. [*Nicola presents himself.*]

CATHERINE [*unmoved by Petkoff's sally*]. Nicola: go to the blue closet and bring your master's old coat here—the braided one he usually wears in the house.

NICOLA. Yes, madam. [*Nicola goes out.*]

PETKOFF. Catherine.

CATHERINE. Yes, Paul?

PETKOFF. I bet you any piece of jewellery you like to order from Sophia against a week's housekeeping money, that the coat isn't there.

CATHERINE. Done, Paul.

PETKOFF [*excited by the prospect of a gamble*]. Come: here's an opportunity for some sport. Who'll bet on it? Bluntschli: I'll give you six to one.

BLUNTSCHLI [*imperturbably*]. It would be robbing you, Major. Madame is sure to be right. [*Without looking up, he passes another batch of papers to Sergius.*]

SERGIUS [*also excited*]. Bravo, Switzerland! Major: I bet my best charger against an Arab mare for Raina that Nicola finds the coat in the blue closet.

PETKOFF [*eagerly*]. Your best char—

CATHERINE [*hastily interrupting him*]. Don't be foolish, Paul. An Arabian mare will cost you 50,000 levas.

RAINA [*suddenly coming out of her picturesque revery*]. Really, mother, if you are going to take the jewellery, I don't see why you should grudge me my Arab.

[*Nicola comes back with the coat and brings it to Petkoff, who can hardly believe his eyes.*]

CATHERINE. Where was it, Nicola?

NICOLA. Hanging in the blue closet, madam.

PETKOFF. Well, I am d—

CATHERINE [*stopping him*]. Paul!

PETKOFF. I could have sworn it wasn't there. Age is beginning to tell on me. I'm getting hallucinations. [*To Nicola.*] Here: help me to change. Excuse me, Bluntschli. [*He begins changing coats, Nicola acting as valet.*] Remember: I didn't take that bet of yours, Sergius. You'd better give Raina that Arab steed yourself, since you've roused her expectations. Eh, Raina? [*He looks round at her; but she is again rapt in the landscape. With a little gush of paternal affection and pride, he points her out to them and says*] She's dreaming, as usual.

SERGIUS. Assuredly she shall not be the loser.

PETKOFF. So much the better for her. *I* shan't come off so cheap, I expect. [*The change is now complete. Nicola goes out with the discarded coat.*] Ah, now I feel at home at last. [*He sits down and takes his newspaper with a grunt of relief.*]

BLUNTSCHLI [*to Sergius, handing a paper*]. That's the last order.

PETKOFF [*jumping up*]. What! finished?

BLUNTSCHLI. Finished. [*Petkoff goes beside Sergius; looks curiously over his left shoulder as he signs; and says with childlike envy*] Haven't you anything for me to sign?

BLUNTSCHLI. Not necessary. His signature will do.

PETKOFF. Ah, well, I think we've done a thundering good day's work. [*He goes away from the table.*] Can I do anything more?

BLUNTSCHLI. You had better both see the fellows that are to take these. [*To Sergius.*] Pack them off at once; and shew them that I've marked on the orders the time they should hand them in by. Tell them that if they stop to drink or tell stories—if they're five minutes late, they'll have the skin taken off their backs.

SERGIUS [*rising indignantly*]. I'll say so. And if one of them is man enough to spit in my face for insulting him, I'll buy his discharge and give him a pension. [*He strides out, his humanity deeply outraged.*]

BLUNTSCHLI [*confidentially*]. Just see that he talks to them properly, Major, will you?

PETKOFF [*officiously*]. Quite right, Bluntschli, quite right. I'll see to it. [*He goes to the door importantly, but hesitates on the threshold.*] By the bye, Catherine, you may as well come, too. They'll be far more frightened of you than of me.

CATHERINE [*putting down her embroidery*]. I daresay I had better. You will only splutter at them. [*She goes out, Petkoff holding the door for her and following her.*]

BLUNTSCHLI. What a country! They make cannons out of cherry trees; and the officers send for their wives to keep discipline! [*He begins to fold and docket the papers. Raina, who has risen from the divan, strolls down the room with her hands clasped behind her, and looks mischievously at him.*]

RAINA. You look ever so much nicer than when we last met. [*He looks up, surprised.*] What have you done to yourself?

BLUNTSCHLI. Washed; brushed; good night's sleep and breakfast. That's all.

RAINA. Did you get back safely that morning?

BLUNTSCHLI. Quite, thanks.

RAINA. Were they angry with you for running away from Sergius's charge?

BLUNTSCHLI. No, they were glad; because they'd all just run away themselves.

RAINA [*going to the table, and leaning over it towards him*]. It must have made a lovely story for them—all that about me and my room.

BLUNTSCHLI. Capital story. But I only told it to one of them—a particular friend.

RAINA. On whose discretion you could absolutely rely?

BLUNTSCHLI. Absolutely.

RAINA. Hm! He told it all to my father and Sergius the day you exchanged the prisoners. [*She turns away and strolls carelessly across to the other side of the room.*]

BLUNTSCHLI [*deeply concerned and half incredulous*]. No! you don't mean that, do you?

RAINA [*turning, with sudden earnestness*]. I do indeed. But they don't know that it was in this house that you hid. If Sergius knew, he would challenge you and kill you in a duel.

BLUNTSCHLI. Bless me! then don't tell him.

RAINA [*full of reproach for his levity*]. Can you realize what it is to me to deceive him? I want to be quite perfect with Sergius—no meanness, no smallness, no deceit. My relation to him is the one really beautiful and noble part of my life. I hope you can understand that.

BLUNTSCHLI [*sceptically*]. You mean that you wouldn't like him to find out that the story about the ice pudding was a—a—a— You know.

RAINA [*wincing*]. Ah, don't talk of it in that flippant way. I lied: I know it. But I did it to save your life. He would have killed you. That was the second time I ever uttered a falsehood. [*Bluntschli rises quickly and looks doubtfully and somewhat severely at her.*] Do you remember the first time?

BLUNTSCHLI. I! No. Was I present?

RAINA. Yes; and I told the officer who was searching for you that you were not present.

BLUNTSCHLI. True. I should have remembered it.

RAINA [*greatly encouraged*]. Ah, it is natural that you should forget it first. It cost you nothing: it cost me a lie!—a lie!! [*She sits down on the ottoman, looking straight before her with her hands clasped on her knee. Bluntschli, quite touched, goes to the ottoman with a particularly reassuring and considerate air, and sits down beside her.*]

BLUNTSCHLI. My dear young lady, don't let this worry you. Remember: I'm a soldier. Now what are the two things that happen to a soldier so often that he comes to think nothing of them? One is hearing people tell lies [*Raina recoils*]: the other is getting his life saved in all sorts of ways by all sorts of people.

RAINA [*rising in indignant protest*]. And so he becomes a creature incapable of faith and of gratitude.

BLUNTSCHLI [*making a wry face*]. Do you like gratitude? I don't. If pity is akin to love, gratitude is akin to the other thing.

RAINA. Gratitude! [*Turning on him.*] If you are incapable of gratitude you are incapable of any noble sentiment. Even animals are grateful. Oh, I see now exactly what you think of me! You were not surprised to hear me lie. To you it was something I probably did every day—every hour. That is how men think of women. [*She walks up the room melodramatically.*]

BLUNTSCHLI [*dubiously*]. There's reason in everything. You said you'd told only two lies in your whole life. Dear young lady: isn't that rather a short allowance? I'm quite a straightforward man myself; but it wouldn't last me a whole morning.

RAINA [*staring haughtily at him*]. Do you know, sir, that you are insulting me?

BLUNTSCHLI. I can't help it. When you get into that noble attitude and speak in that thrilling voice, I admire you; but I find it impossible to believe a single word you say.

RAINA [*superbly*]. Captain Bluntschli!

BLUNTSCHLI [*unmoved*]. Yes?

RAINA [*coming a little towards him, as if she could not believe her senses*]. Do you mean what you said just now? Do you know what you said just now?

BLUNTSCHLI. I do.

RAINA [*gasping*]. I! I!!! [*She points to herself incredulously, meaning "I, Raina Petkoff, tell lies!" He meets her gaze unflinchingly. She suddenly sits down beside him, and*] *adds, with a complete change of manner from the heroic to the familiar]* How did you find me out?

BLUNTSCHLI [*promptly*]. Instinct, dear young lady. Instinct, and experience of the world.

RAINA [*wonderingly*]. Do you know, you are the first man I ever met who did not take me seriously?

BLUNTSCHLI. You mean, don't you, that I am the first man that has ever taken you quite seriously?

RAINA. Yes, I suppose I do mean that. [*Cosily, quite at her ease with him.*] How strange it is to be talked to in such a way! You know, I've always gone on like that—I mean the noble attitude and the thrilling voice. I did it when I was a tiny child to my nurse. She believed in it. I do it before my parents. T h e y believe in it. I do it before Sergius. He believes in it.

BLUNTSCHLI. Yes: he's a little in that line himself, isn't he?

RAINA [*startled*]. Do you think so?

BLUNTSCHLI. You know him better than I do.

RAINA. I wonder—I w o n d e r is he? If I thought that— ! [*Discouraged.*] Ah, well, what does it matter? I suppose, now that you've found me out, you despise me.

BLUNTSCHLI [*warmly, rising*]. No, my dear young lady, no, no, no a thousand times. It's part of your youth—part of your charm. I'm like all the rest of them—the nurse—your parents—Sergius: I'm your infatuated admirer.

RAINA [*pleased*]. Really?

BLUNTSCHLI [*slapping his breast smartly with his hand, German fashion*]. Hand aufs Herz! Really and truly.

RAINA [*very happy*]. But what did you think of me for giving you my portrait?

BLUNTSCHLI [*astonished*]. Your portrait! You never gave me your portrait.

RAINA [*quickly*]. Do you mean to say you never got it?

BLUNTSCHLI. No. [*He sits down beside her, with renewed interest, and says, with some complacency*] When did you send it to me?

RAINA [*indignantly*]. I did not send it to you. [*She turns her head away, and adds, reluctantly*] It was in the pocket of that coat.

BLUNTSCHLI [*pursing his lips and rounding his eyes*]. Oh-o-oh! I never found it. It must be there still.

RAINA [*springing up*]. There still!—for my father to find

the first time he puts his hand in his pocket! Oh, how could you be so stupid?

BLUNTSCHLI [*rising also*]. It doesn't matter: it's only a photograph: how can he tell who it was intended for? Tell him he put it there himself.

RAINA [*impatiently*]. Yes, that is so clever—so clever! What shall I do?

BLUNTSCHLI. Ah, I see. You wrote something on it. That was rash!

RAINA [*annoyed almost to tears*]. Oh, to have done such a thing for you, who care no more—except to laugh at me—oh! Are you sure nobody has touched it?

BLUNTSCHLI. Well, I can't be quite sure. You see I couldn't carry it about with me all the time: one can't take much luggage on active service.

RAINA. What did you do with it?

BLUNTSCHLI. When I got through to Peerot I had to put it in safe keeping somehow. I thought of the railway cloak room; but that's the surest place to get looted in modern warfare. So I pawned it.

RAINA. P a w n e d　i t ! ! !

BLUNTSCHLI. I know it doesn't sound nice; but it was much the safest plan. I redeemed it the day before yesterday. Heaven only knows whether the pawnbroker cleared out the pockets or not.

RAINA [*furious—throwing the words right into his face*]. You have a low, shopkeeping mind. You think of things that would never come into a gentleman's head.

BLUNTSCHLI [*phlegmatically*]. That's the Swiss national character, dear lady.

RAINA. Oh, I wish I had never met you. [*She flounces away and sits at the window fuming.*]

[*Louka comes in with a heap of letters and telegrams on her salver, and crosses, with her bold, free gait, to the table. Her left sleeve is looped up to the shoulder with a brooch, shewing her naked arm, with a broad gilt bracelet covering the bruise.*]

LOUKA [*to Bluntschli*]. For you. [*She empties the salver recklessly on the table.*] The messenger is waiting. [*She is determined not to be civil to a Servian, even if she must bring him his letters.*]

BLUNTSCHLI [*to Raina*]. Will you excuse me: the last postal delivery that reached me was three weeks ago. These are the subsequent accumulations. Four telegrams—a week old. [He opens one.] Oho! Bad news!

RAINA [rising and advancing a little remorsefully]. Bad news?

BLUNTSCHLI. My father's dead. [He looks at the telegram with his lips pursed, musing on the unexpected change in his arrangements.]

RAINA. Oh, how very sad!

BLUNTSCHLI. Yes: I shall have to start for home in an hour. He has left a lot of big hotels behind him to be looked after. [Takes up a heavy letter in a long blue envelope.] Here's a whacking letter from the family solicitor. [He pulls out the enclosures and glances over them.] Great Heavens! Seventy! Two hundred! [In a crescendo of dismay.] Four hundred! Four thousand!! Nine thousand six hundred!!! What on earth shall I do with them all?

RAINA [timidly]. Nine thousand hotels?

BLUNTSCHLI. Hotels! Nonsense. If you only knew!—oh, it's too ridiculous! Excuse me: I must give my fellow orders about starting. [He leaves the room hastily, with the documents in his hand.]

LOUKA [tauntingly]. He has not much heart, that Swiss, though he is so fond of the Servians. He has not a word of grief for his poor father.

RAINA [bitterly]. Grief!—a man who has been doing nothing but killing people for years! What does he care? What does any soldier care? [She goes to the door, evidently restraining her tears with difficulty.]

LOUKA. Major Saranoff has been fighting, too; and he has plenty of heart left. [Raina, at the door, looks haughtily at her and goes out.] Aha! I thought you wouldn't get much feeling out of your soldier. [She is following Raina when Nicola enters with an armful of logs for the fire.]

NICOLA [grinning amorously at her]. I've been trying all the afternoon to get a minute alone with you, my girl. [His countenance changes as he notices her arm.] Why, what fashion is that of wearing your sleeve, child?

LOUKA [proudly]. My own fashion.

NICOLA. Indeed! If the mistress catches you, she'll talk to you. [He throws the logs down on the ottoman, and sits comfortably beside them.]

LOUKA. Is that any reason why you should take it on yourself to talk to me?

NICOLA. Come: don't be so contrary with me. I've some

good news for you. [*He takes out some paper money. Louka, with an eager gleam in her eyes, comes close to look at it.*] See, a twenty leva bill! Sergius gave me that out of pure swagger. A fool and his money are soon parted. There's ten levas more. The Swiss gave me that for backing up the mistress's and Raina's lies about him. He's no fool, he isn't. You should have heard old Catherine downstairs as polite as you please to me, telling me not to mind the Major being a little impatient; for they knew what a good servant I was—after making a fool and a liar of me before them all! The twenty will go to our savings; and you shall have the ten to spend if you'll only talk to me so as to remind me I'm a human being. I get tired of being a servant occasionally.

LOUKA [*scornfully*]. Yes: sell your manhood for thirty levas, and buy me for ten! Keep your money. You were born to be a servant. I was not. When you set up your shop you will only be everybody's servant instead of somebody's servant.

NICOLA [*picking up his logs, and going to the stove*]. Ah, wait till you see. We shall have our evenings to ourselves; and I shall be master in my own house, I promise you. [*He throws the logs down and kneels at the stove.*]

LOUKA. You shall never be master in mine. [*She sits down on Sergius's chair.*]

NICOLA [*turning, still on his knees, and squatting down rather forlornly, on his calves, daunted by her implacable disdain*]. You have a great ambition in you, Louka. Remember: if any luck comes to you, it was I that made a woman of you.

LOUKA. You!

NICOLA [*with dogged self-assertion*]. Yes, me. Who was it made you give up wearing a couple of pounds of false black hair on your head and reddening your lips and cheeks like any other Bulgarian girl? I did. Who taught you to trim your nails, and keep your hands clean, and be dainty about yourself, like a fine Russian lady? Me! do you hear that? me! [*She tosses her head defiantly; and he rises, ill-humoredly, adding more coolly*] I've often thought that if Raina were out of the way, and you just a little less of a fool and Sergius just a little more of one, you might come to be one of my grandest customers, instead of only being my wife and costing me money.

LOUKA. I believe you would rather be my servant than my husband. You would make more out of me. Oh, I know that soul of yours.

NICOLA [*going up close to her for greater emphasis*]. Never you mind my soul; but just listen to my advice. If you want to be a lady, your present behaviour to me won't do at all, unless when we're alone. It's too sharp and impudent; and impudence is a sort of familiarity: it shews affection for me. And don't you try being high and mighty with me either. You're like all country girls: you think it's genteel to treat a servant the way I treat a stable-boy. That's only your ignorance; and don't you forget it. And don't be so ready to defy everybody. Act as if you expected to have your own way, not as if you expected to be ordered about. The way to get on as a lady is the same as the way to get on as a servant: you've got to know your place; that's the secret of it. And you may depend on me to know my place if you get promoted. Think over it, my girl. I'll stand by you: one servant should always stand by another.

LOUKA [*rising impatiently*]. Oh, I must behave in my own way. You take all the courage out of me with your cold-blooded wisdom. Go and put those logs on the fire: that's the sort of thing you understand. [*Before Nicola can retort, Sergius comes in. He checks himself a moment on seeing Louka; then goes to the stove.*]

SERGIUS [*to Nicola*]. I am not in the way of your work, I hope.

NICOLA [*in a smooth, elderly manner*]. Oh, no, sir, thank you kindly. I was only speaking to this foolish girl about her habit of running up here to the library whenever she gets a chance, to look at the books. That's the worst of her education, sir: it gives her habits above her station. [*To Louka.*] Make that table tidy, Louka, for the Major. [*He goes out sedately.*]

[*Louka, without looking at Sergius, begins to arrange the papers on the table. He crosses slowly to her, and studies the arrangement of her sleeve reflectively.*]

SERGIUS. Let me see: is there a mark there? [*He turns up the bracelet and sees the bruise made by his grasp. She stands motionless, not looking at him: fascinated, but on her guard.*] Ffff! Does it hurt?

LOUKA. Yes.

SERGIUS. Shall I cure it?

LOUKA [*instantly withdrawing herself proudly, but still not looking at him*]. No. You cannot cure it now.

SERGIUS [*masterfully*]. Quite sure? [*He makes a movement as if to take her in his arms.*]

LOUKA. Don't trifle with me, please. An officer should not trifle with a servant.

SERGIUS [touching the arm with a merciless stroke of his forefinger]. That was no trifle, Louka.

LOUKA. No. [Looking at him for the first time.] Are you sorry?

SERGIUS [with measured emphasis, folding his arms]. I am never sorry.

LOUKA [wistfully]. I wish I could believe a man could be so unlike a woman as that. I wonder are you really a brave man?

SERGIUS [unaffectedly, relaxing his attitude]. Yes: I am a brave man. My heart jumped like a woman's at the first shot; but in the charge I found that I was brave. Yes: that at least is real about me.

LOUKA. Did you find in the charge that the men whose fathers are poor like mine were any less brave than the men who are rich like you?

SERGIUS [with bitter levity]. Not a bit. They all slashed and cursed and yelled like heroes. Psha! the courage to rage and kill is cheap. I have an English bull terrier who has as much of that sort of courage as the whole Bulgarian nation, and the whole Russian nation at its back. But he lets my groom thrash him, all the same. That's your soldier all over! No, Louka, your poor men can cut throats; but they are afraid of their officers; they put up with insults and blows; they stand by and see one another punished like children—aye, and help to do it when they are ordered. And the officers!—well [with a short, bitter laugh] I am an officer. Oh [fervently] give me the man who will defy to the death any power on earth or in heaven that sets itself up against his own will and conscience: he alone is the brave man.

LOUKA. How easy it is to talk! Men never seem to me to grow up: they all have schoolboy's ideas. You don't know what true courage is.

SERGIUS [ironically]. Indeed! I am willing to be instructed.

LOUKA. Look at me! how much am I allowed to have my own will? I have to get your room ready for you—to sweep and dust, to fetch and carry. How could that degrade me if it did not degrade you to have it done for you? But [with subdued passion] if I were Empress of Russia, above everyone in the world, then—ah, then, though according to you I could shew no courage at all; you should see, you should see.

SERGIUS. What would you do, most noble Empress?

LOUKA. I would marry the man I loved, which no other queen in Europe has the courage to do. If I loved you, though you would be as far beneath me as I am beneath you, I would dare to be the equal of my inferior. Would you dare as much if you loved me? No: if you felt the beginnings of love for me you would not let it grow. You dare not: you would marry a rich man's daughter because you would be afraid of what other people would say of you.

SERGIUS [*carried away*]. You lie: it is not so, by all the stars! If I loved you, and I were the Czar himself, I would set you on the throne by my side. You know that I love another woman, a woman as high above you as heaven is above earth. And you are jealous of her.

LOUKA. I have no reason to be. She will never marry you now. The man I told you of has come back. She will marry the Swiss.

SERGIUS [*recoiling*]. The Swiss!

LOUKA. A man worth ten of you. Then you can come to me; and I will refuse you. You are not good enough for me. [*She turns to the door.*]

SERGIUS [*springing after her and catching her fiercely in his arms*]. I will kill the Swiss; and afterwards I will do as I please with you.

LOUKA [*in his arms, passive and steadfast*]. The Swiss will kill you, perhaps. He has beaten you in love. He may beat you in war.

SERGIUS [*tormentedly*]. Do you think I believe that she —she! whose worst thoughts are higher than your best ones, is capable of trifling with another man behind my back?

LOUKA. Do you think she would believe the Swiss if he told her now that I am in your arms?

SERGIUS [*releasing her in despair*]. Damnation! Oh, damnation! Mockery, mockery everywhere: everything I think is mocked by everything I do. [*He strikes himself frantically on the breast.*] Coward, liar, fool! Shall I kill myself like a man, or live and pretend to laugh at myself? [*She again turns to go.*] Louka! [*She stops near the door.*] Remember: you belong to me.

LOUKA [*quietly*]. What does that mean—an insult?

SERGIUS [*commandingly*]. It means that you love me, and that I have had you here in my arms, and will perhaps have you there again. Whether that is an insult I neither know nor care: take it as you please. But [*vehemently*] I will not be a coward and a trifler. If I choose to love you, I dare marry you, in spite of all Bulgaria. If these hands ever touch you again, they shall touch my affianced bride.

LOUKA. We shall see whether you dare keep your word. But take care. I will not wait long.

SERGIUS [*again folding his arms and standing motionless in the middle of the room*]. Yes, we shall see. And you shall wait my pleasure.

[*Bluntschli, much preoccupied, with his papers still in his hand, enters, leaving the door open for Louka to go out. He goes across to the table, glancing at her as he passes. Sergius, without altering his resolute attitude, watches him steadily. Louka goes out, leaving the door open.*]

BLUNTSCHLI [*absently, sitting at the table as before, and putting down his papers*]. That's a remarkable looking young woman.

SERGIUS [*gravely, without moving*]. Captain Bluntschli.

BLUNTSCHLI. Eh?

SERGIUS. You have deceived me. You are my rival. I brook no rivals. At six o'clock I shall be in the drilling-ground on the Klissoura road, alone, on horseback, with my sabre. Do you understand?

BLUNTSCHLI [*staring, but sitting quite at his ease*]. Oh, thank you: that's a cavalry man's proposal. I'm in the artillery; and I have the choice of weapons. If I go, I shall take a machine gun. And there shall be no mistake about the cartridges this time.

SERGIUS [*flushing, but with deadly coldness*]. Take care, sir. It is not our custom in Bulgaria to allow invitations of that kind to be trifled with.

BLUNTSCHLI [*warmly*]. Pooh! don't talk to me about Bulgaria. You don't know what fighting is. But have it your own way. Bring your sabre along. I'll meet you.

SERGIUS [*fiercely delighted to find his opponent a man of spirit*]. Well said, Switzer. Shall I lend you my best horse?

BLUNTSCHLI. No: damn your horse!—thank you all the same, my dear fellow. [*Raina comes in, and hears the next sentence.*] I shall fight you on foot. Horseback's too dangerous: I don't want to kill you if I can help it.

RAINA [*hurrying forward anxiously*]. I have heard what Captain Bluntschli said, Sergius. You are going to fight. Why? [*Sergius turns away in silence, and goes to the stove, where he stands watching her as she continues, to Bluntschli*] What about?

BLUNTSCHLI. I don't know: he hasn't told me. Better not interfere, dear young lady. No harm will be done: I've often acted as sword instructor. He won't be able to touch me; and I'll not hurt him. It will save explanations. In the morning I shall be off home; and you'll never see me or hear of me again. You and he will then make it up and live happily ever after.

RAINA [*turning away deeply hurt, almost with a sob in her voice*]. I never said I wanted to see you again.

SERGIUS [*striding forward*]. Ha! That is a confession.

RAINA [*haughtily*]. What do you mean?

SERGIUS. You love that man!

RAINA [*scandalized*]. Sergius!

SERGIUS. You allow him to make love to you behind my back, just as you accept me as your affianced husband behind his. Bluntschli: you knew our relations; and you deceived me. It is for that that I call you to account, not for having received favours that I never enjoyed.

BLUNTSCHLI [*jumping up indignantly*]. Stuff! Rubbish! I have received no favours. Why, the young lady doesn't even know whether I'm married or not.

RAINA [*forgetting herself*]. Oh! [*Collapsing on the ottoman.*] Are you?

SERGIUS. You see the young lady's concern, Captain Bluntschli. Denial is useless. You have enjoyed the privilege of being received in her own room, late at night—

BLUNTSCHLI [*interrupting him pepperily*]. Yes; you blockhead! She received me with a pistol at her head. Your cavalry were at my heels. I'd have blown out her brains if she'd uttered a cry.

SERGIUS [*taken aback*]. Bluntschli! Raina: is this true?

RAINA [*rising in wrathful majesty*]. Oh, how dare you, how dare you?

BLUNTSCHLI. Apologize, man, apologize! [*He resumes his seat at the table.*]

SERGIUS [*with the old measured emphasis, folding his arms*]. I n e v e r apologize.

RAINA [*passionately*]. This is the doing of that friend of yours, Captain Bluntschli. It is he who is spreading this horrible story about me. [*She walks about excitedly.*]

BLUNTSCHLI. No: he's dead—burnt alive.

RAINA [*stopping, shocked*]. Burnt alive!

BLUNTSCHLI. Shot in the hip in a wood-yard. Couldn't drag himself out. Your fellows' shells set the timber on fire and burnt him, with half a dozen other poor devils in the same predicament.

RAINA. How horrible!

SERGIUS. And how ridiculous! Oh, war! war! the dream of patriots and heroes! A fraud, Bluntschli, a hollow sham, like love.

RAINA [outraged]. Like love! You say that before me.

BLUNTSCHLI. Come, Saranoff: that matter is explained.

SERGIUS. A hollow sham, I say. Would you have come back here if nothing had passed between you, except at the muzzle of your pistol? Raina is mistaken about our friend who was burnt. He was not my informant.

RAINA. Who then? [Suddenly guessing the truth.] Ah, Louka! my maid, my servant! You were with her this morning all that time after—after— Oh, what sort of god is this I have been worshipping! [He meets her gaze with sardonic enjoyment of her disenchantment. Angered all the more, she goes closer to him, and says, in a lower, intenser tone] Do you know that I looked out of the window as I went upstairs, to have another sight of my hero; and I saw something that I did not understand then. I know now that you were making love to her.

SERGIUS [with grim humor]. You saw that?

RAINA. Only too well. [She turns away, and throws herself on the divan under the centre window, quite overcome.]

SERGIUS [cynically]. Raina: our romance is shattered. Life's a farce.

BLUNTSCHLI [to Raina, goodhumoredly]. You see: he's found himself out now.

SERGIUS. Bluntschli: I have allowed you to call me a blockhead. You may now call me a coward as well. I refuse to fight you. Do you know why?

BLUNTSCHLI. No; but it doesn't matter. I didn't ask the reason when you cried on; and I don't ask the reason now that you cry off. I'm a professional soldier. I fight when I have to, and am very glad to get out of it when I haven't to. You're only an amateur: you think fighting's an amusement.

SERGIUS. You shall hear the reason all the same, my professional. The reason is that it takes two men—real men—men of heart, blood and honor—to make a genuine combat. I could no more fight with you than I could make love to an ugly woman. You've no magnetism: you're not a man, you're a machine.

BLUNTSCHLI [*apologetically*]. Quite true, quite true. I always was that sort of chap. I'm very sorry. But now that you've found that life isn't a farce, but something quite sensible and serious, what further obstacle is there to your happiness?

RAINA [*rising*]. You are very solicitous about my happiness and his. Do you forget his new love—Louka? It is not you that he must fight now, but his rival, Nicola.

SERGIUS. Rival!! [*Striking his forehead.*]

RAINA. Did you not know that they are engaged?

SERGIUS. Nicola! Are fresh abysses opening! Nicola!!

RAINA [*sarcastically*]. A shocking sacrifice, isn't it? Such beauty, such intellect, such modesty, wasted on a middle-aged servant man! Really, Sergius, you cannot stand by and allow such a thing. It would be unworthy of your chivalry.

SERGIUS [*losing all self-control*]. Viper! Viper! [*He rushes to and fro, raging.*]

BLUNTSCHLI. Look here, Saranoff; you're getting the worst of this.

RAINA [*getting angrier*]. Do you realize what he has done, Captain Bluntschli? He has set this girl as a spy on us; and her reward is that he makes love to her.

SERGIUS. False! Monstrous!

RAINA. Monstrous! [*Confronting him.*] Do you deny that she told you about Captain Bluntschli being in my room?

SERGIUS. No; but—

RAINA [*interrupting*]. Do you deny that you were making love to her when she told you?

SERGIUS. No; but I tell you—

RAINA [*cutting him short contemptuously*]. It is unnecessary to tell us anything more. That is quite enough for us. [*She turns her back on him and sweeps majestically back to the window.*]

BLUNTSCHLI [*quietly, as Sergius, in an agony of mortification, sinks on the ottoman, clutching his averted head between his fists*]. I told you you were getting the worst of it, Saranoff.

SERGIUS. Tiger cat!

RAINA [*running excitedly to Bluntschli*]. You hear this man calling me names, Captain Bluntschli?

BLUNTSCHLI. What else can he do, dear lady? He must defend himself somehow. Come [*very persuasively*], don't quarrel. What good does it do? [*Raina, with a gasp, sits down on the ottoman, and after a vain effort to look vexedly at Bluntschli, she falls a victim to her sense of humor, and is attacked with a disposition to laugh.*]

SERGIUS. Engaged to Nicola! [*He rises.*] Ha! ha! [*Going to the stove and standing with his back to it.*] Ah, well, Bluntschli, you are right to take this huge imposture of a world coolly.

RAINA [*to Bluntschli with an intuitive guess at his state of mind*]. I daresay you think us a couple of grown up babies, don't you?

SERGIUS [*grinning a little*]. He does, he does. Swiss civilization nursetending Bulgarian barbarism, eh?

BLUNTSCHLI [*blushing*]. Not at all, I assure you. I'm only very glad to get you two quieted. There now, let's be pleasant and talk it over in a friendly way. Where is this other young lady?

RAINA. Listening at the door, probably.

SERGIUS [*shivering as if a bullet had struck him, and speaking with quiet but deep indignation*]. I will prove that that, at least, is a calumny. [*He goes with dignity to the door and opens it. A yell of fury bursts from him as he looks out. He darts into the passage, and returns dragging in Louka, whom he flings against the table, R., as he cries*] Judge her, Bluntschli—you, the moderate, cautious man: judge the eavesdropper.

[*Louka stands her ground, proud and silent.*]

BLUNTSCHLI [*shaking his head*]. I mustn't judge her. I once listened myself outside a tent when there was a mutiny brewing. It's all a question of the degree of provocation. My life was at stake.

LOUKA. My love was at stake. [*Sergius flinches, ashamed of her in spite of himself.*] I am not ashamed.

RAINA [*contemptuously*]. Your love! Your curiosity, you mean.

LOUKA [*facing her and retorting her contempt with interest*]. My love, stronger than anything you can feel, even for your chocolate cream soldier.

SERGIUS [*with quick suspicion—to Louka*]. What does that mean?

LOUKA [*fiercely*]. It means—

SERGIUS [*interrupting her slightingly*]. Oh, I remember, the ice pudding. A paltry taunt, girl.

[*Major Petkoff enters, in his shirtsleeves.*]

PETKOFF. Excuse my shirtsleeves, gentlemen. Raina: somebody has been wearing that coat of mine: I'll swear it —somebody with bigger shoulders than mine. It's all burst open at the back. Your mother is mending it. I wish she'd make haste. I shall catch cold. [*He looks more attentively at them.*] Is anything the matter?

RAINA. No. [*She sits down at the stove with a tranquil air.*]

SERGIUS. Oh, no! [*He sits down at the end of the table, as at first.*]

BLUNTSCHLI [*who is already seated*]. Nothing, nothing.

PETKOFF [*sitting down on the ottoman in his old place*]. That's all right. [*He notices Louka.*] Anything the matter, Louka?

LOUKA. No, sir.

PETKOFF [*genially*]. That's all right. [*He sneezes.*] Go and ask your mistress for my coat, like a good girl, will you? [*She turns to obey; but Nicola enters with the coat; and she makes a pretence of having business in the room by taking the little table with the hookah away to the wall near the windows.*]

RAINA [*rising quickly, as she sees the coat on Nicola's arm*]. Here it is, papa. Give it to me, Nicola; and do you put some more wood on the fire. [*She takes the coat, and brings it to the Major, who stands up to put it on. Nicola attends to the fire.*]

PETKOFF [*to Raina, teasing her affectionately*]. Aha! Going to be very good to poor old papa just for one day after his return from the wars, eh?

RAINA [*with solemn reproach*]. Ah, how can you say that to me, father?

PETKOFF. Well, well, only a joke, little one. Come, give me a kiss. [*She kisses him.*] Now give me the coat.

RAINA. Now, I am going to put it on for you. Turn your back. [*He turns his back and feels behind him with his arms for the sleeves. She dexterously takes the photograph from the pocket and throws it on the table before Bluntschli, who covers it with a sheet of paper under the very nose of Sergius, who looks on amazed, with his suspicions roused in the highest degree. She then helps Petkoff on with his coat.*] There, dear! Now are you comfortable?

PETKOFF. Quite, little love. Thanks. [*He sits down; and Raina returns to her seat near the stove.*] Oh, by the bye, I've found something funny. What's the meaning of this?

[*He puts his hand into the picked pocket.*] Eh? Hallo! [*He tries the other pocket.*] Well, I could have sworn—[*Much puzzled, he tries the breast pocket.*] I wonder—[*Tries the original pocket.*] Where can it—[*A light flashes on him; he rises, exclaiming*] Your mother's taken it.

RAINA [*very red*]. Taken what?

PETKOFF. Your photograph, with the inscription: "Raina, to her Chocolate Cream Soldier—a souvenir." Now you know there's something more in this than meets the eye; and I'm going to find it out. [*Shouting*] Nicola!

NICOLA [*dropping a log, and turning*]. Sir!

PETKOFF. Did you spoil any pastry of Miss Raina's this morning?

NICOLA. You heard Miss Raina say that I did, sir.

PETKOFF. I know that, you idiot. Was it true?

NICOLA. I am sure Miss Raina is incapable of saying anything that is not true, sir.

PETKOFF. Are you? Then I'm not. [*Turning to the others.*] Come: do you think I don't see it all? [*Goes to Sergius, and slaps him on the shoulder.*] Sergius: you're the chocolate cream soldier, aren't you?

SERGIUS [*starting up*]. I! a chocolate cream soldier! Certainly not.

PETKOFF. Not! [*He looks at them. They are all very serious and very conscious.*] Do you mean to tell me that Raina sends photographic souvenirs to other men?

SERGIUS [*enigmatically*]. The world is not such an innocent place as we used to think, Petkoff.

BLUNTSCHLI [*rising*]. It's all right, Major. I'm the chocolate cream soldier. [*Petkoff and Sergius are equally astonished.*] The gracious young lady saved my life by giving me chocolate creams when I was starving—shall I ever forget their flavour! My late friend Stolz told you the story at Peerot. I was the fugitive.

PETKOFF. You! [*He gasps.*] Sergius: do you remember how those two women went on this morning when we mentioned it? [*Sergius smiles cynically. Petkoff confronts Raina severely.*] You're a nice young woman, aren't you?

RAINA [*bitterly*]. Major Saranoff has changed his mind. And when I wrote that on the photograph, I did not know that Captain Bluntschli was married.

BLUNTSCHLI [*much startled—protesting vehemently*]. I'm not married.

RAINA [*with deep reproach*]. You said you were.

BLUNTSCHLI. I did not. I positively did not. I never was married in my life.

PETKOFF [*exasperated*]. Raina: will you kindly inform me, if I am not asking too much, which gentleman you are engaged to?

RAINA. To neither of them. This young lady [*introducing Louka, who faces them all proudly*] is the object of Major Saranoff's affections at present.

PETKOFF. Louka! Are you mad, Sergius? Why, this girl's engaged to Nicola.

NICOLA [*coming forward*]. I beg your pardon sir. There is a mistake. Louka is not engaged to me.

PETKOFF. Not engaged to you, you scoundrel! Why, you had twenty-five levas from me on the day of your betrothal; and she had that gilt bracelet from Miss Raina.

NICOLA [*with cool unction*]. We gave it out so, sir. But it was only to give Louka protection. She had a soul above her station; and I have been no more than her confidential servant. I intend, as you know, sir, to set up a shop later on in Sofea; and I look forward to her custom and recommendation should she marry into the nobility. [*He goes out with impressive discretion, leaving them all staring after him.*]

PETKOFF [*breaking the silence*]. Well, I am—hm!

SERGIUS. This is either the finest heroism or the most crawling baseness. Which is it, Bluntschli?

BLUNTSCHLI. Never mind whether it's heroism or baseness. Nicola's the ablest man I've met in Bulgaria. I'll make him manager of a hotel if he can speak French and German.

LOUKA [*suddenly breaking out at Sergius*]. I have been insulted by everyone here. You set them the example. You owe me an apology. [*Sergius immediately, like a repeating clock of which the spring has been touched, begins to fold his arms.*]

BLUNTSCHLI [*before he can speak*]. It's no use. He never apologizes.

LOUKA. Not to you, his equal and his enemy. To me, his poor servant, he will not refuse to apologize.

SERGIUS [*approvingly*]. You are right. [*He bends his knee in his grandest manner.*] Forgive me!

LOUKA. I forgive you. [*She timidly gives him her hand, which he kisses.*] That touch makes me your affianced wife.

SERGIUS [*springing up*]. Ah, I forgot that!

LOUKA [*coldly*]. You can withdraw if you like.

SERGIUS. Withdraw! Never! You belong to me! [*He puts his arm about her and draws her to him.*]

[*Catherine comes in and finds Louka in Sergius's arms, and all the rest gazing at them in bewildered astonishment.*]

CATHERINE. What does this mean? [*Sergius releases Louka.*]

PETKOFF. Well, my dear, it appears that Sergius is going to marry Louka instead of Raina. [*She is about to break out indignantly at him: he stops her by exclaiming testily*] Don't blame me: I've nothing to do with it. [*He retreats to the stove.*]

CATHERINE. Marry Louka! Sergius: you are bound by your word to us!

SERGIUS [*folding his arms*]. Nothing binds me.

BLUNTSCHLI [*much pleased by this piece of common sense*]. Saranoff: your hand. My congratulations. These heroics of yours have their practical side after all. [*To Louka.*] Gracious young lady: the best wishes of a good Republican! [*He kisses her hand, to Raina's great disgust.*]

CATHERINE [*threateningly*]. Louka: you have been telling stories.

LOUKA. I have done Raina no harm.

CATHERINE [*haughtily*]. Raina! [*Raina is equally indignant at the liberty.*]

LOUKA. I have a right to call her Raina: she calls me Louka. I told Major Saranoff she would never marry him if the Swiss gentleman came back.

BLUNTSCHLI [*surprised*]. Hallo!

LOUKA [*turning to Raina*]. I thought you were fonder of him than of Sergius. You know best whether I was right.

BLUNTSCHLI. What nonsense! I assure you, my dear Major, my dear Madame, the gracious young lady simply saved my life, nothing else. She never cared two straws for me. Why, bless my heart and soul, look at the young lady and look at me. She, rich, young, beautiful, with her imagination full of fairy princes and noble natures and cavalry charges and goodness knows what! And I, a commonplace Swiss soldier who hardly knows what a decent life is after fifteen years of barracks and battles—a vagabond—a man who has spoiled all his chances in life through an incurably romantic disposition—a man—

SERGIUS [*starting as if a needle had pricked him and interrupting Bluntschli in incredulous amazement*]. Excuse me,

Bluntschli: w h a t did you say had spoiled your chances in life?

BLUNTSCHLI [*promptly*]. An incurably romantic disposition. I ran away from home twice when I was a boy. I went into the army instead of into my father's business. I climbed the balcony of this house when a man of sense would have dived into the nearest cellar. I came sneaking back here to have another look at the young lady when any other man of my age would have sent the coat back—

PETKOFF. My coat!

BLUNTSCHLI. —Yes: that's the coat I mean—would have sent it back and gone quietly home. Do you suppose I am the sort of fellow a young girl falls in love with? Why, look at our ages! I'm thirty-four: I don't suppose the young lady is much over seventeen. [*This estimate produces a marked sensation, all the rest turning and staring at one another. He proceeds innocently.*] All that adventure which was life or death to me, was only a schoolgirl's game to her—chocolate creams and hide and seek. Here's the proof! [*He takes the photograph from the table.*] Now, I ask you, would a woman who took the affair seriously have sent me this and written on it: "Raina, to her chocolate cream soldier—a souvenir"? [*He exhibits the photograph triumphantly, as if it settled the matter beyond all possibility of refutation.*]

PETKOFF. That's what I was looking for. How the deuce did it get there?

BLUNTSCHLI [*to Raina complacently*]. I have put everything right, I hope, gracious young lady!

RAINA [*in uncontrollable vexation*]. I quite agree with your account of yourself. You are a romantic idiot. [*Bluntschli is unspeakably taken aback.*] Next time I hope you will know the difference between a schoolgirl of seventeen and a woman of twenty-three.

BLUNTSCHLI [*stupefied*]. Twenty-three! [*She snaps the photograph contemptuously from his hand; tears it across; and throws the pieces at his feet.*]

SERGIUS [*with grim enjoyment of Bluntschli's discomfiture*]. Bluntschli: my one last belief is gone. Your sagacity is a fraud, like all the other things. You have less sense than even I have.

BLUNTSCHLI [*overwhelmed*]. Twenty-three! Twenty-three!! [*He considers.*] Hm! [*Swiftly making up his mind.*] In that case, Major Petkoff, I beg to propose formally to be-

come a suitor for your daughter's hand, in place of Major
Saranoff retired.

RAINA. You dare!

BLUNTSCHLI. If you were twenty-three when you said
those things to me this afternoon, I shall take them seriously.

CATHERINE [*loftily polite*]. I doubt, sir, whether you quite
realize either my daughter's position or that of Major Sergius
Saranoff, whose place you propose to take. The Petkoffs and
the Saranoffs are known as the richest and most important
families in the country. Our position is almost historical: we
can go back for nearly twenty years.

PETKOFF. Oh, never mind that, Catherine. [*To Bluntschli.*] We should be most happy, Bluntschli, if it were only
a question of your position; but hang it, you know, Raina is
accustomed to a very comfortable establishment. Sergius
keeps twenty horses.

BLUNTSCHLI. But what on earth is the use of twenty
horses? Why, it's a circus.

CATHERINE [*severely*]. My daughter, sir, is accustomed
to a first-rate stable.

RAINA. Hush, mother, you're making me ridiculous.

BLUNTSCHLI. Oh, well, if it comes to a question of an establishment, here goes! [*He goes impetuously to the table
and seizes the papers in the blue envelope.*] How many horses
did you say?

SERGIUS. Twenty, noble Switzer!

BLUNTSCHLI. I have two hundred horses. [*They are
amazed.*] How many carriages?

SERGIUS. Three.

BLUNTSCHLI. I have seventy. Twenty-four of them will
hold twelve inside, besides two on the box, without counting
the driver and conductor. How many tablecloths have you?

SERGIUS. How the deuce do I know?

BLUNTSCHLI. Have you four thousand?

SERGIUS. No.

BLUNTSCHLI. I have. I have nine thousand six hundred
pairs of sheets and blankets, with two thousand four hundred
eider-down quilts. I have ten thousand knives and forks, and
the same quantity of dessert spoons. I have six hundred servants. I have six palatial establishments, besides two livery
stables, a tea garden and a private house. I have four medals
for distinguished services; I have the rank of an officer and
the standing of a gentleman; and I have three native languages. Show me any man in Bulgaria that can offer as much.

PETKOFF [*with childish awe*]. Are you Emperor of Switzerland?

BLUNTSCHLI. My rank is the highest known in Switzerland: I'm a free citizen.

CATHERINE. Then Captain Bluntschli, since you are my daughter's choice, I shall not stand in the way of her happiness. [*Petkoff is about to speak.*] That is Major Petkoff's feeling also.

PETKOFF. Oh, I shall be only too glad. Two hundred horses! Whew!

SERGIUS. What says the lady?

RAINA [*pretending to sulk*]. The lady says that he can keep his tablecloths and his omnibuses. I am not here to be sold to the highest bidder.

BLUNTSCHLI. I won't take that answer. I appealed to you as a fugitive, a beggar, and a starving man. You accepted me. You gave me your hand to kiss, your bed to sleep in, and your roof to shelter me—

RAINA [*interrupting him*]. I did not give them to the Emperor of Switzerland!

BLUNTSCHLI. That's just what I say. [*He catches her hand quickly and looks her straight in the face as he adds, with confident mastery*] Now tell us who you did give them to.

RAINA [*succumbing with a shy smile*]. To my chocolate cream soldier!

BLUNTSCHLI [*with a boyish laugh of delight*]. That'll do. Thank you. [*Looks at his watch and suddenly becomes businesslike.*] Time's up, Major. You've managed those regiments so well that you are sure to be asked to get rid of some of the Infantry of the Teemok division. Send them home by way of Lom Palanka. Saranoff: don't get married until I come back: I shall be here punctually at five in the evening on Tuesday fortnight. Gracious ladies—good evening. [*He makes them a military bow, and goes.*]

SERGIUS. What a man! What a man!

Candida

ACT ONE

A fine October morning in the north east suburbs of London,
a vast district many miles away from the London of Mayfair and St. James's, much less known there than the Paris of the
Rue de Rivoli and the Champs Elysées, and much less narrow,
squalid, fetid and airless in its slums; strong in comfortable,
prosperous middle class life; wide streeted; myriad-populated,
well-served with ugly iron urinals, Radical clubs, tram lines,
and a perpetual stream of yellow cars; enjoying in its main
thoroughfares the luxury of grass-grown "front gardens," un-
trodden by the foot of man save as to the path from the gate
to the hall door; but blighted by an intolerable monotony of
miles and miles of graceless, characterless brick houses, black
iron railings, stony pavements, slaty roofs, and respectably ill
dressed or disreputably poorly dressed people, quite accustomed to the place, and mostly plodding about somebody else's
work, which they would not do if they themselves could help
it. The little energy and eagerness that crop up shew themselves in cockney cupidity and business "push." Even the
policemen and the chapels are not infrequent enough to break
the monotony. The sun is shining cheerfully; there is no fog;
and though the smoke effectually prevents anything, whether
faces and hands or bricks and mortar, from looking fresh and
clean, it is not hanging heavily enough to trouble a Londoner.

This desert of unattractiveness has its oasis. Near the outer
end of the Hackney Road is a park of 217 acres, fenced in,
not by railings, but by a wooden paling, and containing plenty
of greensward, trees, a lake for bathers, flower beds with the
flowers arranged carefully in patterns by the admired cockney
art of carpet gardening and a sandpit, imported from the sea-
side for the delight of the children, but speedily deserted on
its becoming a natural vermin preserve for all the petty fauna
of Kingsland, Hackney and Hoxton. A bandstand, an unfin-

ished forum for religious, anti-religious and political orators, cricket pitches, a gymnasium, and an old fashioned stone kiosk are among its attractions. Wherever the prospect is bounded by trees or rising green grounds, it is a pleasant place. Where the ground stretches flat to the grey palings, with bricks and mortar, sky signs, crowded chimneys and smoke beyond, the prospect makes it desolate and sordid.

　　The best view of Victoria Park is from the front window of St. Dominic's Parsonage, from which not a single chimney is visible. The parsonage is a semi-detached villa with a front garden and a porch. Visitors go up the flight of steps to the porch: tradespeople and members of the family go down by a door under the steps to the basement, with a breakfast room, used for all meals, in front, and the kitchen at the back. Upstairs, on the level of the hall door, is the drawing-room, with its large plate glass window looking on the park. In this room, the only sitting-room that can be spared from the children and the family meals, the parson, the Reverend James Mavor Morell, does his work. He is sitting in a strong round backed revolving chair at the right hand end of a long table, which stands across the window, so that he can cheer himself with the view of the park at his elbow. At the opposite end of the table, adjoining it, is a little table only half the width of the other, with a typewriter on it. His typist is sitting at this machine, with her back to the window. The large table is littered with pamphlets, journals, letters, nests of drawers, an office diary, postage scales and the like. A spare chair for visitors having business with the parson is in the middle, turned to his end. Within reach of his hand is a stationery case, and a cabinet photograph in a frame. Behind him the right hand wall, recessed above the fireplace, is fitted with bookshelves, on which an adept eye can measure the parson's divinity and casuistry by a complete set of Browning's poems and Maurice's Theological Essays, and guess at his politics from a yellow backed Progress and Poverty, Fabian Essays, A Dream of John Ball, Marx's Capital, and half a dozen other literary landmarks in Socialism. Opposite him on the left, near the typewriter, is the door. Further down the room, opposite the fireplace, a bookcase stands on a cellaret, with a sofa near it. There is a generous fire burning; and the hearth, with a comfortable armchair and a japanned flower painted coal scuttle at one side, a miniature chair for a boy or girl on the other, a nicely varnished wooden mantelpiece, with neatly moulded shelves, tiny bits of mirror let into the panels, and a travelling clock in

*a leather case [the inevitable wedding present], and on the
wall above a large autotype of the chief figure in Titian's
Virgin of the Assumption, is very inviting. Altogether the
room is the room of a good housekeeper, vanquished, as far as
the table is concerned, by an untidy man, but elsewhere mistress of the situation. The furniture, in its ornamental aspect,
betrays the style of the advertised "drawing-room suite" of
the pushing suburban furniture dealer; but there is nothing
useless or pretentious in the room. The paper and panelling
are dark, throwing the big cheery window and the park outside into strong relief.*

*The Reverend James Mavor Morell is a Christian Social-
ist clergyman of the Church of England, and an active member of the Guild of St. Matthew and the Christian Social
Union. A vigorous, genial, popular man of forty, robust and
goodlooking, full of energy, with pleasant, hearty, considerate
manners, and a sound, unaffected voice, which he uses with
the clean, athletic articulation of a practised orator, and with
a wide range and perfect command of expression. He is a
first rate clergyman, able to say what he likes to whom he
likes, to lecture people without setting himself up against them,
to impose his authority on them without humiliating them,
and to interfere in their business without impertinence. His
well spring of spiritual enthusiasm and sympathetic emotion
has never run dry for a moment: he still eats and sleeps heartily
enough to win the daily battle between exhaustion and recu-
peration triumphantly. Withal, a great baby, pardonably vain
of his powers and unconsciously pleased with himself. He has
a healthy complexion, a good forehead, with the brows somewhat blunt, and the eyes bright and eager, a mouth resolute,
but not particularly well cut, and a substantial nose, with the
mobile, spreading nostrils of the dramatic orator, but, like all
his features, void of subtlety.*

*The typist, Miss Proserpine Garnett, is a brisk little woman
of about 30, of the lower middle class, neatly but cheaply
dressed in a black merino skirt and a blouse, rather pert and
quick of speech, and not very civil in her manner, but sensitive and affectionate. She is clattering away busily at her
machine whilst Morell opens the last of his morning's letters.
He realizes its contents with a comic groan of despair.*

PROSERPINE. Another lecture?

MORELL. Yes. The Hoxton Freedom Group want me to
address them on Sunday morning [*great emphasis on "Sun-*

day," this being the unreasonable part of the business]. What
are they?

PROSERPINE. Communist Anarchists, I think.

MORELL. Just like Anarchists not to know that they can't
have a parson on Sunday! Tell them to come to church if
they want to hear me: it will do them good. Say I can only
come on Mondays and Thursdays. Have you the diary there?

PROSERPINE [*taking up the diary*]. Yes.

MORELL. Have I any lecture on for next Monday?

PROSERPINE [*referring to diary*]. Tower Hamlets Radical
Club.

MORELL. Well, Thursday then?

PROSERPINE. English Land Restoration League.

MORELL. What next?

PROSERPINE. Guild of St. Matthew on Monday. Independent Labor Party, Greenwich Branch, on Thursday. Monday, Social-Democratic Federation, Mile End Branch. Thursday, first Confirmation class— [*Impatiently.*] Oh, I'd better
tell them you can't come. They're only half a dozen ignorant
and conceited costermongers without five shillings between
them.

MORELL [*amused*]. Ah; but you see they're near relatives
of mine, Miss Garnett.

PROSERPINE [*staring at him*]. Relatives of yours!

MORELL. Yes: we have the same father—in Heaven.

PROSERPINE [*relieved*]. Oh, is that all?

MORELL [*with a sadness which is a luxury to a man whose
voice expresses it so finely*]. Ah, you don't believe it. Everybody says it: nobody believes it—nobody. [*Briskly, getting
back to business.*] Well, well! Come, Miss Proserpine, can't
you find a date for the costers? What about the 25th?: that
was vacant the day before yesterday.

PROSERPINE [*referring to diary*]. Engaged—the Fabian
Society.

MORELL. Bother the Fabian Society! Is the 28th gone,
too?

PROSERPINE. City dinner. You're invited to dine with the
Founder's Company.

MORELL. That'll do; I'll go to the Hoxton Group of Freedom instead. [*She enters the engagement in silence, with implacable disparagement of the Hoxton Anarchists in every line
of her face. Morell bursts open the cover of a copy of* The
Church Reformer, *which has come by post, and glances
through Mr. Stewart Hendlam's leader and the Guild of St.*

*Matthew news. These proceedings are presently enlivened by
the appearance of Morell's curate, the Reverend Alexander
Mill, a young gentleman gathered by Morell from the nearest
University settlement, whither he had come from Oxford to
give the east end of London the benefit of his university training. He is a conceitedly well intentioned, enthusiastic, immature person, with nothing positively unbearable about him except a habit of speaking with his lips carefully closed for half
an inch from each corner, a finicking articulation, and a set of
horribly corrupt vowels, notably ow for o, this being his chief
means of bringing Oxford refinement to bear on Hackney
vulgarity. Morell, whom he has won over by a doglike devotion, looks up indulgently from* The Church Reformer *as he
enters, and remarks*] Well, Lexy! Late again, as usual.

LEXY. I'm afraid so. I wish I could get up in the morning.

MORELL [*exulting in his own energy*]. Ha! ha! [*Whimsically.*] Watch and pray, Lexy: watch and pray.

LEXY. I know. [*Rising wittily to the occasion.*] But how
can I watch and pray when I am asleep? Isn't that so, Miss
Prossy?

PROSERPINE [*sharply*]. Miss Garnett, if you please.

LEXY. I beg your pardon——Miss Garnett.

PROSERPINE. You've got to do all the work to-day.

LEXY. Why?

PROSERPINE. Never mind why. It will do you good to earn
your supper before you eat it, for once in a way, as I do.
Come: don't dawdle. You should have been off on your
rounds half an hour ago.

LEXY [*perplexed*]. Is she in earnest, Morell?

MORELL [*in the highest spirits—his eyes dancing*]. Yes. *I*
am going to dawdle to-day.

LEXY. You! You don't know how.

MORELL [*heartily*]. Ha! ha! Don't I? I'm going to have
this day all to myself—or at least the forenoon. My wife's
coming back: she's due here at 11.45.

LEXY [*surprised*]. Coming back already—with the children? I thought they were to stay to the end of the month.

MORELL. So they are: she's only coming up for two days,
to get some flannel things for Jimmy, and to see how we're
getting on without her.

LEXY [*anxiously*]. But, my dear Morell, if what Jimmy
and Fluffy had was scarlatina, do you think it wise—

MORELL. Scarlatina!—rubbish, German measles. I brought
it into the house myself from the Pycroft Street School. A

parson is like a doctor, my boy: he must face infection as a soldier must face bullets. [*He rises and claps Lexy on the shoulder.*] Catch the measles if you can, Lexy: she'll nurse you; and what a piece of luck that will be for you!—eh?

LEXY [*smiling uneasily*]. It's so hard to understand you about Mrs. Morell—

MORELL [*tenderly*]. Ah, my boy, get married—get married to a good woman; and then you'll understand. That's a foretaste of what will be best in the Kingdom of Heaven we are trying to establish on earth. That will cure you of dawdling. An honest man feels that he must pay Heaven for every hour of happiness with a good spell of hard, unselfish work to make others happy. We have no more right to consume happiness without producing it than to consume wealth without producing it. Get a wife like my Candida; and you'll always be in arrear with your repayment.

[*He pats Lexy affectionately on the back, and is leaving the room when Lexy calls to him.*]

LEXY. Oh, wait a bit: I forgot. [*Morell halts and turns with the door knob in his hand.*] Your father-in-law is coming round to see you. [*Morell shuts the door again, with a complete change of manner.*]

MORELL [*surprised and not pleased*]. Mr. Burgess?

LEXY. Yes. I passed him in the park, arguing with somebody. He gave me good day and asked me to let you know that he was coming.

MORELL [*half incredulous*]. But he hasn't called here for —I may almost say for years. Are you sure, Lexy? You're not joking, are you?

LEXY [*earnestly*]. No, sir, really.

MORELL [*thoughtfully*]. Hm! Time for him to take another look at Candida before she grows out of his knowledge. [*He resigns himself to the inevitable, and goes out. Lexy looks after him with beaming, foolish worship.*]

LEXY. What a good man! What a thorough, loving soul he is!

[*He takes Morell's place at the table, making himself very comfortable as he takes out a cigaret.*]

PROSERPINE [*impatiently, pulling the letter she has been working at off the typewriter and folding it.*] Oh, a man ought to be able to be fond of his wife without making a fool of himself about her.

LEXY [*shocked*]. Oh, Miss Prossy!

PROSERPINE [*rising busily and coming to the stationery*

case to get an envelope, in which she encloses the letter as she speaks]. Candida here, and Candida there, and Candida everywhere! [*She licks the envelope.*] It's enough to drive anyone out of their senses [*thumping the envelope to make it stick*] to hear a perfectly commonplace woman raved about in that absurd manner merely because she's got good hair, and a tolerable figure.

LEXY [*with reproachful gravity*]. I think her extremely beautiful, Miss Garnett. [*He takes the photograph up; looks at it; and adds, with even greater impressiveness*] Extremely beautiful. How fine her eyes are!

PROSERPINE. Her eyes are not a bit better than mine—now! [*He puts down the photograph and stares austerely at her.*] And you know very well that you think me dowdy and second rate enough.

LEXY [*rising majestically*]. Heaven forbid that I should think of any of God's creatures in such a way! [*He moves stiffly away from her across the room to the neighbourhood of the bookcase.*]

PROSERPINE. Thank you. That's very nice and comforting.

LEXY [*saddened by her depravity*]. I had no idea you had any feeling against Mrs. Morell.

PROSERPINE [*indignantly*]. I have no feeling against her. She's very nice, very good-hearted: I'm very fond of her and can appreciate her real qualities far better than any man can. [*He shakes his head sadly and turns to the bookcase, looking along the shelves for a volume. She follows him with intense pepperiness.*] You don't believe me? [*He turns and faces her. She pounces at him with spitfire energy.*] You think I'm jealous. Oh, what a profound knowledge of the human heart you have, Mr. Lexy Mill! How well you know the weaknesses of Woman, don't you! It must be so nice to be a man and have a fine penetrating intellect instead of mere emotions like us, and to know that the reason we don't share your amorous delusions is that we're all jealous of one another! [*She abandons him with a toss of her shoulders, and crosses to the fire to warm her hands.*]

LEXY. Ah, if you women only had the same clue to Man's strength that you have to his weakness, Miss Prossy, there would be no Woman Question.

PROSERPINE [*over her shoulder, as she stoops, holding her hands to the blaze*]. Where did you hear Morell say that? You didn't invent it yourself: you're not clever enough.

LEXY. That's quite true. I am not ashamed of owing him that, as I owe him so many other spiritual truths. He said it at the annual conference of the Women's Liberal Federation. Allow me to add that though they didn't appreciate it, I, a mere man, did. [*He turns to the bookcase again, hoping that this may leave her crushed.*]

PROSERPINE [*putting her hair straight at the little panel of mirror in the mantelpiece*]. Well, when you talk to me, give me your own ideas, such as they are, and not his. You never cut a poorer figure than when you are trying to imitate him.

LEXY [*stung*]. I try to follow his example, not to imitate him.

PROSERPINE [*coming at him again on her way back to her work*]. Yes, you do: you imitate him. Why do you tuck your umbrella under your left arm instead of carrying it in your hand like anyone else? Why do you walk with your chin stuck out before you, hurrying along with that eager look in your eyes—you, who never get up before half past nine in the morning? Why do you say "knoaledge" in church, though you always say "knolledge" in private conversation! Bah! do you think I don't know? [*She goes back to the typewriter.*] Here, come and set about your work: we've wasted enough time for one morning. Here's a copy of the diary for to-day. [*She hands him a memorandum.*]

LEXY [*deeply offended*]. Thank you. [*He takes it and stands at the table with his back to her, reading it. She begins to transcribe her shorthand notes on the typewriter without troubling herself about his feelings. Mr. Burgess enters unannounced. He is a man of sixty, made coarse and sordid by the compulsory selfishness of petty commerce, and later on softened into sluggish bumptiousness by overfeeding and commercial success. A vulgar, ignorant, guzzling man, offensive and contemptuous to people whose labor is cheap, respectful to wealth and rank, and quite sincere and without rancour or envy in both attitudes. Finding him without talent, the world has offered him no decently paid work except ignoble work, and he has become, in consequence, somewhat hoggish. But he has no suspicion of this himself, and honestly regards his commercial prosperity as the inevitable and socially wholesome triumph of the ability, industry, shrewdness and experience in business of a man who in private is easygoing, affectionate and humorously convivial to a fault. Corporeally, he is a podgy man, with a square, clean shaven face and a square beard under his chin; dust colored, with a patch of grey in*] *the centre, and small watery blue eyes with a plaintively sentimental expression, which he transfers easily to his voice by his habit of pompously intoning his sentences.]*

BURGESS [*stopping on the threshold, and looking round*]. They told me Mr. Morell was here.

PROSERPINE [*rising*]. He's upstairs. I'll fetch him for you.

BURGESS [*staring boorishly at her*]. You're not the same young lady as hused to typewrite for him?

PROSERPINE. No.

BURGESS [*assenting*]. No: she was young-er. [*Miss Garnett stolidly stares at him; then she goes out with great dignity. He receives this quite obtusely, and crosses to the hearth-rug, where he turns and spreads himself with his back to the fire.*] Startin' on your rounds, Mr. Mill?

LEXY [*folding his paper and pocketing it*]. Yes: I must be off presently.

BURGESS [*momentously*]. Don't let me detain you, Mr. Mill. What I come about is private between me and Mr. Morell.

LEXY [*huffily*]. I have no intention of intruding, I am sure, Mr. Burgess. Good morning.

BURGESS [*patronizingly*]. Oh, good morning to you. [*Morell returns as Lexy is making for the door.*]

MORELL [*to Lexy*]. Off to work?

LEXY. Yes, sir.

MORELL [*patting him affectionately on the shoulder*]. Take my silk handkerchief and wrap your throat up. There's a cold wind. Away with you.

[*Lexy brightens up, and goes out.*]

BURGESS. Spoilin' your curates, as usu'l, James. Good mornin'. When I pay a man, an' 'is livin' depen's on me, I keep him in his place.

MORELL [*rather shortly*]. I always keep my curates in their places as my helpers and comrades. If you get as much work out of your clerks and warehousemen as I do out of my curates, you must be getting rich pretty fast. Will you take your old chair?

[*He points with curt authority to the arm chair beside the fireplace; then takes the spare chair from the table and sits down in front of Burgess.*]

BURGESS [*without moving*]. Just the same as hever, James!

MORELL. When you last called—it was about three years ago, I think—you said the same thing a little more frankly.

Your exact words then were: "Just as big a fool as ever,
James?"

BURGESS [*soothingly*]. Well, perhaps I did; but [*with conciliatory cheerfulness*] I meant no offence by it. A clorgyman
is privileged to be a bit of a fool, you know: it's on'y becomin'
in his profession that he should. Anyhow, I come here, not
to rake up hold differences, but to let bygones be bygones.
[*Suddenly becoming very solemn, and approaching Morell.*]
James: three year ago, you done me a hill turn. You done me
hout of a contrac'; an' when I gev you 'arsh words in my
nat'ral disappointment, you turned my daughrter again me.
Well, I've come to act the part of a Cherischin. [*Offering his
hand.*] I forgive you, James.

MORELL [*starting up*]. Confound your impudence!

BURGESS [*retreating, with almost lachrymose deprecation
of this treatment*]. Is that becomin' language for a clorgyman,
James?—and you so partic'lar, too?

MORELL [*hotly*]. No, sir, it is not becoming language for
a clergyman. I used the wrong word. I should have said damn
your impudence: that's what St. Paul, or any honest priest,
would have said to you. Do you think I have forgotten that
tender of yours for the contract to supply clothing to the
workhouse?

BURGESS [*in a paroxysm of public spirit*]. I acted in the
interest of the ratepayers, James. It was the lowest tender:
you can't deny it.

MORELL. Yes, the lowest, because you paid worse wages
than any other employer—starvation wages—aye, worse than
starvation wages—to the women who made the clothing.
Your wages would have driven them to the streets to keep
body and soul together. [*Getting angrier and angrier.*] Those
women were my parishioners. I shamed the Guardians out of
accepting your tender: I shamed the ratepayers out of letting
them do it: I shamed everybody but you. [*Boiling over.*] How
dare you, sir, come here and offer to forgive me, and talk
about your daughter, and—

BURGESS. Easy, James, easy, easy. Don't git hinto a fluster
about nothink. I've howned I was wrong.

MORELL [*fuming about*]. Have you? I didn't hear you.

BURGESS. Of course I did. I hown it now. Come: I harsk
your pardon for the letter I wrote you. Is that enough?

MORELL [*snapping his fingers*]. That's nothing. Have you
raised the wages?

BURGESS [*triumphantly*]. Yes.

MORELL [*stopping dead*]. What!

BURGESS [*unctuously*]. I've turned a moddle hemployer. I don't hemploy no women now: they're all sacked; and the work is done by machinery. Not a man 'as less than sixpence a *hour*; and the skilled 'ands gits the Trade Union rate. [*Proudly.*] What 'ave you to say to me now?

MORELL [*overwhelmed*]. Is it possible! Well, there's more joy in heaven over one sinner that repenteth—[*Going to Burgess with an explosion of apologetic cordiality.*] My dear Burgess, I most heartily beg your pardon for my hard thoughts of you. [*Grasps his hand.*] And now, don't you feel the better for the change? Come, confess, you're happier. You look happier.

BURGESS [*ruefully*]. Well, p'raps I do. I s'pose I must, since you notice it. At all events, I git my contrax asseppit [accepted] by the County Council. [*Savagely.*] They dussent 'ave nothink to do with me unless I paid fair wages—curse 'em for a parcel o' meddlin' fools!

MORELL [*dropping his hand, utterly discouraged*]. So that was why you raised the wages! [*He sits down moodily.*]

BURGESS [*severely, in spreading, mounting tones*]. Why else should I do it? What does it lead to but drink and huppishness in workin' men? [*He seats himself magisterially in the easy chair.*] It's hall very well for you, James: it gits you hinto the papers and makes a great man of you; but you never think of the 'arm you do, puttin' money into the pockets of workin' men that they don't know 'ow to spend, and takin' it from people that might be makin' a good huse on it.

MORELL [*with a heavy sigh, speaking with cold politeness*]. What is your business with me this morning? I shall not pretend to believe that you are here merely out of family sentiment.

BURGESS [*obstinately*]. Yes, I ham—just family sentiment and nothink else.

MORELL [*with weary calm*]. I don't believe you!

BURGESS [*rising threateningly*]. Don't say that to me again, James Mavor Morell.

MORELL [*unmoved*]. I'll say it just as often as may be necessary to convince you that it's true. I don't believe you.

BURGESS [*collapsing into an abyss of wounded feeling*]. Oh, well, if you're determined to be unfriendly, I s'pose I'd better go. [*He moves reluctantly towards the door. Morell makes no sign. He lingers.*] I didn't hexpect to find a hunforgivin' spirit in you, James. [*Morell still not responding, he*

*takes a few more reluctant steps doorwards. Then he comes
back whining.*] We huseter git on well enough, spite of our
different opinions. Why are you so changed to me? I give you
my word I come here in pyorr [*pure*] frenliness, not wishin'
to be on bad terms with my hown daughrter's 'usban'. Come,
James: be a Cherischin and shake 'ands. [*He puts his hand
sentimentally on Morell's shoulder.*]

MORELL [*looking up at him thoughtfully*]. Look here,
Burgess. Do you want to be as welcome here as you were
before you lost that contract?

BURGESS. I do, James. I do—honest.

MORELL. Then why don't you behave as you did then?

BURGESS [*cautiously removing his hand*]. 'Ow d'y'mean?

MORELL. I'll tell you. You thought me a young fool then.

BURGESS [*coaxingly*]. No, I didn't, James. I—

MORELL [*cutting him short*]. Yes, you did. And I thought
you an old scoundrel.

BURGESS [*most vehemently deprecating this gross self-
accusation on Morell's part*]. No, you didn't, James. Now
you do yourself a hinjustice.

MORELL. Yes, I did. Well, that did not prevent our getting
on very well together. God made you what I call a scoundrel
as he made me what you call a fool. [*The effect of this observation on Burgess is to remove the keystone of his moral
arch. He becomes bodily weak, and, with his eyes fixed on
Morell in a helpless stare, puts out his hand apprehensively
to balance himself, as if the floor had suddenly sloped under
him. Morell proceeds in the same tone of quiet conviction.*]
It was not for me to quarrel with his handiwork in the one
case more than in the other. So long as you come here honestly
as a self-respecting, thorough, convinced scoundrel, justifying
your scoundrelism, and proud of it, you are welcome. But
[*and now Morell's tone becomes formidable; and he rises and
strikes the back of the chair for greater emphasis*] I won't
have you here snivelling about being a model employer and
a converted man when you're only an apostate with your coat
turned for the sake of a County Council contract. [*He nods
at him to enforce the point; then goes to the hearth-rug, where
he takes up a comfortably commanding position with his back
to the fire, and continues*] No: I like a man to be true to himself, even in wickedness. Come now: either take your hat and
go; or else sit down and give me a good scoundrelly reason
for wanting to be friends with me. [*Burgess, whose emotions
have subsided sufficiently to be expressed by a dazed grin, is*

relieved by this concrete proposition. He ponders it for a moment, and then, slowly and very modestly, sits down in the chair Morell has just left.] That's right. Now, out with it.

BURGESS [*chuckling in spite of himself*]. Well, you are a queer bird, James, and no mistake. But [*almost enthusiastically*] one carnt 'elp likin' you; besides, as I said afore, of course one don't take all a clorgyman says seriously, or the world couldn't go on. Could it now? [*He composes himself for graver discourse, and turning his eyes on Morell proceeds with dull seriousness.*] Well, I don't mind tellin' you, since it's your wish we should be free with one another, that I did think you a bit of a fool once; but I'm beginnin' to think that p'r'aps I was be'ind the times a bit.

MORELL [*delighted*]. Aha! You're finding that out at last, are you?

BURGESS [*portentously*]. Yes, times 'as changed mor'n I could a believed. Five yorr [year] ago, no sensible man would a thought o' takin' up with your ideas. I hused to wonder you was let preach at all. Why, I know a clorgyman that 'as bin kep' hout of his job for yorrs by the Bishop of London, although the pore feller's not a bit more religious than you are. But to-day, if henyone was to offer to bet me a thousan' poun' that you'll end by bein' a bishop yourself, I shouldn't venture to take the bet. You and yore crew are gettin' hinfluential: I can see that. They'll 'ave to give you something someday, if it's only to stop yore mouth. You 'ad the right instinc' arter all, James: the line you took is the payin' line in the long run fur a man o' your sort.

MORELL [*decisively—offering his hand*]. Shake hands, Burgess. Now you're talking honestly. I don't think they'll make me a bishop; but if they do, I'll introduce you to the biggest jobbers I can get to come to my dinner parties.

BURGESS [*who has risen with a sheepish grin and accepted the hand of friendship*]. You will 'ave your joke, James. Our quarrel's made up now, isn't it?

A WOMAN'S VOICE. Say yes, James.

[*Startled, they turn quickly and find that Candida has just come in, and is looking at them with an amused maternal indulgence which is her characteristic expression. She is a woman of 33, well built, well nourished, likely, one guesses, to become matronly later on, but now quite at her best, with the double charm of youth and motherhood. Her ways are those of a woman who has found that she can always manage people by engaging their affection, and who does so frankly*

*and instinctively without the smallest scruple. So far, she is
like any other pretty woman who is just clever enough to make
the most of her sexual attractions for trivially selfish ends; but
Candida's serene brow, courageous eyes, and well set mouth
and chin signify largeness of mind and dignity of character to
ennoble her cunning in the affections. A wisehearted observer,
looking at her, would at once guess that whoever had placed
the Virgin of the Assumption over her hearth did so because
he fancied some spiritual resemblance between them, and yet
would not suspect either her husband or herself of any such
idea, or indeed of any concern with the art of Titian.*

*Just now she is in bonnet and mantle, laden with a strapped
rug with her umbrella stuck through it, a handbag, and a
supply of illustrated papers.]*

MORELL [*shocked at his remissness*]. Candida! Why—
[*looks at his watch, and is horrified to find it so late.*] My
darling! [*Hurrying to her and seizing the rug strap, pouring
forth his remorseful regrets all the time.*] I intended to meet
you at the train. I let the time slip. [*Flinging the rug on the
sofa.*] I was so engrossed by—[*returning to her*]—I forgot—
oh! [*He embraces her with penitent emotion.*]

BURGESS [*a little shamefaced and doubtful of his reception*]. How orr you, Candy? [*She, still in Morell's arms, offers
him her cheek, which he kisses.*] James and me is come to a
unnerstandin'—a honourable unnerstandin'. Ain' we, James?

MORELL [*impetuously*]. Oh, bother your understanding!
You've kept me late for Candida. [*With compassionate fervor.*]
My poor love: how did you manage about the luggage?—
how—

CANDIDA [*stopping him and disengaging herself*]. There,
there, there. I wasn't alone. Eugene came down yesterday;
and we travelled up together.

MORELL [*pleased*]. Eugene!

CANDIDA. Yes: he's struggling with my luggage, poor boy.
Go out, dear, at once; or he will pay for the cab; and I don't
want that. [*Morell hurries out. Candida puts down her handbag; then takes off her mantle and bonnet and puts them on
the sofa with the rug, chatting meanwhile.*] Well, papa, how
are you getting on at home?

BURGESS. The 'ouse ain't worth livin' in since you left it,
Candy. I wish you'd come round and give the gurl a talkin'
to. Who's this Eugene that's come with you?

CANDIDA. Oh, Eugene's one of James's discoveries. He
found him sleeping on the Embankment last June. Haven't

you noticed our new picture [*pointing to the Virgin*]? He gave us that.

BURGESS [*incredulously*]. Garn! D'you mean to tell me—your hown father!—that cab touts or such like, orf the Embankment, buys pictur's like that? [*Severely.*] Don't deceive me, Candy: it's a 'Igh Church pictur; and James chose it hisself.

CANDIDA. Guess again. Eugene isn't a cab tout.

BURGESS. Then wot is he? [*Sarcastically.*] A nobleman, I s'pose.

CANDIDA [*delighted—nodding*]. Yes. His uncle's a peer—a real live earl.

BURGESS [*not daring to believe such good news*]. No!

CANDIDA. Yes. He had a seven day bill for £55 in his pocket when James found him on the Embankment. He thought he couldn't get any money for it until the seven days were up; and he was too shy to ask for credit. Oh, he's a dear boy! We are very fond of him.

BURGESS [*pretending to belittle the aristocracy, but with his eyes gleaming*]. Hm, I thort you wouldn't git a piorr's [peer's] nevvy visitin' in Victoria Park unless he were a bit of a flat. [*Looking again at the picture.*] Of course I don't 'old with that pictur, Candy; but still it's a 'igh class, fust rate work of art: I can see that. Be sure you hintroduce me to him, Candy. [*He looks at his watch anxiously.*] I can only stay about two minutes.

[*Morell comes back with Eugene, whom Burgess contemplates moist-eyed with enthusiasm. He is a strange, shy youth of eighteen, slight, effeminate, with a delicate childish voice, and a hunted, tormented expression and shrinking manner that shew the painful sensitiveness that very swift and acute apprehensiveness produces in youth, before the character has grown to its full strength. Yet everything that his timidity and frailty suggests is contradicted by his face. He is miserably irresolute, does not know where to stand or what to do with his hands and feet, is afraid of Burgess, and would run away into solitude if he dared; but the very intensity with which he feels a perfectly commonplace position shews great nervous force, and his nostrils and mouth shew a fiercely petulant wilfulness, as to the quality of which his great imaginative eyes and fine brow are reassuring. He is so entirely uncommon as to be almost unearthly; and to prosaic people there is something noxious in this unearthliness, just as to poetic people there is something angelic in it. His dress is anarchic. He*

*wears an old blue serge jacket, unbuttoned over a woollen
lawn tennis shirt, with a silk handkerchief for a cravat, trousers
matching the jacket, and brown canvas shoes. In these gar-
ments he has apparently lain in the heather and waded through
the waters; but there is no evidence of his having ever brushed
them.*

*As he catches sight of a stranger on entering, he stops, and
edges along the wall on the opposite side of the room.*]

MORELL [*as he enters*]. Come along: you can spare us
quarter of an hour, at all events. This is my father-in-law,
Mr. Burgess—Mr. Marchbanks.

MARCHBANKS [*nervously backing against the bookcase*].
Glad to meet you, sir.

BURGESS [*crossing to him with great heartiness, whilst
Morell joins Candida at the fire*]. Glad to meet y o u, I'm
shore, Mr. Morchbanks. [*Forcing him to shake hands.*] 'Ow
do you find yoreself this weather? 'Ope you ain't lettin' James
put no foolish ideas into your 'ed?

MARCHBANKS. Foolish ideas! Oh, you mean Socialism.
No.

BURGESS. That's right. [*Again looking at his watch.*] Well,
I must go now: there's no 'elp for it. Yo're not comin' my
way, are you, Mr. Morchbanks?

MARCHBANKS. Which way is that?

BURGESS. Victawriar Pork Station. There's a city train at
12:25.

MORELL. Nonsense. Eugene will stay to lunch with us,
I expect.

MARCHBANKS [*anxiously excusing himself*]. No—I—I—

BURGESS. Well, well, I shan't press you: I bet you'd rather
lunch with Candy. Some night, I 'ope, you'll come and dine
with me at my club, the Freeman Founders in Nortn Folgit.
Come, say you will.

MARCHBANKS. Thank you, Mr. Burgess. Where is Nor-
ton Folgate—down in Surrey, isn't it? [*Burgess, inexpressibly
tickled, begins to splutter with laughter.*]

CANDIDA [*coming to the rescue*]. You'll lose your train,
papa, if you don't go at once. Come back in the afternoon
and tell Mr. Marchbanks where to find the club.

BURGESS [*roaring with glee*]. Down in Surrey—har, har!
that's not a bad one. Well, I never met a man as didn't know
Nortn Folgit before. [*Abashed at his own noisiness.*] Good-
bye, Mr. Morchbanks: I know yo're too 'ighbred to take my
pleasantry in bad part. [*He again offers his hand.*]

MARCHBANKS [*taking it with a nervous jerk*]. Not at all.

BURGESS. Bye, bye, Candy. I'll look in again later on. So long, James.

MORELL. Must you go?

BURGESS. Don't stir. [*He goes out with unabated heartiness.*]

MORELL. Oh, I'll see you out. [*He follows him out. Eugene stares after them apprehensively, holding his breath until Burgess disappears.*]

CANDIDA [*laughing*]. Well, Eugene. [*He turns with a start and comes eagerly towards her, but stops irresolutely as he meets her amused look.*] What do you think of my father?

MARCHBANKS. I—I hardly know him yet. He seems to be a very nice old gentleman.

CANDIDA [*with gentle irony*]. And you'll go to the Free-man Founders to dine with him, won't you?

MARCHBANKS [*miserably, taking it quite seriously*]. Yes, if it will please you.

CANDIDA [*touched*]. Do you know, you are a very nice boy, Eugene, with all your queerness. If you had laughed at my father I shouldn't have minded; but I like you ever so much better for being nice to him.

MARCHBANKS. Ought I to have laughed? I noticed that he said something funny; but I am so ill at ease with strangers; and I never can see a joke! I'm very sorry. [*He sits down on the sofa, his elbows on his knees and his temples between his fists, with an expression of hopeless suffering.*]

CANDIDA [*bustling him goodnaturedly*]. Oh, come! You great baby, you! You are worse than usual this morning. Why were you so melancholy as we came along in the cab?

MARCHBANKS. Oh, that was nothing. I was wondering how much I ought to give the cabman. I know it's utterly silly; but you don't know how dreadful such things are to me—how I shrink from having to deal with strange people. [*Quickly and reassuringly.*] But it's all right. He beamed all over and touched his hat when Morell gave him two shillings. I was on the point of offering him ten. [*Candida laughs heartily. Morell comes back with a few letters and newspapers which have come by the midday post.*]

CANDIDA. Oh, James, dear, he was going to give the cab-man ten shillings—ten shillings for a three minutes' drive—oh, dear!

MORELL [*at the table, glancing through the letters*]. Never mind her, Marchbanks. The overpaying instinct is a generous one: better than the underpaying instinct, and not so common.

MARCHBANKS [*relapsing into dejection*]. No: cowardice, incompetence. Mrs. Morell's quite right.

CANDIDA. Of course she is. [*She takes up her handbag.*] And now I must leave you to James for the present. I suppose you are too much of a poet to know the state a woman finds her house in when she's been away for three weeks. Give me my rug. [*Eugene takes the strapped rug from the couch, and gives it to her. She takes it in her left hand, having the bag in her right.*] Now hang my cloak across my arm. [*He obeys.*] Now my hat. [*He puts it into the hand which has the bag.*] Now open the door for me. [*He hurries up before her and opens the door.*] Thanks. [*She goes out; and Marchbanks shuts the door.*]

MORELL [*still busy at the table*]. You'll stay to lunch, Marchbanks, of course.

MARCHBANKS [*scared*]. I mustn't. [*He glances quickly at Morell, but at once avoids his frank look, and adds, with obvious disingenuousness*] I can't.

MORELL [*over his shoulder*]. You mean you won't.

MARCHBANKS [*earnestly*]. No: I should like to, indeed. Thank you very much. But—but—

MORELL [*breezily, finishing with the letters and coming close to him*]. But—but—but—but—bosh! If you'd like to stay, stay. You don't mean to persuade me you have anything else to do. If you're shy, go and take a turn in the park and write poetry until half past one; and then come in and have a good feed.

MARCHBANKS. Thank you, I should like that very much. But I really mustn't. The truth is, Mrs. Morell told me not to. She said she didn't think you'd ask me to stay to lunch, but that I was to remember, if you did, that you didn't really want me to. [*Plaintively.*] She said I'd understand; but I don't. Please don't tell her I told you.

MORELL [*drolly*]. Oh, is that all? Won't my suggestion that you should take a turn in the park meet the difficulty?

MARCHBANKS. How?

MORELL [*exploding good-humoredly*]. Why, you duffer— [*But this boisterousness jars himself as well as Eugene. He checks himself, and resumes, with affectionate seriousness*] No: I won't put it in that way. My dear lad: in a happy marriage like ours, there is something very sacred in the return of the wife to her home. [*Marchbanks looks quickly at him, half anticipating his meaning.*] An old friend or a truly noble and

sympathetic soul is not in the way on such occasions; but a
chance visitor is. [*The hunted, horror-stricken expression
comes out with sudden vividness in Eugene's face as he
understands. Morell, occupied with his own thought, goes on
without noticing it.*] Candida thought I would rather not have
you here; but she was wrong. I'm very fond of you, my boy,
and I should like you to see for yourself what a happy thing
it is to be married as I am.

MARCHBANKS. Happy!—your marriage! You think that!
You believe that!

MORELL [*buoyantly*]. I know it, my lad. La Rochefou-
cauld said that there are convenient marriages, but no delightful ones. You don't know the comfort of seeing through and
through a thundering liar and rotten cynic like that fellow.
Ha, ha! Now off with you to the park, and write your poem.
Half past one, sharp, mind: we never wait for anybody.

MARCHBANKS [*wildly*]. No: stop; you shan't. I'll force it
into the light.

MORELL [*puzzled*]. Eh? Force what?

MARCHBANKS. I must speak to you. There is something
that must be settled between us.

MORELL [*with a whimsical glance at the clock*]. Now?

MARCHBANKS [*passionately*]. Now. Before you leave this
room. [*He retreats a few steps, and stands as if to bar Morell's way to the door.*]

MORELL [*without moving, and gravely, perceiving now
that there is something serious the matter*]. I'm not going to
leave it, my dear boy: I thought you were. [*Eugene, baffled
by his firm tone, turns his back on him, writhing with anger.
Morell goes to him and puts his hand on his shoulder strongly
and kindly, disregarding his attempt to shake it off.*] Come:
sit down quietly; and tell me what it is. And remember: we
are friends, and need not fear that either of us will be anything but patient and kind to the other, whatever we may
have to say.

MARCHBANKS [*twisting himself round on him*]. Oh, I am
not forgetting myself: I am only [*covering his face desperately
with his hands*] full of horror. [*Then, dropping his hands, and
thrusting his face forward fiercely at Morell, he goes on
threateningly.*] You shall see whether this is a time for patience and kindness. [*Morell, firm as a rock, looks indulgently
at him.*] Don't look at me in that self-complacent way. You
think yourself stronger than I am; but I shall stagger you if
you have a heart in your breast.

MORELL [*powerfully confident*]. Stagger me, my boy. Out with it.

MARCHBANKS. First—

MORELL. First?

MARCHBANKS. I love your wife.

[*Morell recoils, and, after staring at him for a moment in utter amazement, bursts into uncontrollable laughter. Eugene is taken aback, but not disconcerted; and he soon becomes indignant and contemptuous.*]

MORELL [*sitting down to have his laugh out*]. Why, my dear child, of course you do. Everybody loves her: they can't help it. I like it. But [*looking up whimsically at him*] I say, Eugene: do you think yours is a case to be talked about? You're under twenty: she's over thirty. Doesn't it look rather too like a case of calf love?

MARCHBANKS [*vehemently*]. You dare say that of her! You think that way of the love she inspires! It is an insult to her!

MORELL [*rising quickly, in an altered tone*]. To her! Eugene: take care. I have been patient. I hope to remain patient. But there are some things I won't allow. Don't force me to shew you the indulgence I should shew to a child. Be a man.

MARCHBANKS [*with a gesture as if sweeping something behind him*]. Oh, let us put aside all that cant. It horrifies me when I think of the doses of it she has had to endure in all the weary years during which you have selfishly and blindly sacrificed her to minister to your self-sufficiency—you [*turning on him*] who have not one thought—one sense—in common with her.

MORELL [*philosophically*]. She seems to bear it pretty well. [*Looking him straight in the face.*] Eugene, my boy: you are making a fool of yourself—a very great fool of yourself. There's a piece of wholesome plain speaking for you.

MARCHBANKS. Oh, do you think I don't know all that? Do you think that the things people make fools of themselves about are any less real and true than the things they behave sensibly about? [*Morell's gaze wavers for the first time. He instinctively averts his face and stands listening, startled and thoughtful.*] They are more true: they are the only things that are true. You are very calm and sensible and moderate with me because you can see that I am a fool about your wife; just as no doubt that old man who was here just now is very wise over your socialism, because he sees that you are a fool about it. [*Morell's perplexity deepens markedly. Eugene follows up his advantage, plying him fiercely with questions.*] Does that prove you wrong? Does your complacent superiority to me prove that *I* am wrong?

MORELL [*turning on Eugene, who stands his ground*]. Marchbanks: some devil is putting these words into your mouth. It is easy—terribly easy—to shake a man's faith in himself. To take advantage of that to break a man's spirit is devil's work. Take care of what you are doing. Take care.

MARCHBANKS [*ruthlessly*]. I know. I'm doing it on purpose. I told you I should stagger you.

[*They confront one another threateningly for a moment. Then Morell recovers his dignity.*]

MORELL [*with noble tenderness*]. Eugene: listen to me. Some day, I hope and trust, you will be a happy man like me. [*Eugene chafes intolerantly, repudiating the worth of his happiness. Morell, deeply insulted, controls himself with fine forbearance, and continues steadily, with great artistic beauty of delivery*] You will be married; and you will be working with all your might and valor to make every spot on earth as happy as your own home. You will be one of the makers of the Kingdom of Heaven on earth; and—who knows?—you may be a pioneer and master builder where I am only a humble journeyman; for don't think, my boy, that I cannot see in you, young as you are, promise of higher powers than I can ever pretend to. I well know that it is in the poet that the holy spirit of man—the god within him—is most godlike. It should make you tremble to think of that—to think that the heavy burthen and great gift of a poet may be laid upon you.

MARCHBANKS [*unimpressed and remorseless, his boyish crudity of assertion telling sharply against Morell's oratory*]. It does not make me tremble. It is the want of it in others that makes me tremble.

MORELL [*redoubling his force of style under the stimulus of his genuine feeling and Eugene's obduracy*]. Then help to kindle it in them—in me—not to extinguish it. In the future—when you are as happy as I am—I will be your true brother in the faith. I will help you to believe that God has given us a world that nothing but our own folly keeps from being a paradise. I will help you to believe that every stroke of your work is sowing happiness for the great harvest that all—even the humblest—shall one day reap. And last, but trust me, not least, I will help you to believe that your wife loves you and is happy in her home. We need such help, Marchbanks: we need it greatly and always. There are so many things to make us doubt, if once we let our understanding be troubled. Even at home, we sit as if in camp, encompassed by a hostile army of doubts. Will you play the traitor and let them in on me?

MARCHBANKS [*looking round him*]. Is it like this for her here always? A woman, with a great soul, craving for reality, truth, freedom, and being fed on metaphors, sermons, stale perorations, mere rhetoric. Do you think a woman's soul can live on your talent for preaching?

MORELL [*stung*]. Marchbanks: you make it hard for me to control myself. My talent is like yours insofar as it has any real worth at all. It is the gift of finding words for divine truth.

MARCHBANKS [*impetuously*]. It's the gift of the gab, nothing more and nothing less. What has your knack of fine talking to do with the truth, any more than playing the organ has? I've never been in your church; but I've been to your political meetings; and I've seen you do what's called rousing the meeting to enthusiasm: that is, you excited them until they behaved exactly as if they were drunk. And their wives looked on and saw clearly enough what fools they were. Oh, it's an old story: you'll find it in the Bible. I imagine King David, in his fits of enthusiasm, was very like you. [*Stabbing him with the words.*] "But his wife despised him in her heart."

MORELL [*wrathfully*]. Leave my house. Do you hear? [*He advances on him threateningly.*]

MARCHBANKS [*shrinking back against the couch*]. Let me alone. Don't touch me. [*Morell grasps him powerfully by the lappel of his coat: he cowers down on the sofa and screams passionately.*] Stop, Morell, if you strike me, I'll kill myself: I won't bear it. [*Almost in hysterics.*] Let me go. Take your hand away.

MORELL [*with slow, emphatic scorn*]. You little snivelling, cowardly whelp. [*Releasing him.*] Go, before you frighten yourself into a fit.

MARCHBANKS [*on the sofa, gasping, but relieved by the withdrawal of Morell's hand*]. I'm not afraid of you: it's you who are afraid of me.

MORELL [*quietly, as he stands over him*]. It looks like it, doesn't it?

MARCHBANKS [*with petulant vehemence*]. Yes, it does. [*Morell turns away contemptuously. Eugene scrambles to his feet and follows him.*] You think because I shrink from being brutally handled—because [*with tears in his voice*] I can do nothing but cry with rage when I am met with violence—because I can't lift a heavy trunk down from the top of a cab like you—because I can't fight you for your wife as a navvy would: all that makes you think that I'm afraid of you. But you're wrong. If I haven't got what you call British pluck, I haven't British cowardice either: I'm not afraid of a clergyman's ideas. I'll fight your ideas. I'll rescue her from her slavery to them: I'll pit my own ideas against them. You are driving me out of the house because you daren't let her choose between your ideas and mine. You are afraid to let me see her again. [*Morell, angered, turns suddenly on him. He flies to the door in involuntary dread.*] Let me alone, I say. I'm going.

MORELL [*with cold scorn*]. Wait a moment: I am not going to touch you: don't be afraid. When my wife comes back she will want to know why you have gone. And when she finds you are never going to cross our threshold again, she will want to have that explained too. Now I don't wish to distress her by telling her that you have behaved like a blackguard.

MARCHBANKS [*coming back with renewed vehemence*]. You shall—you must. If you give any explanation but the true one, you are a liar and a coward. Tell her what I said; and how you were strong and manly, and shook me as a terrier shakes a rat; and how I shrank and was terrified; and how you called me a snivelling little whelp and put me out of the house. If you don't tell her, I will: I'll write it to her.

MORELL [*taken aback*]. Why do you want her to know this?

MARCHBANKS [*with lyric rapture*]. Because she will understand me, and know that I understand her. If you keep back one word of it from her—if you are not ready to lay the truth at her feet as I am—then you will know to the end of your days that she really belongs to me and not to you. Goodbye. [*Going.*]

MORELL [*terribly disquieted*]. Stop: I will not tell her.

MARCHBANKS [*turning near the door*]. Either the truth or a lie you must tell her, if I go.

MORELL [*temporizing*]. Marchbanks: it is sometimes justifiable.

MARCHBANKS [*cutting him short*]. I know—to lie. It will be useless. Good-bye, Mr. Clergyman.

[*As he turns finally to the door, it opens and Candida enters in housekeeping attire.*]

CANDIDA. Are you going, Eugene? [*Looking more observantly at him.*] Well, dear me, just look at you, going out into the street in that state! You are a poet, certainly. Look at him, James! [*She takes him by the coat, and brings him forward to show him to Morell.*] Look at his collar! look at his tie! look at his hair! One would think somebody had been throttling you. [*The two men guard themselves against betraying their consciousness.*] Here! Stand still. [*She buttons his collar; ties his neckerchief in a bow; and arranges his hair.*] There! Now you look so nice that I think you'd better stay to lunch after all, though I told you you mustn't. It will be ready in half an hour. [*She puts a final touch to the bow. He kisses her hand.*] Don't be silly.

MARCHBANKS. I want to stay, of course—unless the reverend gentleman, your husband, has anything to advance to the contrary.

CANDIDA. Shall he stay, James, if he promises to be a good boy and to help me to lay the table? [*Marchbanks turns his head and looks steadfastly at Morell over his shoulder, challenging his answer.*]

MORELL [*shortly*]. Oh, yes, certainly: he had better. [*He goes to the table and pretends to busy himself with his papers there.*]

MARCHBANKS [*offering his arm to Candida*]. Come and lay the table. [*She takes it and they go to the door together. As they go out he adds*] I am the happiest of men.

MORELL. So was I—an hour ago.

ACT TWO

The same day. The same room. Late in the afternoon. The spare chair for visitors has been replaced at the table, which is, if possible, more untidy than before. Marchbanks, alone and idle, is trying to find out how the typewriter works. Hearing someone at the door, he steals guiltily away to the window and pretends to be absorbed in the view. Miss Garnett, carrying the notebook in which she takes down Morell's letters in shorthand from his dictation, sits down at the typewriter and sets to work transcribing them, much too busy to notice Eugene. Unfortunately the first key she strikes sticks.

PROSERPINE. Bother! You've been meddling with my type-writer, Mr. Marchbanks; and there's not the least use in your trying to look as if you hadn't.

MARCHBANKS [*timidly*]. I'm very sorry, Miss Garnett. I only tried to make it write.

PROSERPINE. Well, you've made this key stick.

MARCHBANKS [*earnestly*]. I assure you I didn't touch the keys. I didn't, indeed. I only turned a little wheel. [*He points irresolutely at the tension wheel.*]

PROSERPINE. Oh, now I understand. [*She sets the machine to rights, talking volubly all the time.*] I suppose you thought it was a sort of barrel-organ. Nothing to do but turn the handle, and it would write a beautiful love letter for you straight off, eh?

MARCHBANKS [*seriously*]. I suppose a machine could be made to write love-letters. They're all the same, aren't they?

PROSERPINE [*somewhat indignantly: any such discussion, except by way of pleasantry, being outside her code of manners*]. How do I know? Why do you ask me?

MARCHBANKS. I beg your pardon. I thought clever people —people who can do business and write letters, and that sort of thing—always had love affairs.

PROSERPINE [*rising, outraged*]. Mr. Marchbanks! [*She looks severely at him, and marches with much dignity to the bookcase.*]

MARCHBANKS [*approaching her humbly*]. I hope I haven't offended you. Perhaps I shouldn't have alluded to your love affairs.

PROSERPINE [*plucking a blue book from the shelf and turning sharply on him*]. I haven't any love affairs. How dare you say such a thing?

MARCHBANKS [*simply*]. Really! Oh, then you are shy, like me. Isn't that so?

PROSERPINE. Certainly I am not shy. What do you mean?

MARCHBANKS [*secretly*]. You must be: that is the reason there are so few love affairs in the world. We all go about longing for love: it is the first need of our natures, the loudest cry of our hearts; but we dare not utter our longing: we are too shy. [*Very earnestly.*] Oh, Miss Garnett, what would you not give to be without fear, without shame—

PROSERPINE [*scandalized*]. Well, upon my word!

MARCHBANKS [*with petulant impatience*]. Ah, don't say those stupid things to me: they don't deceive me: what use are they? Why are you afraid to be your real self with me? I am just like you.

PROSERPINE. Like me! Pray, are you flattering me or flattering yourself? I don't feel quite sure which. [*She turns to go back to the typewriter.*]

MARCHBANKS [*stopping her mysteriously*]. Hush! I go about in search of love; and I find it in unmeasured stores in the bosoms of others. But when I try to ask for it, this horrible shyness strangles me; and I stand dumb, or worse than dumb, saying meaningless things—foolish lies. And I see the affection I am longing for given to dogs and cats and pet birds, because they come and ask for it. [*Almost whispering.*] It must be asked for: it is like a ghost: it cannot speak unless it is first spoken to. [*At his normal pitch, but with deep melancholy.*] All the love in the world is longing to speak; only it dare not, because it is shy, shy, shy. That is the world's tragedy. [*With a deep sigh he sits in the spare chair and buries his face in his hands.*]

PROSERPINE [*amazed, but keeping her wits about her— her point of honor in encounters with strange young men*]. Wicked people get over that shyness occasionally, don't they?

MARCHBANKS [*scrambling up almost fiercely*]. Wicked people means people who have no love: therefore they have no shame. They have the power to ask love because they don't need it: they have the power to offer it because they have none to give. [*He collapses into his seat, and adds, mournfully*] But we, who have love, and long to mingle it with the love of others: we cannot utter a word. [*Timidly.*] You find that, don't you?

PROSERPINE. Look here: if you don't stop talking like this, I'll leave the room, Mr. Marchbanks: I really will. It's not proper.

[*She resumes her seat at the typewriter, opening the blue book and preparing to copy a passage from it.*]

MARCHBANKS [*hopelessly*]. Nothing that's worth saying is proper. [*He rises, and wanders about the room in his lost way, saying*] I can't understand you, Miss Garnett. What am I to talk about?

PROSERPINE [*snubbing him*]. Talk about indifferent things. Talk about the weather.

MARCHBANKS. Would you stand and talk about indifferent things if a child were by, crying bitterly with hunger.

PROSERPINE. I suppose not.

MARCHBANKS. Well: *I* can't talk about indifferent things with my heart crying out bitterly in its hunger.

PROSERPINE. Then hold your tongue.

MARCHBANKS. Yes: that is what it always comes to. We hold our tongues. Does that stop the cry of your heart?— for it does cry: doesn't it? It must, if you have a heart.

PROSERPINE [*suddenly rising with her hand pressed on her heart*]. Oh, it's no use trying to work while you talk like that. [*She leaves her little table and sits on the sofa. Her feelings are evidently strongly worked on.*] It's no business of yours, whether my heart cries or not; but I have a mind to tell you, for all that.

MARCHBANKS. You needn't. I know already that it must.

PROSERPINE. But mind: if you ever say I said so, I'll deny it.

MARCHBANKS [*compassionately*]. Yes, I know. And so you haven't the courage to tell him?

PROSERPINE [*bouncing up*]. Him! Who?

MARCHBANKS. Whoever he is. The man you love. It might be anybody. The curate, Mr. Mill, perhaps.

PROSERPINE [*with disdain*]. Mr. Mill!!! A fine man to break my heart about, indeed! I'd rather have you than Mr. Mill.

MARCHBANKS [*recoiling*]. No, really—I'm very sorry; but you mustn't think of that. I—

PROSERPINE [*testily, crossing to the fire and standing at it with her back to him*]. Oh, don't be frightened: it's not you. It's not any one particular person.

MARCHBANKS. I know. You feel that you could love anybody that offered—

PROSERPINE [*exasperated*]. Anybody that offered! No, I do not. What do you take me for?

MARCHBANKS [*discouraged*]. No use. You won't make me real answers—only those things that everybody says. [*He strays to the sofa and sits down disconsolately.*]

PROSERPINE [*nettled at what she takes to be a disparagement of her manners by an aristocrat*]. Oh, well, if you want original conversation, you'd better go and talk to yourself.

MARCHBANKS. That is what all poets do: they talk to themselves out loud; and the world overhears them. But it's horribly lonely not to hear someone else talk sometimes.

PROSERPINE. Wait until Mr. Morell comes. He'll talk to you. [*Marchbanks shudders.*] Oh, you needn't make wry

faces over him: he can talk better than you. [*With temper.*]
He'd talk your little head off. [*She is going back angrily to
her place, when, suddenly enlightened, he springs up and
stops her.*]

MARCHBANKS. Ah, I understand now!

PROSERPINE [*reddening*]. What do you understand?

MARCHBANKS. Your secret. Tell me: is it really and truly
possible for a woman to love him?

PROSERPINE [*as if this were beyond all bounds*]. Well!!

MARCHBANKS [*passionately*]. No, answer me. I want to
know: I must know. *I* can't understand it. I can see nothing
in him but words, pious resolutions, what people call goodness. You can't love that.

PROSERPINE [*attempting to snub him by an air of cool
propriety*]. I simply don't know what you're talking about. I
don't understand you.

MARCHBANKS [*vehemently*]. You do. You lie—

PROSERPINE. Oh!

MARCHBANKS. You do understand; and you know. [*Determined to have an answer.*] Is it possible for a woman to
love him?

PROSERPINE [*looking him straight in the face*]. Yes. [*He
covers his face with his hands.*] Whatever is the matter with
you! [*He takes down his hands and looks at her. Frightened
at the tragic mask presented to her, she hurries past him at
the utmost possible distance, keeping her eyes on his face
until he turns from her and goes to the child's chair beside
the hearth, where he sits in the deepest dejection. As she
approaches the door, it opens and Burgess enters. On seeing
him, she ejaculates*] Praise heaven, here's somebody! [*and sits
down, reassured, at her table. She puts a fresh sheet of paper
into the typewriter as Burgess crosses to Eugene.*]

BURGESS [*bent on taking care of the distinguished visitor*].
Well: so this is the way they leave you to yourself, Mr.
Morchbanks. I've come to keep you company. [*Marchbanks
looks up at him in consternation, which is quite lost on
him.*] James is receivin' a deppitation in the dinin' room;
and Candy is hupstairs educatin' of a young stitcher gurl
she's hinterusted in. She's settin' there learnin' her to read
out of the "'Ev'nly Twins." [*Condolingly.*] You must find
it lonesome here with no one but the typist to talk to. [*He
pulls round the easy chair above fire, and sits down.*]

PROSERPINE [*highly incensed*]. He'll be all right now
that he has the advantage of your polished conversation:

that's one comfort, anyhow. [*She begins to typewrite with clattering asperity.*]

BURGESS [*amazed at her audacity*]. Hi was not addressin' myself to you, young woman, that I'm awerr of.

PROSERPINE [*tartly, to Marchbanks*]. Did you ever see worse manners, Mr. Marchbanks?

BURGESS [*with pompous severity*]. Mr. Morchbanks is a gentleman and knows his place, which is more than some people do.

PROSERPINE [*fretfully*]. It's well you and I are not ladies and gentlemen: I'd talk to you pretty straight if Mr. Marchbanks wasn't here. [*She pulls the letter out of the machine so crossly that it tears.*] There, now I've spoiled this letter— have to be done all over again. Oh, I can't contain myself— silly old fathead!

BURGESS [*rising, breathless with indignation*]. Ho! I'm a silly ole fat'ead, am I? Ho, indeed [*gasping*]. Hall right, my gurl! Hall right. You just wait till I tell that to your employer. You'll see. I'll teach you: see if I don't.

PROSERPINE. I—

BURGESS [*cutting her short*]. No, you've done it now. No huse a-talkin' to me. I'll let you know who I am. [*Proserpine shifts her paper carriage with a defiant bang, and disdainfully goes on with her work.*] Don't you take no notice of her, Mr. Morchbanks. She's beneath it. [*He sits down again loftily.*]

MARCHBANKS [*miserably nervous and disconcerted*]. Hadn't we better change the subject. I—I don't think Miss Garnett meant anything.

PROSERPINE [*with intense conviction*]. Oh, didn't I though, just!

BURGESS. I wouldn't demean myself to take notice on her.

[*An electric bell rings twice.*]

PROSERPINE [*gathering up her note-book and papers*]. That's for me. [*She hurries out.*]

BURGESS [*calling after her*]. Oh, we can spare you. [*Somewhat relieved by the triumph of having the last word, and yet half inclined to try to improve on it, he looks after her for a moment; then subsides into his seat by Eugene, and addresses him very confidentially.*] Now we're alone, Mr. Morchbanks, let me give you a friendly 'int that I wouldn't give to everybody. 'Ow long 'ave you known my son-in-law James here?

MARCHBANKS. I don't know. I never can remember dates.
A few months, perhaps.

BURGESS. Ever notice anything queer about him?

MARCHBANKS. I don't think so.

BURGESS [*impressively*]. No more you wouldn't. That's
the danger in it. Well, he's mad.

MARCHBANKS. Mad!

BURGESS. Mad as a Morch 'are. You take notice on him
and you'll see.

MARCHBANKS [*beginning*]. But surely that is only because
his opinions—

BURGESS [*touching him with his forefinger on his knee,
and pressing it as if to hold his attention with it*]. That's wot
I used ter think, Mr. Morchbanks. Hi thought long enough
that it was honly 'is opinions; though, mind you, hopinions
becomes vurry serious things when people takes to hactin on
'em as 'e does. But that's not wot I go on. [*He looks round
to make sure that they are alone, and bends over to Eugene's
ear.*] Wot do you think he says to me this mornin' in this
very room?

MARCHBANKS. What?

BURGESS. He sez to me—this is as sure as we're settin'
here now—he sez: "I'm a fool," he sez; "and yore a scounderl"—as cool as possible. Me a scounderl, mind you! And
then shook 'ands with me on it, as if it was to my credit! Do
you mean to tell me that that man's sane?

MORELL [*outside, calling to Proserpine, holding the door
open*]. Get all their names and addresses, Miss Garnett.

PROSERPINE [*in the distance*]. Yes, Mr. Morell.

[*Morell comes in, with the deputation's documents in his
hands.*]

BURGESS [*aside to Marchbanks*]. Yorr he is. Just you keep
your heye on him and see. [*Rising momentously.*] I'm sorry,
James, to 'ave to make a complaint to you. I don't want to
do it; but I feel I oughter, as a matter o' right and dooty.

MORELL. What's the matter.

BURGESS. Mr. Morchbanks will bear me out: he was a
witness. [*Very solemnly.*] Your young woman so far forgot
herself as to call me a silly ole fat'ead.

MORELL [*delighted—with tremendous heartiness*]. Oh,
now, isn't that exactly like Prossy? She's so frank: she
can't contain herself! Poor Prossy! Ha! Ha!

BURGESS [*trembling with rage*]. And do you hexpec me to
put up with it from the like of 'er?

MORELL. Pooh, nonsense! you can't take any notice of it.
Never mind. [*He goes to the cellaret and puts the papers
into one of the drawers.*]

BURGESS. Oh, *I* don't mind. I'm above it. But is it r i g h t?
—that's what I want to know. It is right?

MORELL. That's a question for the Church, not for the
laity. Has it done you any harm, that's the question for you,
eh? Of course, it hasn't. Think no more of it. [*He dismisses
the subject by going to his place at the table and setting to
work at his correspondence.*]

BURGESS [*aside to Marchbanks*]. What did I tell you?
Mad as a 'atter. [*He goes to the table and asks, with the
sickly civility of a hungry man*] When's dinner, James?

MORELL. Not for half an hour yet.

BURGESS [*with plaintive resignation*]. Gimme a nice book
to read over the fire, will you, James: thur's a good chap.

MORELL. What sort of book? A good one?

BURGESS [*with almost a yell of remonstrance*]. Nah-oo!
Summat pleasant, just to pass the time. [*Morell takes an illustrated paper from the table and offers it. He accepts it
humbly.*] Thank yer, James. [*He goes back to his easy chair
at the fire, and sits there at his ease, reading.*]

MORELL [*as he writes*]. Candida will come to entertain you
presently. She has got rid of her pupil. She is filling the lamps.

MARCHBANKS [*starting up in the wildest consternation*].
But that will soil her hands. I can't bear that, Morell: it's a
shame. I'll go and fill them. [*He makes for the door.*]

MORELL. You'd better not. [*Marchbanks stops irresolutely.*] She'd only set you to clean my boots, to save me
the trouble of doing it myself in the morning.

BURGESS [*with grave disapproval*]. Don't you keep a
servant now, James?

MORELL. Yes; but she isn't a slave; and the house looks
as if I kept three. That means that everyone has to lend a
hand. It's not a bad plan: Prossy and I can talk business
after breakfast whilst we're washing up. Washing up's no
trouble when there are two people to do it.

MARCHBANKS [*tormentedly*]. Do you think every woman
is as coarse-grained as Miss Garnett?

BURGESS [*emphatically*]. That's quite right, Mr. Morchbanks. That's q u i t e right. She is corse-grained.

MORELL [*quietly and significantly*]. Marchbanks!

MARCHBANKS. Yes.

MORELL. How many servants does your father keep?

MARCHBANKS. Oh, I don't know. [*He comes back uneasily to the sofa, as if to get as far as possible from Morell's questioning, and sits down in great agony of mind, thinking of the paraffin.*]

MORELL [*very gravely*]. So many that you don't know. [*More aggressively.*] Anyhow, when there's anything coarse-grained to be done, you ring the bell and throw it on to somebody else, eh? That's one of the great facts in your existence, isn't it?

MARCHBANKS. Oh, don't torture me. The one great fact now is that your wife's beautiful fingers are dabbling in paraffin oil, and that you are sitting here comfortably preaching about it—everlasting preaching, preaching, words, words, words.

BURGESS [*intensely appreciating this retort*]. Ha, ha! Devil a better. [*Radiantly.*] 'Ad you there, James, straight.

[*Candida comes in, well aproned, with a reading lamp trimmed, filled, and ready for lighting. She places it on the table near Morell, ready for use.*]

CANDIDA [*brushing her finger tips together with a slight twitch of her nose*]. If you stay with us, Eugene, I think I will hand over the lamps to you.

MARCHBANKS. I will stay on condition that you hand over all the rough work to me.

CANDIDA. That's very gallant; but I think I should like to see how you do it first. [*Turning to Morell.*] James: you've not been looking after the house properly.

MORELL. What have I done—or not done—my love?

CANDIDA [*with serious vexation*]. My own particular pet scrubbing brush has been used for blackleading. [*A heart-breaking wail bursts from Marchbanks. Burgess looks round, amazed. Candida hurries to the sofa.*] What's the matter? Are you ill, Eugene?

MARCHBANKS. No, not ill. Only horror, horror, horror! [*He bows his head on his hands.*]

BURGESS [*shocked*]. What! Got the 'orrors, Mr. Morchbanks! Oh, that's bad, at your age. You must leave it off grajally.

CANDIDA [*reassured*]. Nonsense, papa. It's only poetic horror, isn't it, Eugene? [*Petting him.*]

BURGESS [*abashed*]. Oh, poetic 'orror, is it? I beg your pordon, I'm shore. [*He turns to the fire again, deprecating his hasty conclusion.*]

CANDIDA. What is it, Eugene—the scrubbing brush? [*He

shudders.] Well, there! never mind. [*She sits down beside him.*] Wouldn't you like to present me with a nice new one, with an ivory back inlaid with mother-of-pearl?

MARCHBANKS [*softly and musically, but sadly and longingly*]. No, not a scrubbing brush, but a boat—a tiny shallop to sail away in, far from the world, where the marble floors are washed by the rain and dried by the sun, where the south wind dusts the beautiful green and purple carpets. Or a chariot—to carry us up into the sky, where the lamps are stars, and don't need to be filled with paraffin oil every day.

MORELL [*harshly*]. And where there is nothing to do but to be idle, selfish and useless.

CANDIDA [*jarred*]. Oh, James, how could you spoil it all!

MARCHBANKS [*firing up*]. Yes, to be idle, selfish and useless: that is to be beautiful and free and happy: hasn't every man desired that with all his soul for the woman he loves? That's my ideal: what's yours, and that of all the dreadful people who live in these hideous rows of houses? Sermons and scrubbing brushes! With you to preach the sermon and your wife to scrub.

CANDIDA [*quaintly*]. He cleans the boots, Eugene. You will have to clean them to-morrow for saying that about him.

MARCHBANKS. Oh! don't talk about boots. Your feet should be beautiful on the mountains.

CANDIDA. My feet would not be beautiful on the Hackney Road without boots.

BURGESS [*scandalized*]. Come, Candy, don't be vulgar. Mr. Morchbanks ain't accustomed to it. You're givin' him the 'orrors again. I mean the poetic ones.

[*Morell is silent. Apparently he is busy with his letters: really he is puzzling with misgiving over his new and alarming experience that the surer he is of his moral thrusts, the more swiftly and effectively Eugene parries them. To find himself beginning to fear a man whom he does not respect afflicts him bitterly.*]

[*Miss Garnett comes in with a telegram.*]

PROSERPINE [*handing the telegram to Morell*]. Reply paid. The boy's waiting. [*To Candida, coming back to her machine and sitting down.*] Maria is ready for you now in the kitchen, Mrs. Morell. [*Candida rises.*] The onions have come.

MARCHBANKS [*convulsively*]. Onions!

CANDIDA. Yes, onions. Not even Spanish ones—nasty little red onions. You shall help me to slice them. Come along.

[*She catches him by the wrist and runs out, pulling him after her. Burgess rises in consternation, and stands aghast on the hearth-rug, staring after them.*]

BURGESS. Candy didn't oughter 'andle a peer's nevvy like that. It's goin' too fur with it. Lookee 'ere, James: do 'e often git taken queer like that?

MORELL [*shortly, writing a telegram*]. I don't know.

BURGESS [*sentimentally*]. He talks very pretty. I allus had a turn for a bit of potery. Candy takes arter me that-a-way: huse ter make me tell her fairy stories when she was on'y a little kiddy not that 'igh [*indicating a stature of two feet or thereabouts*].

MORELL [*preoccupied*]. Ah, indeed. [*He blots the telegram, and goes out.*]

PROSERPINE. Used you to make the fairy stories up out of your own head?

[*Burgess, not deigning to reply, strikes an attitude of the haughtiest disdain on the hearth-rug.*]

PROSERPINE [*calmly*]. I should never have supposed you had it in you. By the way, I'd better warn you, since you've taken such a fancy to Mr. Marchbanks. He's mad.

BURGESS. Mad! Wot! 'Im too!!

PROSERPINE. Mad as a March hare. He did frighten me, I can tell you, just before you came in that time. Haven't you noticed the queer things he says?

BURGESS. So that's wot the poetic 'orrors means. Blame me if it didn't come into my head once or twyst that he must be off his chump! [*He crosses the room to the door, lifting up his voice as he goes.*] Well, this is a pretty sort of asylum for a man to be in, with no one but you to take care of him!

PROSERPINE [*as he passes her*]. Yes, what a dreadful thing it would be if anything happened to you!

BURGESS [*loftily*]. Don't you address no remarks to me. Tell your hemployer that I've gone into the garden for a smoke.

PROSERPINE [*mocking*]. Oh!

[*Before Burgess can retort, Morell comes back.*]

BURGESS [*sentimentally*]. Goin' for a turn in the garden to smoke, James.

MORELL [*brusquely*]. Oh, all right, all right. [*Burgess goes out pathetically in the character of the weary old man. Morell stands at the table, turning over his papers, and adding, across to Proserpine, half humorously, half absently*]

Well, Miss Prossy, why have you been calling my father-in-law names?

PROSERPINE [*blushing fiery red, and looking quickly up at him, half scared, half reproachful*]. I— [*She bursts into tears.*]

MORELL [*with tender gaiety, leaning across the table towards her, and consoling her*]. Oh, come, come, come! Never mind, Pross: he is a silly old fathead, isn't he?

[*With an explosive sob, she makes a dash at the door, and vanishes, banging it. Morell, shaking his head resignedly, sighs, and goes wearily to his chair, where he sits down and sets to work, looking old and careworn.*

[*Candida comes in. She has finished her household work and taken off the apron. She at once notices his dejected appearance, and posts herself quietly at the spare chair, looking down at him attentively; but she says nothing.*]

MORELL [*looking up, but with his pen raised ready to resume his work*]. Well? Where is Eugene?

CANDIDA. Washing his hands in the scullery—under the tap. He will make an excellent cook if he can only get over his dread of Maria.

MORELL [*shortly*]. Ha! No doubt. [*He begins writing again.*]

CANDIDA [*going nearer, and putting her hand down softly on his to stop him, as she says*]. Come here, dear. Let me look at you. [*He drops his pen and yields himself at her disposal. She makes him rise and brings him a little away from the table, looking at him critically all the time.*] Turn your face to the light. [*She places him facing the window.*] My boy is not looking well. Has he been overworking?

MORELL. Nothing more than usual.

CANDIDA. He looks very pale, and grey, and wrinkled, and old. [*His melancholy deepens; and she attacks it with wilful gaiety.*] Here [*pulling him towards the easy chair*] you've done enough writing for to-day. Leave Prossy to finish it and come and talk to me.

MORELL. But—

CANDIDA. Yes, I must be talked to sometimes. [*She makes him sit down, and seats herself on the carpet beside his knee.*] Now [*patting his hand*] you're beginning to look better already. Why don't you give up all this tiresome overworking—going out every night lecturing and talking? Of course what you say is all very true and very right; but it does no good: they don't mind what you say to them one little bit. Of course they agree with you; but what's the use of people agreeing with you if they go and do just the opposite of what you tell them the moment your back is turned? Look at our congregation at St. Dominic's! Why do they come to hear you talking about Christianity every Sunday? Why, just because they've been so full of business and money-making for six days that they want to forget all about it and have a rest on the seventh, so that they can go back fresh and make money harder than ever! You positively help them at it instead of hindering them.

MORELL [*with energetic seriousness*]. You know very well, Candida, that I often blow them up soundly for that. But if there is nothing in their church-going but rest and diversion, why don't they try something more amusing—more self-indulgent? There must be some good in the fact that they prefer St. Dominic's to worse places on Sundays.

CANDIDA. Oh, the worst places aren't open; and even if they were, they daren't be seen going to them. Besides, James, dear, you preach so splendidly that it's as good as a play for them. Why do you think the women are so enthusiastic?

MORELL [*shocked*]. Candida!

CANDIDA. Oh, *I* know. You silly boy: you think it's your Socialism and your religion; but if it was that, they'd do what you tell them instead of only coming to look at you. They all have Prossy's complaint.

MORELL. Prossy's complaint! What do you mean, Candida?

CANDIDA. Yes, Prossy, and all the other secretaries you ever had. Why does Prossy condescend to wash up the things, and to peel potatoes and abase herself in all manner of ways for six shillings a week less than she used to get in a city office? She's in love with you, James: that's the reason. They're all in love with you. And you are in love with preaching because you do it so beautifully. And you think it's all enthusiasm for the kingdom of Heaven on earth; and so do they. You dear silly!

MORELL. Candida: what dreadful, what soul-destroying cynicism! Are you jesting? Or—can it be?—are you jealous?

CANDIDA [*with curious thoughtfulness*]. Yes, I feel a little jealous sometimes.

MORELL [*incredulously*]. What! Of Prossy!

CANDIDA [*laughing*]. No, no, no, no. Not jealous of any-

body. Jealous for somebody else, who is not loved as he
ought to be.

MORELL. Me!

CANDIDA. You! Why, you're spoiled with love and worship: you get far more than is good for you. No: I mean
Eugene.

MORELL [startled]. Eugene!

CANDIDA. It seems unfair that all the love should go to
you, and none to him, although he needs it so much more
than you do. [A convulsive movement shakes him in spite
of himself.] What's the matter? Am I worrying you?

MORELL [hastily]. Not at all. [Looking at her with troubled intensity.] You know that I have perfect confidence in
you, Candida.

CANDIDA. You vain thing! Are you so sure of your irresistible attractions?

MORELL. Candida: you are shocking me. I never thought
of my attractions. I thought of your goodness—your purity.
That is what I confide in.

CANDIDA. What a nasty, uncomfortable thing to say to
me! Oh, you are a clergyman, James—a thorough clergyman.

MORELL [turning away from her, heart-stricken]. So Eugene says.

CANDIDA [with lively interest, leaning over to him with
her arms on his knee]. Eugene's always right. He's a wonderful boy: I have grown fonder and fonder of him all the time
I was away. Do you know, James, that though he has not
the least suspicion of it himself, he is ready to fall madly in
love with me?

MORELL [grimly]. Oh, he has no suspicion of it himself,
hasn't he?

CANDIDA. Not a bit. [She takes her arms from his knee,
and turns thoughtfully, sinking into a more restful attitude
with her hands in her lap.] Some day he will know—when he
is grown up and experienced, like you. And he will know
that I must have known. I wonder what he will think of me
then.

MORELL. No evil, Candida. I hope and trust, no evil.

CANDIDA [dubiously]. That will depend.

MORELL [bewildered]. Depend!

CANDIDA [looking at him]. Yes: it will depend on what
happens to him. [He looks vacantly at her.] Don't you see?
It will depend on how he comes to learn what love really is.

I mean on the sort of woman who will teach it to him.

MORELL [*quite at a loss*]. Yes. No. I don't know what you mean.

CANDIDA [*explaining*]. If he learns it from a good woman, then it will be all right: he will forgive me.

MORELL. Forgive!

CANDIDA. But suppose he learns it from a bad woman, as so many men do, especially poetic men, who imagine all women are angels! Suppose he only discovers the value of love when he has thrown it away and degraded himself in his ignorance. Will he forgive me then, do you think?

MORELL. Forgive you for what?

CANDIDA [*realizing how stupid he is, and a little disappointed, though quite tenderly so*]. Don't you understand? [*He shakes his head. She turns to him again, so as to explain with the fondest intimacy.*] I mean, will he forgive me for not teaching him myself? For abandoning him to the bad women for the sake of my goodness—my purity, as you call it? Ah, James, how little you understand me, to talk of your confidence in my goodness and purity! I would give them both to poor Eugene as willingly as I would give my shawl to a beggar dying of cold, if there were nothing else to restrain me. Put your trust in my love for you, James, for if that went, I should care very little for your sermons—mere phrases that you cheat yourself and others with every day. [*She is about to rise.*]

MORELL. His words!

CANDIDA [*checking herself quickly in the act of getting up, so that she is on her knees, but upright*]. Whose words?

MORELL. Eugene's.

CANDIDA [*delighted*]. He is always right. He understands you; he understands me; he understands Prossy; and you, James—you understand nothing. [*She laughs, and kisses him to console him. He recoils as if stung, and springs up.*]

MORELL. How can you bear to do that when—oh, Candida [*with anguish in his voice*], I had rather you had plunged a grappling iron into my heart than given me that kiss.

CANDIDA [*rising, alarmed*]. My dear: what's the matter?

MORELL [*frantically waving her off*]. Don't touch me.

CANDIDA [*amazed*]. James!

[*They are interrupted by the entrance of Marchbanks, with Burgess, who stops near the door, staring, whilst Eugene hurries forward between them.*]

MARCHBANKS. Is anything the matter?

MORELL [*deadly white, putting an iron constraint on himself*]. Nothing but this: that either you were right this morning, or Candida is mad.

BURGESS [*in loudest protest*]. Wot! Candy mad too! Oh, come, come, come! [*He crosses the room to the fireplace, protesting as he goes, and knocks the ashes out of his pipe on the bars. Morell sits down desperately, leaning forward to hide his face, and interlacing his fingers rigidly to keep them steady.*]

CANDIDA [*to Morell, relieved and laughing*]. Oh, you're only shocked! Is that all? How conventional all you unconventional people are!

BURGESS. Come: be'ave yourself, Candy. What'll Mr. Morchbanks think of you?

CANDIDA. This comes of James teaching me to think for myself, and never to hold back out of fear of what other people may think of me. It works beautifully as long as I think the same things as he does. But now, because I have just thought something different!—look at him—just look! [*She points to Morell, greatly amused. Eugene looks, and instantly presses his hand on his heart, as if some deadly pain had shot through it, and sits down on the sofa like a man witnessing a tragedy.*]

BURGESS [*on the hearth-rug*]. Well, James, you certainly ain't as himpressive lookin' as usu'l.

MORELL [*with a laugh which is half a sob*]. I suppose not. I beg all your pardons: I was not conscious of making a fuss. [*Pulling himself together.*] Well, well, well, well, well! [*He goes back to his place at the table, setting to work at his papers again with resolute cheerfulness.*]

CANDIDA [*going to the sofa and sitting beside Marchbanks, still in a bantering humor*]. Well, Eugene, why are you so sad? Did the onions make you cry?

[*Morell cannot prevent himself from watching them.*]

MARCHBANKS [*aside to her*]. It is your cruelty. I hate cruelty. It is a horrible thing to see one person make another suffer.

CANDIDA [*petting him ironically*]. Poor boy, have I been cruel? Did I make it slice nasty little red onions?

MARCHBANKS [*earnestly*]. Oh, stop, stop: I don't mean myself. You have made him suffer frightfully. I feel his pain in my own heart. I know that it is not your fault—it is something that must happen; but don't make light of it. I shudder when you torture him and laugh.

CANDIDA [*incredulously*]. *I* torture James! Nonsense, Eugene: how you exaggerate! Silly! [*She looks round at Morell, who hastily resumes his writing. She goes to him and stands behind his chair, bending over him.*] Don't work any more, dear. Come and talk to us.

MORELL [*affectionately but bitterly*]. Ah no: I can't talk. I can only preach.

CANDIDA [*caressing him*]. Well, come and preach.

BURGESS [*strongly remonstrating*]. Aw, no, Candy. 'Ang it all!

[*Lexy Mill comes in, looking anxious and important.*]

LEXY [*hastening to shake hands with Candida*]. How do you do, Mrs. Morell? So glad to see you back again.

CANDIDA. Thank you, Lexy. You know Eugene, don't you?

LEXY. Oh, yes. How do you do, Marchbanks?

MARCHBANKS. Quite well, thanks.

LEXY [*to Morell*]. I've just come from the Guild of St. Matthew. They are in the greatest consternation about your telegram. There's nothing wrong, is there?

CANDIDA. What did you telegraph about, James?

LEXY [*to Candida*]. He was to have spoken for them tonight. They've taken the large hall in Mare Street and spent a lot of money on posters. Morell's telegram was to say he couldn't come. It came on them like a thunderbolt.

CANDIDA [*surprised, and beginning to suspect something wrong*]. Given up an engagement to speak!

BURGESS. First time in his life, I'll bet. Ain't it, Candy?

LEXY [*to Morell*]. They decided to send an urgent telegram to you asking whether you could not change your mind. Have you received it?

MORELL [*with restrained impatience*]. Yes, yes: I got it.

LEXY. It was reply paid.

MORELL. Yes, I know. I answered it. I can't go.

CANDIDA. But why, James?

MORELL [*almost fiercely*]. Because I don't choose. These people forget that I am a man: they think I am a talking machine to be turned on for their pleasure every evening of my life. May I not have o n e night at home, with my wife, and my friends?

[*They are all amazed at this outburst, except Eugene. His expression remains unchanged.*]

CANDIDA. Oh, James, you know you'll have an attack of bad conscience to-morrow; and *I* shall have to suffer for that.

LEXY [*intimidated, but urgent*]. I know, of course, that they make the most unreasonable demands on you. But they have been telegraphing all over the place for another speaker: and they can get nobody but the President of the Agnostic League.

MORELL [*promptly*]. Well, an excellent man. What better do they want?

LEXY. But he always insists so powerfully on the divorce of Socialism from Christianity. He will undo all the good we have been doing. Of course you know best; but— [*He hesitates.*]

CANDIDA [*coaxingly*]. Oh, do go, James. We'll all go.

BURGESS [*grumbling*]. Look 'ere, Candy! I say! Let's stay at home by the fire, comfortable. He won't need to be more'n a couple-o'-hour away.

CANDIDA. You'll be just as comfortable at the meeting. We'll all sit on the platform and be great people.

EUGENE [*terrified*]. Oh, please don't let us go on the platform. No—everyone will stare at us—I couldn't. I'll sit at the back of the room.

CANDIDA. Don't be afraid. They'll be too busy looking at James to notice you.

MORELL [*turning his head and looking meaningly at her over his shoulder*]. Prossy's complaint, Candida! Eh?

CANDIDA [*gaily*]. Yes.

BURGESS [*mystified*]. Prossy's complaint. Wot are you talking about, James?

MORELL [*not heeding him, rises; goes to the door; and holds it open, shouting in a commanding voice*]. Miss Garnett.

PROSERPINE [*in the distance*]. Yes, Mr. Morell. Coming.

[*They all wait, except Burgess, who goes stealthily to Lexy and draws him aside.*]

BURGESS. Listen here, Mr. Mill. Wot's Prossy's complaint? Wot's wrong with 'er?

LEXY [*confidentially*]. Well, I don't exactly know; but she spoke very strangely to me this morning. I'm afraid she's a little out of her mind sometimes.

BURGESS [*overwhelmed*]. Why, it must be catchin'! Four in the same 'ouse! [*He goes back to the hearth, quite lost before the instability of the human intellect in a clergyman's house.*]

PROSERPINE [*appearing on the threshold*]. What is it, Mr. Morell?

MORELL. Telegraph to the Guild of St. Matthew that I am coming.

PROSERPINE [*surprised*]. Don't they expect you?

MORELL [*peremptorily*]. Do as I tell you.

[*Proserpine, frightened, sits down at her typewriter, and obeys. Morell goes across to Burgess, Candida watching his movements all the time with growing wonder and misgiving.*]

MORELL. Burgess: you don't want to come?

BURGESS [*in deprecation*]. Oh, don't put it like that, James. It's only that it ain't Sunday, you know.

MORELL. I'm sorry. I thought you might like to be introduced to the chairman. He's on the Works Committee of the County Council and has some influence in the matter of contracts. [*Burgess wakes up at once. Morell, expecting as much, waits a moment, and says*] Will you come?

BURGESS [*with enthusiasm*]. Course I'll come, James. Ain' it always a pleasure to 'ear you.

MORELL [*turning from him*]. I shall want you to take some notes at the meeting, Miss Garnett, if you have no other engagement. [*She nods, afraid to speak.*] You are coming, Lexy, I suppose.

LEXY. Certainly.

CANDIDA. We are all coming, James.

MORELL. No: you are not coming; and Eugene is not coming. You will stay here and entertain him—to celebrate your return home. [*Eugene rises, breathless.*]

CANDIDA. But James—

MORELL [*authoritatively*]. I insist. You do not want to come; and he does not want to come. [*Candida is about to protest.*] Oh, don't concern yourselves: I shall have plenty of people without you: your chairs will be wanted by unconverted people who have never heard me before.

CANDIDA [*troubled*]. Eugene: wouldn't you like to come?

MORELL. I should be afraid to let myself go before Eugene: he is so critical of sermons. [*Looking at him.*] He knows I am afraid of him: he told me as much this morning. Well, I shall shew him how much afraid I am by leaving him here in your custody, Candida.

MARCHBANKS [*to himself, with vivid feeling*]. That's brave. That's beautiful. [*He sits down again listening with parted lips.*]

CANDIDA [*with anxious misgiving*]. But—but— Is anything the matter, James? [*Greatly troubled.*] I can't understand—

MORELL. Ah, I thought it was *I* who couldn't understand, dear. [*He takes her tenderly in his arms and kisses her on the forehead; then looks round quietly at Marchbanks.*]

ACT THREE

Late in the evening. Past ten. The curtains are drawn, and the lamps lighted. The typewriter is in its case; the large table has been cleared and tidied; everything indicates that the day's work is done.

Candida and Marchbanks are seated at the fire. The reading lamp is on the mantelshelf above Marchbanks, who is sitting on the small chair reading aloud from a manuscript. A little pile of manuscripts and a couple of volumes of poetry are on the carpet beside him. Candida is in the easy chair with the poker, a light brass one, upright in her hand. She is leaning back and looking at the point of it curiously, with her feet stretched towards the blaze and her heels resting on the fender, profoundly unconscious of her appearance and surroundings.

MARCHBANKS [*breaking off in his recitation*]. Every poet that ever lived has put that thought into a sonnet. He must: he can't help it. [*He looks to her for assent, and notices her absorption in the poker.*] Haven't you been listening? [*No response.*] Mrs. Morell!

CANDIDA [*starting*]. Eh?

MARCHBANKS. Haven't you been listening?

CANDIDA [*with a guilty excess of politeness*]. Oh, yes. It's very nice. Go on, Eugene. I'm longing to hear what happens to the angel.

MARCHBANKS [*crushed—the manuscript dropping from his hand to the floor*]. I beg your pardon for boring you.

CANDIDA. But you are not boring me, I assure you. Please go on. Do, Eugene.

MARCHBANKS. I finished the poem about the angel quarter of an hour ago. I've read you several things since.

CANDIDA [*remorsefully*]. I'm so sorry, Eugene. I think the poker must have fascinated me. [*She puts it down.*]

MARCHBANKS. It made me horribly uneasy.

CANDIDA. Why didn't you tell me? I'd have put it down at once.

MARCHBANKS. I was afraid of making you uneasy, too. It looked as if it were a weapon. If I were a hero of old, I should have laid my drawn sword between us. If Morell had come in he would have thought you had taken up the poker because there was no sword between us.

CANDIDA [*wondering*]. What? [*With a puzzled glance at him.*] I can't quite follow that. Those sonnets of yours have perfectly addled me. Why should there be a sword between us?

MARCHBANKS [*evasively*]. Oh, never mind. [*He stoops to pick up the manuscript.*]

CANDIDA. Put that down again, Eugene. There are limits to my appetite for poetry—even your poetry. You've been reading to me for more than two hours—ever since James went out. I want to talk.

MARCHBANKS [*rising, scared*]. No: I mustn't talk. [*He looks round him in his lost way, and adds, suddenly*] I think I'll go out and take a walk in the park. [*Making for the door.*]

CANDIDA. Nonsense: it's shut long ago. Come and sit down on the hearth-rug, and talk moonshine as you usually do. I want to be amused. Don't you want to?

MARCHBANKS [*in half terror, half rapture*]. Yes.

CANDIDA. Then come along. [*She moves her chair back a little to make room. He hesitates; then timidly stretches himself on the hearth-rug, face upwards, and throws back his head across her knees, looking up at her.*]

MARCHBANKS. Oh, I've been so miserable all the evening, because I was doing right. Now I'm doing wrong; and I'm happy.

CANDIDA [*tenderly amused at him*]. Yes: I'm sure you feel a great grown up wicked deceiver—quite proud of yourself, aren't you?

MARCHBANKS [*raising his head quickly and turning a little to look round at her*]. Take care. I'm ever so much older than you, if you only knew. [*He turns quite over on his knees, with his hands clasped and his arms on her lap, and speaks with growing impulse, his blood beginning to stir.*] May I say some wicked things to you?

CANDIDA [*without the least fear or coldness, quite nobly, and with perfect respect for his passion, but with a touch of her wise-hearted maternal humor*]. No. But you may say anything you really and truly feel. Anything at all, no matter what it is. I am not afraid, so long as it is your real self that speaks, and not a mere attitude—a gallant attitude, or a wicked attitude, or even a poetic attitude. I put you on your honor and truth. Now say whatever you want to.

MARCHBANKS [*the eager expression vanishing utterly from his lips and nostrils as his eyes light up with pathetic spirituality*]. Oh, now I can't say anything: all the words I know belong to some attitude or other—all except one.

CANDIDA. What one is that?

MARCHBANKS [*softly, losing himself in the music of the name*]. Candida, Candida, Candida, Candida, Candida. I must say that now, because you have put me on my honor and truth; and I never think or feel Mrs. Morell: it is always Candida.

CANDIDA. Of course. And what have you to say to Candida?

MARCHBANKS. Nothing, but to repeat your name a thousand times. Don't you feel that every time is a prayer to you?

CANDIDA. Doesn't it make you happy to be able to pray?

MARCHBANKS. Yes, very happy.

CANDIDA. Well, that happiness is the answer to your prayer. Do you want anything more?

MARCHBANKS [*in beatitude*]. No: I have come into heaven, where want is unknown.

[*Morell comes in. He halts on the threshold, and takes in the scene at a glance.*]

MORELL [*grave and self-contained*]. I hope I don't disturb you.

[*Candida starts up violently, but without the smallest embarrassment, laughing at herself. Eugene, still kneeling, saves himself from falling by putting his hands on the seat of the chair, and remains there, staring open mouthed at Morell.*]

CANDIDA [*as she rises*]. Oh, James, how you startled me! I was so taken up with Eugene that I didn't hear your latchkey. How did the meeting go off? Did you speak well?

MORELL. I have never spoken better in my life.

CANDIDA. That was first rate! How much was the collection?

MORELL. I forgot to ask.

CANDIDA [*to Eugene*]. He must have spoken splendidly, or he would never have forgotten that. [*To Morell.*] Where are all the others?

MORELL. They left long before I could get away: I thought I should never escape. I believe they are having supper somewhere.

CANDIDA [*in her domestic business tone*]. Oh; in that case, Maria may go to bed. I'll tell her. [*She goes out to the kitchen.*]

MORELL [*looking sternly down at Marchbanks*]. Well?

MARCHBANKS [*squatting cross-legged on the hearth-rug, and actually at ease with Morell—even impishly humorous*]. Well?

MORELL. Have you anything to tell me?

MARCHBANKS. Only that I have been making a fool of myself here in private whilst you have been making a fool of yourself in public.

MORELL. Hardly in the same way, I think.

MARCHBANKS [*scrambling up—eagerly*]. The very, very, very same way. I have been playing the good man just like you. When you began your heroics about leaving me here with Candida—

MORELL [*involuntarily*]. Candida?

MARCHBANKS. Oh, yes: I've got that far. Heroics are infectious: I caught the disease from you. I swore not to say a word in your absence that I would not have said a month ago in your presence.

MORELL. Did you keep your oath?

MARCHBANKS [*suddenly perching himself grotesquely on the easy chair*]. I was ass enough to keep it until about ten minutes ago. Up to that moment I went on desperately reading to her—reading my own poems—anybody's poems—to stave off a conversation. I was standing outside the gate of Heaven, and refusing to go in. Oh, you can't think how heroic it was, and how uncomfortable! Then—

MORELL [*steadily controlling his suspense*]. Then?

MARCHBANKS [*prosaically slipping down into a quite ordinary attitude in the chair*]. Then she couldn't bear being read to any longer.

MORELL. And you approached the gate of Heaven at last?

MARCHBANKS. Yes.

MORELL. Well? [*Fiercely.*] Speak, man: have you no feeling for me?

MARCHBANKS [*softly and musically*]. Then she became an angel; and there was a flaming sword that turned every way, so that I couldn't go in; for I saw that that gate was really the gate of Hell.

MORELL [*triumphantly*]. She repulsed you!

MARCHBANKS [*rising in wild scorn*]. No, you fool: if she had done that I should never have seen that I was in Heaven already. Repulsed me! You think that would have saved me —virtuous indignation! Oh, you are not worthy to live in the same world with her. [*He turns away contemptuously to the other side of the room.*]

MORELL [*who has watched him quietly without changing his place*]. Do you think you make yourself more worthy by reviling me, Eugene?

MARCHBANKS. Here endeth the thousand and first lesson. Morell: I don't think much of your preaching after all: I believe I could do it better myself. The man I want to meet is the man that Candida married.

MORELL. The man that—? Do you mean me?

MARCHBANKS. I don't mean the Reverend James Mavor Morell, moralist and windbag. I mean the real man that the Reverend James must have hidden somewhere inside his black coat—the man that Candida loved. You can't make a woman like Candida love you by merely buttoning your collar at the back instead of in front.

MORELL [*boldly and steadily*]. When Candida promised to marry me, I was the same moralist and windbag that you now see. I wore my black coat; and my collar was buttoned behind instead of in front. Do you think she would have loved me any the better for being insincere in my profession?

MARCHBANKS [*on the sofa hugging his ankles*]. Oh, she forgave you, just as she forgives me for being a coward, and a weakling, and what you call a snivelling little whelp and all the rest of it. [*Dreamily.*] A woman like that has divine insight: she loves our souls, and not our follies and vanities and illusions, or our collars and coats, or any other of the rags and tatters we are rolled up in. [*He reflects on this for an instant; then turns intently to question Morell.*] What I want to know is how you got past the flaming sword that stopped me.

MORELL [*meaningly*]. Perhaps because I was not interrupted at the end of ten minutes.

MARCHBANKS [*taken aback*]. What!

MORELL. Man can climb to the highest summits; but he cannot dwell there long.

MARCHBANKS. It's false: there can he dwell for ever and

there only. It's in the other moments that he can find no rest, no sense of the silent glory of life. Where would you have me spend my moments, if not on the summits?

MORELL. In the scullery, slicing onions and filling lamps.

MARCHBANKS. Or in the pulpit, scrubbing cheap earthenware souls?

MORELL. Yes, that, too. It was there that I earned my golden moment, and the right, in that moment, to ask her to love me. *I* did not take the moment on credit; nor did I use it to steal another man's happiness.

MARCHBANKS [*rather disgustedly, trotting back towards the fireplace*]. I have no doubt you conducted the transaction as honestly as if you were buying a pound of cheese. [*He stops on the brink of the hearth-rug and adds, thoughtfully, to himself, with his back turned to Morell*] I could only go to her as a beggar.

MORELL [*starting*]. A beggar dying of cold—asking for her shawl?

MARCHBANKS [*turning, surprised*]. Thank you for touching up my poetry. Yes, if you like, a beggar dying of cold asking for her shawl.

MORELL [*excitedly*]. And she refused. Shall I tell you why she refused? I can tell you, on her own authority. It was because of—

MARCHBANKS. She didn't refuse.

MORELL. No!

MARCHBANKS. She offered me all I chose to ask for, her shawl, her wings, the wreath of stars on her head, the lilies in her hand, the crescent moon beneath her feet—

MORELL [*seizing him*]. Out with the truth, man; my wife is my wife: I want no more of your poetic fripperies. I know well that if I have lost her love and you have gained it, no law will bind her.

MARCHBANKS [*quaintly, without fear or resistance*]. Catch me by the shirt collar, Morell: she will arrange it for me afterwards as she did this morning. [*With quiet rapture.*] I shall feel her hands touch me.

MORELL. You young imp, do you know how dangerous it is to say that to me? Or [*with a sudden misgiving*] has something made you brave?

MARCHBANKS. I'm not afraid now. I disliked you before: that was why I shrank from your touch. But I saw to-day—when she tortured you—that you love her. Since then I have been your friend: you may strangle me if you like.

MORELL [*releasing him*]. Eugene: if that is not a heartless lie—if you have a spark of human feeling left in you—will you tell me what has happened during my absence?

MARCHBANKS. What happened! Why, the flaming sword—[*Morell stamps with impatience.*] Well, in plain prose, I loved her so exquisitely that I wanted nothing more than the happiness of being in such love. And before I had time to come down from the highest summits, you came in.

MORELL [*suffering deeply*]. So it is still unsettled—still the misery of doubt.

MARCHBANKS. Misery! I am the happiest of men. I desire nothing now but her happiness. [*With dreamy enthusiasm.*] Oh, Morell, let us both give her up. Why should she have to choose between a wretched little nervous disease like me, and a pig-headed parson like you? Let us go on a pilgrimage, you to the east and I to the west, in search of a worthy lover for her—some beautiful archangel with purple wings—

MORELL. Some fiddlestick. Oh, if she is mad enough to leave me for you, who will protect her? Who will help her? who will work for her? who will be a father to her children? [*He sits down distractedly on the sofa, with his elbows on his knees and his head propped on his clenched fists.*]

MARCHBANKS [*snapping his fingers wildly*]. She does not ask those silly questions. It is she who wants somebody to protect, to help, to work for—somebody to give her children to protect, to help and to work for. Some grown up man who has become as a little child again. Oh, you fool, you fool, you triple fool! I am the man, Morell: I am the man. [*He dances about excitedly, crying*] You don't understand what a woman is. Send for her, Morell: send for her and let her choose between— [*The door opens and Candida enters. He stops as if petrified.*]

CANDIDA [*amazed, on the threshold*]. What on earth are you at, Eugene?

MARCHBANKS [*oddly*]. James and I are having a preaching match; and he is getting the worst of it. [*Candida looks quickly round at Morell. Seeing that he is distressed, she hurries down to him, greatly vexed, speaking with vigorous reproach to Marchbanks.*]

CANDIDA. You have been annoying him. Now I won't have it, Eugene: do you hear? [*Putting her hand on Morell's shoulder and quite forgetting her wifely tact in her annoyance.*] My boy shall not be worried: I will protect him.

MORELL [*rising proudly*]. Protect!

CANDIDA [*not heeding him—to Eugene*]. What have you been saying?

MARCHBANKS [*appalled*]. Nothing—I—

CANDIDA. Eugene! Nothing?

MARCHBANKS [*piteously*]. I mean—I—I'm very sorry. I won't do it again: indeed I won't. I'll let him alone.

MORELL [*indignantly, with an aggressive movement towards Eugene*]. Let me alone! You young—

CANDIDA [*stopping him*]. Sh—no, let me deal with him, James.

MARCHBANKS. Oh, you're not angry with me, are you?

CANDIDA [*severely*]. Yes, I am—very angry. I have a great mind to pack you out of the house.

MORELL [*taken aback by Candida's vigor, and by no means relishing the sense of being rescued by her from another man*]. Gently, Candida, gently. I am able to take care of myself.

CANDIDA [*petting him*]. Yes, dear: of course you are. But you mustn't be annoyed and made miserable.

MARCHBANKS [*almost in tears, turning to the door*]. I'll go.

CANDIDA. Oh, you needn't go: I can't turn you out at this time of night. [*Vehemently.*] Shame on you! For shame!

MARCHBANKS [*desperately*]. But what have I done?

CANDIDA. I know what you have done—as well as if I had been here all the time. Oh, it was unworthy! You are like a child: you cannot hold your tongue.

MARCHBANKS. I would die ten times over sooner than give you a moment's pain.

CANDIDA [*with infinite contempt for this puerility*]. Much good your dying would do me!

MORELL. Candida, my dear: this altercation is hardly quite seemly. It is a matter between two men; and I am the right person to settle it.

CANDIDA. Two men! Do you call that a man? [*To Eugene.*] You bad boy!

MARCHBANKS [*gathering a whimsically affectionate courage from the scolding*]. If I am to be scolded like this, I must make a boy's excuse. He began it. And he's bigger than I am.

CANDIDA [*losing confidence a little as her concern for Morell's dignity takes the alarm*]. That can't be true. [*To Morell.*] You didn't begin it, James, did you?

MORELL [*contemptuously*]. No.

MARCHBANKS [*indignant*]. Oh!

MORELL [*to Eugene*]. You began it—this morning. [*Candida, instantly connecting this with his mysterious allusion in the afternoon to something told him by Eugene in the morning, looks quickly at him, wrestling with the enigma. Morell proceeds with the emphasis of offended superiority.*] But your other point is true. I am certainly the bigger of the two, and, I hope, the stronger, Candida. So you had better leave the matter in my hands.

CANDIDA [*again soothing him*]. Yes, dear; but— [*Troubled.*] I don't understand about this morning.

MORELL [*gently snubbing her*]. You need not understand, my dear.

CANDIDA. But, James, I— [*The street bell rings.*] Oh, bother! Here they all come. [*She goes out to let them in.*]

MARCHBANKS [*running to Morell*]. Oh, Morell, isn't it dreadful? She's angry with us: she hates me. What shall I do?

MORELL [*with quaint desperation, clutching himself by the hair*]. Eugene: my head is spinning round. I shall begin to laugh presently. [*He walks up and down the middle of the room.*]

MARCHBANKS [*following him anxiously*]. No, no: she'll think I've thrown you into hysterics. Don't laugh.

[*Boisterous voices and laughter are heard approaching. Lexy Mill, his eyes sparkling, and his bearing denoting unwonted elevation of spirit, enters with Burgess, who is greasy and self-complacent, but has all his wits about him. Miss Garnett, with her smartest hat and jacket on, follows them; but though her eyes are brighter than before, she is evidently a prey to misgiving. She places herself with her back to her typewriting table, with one hand on it to rest herself, passes the other across her forehead as if she were a little tired and giddy. Marchbanks relapses into shyness and edges away into the corner near the window, where Morell's books are.*]

MILL [*exhilaratedly*]. Morell: I must congratulate you. [*Grasping his hand.*] What a noble, splendid, inspired address you gave us! You surpassed yourself.

BURGESS. So you did, James. It fair kep' me awake to the last word. Didn't it, Miss Gornett?

PROSERPINE [*worriedly*]. Oh, I wasn't minding you: I was trying to make notes. [*She takes out her note-book, and looks at her stenography, which nearly makes her cry.*]

MORELL. Did I go too fast, Pross?

PROSERPINE. Much too fast. You know I can't do more than a hundred words a minute. [*She relieves her feelings by throwing her note-book angrily beside her machine, ready for use next morning.*]

MORELL [*soothingly*]. Oh, well, well, never mind, never mind, never mind. Have you all had supper?

LEXY. Mr. Burgess has been kind enough to give us a really splendid supper at the Belgrave.

BURGESS [*with effusive magnanimity*]. Don't mention it, Mr. Mill. [*Modestly.*] You're 'arty welcome to my little treat.

PROSERPINE. We had champagne! I never tasted it before. I feel quite giddy.

MORELL [*surprised*]. A champagne supper! That was very handsome. Was it my eloquence that produced all this extravagance?

MILL [*rhetorically*]. Your eloquence, and Mr. Burgess's goodness of heart. [*With a fresh burst of exhilaration.*] And what a very fine fellow the chairman is, Morell! He came to supper with us.

MORELL [*with long drawn significance, looking at Burgess*]. O-o-o-h, the chairman. Now I understand.

[*Burgess, covering a lively satisfaction in his diplomatic cunning with a deprecatory cough, retires to the hearth. Lexy folds his arms and leans against the cellaret in a high-spirited attitude. Candida comes in with glasses, lemons, and a jug of hot water on a tray.*]

CANDIDA. Who will have some lemonade? You know our rules: total abstinence. [*She puts the tray on the table, and takes up the lemon squeezers, looking enquiringly round at them.*]

MORELL. No use, dear. They've all had champagne. Pross has broken her pledge.

CANDIDA [*to Proserpine*]. You don't mean to say you've been drinking champagne!

PROSERPINE [*stubbornly*]. Yes, I do. I'm only a beer teetotaller, not a champagne teetotaller. I don't like beer. Are there any letters for me to answer, Mr. Morell?

MORELL. No more to-night.

PROSERPINE. Very well. Good-night, everybody.

LEXY [*gallantly*]. Had I not better see you home, Miss Garnett?

PROSERPINE. No, thank you. I shan't trust myself with

anybody to-night. I wish I hadn't taken any of that stuff.
[*She walks straight out.*]

BURGESS [*indignantly*]. Stuff, indeed! That gurl dunno
wot champagne is! Pommery and Greeno at twelve and six
a bottle. She took two glasses a'most straight hoff.

MORELL [*a little anxious about her*]. Go and look after
her, Lexy.

LEXY [*alarmed*]. But if she should really be— Suppose
she began to sing in the street, or anything of that sort.

MORELL. Just so: she may. That's why you'd better see
her safely home.

CANDIDA. Do, Lexy: there's a good fellow. [*She shakes
his hand and pushes him gently to the door.*]

LEXY. It's evidently my duty to go. I hope it may not
be necessary. Good-night, Mrs. Morell. [*To the rest.*] Good-
night. [*He goes. Candida shuts the door.*]

BURGESS. He was gushin' with hextra piety hisself arter
two sips. People can't drink like they huster. [*Dismissing
the subject and bustling away from the hearth.*] Well, James:
it's time to lock up. Mr. Morchbanks: shall I 'ave the pleasure of your company for a bit of the way home?

MARCHBANKS [*affrightedly*]. Yes: I'd better go. [*He
hurries across to the door; but Candida places herself before
it, barring his way.*]

CANDIDA [*with quiet authority*]. You sit down. You're
not going yet.

MARCHBANKS [*quailing*]. No: I—I didn't mean to. [*He
comes back into the room and sits down abjectly on the sofa.*]

CANDIDA. Mr. Marchbanks will stay the night with us,
papa.

BURGESS. Oh, well, I'll say good-night. So long, James.
[*He shakes hands with Morell and goes on to Eugene.*] Make
'em give you a night light by your bed, Mr. Morchbanks:
it'll comfort you if you wake up in the night with a touch of
that complaint of yores. Good-night.

MARCHBANKS. Thank you: I will. Good-night, Mr. Burgess. [*They shake hands and Burgess goes to the door.*]

CANDIDA [*intercepting Morell, who is following Burgess*].
Stay here, dear: I'll put on papa's coat for him. [*She goes out
with Burgess.*]

MARCHBANKS. Morell: there's going to be a terrible
scene. Aren't you afraid?

MORELL. Not in the least.

MARCHBANKS. I never envied you your courage before. [*He rises timidly and puts his hand appealingly on Morell's forearm.*] Stand by me, won't you?

MORELL [*casting him off gently, but resolutely*]. Each for himself, Eugene. She must choose between us now. [*He goes to the other side of the room as Candida returns. Eugene sits down again on the sofa like a guilty schoolboy on his best behaviour.*]

CANDIDA [*between them, addressing Eugene*]. Are you sorry?

MARCHBANKS [*earnestly*]. Yes, heartbroken.

CANDIDA. Well, then, you are forgiven. Now go off to bed like a good little boy: I want to talk to James about you.

MARCHBANKS [*rising in great consternation*]. Oh, I can't do that, Morell. I must be here. I'll not go away. Tell her.

CANDIDA [*with quick suspicion*]. Tell me what? [*His eyes avoid hers furtively. She turns and mutely transfers the question to Morell.*]

MORELL [*bracing himself for the catastrophe*]. I have nothing to tell her, except [*here his voice deepens to a measured and mournful tenderness*] that she is my greatest treasure on earth—if she is really mine.

CANDIDA [*coldly, offended by his yielding to his orator's instinct and treating her as if she were the audience at the Guild of St. Matthew*]. I am sure Eugene can say no less, if that is all.

MARCHBANKS [*discouraged*]. Morell: she's laughing at us.

MORELL [*with a quick touch of temper*]. There is nothing to laugh at. Are you laughing at us, Candida?

CANDIDA [*with quiet anger*]. Eugene is very quick-witted, James. I hope I am going to laugh; but I am not sure that I am not going to be very angry. [*She goes to the fireplace, and stands there leaning with her arm on the mantelpiece, and her foot on the fender, whilst Eugene steals to Morell and plucks him by the sleeve.*]

MARCHBANKS [*whispering*]. Stop, Morell. Don't let us say anything.

MORELL [*pushing Eugene away without deigning to look at him*]. I hope you don't mean that as a threat, Candida.

CANDIDA [*with emphatic warning*]. Take care, James. Eugene: I asked you to go. Are you going?

MORELL [*putting his foot down*]. He shall not go. I wish him to remain.

MARCHBANKS. I'll go. I'll do whatever you want. [*He turns to the door.*]

CANDIDA. Stop! [*He obeys.*] Didn't you hear James say he wished you to stay? James is master here. Don't you know that?

MARCHBANKS [*flushing with a young poet's rage against tyranny*]. By what right is he master?

CANDIDA [*quietly*]. Tell him, James.

MORELL [*taken aback*]. My dear: I don't know of any right that makes me master. I assert no such right.

CANDIDA [*with infinite reproach*]. You don't know! Oh, James, James! [*To Eugene, musingly.*] I wonder do you understand, Eugene! No: you're too young. Well, I give you leave to stay—to stay and learn. [*She comes away from the hearth and places herself between them.*] Now, James: what's the matter? Come: tell me.

MARCHBANKS [*whispering tremulously across to him*]. Don't.

CANDIDA. Come. Out with it!

MORELL [*slowly*]. I meant to prepare your mind carefully, Candida, so as to prevent misunderstanding.

CANDIDA. Yes, dear: I am sure you did. But never mind: I shan't misunderstand.

MORELL. Well—er— [*He hesitates, unable to find the long explanation which he supposed to be available.*]

CANDIDA. Well?

MORELL [*baldly*]. Eugene declares that you are in love with him.

MARCHBANKS [*frantically*]. No, no, no, no, never. I did not, Mrs. Morell: it's not true. I said I loved you, and that he didn't. I said that I understood you, and that he couldn't. And it was not after what passed there before the fire that I spoke: it was not, on my word. It was this morning.

CANDIDA [*enlightened*]. This morning!

MARCHBANKS. Yes. [*He looks at her, pleading for credence, and then adds, simply*] That was what was the matter with my collar.

CANDIDA [*after a pause; for she does not take in his meaning at once*]. His collar! [*She turns to Morell, shocked.*] Oh, James: did you—[*she stops*]?

MORELL [*ashamed*]. You know, Candida, that I have a temper to struggle with. And he said [*shuddering*] that you despised me in your heart.

CANDIDA [*turning quickly on Eugene*]. Did you say that?

MARCHBANKS [*terrified*]. No!

CANDIDA [*severely*]. Then James has just told me a falsehood. Is that what you mean?

MARCHBANKS. No, no: I—I—[*blurting out the explanation desperately*]—it was David's wife. And it wasn't at home: it was when she saw him dancing before all the people.

MORELL [*taking the cue with a debater's adroitness*]. Dancing before all the people, Candida; and thinking he was moving their hearts by his mission when they were only suffering from—Prossy's complaint. [*She is about to protest: he raises his hand to silence her, exclaiming*] Don't try to look indignant, Candida—

CANDIDA [*interjecting*]. Try!

MORELL [*continuing*]. Eugene was right. As you told me a few hours after, he is always right. He said nothing that you did not say far better yourself. He is the poet, who sees everything; and I am the poor parson, who understands nothing.

CANDIDA [*remorsefully*]. Do you mind what is said by a foolish boy, because I said something like it again in jest?

MORELL. That foolish boy can speak with the inspiration of a child and the cunning of a serpent. He has claimed that you belong to him and not to me; and, rightly or wrongly, I have come to fear that it may be true. I will not go about tortured with doubts and suspicions. I will not live with you and keep a secret from you. I will not suffer the intolerable degradation of jealousy. We have agreed—he and I—that you shall choose between us now. I await your decision.

CANDIDA [*slowly recoiling a step, her heart hardened by his rhetoric in spite of the sincere feeling behind it*]. Oh! I am to choose, am I? I suppose it is quite settled that I must belong to one or the other.

MORELL [*firmly*]. Quite. You must choose definitely.

MARCHBANKS [*anxiously*]. Morell: you don't understand. She means that she belongs to herself.

CANDIDA [*turning on him*]. I mean that and a good deal more, Master Eugene, as you will both find out presently. And pray, my lords and masters, what have you to offer for my choice? I am up for auction, it seems. What do you bid, James?

MORELL [*reproachfully*]. Cand— [*He breaks down: his*

*eyes and throat fill with tears: the orator becomes the
wounded animal.*] I can't speak—

CANDIDA [*impulsively going to him*]. Ah, dearest—

MARCHBANKS [*in wild alarm*]. Stop: it's not fair. You
mustn't show her that you suffer, Morell. I am on the rack,
too; but I am not crying.

MORELL [*rallying all his forces*]. Yes: you are right. It
is not for pity that I am bidding. [*He disengages himself from
Candida.*]

CANDIDA [*retreating, chilled*]. I beg your pardon, James;
I did not mean to touch you. I am waiting to hear your bid.

MORELL [*with proud humility*]. I have nothing to offer
you but my strength for your defence, my honesty of purpose for your surety, my ability and industry for your livelihood, and my authority and position for your dignity. That
is all it becomes a man to offer to a woman.

CANDIDA [*quite quietly*]. And you, Eugene? What do you
offer?

MARCHBANKS. My weakness! my desolation! my heart's
need!

CANDIDA [*impressed*]. That's a good bid, Eugene. Now I
know how to make my choice.

[*She pauses and looks curiously from one to the other, as
if weighing them. Morell, whose lofty confidence has changed
into heartbreaking dread at Eugene's bid, loses all power of
concealing his anxiety. Eugene, strung to the highest tension,
does not move a muscle.*]

MORELL [*in a suffocated voice—the appeal bursting from
the depths of his anguish*]. Candida!

MARCHBANKS [*aside, in a flash of contempt*]. Coward!

CANDIDA [*significantly*]. I give myself to the weaker of the
two.

[*Eugene divines her meaning at once: his face whitens like
steel in a furnace that cannot melt it.*]

MORELL [*bowing his head with the calm of collapse*]. I
accept your sentence, Candida.

CANDIDA. Do you understand, Eugene?

MARCHBANKS. Oh, I feel I'm lost. He cannot bear the
burden.

MORELL [*incredulously, raising his head with prosaic ab-
ruptness*]. Do you mean me, Candida?

CANDIDA [*smiling a little*]. Let us sit and talk comfortably over it like three friends. [*To Morell.*] Sit down, dear.

[*Morell takes the chair from the fireside—the children's chair.*] Bring me that chair, Eugene. [*She indicates the easy chair. He fetches it silently, even with something like cold strength, and places it next Morell, a little behind him. She sits down. He goes to the sofa and sits there, still silent and in-scrutable. When they are all settled she begins, throwing a spell of quietness on them by her calm, sane, tender tone.*] You remember what you told me about yourself, Eugene: how nobody has cared for you since your old nurse died: how those clever, fashionable sisters and successful brothers of yours were your mother's and father's pets: how miserable you were at Eton: how your father is trying to starve you into returning to Oxford: how you have had to live without comfort or welcome or refuge, always lonely, and nearly always disliked and misunderstood, poor boy!

MARCHBANKS [*faithful to the nobility of his lot*]. I had my books. I had Nature. And at last I met you.

CANDIDA. Never mind that just at present. Now I want you to look at this other boy here—my boy—spoiled from his cradle. We go once a fortnight to see his parents. You should come with us, Eugene, and see the pictures of the hero of that household. James as a baby! the most wonderful of all babies. James holding his first school prize, won at the ripe age of eight! James as the captain of his eleven! James in his first frock coat! James under all sorts of glorious circum-stances! You know how strong he is (I hope he didn't hurt you)—how clever he is—how happy! [*With deepening grav-ity.*] Ask James's mother and his three sisters what it cost to save James the trouble of doing anything but be strong and clever and happy. Ask me what it costs to be James's mother and three sisters and wife and mother to his children all in one. Ask Prossy and Maria how troublesome the house is even when we have no visitors to help us to slice the onions. Ask the tradesmen who want to worry James and spoil his beautiful sermons who it is that puts them off. When there is money to give, he gives it: when there is money to refuse, I refuse it. I build a castle of comfort and indul-gence and love for him, and stand sentinel always to keep little vulgar cares out. I make him master here, though he does not know it, and could not tell you a moment ago how it came to be so. [*With sweet irony.*] And when he thought I might go away with you, his only anxiety was what should become of me! And to tempt me to stay he offered me [*leaning forward to stroke his hair caressingly at each phrase*] his strength for my defence, his industry for my livelihood, his position for my dignity, his— [*Relenting.*] Ah, I am mixing up your beautiful sentences and spoiling them, am I not, darling? [*She lays her cheek fondly against his.*]

MORELL [*quite overcome, kneeling beside her chair and embracing her with boyish ingenuousness*]. It's all true, every word. What I am you have made me with the labor of your hands and the love of your heart! You are my wife, my mother, my sisters: you are the sum of all loving care to me.

CANDIDA [*in his arms, smiling, to Eugene*]. Am I your mother and sisters to you, Eugene?

MARCHBANKS [*rising with a fierce gesture of disgust*]. Ah, never. Out, then, into the night with me!

CANDIDA [*rising quickly and intercepting him*]. You are not going like that, Eugene?

MARCHBANKS [*with the ring of a man's voice—no longer a boy's—in the words*]. I know the hour when it strikes. I am impatient to do what must be done.

MORELL [*rising from his knee, alarmed*]. Candida: don't let him do anything rash.

CANDIDA [*confident, smiling at Eugene*]. Oh, there is no fear. He has learnt to live without happiness.

MARCHBANKS. I no longer desire happiness: life is nobler than that. Parson James: I give you my happiness with both hands: I love you because you have filled the heart of the woman I loved. Good-bye. [*He goes towards the door.*]

CANDIDA. One last word. [*He stops, but without turning to her.*] How old are you, Eugene?

MARCHBANKS. As old as the world now. This morning I was eighteen.

CANDIDA [*going to him, and standing behind him with one hand caressingly on his shoulder*]. Eighteen! Will you, for my sake, make a little poem out of the two sentences I am going to say to you? And will you promise to repeat it to yourself whenever you think of me?

MARCHBANKS [*without moving*]. Say the sentences.

CANDIDA. When I am thirty, she will be forty-five. When I am sixty, she will be seventy-five.

MARCHBANKS [*turning to her*]. In a hundred years, we shall be the same age. But I have a better secret than that in my heart. Let me go now. The night outside grows impatient.

CANDIDA. Good-bye. [*She takes his face in her hands; and as he divines her intention and bends his knee, she kisses his forehead. Then he flies out into the night. She turns to Morell, holding out her arms to him.*] Ah, James! [*They embrace. But they do not know the secret in the poet's heart.*]

Man and Superman

TO ARTHUR BINGHAM WALKLEY

My dear Walkley

You once asked me why I did not write a Don Juan play. The levity with which you assumed this frightful responsibility has probably by this time enabled you to forget it; but the day of reckoning has arrived: here is your play! I say your play, because *qui facit per alium facit per se.* Its profits, like its labor, belong to me: its morals, its manners, its philosophy, its influence on the young, are for you to justify. You were of mature age when you made the suggestion; and you knew your man. It is hardly fifteen years since, as twin pioneers of the New Journalism of that time, we two, cradled in the same new sheets, made an epoch in the criticism of the theatre and the opera house by making it a pretext for a propaganda of our own views of life. So you cannot plead ignorance of the character of the force you set in motion. You meant me to *épater le bourgeois;* and if he protests, I hereby refer him to you as the accountable party.

I warn you that if you attempt to repudiate your responsibility, I shall suspect you of finding the play too decorous for your taste. The fifteen years have made me older and graver. In you I can detect no such becoming change. Your levities and audacities are like the loves and comforts prayed for by Desdemona: they increase, even as your days do grow. No mere pioneering journal dares meddle with them now: the stately *Times* itself is alone sufficiently above suspicion to act as your chaperone; and even the *Times* must sometimes thank its stars that new plays are not produced every day, since after each such event its gravity is compromised, its platitude turned to epigram, its portentousness to wit, its propriety to elegance, and even its decorum into naughtiness by criticisms which the traditions of the paper

do not allow you to sign at the end, but which you take care
to sign with the most extravagant flourishes between the lines.
I am not sure that this is not a portent of Revolution. In
eighteenth-century France the end was at hand when men
bought the *Encyclopedia* and found Diderot there. When I
buy the *Times* and find you there, my prophetic ear catches
a rattle of twentieth-century tumbrils.

However, that is not my present anxiety. The question
is, will you not be disappointed with a Don Juan play in
which not one of that hero's *mille e tre* adventures is brought
upon the stage? To propitiate you, let me explain myself.
You will retort that I never do anything else: it is your favorite jibe at me that what I call drama is nothing but explanation. But you must not expect me to adopt your inex-
plicable, fantastic, petulant, fastidious ways: you must take
me as I am, a reasonable, patient, consistent, apologetic, la-
borious person, with the temperament of a schoolmaster and
the pursuits of a vestryman. No doubt that literary knack of
mine which happens to amuse the British public distracts attention from my character; but the character is there none
the less, solid as bricks. I have a conscience; and conscience
is always anxiously explanatory. You, on the contrary, feel
that a man who discusses his conscience is much like a woman
who discusses her modesty. The only moral force you condescend to parade is the force of your wit: the only demand
you make in public is the demand of your artistic temperament for symmetry, elegance, style, grace, refinement, and
the cleanliness which comes next to godliness if not before it.
But my conscience is the genuine pulpit article: it annoys me
to see people comfortable when they ought to be uncomfortable; and I insist on making them think in order to bring
them to conviction of sin. If you don't like my preaching you
must lump it. I really cannot help it.

In the preface to my *Plays for Puritans* I explained the
predicament of our contemporary English drama, forced to
deal almost exclusively with cases of sexual attraction, and
yet forbidden to exhibit the incidents of that attraction or
even to discuss its nature. Your suggestion that I should
write a Don Juan play was virtually a challenge to me to
treat this subject myself dramatically. The challenge was difficult enough to be worth accepting, because, when you come
to think of it, though we have plenty of dramas with heroes
and heroines who are in love and must accordingly marry or
perish at the end of the play, or about people whose rela-

tions with one another have been complicated by the marriage laws, not to mention the looser sort of plays which trade on the tradition that illicit love affairs are at once vicious and delightful, we have no modern English plays in which the natural attraction of the sexes for one another is made the mainspring of the action. That is why we insist on beauty in our performers, differing herein from the countries our friend William Archer holds up as examples of seriousness to our childish theatres. There the Juliets and Isoldes, the Romeos and Tristans, might be our mothers and fathers. Not so the English actress. The heroine she impersonates is not allowed to discuss the elemental relations of men and women: all her romantic twaddle about novelet-made love, all her purely legal dilemmas as to whether she was married or "betrayed," quite miss our hearts and worry our minds. To console ourselves we must just look at her. We do so; and her beauty feeds our starving emotions. Sometimes we grumble ungallantly at the lady because she does not act as well as she looks. But in a drama which, with all its preoccupation with sex, is really void of sexual interest, good looks are more desired than histrionic skill.

Let me press this point on you, since you are too clever to raise the fool's cry of paradox whenever I take hold of a stick by the right instead of the wrong end. Why are our occasional attempts to deal with the sex problem on the stage so repulsive and dreary that even those who are most determined that sex questions shall be held open and their discussion kept free, cannot pretend to relish these joyless attempts at social sanitation? Is it not because at bottom they are utterly sexless? What is the usual formula for such plays? A woman has, on some past occasion, been brought into conflict with the law which regulates the relations of the sexes. A man, by falling in love with her, or marrying her, is brought into conflict with the social convention which discountenances the woman. Now the conflicts of individuals with law and convention can be dramatized like all other human conflicts; but they are purely judicial; and the fact that we are much more curious about the suppressed relations between the man and the woman than about the relations between both and our courts of law and private juries of matrons, produces that sensation of evasion, of dissatisfaction, of fundamental irrelevance, of shallowness, of useless disagreeableness, of total failure to edify and partial failure to interest, which is as familiar to you in the theatres as it was to me when I, too, frequented those uncomfortable buildings, and found our popular playwrights in the mind to (as they thought) emulate Ibsen.

I take it that when you asked me for a Don Juan play you did not want that sort of thing. Nobody does: the successes such plays sometimes obtain are due to the incidental conventional melodrama with which the experienced popular author instinctively saves himself from failure. But what did you want? Owing to your unfortunate habit—you now, I hope, feel its inconvenience—of not explaining yourself, I have had to discover this for myself. First, then, I have had to ask myself, what is a Don Juan? Vulgarly, a libertine. But your dislike of vulgarity is pushed to the length of a defect (universality of character is impossible without a share of vulgarity); and even if you could acquire the taste, you would find yourself overfed from ordinary sources without troubling me. So I took it that you demanded a Don Juan in the philosophic sense.

Philosophically, Don Juan is a man who, though gifted enough to be exceptionally capable of distinguishing between good and evil, follows his own instincts without regard to the common, statute, or canon law; and therefore, whilst gaining the ardent sympathy of our rebellious instincts (which are flattered by the brilliancies with which Don Juan associates them), finds himself in mortal conflict with existing institutions, and defends himself by fraud and force as unscrupulously as a farmer defends his crops by the same means against vermin. The prototypic Don Juan, invented early in the sixteenth century by a Spanish monk, was presented, according to the ideas of that time, as the enemy of God, the approach of whose vengeance is felt throughout the drama, growing in menace from minute to minute. No anxiety is caused on Don Juan's account by any minor antagonist: he easily eludes the police, temporal and spiritual; and when an indignant father seeks private redress with the sword, Don Juan kills him without an effort. Not until the slain father returns from heaven as the agent of God, in the form of his own statue, does he prevail against his slayer and cast him into hell. The moral is a monkish one: repent and reform now; for tomorrow it may be too late. This is really the only point on which Don Juan is sceptical; for he is a devout believer in an ultimate hell, and risks damnation only because, as he is young, it seems so far off that repentance can be postponed until he has amused himself to his heart's content.

But the lesson intended by an author is hardly ever the lesson the world chooses to learn from his book. What attracts and impresses us in *El Burlador de Sevilla* is not the immediate urgency of repentance, but the heroism of daring to be the enemy of God. From Prometheus to my own *Devil's Disciple,* such enemies have always been popular. Don Juan became such a pet that the world could not bear his damnation. It reconciled him sentimentally to God in a second version, and clamored for his canonization for a whole century, thus treating him as English journalism has treated that comic foe of the gods, Punch. Molière's Don Juan casts back to the original in point of impenitence; but in piety he falls off greatly. True, he also proposes to repent; but in what terms! *"Oui, ma foi! il faut s'amender. Encore vingt ou trente ans de cette vie-ci, et puis nous songerons à nous."* After Molière comes the artist-enchanter, the master of masters, Mozart, who reveals the hero's spirit in magical harmonies, elfin tones, and elate darting rhythms as of summer lightning made audible. Here you have freedom in love and in morality mocking exquisitely at slavery to them, and interesting you, attracting you, tempting you, inexplicably forcing you to range the hero with his enemy the statue on a transcendant plane, leaving the prudish daughter and her priggish lover on a crockery shelf below to live piously ever after.

After these completed works Byron's fragment does not count for much philosophically. Our vagabond libertines are no more interesting from that point of view than the sailor who has a wife in every port; and Byron's hero is, after all, only a vagabond libertine. And he is dumb: he does not discuss himself with a Sganarelle-Leporello or with the fathers or brothers of his mistresses: he does not even, like Casanova, tell his own story. In fact he is not a true Don Juan at all; for he is no more an enemy of God than any romantic and adventurous young sower of wild oats. Had you and I been in his place at his age, who knows whether we might not have done as he did, unless indeed your fastidiousness had saved you from the Empress Catherine. Byron was as little of a philosopher as Peter the Great: both were instances of that rare and useful, but unedifying variation, an energetic genius born without the prejudices or superstitions of his contemporaries. The resultant unscrupulous freedom of thought made

Byron a greater poet than Wordsworth just as it made Peter a greater king than George III; but as it was, after all, only a negative qualification, it did not prevent Peter from being an appalling blackguard and an arrant poltroon, nor did it enable Byron to become a religious force like Shelley. Let us, then, leave Byron's Don Juan out of account. Mozart's is the last of the true Don Juans; for by the time he was of age, his cousin Faust had, in the hands of Goethe, taken his place and carried both his warfare and his reconciliation with the gods far beyond mere lovemaking into politics, high art, schemes for reclaiming new continents from the ocean, and recognition of an eternal womanly principle in the universe. Goethe's *Faust* and Mozart's *Don Juan* were the last words of the eighteenth century on the subject; and by the time the polite critics of the nineteenth century, ignoring William Blake as superficially as the eighteenth had ignored Hogarth or the seventeenth Bunyan, had got past the Dickens-Macaulay Dumas-Guizot stage and the Stendhal-Meredith-Turgenieff stage, and were confronted with philosophic fiction by such pens as Ibsen's and Tolstoy's, Don Juan had changed his sex and become Doña Juana, breaking out of the Doll's House and asserting herself as an individual instead of a mere item in a moral pageant.

Now it is all very well for you at the beginning of the twentieth century to ask me for a Don Juan play; but you will see from the foregoing survey that Don Juan is a full century out of date for you and for me; and if there are millions of less literate people who are still in the eighteenth century, have they not Molière and Mozart, upon whose art no human hand can improve? You would laugh at me if at this time of day I dealt in duels and ghosts and "womanly" women. As to mere libertinism, you would be the first to remind me that the *Festin de Pierre* of Molière is not a play for amorists, and that one bar of the voluptuous sentimentality of Gounod or Bizet would appear as a licentious stain on the score of *Don Giovanni*. Even the more abstract parts of the Don Juan play are dilapidated past use: for instance, Don Juan's supernatural antagonist hurled those who refuse to repent into lakes of burning brimstone, there to be tormented by devils with horns and tails. Of that antagonist, and of that conception of repentance, how much is left that could be used in a play by me dedicated to you? On the other hand, those forces of middle class public opinion which hardly existed for a Spanish nobleman in the days of the first Don

Juan, are now triumphant everywhere. Civilized society is one huge bourgeoisie: no nobleman dares now shock his greengrocer. The women, *"marchesane, principesse, cameriere, cittadine"* and all, are become equally dangerous: the sex is aggressive, powerful: when women are wronged they do not group themselves pathetically to sing *"Protegga il giusto cielo"*: they grasp formidable legal and social weapons, and retaliate. Political parties are wrecked and public careers undone by a single indiscretion. A man had better have all the statues in London to supper with him, ugly as they are, than be brought to the bar of the Nonconformist Conscience by Donna Elvira. Excommunication has become almost as serious a business as it was in the tenth century.

As a result, Man is no longer, like Don Juan, victor in the duel of sex. Whether he has ever really been may be doubted: at all events the enormous superiority of Woman's natural position in this matter is telling with greater and greater force. As to pulling the Nonconformist Conscience by the beard as Don Juan plucked the beard of the Commandant's statue in the convent of San Francisco, that is out of the question nowadays: prudence and good manners alike forbid it to a hero with any mind. Besides, it is Don Juan's own beard that is in danger of plucking. Far from relapsing into hypocrisy, as Sganarelle feared, he has unexpectedly discovered a moral in his immorality. The growing recognition of his new point of view is heaping responsibility on him. His former jests he has had to take as seriously as I have had to take some of the jests of Mr. W. S. Gilbert. His scepticism, once his least tolerated quality, has now triumphed so completely that he can no longer assert himself by witty negations, and must, to save himself from cipherdom, find an affirmative position. His thousand and three affairs of gallantry, after becoming, at most, two immature intrigues leading to sordid and prolonged complications and humiliations, have been discarded altogether as unworthy of his philosophic dignity and compromising to his newly acknowledged position as the founder of a school. Instead of pretending to read Ovid he does actually read Schopenhauer and Nietzsche, studies Westermarck, and is concerned for the future of the race instead of for the freedom of his own instincts. Thus his profligacy and his dare-devil airs have gone the way of his sword and mandoline into the rag shop of anachronisms and superstitions. In fact, he is now more Hamlet than Don Juan; for though the lines put into the actor's mouth to indi-

cate to the pit that Hamlet is a philosopher are for the most
part mere harmonious platitude which, with a little debase-
ment of the word-music, would be properer to Pecksniff, yet
if you separate the real hero, inarticulate and unintelligible
to himself except in flashes of inspiration, from the performer
who has to talk at any cost through five acts; and if you also
do what you must always do in Shakespeare's tragedies: that
is, dissect out the absurd sensational incidents and physical
violences of the borrowed story from the genuine Shakespearian tissue, you will get a true Promethean foe of the
gods, whose instinctive attitude towards women much re-
sembles that to which Don Juan is now driven. From this
point of view Hamlet was a developed Don Juan whom
Shakespeare palmed off as a reputable man just as he palmed
poor Macbeth off as a murderer. Today the palming off is no
longer necessary (at least on your plane and mine) because
Don Juanism is no longer misunderstood as mere Casa-
novism. Don Juan himself is almost ascetic in his desire to
avoid that misunderstanding; and so my attempt to bring
him up to date by launching him as a modern Englishman
into a modern English environment has produced a figure
superficially quite unlike the hero of Mozart.

And yet I have not the heart to disappoint you wholly
of another glimpse of the Mozartian *dissoluto punito* and
his antagonist the statue. I feel sure you would like to know
more of the statue—to draw him out when he is off duty,
so to speak. To gratify you, I have resorted to the trick of
the strolling theatrical manager who advertises the panto-
mime of Sinbad the Sailor with a stock of second-hand picture posters designed for Ali Baba. He simply thrusts a
few oil jars into the valley of diamonds, and so fulfils the
promise held out by the hoardings to the public eye. I have
adapted this simple device to our occasion by thrusting into
my perfectly modern three-act play a totally extraneous act
in which my hero, enchanted by the air of the Sierra, has a
dream in which his Mozartian ancestor appears and philoso-
phizes at great length in a Shavio-Socratic dialogue with
the lady, the statue, and the devil.

But this pleasantry is not the essence of the play. Over
this essence I have no control. You propound a certain social
substance, sexual attraction to wit, for dramatic distillation;
and I distil it for you. I do not adulterate the product with
aphrodisiacs nor dilute it with romance and water; for I am
merely executing your commission, not producing a popular

play for the market. You must therefore (unless, like most wise men, you read the play first and the preface afterwards) prepare yourself to face a trumpery story of modern London life, a life in which, as you know, the ordinary man's main business is to get means to keep up the position and habits of a gentleman, and the ordinary woman's business is to get married. In 9,999 cases out of 10,000, you can count on their doing nothing, whether noble or base, that conflicts with these ends; and that assurance is what you rely on as their religion, their morality, their principles, their patriotism, their reputation, their honor and so forth.

On the whole, this is a sensible and satisfactory foundation for society. Money means nourishment and marriage means children; and that men should put nourishment first and women children first is, broadly speaking, the law of Nature and not the dictate of personal ambition. The secret of the prosaic man's success, such as it is, is the simplicity with which he pursues these ends: the secret of the artistic man's failure, such as that is, is the versatility with which he strays in all directions after secondary ideals. The artist is either a poet or a scallawag: as poet, he cannot see, as the prosaic man does, that chivalry is at bottom only romantic suicide: as scallawag, he cannot see that it does not pay to sponge and beg and lie and brag and neglect his person. Therefore do not misunderstand my plain statement of the fundamental constitution of London society as an Irishman's reproach to your nation. From the day I first set foot on this foreign soil I knew the value of the prosaic qualities of which Irishmen teach Englishmen to be ashamed as well as I knew the vanity of the poetic qualities of which Englishmen teach Irishmen to be proud. For the Irishman instinctively disparages the quality which makes the Englishman dangerous to him; and the Englishman instinctively flatters the fault that makes the Irishman harmless and amusing to him. What is wrong with the prosaic Englishman is what is wrong with the prosaic men of all countries: stupidity. The vitality which places nourishment and children first, heaven and hell a somewhat remote second, and the health of society as an organic whole nowhere, may muddle successfully through the comparatively tribal stages of gregariousness; but in nineteenth-century nations and twentieth-century empires the determination of every man to be rich at all costs, and of every woman to be married at all costs, must, without a highly scientific social organization, produce a ruinous development of poverty, celibacy, prostitution, infant mortality, adult degeneracy, and everything that wise men most dread. In short, there is no future for men, however brimming with crude vitality, who are neither intelligent nor politically educated enough to be socialists. So do not misunderstand me in the other direction either: if I appreciate the vital qualities of the Englishman as I appreciate the vital qualities of the bee, I do not guarantee the Englishman against being, like the bee (or the Canaanite) smoked out and unloaded of his honey by beings inferior to himself in simple acquisitiveness, combativeness, and fecundity, but superior to him in imagination and cunning.

The Don Juan play, however, is to deal with sexual attraction, and not with nutrition, and to deal with it in a society in which the serious business of sex is left by men to women, as the serious business of nutrition is left by women to men. That the men, to protect themselves against a too aggressive prosecution of the women's business, have set up a feeble romantic convention that the initiative in sex business must always come from the man, is true; but the pretence is so shallow that even in the theatre, that last sanctuary of unreality, it imposes only on the inexperienced. In Shakespeare's plays the woman always takes the initiative. In his problem plays and his popular plays alike the love interest is the interest of seeing the woman hunt the man down. She may do it by blandishment, like Rosalind, or by stratagem, like Mariana; but in every case the relation between the woman and the man is the same: she is the pursuer and contriver, he the pursued and disposed of. When she is baffled, like Ophelia, she goes mad and commits suicide; and the man goes straight from her funeral to a fencing match. No doubt Nature, with very young creatures, may save the woman the trouble of scheming: Prospero knows that he has only to throw Ferdinand and Miranda together and they will mate like a pair of doves; and there is no need for Perdita to capture Florizel as the lady doctor in *All's Well That Ends Well* (an early Ibsenite heroine) captures Bertram. But the mature cases all illustrate the Shakespearian law. The one apparent exception, Petruchio, is not a real one: he is most carefully characterized as a purely commercial matrimonial adventurer. Once he is assured that Katharine has money, he undertakes to marry her before he has seen her. In real life we find not only Petruchios, but Mantalinis and Dobbins who pursue women with appeals to their pity or

jealousy or vanity, or cling to them in a romantically infatuated way. Such effeminates do not count in the world
scheme: even Bunsby dropping like a fascinated bird into
the jaws of Mrs. MacStinger is by comparison a true tragic
object of pity and terror. I find in my own plays that Woman,
projecting herself dramatically by my hands (a process over
which I assure you I have no more real control than I have
over my wife), behaves just as Woman did in the plays of
Shakespeare.

And so your Don Juan has come to birth as a stage
projection of the tragi-comic love chase of the man by the
woman; and my Don Juan is the quarry instead of the
huntsman. Yet he is a true Don Juan, with a sense of reality
that disables convention, defying to the last the fate which
finally overtakes him. The woman's need of him to enable
her to carry on Nature's most urgent work, does not prevail
against him until his resistance gathers her energy to a
climax at which she dares to throw away her customary
exploitations of the conventional affectionate and dutiful
poses, and claim him by natural right for a purpose that far
transcends their mortal personal purposes.

Among the friends to whom I have read this play in
manuscript are some of our own sex who are shocked at
the "unscrupulousness," meaning the total disregard of masculine fastidiousness, with which the woman pursues her purpose. It does not occur to them that if women were as fastidious as men, morally or physically, there would be an end
of the race. Is there anything meaner than to throw necessary work upon other people and then disparage it as unworthy and indelicate. We laugh at the haughty American
nation because it makes the Negro clean its boots and then
proves the moral and physical inferiority of the Negro by the
fact that he is a shoeblack; but we ourselves throw the whole
drudgery of creation on one sex, and then imply that no
female of any womanliness or delicacy would initiate any
effort in that direction. There are no limits to male hypocrisy
in this matter. No doubt there are moments when man's
sexual immunities are made acutely humiliating to him.
When the terrible moment of birth arrives, its supreme importance and its superhuman effort and peril, in which the
father has no part, dwarf him into the meanest insignifi-
cance: he slinks out of the way of the humblest petticoat,
happy if he be poor enough to be pushed out of the house
to outface his ignominy by drunken rejoicings. But when

the crisis is over he takes his revenge, swaggering as the breadwinner, and speaking of Woman's "sphere" with condescension, even with chivalry, as if the kitchen and the nursery were less important than the office in the city. When his swagger is exhausted he drivels into erotic poetry or sentimental uxoriousness; and the Tennysonian King Arthur posing at Guinevere becomes Don Quixote grovelling before Dulcinea. You must admit that here Nature beats Comedy out of the field: the wildest hominist or feminist farce is insipid after the most commonplace "slice of life." The pretence that women do not take the initiative is part of the farce. Why, the whole world is strewn with snares, traps, gins and pitfalls for the capture of men by women. Give women the vote, and in five years there will be a crushing tax on bachelors. Men, on the other hand, attach penalties to marriage, depriving women of property, of the franchise, of the free use of their limbs, of that ancient symbol of immortality, the right to make oneself at home in the house of God by taking off the hat, of everything that he can force Woman to dispense with without compelling himself to dispense with her. All in vain. Woman must marry because the race must perish without her travail: if the risk of death and the certainty of pain, danger and unutterable discomforts cannot deter her, slavery and swaddled ankles will not. And yet we assume that the force that carries women through all these perils and hardships, stops abashed before the primnesses of our behavior for young ladies. It is assumed that the woman must wait, motionless, until she is wooed. Nay, she often does wait motionless. That is how the spider waits for the fly. But the spider spins her web. And if the fly, like my hero, shews a strength that promises to extricate him, how swiftly does she abandon her pretence of passiveness, and openly fling coil after coil about him until he is secured for ever!

If the really impressive books and other art-works of the world were produced by ordinary men, they would express more fear of women's pursuit than love of their illusory beauty. But ordinary men cannot produce really impressive art-works. Those who can are men of genius: that is, men selected by Nature to carry on the work of building up an intellectual consciousness of her own instinctive purpose. Accordingly, we observe in the man of genius all the unscrupulousness and all the "self-sacrifice" (the two things are the same) of Woman. He will risk the stake and the cross; starve,

when necessary, in a garret all his life; study women and
live on their work and care as Darwin studied worms and
lived upon sheep; work his nerves into rags without payment, a sublime altruist in his disregard of himself, an atro-
cious egoist in his disregard of others. Here Woman meets
a purpose as impersonal, as irresistible as her own; and the
clash is sometimes tragic. When it is complicated by the
genius being a woman, then the game is one for a king of
critics: your George Sand becomes a mother to gain experience for the novelist and to develop her, and gobbles up
men of genius, Chopins, Mussets and the like, as mere hors
d'œuvres.

I state the extreme case, of course; but what is true of
the great man who incarnates the philosophic consciousness
of Life and the woman who incarnates its fecundity, is true
in some degree of all geniuses and all women. Hence it is
that the world's books get written, its pictures painted, its
statues modelled, its symphonies composed, by people who
are free of the otherwise universal dominion of the tyranny
of sex. Which leads us to the conclusion, astonishing to the
vulgar, that art, instead of being before all things the expression of the normal sexual situation, is really the only
department in which sex is a superseded and secondary power,
with its consciousness so confused and its purpose so per-
verted, that its ideas are mere fantasy to common men.
Whether the artist becomes poet or philosopher, moralist or
founder of a religion, his sexual doctrine is nothing but a
barren special pleading for pleasure, excitement, and knowledge when he is young, and for contemplative tranquillity
when he is old and satiated. Romance and Asceticism, Amor-
ism and Puritanism are equally unreal in the great Philistine
world. The world shewn us in books, whether the books be
confessed epics or professed gospels, or in codes, or in political orations, or in philosophic systems, is not the main world
at all: it is only the self-consciousness of certain abnormal
people who have the specific artistic talent and temperament. A serious matter this for you and me, because the
man whose consciousness does not correspond to that of
the majority is a madman; and the old habit of worshipping
madmen is giving way to the new habit of locking them up.
And since what we call education and culture is for the most
part nothing but the substitution of reading for experience, of
literature for life, of the obsolete fictitious for the contemporary real, education, as you no doubt observed at Oxford,

destroys, by supplantation, every mind that is not strong enough to see through the imposture and to use the great Masters of Arts as what they really are and no more: that is, patentees of highly questionable methods of thinking, and manufacturers of highly questionable, and for the majority but half valid representations of life. The schoolboy who uses his Homer to throw at his fellow's head makes perhaps the safest and most rational use of him; and I observe with reassurance that you occasionally do the same, in your prime, with your Aristotle.

Fortunately for us, whose minds have been so overwhelmingly sophisticated by literature, what produces all these treatises and poems and scriptures of one sort or another is the struggle of Life to become divinely conscious of itself instead of blindly stumbling hither and thither in the line of least resistance. Hence there is a driving towards truth in all books on matters where the writer, though exceptionally gifted, is normally constituted, and has no private axe to grind. Copernicus had no motive for misleading his fellowmen as to the place of the sun in the solar system: he looked for it as honestly as a shepherd seeks his path in a mist. But Copernicus would not have written love stories scientifically. When it comes to sex relations, the man of genius does not share the common man's danger of capture, nor the woman of genius the common woman's overwhelming specialization. And that is why our scriptures and other art works, when they deal with love, turn from honest attempts at science in physics to romantic nonsense, erotic ecstasy, or the stern asceticism of satiety ("the road of excess leads to the palace of wisdom" said William Blake; for "you never know what is enough unless you know what is more than enough").

There is a political aspect of this sex question which is too big for my comedy, and too momentous to be passed over without culpable frivolity. It is impossible to demonstrate that the initiative in sex transactions remains with Woman, and has been confirmed to her, so far, more and more by the suppression of rapine and discouragement of importunity, without being driven to very serious reflections on the fact that this initiative is politically the most important of all the initiatives, because our political experiment of democracy, the last refuge of cheap misgovernment, will ruin us if our citizens are ill bred.

When we two were born, this country was still dominated by a selected class bred by political marriages. The

commercial class had not then completed the first twenty-five
years of its new share of political power; and it was itself
selected by money qualification, and bred, if not by political
marriage, at least by a pretty rigorous class marriage. Aristocracy and plutocracy still furnish the figureheads of politics; but they are now dependent on the votes of the pro-
miscuously bred masses. And this, if you please, at the very
moment when the political problem, having suddenly ceased
to mean a very limited and occasional interference, mostly
by way of jobbing public appointments, in the mismanage-
ment of a tight but parochial little island, with occasional
meaningless prosecution of dynastic wars, has become the industrial reorganization of Britain, the construction of a practically international Commonwealth, and the partition of the
whole of Africa and perhaps the whole of Asia by the civilized Powers. Can you believe that the people whose conceptions of society and conduct, whose power of attention and
scope of interest, are measured by the British theatre as you
know it today, can either handle this colossal task themselves,
or understand and support the sort of mind and character
that is (at least comparatively) capable of handling it? For
remember: what our voters are in the pit and gallery they
are also in the polling booth. We are all now under what
Burke called "the hoofs of the swinish multitude." Burke's
language gave great offence because the implied exceptions
to its universal application made it a class insult; and it certainly was not for the pot to call the kettle black. The aristocracy he defended, in spite of the political marriages by
which it tried to secure breeding for itself, had its mind un-
dertrained by silly schoolmasters and governesses, its character corrupted by gratuitous luxury, its self-respect adulterated
to complete spuriousness by flattery and flunkeyism. It is no
better today and never will be any better: our very peasants
have something morally hardier in them that culminates occasionally in a Bunyan, a Burns, or a Carlyle. But observe,
this aristocracy, which was overpowered from 1832 to 1885
by the middle class, has come back to power by the votes of
"the swinish multitude." Tom Paine has triumphed over
Edmund Burke; and the swine are now courted electors. How
many of their own class have these electors sent to parliament? Hardly a dozen out of 670, and these only under the
persuasion of conspicuous personal qualifications and popular
eloquence. The multitude thus pronounces judgment on its
own units: it admits itself unfit to govern, and will vote only

for a man morphologically and generically transfigured by
palatial residence and equipage, by transcendent tailoring, by
the glamor of aristocratic kinship. Well, we two know these
transfigured persons, these college passmen, these well
groomed monocular Algys and Bobbies, these cricketers to
whom age brings golf instead of wisdom, these plutocratic
products of "the nail and sarspan business as he got his money
by." Do you know whether to laugh or cry at the notion
that they, poor devils! will drive a team of continents as they
drive a four-in-hand; turn a jostling anarchy of casual trade
and speculation into an ordered productivity; and federate
our colonies into a world-Power of the first magnitude? Give
these people the most perfect political constitution and the
soundest political program that benevolent omniscience can
devise for them, and they will interpret it into mere fashionable folly or canting charity as infallibly as a savage con-
verts the philosophical theology of a Scotch missionary into
crude African idolatry.

I do not know whether you have any illusions left on the
subject of education, progress, and so forth. I have none. Any
pamphleteer can shew the way to better things; but when
there is no will there is no way. My nurse was fond of re-
marking that you cannot make a silk purse out of a sow's
ear; and the more I see of the efforts of our churches and
universities and literary sages to raise the mass above its
own level, the more convinced I am that my nurse was right.
Progress can do nothing but make the most of us all as we
are, and that most would clearly not be enough even if those
who are already raised out of the lowest abysses would allow
the others a chance. The bubble of Heredity has been
pricked: the certainty that acquirements are negligible as elements in practical heredity has demolished the hopes of the
educationists as well as the terrors of the degeneracy mon-
gers; and we know now that there is no hereditary "governing
class" any more than a hereditary hooliganism. We must
either breed political capacity or be ruined by Democracy,
which was forced on us by the failure of the older alternatives. Yet if Despotism failed only for want of a
capable benevolent despot, what chance has Democracy,
which requires a whole population of capable voters: that is,
of political critics who, if they cannot govern in person for
lack of spare energy or specific talent for administration, can
at least recognize and appreciate capacity and benevolence
in others, and so govern through capably benevolent repre-

sentatives? Where are such voters to be found today? Nowhere. Promiscuous breeding has produced a weakness of
character that is too timid to face the full stringency of
a thoroughly competitive struggle for existence and too lazy
and petty to organize the commonwealth co-operatively.
Being cowards, we defeat natural selection under cover of
philanthropy: being sluggards, we neglect artificial selection
under cover of delicacy and morality.

Yet we must get an electorate of capable critics or collapse as Rome and Egypt collapsed. At this moment the Roman decadent phase of *panem et circenses* is being inaugu-
rated under our eyes. Our newspapers and melodramas are
blustering about our imperial destiny; but our eyes and hearts
turn eagerly to the American millionaire. As his hand goes
down to his pocket, our fingers go up to the brims of our
hats by instinct. Our ideal prosperity is not the prosperity of
the industrial north, but the prosperity of the Isle of Wight,
of Folkestone and Ramsgate, of Nice and Monte Carlo. That
is the only prosperity you see on the stage, where the work-
ers are all footmen, parlormaids, comic lodging-letters and
fashionable professional men, whilst the heroes and heroines
are miraculously provided with unlimited dividends, and eat
gratuitously, like the knights in Don Quixote's books of
chivalry. The city papers prate of the competition of Bombay
with Manchester and the like. The real competition is the
competition of Regent Street with the Rue de Rivoli, of
Brighton and the south coast with the Riviera, for the spending money of the American Trusts. What is all this growing
love of pageantry, this effusive loyalty, this officious rising
and uncovering at a wave from a flag or a blast from a brass
band? Imperialism? Not a bit of it. Obsequiousness, servility,
cupidity roused by the prevailing smell of money. When Mr.
Carnegie rattled his millions in his pockets all England became one rapacious cringe. Only, when Rhodes (who had
probably been reading my *Socialism for Millionaires*) left
word that no idler was to inherit his estate, the bent backs
straightened mistrustfully for a moment. Could it be that
the Diamond King was no gentleman after all? However, it
was easy to ignore a rich man's solecism. The ungentlemanly
clause was not mentioned again; and the backs soon bowed
themselves back into their natural shape.

But I hear you asking me in alarm whether I have actually put all this tub thumping into a Don Juan comedy. I
have not. I have only made my Don Juan a political pam-

phleteer, and given you his pamphlet in full by way of ap-
pendix. You will find it at the end of the book. I am sorry
to say that it is a common practice with romancers to announce their hero as a man of extraordinary genius, and to
leave his works entirely to the reader's imagination; so that
at the end of the book you whisper to yourself ruefully that
but for the author's solemn preliminary assurance you should
hardly have given the gentleman credit for ordinary good
sense. You cannot accuse me of this pitiable barrenness, this
feeble evasion. I not only tell you that my hero wrote a revolutionists' handbook: I give you the handbook at full length
for your edification if you care to read it. And in that handbook you will find the politics of the sex question as I conceive Don Juan's descendant to understand them. Not that
I disclaim the fullest responsibility for his opinions and for
those of all my characters, pleasant and unpleasant. They
are all right from their several points of view; and their
points of view are, for the dramatic moment, mine also. This
may puzzle the people who believe that there is such a thing
as an absolutely right point of view, usually their own. It
may seem to them that nobody who doubts this can be in
a state of grace. However that may be, it is certainly true
that nobody who agrees with them can possibly be a dramatist, or indeed anything else that turns upon a knowledge of
mankind. Hence it has been pointed out that Shakespeare
had no conscience. Neither have I, in that sense.

You may, however, remind me that this digression of
mine into politics was preceded by a very convincing demonstration that the artist never catches the point of view of the
common man on the question of sex, because he is not in
the same predicament. I first prove that anything I write on
the relation of the sexes is sure to be misleading; and then
I proceed to write a Don Juan play. Well, if you insist on
asking me why I behave in this absurd way, I can only reply
that you asked me to, and that in any case my treatment of
the subject may be valid for the artist, amusing to the amateur, and at least intelligible and therefore possibly suggestive to the Philistine. Every man who records his illusions is
providing data for the genuinely scientific psychology which
the world still waits for. I plank down my view of the existing relations of men to women in the most highly civilized
society for what it is worth. It is a view like any other view
and no more, neither true nor false, but, I hope, a way of
looking at the subject which throws into the familiar order of

cause and effect a sufficient body of fact and experience to
be interesting to you, if not to the playgoing public of London. I have certainly shewn little consideration for that public in this enterprise; but I know that it has the friendliest disposition towards you and me as far as it has any consciousness of our existence, and quite understands that what I
write for you must pass at a considerable height over its
simple romantic head. It will take my books as read and
my genius for granted, trusting me to put forth work of
such quality as shall bear out its verdict. So we may disport
ourselves on our own plane to the top of our bent; and if
any gentleman points out that neither this epistle dedicatory
nor the dream of Don Juan in the third act of the ensuing
comedy is suitable for immediate production at a popular
theatre we need not contradict him. Napoleon provided Talma
with a pit of kings, with what effect on Talma's acting is not
recorded. As for me, what I have always wanted is a pit of
philosophers; and this is a play for such a pit.

I should make formal acknowledgment to the authors
whom I have pillaged in the following pages if I could
recollect them all. The theft of the brigand-poetaster from
Sir Arthur Conan Doyle is deliberate; and the metamorphosis
of Leporello into Enry Straker, motor engineer and New
Man, is an intentional dramatic sketch for the contemporary
embryo of Mr. H. G. Wells's anticipation of the efficient engineering class which will, he hopes, finally sweep the jab-
berers out of the way of civilization. Mr. Barrie has also,
whilst I am correcting my proofs, delighted London with a
servant who knows more than his masters. The conception
of Mendoza Limited I trace back to a certain West Indian
colonial secretary, who, at a period when he and I and Mr.
Sidney Webb were sowing our political wild oats as a sort
of Fabian Three Musketeers, without any prevision of the
surprising respectability of the crop that followed, recommended Webb, the encyclopedic and inexhaustible, to form
himself into a company for the benefit of the shareholders.
Octavius I take over unaltered from Mozart; and I hereby
authorize any actor who impersonates him, to sing *"Dalla
sua pace"* (if he can) at any convenient moment during the
representation. Ann was suggested to me by the fifteenth
century Dutch morality called Everyman, which Mr. William
Poel has lately resuscitated so triumphantly. I trust he will
work that vein further, and recognize that Elizabethan Renas-
cence fustian is no more bearable after medieval poesy than

Scribe after Ibsen. As I sat watching Everyman at the
Charterhouse, I said to myself Why not Everywoman? Ann
was the result: every woman is not Ann; but Ann is Everywoman.

That the author of Everyman was no mere artist, but
an artist-philosopher, and that the artist-philosophers are the
only sort of artists I take quite seriously, will be no news to
you. Even Plato and Boswell, as the dramatists who invented
Socrates and Dr. Johnson, impress me more deeply than the
romantic playwrights. Ever since, as a boy, I first breathed
the air of the transcendental regions as a performance of
Mozart's *Zauberflöte*, I have been proof against the garish
splendors and alcoholic excitements of the ordinary stage
combinations of Tappertitian romance with the police intelligence. Bunyan, Blake, Hogarth, and Turner (these four
apart and above all the English classics), Goethe, Shelley,
Schopenhauer, Wagner, Ibsen, Morris, Tolstoy, and Nietzsche
are among the writers whose peculiar sense of the world I
recognize as more or less akin to my own. Mark the word
peculiar. I read Dickens and Shakespeare without shame or
stint; but their pregnant observations and demonstrations of
life are not co-ordinated into any philosophy or religion: on
the contrary, Dickens's sentimental assumptions are violently
contradicted by his observations; and Shakespeare's pessimism
is only his wounded humanity. Both have the specific genius
of the fictionist and the common sympathies of human feeling and thought in pre-eminent degree. They are often saner
and shrewder than the philosophers just as Sancho Panza
was often saner and shrewder than Don Quixote. They clear
away vast masses of oppressive gravity by their sense of the
ridiculous, which is at bottom a combination of sound moral
judgment with lighthearted good humor. But they are concerned with the diversities of the world instead of with its
unities: they are so irreligious that they exploit popular religion for professional purposes without delicacy or scruple
(for example, Sydney Carton and the ghost in Hamlet!):
they are anarchical, and cannot balance their exposures of
Angelo and Dogberry, Sir Leicester Dedlock and Mr. Tite
Barnacle, with any portrait of a prophet or a worthy leader:
they have no constructive ideas: they regard those who have
them as dangerous fanatics: in all their fictions there is no
leading thought or inspiration for which any man could
conceivably risk the spoiling of his hat in a shower, much
less his life. Both are alike forced to borrow motives for the

more strenuous actions of their personages from the common
stockpot of melodramatic plots; so that Hamlet has to be
stimulated by the prejudices of a policeman and Macbeth
by the cupidities of a bushranger. Dickens, without the excuse of having to manufacture motives for Hamlets and Macbeths, superfluously punts his crew down the stream of his
monthly parts by mechanical devices which I leave you to
describe, my own memory being quite baffled by the simplest
question as to Monks in *Oliver Twist*, or the long lost parentage of Smike, or the relations between the Dorrit and
Clennam families so inopportunely discovered by Monsieur
Rigaud Blandois. The truth is, the world was to Shakespeare
a great "stage of fools" on which he was utterly bewildered.
He could see no sort of sense in living at all; and Dickens
saved himself from the despair of the dream in The Chimes
by taking the world for granted and busying himself with its
details. Neither of them could do anything with a serious
positive character: they could place a human figure before
you with perfect verisimilitude; but when the moment came
for making it live and move, they found, unless it made them
laugh, that they had a puppet on their hands, and had to
invent some artificial external stimulus to make it work. This
is what is the matter with Hamlet all through: he has no will
except in his bursts of temper. Foolish Bardolaters make a
virtue of this after their fashion: they declare that the play
is the tragedy of irresolution; but all Shakespeare's projections of the deepest humanity he knew have the same defect:
their characters and manners are lifelike; but their actions
are forced on them from without, and the external force is
grotesquely inappropriate except when it is quite conventional,
as in the case of Henry V. Falstaff is more vivid than any of
these serious reflective characters, because he is self-acting:
his motives are his own appetites and instincts and humors.
Richard III, too, is delightful as the whimsical comedian who
stops a funeral to make love to the corpse's widow; but when,
in the next act, he is replaced by a stage villain who smothers
babies and offs with people's heads, we are revolted at the imposture and repudiate the changeling. Faulconbridge, Coriolanus, Leontes are admirable descriptions of instinctive temperaments: indeed the play of *Coriolanus* is the greatest of
Shakespeare's comedies; but description is not philosophy;
and comedy neither compromises the author nor reveals him.
He must be judged by those characters into which he puts
what he knows of himself, his Hamlets and Macbeths and

Lears and Prosperos. If these characters are agonizing in a void about factitious melodramatic murders and revenges and the like, whilst the comic characters walk with their feet on solid ground, vivid and amusing, you know that the author has much to shew and nothing to teach. The comparison between Falstaff and Prospero is like the comparison between Micawber and David Copperfield. At the end of the book you know Micawber, whereas you only know what has happened to David, and are not interested enough in him to wonder what his politics or religion might be if anything so stupendous as a religious or political idea, or a general idea of any sort, were to occur to him. He is tolerable as a child; but he never becomes a man, and might be left out of his own biography altogether but for his usefulness as a stage confidant, a Horatio or "Charles his friend"—what they call on the stage a feeder.

Now you cannot say this of the works of the artist-philosophers. You cannot say it, for instance, of *The Pilgrim's Progress*. Put your Shakespearian hero and coward, Henry V and Pistol or Parolles, beside Mr. Valiant and Mr. Fearing, and you have a sudden revelation of the abyss that lies between the fashionable author who could see nothing in the world but personal aims and the tragedy of their disappointment or the comedy of their incongruity, and the field preacher who achieved virtue and courage by identifying himself with the purpose of the world as he understood it. The contrast is enormous: Bunyan's coward stirs your blood more than Shakespeare's hero, who actually leaves you cold and secretly hostile. You suddenly see that Shakespeare, with all his flashes and divinations, never understood virtue and courage, never conceived how any man who was not a fool could, like Bunyan's hero, look back from the brink of the river of death over the strife and labor of his pilgrimage, and say "yet do I not repent me"; or, with the panache of a millionaire, bequeath "my sword to him that shall succeed me in my pilgrimage, and my courage and skill to him that can get it." This is the true joy in life, the being used for a purpose recognized by yourself as a mighty one; the being thoroughly worn out before you are thrown on the scrap heap; the being a force of Nature instead of a feverish selfish little clod of ailments and grievances complaining that the world will not devote itself to making you happy. And also the only real tragedy in life is the being used by personally minded men for purposes which you recognize to be

base. All the rest is at worst mere misfortune or mortality:
this alone is misery, slavery, hell on earth; and the revolt
against it is the only force that offers a man's work to the poor
artist, whom our personally minded rich people would so
willingly employ as pander, buffoon, beauty monger, senti-
mentalizer and the like.

It may seem a long step from Bunyan to Nietzsche; but
the difference between their conclusions is purely formal.
Bunyan's perception that righteousness is filthy rags, his
scorn for Mr. Legality in the village of Morality, his defiance
of the Church as the supplanter of religion, his insistence
on courage as the virtue of virtues, his estimate of the career
of the conventionally respectable and sensible Worldly Wiseman as no better at bottom than the life and death of Mr.
Badman: all this, expressed by Bunyan in the terms of a
tinker's theology, is what Nietzsche has expressed in terms of
post-Darwinian, post-Schopenhauerian philosophy; Wagner
in terms of polytheistic mythology; and Ibsen in terms of mid-
nineteenth century Parisian dramaturgy. Nothing is new in
these matters except their novelties: for instance, it is a novelty to call Justification by Faith "Wille," and Justification
by Works "Vorstellung." The sole use of the novelty is that
you and I buy and read Schopenhauer's treatise on Will and
Representation when we should not dream of buying a set of
sermons on Faith versus Works. At bottom the controversy is
the same, and the dramatic results are the same. Bunyan
makes no attempt to present his pilgrims as more sensible or
better conducted than Mr. Worldly Wiseman. Mr. W. W.'s
worst enemies, as Mr. Embezzler, Mr. Never-go-to-Church-
on-Sunday, Mr. Bad Form, Mr. Murderer, Mr. Burglar, Mr.
Co-respondent, Mr. Blackmailer, Mr. Cad, Mr. Drunkard,
Mr. Labor Agitator and so forth, can read the *Pilgrim's
Progress* without finding a word said against them; whereas
the respectable people who snub them and put them in prison,
such as Mr. W. W. himself and his young friend Civility;
Formalist and Hypocrisy; Wildhead, Inconsiderate, and Prag-
matick (who were clearly young university men of good
family and high feeding); that brisk lad Ignorance, Talka-
tive, By-Ends of Fairspeech and his mother-in-law Lady
Feigning, and other reputable gentlemen and citizens, catch
it very severely. Even Little Faith, though he gets to heaven
at last, is given to understand that it served him right to be
mobbed by the brothers Faint Heart, Mistrust, and Guilt, all
three recognized members of respectable society and veritable

pillars of the law. The whole allegory is a consistent attack
on morality and respectability, without a word that one can
remember against vice and crime. Exactly what is complained
of in Nietzsche and Ibsen, is it not? And also exactly what
would be complained of in all the literature which is great
enough and old enough to have attained canonical rank,
officially or unofficially, were it not that books are admitted
to the canon by a compact which confesses their greatness in
consideration of abrogating their meaning; so that the reverend rector can agree with the prophet Micah as to his
inspired style without being committed to any complicity in
Micah's furiously Radical opinions. Why, even I, as I force
myself, pen in hand, into recognition and civility, find all
the force of my onslaught destroyed by a simple policy of
nonresistance. In vain do I redouble the violence of the language in which I proclaim my heterodoxies. I rail at the
theistic credulity of Voltaire, the amoristic superstition of
Shelley, the revival of tribal soothsaying and idolatrous rites
which Huxley called Science and mistook for an advance
on the Pentateuch, no less than at the welter of ecclesiastical
and professional humbug which saves the face of the stupid
system of violence and robbery which we call Law and Industry. Even atheists reproach me with infidelity and anarchists with nihilism because I cannot endure their moral
tirades. And yet, instead of exclaiming "Send this inconceivable Satanist to the stake," the respectable newspapers pith me
by announcing "another book by this brilliant and thoughtful writer." And the ordinary citizen, knowing that an author
who is well spoken of by a respectable newspaper must be
all right, reads me, as he reads Micah, with undisturbed
edification from his own point of view. It is narrated that
in the eighteen-seventies an old lady, a very devout Method-
ist, moved from Colchester to a house in the neighborhood
of the City Road, in London, where, mistaking the Hall of
Science for a chapel, she sat at the feet of Charles Bradlaugh
for many years, entranced by his eloquence, without questioning his orthodoxy or moulting a feather of her faith. I
fear I shall be defrauded of my just martyrdom in the same
way.

However, I am digressing, as a man with a grievance
always does. And after all, the main thing in determining the
artistic quality of a book is not the opinions it propagates,
but the fact that the writer has opinions. The old lady from
Colchester was right to sun her simple soul in the energetic

radiance of Bradlaugh's genuine beliefs and disbeliefs rather than in the chill of such mere painting of light and heat as elocution and convention can achieve. My contempt for belles-lettres, and for amateurs who become the heroes of the fanciers of literary virtuosity, is not founded on any illusion of mind as to the permanence of those forms of thought (call them opinions) by which I strive to communicate my bent to my fellows. To younger men they are already outmoded; for though they have no more lost their logic than an eighteenth century pastel has lost its drawing or its color, yet, like the pastel, they grow indefinably shabby, and will grow shabbier until they cease to count at all, when my books will either perish, or, if the world is still poor enough to want them, will have to stand, with Bunyan's, by quite amorphous qualities of temper and energy. With this conviction I cannot be a bellettrist. No doubt I must recognize, as even the Ancient Mariner did, that I must tell my story entertainingly if I am to hold the wedding guest spellbound in spite of the siren sounds of the loud bassoon. But "for art's sake" alone I would not face the toil of writing a single sentence. I know that there are men who, having nothing to say and nothing to write, are nevertheless so in love with oratory and with literature that they keep desperately repeating as much as they can understand of what others have said or written aforetime. I know that the leisurely tricks which their want of conviction leaves them free to play with the diluted and mis-apprehended message supply them with a pleasant parlor game which they call style. I can pity their dotage and even sympathize with their fancy. But a true original style is never achieved for its own sake: a man may pay from a shilling to a guinea, according to his means, to see, hear, or read another man's act of genius; but he will not pay with his whole life and soul to become a mere virtuoso in litera-ture, exhibiting an accomplishment which will not even make money for him, like fiddle playing. Effectiveness of assertion is the Alpha and Omega of style. He who has nothing to assert has no style and can have none: he who has something to assert will go as far in power of style as its momentousness and his conviction will carry him. Disprove his assertion after it is made, yet its style remains. Darwin has no more de-stroyed the style of Job nor of Handel than Martin Luther de-stroyed the style of Giotto. All the assertions get disproved sooner or later; and so we find the world full of a magnificent débris of artistic fossils, with the matter-of-fact credibility

gone clean out of them, but the form still splendid. And that
is why the old masters play the deuce with our mere susceptibles. Your Royal Academician thinks he can get the style
of Giotto without Giotto's beliefs, and correct his perspective
into the bargain. Your man of letters thinks he can get Bunyan's or Shakespeare's style without Bunyan's conviction or
Shakespeare's apprehension, especially if he takes care not
to split his infinitives. And so with your Doctors of Music,
who, with their collections of discords duly prepared and
resolved or retarded or anticipated in the manner of the great
composers, think they can learn the art of Palestrina from
Cherubini's treatise. All this academic art is far worse than
the trade in sham antique furniture; for the man who sells
me an oaken chest which he swears was made in the thirteenth century, though as a matter of fact he made it himself only yesterday, at least does not pretend that there are
any modern ideas in it, whereas your academic copier of
fossils offers them to you as the latest outpouring of the
human spirit, and, worst of all, kidnaps young people as
pupils and persuades them that his limitations are rules, his
observances dexterities, his timidities good taste, and his emp-
tinesses purities. And when he declares that art should not
be didactic, all the people who have nothing to teach and
all the people who don't want to learn agree with him emphatically.

I pride myself on not being one of these susceptibles.
If you study the electric light with which I supply you in
that Bumbledonian public capacity of mine over which you
make merry from time to time, you will find that your
house contains a great quantity of highly susceptible copper
wire which gorges itself with electricity and gives you no
light whatever. But here and there occurs a scrap of intensely insusceptible, intensely resistant material; and that
stubborn scrap grapples with the current and will not let it
through until it has made itself useful to you as those two
vital qualities of literature, light and heat. Now if I am to
be no mere copper wire amateur but a luminous author, I
must also be a most intensely refractory person, liable to go
out and to go wrong at inconvenient moments, and with incendiary possibilities. These are the faults of my qualities;
and I assure you that I sometimes dislike myself so much
that when some irritable reviewer chances at that moment
to pitch into me with zest, I feel unspeakably relieved and
obliged. But I never dream of reforming, knowing that I

must take myself as I am and get what work I can out of myself. All this you will understand; for there is community of material between us: we are both critics of life as well as of art; and you have perhaps said to yourself when I have passed your windows "There, but for the grace of God, go I." An awful and chastening reflection, which shall be the closing cadence of this immoderately long letter from yours faithfully,

G. BERNARD SHAW.

Woking, 1903.

ACT ONE

Roebuck Ramsden *is in his study, opening the morning's letters. The study, handsomely and solidly furnished, proclaims the man of means. Not a speck of dust is visible: it is clear that there are at least two housemaids and a parlormaid downstairs, and a housekeeper upstairs who does not let them spare elbow-grease. Even the top of Roebuck's head is polished: on a sunshiny day he could heliograph his orders to distant camps by merely nodding. In no other respect, however, does he suggest the military man. It is in active civil life that men get his broad air of importance, his dignified expectation of deference, his determinate mouth disarmed and refined since the hour of his success by the withdrawal of opposition and the concession of comfort and precedence and power. He is more than a highly respectable man: he is marked out as a president of highly respectable men, a chairman among directors, an alderman among councillors, a mayor among aldermen. Four tufts of iron-grey hair, which will soon be as white as isinglass, and are in other respects not at all unlike it, grow in two symmetrical pairs above his ears and at the angles of his spreading jaws. He wears a black frock coat, a white waistcoat (it is bright spring weather), and trousers, neither black nor perceptibly blue, of one of those indefinitely mixed hues which the modern clothier has produced to harmonize with the religions of respectable men. He has not been out of doors yet to-day; so he still wears his slippers, his boots being ready for him on the hearthrug. Surmising that he has no valet, and seeing that he has no secretary with a shorthand notebook and a typewriter, one meditates on how little our great burgess domesticity* has been disturbed by new fashions and methods, or by the enterprise of the railway and hotel companies which sell you a Saturday to Monday of life at Folkestone as a real gentleman for two guineas, first class fares both ways included.

How old is Roebuck? The question is important on the threshold of a drama of ideas; for under such circumstances everything depends on whether his adolescence belonged to the sixties or to the eighties. He was born, as a matter of fact, in 1839, and was a Unitarian and Free Trader from his boyhood, and an Evolutionist from the publication of the Origin of Species. Consequently he has always classed himself as an advanced thinker and fearlessly outspoken reformer.

Sitting at his writing table, he has on his right the windows giving on Portland Place. Through these, as through a proscenium, the curious spectator may contemplate his profile as well as the blinds will permit. On his left is the inner wall, with a stately bookcase, and the door not quite in the middle, but somewhat further from him. Against the wall opposite him are two busts on pillars: one, to his left, of John Bright; the other, to his right, of Mr. Herbert Spencer. Between them hang an engraved portrait of Richard Cobden; enlarged photographs of Martineau, Huxley, and George Eliot; autotypes of allegories by Mr. G. F. Watts (for Roebuck believes in the fine arts with all the earnestness of a man who does not understand them), and an impression of Dupont's engraving of Delaroche's Beaux Arts hemicycle, representing the great men of all ages. On the wall behind him, above the mantelshelf, is a family portrait of impenetrable obscurity.

A chair stands near the writing table for the convenience of business visitors. Two other chairs are against the wall between the busts.

A parlormaid enters with a visitor's card. Roebuck takes it, and nods, pleased. Evidently a welcome caller.

RAMSDEN. Shew him up.

The parlormaid goes out and returns with the visitor.

THE MAID. Mr. Robinson.

Mr. Robinson is really an uncommonly nice looking young fellow. He must, one thinks, be the jeune premier; for it is not in reason to suppose that a second such attractive male figure should appear in one story. The slim, shapely frame, the elegant suit of new mourning, the small head and regular features, the pretty little moustache, the frank clear eyes,

*the wholesome bloom on the youthful complexion, the well
brushed glossy hair, not curly, but of fine texture and good
dark color, the arch of good nature in the eyebrows, the
erect forehead and neatly pointed chin, all announce the
man who will love and suffer later on. And that he will not
do so without sympathy is guaranteed by an engaging sincerity and eager modest serviceableness which stamp him
as a man of amiable nature. The moment he appears, Ramsden's face expands into fatherly liking and welcome, an expression which drops into one of decorous grief as the young
man approaches him with sorrow in his face as well as in
his black clothes. Ramsden seems to know the nature of the
bereavement. As the visitor advances silently to the writing
table, the old man rises and shakes his hand across it without a word: a long, affectionate shake which tells the story
of a recent sorrow common to both.*

RAMSDEN [*concluding the handshake and cheering up*]
Well, well, Octavius, it's the common lot. We must all face
it some day. Sit down.

*Octavius takes the visitor's chair. Ramsden replaces himself
in his own.*

OCTAVIUS. Yes: we must face it, Mr. Ramsden. But I
owed him a great deal. He did everything for me that my
father could have done if he had lived.

RAMSDEN. He had no son of his own, you see.

OCTAVIUS. But he had daughters; and yet he was as good
to my sister as to me. And his death was so sudden! I always intended to thank him—to let him know that I had
not taken all his care of me as a matter of course, as any
boy takes his father's care. But I waited for an opportunity;
and now he is dead—dropped without a moment's warning.
He will never know what I felt. [*He takes out his handkerchief and cries unaffectedly*.]

RAMSDEN. How do we know that, Octavius? He may
know it: we cannot tell. Come! dont grieve. [*Octavius masters
himself and puts up his handkerchief*]. Thats right. Now let me
tell you something to console you. The last time I saw him—
it was in this very room—he said to me: "Tavy is a generous
lad and the soul of honor; and when I see how little consideration other men get from their sons, I realize how much
better than a son hes been to me." There! Doesnt that do
you good?

OCTAVIUS. Mr. Ramsden: he used to say to me that he

had met only one man in the world who was the soul of honor, and that was Roebuck Ramsden.

RAMSDEN. Oh, that was his partiality: we were very old friends, you know. But there was something else he used to say about you. I wonder whether I ought to tell you or not!

OCTAVIUS. You know best.

RAMSDEN. It was something about his daughter.

OCTAVIUS [*eagerly*] About Ann! Oh, do tell me that, Mr. Ramsden.

RAMSDEN. Well, he said he was glad, after all, you were not his son, because he thought that someday Annie and you —[*Octavius blushes vividly.*] Well, perhaps I shouldn't have told you. But he was in earnest.

OCTAVIUS. Oh, if only I thought I had a chance! You know, Mr. Ramsden, I don't care about money or about what people call position; and I can't bring myself to take an interest in the business of struggling for them. Well, Ann has a most exquisite nature; but she is so accustomed to be in the thick of that sort of thing that she thinks a man's character incomplete if he is not ambitious. She knows that if she married me she would have to reason herself out of being ashamed of me for not being a big success of some kind.

RAMSDEN [*getting up and planting himself with his back to the fireplace*] Nonsense, my boy, nonsense! You're too modest. What does she know about the real value of men at her age? [*More seriously*] Besides, she's a wonderfully dutiful girl. Her father's wish would be sacred to her. Do you know that since she grew up to years of discretion, I don't believe she has ever once given her own wish as a reason for doing anything or not doing it. It's always "Father wishes me to," or "Mother wouldn't like it." It's really almost a fault in her. I have often told her she must learn to think for herself.

OCTAVIUS [*shaking his head*] I couldn't ask her to marry me because her father wished it, Mr. Ramsden.

RAMSDEN. Well, perhaps not. No: of course not. I see that. No: you certainly couldn't. But when you win her on your own merits, it will be a great happiness to her to fulfil her father's desire as well as her own. Eh? Come! you'll ask her, won't you?

OCTAVIUS [*with sad gaiety*] At all events I promise you I shall never ask anyone else.

RAMSDEN. Oh, you shan't need to. She'll accept you, my boy—although [*here he suddenly becomes very serious indeed*] you have one great drawback.

OCTAVIUS [*anxiously*] What drawback is that, Mr. Ramsden? I should rather say which of my many drawbacks?

RAMSDEN. I'll tell you, Octavius. [*He takes from the table a book bound in red cloth*]. I have in my hand a copy of the most infamous, the most scandalous, the most mischievous, the most blackguardly book that ever escaped burning at the hands of the common hangman. I have not read it: I would not soil my mind with such filth; but I have read what the papers say of it. The title is quite enough for me. [*He reads it*]. The Revolutionist's Handbook and Pocket Companion. By John Tanner, M.I.R.C., Member of the Idle Rich Class.

OCTAVIUS [*smiling*] But Jack—

RAMSDEN [*testily*] For goodness' sake, don't call him Jack under my roof [*he throws the book violently down on the table. Then, somewhat relieved, he comes past the table to Octavius, and addresses him at close quarters with impressive gravity*]. Now, Octavius, I know that my dead friend was right when he said you were a generous lad. I know that this man was your schoolfellow, and that you feel bound to stand by him because there was a boyish friendship between you. But I ask you to consider the altered circumstances. You were treated as a son in my friend's house. You lived there; and your friends could not be turned from the door. This man Tanner was in and out there on your account almost from his childhood. He addresses Annie by her Christian name as freely as you do. Well, while her father was alive, that was her father's business, not mine. This man Tanner was only a boy to him: his opinions were something to be laughed at, like a man's hat on a child's head. But now Tanner is a grown man and Annie a grown woman. And her father is gone. We don't as yet know the exact terms of his will; but he often talked it over with me; and I have no more doubt than I have that you're sitting there that the will appoints me Annie's trustee and guardian. [*Forcibly*] Now I tell you, once for all, I can't and I won't have Annie placed in such a position that she must, out of regard for you, suffer the intimacy of this fellow Tanner. It's not fair: it's not right: it's not kind. What are you going to do about it?

OCTAVIUS. But Ann herself has told Jack that whatever his opinions are, he will always be welcome because he knew her dear father.

RAMSDEN [*out of patience*] That girl's mad about her duty to her parents. [*He starts off like a goaded ox in the direction of John Bright, in whose expression there is no sympathy for him. As he speaks he fumes down to Herbert Spencer, who receives him still more coldly*]. Excuse me, Octavius; but there are limits to social toleration. You know that I am not a bigoted or prejudiced man. You know that I am plain Roebuck Ramsden when other men who have done less have got handles to their names, because I have stood for equality and liberty of conscience while they were truckling to the Church and to the aristocracy. Whitefield and I lost chance after chance through our advanced opinions. But I draw the line at Anarchism and Free Love and that sort of thing. If I am to be Annie's guardian, she will have to learn that she has a duty to me. I won't have it: I will not have it. She must forbid John Tanner the house; and so must you.

The parlormaid returns.

OCTAVIUS. But—

RAMSDEN [*calling his attention to the servant*] Ssh! Well?

THE MAID. Mr. Tanner wishes to see you, sir.

RAMSDEN. Mr. Tanner!

OCTAVIUS. Jack!

RAMSDEN. How dare Mr. Tanner call on me! Say I cannot see him.

OCTAVIUS [*hurt*] I am sorry you are turning my friend from your door like that.

THE MAID [*calmly*] He's not at the door, sir. He's upstairs in the drawingroom with Miss Ramsden. He came with Mrs. Whitefield and Miss Ann and Miss Robinson, sir. [*Ramsden's feelings are beyond words.*]

OCTAVIUS [*grinning*] That's very like Jack, Mr. Ramsden. You must see him, even if it's only to turn him out.

RAMSDEN [*hammering out his words with suppressed fury*] Go upstairs and ask Mr. Tanner to be good enough to step down here. [*The parlormaid goes out; and Ramsden returns to the fireplace, as to a fortified position*]. I must say that of all the confounded pieces of impertinence—well, if these are Anarchist manners, I hope you like them. And Annie with him! Annie! A— [*he chokes*].

OCTAVIUS. Yes: that's what surprises me. He's so desperately afraid of Ann. There must be something the matter.

Mr. John Tanner suddenly opens the door and enters. He is too young to be described simply as a big man with a beard. But it is already plain that middle life will find him in that category. He has still some of the slimness of youth; but youthfulness is not the effect he aims at: his frock coat would befit a prime minister; and a certain high chested car-

*riage of the shoulders, a lofty pose of the head; and the
Olympian majesty with which a mane, or rather a huge wisp,
of hazel colored hair is thrown back from an imposing brow,
suggest Jupiter rather than Apollo. He is prodigiously fluent
of speech, restless, excitable [mark the snorting nostril and
the restless blue eye, just the thirty-secondth of an inch too
wide open], possibly a little mad. He is carefully dressed, not
from the vanity that cannot resist finery, but from a sense
of the importance of everything he does which leads him to
make as much of paying a call as other men do of getting
married or laying a foundation stone. A sensitive, susceptible,
exaggerative, earnest man: a megalomaniac, who would be
lost without a sense of humor.*

*Just at present the sense of humor is in abeyance. To say
that he is excited is nothing: all his moods are phases of excitement. He is now in the panic-stricken phase; and he walks
straight up to Ramsden as if with the fixed intention of shooting him on his own hearthrug. But what he pulls from his
breast pocket is not a pistol, but a foolscap document which
he thrusts under the indignant nose of Ramsden as he exclaims—*

TANNER. Ramsden: do you know what that is?

RAMSDEN [*loftily*] No, sir.

TANNER. It's a copy of Whitefield's will. Ann got it this
morning.

RAMSDEN. When you say Ann, you mean, I presume,
Miss Whitefield.

TANNER. I mean our Ann, your Ann, Tavy's Ann, and
now, Heaven help me, my Ann!

OCTAVIUS [*rising, very pale*] What do you mean?

TANNER. Mean! [*He holds up the will*]. Do you know who
is appointed Ann's guardian by this will?

RAMSDEN [*coolly*] I believe I am.

TANNER. You! You and I, man. I! I!! I!!! Both of us!
[*He flings the will down on the writing table*].

RAMSDEN. You! Impossible.

TANNER. It's only too hideously true. [*He throws himself into Octavius's chair*]. Ramsden: get me out of it somehow. You don't know Ann as well as I do. She'll commit
every crime a respectable woman can; and she'll justify every one of them by saying that it was the wish of her guardians. She'll put everything on us; and we shall have no more
control over her than a couple of mice over a cat.

OCTAVIUS. Jack: I wish you wouldn't talk like that about Ann.

TANNER. This chap's in love with her: that's another complication. Well, she'll either jilt him and say I didn't approve of him, or marry him and say you ordered her to. I tell you, this is the most staggering blow that has ever fallen on a man of my age and temperament.

RAMSDEN. Let me see that will, sir. [*He goes to the writing table and picks it up*]. I cannot believe that my old friend Whitefield would have shewn such a want of confidence in me as to associate me with— [*His countenance falls as he reads*].

TANNER. It's all my own doing: that's the horrible irony of it. He told me one day that you were to be Ann's guardian; and like a fool I began arguing with him about the folly of leaving a young woman under the control of an old man with obsolete ideas.

RAMSDEN [*stupended*] My ideas obsolete ! ! ! ! ! ! !

TANNER. Totally. I had just finished an essay called Down with Government by the Greyhaired; and I was full of arguments and illustrations. I said the proper thing was to combine the experience of an old hand with the vitality of a young one. Hang me if he didn't take me at my word and alter his will—it's dated only a fortnight after that conversation—appointing me as joint guardian with you!

RAMSDEN [*pale and determined*] I shall refuse to act.

TANNER. What's the good of that? I've been refusing all the way from Richmond; but Ann keeps on saying that of course she's only an orphan; and that she can't expect the people who were glad to come to the house in her father's time to trouble much about her now. That's the latest game. An orphan! It's like hearing an ironclad talk about being at the mercy of the winds and waves.

OCTAVIUS. This is not fair, Jack. She is an orphan. And you ought to stand by her.

TANNER. Stand by her! What danger is she in? She has the law on her side; she has popular sentiment on her side; she has plenty of money and no conscience. All she wants with me is to load up all her moral responsibilities on me, and do as she likes at the expense of my character. I can't control her; and she can compromise me as much as she likes. I might as well be her husband.

RAMSDEN. You can refuse to accept the guardianship. *I* shall certainly refuse to hold it jointly with you.

TANNER. Yes; and what will she say to that? what does she say to it? Just that her father's wishes are sacred to her, and that she shall always look up to me as her guardian whether I care to face the responsibility or not. Refuse! You might as well refuse to accept the embraces of a boa constrictor when once it gets round your neck.

OCTAVIUS. This sort of talk is not kind to me, Jack.

TANNER [*rising and going to Octavius to console him, but still lamenting*] If he wanted a young guardian, why didn't he appoint Tavy?

RAMSDEN. Ah! why indeed?

OCTAVIUS. I will tell you. He sounded me about it; but I refused the trust because I loved her. I had no right to let myself be forced on her as a guardian by her father. He spoke to her about it; and she said I was right. You know I love her, Mr. Ramsden; and Jack knows it too. If Jack loved a woman, I would not compare her to a boa constrictor in his presence, however much I might dislike her [*he sits down between the busts and turns his face to the wall*].

RAMSDEN. I do not believe that Whitefield was in his right senses when he made that will. You have admitted that he made it under your influence.

TANNER. You ought to be pretty well obliged to me for my influence. He leaves you two thousand five hundred for your trouble. He leaves Tavy a dowry for his sister and five thousand for himself.

OCTAVIUS [*his tears flowing afresh*] Oh, I can't take it. He was too good to us.

TANNER. You won't get it, my boy, if Ramsden upsets the will.

RAMSDEN. Ha! I see. You have got me in a cleft stick.

TANNER. He leaves me nothing but the charge of Ann's morals, on the ground that I have already more money than is good for me. That shews that he had his wits about him, doesn't it?

RAMSDEN [*grimly*] I admit that.

OCTAVIUS [*rising and coming from his refuge by the wall*] Mr. Ramsden: I think you are prejudiced against Jack. He is a man of honor, and incapable of abusing—

TANNER. Don't, Tavy: you'll make me ill. I am not a man of honor: I am a man struck down by a dead hand. Tavy: you must marry her after all and take her off my hands. And I had set my heart on saving you from her!

OCTAVIUS. Oh, Jack, you talk of saving me from my highest happiness.

TANNER. Yes, a lifetime of happiness. If it were only the first half hour's happiness, Tavy, I would buy it for you with my last penny. But a lifetime of happiness! No man alive could bear it: it would be hell on earth.

RAMSDEN [*violently*] Stuff, sir. Talk sense; or else go and waste someone else's time: I have something better to do than listen to your fooleries [*he positively kicks his way to his table and resumes his seat*].

TANNER. You hear him, Tavy! Not an idea in his head later than eighteen sixty. We can't leave Ann with no other guardian to turn to.

RAMSDEN. I am proud of your contempt for my character and opinions, sir. Your own are set forth in that book, I believe.

TANNER [*eagerly going to the table*] What! You've got my book! What do you think of it?

RAMSDEN. Do you suppose I would read such a book, sir?

TANNER. Then why did you buy it?

RAMSDEN. I did not buy it, sir. It has been sent me by some foolish lady who seems to admire your views. I was about to dispose of it when Octavius interrupted me. I shall do so now, with your permission. [*He throws the book into the waste paper basket with such vehemence that Tanner recoils under the impression that it is being thrown at his head*].

TANNER. You have no more manners than I have myself. However, that saves ceremony between us. [*He sits down again*]. What do you intend to do about this will?

OCTAVIUS. May I make a suggestion?

RAMSDEN. Certainly, Octavius.

OCTAVIUS. Aren't we forgetting that Ann herself may have some wishes in this matter?

RAMSDEN. I quite intend that Annie's wishes shall be consulted in every reasonable way. But she is only a woman, and a young and inexperienced woman at that.

TANNER. Ramsden: I begin to pity you.

RAMSDEN [*hotly*] I don't want to know how you feel towards me, Mr. Tanner.

TANNER. Ann will do just exactly what she likes. And what's more, she'll force us to advise her to do it; and she'll put the blame on us if it turns out badly. So, as Tavy is longing to see her—

OCTAVIUS [*shyly*] I am not, Jack.

TANNER. You lie, Tavy: you are. So let's have her down from the drawingroom and ask her what she intends us to do. Off with you, Tavy, and fetch her. [*Tavy turns to go*]. And don't be long; for the strained relations between myself and Ramsden will make the interval rather painful [*Ramsden compresses his lips, but says nothing*].

OCTAVIUS. Never mind him, Mr. Ramsden. He's not serious. [*He goes out*].

RAMSDEN [*very deliberately*] Mr. Tanner: you are the most impudent person I have ever met.

TANNER [*seriously*] I know it, Ramsden. Yet even I cannot wholly conquer shame. We live in an atmosphere of shame. We are ashamed of everything that is real about us; ashamed of ourselves, of our relatives, of our incomes, of our accents, of our opinions, of our experience, just as we are ashamed of our naked skins. Good Lord, my dear Ramsden, we are ashamed to walk, ashamed to ride in an omnibus, ashamed to hire a hansom instead of keeping a carriage, ashamed of keeping one horse instead of two and a groom-gardener instead of a coachman and footman. The more things a man is ashamed of, the more respectable he is. Why, you're ashamed to buy my book, ashamed to read it: the only thing you're not ashamed of is to judge me for it without having read it; and even that only means that you're ashamed to have heterodox opinions. Look at the effect I produce because my fairy godmother withheld from me this gift of shame. I have every possible virtue that a man can have except—

RAMSDEN. I am glad you think so well of yourself.

TANNER. All you mean by that is that you think I ought to be ashamed of talking about my virtues. You don't mean that I haven't got them: you know perfectly well that I am as sober and honest a citizen as yourself, as truthful personally, and much more truthful politically and morally.

RAMSDEN [*touched on his most sensitive point*] I deny that. I will not allow you or any man to treat me as if I were a mere member of the British public. I detest its prejudices; I scorn its narrowness; I demand the right to think for myself. You pose as an advanced man. Let me tell you that I was an advanced man before you were born.

TANNER. I knew it was a long time ago.

RAMSDEN. I am as advanced as ever I was. I defy you to prove that I have ever hauled down the flag. I am more advanced than ever I was. I grow more advanced every day.

TANNER. More advanced in years, Polonius.

RAMSDEN. Polonius! So you are Hamlet, I suppose.

TANNER. No: I am only the most impudent person you've ever met. That's your notion of a thoroughly bad character. When you want to give me a piece of your mind, you ask yourself, as a just and upright man, what is the worst you can fairly say of me. Thief, liar, forger, adulterer, perjurer, glutton, drunkard? Not one of these names fits me. You have to fall back on my deficiency in shame. Well, I admit it. I even congratulate myself; for if I were ashamed of my real self, I should cut as stupid a figure as any of the rest of you. Cultivate a little impudence, Ramsden; and you will become quite a remarkable man.

RAMSDEN. I have no—

TANNER. You have no desire for that sort of notoriety. Bless you, I knew that answer would come as well as I know that a box of matches will come out of an automatic machine when I put a penny in the slot: you would be ashamed to say anything else.

The crushing retort for which Ramsden has been visibly collecting his forces is lost for ever; for at this point Octavius returns with Miss Ann Whitefield and her mother; and Ramsden springs up and hurries to the door to receive them. Whether Ann is good-looking or not depends upon your taste; also and perhaps chiefly on your age and sex. To Octavius she is an enchantingly beautiful woman, in whose presence the world becomes transfigured, and the puny limits of individual consciousness are suddenly made infinite by a mystic memory of the whole life of the race to its beginnings in the east, or even back to the paradise from which it fell. She is to him the reality of romance, the inner good sense of nonsense, the unveiling of his eyes, the freeing of his soul, the abolition of time, place and circumstance, the etherealization of his blood into rapturous rivers of the very water of life itself, the revelation of all the mysteries and the sanctification of all the dogmas. To her mother she is, to put it as moderately as possible, nothing whatever of the kind. Not that Octavius's admiration is in any way ridiculous or discreditable. Ann is a well formed creature, as far as that goes; and she is perfectly ladylike, graceful, and comely, with ensnaring eyes and hair. Besides, instead of making herself

*an eyesore, like her mother, she has devised a mourning cos-
tume of black and violet silk which does honor to her late
father and reveals the family tradition of brave unconven-
tionality by which Ramsden sets such store.*

*But all this is beside the point as an explanation of Ann's
charm. Turn up her nose, give a cast to her eye, replace her
black and violet confection by the apron and feathers of a
flower girl, strike all the aitches out of her speech, and Ann
would still make men dream. Vitality is as common as
humanity; but, like humanity, it sometimes rises to genius;
and Ann is one of the vital geniuses. Not at all, if you please,
an oversexed person: that is a vital defect, not a true excess.
She is a perfectly respectable, perfectly self-controlled woman,
and looks it; though her pose is fashionably frank and impulsive. She inspires confidence as a person who will do
nothing she does not mean to do; also some fear, perhaps, as
a woman who will probably do everything she means to do
without taking more account of other people than may be
necessary and what she calls right. In short, what the weaker
of her own sex sometimes call a cat.*

*Nothing can be more decorous than her entry and her
reception by Ramsden, whom she kisses. The late Mr. Whitefield would be gratified almost to impatience by the long
faces of the men [except Tanner, who is fidgety], the silent
handgrasps, the sympathetic placing of chairs, the sniffing
of the widow, and the liquid eye of the daughter, whose
heart, apparently, will not let her control her tongue to
speech. Ramsden and Octavius take the two chairs from
the wall, and place them for the two ladies; but Ann comes
to Tanner and takes his chair, which he offers with a brusque
gesture, subsequently relieving his irritation by sitting down
on the corner of the writing table with studied indecorum.
Octavius gives Mrs. Whitefield a chair next Ann, and himself takes the vacant one which Ramsden has placed under
the nose of the effigy of Mr. Herbert Spencer.*

*Mrs. Whitefield, by the way, is a little woman, whose faded
flaxen hair looks like straw on an egg. She has an expression
of muddled shrewdness, a squeak of protest in her voice, and
an odd air of continually elbowing away some larger person
who is crushing her into a corner. One guesses her as one of
those women who are conscious of being treated as silly and
negligible, and who, without having strength enough to assert
themselves effectually, at any rate never submit to their fate.*

*There is a touch of chivalry in Octavius's scrupulous attention
to her, even whilst his whole soul is absorbed by Ann.*

*Ramsden goes solemnly back to his magisterial seat at the
writing table, ignoring Tanner, and opens the proceedings.*

RAMSDEN. I am sorry, Annie, to force business on you
at a sad time like the present. But your poor dear father's
will has raised a very serious question. You have read it, I
believe?

*Ann assents with a nod and a catch of her breath, too much
affected to speak.*

I must say I am surprised to find Mr. Tanner named as
joint guardian and trustee with myself of you and Rhoda.
[*A pause. They all look portentous; but they have nothing to
say. Ramsden, a little ruffled by the lack of any response,
continues*] I don't know that I can consent to act under such
conditions. Mr. Tanner has, I understand, some objection
also; but I do not profess to understand its nature: he will
no doubt speak for himself. But we are agreed that we can
decide nothing until we know your views. I am afraid I
shall have to ask you to choose between my sole guardianship
and that of Mr. Tanner; for I fear it is impossible for us to
undertake a joint arrangement.

ANN [*in a low musical voice*] Mamma—

MRS. WHITEFIELD [*hastily*] Now, Ann, I do beg you not
to put it on me. I have no opinion on the subject; and if I
had, it would probably not be attended to. I am quite content with whatever you three think best.

*Tanner turns his head and looks fixedly at Ramsden, who
angrily refuses to receive this mute communication.*

ANN [*resuming in the same gentle voice, ignoring her
mother's bad taste*] Mamma knows that she is not strong
enough to bear the whole responsibility for me and Rhoda
without some help and advice. Rhoda must have a guardian;
and though I am older, I do not think any young unmarried
woman should be left quite to her own guidance. I hope
you agree with me, Granny?

TANNER [*starting*] Granny! Do you intend to call your
guardians Granny?

ANN. Don't be foolish, Jack. Mr. Ramsden has always
been Grandpapa Roebuck to me: I am Granny's Annie; and
he is Annie's Granny. I christened him so when I first
learned to speak.

RAMSDEN [*sarcastically*] I hope you are satisfied, Mr.
Tanner. Go on, Annie: I quite agree with you.

ANN. Well, if I am to have a guardian, can I set aside anybody whom my dear father appointed for me?

RAMSDEN [*biting his lip*] You approve of your father's choice, then?

ANN. It is not for me to approve or disapprove. I accept it. My father loved me and knew best what was good for me.

RAMSDEN. Of course I understand your feeling, Annie. It is what I should have expected of you; and it does you credit. But it does not settle the question so completely as you think. Let me put a case to you. Suppose you were to discover that I had been guilty of some disgraceful action— that I was not the man your poor dear father took me for! Would you still consider it right that I should be Rhoda's guardian?

ANN. I can't imagine you doing anything disgraceful, Granny.

TANNER [*to Ramsden*] You haven't done anything of the sort, have you?

RAMSDEN [*indignantly*] No sir.

MRS. WHITEFIELD [*placidly*] Well, then, why suppose it?

ANN. You see, Granny, Mamma would not like me to suppose it.

RAMSDEN [*much perplexed*] You are both so full of natural and affectionate feeling in these family matters that it is very hard to put the situation fairly before you.

TANNER. Besides, my friend, you are not putting the situation fairly before them.

RAMSDEN [*sulkily*] Put it yourself, then.

TANNER. I will. Ann: Ramsden thinks I am not fit to be your guardian; and I quite agree with him. He considers that if your father had read my book, he wouldn't have appointed me. That book is the disgraceful action he has been talking about. He thinks it's your duty for Rhoda's sake to ask him to act alone and to make me withdraw. Say the word; and I will.

ANN. But I haven't read your book, Jack.

TANNER [*diving at the waste-paper basket and fishing the book out for her*] Then read it at once and decide.

RAMSDEN [*vehemently*] If I am to be your guardian, I positively forbid you to read that book, Annie. [*He smites the table with his fist and rises*].

ANN. Of course not if you don't wish it. [*She puts the book on the table*].

TANNER. If one guardian is to forbid you to read the other guardian's book, how are we to settle it? Suppose I order you to read it! What about your duty to me?

ANN [*gently*] I am sure you would never purposely force me into a painful dilemma, Jack.

RAMSDEN [*irritably*] Yes, yes, Annie: this is all very well, and, as I said, quite natural and becoming. But you must make a choice one way or the other. We are as much in a dilemma as you.

ANN. I feel that I am too young, too inexperienced, to decide. My father's wishes are sacred to me.

MRS. WHITEFIELD. If you two men won't carry them out I must say it is rather hard that you should put the responsibility on Ann. It seems to me that people are always putting things on other people in this world.

RAMSDEN. I am sorry you take it in that way.

ANN [*touchingly*] Do you refuse to accept me as your ward, Granny?

RAMSDEN. No: I never said that. I greatly object to act with Mr. Tanner: that's all.

MRS. WHITEFIELD. Why? What's the matter with poor Jack?

TANNER. My views are too advanced for him.

RAMSDEN [*indignantly*] They are not. I deny it.

ANN. Of course not. What nonsense! Nobody is more advanced than Granny. I am sure it is Jack himself who has made all the difficulty. Come, Jack! be kind to me in my sorrow. You don't refuse to accept me as your ward, do you?

TANNER [*gloomily*] No. I let myself in for it; so I suppose I must face it. [*He turns away to the bookcase, and stands there, moodily studying the titles of the volumes*].

ANN [*rising and expanding with subdued but gushing delight*] Then we are all agreed; and my dear father's will is to be carried out. You don't know what a joy that is to me and to my mother! [*She goes to Ramsden and presses both his hands, saying*] And I shall have my dear Granny to help and advise me. [*She casts a glance at Tanner over her shoulder*]. And Jack the Giant Killer. [*She goes past her mother to Octavius*] And Jack's inseparable friend Ricky-ticky-tavy [*he blushes and looks inexpressibly foolish*].

MRS. WHITEFIELD [*rising and shaking her widow's weeds straight*] Now that you are Ann's guardian, Mr. Ramsden, I wish you would speak to her about her habit of giving people nicknames. They can't be expected to like it. [*She moves towards the door*].

ANN. How can you say such a thing, Mamma! [*Glowing with affectionate remorse*] Oh, I wonder can you be right! Have I been inconsiderate? [*She turns to Octavius, who is sitting astride his chair with his elbows on the back of it. Putting her hand on his forehead she turns his face up suddenly*]. Do you want to be treated like a grown up man? Must I call you Mr. Robinson in future?

OCTAVIUS [*earnestly*] Oh please call me Ricky-ticky-tavy. "Mr. Robinson" would hurt me cruelly. [*She laughs and pats his cheek with her finger; then comes back to Ramsden*]. You know I'm beginning to think that Granny is rather a piece of impertinence. But I never dreamt of its hurting you.

RAMSDEN [*breezily, as he pats her affectionately on the back*] My dear Annie, nonsense. I insist on Granny. I won't answer to any other name than Annie's Granny.

ANN [*gratefully*] You all spoil me, except Jack.

TANNER [*over his shoulder, from the bookcase*] I think you ought to call me Mr. Tanner.

ANN [*gently*] No you don't, Jack. That's like the things you say on purpose to shock people: those who know you pay no attention to them. But, if you like, I'll call you after your famous ancestor Don Juan.

RAMSDEN. Don Juan!

ANN [*innocently*] Oh, is there any harm in it? I didn't know. Then I certainly won't call you that. May I call you Jack until I can think of something else?

TANNER. Oh, for Heaven's sake don't try to invent anything worse. I capitulate. I consent to Jack. I embrace Jack. Here endeth my first and last attempt to assert my authority.

ANN. You see, Mamma, they all really like to have pet names.

MRS. WHITEFIELD. Well, I think you might at least drop them until we are out of mourning.

ANN [*reproachfully, stricken to the soul*] Oh, how could you remind me, mother? [*She hastily leaves the room to conceal her emotion*].

MRS. WHITEFIELD. Of course. My fault as usual! [*She follows Ann*].

TANNER [*coming from the bookcase*] Ramsden: we're beaten—smashed—nonentitized, like her mother.

RAMSDEN. Stuff, sir. [*He follows Mrs. Whitefield out of the room*].

TANNER [*left alone with Octavius, stares whimsically at him*] Tavy: do you want to count for something in the world?

OCTAVIUS. I want to count for something as a poet: I want to write a great play.

TANNER. With Ann as the heroine?

OCTAVIUS. Yes: I confess it.

TANNER. Take care, Tavy. The play with Ann as the heroine is all right; but if you're not very careful, by Heaven she'll marry you.

OCTAVIUS [*sighing*] No such luck, Jack!

TANNER. Why, man, your head is in the lioness's mouth: you are half swallowed already—in three bites—Bite One, Ricky; Bite Two, Ticky; Bite Three, Tavy; and down you go.

OCTAVIUS. She is the same to everybody, Jack: you know her ways.

TANNER. Yes: she breaks everybody's back with the stroke of her paw; but the question is, which of us will she eat? My own opinion is that she means to eat you.

OCTAVIUS [*rising, pettishly*] It's horrible to talk like that about her when she is upstairs crying for her father. But I do so want her to eat me that I can bear your brutalities because they give me hope.

TANNER. Tavy; that's the devilish side of a woman's fascination: she makes you will your own destruction.

OCTAVIUS. But it's not destruction: it's fulfilment.

TANNER. Yes, of her purpose; and that purpose is neither her happiness nor yours, but Nature's. Vitality in a woman is a blind fury of creation. She sacrifices herself to it: do you think she will hesitate to sacrifice you?

OCTAVIUS. Why, it is just because she is self-sacrificing that she will not sacrifice those she loves.

TANNER. That is the profoundest of mistakes, Tavy. It is the self-sacrificing women that sacrifice others most recklessly. Because they are unselfish, they are kind in little things. Because they have a purpose which is not their own purpose, but that of the whole universe, a man is nothing to them but an instrument of that purpose.

OCTAVIUS. Don't be ungenerous, Jack. They take the tenderest care of us.

TANNER. Yes, as a soldier takes care of his rifle or a musician of his violin. But do they allow us any purpose or freedom of our own? Will they lend us to one another? Can the strongest man escape from them when once he is appropriated? They tremble when we are in danger, and weep when we die; but the tears are not for us, but for a father wasted, a son's breeding thrown away. They accuse us of treating them as a mere means to our pleasure; but how can so feeble and transient a folly as a man's selfish pleasure enslave a woman as the whole purpose of Nature embodied in a woman can enslave a man?

OCTAVIUS. What matter, if the slavery makes us happy?

TANNER. No matter at all if you have no purpose of your own, and are, like most men, a mere breadwinner. But you, Tavy, are an artist: that is, you have a purpose as absorbing and as unscrupulous as a woman's purpose.

OCTAVIUS. Not unscrupulous.

TANNER. Quite unscrupulous. The true artist will let his wife starve, his children go barefoot, his mother drudge for his living at seventy, sooner than work at anything but his art. To women he is half vivisector, half vampire. He gets into intimate relations with them to study them, to strip the mask of convention from them, to surprise their inmost secrets, knowing that they have the power to rouse his deepest creative energies, to rescue him from his cold reason, to make him see visions and dream dreams, to inspire him, as he calls it. He persuades women that they may do this for their own purpose whilst he really means them to do it for his. He steals the mother's milk and blackens it to make printer's ink to scoff at her and glorify ideal women with. He pretends to spare her the pangs of child-bearing so that he may have for himself the tenderness and fostering that belong of right to her children. Since marriage began, the great artist has been known as a bad husband. But he is worse: he is a child-robber, a blood-sucker, a hypocrite and a cheat. Perish the race and wither a thousand women if only the sacrifice of them enable him to act Hamlet better, to paint a finer picture, to write a deeper poem, a greater play, a profounder philosophy! For mark you, Tavy, the artist's work is to shew us ourselves as we really are. Our minds are nothing but this knowledge of ourselves; and he who adds a jot to such knowledge creates new mind as surely as any woman creates new men. In the rage of that creation he is as ruthless as the woman, as dangerous to her as she to him, and as horribly fascinating. Of all human struggles there is none so treacherous and remorseless as the struggle between the artist man and the mother woman. Which shall use up the other? that is the issue between them. And it is all the deadlier because, in your romanticist cant, they love one another.

OCTAVIUS. Even if it were so—and I don't admit it for a moment—it is out of the deadliest struggles that we get the noblest characters.

TANNER. Remember that the next time you meet a grizzly bear or a Bengal tiger, Tavy.

OCTAVIUS. I meant where there is love, Jack.

TANNER. Oh, the tiger will love you. There is no love sincerer than the love of food. I think Ann loves you that way: she patted your cheek as if it were a nicely underdone chop.

OCTAVIUS. You know, Jack, I should have to run away from you if I did not make it a fixed rule not to mind anything you say. You come out with perfectly revolting things sometimes.

Ramsden returns, followed by Ann. They come in quickly, with their former leisurely air of decorous grief changed to one of genuine concern, and, on Ramsden's part, of worry. He comes between the two men, intending to address Octavius, but pulls himself up abruptly as he sees Tanner.

RAMSDEN. I hardly expected to find you still here, Mr. Tanner.

TANNER. Am I in the way? Good morning, fellow guardian [*he goes towards the door*].

ANN. Stop, Jack. Granny: he must know, sooner or later.

RAMSDEN. Octavius: I have a very serious piece of news for you. It is of the most private and delicate nature—of the most painful nature too, I am sorry to say. Do you wish Mr. Tanner to be present whilst I explain?

OCTAVIUS [*turning pale*] I have no secrets from Jack.

RAMSDEN. Before you decide that finally, let me say that the news concerns your sister, and that it is terrible news.

OCTAVIUS. Violet! What has happened? Is she—dead?

RAMSDEN. I am not sure that it is not even worse than that.

OCTAVIUS. Is she badly hurt? Has there been an accident?

RAMSDEN. No: nothing of that sort.

TANNER. Ann: will you have the common humanity to tell us what the matter is?

ANN [*half whispering*] I can't. Violet has done something dreadful. We shall have to get her away somewhere. [*She flutters to the writing table and sits in Ramsden's chair, leaving the three men to fight it out between them*].

OCTAVIUS [*enlightened*] Is that what you meant, Mr. Ramsden?

RAMSDEN. Yes. [*Octavius sinks upon a chair, crushed*]. I am afraid there is no doubt that Violet did not really go to Eastbourne three weeks ago when we thought she was with the Parry Whitefields. And she called on a strange doctor yesterday with a wedding ring on her finger. Mrs. Parry Whitefield met her there by chance; and so the whole thing came out.

OCTAVIUS [*rising with his fists clenched*] Who is the scoundrel?

ANN. She won't tell us.

OCTAVIUS [*collapsing into the chair again*] What a frightful thing!

TANNER [*with angry sarcasm*] Dreadful. Appalling. Worse than death, as Ramsden says. [*He comes to Octavius*]. What would you not give, Tavy, to turn it into a railway accident, with all her bones broken, or something equally respectable and deserving of sympathy?

OCTAVIUS. Don't be brutal, Jack.

TANNER. Brutal! Good Heavens, man, what are you crying for? Here is a woman whom we all supposed to be making bad water color sketches, practising Grieg and Brahms, gadding about to concerts and parties, wasting her life and her money. We suddenly learn that she has turned from these sillinesses to the fulfilment of her highest purpose and greatest function—to increase, multiply and replenish the earth. And instead of admiring her courage and rejoicing in her instinct; instead of crowning the completed womanhood and raising the triumphal strain of "Unto us a child is born: unto us a son is given," here you are—you who have been as merry as grigs in your mourning for the dead—all pulling long faces and looking as ashamed and disgraced as if the girl had committed the vilest of crimes.

RAMSDEN [*roaring with rage*] I will not have these abominations uttered in my house [*he smites the writing table with his fist*].

TANNER. Look here: if you insult me again I'll take you at your word and leave your house. Ann: where is Violet now?

ANN. Why? Are you going to her?

TANNER. Of course I am going to her. She wants help; she wants money; she wants respect and congratulation; she wants every chance for her child. She does not seem likely to get it from you: she shall from me. Where is she?

ANN. Don't be so headstrong, Jack. She's upstairs.

TANNER. What! Under Ramsden's sacred roof! Go and do your miserable duty, Ramsden. Hunt her out into the street. Cleanse your threshold from her contamination. Vindicate the purity of your English home. I'll go for a cab.

ANN [*alarmed*] Oh, Granny, you mustn't do that.

OCTAVIUS [*broken-heartedly, rising*] I'll take her away, Mr. Ramsden. She had no right to come to your house.

RAMSDEN [*indignantly*] But I am only too anxious to help her. [*Turning on Tanner*] How dare you, sir, impute such monstrous intentions to me? I protest against it. I am ready to put down my last penny to save her from being driven to run to you for protection.

TANNER [*subsiding*] It's all right, then. He's not going to act up to his principles. It's agreed that we all stand by Violet.

OCTAVIUS. But who is the man? He can make reparation by marrying her; and he shall, or he shall answer for it to me.

RAMSDEN. He shall, Octavius. There you speak like a man.

TANNER. Then you don't think him a scoundrel, after all?

OCTAVIUS. Not a scoundrel! He is a heartless scoundrel.

RAMSDEN. A damned scoundrel. I beg your pardon, Annie; but I can say no less.

TANNER. So we are to marry your sister to a damned scoundrel by way of reforming her character! On my soul, I think you are all mad.

ANN. Don't be absurd, Jack. Of course you are quite right, Tavy; but we don't know who he is: Violet won't tell us.

TANNER. What on earth does it matter who he is? He's done his part; and Violet must do the rest.

RAMSDEN [*beside himself*]. Stuff! lunacy! There is a rascal in our midst, a libertine, a villain worse than a murderer; and we are not to learn who he is! In our ignorance we are to shake him by the hand; to introduce him into our homes; to trust our daughters with him; to—to——

ANN [*coaxingly*] There, Granny, don't talk so loud. It's most shocking: we must all admit that; but if Violet won't tell us, what can we do? Nothing. Simply nothing.

RAMSDEN. Hmph! I'm not so sure of that. If any man

has paid Violet any special attention, we can easily find that out. If there is any man of notoriously loose principles among us—

TANNER. Ahem!

RAMSDEN [*raising his voice*] Yes sir, I repeat, if there is any man of notoriously loose principles among us—

TANNER. Or any man notoriously lacking in self-control.

RAMSDEN [*aghast*] Do you dare to suggest that *I* am capable of such an act?

TANNER. My dear Ramsden, this is an act of which every man is capable. That is what comes of getting at cross purposes with Nature. The suspicion you have just flung at me clings to us all. It's a sort of mud that sticks to the judge's ermine or the cardinal's robe as fast as to the rags of the tramp. Come, Tavy: don't look so bewildered: it might have been me: it might have been Ramsden; just as it might have been anybody. If it had, what could we do but lie and protest—as Ramsden is going to protest.

RAMSDEN [*choking*] I—I—I—

TANNER. Guilt itself could not stammer more confusedly. And yet you know perfectly well he's innocent, Tavy.

RAMSDEN [*exhausted*] I am glad you admit that, sir. I admit, myself, that there is an element of truth in what you say, grossly as you may distort it to gratify your malicious humor. I hope, Octavius, no suspicion of me is possible in your mind.

OCTAVIUS. Of you! No, not for a moment.

TANNER [*drily*] I think he suspects me just a little.

OCTAVIUS. Jack: you couldn't—you wouldn't—

TANNER. Why not?

OCTAVIUS [*appalled*] Why not!

TANNER. Oh, well, I'll tell you why not. First, you would feel bound to quarrel with me. Second, Violet doesn't like me. Third, if I had the honor of being the father of Violet's child, I should boast of it instead of denying it. So be easy: our friendship is not in danger.

OCTAVIUS. I should have put away the suspicion with horror if only you would think and feel naturally about it. I beg your pardon.

TANNER. My pardon! nonsense! And now let's sit down and have a family council. [*He sits down. The rest follow his example, more or less under protest*]. Violet is going to do the State a service; consequently she must be packed

abroad like a criminal until it's over. What's happening upstairs?

ANN. Violet is in the housekeeper's room—by herself,
of course.

TANNER. Why not in the drawingroom?

ANN. Don't be absurd, Jack. Miss Ramsden is in the
drawingroom with my mother, considering what to do.

TANNER. Oh! the housekeeper's room is the peniten-
tiary, I suppose; and the prisoner is waiting to be brought before her judges. The old cats!

ANN. Oh, Jack!

RAMSDEN. You are at present a guest beneath the roof
of one of the old cats, sir. My sister is the mistress of this
house.

TANNER. She would put me in the housekeeper's room,
too, if she dared, Ramsden. However, I withdraw cats. Cats
would have more sense. Ann: as your guardian, I order you
to go to Violet at once and be particularly kind to her.

ANN. I have seen her, Jack. And I am sorry to say I
am afraid she is going to be rather obstinate about going
abroad. I think Tavy ought to speak to her about it.

OCTAVIUS. How can I speak to her about such a thing
[*he breaks down*]?

ANN. Don't break down, Ricky. Try to bear it for all
our sakes.

RAMSDEN. Life is not all plays and poems, Octavius.
Come! face it like a man.

TANNER [*chafing again*] Poor dear brother! Poor dear
friends of the family! Poor dear Tabbies and Grimalkins!
Poor dear everybody except the woman who is going to risk
her life to create another life! Tavy: don't you be a selfish
ass. Away with you and talk to Violet; and bring her down
here if she cares to come. [*Octavius rises*]. Tell her we'll
stand by her.

RAMSDEN [*rising*] No, sir—

TANNER. [*rising also and interrupting him*] Oh, we understand: it's against your conscience; but still you'll do it.

OCTAVIUS. I assure you all, on my word, I never meant
to be selfish. It's so hard to know what to do when one
wishes earnestly to do right.

TANNER. My dear Tavy, your pious English habit of regarding the world as a moral gymnasium built expressly to
strengthen your character in, occasionally leads you to think
about your own confounded principles when you should be

thinking about other people's necessities. The need of the
present hour is a happy mother and a healthy baby. Bend
your energies on that; and you will see your way clearly
enough.

Octavius, much perplexed, goes out.

RAMSDEN [*facing Tanner impressively*] And Morality,
sir? What is to become of that?

TANNER. Meaning a weeping Magdalen and an innocent
child branded with her shame. Not in our circle, thank you.
Morality can go to its father the devil.

RAMSDEN. I thought so, sir. Morality sent to the devil to
please our libertines, male and female. That is to be the
future of England, is it?

TANNER. Oh, England will survive your disapproval.
Meanwhile, I understand that you agree with me as to the
practical course we are to take?

RAMSDEN. Not in your spirit, sir. Not for your reasons.

TANNER. You can explain that if anybody calls you to
account, here or hereafter. [*He turns away, and plants himself in front of Mr. Herbert Spencer, at whom he stares
gloomily*].

ANN [*rising and coming to Ramsden*] Granny: hadn't
you better go up to the drawingroom and tell them what we
intend to do?

RAMSDEN [*looking pointedly at Tanner*] I hardly like to
leave you alone with this gentleman. Will you not come with
me?

ANN. Miss Ramsden would not like to speak about it
before me, Granny. I ought not to be present.

RAMSDEN. You are right: I should have thought of that.
You are a good girl, Annie.

*He pats her on the shoulder. She looks up at him with
beaming eyes; and he goes out, much moved. Having disposed
of him, she looks at Tanner. His back being turned to her, she
gives a moment's attention to her personal appearance, then
softly goes to him and speaks almost into his ear.*

ANN. Jack [*he turns with a start*]: are you glad that you
are my guardian? You don't mind being made responsible
for me, I hope.

TANNER. The latest addition to your collection of scape-
goats, eh?

ANN. Oh, that stupid old joke of yours about me! Do
please drop it. Why do you say things that you know must
pain me? I do my best to please you, Jack: I suppose I

may tell you so now that you are my guardian. You will make me so unhappy if you refuse to be friends with me.

TANNER [*studying her as gloomily as he studied the bust*] You need not go begging for my regard. How unreal our moral judgments are! You seem to me to have absolutely no conscience—only hypocrisy; and you can't see the difference—yet there is a sort of fascination about you. I always attend to you, somehow. I should miss you if I lost you.

ANN [*tranquilly slipping her arm into his and walking about with him*] But isn't that only natural, Jack? We have known each other since we were children. Do you remember—

TANNER [*abruptly breaking loose*] Stop! I remember everything.

ANN. Oh, I daresay we were often very silly; but—

TANNER. I won't have it, Ann. I am no more that schoolboy now than I am the dotard of ninety I shall grow into if I live long enough. It is over: let me forget it.

ANN. Wasn't it a happy time? [*She attempts to take his arm again*].

TANNER. Sit down and behave yourself. [*He makes her sit down in the chair next the writing table*]. No doubt it was a happy time for you. You were a good girl and never compromised yourself. And yet the wickedest child that ever was slapped could hardly have had a better time. I can understand the success with which you bullied the other girls: your virtue imposed on them. But tell me this: did you ever know a good boy?

ANN. Of course. All boys are foolish sometimes; but Tavy was always a really good boy.

TANNER [*struck by this*] Yes: you're right. For some reason you never tempted Tavy.

ANN. Tempted! Jack!

TANNER. Yes, my dear Lady Mephistopheles, tempted. You were insatiably curious as to what a boy might be capable of, and diabolically clever at getting through his guard and surprising his inmost secrets.

ANN. What nonsense! All because you used to tell me long stories of the wicked things you had done—silly boys' tricks! And you call such things inmost secrets! Boys' secrets are just like men's; and you know what they are!

TANNER [*obstinately*] No I don't. What are they, pray?

ANN. Why, the things they tell everybody, of course.

TANNER. Now I swear I told you things I told no one

else. You lured me into a compact by which we were to have no secrets from one another. We were to tell one another everything. I didn't notice that you never told me anything.

ANN. You didn't want to talk about me, Jack. You wanted to talk about yourself.

TANNER. Ah, true, horribly true. But what a devil of a child you must have been to know that weakness and to play on it for the satisfaction of your own curiosity! I wanted to brag to you, to make myself interesting. And I found myself doing all sorts of mischievous things simply to have something to tell you about. I fought with boys I didn't hate; I lied about things I might just as well have told the truth about; I stole things I didn't want; I kissed little girls I didn't care for. It was all bravado: passionless and therefore unreal.

ANN. I never told of you, Jack.

TANNER. No; but if you had wanted to stop me you would have told of me. You wanted me to go on.

ANN [flashing out] Oh, that's not true: it's not true, Jack. I never wanted you to do those dull, disappointing, brutal, stupid, vulgar things. I always hoped that it would be something really heroic at last. [Recovering herself] Excuse me, Jack; but the things you did were never a bit like the things I wanted you to do. They often gave me great uneasiness; but I could not tell on you and get you into trouble. And you were only a boy. I knew you would grow out of them. Perhaps I was wrong.

TANNER [sardonically] Do not give way to remorse, Ann. At least nineteen twentieths of the exploits I confessed to you were pure lies. I soon noticed that you didn't like the true stories.

ANN. Of course I knew that some of the things couldn't have happened. But—

TANNER. You are going to remind me that some of the most disgraceful ones did.

ANN [fondly, to his great terror] I don't want to remind you of anything. But I knew the people they happened to, and heard about them.

TANNER. Yes; but even the true stories were touched up for telling. A sensitive boy's humiliations may be very good fun for ordinary thickskinned grown-ups; but to the boy himself they are so acute, so ignominious, that he cannot confess them—cannot but deny them passionately. However, perhaps it was as well for me that I romanced a bit; for, on the one occasion when I told you the truth, you threatened to tell of me.

ANN. Oh, never. Never once.

TANNER. Yes, you did. Do you remember a dark-eyed girl named Rachel Rosetree? [*Ann's brows contract for an instant involuntarily*]. I got up a love affair with her; and we met one night in the garden and walked about very uncomfortably with our arms round one another, and kissed at parting, and were most conscientiously romantic. If that love affair had gone on, it would have bored me to death; but it didn't go on; for the next thing that happened was that Rachel cut me because she found out that I had told you. How did she find it out? From you. You went to her and held the guilty secret over her head, leading her a life of abject terror and humiliation by threatening to tell on her.

ANN. And a very good thing for her, too. It was my duty to stop her misconduct; and she is thankful to me for it now.

TANNER. Is she?

ANN. She ought to be, at all events.

TANNER. It was not your duty to stop my misconduct, I suppose.

ANN. I did stop it by stopping her.

TANNER. Are you sure of that? You stopped my telling you about my adventures; but how do you know that you stopped the adventures?

ANN. Do you mean to say that you went on in the same way with other girls?

TANNER. No. I had enough of that sort of romantic tomfoolery with Rachel.

ANN [*unconvinced*] Then why did you break off our confidences and become quite strange to me?

TANNER [*enigmatically*] It happened just then that I got something that I wanted to keep all to myself instead of sharing it with you.

ANN. I am sure I shouldn't have asked for any of it if you had grudged it.

TANNER. It wasn't a box of sweets, Ann. It was something you'd never have let me call my own.

ANN [*incredulously*] What?

TANNER. My soul.

ANN. Oh, do be sensible, Jack. You know you're talking nonsense.

TANNER. The most solemn earnest, Ann. You didn't notice at that time that you were getting a soul too. But you were. It was not for nothing that you suddenly found you had a moral duty to chastise and reform Rachel. Up to that time you had traded pretty extensively in being a good child; but you had never set up a sense of duty to others. Well, I set one up too. Up to that time I had played the boy buccaneer with no more conscience than a fox in a poultry farm. But now I began to have scruples, to feel obligations, to find that veracity and honor were no longer goody-goody expressions in the mouths of grown up people, but compelling principles in myself.

ANN [quietly] Yes, I suppose you're right. You were beginning to be a man, and I to be a woman.

TANNER. Are you sure it was not that we were beginning to be something more? What does the beginning of manhood and womanhood mean in most people's mouths? You know: it means the beginning of love. But love began long before that for me. Love played its part in the earliest dreams and follies and romances I can remember—may I say the earliest follies and romances we can remember?—though we did not understand it at the time. No: the change that came to me was the birth in me of moral passion; and I declare that according to my experience moral passion is the only real passion.

ANN. All passions ought to be moral, Jack.

TANNER. Ought! Do you think that anything is strong enough to impose oughts on a passion except a stronger passion still?

ANN. Our moral sense controls passion, Jack. Don't be stupid.

TANNER. Our moral sense! And is that not a passion? Is the devil to have all the passions as well as all the good tunes? If it were not a passion—if it were not the mightiest of the passions, all the other passions would sweep it away like a leaf before a hurricane. It is the birth of that passion that turns a child into a man.

ANN. There are other passions, Jack. Very strong ones.

TANNER. All the other passions were in me before; but they were idle and aimless—mere childish greedinesses and cruelties, curiosities and fancies, habits and superstitions, grotesque and ridiculous to the mature intelligence. When they suddenly began to shine like newly lit flames it was by no light of their own, but by the radiance of the dawning moral passion. That passion dignified them, gave them conscience and meaning, found them a mob of appetites and organized them into an army of purposes and principles. My soul was born of that passion.

ANN. I noticed that you got more sense. You were a dreadfully destructive boy before that.

TANNER. Destructive! Stuff! I was only mischievous.

ANN. Oh Jack, you were very destructive. You ruined all the young fir trees by chopping off their leaders with a wooden sword. You broke all the cucumber frames with your catapult. You set fire to the common: the police arrested Tavy for it because he ran away when he couldn't stop you. You—

TANNER. Pooh! pooh! pooh! these were battles, bombardments, stratagems to save our scalps from the red Indians. You have no imagination, Ann. I am ten times more destructive now than I was then. The moral passion has taken my destructiveness in hand and directed it to moral ends. I have become a reformer, and, like all reformers, an iconoclast. I no longer break cucumber frames and burn gorse bushes: I shatter creeds and demolish idols.

ANN [bored] I am afraid I am too feminine to see any sense in destruction. Destruction can only destroy.

TANNER. Yes. That is why it is so useful. Construction cumbers the ground with institutions made by busybodies. Destruction clears it and gives us breathing space and liberty.

ANN. It's no use, Jack. No woman will agree with you there.

TANNER. That's because you confuse construction and destruction with creation and murder. They're quite different: I adore creation and abhor murder. Yes: I adore it in tree and flower, in bird and beast, even in you. [A flush of interest and delight suddenly chases the growing perplexity and boredom from her face]. It was the creative instinct that led you to attach me to you by bonds that have left their mark on me to this day. Yes, Ann: the old childish compact between us was an unconscious love compact—

ANN. Jack!

TANNER. Oh, don't be alarmed—

ANN. I am not alarmed.

TANNER [whimsically] Then you ought to be: where are your principles?

ANN. Jack: are you serious or are you not?

TANNER. Do you mean about the moral passion?

ANN. No, no; the other one. [*Confused*] Oh! you are so silly: one never knows how to take you.

TANNER. You must take me quite seriously. I am your guardian; and it is my duty to improve your mind.

ANN. The love compact is over, then, is it? I suppose you grew tired of me?

TANNER. No; but the moral passion made our childish relations impossible. A jealous sense of my new individuality arose in me—

ANN. You hated to be treated as a boy any longer. Poor Jack!

TANNER. Yes, because to be treated as a boy was to be taken on the old footing. I had become a new person; and those who knew the old person laughed at me. The only man who behaved sensibly was my tailor: he took my measure anew every time he saw me, whilst all the rest went on with their old measurements and expected them to fit me.

ANN. You became frightfully self-conscious.

TANNER. When you go to heaven, Ann, you will be frightfully conscious of your wings for the first year or so. When you meet your relatives there, and they persist in treating you as if you were still a mortal, you will not be able to bear them. You will try to get into a circle which has never known you except as an angel.

ANN. So it was only your vanity that made you run away from us after all?

TANNER. Yes, only my vanity, as you call it.

ANN. You need not have kept away from me on that account.

TANNER. From you above all others. You fought harder than anybody against my emancipation.

ANN [*earnestly*] Oh, how wrong you are! I would have done anything for you.

TANNER. Anything except let me get loose from you. Even then you had acquired by instinct that damnable woman's trick of heaping obligations on a man, of placing yourself so entirely and helplessly at his mercy that at last he dare not take a step without running to you for leave. I know a poor wretch whose one desire in life is to run away from his wife. She prevents him by threatening to throw herself in front of the engine of the train he leaves her in. That is what all women do. If we try to go where you do not want us to go there is no law to prevent us; but when we take the first step your breasts are under our foot as it descends: your bodies are under our wheels as we start. No woman shall ever enslave me in that way.

ANN. But, Jack, you cannot get through life without considering other people a little.

TANNER. Ay; but what other people? It is this consideration of other people—or rather this cowardly fear of them which we call consideration—that makes us the sentimental slaves we are. To consider you, as you call it, is to substitute your will for my own. How if it be a baser will than mine? Are women taught better than men or worse? Are mobs of voters taught better than statesmen or worse? Worse, of course, in both cases. And then what sort of world are you going to get, with its public men considering its voting mobs, and its private men considering their wives? What does Church and State mean nowadays? The Woman and the Ratepayer.

ANN [*placidly*] I am so glad you understand politics, Jack: it will be most useful to you if you go into parliament [*he collapses like a pricked bladder*]. But I am sorry you thought my influence a bad one.

TANNER. I don't say it was a bad one. But bad or good, I didn't choose to be cut to your measure. And I won't be cut to it.

ANN. Nobody wants you to, Jack. I assure you—really on my word—I don't mind your queer opinions one little bit. You know we have all been brought up to have advanced opinions. Why do you persist in thinking me so narrow minded?

TANNER. That's the danger of it. I know you don't mind, because you've found out that it doesn't matter. The boa constrictor doesn't mind the opinions of a stag one little bit when once she has got her coils round it.

ANN [*rising in sudden enlightenment*] O-o-o-o-oh! *now* I understand why you warned Tavy that I am a boa constrictor. Granny told me. [*She laughs and throws her boa round his neck*]. Doesn't it feel nice and soft, Jack?

TANNER [*in the toils*] You scandalous woman, will you throw away even your hypocrisy?

ANN. I am never hypocritical with you, Jack. Are you angry? [*She withdraws the boa and throws it on a chair*]. Perhaps I shouldn't have done that.

TANNER [*contemptuously*] Pooh, prudery! Why should you not, if it amuses you?

ANN [*shyly*] Well, because—because I suppose what you

really mean by the boa constrictor was this [*she puts her arms round his neck*].

TANNER [*staring at her*] Magnificent audacity! [*She laughs and pats his cheeks*]. Now just to think that if I mentioned this episode not a soul would believe me except the people who would cut me for telling, whilst if you accused me of it nobody would believe my denial!

ANN [*taking her arms away with perfect dignity*] You are incorrigible, Jack. But you should not jest about our affection for one another. Nobody could possibly misunderstand it. You do not misunderstand it, I hope.

TANNER. My blood interprets for me, Ann. Poor Ricky Ticky Tavy!

ANN [*looking quickly at him as if this were a new light*] Surely you are not so absurd as to be jealous of Tavy.

TANNER. Jealous! Why should I be? But I don't wonder at your grip of him. I feel the coils tightening round my very self, though you are only playing with me.

ANN. Do you think I have designs on Tavy?

TANNER. I know you have.

ANN [*earnestly*] Take care, Jack. You may make Tavy very unhappy if you mislead him about me.

TANNER. Never fear: he will not escape you.

ANN. I wonder are you really a clever man!

TANNER. Why this sudden misgiving on the subject?

ANN. You seem to understand all the things I don't understand; but you are a perfect baby in the things I do understand.

TANNER. I understand how Tavy feels for you, Ann: you may depend on that, at all events.

ANN. And you think you understand how I feel for Tavy, don't you?

TANNER. I know only too well what is going to happen to poor Tavy.

ANN. I should laugh at you, Jack, if it were not for poor papa's death. Mind! Tavy will be very unhappy.

TANNER. Yes; but he won't know it, poor devil. He is a thousand times too good for you. That's why he is going to make the mistake of his life about you.

ANN. I think men make more mistakes by being too clever than by being too good [*she sits down, with a trace of contempt for the whole male sex in the elegant carriage of her shoulders*].

TANNER. Oh, I know you don't care very much about

Tavy. But there is always one who kisses and one who only allows the kiss. Tavy will kiss; and you will only turn the cheek. And you will throw him over if anybody better turns up.

ANN [*offended*] You have no right to say such things, Jack. They are not true, and not delicate. If you and Tavy choose to be stupid about me, that is not my fault.

TANNER [*remorsefully*] Forgive my brutalities, Ann. They are levelled at this wicked world, not at you. [*She looks up at him, pleased and forgiving. He becomes cautious at once*]. All the same, I wish Ramsden would come back. I never feel safe with you: there is a devilish charm—or no: not a charm, a subtle interest [*she laughs*]—Just so: you know it; and you triumph in it. Openly and shamelessly triumph in it!

ANN. What a shocking flirt you are, Jack!

TANNER. A flirt! ! I ! ! !

ANN. Yes, a flirt. You are always abusing and offending people; but you never really mean to let go your hold of them.

TANNER. I will ring the bell. This conversation has already gone further than I intended.

Ramsden and Octavius come back with Miss Ramsden, a hardheaded old maiden lady in a plain brown silk gown, with enough rings, chains and brooches to shew that her plainness of dress is a matter of principle, not of poverty. She comes into the room very determinedly: the two men, perplexed and downcast, following her. Ann rises and goes eagerly to meet her. Tanner retreats to the wall between the busts and pretends to study the pictures. Ramsden goes to his table as usual; and Octavius clings to the neighborhood of Tanner.

MISS RAMSDEN [*almost pushing Ann aside as she comes to Mrs. Whitefield's chair and plants herself there resolutely*] I wash my hands of the whole affair.

OCTAVIUS [*very wretched*] I know you wish me to take Violet away, Miss Ramsden. I will. [*He turns irresolutely to the door*].

RAMSDEN. No no—

MISS RAMSDEN. What is the use of saying no, Roebuck? Octavius knows that I would not turn any truly contrite and repentant woman from your doors. But when a woman is not only wicked, but intends to go on being wicked, she and I part company.

ANN. Oh, Miss Ramsden, what do you mean? What has Violet said?

RAMSDEN. Violet is certainly very obstinate. She won't leave London. I don't understand her.

MISS RAMSDEN. I do. It's as plain as the nose on your face, Roebuck, that she won't go because she doesn't want to be separated from this man, whoever he is.

ANN. Oh, surely, surely! Octavius: did you speak to her?

OCTAVIUS. She won't tell us anything. She won't make any arrangement until she has consulted somebody. It can't be anybody else than the scoundrel who has betrayed her.

TANNER [to Octavius] Well, let her consult him. He will be glad enough to have her sent abroad. Where is the difficulty?

MISS RAMSDEN [taking the answer out of Octavius's mouth] The difficulty, Mr. Jack, is that when I offered to help her I didn't offer to become her accomplice in her wickedness. She either pledges her word never to see that man again, or else she finds some new friends; and the sooner the better. The parlormaid appears at the door. Ann hastily resumes her seat, and looks as unconcerned as possible. Octavius instinctively imitates her.

THE MAID. The cab is at the door, ma'am.

MISS RAMSDEN. What cab?

THE MAID. For Miss Robinson.

MISS RAMSDEN. Oh! [Recovering herself] All right. [The maid withdraws]. She has sent for a cab.

TANNER. I wanted to send for that cab half an hour ago.

MISS RAMSDEN. I am glad she understands the position she has placed herself in.

RAMSDEN. I don't like her going away in this fashion, Susan. We had better not do anything harsh.

OCTAVIUS. No: thank you again and again; but Miss Ramsden is quite right. Violet cannot expect to stay.

ANN. Hadn't you better go with her, Tavy?

OCTAVIUS. She won't have me.

MISS RAMSDEN. Of course she won't. She's going straight to that man.

TANNER. As a natural result of her virtuous reception here.

RAMSDEN [much troubled] There, Susan! You hear! and there's some truth in it. I wish you could reconcile it with your principles to be a little patient with this poor girl. She's very young; and there's a time for everything.

MISS RAMSDEN. Oh, she will get all the sympathy she wants from the men. I'm surprised at you, Roebuck.

TANNER. So am I, Ramsden, most favorably.

Violet appears at the door. She is as impenitent and self-possessed a young lady as one would desire to see among the best behaved of her sex. Her small head and tiny resolute mouth and chin; her haughty crispness of speech and trimness of carriage; the ruthless elegance of her equipment, which includes a very smart hat with a dead bird in it, mark a personality which is as formidable as it is exquisitely pretty. She is not a siren, like Ann: admiration comes to her without any compulsion or even interest on her part; besides, there is some fun in Ann, but in this woman none, perhaps no mercy either: if anything restrains her, it is intelligence and pride, not compassion. Her voice might be the voice of a schoolmistress addressing a class of girls who had disgraced themselves, as she proceeds with complete composure and some disgust to say what she has come to say.

VIOLET. I have only looked in to tell Miss Ramsden that she will find her birthday present to me, the filigree bracelet, in the housekeeper's room.

TANNER. Do come in, Violet, and talk to us sensibly.

VIOLET. Thank you: I have had quite enough of the family conversation this morning. So has your mother, Ann: she has gone home crying. But at all events, I have found out what some of my pretended friends are worth. Good bye.

TANNER. No, no: one moment. I have something to say which I beg you to hear. [*She looks at him without the slightest curiosity, but waits, apparently as much to finish getting her glove on as to hear what he has to say*]. I am altogether on your side in this matter. I congratulate you, with the sincerest respect, on having the courage to do what you have done. You are entirely in the right; and the family is entirely in the wrong.

Sensation. Ann and Miss Ramsden rise and turn towards the two. Violet, more surprised than any of the others, forgets her glove, and comes forward into the middle of the room, both puzzled and displeased. Octavius alone does not move or raise his head: he is overwhelmed with shame.

ANN [*pleading to Tanner to be sensible*] Jack!

MISS RAMSDEN [*outraged*] Well, I must say!

VIOLET [*sharply to Tanner*] Who told you?

TANNER. Why, Ramsden and Tavy of course. Why should they not?

VIOLET. But they don't know.

TANNER. Don't know what?

VIOLET. They don't know that I am in the right, I mean.

TANNER. Oh, they know it in their hearts, though they think themselves bound to blame you by their silly superstitions about morality and propriety and so forth. But I know, and the whole world really knows, though it dare not say so, that you were right to follow your instinct; that vitality and bravery are the greatest qualities a woman can have, and motherhood her solemn initiation into womanhood; and that the fact of your not being legally married matters not one scrap either to your own worth or to our real regard for you.

VIOLET [flushing with indignation] Oh! You think me a wicked woman, like the rest. You think I have not only been vile, but that I share your abominable opinions. Miss Ramsden: I have borne your hard words because I knew you would be sorry for them when you found out the truth. But I won't bear such a horrible insult as to be complimented by Jack on being one of the wretches of whom he approves. I have kept my marriage a secret for my husband's sake. But now I claim my right as a married woman not to be insulted.

OCTAVIUS [raising his head with inexpressible relief] You are married!

VIOLET. Yes; and I think you might have guessed it. What business had you all to take it for granted that I had no right to wear my wedding ring? Not one of you even asked me: I cannot forget that.

TANNER [in ruins] I am utterly crushed. I meant well. I apologize—abjectly apologize.

VIOLET. I hope you will be more careful in future about the things you say. Of course one does not take them seriously; but they are very disagreeable, and rather in bad taste, I think.

TANNER [bowing to the storm] I have no defence: I shall know better in future than to take any woman's part. We have all disgraced ourselves in your eyes, I am afraid, except Ann. She befriended you. For Ann's sake, forgive us.

VIOLET. Yes: Ann has been very kind; but then Ann knew.

TANNER. Oh!

MISS RAMSDEN [*stiffly*] And who, pray, is the gentleman who does not acknowledge his wife?

VIOLET [*promptly*] That is my business, Miss Ramsden, and not yours. I have my reasons for keeping my marriage a secret for the present.

RAMSDEN. All I can say is that we are extremely sorry, Violet. I am shocked to think of how we have treated you.

OCTAVIUS [*awkwardly*] I beg your pardon, Violet. I can say no more.

MISS RAMSDEN [*still loth to surrender*] Of course what you say puts a very different complexion on the matter. All the same, I owe it to myself—

VIOLET [*cutting her short*] You owe me an apology, Miss Ramsden: that's what you owe both to yourself and to me. If you were a married woman you would not like sitting in the housekeeper's room and being treated like a naughty child by young girls and old ladies without any serious duties and responsibilities.

TANNER. Don't hit us when we're down, Violet. We seem to have made fools of ourselves; but really it was you who made fools of us.

VIOLET. It was no business of yours, Jack, in any case.

TANNER. No business of mine! Why, Ramsden as good as accused me of being the unknown gentleman.

Ramsden makes a frantic demonstration; but Violet's cool keen anger extinguishes it.

VIOLET. You! Oh, how infamous! how abominable! how disgracefully you have all been talking about me! If my husband knew it he would never let me speak to any of you again. [*To Ramsden*] I think you might have spared me that, at least.

RAMSDEN. But I assure you I never—at least it is a monstrous perversion of something I said that—

MISS RAMSDEN. You needn't apologize, Roebuck. She brought it all on herself. It is for her to apoligize for having deceived us.

VIOLET. I can make allowances for you, Miss Ramsden: you cannot understand how I feel on this subject, though I should have expected rather better taste from people of greater experience. However, I quite feel that you have all placed yourselves in a very painful position; and the most truly considerate thing for me to do is to go at once. Good morning.

She goes, leaving them staring.

MISS RAMSDEN. Well, I must say!

RAMSDEN [*plaintively*] I don't think she is quite fair to us.

TANNER. You must cower before the wedding ring like the rest of us, Ramsden. The cup of our ignominy is full.

ACT TWO

On the carriage drive in the park of a country house near Richmond a motor car has broken down. It stands in front of a clump of trees round which the drive sweeps to the house, which is partly visible through them: indeed Tanner, standing in the drive with the car on his right hand, could get an unobstructed view of the west corner of the house on his left were he not far too much interested in a pair of supine legs in blue serge trousers which protrude from beneath the machine. He is watching them intently with bent back and hands supported on his knees. His leathern overcoat and peaked cap proclaim him one of the dismounted passengers.

THE LEGS. Aha! I got him.

TANNER. All right now?

THE LEGS. Aw right now.

Tanner stoops and takes the legs by the ankles, drawing their owner forth like a wheelbarrow, walking on his hands, with a hammer in his mouth. He is a young man in a neat suit of blue serge, clean shaven, dark eyed, square fingered, with short well brushed black hair and rather irregular sceptically turned eyebrows. When he is manipulating the car his movements are swift and sudden, yet attentive and deliberate. With Tanner and Tanner's friends his manner is not in the least deferential, but cool and reticent, keeping them quite effectually at a distance whilst giving them no excuse for complaining of him. Nevertheless he has a vigilant eye on them always, and that, too, rather cynically, like a man who knows the world well from its seamy side. He speaks slowly and with a touch of sarcasm; and as he does not at all affect the gentleman in his speech, it may be inferred that his smart appearance is a mark of respect to himself and his own class, not to that which employs him.

He now gets into the car to test his machinery and put his cap and overcoat on again. Tanner takes off his leathern

*overcoat and pitches it into the car. The chauffeur (or auto-
mobilist or motoreer or whatever England may presently decide to call him) looks round inquiringly in the act of stow-
ing away his hammer.*

THE CHAUFFEUR. Had enough of it, eh?

TANNER. I may as well walk to the house and stretch
my legs and calm my nerves a little. [*Looking at his watch*]
I suppose you know that we have come from Hyde Park
Corner to Richmond in twenty-one minutes.

THE CHAUFFEUR. I'd ha done it under fifteen if I'd had
a clear road all the way.

TANNER. Why do you do it? Is it for love of sport or
for the fun of terrifying your unfortunate employer?

THE CHAUFFEUR. What are you afraid of?

TANNER. The police, and breaking my neck.

THE CHAUFFEUR. Well, if you like easy going, you can
take a bus, you know. It's cheaper. You pay me to save your
time and give you the value of your thousand pound car.
[*He sits down calmly*].

TANNER. I am the slave of that car and of you too. I
dream of the accursed thing at night.

THE CHAUFFEUR. You'll get over that. If you're going
up to the house, may I ask how long you're goin to stay
there? Because if you mean to put in the whole morning
talkin to the ladies, I'll put the car in the stables and make
myself comfortable. If not, I'll keep the car on the go about
here til you come.

TANNER. Better wait here. We shan't be long. There's
a young American gentleman, a Mr. Malone, who is driving
Mr. Robinson down in his new American steam car.

THE CHAUFFEUR [*springing up and coming hastily out of
the car to Tanner*] American steam car! Wot! racin us down
from London!

TANNER. Perhaps they're here already.

THE CHAUFFEUR. If I'd known it! [*With deep reproach*]
Why didn't you tell me, Mr. Tanner?

TANNER. Because I've been told that this car is capable
of 84 miles an hour; and I already know what you are
capable of when there is a rival car on the road. No, Henry:
there are things it is not good for you to know; and this was
one of them. However, cheer up: we are going to have a
day after your own heart. The American is to take Mr.
Robinson and his sister and Miss Whitefield. We are to take
Miss Rhoda.

THE CHAUFFEUR [*consoled, and musing on another matter*] That's Miss Whitefield's sister, isn't it?

TANNER. Yes.

THE CHAUFFEUR. And Miss Whitefield herself is goin in the other car? Not with you?

TANNER. Why the devil should she come with me? Mr. Robinson will be in the other car. [*The Chauffeur looks at Tanner with cool incredulity, and turns to the car, whistling a popular air softly to himself. Tanner, a little annoyed, is about to pursue the subject when he hears the footsteps of Octavius on the gravel. Octavius is coming from the house, dressed for motoring, but without his overcoat*]. We've lost the race, thank Heaven: here's Mr. Robinson. Well, Tavy, is the steam car a success?

OCTAVIUS. I think so. We came from Hyde Park Corner here in seventeen minutes. [*The Chauffeur, furious, kicks the car with a groan of vexation*]. How long were you?

TANNER. Oh, about three quarters of an hour or so.

THE CHAUFFEUR [*remonstrating*] Now, now, Mr. Tanner, come now! We could ha done it easy under fifteen.

TANNER. By the way, let me introduce you. Mr. Octavius Robinson: Mr. Enry Straker.

STRAKER. Pleased to meet you, sir. Mr. Tanner is gittin at you with is Enry Straker, you know. You call it Henery. But I don't mind, bless you.

TANNER. You think it's simply bad taste in me to chaff him, Tavy. But you're wrong. This man takes more trouble to drop his aitches than ever his father did to pick them up. It's a mark of caste to him. I have never met anybody more swollen with the pride of class than Enry is.

STRAKER. Easy, easy! A little moderation, Mr. Tanner.

TANNER. A little moderation, Tavy, you observe. You would tell me to draw it mild. But this chap has been educated. What's more, he knows that we haven't. What was that Board School of yours, Straker?

STRAKER. Sherbrooke Road.

TANNER. Sherbrooke Road! Would any of us say Rugby! Harrow! Eton! in that tone of intellectual snobbery? Sherbrooke Road is a place where boys learn something: Eton is a boy farm where we are sent because we are nuisances at home, and because in after life, whenever a Duke is mentioned, we can claim him as an old schoolfellow.

STRAKER. You don't know nothing about it, Mr. Tanner. It's not the Board School that does it: it's the Polytechnic.

TANNER. His university, Octavius. Not Oxford, Cambridge, Durham, Dublin or Glasgow. Not even those Nonconformist holes in Wales. No, Tavy. Regent Street, Chelsea, the Borough—I don't know half their confounded names: these are his universities, not mere shops for selling class limitations like ours. You despise Oxford, Enry, don't you?

STRAKER. No, I don't. Very nice sort of place, Oxford, I should think, for people that like that sort of place. They teach you to be a gentleman there. In the Polytechnic they teach you to be an engineer or such like. See?

TANNER. Sarcasm, Tavy, sarcasm! Oh, if you could only see into Enry's soul, the depth of his contempt for a gentleman, the arrogance of his pride in being an engineer, would appal you. He positively likes the car to break down because it brings out my gentlemanly helplessness and his workmanlike skill and resource.

STRAKER. Never you mind him, Mr. Robinson. He likes to talk. We know him, don't we?

OCTAVIUS [earnestly] But there's a great truth at the bottom of what he says. I believe most intensely in the dignity of labor.

STRAKER [unimpressed] That's because you never done any, Mr. Robinson. My business is to do away with labor. You'll get more out of me and a machine than you will out of twenty laborers, and not so much to drink either.

TANNER. For Heaven's sake, Tavy, don't start him on political economy. He knows all about it; and we don't. You're only a poetic Socialist, Tavy: he's a scientific one.

STRAKER [unperturbed] Yes. Well, this conversation is very improvin; but I've got to look after the car; and you two want to talk about your ladies. I know. [He retires to busy himself about the car; and presently saunters off towards the house].

TANNER. That's a very momentous social phenomenon.

OCTAVIUS. What is?

TANNER. Straker is. Here have we literary and cultured persons been for years setting up a cry of the New Woman whenever some unusually old fashioned female came along; and never noticing the advent of the New Man. Straker's the New Man.

OCTAVIUS. I see nothing new about him, except your way of chaffing him. But I don't want to talk about him just now. I want to speak to you about Ann.

TANNER. Straker knew even that. He learnt it at the

Polytechnic, probably. Well, what about Ann? Have you proposed to her?

OCTAVIUS [*self-reproachfully*] I was brute enough to do so last night.

TANNER. Brute enough! What do you mean?

OCTAVIUS [*dithyrambically*] Jack: we men are all coarse: we never understand how exquisite a woman's sensibilities are. How could I have done such a thing!

TANNER. Done what, you maudlin idiot?

OCTAVIUS. Yes, I am an idiot. Jack: if you had heard her voice! if you had seen her tears! I have lain awake all night thinking of them. If she had reproached me, I could have borne it better.

TANNER. Tears! that's dangerous. What did she say?

OCTAVIUS. She asked me how she could think of anything now but her dear father. She stifled a sob—[*he breaks down*].

TANNER [*patting him on the back*] Bear it like a man, Tavy, even if you feel it like an ass. It's the old game: she's not tired of playing with you yet.

OCTAVIUS [*impatiently*] Oh, don't be a fool, Jack. Do you suppose this eternal shallow cynicism of yours has any real bearing on a nature like hers?

TANNER. Hm! Did she say anything else?

OCTAVIUS. Yes; and that is why I expose myself and her to your ridicule by telling you what passed.

TANNER [*remorsefully*] No, dear Tavy, not ridicule, on my honor! However, no matter. Go on.

OCTAVIUS. Her sense of duty is so devout, so perfect, so—

TANNER. Yes: I know. Go on.

OCTAVIUS. You see, under this new arrangement, you and Ramsden are her guardians; and she considers that all her duty to her father is now transferred to you. She said she thought I ought to have spoken to you both in the first instance. Of course she is right; but somehow it seems rather absurd that I am to come to you and formally ask to be received as a suitor for your ward's hand.

TANNER. I am glad that love has not totally extinguished your sense of humor, Tavy.

OCTAVIUS. That answer won't satisfy her.

TANNER. My official answer is, obviously, Bless you, my children: may you be happy!

OCTAVIUS. I wish you would stop playing the fool about this. If it is not serious to you, it is to me, and to her.

TANNER. You know very well that she is as free to choose as you are.

OCTAVIUS. She does not think so.

TANNER. Oh, doesn't she! just! However, say what you want me to do?

OCTAVIUS. I want you to tell her sincerely and earnestly what you think about me. I want you to tell her that you can trust her to me—that is, if you feel you can.

TANNER. I have no doubt that I can trust her to you. What worries me is the idea of trusting you to her. Have you read Maeterlinck's book about the bee?

OCTAVIUS [*keeping his temper with difficulty*] I am not discussing literature at present.

TANNER. Be just a little patient with me. *I* am not discussing literature: the book about the bee is natural history. It's an awful lesson to mankind. You think that you are Ann's suitor; that you are the pursuer and she the pursued; that it is your part to woo, to persuade, to prevail, to overcome. Fool: it is you who are the pursued, the marked down quarry, the destined prey. You need not sit looking longingly at the bait through the wires of the trap: the door is open, and will remain so until it shuts behind you for ever.

OCTAVIUS. I wish I could believe that, vilely as you put it.

TANNER. Why, man, what other work has she in life but to get a husband? It is a woman's business to get married as soon as possible, and a man's to keep unmarried as long as he can. You have your poems and your tragedies to work at: Ann has nothing.

OCTAVIUS. I cannot write without inspiration. And nobody can give me that except Ann.

TANNER. Well, hadn't you better get it from her at a safe distance? Petrarch didn't see half as much of Laura, nor Dante of Beatrice, as you see of Ann now; and yet they wrote first-rate poetry—at least so I'm told. They never exposed their idolatry to the test of domestic familiarity; and it lasted them to their graves. Marry Ann; and at the end of a week you'll find no more inspiration in her than in a plate of muffins.

OCTAVIUS. You think I shall tire of her!

TANNER. Not at all: you don't get tired of muffins. But you don't find inspiration in them; and you won't in her when she ceases to be a poet's dream and becomes a solid eleven stone wife. You'll be forced to dream about somebody else; and then there will be a row.

OCTAVIUS. This sort of talk is no use, Jack. You don't understand. You have never been in love.

TANNER. I! I have never been out of it. Why, I am in love even with Ann. But I am neither the slave of love nor its dupe. Go to the bee, thou poet: consider her ways and be wise. By Heaven, Tavy, if women could do without our work, and we ate their children's bread instead of making it, they would kill us as the spider kills her mate or as the bees kill the drone. And they would be right if we were good for nothing but love.

OCTAVIUS. Ah, if we were only good enough for Love! There is nothing like Love: there is nothing else but Love: without it the world would be a dream of sordid horror.

TANNER. And this—this is the man who asks me to give him the hand of my ward! Tavy: I believe we were changed in our cradles, and that you are the real descendant of Don Juan.

OCTAVIUS. I beg you not to say anything like that to Ann.

TANNER. Don't be afraid. She has marked you for her own; and nothing will stop her now. You are doomed. [Straker comes back with a newspaper]. Here comes the New Man, demoralizing himself with a halfpenny paper as usual.

STRAKER. Now would you believe it, Mr. Robinson, when we're out motoring we take in two papers, the Times for him, the Leader or the Echo for me. And do you think I ever see my paper? Not much. He grabs the Leader and leaves me to stodge myself with his Times.

OCTAVIUS. Are there no winners in the Times?

TANNER. Enry don't old with bettin, Tavy. Motor records are his weakness. What's the latest?

STRAKER. Paris to Biskra at forty mile an hour average, not countin the Mediterranean.

TANNER. How many killed?

STRAKER. Two silly sheep. What does it matter? Sheep don't cost such a lot: they were glad to ave the price without the trouble o sellin em to the butcher. All the same, d'y'see, there'll be a clamor agin it ·presently; and then the French Government'll stop it; an our chance'll be gone, see? That's what makes me fairly mad: Mr. Tanner won't do a good run while he can.

TANNER. Tavy: do you remember my uncle James?

OCTAVIUS. Yes. Why?

TANNER. Uncle James had a first rate cook: he couldn't digest anything except what she cooked. Well, the poor man was shy and hated society. But his cook was proud of her skill, and wanted to serve up dinners to princes and ambassadors. To prevent her from leaving him, that poor old man had to give a big dinner twice a month, and suffer agonies of awkwardness. Now here am I; and here is this chap Enry Straker, the New Man. I loathe travelling; but I rather like Enry. He cares for nothing but tearing along in a leather coat and goggles, with two inches of dust all over him, at sixty miles an hour and the risk of his life and mine. Except, of course, when he is lying on his back in the mud under the machine trying to find out where it has given way. Well, if I don't give him a thousand mile run at least once a fortnight I shall lose him. He will give me the sack and go to some American millionaire; and I shall have to put up with a nice respectful groom-gardener-amateur, who will touch his hat and know his place. I am Enry's slave, just as Uncle James was his cook's slave.

STRAKER [*exasperated*] Garn! I wish I had a car that would go as fast as you can talk, Mr. Tanner. What I say is that you lose money by a motor car unless you keep it workin. Might as well ave a pram and a nussmaid to wheel you in it as that car and me if you don't git the last inch out of us both.

TANNER [*soothingly*] All right, Henry, all right. We'll go out for half an hour presently.

STRAKER [*in disgust*] Arf an ahr! [*He returns to his machine; seats himself in it; and turns up a fresh page of his paper in search of more news*].

OCTAVIUS. Oh, that reminds me. I have a note for you from Rhoda. [*He gives Tanner a note*].

TANNER [*opening it*] I rather think Rhoda is heading for a row with Ann. As a rule there is only one person an English girl hates more than she hates her mother; and that's her eldest sister. But Rhoda positively prefers her mother to Ann. She— [*indignantly*] Oh, I say!

OCTAVIUS. What's the matter?

TANNER. Rhoda was to have come with me for a ride in the motor car. She says Ann has forbidden her to go out with me.

Straker suddenly begins whistling his favorite air with remarkable deliberation. Surprised by this burst of larklike melody, and jarred by a sardonic note in its cheerfulness, they turn and look inquiringly at him. But he is busy with his paper; and nothing comes of their movement.

OCTAVIUS [*recovering himself*] Does she give any reason?

TANNER. Reason! An insult is not a reason. Ann forbids her to be alone with me on any occasion. Says I am not a fit person for a young girl to be with. What do you think of your paragon now?

OCTAVIUS. You must remember that she has a very heavy responsibility now that her father is dead. Mrs. Whitefield is too weak to control Rhoda.

TANNER [*staring at him*] In short, you agree with Ann.

OCTAVIUS. No; but I think I understand her. You must admit that your views are hardly suited for the formation of a young girl's mind and character.

TANNER. I admit nothing of the sort. I admit that the formation of a young lady's mind and character usually consists in telling her lies; but I object to the particular lie that I am in the habit of abusing the confidence of girls.

OCTAVIUS. Ann doesn't say that, Jack.

TANNER. What else does she mean?

STRAKER [*catching sight of Ann coming from the house*] Miss Whitefield, gentlemen. [*He dismounts and strolls away down the avenue with the air of a man who knows he is no longer wanted*].

ANN [*coming between Octavius and Tanner*] Good morning, Jack. I have come to tell you that poor Rhoda has got one of her headaches and cannot go out with you to-day in the car. It is a cruel disappointment to her, poor child!

TANNER. What do you say now, Tavy.

OCTAVIUS. Surely you cannot misunderstand, Jack. Ann is shewing you the kindest consideration, even at the cost of deceiving you.

ANN. What do you mean?

TANNER. Would you like to cure Rhoda's headache, Ann?

ANN. Of course.

TANNER. Then tell her what you said just now; and add that you arrived about two minutes after I had received her letter and read it.

ANN. Rhoda has written to you!

TANNER. With full particulars.

OCTAVIUS. Never mind him, Ann. You were right—quite right. Ann was only doing her duty, Jack; and you know it. Doing it in the kindest way, too.

ANN [*going to Octavius*] How kind you are, Tavy! How helpful! How well you understand!

Octavius beams.

TANNER. Ay: tighten the coils. You love her, Tavy, don't you?

OCTAVIUS. She knows I do.

ANN. Hush. For shame, Tavy!

TANNER. Oh, I give you leave. I am your guardian; and I commit you to Tavy's care for the next hour. I am off for a turn in the car.

ANN. No, Jack. I must speak to you about Rhoda. Ricky: will you go back to the house and entertain your American friend. He's rather on Mamma's hands so early in the morning. She wants to finish her housekeeping.

OCTAVIUS. I fly, dearest Ann [*he kisses her hand*].

ANN [*tenderly*] Ricky Ticky Tavy!

He looks at her with an eloquent blush, and runs off.

TANNER [*bluntly*] Now look here, Ann. This time you've landed yourself; and if Tavy were not in love with you past all salvation he'd have found out what an incorrigible liar you are.

ANN. You misunderstand, Jack. I didn't dare tell Tavy the truth.

TANNER. No: your daring is generally in the opposite direction. What the devil do you mean by telling Rhoda that I am too vicious to associate with her? How can I ever have any human or decent relations with her again, now that you have poisoned her mind in that abominable way?

ANN. I know you are incapable of behaving badly—

TANNER. Then why did you lie to her?

ANN. I had to.

TANNER. Had to!

ANN. Mother made me.

TANNER [*his eye flashing*] Ha! I might have known it. The mother! Always the mother!

ANN. It was that dreadful book of yours. You know how timid mother is. All timid women are conventional: we must be conventional, Jack, or we are so cruelly, so vilely misunderstood. Even you, who are a man, cannot say what you think without being misunderstood and vilified—yes: I admit it: I have had to vilify you. Do you want to have poor Rhoda misunderstood and vilified in the same way? Would it be right for mother to let her expose herself to such treatment before she is old enough to judge for herself?

TANNER. In short, the way to avoid misunderstanding is for everybody to lie and slander and insinuate and pretend as hard as they can. That is what obeying your mother comes to.

ANN. I love my mother, Jack.

TANNER [*working himself up into a sociological rage*] Is that any reason why you are not to call your soul your own? Oh, I protest against this vile abjection of youth to age! Look at fashionable society as you know it. What does it pretend to be? An exquisite dance of nymphs. What is it? A horrible procession of wretched girls, each in the claws of a cynical, cunning, avaricious, disillusioned, ignorantly experienced, foul-minded old woman whom she calls mother, and whose duty it is to corrupt her mind and sell her to the highest bidder. Why do these unhappy slaves marry anybody, however old and vile, sooner than not marry at all? Because marriage is their only means of escape from these decrepit fiends who hide their selfish ambitions, their jealous hatreds of the young rivals who have supplanted them, under the mask of maternal duty and family affection. Such things are abominable: the voice of nature proclaims for the daughter a father's care and for the son a mother's. The law for father and son and mother and daughter is not the law of love: it is the law of revolution, of emancipation, of final supersession of the old and worn-out by the young and capable. I tell you, the first duty of manhood and womanhood is a Declaration of Independence: the man who pleads his father's authority is no man: the woman who pleads her mother's authority is unfit to bear citizens to a free people.

ANN [*watching him with quiet curiosity*] I suppose you will go in seriously for politics some day, Jack.

TANNER [*heavily let down*] Eh? What? Wh—? [*Collecting his scattered wits*] What has that got to do with what I have been saying?

ANN. You talk so well.

TANNER. Talk! Talk! It means nothing to you but talk. Well, go back to your mother, and help her to poison Rhoda's imagination as she has poisoned yours. It is the tame elephants who enjoy capturing the wild ones.

ANN. I am getting on. Yesterday I was a boa constrictor: to-day I am an elephant.

TANNER. Yes. So pack your trunk and begone: I have no more to say to you.

ANN. You are so utterly unreasonable and impracticable. What can I do?

TANNER. Do! Break your chains. Go your way according to your own conscience and not according to your mother's. Get your mind clean and vigorous; and learn to enjoy a fast ride in a motor car instead of seeing nothing in it but an excuse for a detestable intrigue. Come with me to Marseilles and across to Algiers and to Biskra, at sixty miles an hour. Come right down to the Cape if you like. That will be a Declaration of Independence with a vengeance. You can write a book about it afterwards. That will finish your mother and make a woman of you.

ANN [*thoughtfully*] I don't think there would be any harm in that, Jack. You are my guardian: you stand in my father's place, by his own wish. Nobody could say a word against our travelling together. It would be delightful: thank you a thousand times, Jack. I'll come.

TANNER [*aghast*] You'll come ! ! !

ANN. Of course.

TANNER. But—[*he stops, utterly appalled; then resumes feebly*] No: look here, Ann: if there's no harm in it there's no point in doing it.

ANN. How absurd you are! You don't want to compromise me, do you?

TANNER. Yes: that's the whole sense of my proposal.

ANN. You are talking the greatest nonsense; and you know it. You would never do anything to hurt me.

TANNER. Well, if you don't want to be compromised, don't come.

ANN [*with simple earnestness*] Yes, I will come, Jack, since you wish it. You are my guardian; and I think we ought to see more of one another and come to know one another better. [*Gratefully*] It's very thoughtful and very kind of you, Jack, to offer me this lovely holiday, especially after what I said about Rhoda. You really are good—much better than you think. When do we start?

TANNER. But——

The conversation is interrupted by the arrival of Mrs. Whitefield from the house. She is accompanied by the American gentleman, and followed by Ramsden and Octavius.

Hector Malone is an Eastern American; but he is not at all ashamed of his nationality. This makes English people of fashion think well of him, as of a young fellow who is manly enough to confess to an obvious disadvantage without any attempt to conceal or extenuate it. They feel that he ought not to be made to suffer for what is clearly not his fault, and make a point of being specially kind to him. His chivalrous manners to women, and his elevated moral sentiments, being both gratuitous and unusual, strike them as being a little unfortunate; and though they find his vein of easy humor rather amusing when it has ceased to puzzle them [as it does at first], they have had to make him understand that he really must not tell anecdotes unless they are strictly personal and scandalous, and also that oratory is an accomplishment which belongs to a cruder stage of civilization than that in which his migration has landed him. On these points Hector is not quite convinced: he still thinks that the British are apt to make merits of their stupidities, and to represent their various incapacities as points of good breeding. English life seems to him to suffer from a lack of edifying rhetoric [which he calls moral tone]; English behavior to shew a want of respect for womanhood; English pronunciation to fail very vulgarly in tackling such words as world, girl, bird, etc.; English society to be plain spoken to an extent which stretches occasionally to intolerable coarseness; and English intercourse to need enlivening by games and stories and other pastimes; so he does not feel called upon to acquire these defects after taking great pains to cultivate himself in a first rate manner before venturing across the Atlantic. To this culture he finds English people either totally indifferent, as they very commonly are to all culture, or else politely evasive, the truth being that Hector's culture is nothing but a state of saturation with our literary exports of thirty years ago, reimported by him to be unpacked at a moment's notice and hurled at the head of English literature, science and art, at every conversational opportunity. The dismay set up by these sallies encourages him in his belief that he is helping to educate England. When he finds people chattering harmlessly about Anatole France and Nietzsche, he devastates them with Matthew Arnold, the Autocrat of the Breakfast Table, and even Macaulay; and as he is devoutly religious at bottom, he first leads the unwary, by humorous irreverences, to leave popular theology out of account in discussing moral questions with him, and then scatters them in confusion by demanding whether the carrying out of his ideals of conduct was not the manifest object of God Almighty in creating honest men and pure women. The engaging freshness of his personality and the dumbfoundering staleness of his culture make it extremely difficult to decide whether he is

*worth knowing; for whilst his company is undeniably pleasant
and enlivening, there is intellectually nothing new to be got
out of him, especially as he despises politics, and is careful
not to talk commercial shop, in which department he is probably much in advance of his English capitalist friends. He
gets on best with romantic Christians of the amoristic sect:
hence the friendship which has sprung up between him and
Octavius.*

*In appearance Hector is a neatly built young man of twenty-
four, with a short, smartly trimmed black beard, clear, well
shaped eyes, and an ingratiating vivacity of expression. He is,
from the fashionable point of view, faultlessly dressed. As he
comes along the drive from the house with Mrs. Whitefield he
is sedulously making himself agreeable and entertaining, and
thereby placing on her slender wit a burden it is unable to
bear. An Englishman would let her alone, accepting boredom
and indifference as their common lot; and the poor lady wants
to be either let alone or let prattle about the things that interest her.*

*Ramsden strolls over to inspect the motor car. Octavius
joins Hector.*

ANN [*pouncing on her mother joyously*] Oh, mamma,
what do you think! Jack is going to take me to Nice in his
motor car. Isn't it lovely? I am the happiest person in London.

TANNER [*desperately*] Mrs. Whitefield objects. I am sure
she objects. Doesn't she, Ramsden?

RAMSDEN. I should think it very likely indeed.

ANN. You don't object, do you, mother?

MRS. WHITEFIELD. *I* object! Why should I? I think it will
do you good, Ann. [*Trotting over to Tanner*] I meant to ask
you to take Rhoda out for a run occasionally: she is too much
in the house; but it will do when you come back.

TANNER. Abyss beneath abyss of perfidy!

ANN [*hastily, to distract attention from this outburst*] Oh,
I forgot: you have not met Mr. Malone. Mr. Tanner, my
guardian: Mr. Hector Malone.

HECTOR. Pleased to meet you, Mr. Tanner. I should like
to suggest an extension of the travelling party to Nice, if I
may.

ANN. Oh, we're all coming. That's understood, isn't it?

HECTOR. I also am the modest possessor of a motor car.
If Miss Robinson will allow me the privilege of taking her,
my car is at her service.

OCTAVIUS. Violet!

General constraint.

ANN [*subduedly*] Come, mother: we must leave them to talk over the arrangements. I must see to my travelling kit. *Mrs. Whitefield looks bewildered; but Ann draws her discreetly away; and they disappear round the corner towards the house.*

HECTOR. I think I may go so far as to say that I can depend on Miss Robinson's consent.

Continued embarrassment.

OCTAVIUS. I'm afraid we must leave Violet behind. There are circumstances which make it impossible for her to come on such an expedition.

HECTOR [*amused and not at all convinced*] Too American, eh? Must the young lady have a chaperone?

OCTAVIUS. It's not that, Malone—at least not altogether.

HECTOR. Indeed! May I ask what other objection applies?

TANNER [*impatiently*] Oh, tell him, tell him. We shall never be able to keep the secret unless everybody knows what it is. Mr Malone: if you go to Nice with Violet, you go with another man's wife. She is married.

HECTOR [*thunderstruck*] You don't tell me so!

TANNER. We do. In confidence.

RAMSDEN [*with an air of importance, lest Malone should suspect a misalliance*] Her marriage has not yet been made known: she desires that it shall not be mentioned for the present.

HECTOR. I shall respect the lady's wishes. Would it be indiscreet to ask who her husband is, in case I should have an opportunity of consulting him about this trip?

TANNER. We don't know who he is.

HECTOR [*retiring into his shell in a very marked manner*] In that case, I have no more to say.

They become more embarrassed than ever.

OCTAVIUS. You must think this very strange.

HECTOR. A little singular. Pardon me for saying so.

RAMSDEN [*half apologetic, half huffy*] The young lady was married secretly; and her husband has forbidden her, it seems, to declare his name. It is only right to tell you, since you are interested in Miss—er—in Violet.

OCTAVIUS [*sympathetically*] I hope this is not a disappointment to you.

HECTOR [*softened, coming out of his shell again*] Well: it is a blow. I can hardly understand how a man can leave his wife in such a position. Surely it's not customary. It's not manly. It's not considerate.

OCTAVIUS. We feel that, as you may imagine, pretty deeply.

RAMSDEN [testily] It is some young fool who has not enough experience to know what mystifications of this kind lead to.

HECTOR [with strong symptoms of moral repugnance] I hope so. A man need be very young and pretty foolish too to be excused for such conduct. You take a very lenient view, Mr. Ramsden. Too lenient to my mind. Surely marriage should ennoble a man.

TANNER [sardonically] Ha!

HECTOR. Am I to gather from that cacchination that you don't agree with me, Mr. Tanner?

TANNER [drily] Get married and try. You may find it delightful for a while: you certainly won't find it ennobling. The greatest common measure of a man and a woman is not necessarily greater than the man's single measure.

HECTOR. Well, we think in America that a woman's moral number is higher than a man's, and that the purer nature of a woman lifts a man right out of himself, and makes him better than he was.

OCTAVIUS [with conviction] So it does.

TANNER. No wonder American women prefer to live in Europe! It's more comfortable than standing all their lives on an altar to be worshipped. Anyhow, Violet's husband has not been ennobled. So what's to be done?

HECTOR [shaking his head] I can't dismiss that man's conduct as lightly as you do, Mr. Tanner. However, I'll say no more. Whoever he is, he's Miss Robinson's husband; and I should be glad for her sake to think better of him.

OCTAVIUS [touched; for he divines a secret sorrow] I'm very sorry, Malone. Very sorry.

HECTOR [gratefully] You're a good fellow, Robinson. Thank you.

TANNER. Talk about something else. Violet's coming from the house.

HECTOR. I should esteem it a very great favor, gentlemen, if you would take the opportunity to let me have a few words with the lady alone. I shall have to cry off this trip; and it's rather a delicate—

RAMSDEN [glad to escape] Say no more. Come, Tanner.

Come, Tavy. [*He strolls away into the park with Octavius and Tanner, past the motor car*].

Violet comes down the avenue to Hector.

VIOLET. Are they looking?

HECTOR. No.

She kisses him.

VIOLET. Have you been telling lies for my sake?

HECTOR. Lying! Lying hardly describes it. I overdo it. I get carried away in an ecstasy of mendacity. Violet: I wish you'd let me own up.

VIOLET [*instantly becoming serious and resolute*] No, no, Hector: you promised me not to.

HECTOR. I'll keep my promise until you release me from it. But I feel mean, lying to those men, and denying my wife. Just dastardly.

VIOLET. I wish your father were not so unreasonable.

HECTOR. He's not unreasonable. He's right from his point of view. He has a prejudice against the English middle class.

VIOLET. It's too ridiculous. You know how I dislike saying such things to you, Hector; but if I were to—oh, well, no matter.

HECTOR. I know. If you were to marry the son of an English manufacturer of office furniture, your friends would consider it a misalliance. And here's my silly old dad, who is the biggest office furniture man in the world, would shew me the door for marrying the most perfect lady in England merely because she has no handle to her name. Of course it's just absurd. But I tell you, Violet, I don't like deceiving him. I feel as if I was stealing his money. Why won't you let me own up?

VIOLET. We can't afford it. You can be as romantic as you please about love, Hector; but you mustn't be romantic about money.

HECTOR [*divided between his uxoriousness and his habitual elevation of moral sentiment*] That's very English. [*Appealing to her impulsively*] Violet: dad's bound to find us out someday.

VIOLET. Oh yes, later on of course. But don't let's go over this every time we meet, dear. You promised—

HECTOR. All right, all right, I—

VIOLET [*not to be silenced*] It is I and not you who suffer by this concealment; and as to facing a struggle and poverty and all that sort of thing I simply will not do it. It's too silly.

HECTOR. You shall not. I'll sort of borrow the money

from my dad until I get on my own feet; and then I can own up and pay up at the same time.

VIOLET [*alarmed and indignant*] Do you mean to work? Do you want to spoil our marriage?

HECTOR. Well, I don't mean to let marriage spoil my character. Your friend Mr. Tanner has got the laugh on me a bit already about that; and—

VIOLET. The beast! I hate Jack Tanner.

HECTOR [*magnanimously*] Oh, he's all right: he only needs the love of a good woman to ennoble him. Besides, he's proposed a motoring trip to Nice; and I'm going to take you.

VIOLET. How jolly!

HECTOR. Yes; but how are we going to manage? You see, they've warned me off going with you, so to speak. They've told me in confidence that you're married. That's just the most overwhelming confidence I've ever been honored with.

Tanner returns with Straker, who goes to his car.

TANNER. Your car is a great success, Mr. Malone. Your engineer is showing it off to Mr. Ramsden.

HECTOR [*eagerly—forgetting himself*] Let's come, Vi.

VIOLET [*coldly, warning him with her eyes*] I beg your pardon, Mr. Malone, I did not quite catch—

HECTOR [*recollecting himself*] I ask to be allowed the pleasure of shewing you my little American steam car, Miss Robinson.

VIOLET. I shall be very pleased. [*They go off together down the avenue*].

TANNER. About this trip, Straker.

STRAKER [*preoccupied with the car*] Yes?

TANNER. Miss Whitefield is supposed to be coming with me

STRAKER. So I gather.

TANNER. Mr. Robinson is to be one of the party.

STRAKER. Yes.

TANNER. Well, if you can manage so as to be a good deal occupied with me, and leave Mr. Robinson a good deal occupied with Miss Whitefield, he will be deeply grateful to you.

STRAKER [*looking round at him*] Evidently.

TANNER. "Evidently"! Your grandfather would have simply winked.

STRAKER. My grandfather would have touched his at.

TANNER. And I should have given your good nice respect-ful grandfather a sovereign.

STRAKER. Five shillins, more likely. [*He leaves the car and approaches Tanner*]. What about the lady's views?

TANNER. She is just as willing to be left to Mr. Robinson as Mr. Robinson is to be left to her. [*Straker looks at his principal with cool scepticism; then turns to the car whistling his favorite air*]. Stop that aggravating noise. What do you mean by it? [*Straker calmly resumes the melody and finishes it. Tanner politely hears it out before he again addresses Straker, this time with elaborate seriousness*]. Enry: I have ever been a warm advocate of the spread of music among the masses; but I object to your obliging the company when-ever Miss Whitefield's name is mentioned. You did it this morning, too.

STRAKER [*obstinately*] It's not a bit o use. Mr. Robinson may as well give it up first as last.

TANNER. Why?

STRAKER. Garn! You know why. Course it's not my busi-ness; but you needn't start kiddin me about it.

TANNER. I am not kidding. I don't know why.

STRAKER [*cheerfully sulky*] Oh, very well. All right. It ain't my business.

TANNER [*impressively*] I trust, Enry, that, as between employer and engineer, I shall always know how to keep my proper distance, and not intrude my private affairs on you. Even our business arrangements are subject to the approval of your Trade Union. But don't abuse your advantages. Let me remind you that Voltaire said that what was too silly to be said could be sung.

STRAKER. It wasn't Voltaire: it was Bow Mar Shay.

TANNER. I stand corrected: Beaumarchais of course. Now you seem to think that what is too delicate to be said can be whistled. Unfortunately your whistling, though melodious, is unintelligible. Come! there's nobody listening: neither my genteel relatives nor the secretary of your confounded Union. As man to man, Enry, why do you think that my friend has no chance with Miss Whitefield?

STRAKER. Cause she's arter summun else.

TANNER. Bosh! who else?

STRAKER. You.

TANNER. Me!!!

STRAKER. Mean to tell me you didn't know? Oh, come, Mr. Tanner!

TANNER [*in fierce earnest*] Are you playing the fool, or do you mean it?

STRAKER [*with a flash of temper*] I'm not playin no fool. [*More coolly*] Why, it's as plain as the nose on your face. If you ain't spotted that, you don't know much about these sort of things. [*Serene again*] Ex-cuse me, you know, Mr. Tanner; but you asked me as man to man; and I told you as man to man.

TANNER [*wildly appealing to the heavens*] Then I—*I* am the bee, the spider, the marked down victim, the destined prey.

STRAKER. I dunno about the bee and the spider. But the marked down victim, that's what you are and no mistake; and a jolly good job for you, too, I should say.

TANNER [*momentously*] Henry Straker: the golden moment of your life has arrived.

STRAKER. What d'y' mean?

TANNER. That record to Biskra.

STRAKER [*eagerly*] Yes?

TANNER. Break it.

STRAKER [*rising to the height of his destiny*] D'y'mean it?

TANNER. I do.

STRAKER. When?

TANNER. Now. Is that machine ready to start?

STRAKER [*quailing*] But you can't—

TANNER [*cutting him short by getting into the car*] Off we go. First to the bank for money; then to my rooms for my kit; then to your rooms for your kit; then break the record from London to Dover or Folkestone; then across the channel and away like mad to Marseilles, Gibraltar, Genoa, any port from which we can sail to a Mahometan country where men are protected from women.

STRAKER. Garn! you're kiddin.

TANNER [*resolutely*] Stay behind then. If you won't come I'll do it alone. [*He starts the motor*].

STRAKER [*running after him*] Here! Mister! arf a mo! steady on! [*He scrambles in as the car plunges forward*].

ACT THREE

Evening in the Sierra Nevada. Rolling slopes of brown, with olive trees instead of apple trees in the cultivated patches, and occasional prickly pears instead of gorse and bracken in the wilds. Higher up, tall stone peaks and precipices, all handsome and distinguished. No wild nature here: rather a most aristocratic mountain landscape made by a fastidious artist-creator. No vulgar profusion of vegetation: even a touch of aridity in the frequent patches of stones: Spanish magnificence and Spanish economy everywhere.

Not very far north of a spot at which the high road over one of the passes crosses a tunnel on the railway from Malaga to Granada, is one of the mountain amphitheatres of the Sierra. Looking at it from the wide end of the horse-shoe, one sees, a little to the right, in the face of the cliff, a romantic cave which is really an abandoned quarry, and towards the left a little hill, commanding a view of the road, which skirts the amphitheatre on the left, maintaining its higher level on embankments and an occasional stone arch. On the hill, watching the road, is a man who is either a Spaniard or a Scotchman. Probably a Spaniard, since he wears the dress of a Spanish goatherd and seems at home in the Sierra Nevada, but very like a Scotchman for all that. In the hollow, on the slope leading to the quarry-cave, are about a dozen men who, as they recline at their ease round a heap of smouldering white ashes of dead leaf and brushwood, have an air of being conscious of themselves as picturesque scoundrels honoring the Sierra by using it as an effective pictorial background. As a matter of artistic fact they are not picturesque; and the mountains tolerate them as lions tolerate lice. An English policeman or Poor Law Guardian would recognize them as a selected band of tramps and ablebodied paupers.

This description of them is not wholly contemptuous. Whoever has intelligently observed the tramp, or visited the ablebodied ward of a workhouse, will admit that our social failures are not all drunkards and weaklings. Some of them are men who do not fit the class they were born into. Precisely the same qualities that make the educated gentleman an artist may make an uneducated manual laborer an ablebodied pauper. There are men who fall helplessly into the workhouse because they are good for nothing; but there are also men who are there because they are strongminded enough to disregard the social convention [obviously not a disinterested one on the part of the ratepayer] which bids a man live by heavy and badly paid drudgery when he has the alternative of walking into the workhouse, announcing himself as a destitute person, and legally compelling the Guardians to feed, clothe and house him better than he could feed, clothe and house himself without great exertion. When a man who is born a poet refuses a stool in a stockbroker's office, and starves in a garret, sponging on a poor landlady or on his friends and relatives sooner than work against his grain; or when a lady, because she is a lady, will face any extremity of parasitic dependence rather than take a situation as cook or parlormaid, we make large allowances for them. To such allowances the ablebodied pauper, and his nomadic variant the tramp, are equally entitled.

Further, the imaginative man, if his life is to be tolerable to him, must have leisure to tell himself stories, and a position which lends itself to imaginative decoration. The ranks of unskilled labor offer no such positions. We misuse our laborers horribly; and when a man refuses to be misused, we have no right to say that he is refusing honest work. Let us be frank in this matter before we go on with our play; so that we may enjoy it without hypocrisy. If we were reasoning, farsighted people, four fifths of us would go straight to the Guardians for relief, and knock the whole social system to pieces with most beneficial reconstructive results. The reason we do not do this is because we work like bees or ants, by instinct or habit, not reasoning about the matter at all. Therefore when a man comes along who can and does reason, and who, applying the Kantian test to his conduct, can truly say to us, If everybody did as I do, the world would be compelled to reform itself industrially, and abolish slavery and squalor, which exist only because everybody does as you do, let us honor that man and seriously consider the advisability of following his example. Such a man is the able-bodied, able-minded pauper. Were he a gentleman doing his best to get a pension or a sinecure instead of sweeping a crossing, nobody would blame him for deciding that so long as the alternative lies between living mainly at the expense of the community and allowing the community to live mainly at his, it would be folly to accept what is to him personally the greater of the two evils.

We may therefore contemplate the tramps of the Sierra without prejudice, admitting cheerfully that our objects— briefly, to be gentlemen of fortune—are much the same as theirs, and the difference in our position and methods merely accidental. One or two of them, perhaps, it would be wiser to kill without malice in a friendly and frank manner; for there are bipeds, just as there are quadrupeds, who are too dangerous to be left unchained and unmuzzled; and these cannot

*fairly expect to have other men's lives wasted in the work of
watching them. But as society has not the courage to kill them,
and, when it catches them, simply wreaks on them some
superstitious expiatory rites of torture and degradation, and
then lets them loose with heightened qualifications for mischief, it is just as well that they are at large in the Sierra, and
in the hands of a chief who looks as if he might possibly, on
provocation, order them to be shot.*

*This chief, seated in the centre of the group on a squared
block of stone from the quarry, is a tall strong man, with a
striking cockatoo nose, glossy black hair, pointed beard, upturned moustache, and a Mephistophelean affectation which is
fairly imposing, perhaps because the scenery admits of a
larger swagger than Piccadilly, perhaps because of a certain
sentimentality in the man which gives him that touch of grace
which alone can excuse deliberate picturesqueness. His eyes
and mouth are by no means rascally; he has a fine voice and
a ready wit; and whether he is really the strongest man in the
party or not, he looks it. He is certainly the best fed, the best
dressed, and the best trained. The fact that he speaks English
is not unexpected, in spite of the Spanish landscape; for with
the exception of one man who might be guessed as a bull-
fighter ruined by drink, and one unmistakable Frenchman,
they are all cockney or American; therefore, in a land of
cloaks and sombreros, they mostly wear seedy overcoats,
woollen mufflers, hard hemispherical hats, and dirty brown
gloves. Only a very few dress after their leader, whose broad
sombrero with a cock's feather in the band, and voluminous
cloak descending to his high boots, are as un-English as possible. None of them are armed; and the ungloved ones keep
their hands in their pockets because it is their national belief
that it must be dangerously cold in the open air with the
night coming on. [It is as warm an evening as any reasonable
man could desire].*

*Except the bullfighting inebriate there is only one person in
the company who looks more than, say, thirty-three. He is a
small man with reddish whiskers, weak eyes, and the anxious
look of a small tradesman in difficulties. He wears the only
tall hat visible: it shines in the sunset with the sticky glow of
some sixpenny patent hat reviver, often applied and constantly
tending to produce a worse state of the original surface than
the ruin it was applied to remedy. He has a collar and cuffs of
celluloid; and his brown Chesterfield overcoat, with velvet
collar, is still presentable. He is pre-eminently the respectable*

*man of the party, and is certainly over forty, possibly over
fifty. He is the corner man on the leader's right, opposite
three men in scarlet ties on his left. One of these three is the
Frenchman. Of the remaining two, who are both English, one
is argumentative, solemn, and obstinate; the other rowdy and
mischievous.*

*The chief, with a magnificent fling of the end of his cloak
across his left shoulder, rises to address them. The applause
which greets him shews that he is a favorite orator.*

THE CHIEF. Friends and fellow brigands. I have a proposal to make to this meeting. We have now spent three evenings in discussing the question Have Anarchists or Social-
Democrats the most personal courage? We have gone into the
principles of Anarchism and Social-Democracy at great length.
The cause of Anarchy has been ably represented by our
one Anarchist, who doesn't know what Anarchism means
[*laughter*]—

THE ANARCHIST [*rising*] A point of order, Mendoza—

MENDOZA [*forcibly*] No, by thunder: your last point of
order took half an hour. Besides, Anarchists don't believe in
order.

THE ANARCHIST [*mild, polite but persistent: he is, in fact,
the respectable looking elderly man in the celluloid collar and
cuffs*] That is a vulgar error. I can prove—

MENDOZA. Order, order.

THE OTHERS [*shouting*] Order, order. Sit down. Chair!
Shut up.

The Anarchist is suppressed.

MENDOZA. On the other hand we have three Social-
Democrats among us. They are not on speaking terms; and
they have put before us three distinct and incompatible views
of Social-Democracy.

THE THREE MEN IN SCARLET TIES. 1. Mr. Chairman, I
protest. A personal explanation. 2. It's a lie. I never said so.
Be fair, Mendoza. 3. Je demande la parole. C'est absolument
faux. C'est faux! faux!! faux!!! Assas-s-s-s-sin!!!!!!

MENDOZA. Order, order.

THE OTHERS. Order, order, order! Chair!

The Social-Democrats are suppressed.

MENDOZA. Now, we tolerate all opinions here. But after
all, comrades, the vast majority of us are neither Anarchists
nor Socialists, but gentlemen and Christians.

THE MAJORITY [*shouting assent*] Hear, hear! So we are. Right.

THE ROWDY SOCIAL-DEMOCRAT [*smarting under suppression*] You ain't no Christian. You're a Sheeny, you are.

MENDOZA [*with crushing magnanimity*] My friend: *I* am an exception to all rules. It is true that I have the honor to be a Jew; and when the Zionists need a leader to reassemble our race on its historic soil of Palestine, Mendoza will not be the last to volunteer [*sympathetic applause—hear, hear, &c.*]. But I am not a slave to any superstition. I have swallowed all the formulas, even that of Socialism; though, in a sense, once a Socialist, always a Socialist.

THE SOCIAL-DEMOCRATS. Hear, hear!

MENDOZA. But I am well aware that the ordinary man—even the ordinary brigand, who can scarcely be called an ordinary man [Hear, hear!]—is not a philosopher. Common sense is good enough for him; and in our business affairs common sense is good enough for me. Well, what is our business here in the Sierra Nevada, chosen by the Moors as the fairest spot in Spain? Is it to discuss abstruse questions of political economy? No: it is to hold up motor cars and secure a more equitable distribution of wealth.

THE SULKY SOCIAL-DEMOCRAT. All made by labor, mind you.

MENDOZA [*urbanely*] Undoubtedly. All made by labor, and on its way to be squandered by wealthy vagabonds in the dens of vice that disfigure the sunny shores of the Mediterranean. We intercept that wealth. We restore it to circulation among the class that produced it and that chiefly needs it—the working class. We do this at the risk of our lives and liberties, by the exercise of the virtues of courage, endurance, foresight, and abstinence—especially abstinence. I myself have eaten nothing but prickly pears and broiled rabbit for three days.

THE SULKY SOCIAL-DEMOCRAT [*stubbornly*] No more ain't we.

MENDOZA [*indignantly*] Have I taken more than my share?

THE SULKY SOCIAL-DEMOCRAT [*unmoved*] Why should you?

THE ANARCHIST. Why should he not? To each according to his needs: from each according to his means.

THE FRENCHMAN [*shaking his fist at the Anarchist*] Fumiste!

MENDOZA [*diplomatically*] I agree with both of you.

THE GENUINELY ENGLISH BRIGANDS. Hear, hear! Bravo, Mendoza!

MENDOZA. What I say is, let us treat one another as gentlemen, and strive to excel in personal courage only when we take the field.

THE ROWDY SOCIAL-DEMOCRAT [*derisively*] Shikespear.

A whistle comes from the goatherd on the hill. He springs up and points excitedly forward along the road to the north.

THE GOATHERD. Automobile! Automobile! [*He rushes down the hill and joins the rest, who all scramble to their feet*].

MENDOZA [*in ringing tones*] To arms! Who has the gun?

THE SULKY SOCIAL-DEMOCRAT [*handing a rifle to Mendoza*] Here.

MENDOZA. Have the nails been strewn in the road?

THE ROWDY SOCIAL-DEMOCRAT. Two ahnces of em.

MENDOZA. Good! [*To the Frenchman*] With me, Duval. If the nails fail, puncture their tires with a bullet. [*He gives the rifle to Duval, who follows him up the hill. Mendoza produces an opera glass. The others hurry across to the road and disappear to the north*].

MENDOZA [*on the hill, using his glass*] Two only, a capitalist and his chauffeur. They look English.

DUVAL. Angliche! Aoh yess. Cochons! [*Handling the rifle*] Faut tirer, n'est-ce-pas?

MENDOZA. No: the nails have gone home. Their tire is down: they stop.

DUVAL [*shouting to the others*] Fondez sur eux, nom de Dieu!

MENDOZA [*rebuking his excitement*] Du calme, Duval: keep your hair on. They take it quietly. Let us descend and receive them.

Mendoza descends, passing behind the fire and coming forward, whilst Tanner and Straker, in their motoring goggles, leather coats, and caps, are led in from the road by the brigands.

TANNER. Is this the gentleman you describe as your boss? Does he speak English?

THE ROWDY SOCIAL-DEMOCRAT. Course he does. Y' downt suppowz we Hinglishmen lets ahrselves be bossed by a bloomin Spenniard, do you?

MENDOZA [*with dignity*] Allow me to introduce myself: Mendoza, President of the League of the Sierra! [*Posing loftily*] I am a brigand: I live by robbing the rich.

TANNER [*promptly*] I am a gentleman: I live by robbing the poor. Shake hands.

THE ENGLISH SOCIAL-DEMOCRATS. Hear, hear!

General laughter and good humor. Tanner and Mendoza shake hands. The Brigands drop into their former places.

STRAKER. Ere! where do I come in?

TANNER [*introducing*] My friend and chauffeur.

THE SULKY SOCIAL-DEMOCRAT [*suspiciously*] Well, which is he? friend or show-foor? It makes all the difference, you know.

MENDOZA [*explaining*] We should expect ransom for a friend. A professional chauffeur is free of the mountains. He even takes a trifling percentage of his principal's ransom if he will honor us by accepting it.

STRAKER. I see. Just to encourage me to come this way again. Well, I'll think about it.

DUVAL [*impulsively rushing across to Straker*] Mon frère! [*He embraces him rapturously and kisses him on both cheeks*].

STRAKER [*disgusted*] Ere, git out: don't be silly. Who are you, pray?

DUVAL. Duval: Social-Democrat.

STRAKER. Oh, you're a Social-Democrat, are you?

THE ANARCHIST. He means that he has sold out to the parliamentary humbugs and the bourgeoisie. Compromise! that is his faith.

DUVAL [*furiously*] I understand what he say. He say Bourgeois. He say Compromise. Jamais de la vie! Misérable menteur—

STRAKER. See here, Captain Mendoza, ow much o this sort o thing do you put up with here? Are we avin a pleasure trip in the mountains, or are we at a Socialist meetin?

THE MAJORITY. Hear, hear! Shut up. Chuck it. Sit down, &c. &c. [*The Social-Democrats and the Anarchist are hustled into the background. Straker, after superintending this proceeding with satisfaction, places himself on Mendoza's left, Tanner being on his right*].

MENDOZA. Can we offer you anything? Broiled rabbit and prickly pears—

TANNER. Thank you: we have dined.

MENDOZA [*to his followers*] Gentlemen: business is over for the day. Go as you please until morning.

The Brigands disperse into groups lazily. Some go into the cave. Others sit down or lie down to sleep in the open. A few produce a pack of cards and move off towards the road; for it is now starlight; and they know that motor cars have lamps which can be turned to account for lighting a card party.

STRAKER [*calling after them*] Don't none of you go fooling with that car, d'ye hear?

MENDOZA. No fear, Monsieur le Chauffeur. The first one we captured cured us of that.

STRAKER [*interested*] What did it do?

MENDOZA. It carried three brave comrades of ours, who did not know how to stop it, into Granada, and capsized them opposite the police station. Since then we never touch one without sending for the chauffeur. Shall we chat at our ease?

TANNER. By all means.

Tanner, Mendoza, and Straker sit down on the turf by the fire. Mendoza delicately waives his presidential dignity, of which the right to sit on the squared stone block is the appanage, by sitting on the ground like his guests, and using the stone only as a support for his back.

MENDOZA. It is the custom in Spain always to put off business until to-morrow. In fact, you have arrived out of office hours. However, if you would prefer to settle the question of ransom at once, I am at your service.

TANNER. To-morrow will do for me. I am rich enough to pay anything in reason.

MENDOZA [*respectfully, much struck by this admission*] You are a remarkable man, sir. Our guests usually describe themselves as miserably poor.

TANNER. Pooh! Miserably poor people don't own motor cars.

MENDOZA. Precisely what we say to them.

TANNER. Treat us well: we shall not prove ungrateful.

STRAKER. No prickly pears and broiled rabbits, you know. Don't tell me you can't do us a bit better than that if you like.

MENDOZA. Wine, kids, milk, cheese and bread can be procured for ready money.

STRAKER [*graciously*] Now you're talking.

TANNER. Are you all Socialists here, may I ask?

MENDOZA [*repudiating this humiliating misconception*] Oh no, no, no: nothing of the kind, I assure you. We naturally have modern views as to the justice of the existing distribution of wealth: otherwise we should lose our self-respect. But nothing that you could take exception to, except two or three faddists.

TANNER. I had no intention of suggesting anything discreditable. In fact, I am a bit of a Socialist myself.

STRAKER [drily] Most rich men are, I notice.

MENDOZA. Quite so. It has reached us, I admit. It is in the air of the century.

STRAKER. Socialism must be looking up a bit if your chaps are taking to it.

MENDOZA. That is true, sir. A movement which is confined to philosophers and honest men can never exercise any real political influence: there are too few of them. Until a movement shews itself capable of spreading among brigands, it can never hope for a political majority.

TANNER. But are your brigands any less honest than ordinary citizens?

MENDOZA. Sir: I will be frank with you. Brigandage is abnormal. Abnormal professions attract two classes: those who are not good enough for ordinary bourgeois life and those who are too good for it. We are dregs and scum, sir: the dregs very filthy, the scum very superior.

STRAKER. Take care! some o the dregs'll hear you.

MENDOZA. It does not matter: each brigand thinks himself scum, and likes to hear the others called dregs.

TANNER. Come! you are a wit. [Mendoza inclines his head, flattered]. May one ask you a blunt question?

MENDOZA. As blunt as you please.

TANNER. How does it pay a man of your talent to shepherd such a flock as this on broiled rabbit and prickly pears? I have seen men less gifted, and I'll swear less honest, supping at the Savoy on foie gras and champagne.

MENDOZA. Pooh! they have all had their turn at the broiled rabbit, just as I shall have my turn at the Savoy. Indeed, I have had a turn there already—as waiter.

TANNER. A waiter! You astonish me!

MENDOZA [reflectively] Yes: I, Mendoza of the Sierra, was a waiter. Hence, perhaps, my cosmopolitanism. [With sudden intensity] Shall I tell you the story of my life?

STRAKER [apprehensively] If it ain't too long, old chap—

TANNER [interrupting him] Tsh-sh: you are a Philistine, Henry: you have no romance in you. [To Mendoza] You interest me extremely, President. Never mind Henry: he can go to sleep.

MENDOZA. The woman I loved—

STRAKER. Oh, this is a love story, is it? Right you are.

Go on: I was only afraid you were going to talk about yourself.

MENDOZA. Myself! I have thrown myself away for her sake: that is why I am here. No matter: I count the world well lost for her. She had, I pledge you my word, the most magnificent head of hair I ever saw. She had humor; she had intellect; she could cook to perfection; and her highly strung temperament made her uncertain, incalculable, variable, capricious, cruel, in a word, enchanting.

STRAKER. A six shillin novel sort o woman, all but the cookin. Er name was Lady Gladys Plantagenet, wasn't it?

MENDOZA. No, sir: she was not an earl's daughter. Photography, reproduced by the half-tone process, has made me familiar with the appearance of the daughters of the English peerage; and I can honestly say that I would have sold the lot, faces, dowries, clothes, titles, and all, for a smile from this woman. Yet she was a woman of the people, a worker: otherwise—let me reciprocate your bluntness—I should have scorned her.

TANNER. Very properly. And did she respond to your love?

MENDOZA. Should I be here if she did? She objected to marry a Jew.

TANNER. On religious grounds?

MENDOZA. No: she was a freethinker. She said that every Jew considers in his heart that English people are dirty in their habits.

TANNER [surprised] Dirty!

MENDOZA. It shewed her extraordinary knowledge of the world; for it is undoubtedly true. Our elaborate sanitary code makes us unduly contemptuous of the Gentile.

TANNER. Did you ever hear that, Henry?

STRAKER. I've heard my sister say so. She was cook in a Jewish family once.

MENDOZA. I could not deny it; neither could I eradicate the impression it made on her mind. I could have got round any other objection; but no woman can stand a suspicion of indelicacy as to her person. My entreaties were in vain: she always retorted that she wasn't good enough for me, and recommended me to marry an accursed barmaid named Rebecca Lazarus, whom I loathed. I talked of suicide: she offered me a packet of beetle poison to do it with. I hinted at murder: she went into hysterics; and as I am a living man I went to America so that she might sleep without dreaming that I was stealing upstairs to cut her throat. In America I went out west and fell in with a man who was wanted by the police for holding up trains. It was he who had the idea of holding up motors cars in the South of Europe: a welcome idea to a desperate and disappointed man. He gave me some valuable introductions to capitalists of the right sort. I formed a syndicate; and the present enterprise is the result. I became leader, as the Jew always becomes leader, by his brains and imagination. But with all my pride of race I would give everything I possess to be an Englishman. I am like a boy: I cut her name on the trees and her initials on the sod. When I am alone I lie down and tear my wretched hair and cry Louisa—

STRAKER [*startled*] Louisa!

MENDOZA. It is her name—Louisa—Louisa Straker—

TANNER. Straker!

STRAKER [*scrambling up on his knees most indignantly*] Look here: Louisa Straker is my sister, see? Wot do you mean by gassin about her like this? Wotshe got to do with you?

MENDOZA. A dramatic coincidence! You are Enry, her favorite brother!

STRAKER. Oo are you callin Enry? What call have you to take a liberty with my name or with hers? For two pins I'd punch your fat ed, so I would.

MENDOZA [*with grandiose calm*] If I let you do it, will you promise to brag of it afterwards to her? She will be reminded of her Mendoza: that is all I desire.

TANNER. This is genuine devotion, Henry. You should respect it.

STRAKER [*fiercely*] Funk, more likely.

MENDOZA [*springing to his feet*] Funk! Young man: I come of a famous family of fighters; and as your sister well knows, you would have as much chance against me as a perambulator against your motor car.

STRAKER [*secretly daunted, but rising from his knees with an air of reckless pugnacity*] I ain't afraid of you. With your Louisa! Louisa! Miss Straker is good enough for you, I should think.

MENDOZA. I wish you could persuade her to think so.

STRAKER [*exasperated*] Here—

TANNER [*rising quickly and interposing*] Oh come, Henry: even if you could fight the President you can't fight the whole League of the Sierra. Sit down again and be friendly. A cat may look at a king; and even a President of brigands may look at your sister. All this family pride is really very old fashioned.

STRAKER [*subdued, but grumbling*] Let him look at her. But wot does he mean by makin out that she ever looked at im? [*Reluctantly resuming his couch on the turf*] Ear him talk, one ud think she was keepin company with him. [*He turns his back on them and composes himself to sleep*].

MENDOZA [*to Tanner, becoming more confidential as he finds himself virtually alone with a sympathetic listener in the still starlight of the mountains; for all the rest are asleep by this time*] It was just so with her, sir. Her intellect reached forward into the twentieth century: her social prejudices and family affections reached back into the dark ages. Ah, sir, how the words of Shakespeare seem to fit every crisis in our emotions!

> I loved Louisa: 40,000 brothers
> Could not with all their quantity of love
> Make up my sum.

And so on. I forget the rest. Call it madness if you will—infatuation. I am an able man, a strong man: in ten years I should have owned a first-class hotel. I met her; and—you see!—I am a brigand, an outcast. Even Shakespeare cannot do justice to what I feel for Louisa. Let me read you some lines that I have written about her myself. However slight their literary merit may be, they express what I feel better than any casual words can. [*He produces a packet of hotel bills scrawled with manuscript, and kneels at the fire to decipher them, poking it with a stick to make it glow*].

TANNER [*slapping him rudely on the shoulder*] Put them in the fire, President.

MENDOZA [*startled*] Eh?

TANNER. You are sacrificing your career to a monomania.

MENDOZA. I know it.

TANNER. No you don't. No man would commit such a crime against himself if he really knew what he was doing. How can you look round at these august hills, look up at this divine sky, taste this finely tempered air, and then talk like a literary hack on a second floor in Bloomsbury?

MENDOZA [*shaking his head*] The Sierra is no better than Bloomsbury when once the novelty has worn off. Besides, these mountains make you dream of women—of women with magnificent hair.

TANNER. Of Louisa, in short. They will not make me dream of women, my friend: I am heartwhole.

MENDOZA. Do not boast until morning, sir. This is a strange country for dreams.

TANNER. Well, we shall see. Goodnight. [*He lies down and composes himself to sleep*].

Mendoza, with a sigh, follows his example; and for a few moments there is peace in the Sierra. Then Mendoza sits up suddenly and says pleadingly to Tanner—

MENDOZA. Just allow me to read a few lines before you go to sleep. I should really like your opinion of them.

TANNER [*drowsily*] Go on. I am listening.

MENDOZA. I saw thee first in Whitsun week
      Louisa, Louisa—

TANNER [*rousing himself*] My dear President, Louisa is a very pretty name; but it really doesn't rhyme well to Whitsun week.

MENDOZA. Of course not. Louisa is not the rhyme, but the refrain.

TANNER [*subsiding*] Ah, the refrain. I beg your pardon. Go on.

MENDOZA. Perhaps you do not care for that one: I think you will like this better. [*He recites, in rich soft tones, and in slow time*]

Louisa, I love thee.
I love thee, Louisa.
Louisa, Louisa, Louisa, I love thee.
One name and one phrase make my music, Louisa.
Louisa, Louisa, Louisa, I love thee.

Mendoza thy lover,
Thy lover, Mendoza,
Mendoza adoringly lives for Louisa.
There's nothing but that in the world for Mendoza.
Louisa, Louisa, Mendoza adores thee.

[*Affected*] There is no merit in producing beautiful lines upon such a name. Louisa is an exquisite name, is it not?

TANNER [*all but asleep, responds with a faint groan*].

MENDOZA. O wert thou, Louisa,
      The wife of Mendoza,
      Mendoza's Louisa, Louisa Mendoza,

How blest were the life of Louisa's Mendoza!
How painless his longing of love for Louisa!

That is real poetry—from the heart—from the heart of
hearts. Don't you think it will move her?
No answer.

[*Resignedly*] Asleep, as usual. Doggerel to all the world:
heavenly music to me! Idiot that I am to wear my heart on
my sleeve! [*He composes himself to sleep, murmuring*]
Louisa, I love thee; I love thee, Louisa; Louisa, Louisa,
Louisa, I—

*Straker snores; rolls over on his side; and relapses into sleep.
Stillness settles on the Sierra; and the darkness deepens. The
fire has again buried itself in white ash and ceased to glow.
The peaks shew unfathomably dark against the starry firma-
ment; but now the stars dim and vanish; and the sky seems
to steal away out of the universe. Instead of the Sierra there
is nothing; omnipresent nothing. No sky, no peaks, no light,
no sound, no time nor space, utter void. Then somewhere the
beginning of a pallor, and with it a faint throbbing buzz as
of a ghostly violoncello palpitating on the same note endlessly. A couple of ghostly violins presently take advantage of
this bass and therewith the pallor reveals a man in the void,*

*an incorporeal but visible man, seated, absurdly enough, on
nothing. For a moment he raises his head as the music passes
him by. Then, with a heavy sigh, he droops in utter dejection; and the violins, discouraged, retrace their melody in
despair and at last give it up, extinguished by wailings from
uncanny wind instruments, thus:—*

*It is all very odd. One recognizes the Mozartian strain;
and on this hint, and by the aid of certain sparkles of violet*

light in the pallor, the man's costume explains itself as that of a Spanish nobleman of the XV–XVI century. Don Juan, of course; but where? why? how? Besides, in the brief lifting of his face, now hidden by his hat brim, there was a curious suggestion of Tanner. A more critical, fastidious, handsome face, paler and colder, without Tanner's impetuous credulity and enthusiasm, and without a touch of his modern pluto-cratic vulgarity, but still a resemblance, even an identity. The name too: Don Juan Tenorio, John Tanner. Where on earth —or elsewhere—have we got to from the XX century and the Sierra?

Another pallor in the void, this time not violet, but a dis-agreeable smoky yellow. With it, the whisper of a ghostly clarionet turning this tune into infinite sadness:

The yellowish pallor moves: there is an old crone wandering in the void, bent and toothless; draped, as well as one can guess, in the coarse brown frock of some religious order. She wanders and wanders in her slow hopeless way, much as a wasp flies in its rapid busy way, until she blunders against the thing she seeks: companionship. With a sob of relief the poor old creature clutches at the presence of the man and addresses him in her dry unlovely voice, which can still express pride and resolution as well as suffering.

THE OLD WOMAN. Excuse me; but I am so lonely; and this place is so awful.

DON JUAN. A new comer?

THE OLD WOMAN. Yes: I suppose I died this morning. I confessed; I had extreme unction; I was in bed with my family about me and my eyes fixed on the cross. Then it grew dark; and when the light came back it was this light by which I walk seeing nothing. I have wandered for hours in horrible loneliness.

DON JUAN [*sighing*] Ah! you have not yet lost the sense of time. One soon does, in eternity.

THE OLD WOMAN. Where are we?

DON JUAN. In hell.

THE OLD WOMAN [*proudly*] Hell! I in hell! How dare you?

DON JUAN [*unimpressed*] Why not, Señora?

THE OLD WOMAN. You do not know to whom you are

speaking. I am a lady, and a faithful daughter of the Church.

DON JUAN. I do not doubt it.

THE OLD WOMAN. But how then can I be in hell? Purgatory, perhaps: I have not been perfect: who has? But hell! oh, you are lying.

DON JUAN. Hell, Señora, I assure you; hell at its best: that is, its most solitary—though perhaps you would prefer company.

THE OLD WOMAN. But I have sincerely repented; I have confessed—

DON JUAN. How much?

THE OLD WOMAN. More sins than I really committed. I loved confession.

DON JUAN. Ah, that is perhaps as bad as confessing too little. At all events, Señora, whether by oversight or intention, you are certainly damned, like myself; and there is nothing for it now but to make the best of it.

THE OLD WOMAN [*indignantly*] Oh! and I might have been so much wickeder! All my good deeds wasted! It is unjust.

DON JUAN. No: you were fully and clearly warned. For your bad deeds, vicarious atonement, mercy without justice. For your good deeds, justice without mercy. We have many good people here.

THE OLD WOMAN. Were you a good man?

DON JUAN. I was a murderer.

THE OLD WOMAN. A murderer! Oh, how dare they send me to herd with murderers! I was not as bad as that: I was a good woman. There is some mistake: where can I have it set right?

DON JUAN. I do not know whether mistakes can be corrected here. Probably they will not admit a mistake even if they have made one.

THE OLD WOMAN. But whom can I ask?

DON JUAN. I should ask the Devil, Señora: he understands the ways of this place, which is more than I ever could.

THE OLD WOMAN. The Devil! *I* speak to the Devil!

DON JUAN. In hell, Señora, the Devil is the leader of the best society.

THE OLD WOMAN. I tell you, wretch, I know I am not in hell.

DON JUAN. How do you know?

THE OLD WOMAN. Because I feel no pain.

DON JUAN. Oh, then there is no mistake: you are intentionally damned.

THE OLD WOMAN. Why do you say that?

DON JUAN. Because hell, Señora, is a place for the wicked. The wicked are quite comfortable in it: it was made for them. You tell me you feel no pain. I conclude you are one of those for whom Hell exists.

THE OLD WOMAN. Do you feel no pain?

DON JUAN. I am not one of the wicked, Señora; therefore it bores me, bores me beyond description, beyond belief.

THE OLD WOMAN. Not one of the wicked! You said you were a murderer.

DON JUAN. Only a duel. I ran my sword through an old man who was trying to run his through me.

THE OLD WOMAN. If you were a gentleman, that was not a murder.

DON JUAN. The old man called it murder, because he was, he said, defending his daughter's honor. By this he meant that because I foolishly fell in love with her and told her so, she screamed; and he tried to assassinate me after calling me insulting names.

THE OLD WOMAN. You were like all men. Libertines and murderers all, all, all!

DON JUAN. And yet we meet here, dear lady.

THE OLD WOMAN. Listen to me. My father was slain by just such a wretch as you, in just such a duel, for just such a cause. I screamed: it was my duty. My father drew on my assailant: his honor demanded it. He fell: that was the reward of honor. I am here: in hell, you tell me: that is the reward of duty. Is there justice in heaven?

DON JUAN. No; but there is justice in hell: heaven is far above such idle human personalities. You will be welcome in hell, Señora. Hell is the home of honor, duty, justice, and the rest of the seven deadly virtues. All the wickedness on earth is done in their name: where else but in hell should they have their reward? Have I not told you that the truly damned are those who are happy in hell?

THE OLD WOMAN. And are you happy here?

DON JUAN [springing to his feet] No; and that is the enigma on which I ponder in darkness. Why am I here? I, who repudiated all duty, trampled honor underfoot, and laughed at justice!

THE OLD WOMAN. Oh, what do I care why you are here?

Why am *I* here? I, who sacrificed all my inclinations to womanly virtue and propriety!

DON JUAN. Patience, lady: you will be perfectly happy and at home here. As saith the poet, "Hell is a city much like Seville."

THE OLD WOMAN. Happy! here! where I am nothing! where I am nobody!

DON JUAN. Not at all: you are a lady; and wherever ladies are is hell. Do not be surprised or terrified: you will find everything here that a lady can desire, including devils who will serve you from sheer love of servitude, and magnify your importance for the sake of dignifying their service—the best of servants.

THE OLD WOMAN. My servants will be devils!

DON JUAN. Have you ever had servants who were not devils?

THE OLD WOMAN. Never: they were devils, perfect devils, all of them. But that is only a manner of speaking. I thought you meant that my servants here would be real devils.

DON JUAN. No more real devils than you will be a real lady. Nothing is real here. That is the horror of damnation.

THE OLD WOMAN. Oh, this is all madness. This is worse than fire and the worm.

DON JUAN. For you, perhaps, there are consolations. For instance: how old were you when you changed from time to eternity?

THE OLD WOMAN. Do not ask me how old I was—as if I were a thing of the past. I am 77.

DON JUAN. A ripe age, Señora. But in hell old age is not tolerated. It is too real. Here we worship Love and Beauty. Our souls being entirely damned, we cultivate our hearts. As a lady of 77, you would not have a single acquaintance in hell.

THE OLD WOMAN. How can I help my age, man?

DON JUAN. You forget that you have left your age behind you in the realm of time. You are no more 77 than you are 7 or 17 or 27.

THE OLD WOMAN. Nonsense!

DON JUAN. Consider, Señora: was not this true even when you lived on earth? When you were 70, were you really older underneath your wrinkles and your grey hairs than when you were 30?

THE OLD WOMAN. No, younger: at 30 I was a fool. But of what use is it to feel younger and look older?

DON JUAN. You see, Señora, the look was only an illusion. Your wrinkles lied, just as the plump smooth skin of many a stupid girl of 17, with heavy spirits and decrepit ideas, lies about her age. Well, here we have no bodies: we see each other as bodies only because we learnt to think about one another under that aspect when we were alive; and we still think in that way, knowing no other. But we can appear to one another at what age we choose. You have but to will any of your old looks back, and back they will come.

THE OLD WOMAN. It cannot be true.

DON JUAN. Try.

THE OLD WOMAN. Seventeen!

DON JUAN. Stop. Before you decide, I had better tell you that these things are a matter of fashion. Occasionally we have a rage for 17; but it does not last long. Just at present the fashionable age is 40—or say 37; but there are signs of a change. If you were at all good-looking at 27, I should suggest your trying that, and setting a new fashion.

THE OLD WOMAN. I do not believe a word you are saying. However, 27 be it. [Whisk! the old woman becomes a young one, and so handsome that in the radiance into which her dull yellow halo has suddenly lightened one might almost mistake her for Ann Whitefield].

DON JUAN. Doña Ana de Ulloa!

ANA. What? You know me!

DON JUAN. And you forget me!

ANA. I cannot see your face. [He raises his hat]. Don Juan Tenorio! Monster! You who slew my father! even here you pursue me.

DON JUAN. I protest I do not pursue you. Allow me to withdraw [going].

ANA [seizing his arm] You shall not leave me alone in this dreadful place.

DON JUAN. Provided my staying be not interpreted as pursuit.

ANA [releasing him] You may well wonder how I can endure your presence. My dear, dear father!

DON JUAN. Would you like to see him?

ANA. My father here! ! !

DON JUAN. No: he is in heaven.

ANA. I knew it. My noble father! He is looking down on us now. What must he feel to see his daughter in this place, and in conversation with his murderer!

DON JUAN. By the way, if we should meet him—

ANA. How can we meet him? He is in heaven.

DON JUAN. He condescends to look in upon us here from time to time. Heaven bores him. So let me warn you that if you meet him he will be mortally offended if you speak of me as his murderer! He maintains that he was a much better swordsman than I, and that if his foot had not slipped he would have killed me. No doubt he is right: I was not a good fencer. I never dispute the point; so we are excellent friends.

ANA. It is no dishonor to a soldier to be proud of his skill in arms.

DON JUAN. You would rather not meet him, probably.

ANA. How dare you say that?

DON JUAN. Oh, that is the usual feeling here. You may remember that on earth—though of course we never confessed it—the death of anyone we knew, even those we liked best, was always mingled with a certain satisfaction at being finally done with them.

ANA. Monster! Never, never.

DON JUAN [placidly] I see you recognize the feeling. Yes: a funeral was always a festivity in black, especially the funeral of a relative. At all events, family ties are rarely kept up here. Your father is quite accustomed to this: he will not expect any devotion from you.

ANA. Wretch: I wore mourning for him all my life.

DON JUAN. Yes: it became you. But a life of mourning is one thing: an eternity of it quite another. Besides, here you are as dead as he. Can anything be more ridiculous than one dead person mourning for another? Do not look shocked, my dear Ana; and do not be alarmed: there is plenty of humbug in hell (indeed there is hardly anything else); but the humbug of death and age and change is dropped because here we are all dead and all eternal. You will pick up our ways soon.

ANA. And will all the men call me their dear Ana?

DON JUAN. No. That was a slip of the tongue. I beg your pardon.

ANA [almost tenderly] Juan: did you really love me when you behaved so disgracefully to me?

DON JUAN [impatiently] Oh, I beg you not to begin talking about love. Here they talk of nothing else but love— its beauty, its holiness, its spirituality, its devil knows what! —excuse me; but it does so bore me. They don't know what they're talking about. I do. They think they have achieved the perfection of love because they have no bodies. Sheer imaginative debauchery! Faugh!

ANA. Has even death failed to refine your soul, Juan? Has the terrible judgment of which my father's statue was the minister taught you no reverence?

DON JUAN. How is that very flattering statue, by the way? Does it still come to supper with naughty people and cast them into this bottomless pit?

ANA. It has been a great expense to me. The boys in the monastery school would not let it alone: the mischievous ones broke it; and the studious ones wrote their names on it. Three new noses in two years, and fingers without end. I had to leave it to its fate at last; and now I fear it is shockingly mutilated. My poor father!

DON JUAN. Hush! Listen! [*Two great chords rolling on syncopated waves of sound break forth: D minor and its dominant: a sound of dreadful joy to all musicians.*] Ha! Mozart's statue music. It is your father. You had better disappear until I prepare him. [*She vanishes.*]

From the void comes a living statue of white marble, designed to represent a majestic old man. But he waives his majesty with infinite grace; walks with a feather-like step; and makes every wrinkle in his war worn visage brim over with holiday joyousness. To his sculptor he owes a perfectly trained figure, which he carries erect and trim; and the ends of his moustache curl up, elastic as watchsprings, giving him an air which, but for its Spanish dignity, would be called jaunty. He is on the pleasantest terms with Don Juan. His voice, save for a much more distinguished intonation, is so like the voice of Roebuck Ramsden that it calls attention to the fact that they are not unlike one another in spite of their very different fashions of shaving.

DON JUAN. Ah, here you are, my friend. Why don't you learn to sing the splendid music Mozart has written for you?

THE STATUE. Unluckily he has written it for a bass voice. Mine is a counter tenor. Well: have you repented yet?

DON JUAN. I have too much consideration for you to repent, Don Gonzalo. If I did, you would have no excuse for coming from Heaven to argue with me.

THE STATUE. True. Remain obdurate, my boy. I wish I had killed you, as I should have done but for an accident. Then I should have come here; and you would have had a statue and a reputation for piety to live up to. Any news?

DON JUAN. Yes: your daughter is dead.

THE STATUE [*puzzled*] My daughter? [*Recollecting*] Oh!
the one you were taken with. Let me see: what was her name?

DON JUAN. Ana.

THE STATUE. To be sure: Ana. A goodlooking girl, if I
recollect aright. Have you warned Whatshisname—her husband?

DON JUAN. My friend Ottavio? No: I have not seen him
since Ana arrived.

Ana comes indignantly to light.

ANA. What does this mean? Ottavio here and your friend!
And you, father, have forgotten my name. You are indeed
turned to stone.

THE STATUE. My dear: I am so much more admired in
marble than I ever was in my own person that I have retained
the shape the sculptor gave me. He was one of the first men
of his day: you must acknowledge that.

ANA. Father! Vanity! personal vanity! from you!

THE STATUE. Ah, you outlived that weakness, my daughter: you must be nearly 80 by this time. I was cut off (by an
accident) in my 64th year, and am considerably your junior
in consequence. Besides, my child, in this place, what our
libertine friend here would call the farce of parental wisdom
is dropped. Regard me, I beg, as a fellow creature, not as
a father.

ANA. You speak as this villain speaks.

THE STATUE. Juan is a sound thinker, Ana. A bad fencer,
but a sound thinker.

ANA [*horror creeping upon her*] I begin to understand.
These are devils, mocking me. I had better pray.

THE STATUE [*consoling her*] No, no, no, my child: do
not pray. If you do, you will throw away the main advantage
of this place. Written over the gate here are the words "Leave
every hope behind, ye who enter." Only think what a relief
that is! For what is hope? A form of moral responsibility.
Here there is no hope, and consequently no duty, no work,
nothing to be gained by praying, nothing to be lost by doing
what you like. Hell, in short, is a place where you have nothing to do but amuse yourself. [*Don Juan sighs deeply*]. You
sigh, friend Juan; but if you dwelt in heaven, as I do, you
would realize your advantages.

DON JUAN. You are in good spirits to-day, Commander.
You are positively brilliant. What is the matter?

THE STATUE. I have come to a momentous decision, my

boy. But first, where is our friend the Devil? I must consult
him in the matter. And Ana would like to make his acquaintance, no doubt.

ANA. You are preparing some torment for me.

DON JUAN. All that is superstition, Ana. Reassure yourself. Remember: the devil is not so black as he is painted.

THE STATUE. Let us give him a call.

*At the wave of the statue's hand the great chords roll out
again; but this time Mozart's music gets grotesquely adulterated with Gounod's. A scarlet halo begins to glow; and into it
the Devil rises, very Mephistophelean, and not at all unlike
Mendoza, though not so interesting. He looks older; is getting
prematurely bald; and, in spite of an effusion of goodnature
and friendliness, is peevish and sensitive when his advances
are not reciprocated. He does not inspire much confidence in
his powers of hard work or endurance, and is, on the whole,
a disagreeably self-indulgent looking person; but he is clever
and plausible, though perceptibly less well bred than the two
other men, and enormously less vital than the woman.*

THE DEVIL [*heartily*] Have I the pleasure of again receiving a visit from the illustrious Commander of Calatrava?
[*Coldly*] Don Juan, your servant. [*Politely*] And a strange
lady? My respects, Señora.

ANA. Are you—

THE DEVIL [*bowing*] Lucifer, at your service.

ANA. I shall go mad.

THE DEVIL [*gallantly*] Ah, Señora, do not be anxious.
You come to us from earth, full of the prejudices and terrors
of that priest-ridden place. You have heard me ill spoken of;
and yet, believe me, I have hosts of friends there.

ANA. Yes: you reign in their hearts.

THE DEVIL [*shaking his head*] You flatter me, Señora;
but you are mistaken. It is true that the world cannot get
on without me; but it never gives me credit for that: in its
heart it mistrusts and hates me. Its sympathies are all with
misery, with poverty, with starvation of the body and of the
heart. I call on it to sympathize with joy, with love, with
happiness, with beauty—

DON JUAN [*nauseated*] Excuse me: I am going. You know
I cannot stand this.

THE DEVIL [*angrily*] Yes: I know that you are no friend
of mine.

THE STATUE. What harm is he doing you, Juan? It seems

to me that he was talking excellent sense when you interrupted him.

THE DEVIL [*warmly shaking the statue's hand*] Thank you, my friend: thank you. You have always understood me: he has always disparaged and avoided me.

DON JUAN. I have treated you with perfect courtesy.

THE DEVIL. Courtesy! What is courtesy? I care nothing for mere courtesy. Give me warmth of heart, true sincerity, the bond of sympathy with love and joy—

DON JUAN. You are making me ill.

THE DEVIL. There! [*Appealing to the statue*] You hear, sir! Oh, by what irony of fate was this cold selfish egotist sent to my kingdom, and you taken to the icy mansions of the sky!

THE STATUE. I can't complain. I was a hypocrite; and it served me right to be sent to heaven.

THE DEVIL. Why, sir, do you not join us, and leave a sphere for which your temperament is too sympathetic, your heart too warm, your capacity for enjoyment too generous?

THE STATUE. I have this day resolved to do so. In future, excellent Son of the Morning, I am yours. I have left Heaven for ever.

THE DEVIL [*again grasping his hand*] Ah, what an honor for me! What a triumph for our cause! Thank you, thank you. And now, my friend—I may call you so at last—could you not persuade him to take the place you have left vacant above?

THE STATUE [*shaking his head*] I cannot conscientiously recommend anybody with whom I am on friendly terms to deliberately make himself dull and uncomfortable.

THE DEVIL. Of course not; but are you sure he would be uncomfortable? Of course you know best: you brought him here originally; and we had the greatest hopes of him. His sentiments were in the best taste of our best people. You remember how he sang? [*He begins to sing in a nasal operatic baritone, tremulous from an eternity of misuse in the French manner.*]

Vivan le femmine!
Viva il buon vino!

THE STATUE [*taking up the tune an octave higher in his counter tenor*]

Sostegno e gloria
D'umanità.

THE DEVIL. Precisely. Well, he never sings for us now.

DON JUAN. Do you complain of that? Hell is full of musical amateurs: music is the brandy of the damned. May not one lost soul be permitted to abstain?

THE DEVIL. You dare blaspheme against the sublimest of the arts!

DON JUAN [*with cold disgust*] You talk like a hysterical woman fawning on a fiddler.

THE DEVIL. I am not angry. I merely pity you. You have no soul; and you are unconscious of all that you lose. Now you, Señor Commander, are a born musician. How well you sing! Mozart would be delighted if he were still here; but he moped and went to heaven. Curious how these clever men, whom you would have supposed born to be popular here, have turned out social failures, like Don Juan!

DON JUAN. I am really very sorry to be a social failure.

THE DEVIL. Not that we don't admire your intellect, you know. We do. But I look at the matter from your own point of view. You don't get on with us. The place doesn't suit you. The truth is, you have—I won't say no heart; for we know that beneath all your affected cynicism you have a warm one—

DON JUAN [*shrinking*] Don't, please don't.

THE DEVIL [*nettled*] Well, you've no capacity for enjoyment. Will that satisfy you?

DON JUAN. It is a somewhat less insufferable form of cant than the other. But if you'll allow me, I'll take refuge, as usual, in solitude.

THE DEVIL. Why not take refuge in Heaven? That's the proper place for you. [*To Ana*] Come, Señora! could you not persuade him for his own good to try change of air?

ANA. But can he go to Heaven if he wants to?

THE DEVIL. What's to prevent him?

ANA. Can anybody—can *I* go to Heaven if I want to?

THE DEVIL [*rather contemptuously*] Certainly, if your taste lies that way.

ANA. But why doesn't everybody go to Heaven, then?

THE STATUE [*chuckling*] *I* can tell you that, my dear. It's because heaven is the most angelically dull place in all creation: that's why.

THE DEVIL. His excellency the Commander puts it with military bluntness; but the strain of living in Heaven is intolerable. There is a notion that I was turned out of it; but as a matter of fact nothing could have induced me to stay there. I simply left it and organized this place.

THE STATUE. I don't wonder at it. Nobody could stand an eternity of heaven.

THE DEVIL. Oh, it suits some people. Let us be just, Commander: it is a question of temperament. I don't admire the heavenly temperament: I don't understand it: I don't know that I particularly want to understand it; but it takes all sorts to make a universe. There is no accounting for tastes: there are people who like it. I think Don Juan would like it.

DON JUAN. But—pardon my frankness—could you really go back there if you desired to; or are the grapes sour?

THE DEVIL. Back there! I often go back there. Have you never read the book of Job? Have you any canonical authority for assuming that there is any barrier between our circle and the other one?

ANA. But surely there is a great gulf fixed.

THE DEVIL. Dear lady: a parable must not be taken literally. The gulf is the difference between the angelic and the diabolic temperament. What more impassable gulf could you have? Think of what you have seen on earth. There is no physical gulf between the philosopher's class room and the bull ring; but the bull fighters do not come to the class room for all that. Have you ever been in the country where I have the largest following—England? There they have great racecourses, and also concert rooms where they play the classical compositions of his Excellency's friend Mozart. Those who go to the racecourses can stay away from them and go to the classical concerts instead if they like: there is no law against it; for Englishmen never will be slaves: they are free to do whatever the Government and public opinion allow them to do. And the classical concert is admitted to be a higher, more cultivated, poetic, intellectual, ennobling place than the racecourse. But do the lovers of racing desert their sport and flock to the concert room? Not they. They would suffer there all the weariness the Commander has suffered in heaven. There is the great gulf of the parable between the two places. A mere physical gulf they could bridge; or at least I could bridge it for them (the earth is full of Devil's Bridges); but the gulf of dislike is impassable and eternal. And that is the only gulf that separates my friends here from those who are invidiously called the blest.

ANA. I shall go to heaven at once.

THE STATUE. My child: one word of warning first. Let me complete my friend Lucifer's similitude of the classical concert. At every one of those concerts in England you will find rows of weary people who are there, not because they really like classical music, but because they think they ought to like it. Well, there is the same thing in heaven. A number of people sit there in glory, not because they are happy, but because they think they owe it to their position to be in heaven. They are almost all English.

THE DEVIL. Yes: the Southerners give it up and join me just as you have done. But the English really do not seem to know when they are thoroughly miserable. An Englishman thinks he is moral when he is only uncomfortable.

THE STATUE. In short, my daughter, if you go to Heaven without being naturally qualified for it, you will not enjoy yourself there.

ANA. And who dares say that I am not naturally qualified for it? The most distinguished princes of the Church have never questioned it. I owe it to myself to leave this place at once.

THE DEVIL [offended] As you please, Señora. I should have expected better taste from you.

ANA. Father: I shall expect you to come with me. You cannot stay here. What will people say?

THE STATUE. People! Why, the best people are here—princes of the church and all. So few go to Heaven, and so many come here, that the blest, once called a heavenly host, are a continually dwindling minority. The saints, the fathers, the elect of long ago are the cranks, the faddists, the outsiders of to-day.

THE DEVIL. It is true. From the beginning of my career I knew that I should win in the long run by sheer weight of public opinion, in spite of the long campaign of misrepresentation and calumny against me. At bottom the universe is a constitutional one; and with such a majority as mine I cannot be kept permanently out of office.

DON JUAN. I think, Ana, you had better stay here.

ANA [jealously] You do not want me to go with you.

DON JUAN. Surely you do not want to enter Heaven in the company of a reprobate like me.

ANA. All souls are equally precious. You repent, do you not?

DON JUAN. My dear Ana, you are silly. Do you suppose heaven is like earth, where people persuade themselves that what is done can be undone by repentance; that what is spoken can be unspoken by withdrawing it; that what is true can be annihilated by a general agreement to give it the lie? No: heaven is the home of the masters of reality: that is why I am going thither.

ANA. Thank you: I am going to heaven for happiness. I have had quite enough of reality on earth.

DON JUAN. Then you must stay here; for hell is the home of the unreal and of the seekers for happiness. It is the only refuge from heaven, which is, as I tell you, the home of the masters of reality, and from earth, which is the home of the slaves of reality. The earth is a nursery in which men and women play at being heroes and heroines, saints and sinners; but they are dragged down from their fool's paradise by their bodies: hunger and cold and thirst, age and decay and disease, death above all, make them slaves of reality: thrice a day meals must be eaten and digested: thrice a century a new generation must be engendered: ages of faith, of romance, and of science are all driven at last to have but one prayer "Make me a healthy animal." But here you escape this tyranny of the flesh; for here you are not an animal at all: you are a ghost, an appearance, an illusion, a convention, deathless, ageless: in a word, bodiless. There are no social questions here, no political questions, no religious questions, best of all, perhaps, no sanitary questions. Here you call your appearance beauty, your emotions love, your sentiments heroism, your aspirations virtue, just as you did on earth; but here there are no hard facts to contradict you, no ironic contrast of your needs with your pretensions, no human comedy, nothing but a perpetual romance, a universal melodrama. As our German friend put it in his poem, "the poetically nonsensical here is good sense; and the Eternal Feminine draws us ever upward and on"—without getting us a step farther. And yet you want to leave this paradise!

ANA. But if Hell be so beautiful as this, how glorious must heaven be!

The Devil, the Statue, and Don Juan all begin to speak at once in violent protest; then stop, abashed.

DON JUAN. I beg your pardon.

THE DEVIL. Not at all. I interrupted you.

THE STATUE. You were going to say something.

DON JUAN. After you, gentlemen.

THE DEVIL [*to Don Juan*] You have been so eloquent on the advantages of my dominions that I leave you to do equal justice to the drawbacks of the alternative establishment.

DON JUAN. In Heaven, as I picture it, dear lady, you live and work instead of playing and pretending. You face things as they are; you escape nothing but glamor; and your steadfastness and your peril are your glory. If the play still goes on here and on earth, and all the world is a stage, Heaven is at least behind the scenes. But Heaven cannot be described by metaphor. Thither I shall go presently, because there I hope to escape at last from lies and from the tedious, vulgar pursuit of happiness, to spend my eons in contemplation—

THE STATUE. Ugh!

DON JUAN. Señor Commander: I do not blame your disgust: a picture gallery is a dull place for a blind man. But even as you enjoy the contemplation of such romantic mirages as beauty and pleasure; so would I enjoy the contemplation of that which interests me above all things: namely, Life: the force that ever strives to attain greater power of contemplating itself. What made this brain of mine, do you think? Not the need to move my limbs; for a rat with half my brains moves as well as I. Not merely the need to do, but the need to know what I do, lest in my blind efforts to live I should be slaying myself.

THE STATUE. You would have slain yourself in your blind efforts to fence but for my foot slipping, my friend.

DON JUAN. Audacious ribald: your laughter will finish in hideous boredom before morning.

THE STATUE. Ha ha! Do you remember how I frightened you when I said something like that to you from my pedestal in Seville? It sounds rather flat without my trombones.

DON JUAN. They tell me it generally sounds flat with them, Commander.

ANA. Oh, do not interrupt with these frivolities, father. Is there nothing in Heaven but contemplation, Juan?

DON JUAN. In the Heaven I seek, no other joy. But there is the work of helping Life in its struggle upward. Think of how it wastes and scatters itself, how it raises up obstacles to itself and destroys itself in its ignorance and blindness. It needs a brain, this irresistible force, lest in its ignorance it should resist itself. What a piece of work is man! says the poet. Yes: but what a blunderer! Here is the highest miracle of organization yet attained by life, the most intensely alive thing that exists, the most conscious of all the organisms; and yet, how wretched are his brains! Stupidity made sordid and cruel by the realities learnt from toil and poverty: Imagina-

tion resolved to starve sooner than face these realities, piling
up illusions to hide them, and calling itself cleverness, genius!
And each accusing the other of its own defect: Stupidity
accusing Imagination of folly, and Imagination accusing
Stupidity of ignorance: whereas, alas! Stupidity has all the
knowledge, and Imagination all the intelligence.

THE DEVIL. And a pretty kettle of fish they make of it
between them. Did I not say, when I was arranging that
affair of Faust's, that all Man's reason has done for him is
to make him beastlier than any beast. One splendid body
is worth the brains of a hundred dyspeptic, flatulent philosophers.

DON JUAN. You forget that brainless magnificence of
body has been tried. Things immeasurably greater than man
in every respect but brain have existed and perished. The
megatherium, the icthyosaurus have paced the earth with
seven-league steps and hidden the day with cloud vast wings.
Where are they now? Fossils in museums, and so few and
imperfect at that, that a knuckle bone or a tooth of one of
them is prized beyond the lives of a thousand soldiers. These
things lived and wanted to live; but for lack of brains they
did not know how to carry out their purpose, and so destroyed
themselves.

THE DEVIL. And is Man any the less destroying himself
for all this boasted brain of his? Have you walked up and
down upon the earth lately? I have; and I have examined
Man's wonderful inventions. And I tell you that in the arts
of life man invents nothing; but in the arts of death he out-
does Nature herself, and produces by chemistry and machinery
all the slaughter of plague, pestilence and famine. The peasant
I tempt to-day eats and drinks what was eaten and drunk by
the peasants of ten thousand years ago; and the house he lives
in has not altered as much in a thousand centuries as the
fashion of a lady's bonnet in a score of weeks. But when he
goes out to slay, he carries a marvel of mechanism that lets
loose at the touch of his finger all the hidden molecular
energies, and leaves the javelin, the arrow, the blowpipe of
his fathers far behind. In the arts of peace Man is a bungler.
I have seen his cotton factories and the like, with machinery
that a greedy dog could have invented if it had wanted money
instead of food. I know his clumsy typewriters and bungling
locomotives and tedious bicycles: they are toys compared to
the Maxim gun, the submarine torpedo boat. There is nothing
in Man's industrial machinery but his greed and sloth: his

heart is in his weapons. This marvellous force of Life of which you boast is a force of Death: Man measures his strength by his destructiveness. What is his religion? An excuse for hating me. What is his law? An excuse for hanging you. What is his morality? Gentility! an excuse for consuming without producing. What is his art? An excuse for gloating over pictures of slaughter. What are his politics? Either the worship of a despot because a despot can kill, or parliamentary cockfighting. I spent an evening lately in a certain celebrated legislature, and heard the pot lecturing the kettle for its blackness, and ministers answering questions. When I left I chalked up on the door the old nursery saying "Ask no questions and you will be told no lies." I bought a sixpenny family magazine, and found it full of pictures of young men shooting and stabbing one another. I saw a man die: he was a London bricklayer's laborer with seven children. He left seventeen pounds club money; and his wife spent it all on his funeral and went into the workhouse with the children next day. She would not have spent sevenpence on her children's schooling: the law had to force her to let them be taught gratuitously; but on death she spent all she had. Their imagination glows, their energies rise up at the idea of death, these people: they love it; and the more horrible it is the more they enjoy it. Hell is a place far above their comprehension: they derive their notion of it from two of the greatest fools that ever lived, an Italian and an Englishman. The Italian described it as a place of mud, frost, filth, fire, and venomous serpents: all torture. This ass, when he was not lying about me, was maundering about some woman whom he saw once in the street. The Englishman described me as being expelled from Heaven by cannons and gunpowder; and to this day every Briton believes that the whole of his silly story is in the Bible. What else he says I do not know; for it is all in a long poem which neither I nor anyone else ever succeeded in wading through. It is the same in everything. The highest form of literature is the tragedy, a play in which everybody is murdered at the end. In the old chronicles you read of earthquakes and pestilences, and are told that these shewed the power and majesty of God and the littleness of Man. Nowadays the chronicles describe battles. In a battle two bodies of men shoot at one another with bullets and explosive shells until one body runs away, when the others chase the fugitives on horseback and cut them to pieces as they fly. And this, the chronicle concludes, shews the greatness and majesty of empires, and the littleness of the van-

quished. Over such battles the people run about the streets
yelling with delight, and egg their Governments on to spend
hundreds of millions of money in the slaughter, whilst the
strongest Ministers dare not spend an extra penny in the pound
against the poverty and pestilence through which they themselves daily walk. I could give you a thousand instances; but
they all come to the same thing: the power that governs the
earth is not the power of Life but of Death; and the inner
need that has nerved Life to the effort of organizing itself into
the human being is not the need for higher life but for a more
efficient engine of destruction. The plague, the famine, the
earthquake, the tempest were too spasmodic in their action;
the tiger and crocodile were too easily satiated and not cruel
enough: something more constantly, more ruthlessly, more
ingeniously destructive was needed; and that something was
Man, the inventor of the rack, the stake, the gallows, and the
electrocutor; of the sword and gun; above all, of justice, duty,
patriotism and all the other isms by which even those who
are clever enough to be humanely disposed are persuaded to
become the most destructive of all the destroyers.

DON JUAN. Pshaw! all this is old. Your weak side, my
diabolic friend, is that you have always been a gull: you take
Man at his own valuation. Nothing would flatter him more
than your opinion of him. He loves to think of himself as
bold and bad. He is neither one nor the other: he is only a
coward. Call him tyrant, murderer, pirate, bully; and he will
adore you, and swagger about with the consciousness of having the blood of the old sea kings in his veins. Call him liar
and thief; and he will only take an action against you for
libel. But call him coward; and he will go mad with rage: he
will face death to outface that stinging truth. Man gives every
reason for his conduct save one, every excuse for his crimes
save one, every plea for his safety save one; and that one is
his cowardice. Yet all his civilization is founded on his
cowardice, on his abject tameness, which he calls his respectability. There are limits to what a mule or an ass will stand;
but Man will suffer himself to be degraded until his vileness
becomes so loathsome to his oppressors that they themselves
are forced to reform it.

THE DEVIL. Precisely. And these are the creatures in
whom you discover what you call a Life Force!

DON JUAN. Yes; for now comes the most surprising part
of the whole business.

THE STATUE. What's that?

DON JUAN. Why, that you can make any of these cowards brave by simply putting an idea into his head.

THE STATUE. Stuff! As an old soldier I admit the cowardice: it's as universal as sea sickness, and matters just as little. But that about putting an idea into a man's head is stuff and nonsense. In a battle all you need to make you fight is a little hot blood and the knowledge that it's more dangerous to lose than to win.

DON JUAN. That is perhaps why battles are so useless. But men never really overcome fear until they imagine they are fighting to further a universal purpose—fighting for an idea, as they call it. Why was the Crusader braver than the pirate? Because he fought, not for himself, but for the Cross. What force was it that met him with a valor as reckless as his own? The force of men who fought, not for themselves, but for Islam. They took Spain from us, though we were fighting for our very hearths and homes; but when we, too, fought for that mighty idea, a Catholic Church, we swept them back to Africa.

THE DEVIL [ironically] What! you a Catholic, Señor Don Juan! A devotee! My congratulations.

THE STATUE [seriously] Come come! as a soldier, I can listen to nothing against the Church.

DON JUAN. Have no fear, Commander: this idea of a Catholic Church will survive Islam, will survive the Cross, will survive even that vulgar pageant of incompetent schoolboyish gladiators which you call the Army.

THE STATUE. Juan: you will force me to call you to account for this.

DON JUAN. Useless: I cannot fence. Every idea for which Man will die will be a Catholic idea. When the Spaniard learns at last that he is no better than the Saracen, and his prophet no better than Mahomet, he will arise, more Catholic than ever, and die on a barricade across the filthy slum he starves in, for universal liberty and equality.

THE STATUE. Bosh!

DON JUAN. What you call bosh is the only thing men dare die for. Later on, Liberty will not be Catholic enough: men will die for human perfection, to which they will sacrifice all their liberty gladly.

THE DEVIL. Ay: they will never be at a loss for an excuse for killing one another.

DON JUAN. What of that? It is not death that matters, but the fear of death. It is not killing and dying that degrades us, but base living, and accepting the wages and profits of degradation. Better ten dead men than one live slave or his master. Men shall yet rise up, father against son and brother against brother, and kill one another for the great Catholic idea of abolishing slavery.

THE DEVIL. Yes, when the Liberty and Equality of which you prate shall have made free white Christians cheaper in the labor market than black heathen slaves sold by auction at the block.

DON JUAN. Never fear! the white laborer shall have his turn too. But I am not now defending the illusory forms the great ideas take. I am giving you examples of the fact that this creature Man, who in his own selfish affairs is a coward to the backbone, will fight for an idea like a hero. He may be abject as a citizen; but he is dangerous as a fanatic. He can only be enslaved whilst he is spiritually weak enough to listen to reason. I tell you, gentlemen, if you can shew a man a piece of what he now calls God's work to do, and what he will later on call by many new names, you can make him entirely reckless of the consequences to himself personally.

ANA. Yes: he shirks all his responsibilities, and leaves his wife to grapple with them.

THE STATUE. Well said, daughter. Do not let him talk you out of your common sense.

THE DEVIL. Alas! Señor Commander, now that we have got on to the subject of Woman, he will talk more than ever. However, I confess it is for me the one supremely interesting subject.

DON JUAN. To a woman, Señora, man's duties and responsibilities begin and end with the task of getting bread for her children. To her, Man is only a means to the end of getting children and rearing them.

ANA. Is that your idea of a woman's mind? I call it cynical and disgusting materialism.

DON JUAN. Pardon me, Ana: I said nothing about a woman's whole mind. I spoke of her view of Man as a separate sex. It is no more cynical than her view of herself as above all things a Mother. Sexually, Woman is Nature's contrivance for perpetuating its highest achievement. Sexually, Man is Woman's contrivance for fulfilling Nature's behest in the most economical way. She knows by instinct that far back in the evolutional process she invented him, differentiated him, created him in order to produce something better than the single-sexed process can produce. Whilst he fulfils the purpose for which she made him, he is welcome to his dreams, his follies, his ideals, his heroisms, provided that the keystone of them all is the worship of woman, of motherhood, of the family, of the hearth. But how rash and dangerous it was to invent a separate creature whose sole function was her own impregnation! For mark what has happened. First, Man has multiplied on her hands until there are as many men as women; so that she has been unable to employ for her purposes more than a fraction of the immense energy she has left at his disposal by saving him the exhausting labor of gestation. This superfluous energy has gone to his brain and to his muscle. He has become too strong to be controlled by her bodily, and too imaginative and mentally vigorous to be content with mere self-reproduction. He has created civilization without consulting her, taking her domestic labor for granted as the foundation of it.

ANA. That is true, at all events.

THE DEVIL. Yes; and this civilization! what is it, after all?

DON JUAN. After all, an excellent peg to hang your cynical commonplaces on; but before all, it is an attempt on Man's part to make himself something more than the mere instrument of Woman's purpose. So far, the result of Life's continual effort not only to maintain itself, but to achieve higher and higher organization and completer self-consciousness, is only, at best, a doubtful campaign between its forces and those of Death and Degeneration. The battles in this campaign are mere blunders, mostly won, like actual military battles, in spite of the commanders.

THE STATUE. That is a dig at me. No matter: go on, go on.

DON JUAN. It is a dig at a much higher power than you, Commander. Still, you must have noticed in your profession that even a stupid general can win battles when the enemy's general is a little stupider.

THE STATUE [*very seriously*] Most true, Juan, most true. Some donkeys have amazing luck.

DON JUAN. Well, the Life Force is stupid; but it is not so stupid as the forces of Death and Degeneration. Besides, these are in its pay all the time. And so Life wins, after a fashion. What mere copiousness of fecundity can supply and mere greed preserve, we possess. The survival of whatever form of civilization can produce the best rifle and the best fed riflemen is assured.

THE DEVIL. Exactly! the survival, not of the most effective means of Life but of the most effective means of Death. You always come back to my point, in spite of your wrigglings and evasions and sophistries, not to mention the intolerable length of your speeches.

DON JUAN. Oh come! who began making long speeches? However, if I overtax your intellect, you can leave us and seek the society of love and beauty and the rest of your favorite boredoms.

THE DEVIL [*much offended*] This is not fair, Don Juan, and not civil. I am also on the intellectual plane. Nobody can appreciate it more than I do. I am arguing fairly with you, and, I think, utterly refuting you. Let us go on for another hour if you like.

DON JUAN. Good: let us.

THE STATUE. Not that I see any prospect of your coming to any point in particular, Juan. Still, since in this place, instead of merely killing time we have to kill eternity, go ahead by all means.

DON JUAN [*somewhat impatiently*] My point, you marbleheaded old masterpiece, is only a step ahead of you. Are we agreed that Life is a force which has made innumerable experiments in organizing itself; that the mammoth and the man, the mouse and the megatherium, the flies and the fleas and the Fathers of the Church, are all more or less successful attempts to build up that raw force into higher and higher individuals, the ideal individual being omnipotent, omniscient, infallible, and withal completely, unilludedly self-conscious: in short, a god?

THE DEVIL. I agree, for the sake of argument.

THE STATUE. I agree, for the sake of avoiding argument.

ANA. I most emphatically disagree as regards the Fathers of the Church; and I must beg you not to drag them into the argument.

DON JUAN. I did so purely for the sake of alliteration, Ana; and I shall make no further allusion to them. And now, since we are, with that exception, agreed so far, will you not agree with me further that Life has not measured the success of its attempts at godhead by the beauty or bodily perfection of the result, since in both these respects the birds, as our friend Aristophanes long ago pointed out, are so extraordinarily superior, with their power of flight and their lovely plumage, and, may I add, the touching poetry of their loves and nestings, that it is inconceivable that Life, having once produced them, should, if love and beauty were her object, start off on another line and labor at the clumsy elephant and the hideous ape, whose grandchildren we are?

ANA. Aristophanes was a heathen; and you, Juan, I am afraid, are very little better.

THE DEVIL. You conclude, then, that Life was driving at clumsiness and ugliness?

DON JUAN. No, perverse devil that you are, a thousand times no. Life was driving at brains—at its darling object: an organ by which it can attain not only self-consciousness but self-understanding.

THE STATUE. This is metaphysics, Juan. Why the devil should—[to The Devil] I beg your pardon.

THE DEVIL. Pray don't mention it. I have always regarded the use of my name to secure additional emphasis as a high compliment to me. It is quite at your service, Commander.

THE STATUE. Thank you: that's very good of you. Even in heaven, I never quite got out of my old military habits of speech. What I was going to ask Juan was why Life should bother itself about getting a brain. Why should it want to understand itself? Why not be content to enjoy itself?

DON JUAN. Without a brain, Commander, you would enjoy yourself without knowing it, and so lose all the fun.

THE STATUE. True, most true. But I am quite content with brain enough to know that I'm enjoying myself. I don't want to understand why. In fact, I'd rather not. My experience is that one's pleasures don't bear thinking about.

DON JUAN. That is why intellect is so unpopular. But to Life, the force behind the Man, intellect is a necessity, because without it he blunders into death. Just as Life, after ages of struggle, evolved that wonderful bodily organ the eye, so that the living organism could see where it was going and what was coming to help or threaten it, and thus avoid a thousand dangers that formerly slew it, so it is evolving today a mind's eye that shall see, not the physical world, but the purpose of Life, and thereby enable the individual to work for that purpose instead of thwarting and baffling it by setting up shortsighted personal aims as at present. Even as it is, only one sort of man has ever been happy, has ever been universally respected among all the conflicts of interests and illusions.

THE STATUE. You mean the military man.

DON JUAN. Commander: I do not mean the military man. When the military man approaches, the world locks up its spoons and packs off its womankind. No: I sing, not arms and the hero, but the philosophic man: he who seeks in contemplation to discover the inner will of the world, in invention to discover the means of fulfilling that will, and in action to do that will by the so-discovered means. Of all other sorts of men I declare myself tired. They are tedious failures. When I was on earth, professors of all sorts prowled round me feeling for an unhealthy spot in me on which they could fasten. The doctors of medicine bade me consider what I must do to save my body, and offered me quack cures for imaginary diseases. I replied that I was not a hypochondriac; so they called me Ignoramus and went their way. The doctors of divinity bade me consider what I must do to save my soul; but I was not a spiritual hypochondriac any more than a bodily one, and would not trouble myself about that either; so they called me Atheist and went their way. After them came the politician, who said there was only one purpose in Nature, and that was to get him into parliament. I told him I did not care whether he got into parliament or not; so he called me Mugwump and went his way. Then came the romantic man, the Artist, with his love songs and his paintings and his poems; and with him I had great delight for many years, and some profit; for I cultivated my senses for his sake; and his songs taught me to hear better, his paintings to see better, and his poems to feel more deeply. But he led me at last into the worship of Woman.

ANA. Juan!

DON JUAN. Yes: I came to believe that in her voice was all the music of the song, in her face all the beauty of the painting, and in her soul all the emotion of the poem.

ANA. And you were disappointed, I suppose. Well, was it her fault that you attributed all these perfections to her?

DON JUAN. Yes, partly. For with a wonderful instinctive cunning, she kept silent and allowed me to glorify her; to mistake my own visions, thoughts, and feelings for hers. Now my friend the romantic man was often too poor or too timid to approach those women who were beautiful or refined enough to seem to realize his ideal; and so he went to his grave believing in his dream. But I was more favored by nature and circumstance. I was of noble birth and rich; and when my person did not please, my conversation flattered, though I generally found myself fortunate in both.

THE STATUE. Coxcomb!

DON JUAN. Yes; but even my coxcombry pleased. Well, I found that when I had touched a woman's imagination, she would allow me to persuade myself that she loved me; but when my suit was granted she never said "I am happy: my love is satisfied": she always said, first, "At last, the barriers are down," and second, "When will you come again?"

ANA. That is exactly what men say.

DON JUAN. I protest I never said it. But all women say it. Well, these two speeches always alarmed me; for the first meant that the lady's impulse had been solely to throw down my fortifications and gain my citadel; and the second openly announced that henceforth she regarded me as her property, and counted my time as already wholly at her disposal.

THE DEVIL. That is where your want of heart came in.

THE STATUE [shaking his head] You shouldn't repeat what a woman says, Juan.

ANA [severely] It should be sacred to you.

THE STATUE. Still, they certainly do always say it. I never minded the barriers; but there was always a slight shock about the other, unless one was very hard hit indeed.

DON JUAN. Then the lady, who had been happy and idle enough before, became anxious, preoccupied with me, always intriguing, conspiring, pursuing, watching, waiting, bent wholly on making sure of her prey—I being the prey, you understand. Now this was not what I had bargained for. It may have been very proper and very natural; but it was not music, painting, poetry and joy incarnated in a beautiful woman. I ran away from it. I ran away from it very often: in fact I became famous for running away from it.

ANA. Infamous, you mean.

DON JUAN. I did not run away from you. Do you blame me for running away from the others?

ANA. Nonsense, man. You are talking to a woman of 77 now. If you had had the chance, you would have run away from me too—if I had let you. You would not have found it so easy with me as with some of the others. If men will not be faithful to their home and their duties, they must be made to be. I daresay you all want to marry lovely incarnations of music and painting and poetry. Well, you can't have them, because they don't exist. If flesh and blood is not good enough for you you must go without: that's all. Women have to put up with flesh-and-blood husbands—and little enough of that too, sometimes; and you will have to put up with flesh-and-blood wives. [The Devil looks dubious. The Statue makes a wry face]. I see you don't like that, any of you; but it's true, for all that; so if you don't like it you can lump it.

DON JUAN. My dear lady, you have put my whole case

against romance into a few sentences. That is just why I turned my back on the romantic man with the artist nature, as he called his infatuation. I thanked him for teaching me to use my eyes and ears; but I told him that his beauty worshipping and happiness hunting and woman idealizing was not worth a dump as a philosophy of life; so he called me Philistine and went his way.

ANA. It seems that Woman taught you something, too, with all her defects.

DON JUAN. She did more: she interpreted all the other teaching for me. Ah, my friends, when the barriers were down for the first time, what an astounding illumination! I had been prepared for infatuation, for intoxication, for all the illusions of love's young dream; and lo! never was my perception clearer, nor my criticism more ruthless. The most jealous rival of my mistress never saw every blemish in her more keenly than I. I was not duped: I took her without chloroform.

ANA. But you did take her.

DON JUAN. That was the revelation. Up to that moment I had never lost the sense of being my own master; never consciously taken a single step until my reason had examined and approved it. I had come to believe that I was a purely rational creature: a thinker! I said, with the foolish philosopher, "I think; therefore I am." It was Woman who taught me to say "I am; therefore I think." And also "I would think more; therefore I must be more."

THE STATUE. This is extremely abstract and metaphysical, Juan. If you would stick to the concrete, and put your discoveries in the form of entertaining anecdotes about your adventures with women, your conversation would be easier to follow.

DON JUAN. Bah! what need I add? Do you not understand that when I stood face to face with Woman, every fibre in my clear critical brain warned me to spare her and save myself. My morals said No. My conscience said No. My chivalry and pity for her said No. My prudent regard for myself said No. My ear, practised on a thousand songs and symphonies; my eye, exercised on a thousand paintings; tore her voice, her features, her color to shreds. I caught all those tell-tale resemblances to her father and mother by which I knew what she would be like in thirty years time. I noted the gleam of gold from a dead tooth in the laughing mouth: I made curious observations of the strange odors of the chemistry of the nerves. The visions of my romantic reveries, in which I had trod the plains of heaven with a deathless, ageless creature of coral and ivory, deserted me in that supreme hour. I remembered them and desperately strove to recover their illusion; but they now seemed the emptiest of inventions: my judgment was not to be corrupted: my brain still said No on every issue. And whilst I was in the act of framing my excuse to the lady, Life seized me and threw me into her arms as a sailor throws a scrap of fish into the mouth of a seabird.

THE STATUE. You might as well have gone without thinking such a lot about it, Juan. You are like all the clever men: you have more brains than is good for you.

THE DEVIL. And were you not the happier for the experience, Señor Don Juan?

DON JUAN. The happier, no: the wiser, yes. That moment introduced me for the first time to myself, and, through myself, to the world. I saw then how useless it is to attempt to impose conditions on the irresistible force of Life; to preach prudence, careful selection, virtue, honor, chastity—

ANA. Don Juan: a word against chastity is an insult to me.

DON JUAN. I say nothing against your chastity, Señora, since it took the form of a husband and twelve children. What more could you have done had you been the most abandoned of women?

ANA. I could have had twelve husbands and no children: that's what I could have done, Juan. And let me tell you that that would have made all the difference to the earth which I replenished.

THE STATUE. Bravo Ana! Juan: you are floored, quelled, annihilated.

DON JUAN. No; for though that difference is the true essential difference—Doña Ana has, I admit, gone straight to the real point—yet it is not a difference of love or chastity, or even constancy; for twelve children by twelve different husbands would have replenished the earth perhaps more effectively. Suppose my friend Ottavio had died when you were thirty, you would never have remained a widow: you were too beautiful. Suppose the successor of Ottavio had died when you were forty, you would still have been irresistible; and a woman who marries twice marries three times if she becomes free to do so. Twelve lawful children borne by one highly respectable lady to three different fathers is not impossible nor condemned by public opinion. That such a lady may be more law abiding than the poor girl whom we used to spurn into the gutter for bearing one unlawful infant is no doubt true; but dare you say she is less self-indulgent?

ANA. She is less virtuous: that is enough for me.

DON JUAN. In that case, what is virtue but the Trade Unionism of the married? Let us face the facts, dear Ana. The Life Force respects marriage only because marriage is a contrivance of its own to secure the greatest number of children and the closest care of them. For honor, chastity and all the rest of your moral figments it cares not a rap. Marriage is the most licentious of human institutions—

ANA. Juan!

THE STATUE [protesting] Really!—

DON JUAN [determinedly] I say the most licentious of human institutions: that is the secret of its popularity. And a woman seeking a husband is the most unscrupulous of all the beasts of prey. The confusion of marriage with morality has done more to destroy the conscience of the human race than any other single error. Come, Ana! do not look shocked: you know better than any of us that marriage is a mantrap baited with simulated accomplishments and delusive idealizations. When your sainted mother, by dint of scoldings and punishments, forced you to learn how to play half a dozen pieces on the spinet—which she hated as much as you did—had she any other purpose than to delude your suitors into the belief that your husband would have in his home an angel who would fill it with melody, or at least play him to sleep after dinner? You married my friend Ottavio: well, did you ever open the spinet from the hour when the Church united him to you?

ANA. You are a fool, Juan. A young married woman has something else to do than sit at the spinet without any support for her back; so she gets out of the habit of playing.

DON JUAN. Not if she loves music. No: believe me, she only throws away the bait when the bird is in the net.

ANA [bitterly] And men, I suppose, never throw off the mask when their bird is in the net. The husband never becomes negligent, selfish, brutal—oh never!

DON JUAN. What do these recriminations prove, Ana? Only that the hero is as gross an imposture as the heroine.

ANA. It is all nonsense: most marriages are perfectly comfortable.

DON JUAN. "Perfectly" is a strong expression, Ana. What you mean is that sensible people make the best of one another. Send me to the galleys and chain me to the felon whose

number happens to be next before mine; and I must accept
the inevitable and make the best of the companionship. Many
such companionships, they tell me, are touchingly affectionate;
and most are at least tolerably friendly. But that does not
make a chain a desirable ornament nor the galleys an abode
of bliss. Those who talk most about the blessings of marriage
and the constancy of its vows are the very people who declare
that if the chain were broken and the prisoners left free to
choose, the whole social fabric would fly asunder. You cannot
have the argument both ways. If the prisoner is happy, why
lock him in? If he is not, why pretend that he is?

ANA. At all events, let me take an old woman's privilege
again, and tell you flatly that marriage peoples the world and
debauchery does not.

DON JUAN. How if a time come when this shall cease
to be true? Do you not know that where there is a will there
is a way—that whatever Man really wishes to do he will
finally discover a means of doing? Well, you have done your
best, you virtuous ladies, and others of your way of thinking,
to bend Man's mind wholly towards honorable love as the
highest good, and to understand by honorable love romance
and beauty and happiness in the possession of beautiful,
refined, delicate, affectionate women. You have taught women
to value their own youth, health, shapeliness, and refinement
above all things. Well, what place have squalling babies and
household cares in this exquisite paradise of the senses and
emotions? Is it not the inevitable end of it all that the human
will shall say to the human brain: Invent me a means by
which I can have love, beauty, romance, emotion, passion
without their wretched penalties, their expenses, their worries,
their trials, their illnesses and agonies and risks of death, their
retinue of servants and nurses and doctors and schoolmasters.

THE DEVIL. All this, Señor Don Juan, is realized here in
my realm.

DON JUAN. Yes, at the cost of death. Man will not take
it at that price: he demands the romantic delights of your
hell whilst he is still on earth. Well, the means will be found:
the brain will not fail when the will is in earnest. The day is
coming when great nations will find their numbers dwindling
from census to census; when the six roomed villa will rise in
price above the family mansion; when the viciously reckless
poor and the stupidly pious rich will delay the extinction of
the race only by degrading it; whilst the boldly prudent, the
thriftily selfish and ambitious, the imaginative and poetic, the

lovers of money and solid comfort, the worshippers of success, of art, and of love, will all oppose to the Force of Life the device of sterility.

THE STATUE. That is all very eloquent, my young friend; but if you had lived to Ana's age, or even to mine, you would have learned that the people who get rid of the fear of poverty and children and all the other family troubles, and devote themselves to having a good time of it, only leave their minds free for the fear of old age and ugliness and impotence and death. The childless laborer is more tormented by his wife's idleness and her constant demands for amusement and distraction than he could be by twenty children; and his wife is more wretched than he. I have had my share of vanity; for as a young man I was admired by women; and as a statue I am praised by art critics. But I confess that had I found nothing to do in the world but wallow in these delights I should have cut my throat. When I married Ana's mother—or perhaps, to be strictly correct, I should rather say when I at last gave in and allowed Ana's mother to marry me—I knew that I was planting thorns in my pillow, and that marriage for me, a swaggering young officer thitherto unvanquished, meant defeat and capture.

ANA [scandalized] Father!

THE STATUE. I am sorry to shock you, my love; but since Juan has stripped every rag of decency from the discussion I may as well tell the frozen truth.

ANA. Hmf! I suppose I was one of the thorns.

THE STATUE. By no means: you were often a rose. You see, your mother had most of the trouble you gave.

DON JUAN. Then may I ask, Commander, why you have left Heaven to come here and wallow, as you express it, in sentimental beatitudes which you confess would once have driven you to cut your throat?

THE STATUE [struck by this] Egad, that's true.

THE DEVIL [alarmed] What! You are going back from your word! [To Don Juan] And all your philosophizing has been nothing but a mask for proselytizing! [To the Statue] Have you forgotten already the hideous dulness from which I am offering you a refuge here? [To Don Juan] And does your demonstration of the approaching sterilization and extinction of mankind lead to anything better than making the most of those pleasures of art and love which you yourself admit refined you, elevated you, developed you?

DON JUAN. I never demonstrated the extinction of mankind. Life cannot will its own extinction either in its blind amorphous state or in any of the forms into which it has organized itself. I had not finished when His Excellency interrupted me.

THE STATUE. I begin to doubt whether you ever will finish, my friend. You are extremely fond of hearing yourself talk.

DON JUAN. True; but since you have endured so much, you may as well endure to the end. Long before this sterilization which I described becomes more than a clearly foreseen possibility, the reaction will begin. The great central purpose of breeding the race, ay, breeding it to heights now deemed superhuman: that purpose which is now hidden in a mephitic cloud of love and romance and prudery and fastidiousness, will break through into clear sunlight as a purpose no longer to be confused with the gratification of personal fancies, the impossible realization of boys' and girls' dreams of bliss, or the need of older people for companionship or money. The plain-spoken marriage services of the vernacular Churches will no longer be abbreviated and half suppressed as indelicate. The sober decency, earnestness and authority of their declaration of the real purpose of marriage will be honored and accepted, whilst their romantic vowings and pledgings and until-death-do-us-partings and the like will be expunged as unbearable frivolities. Do my sex the justice to admit, Señora, that we have always recognized that the sex relation is not a personal or friendly relation at all.

ANA. Not a personal or friendly relation! What relation is more personal? more sacred? more holy?

DON JUAN. Sacred and holy, if you like, Ana, but not personally friendly. Your relation to God is sacred and holy: dare you call it personally friendly? In the sex relation the universal creative energy, of which the parties are both the helpless agents, over-rides and sweeps away all personal considerations and dispenses with all personal relations. The pair may be utter strangers to one another, speaking different languages, differing in race and color, in age and disposition, with no bond between them but a possibility of that fecundity for the sake of which the Life Force throws them into one another's arms at the exchange of a glance. Do we not recognize this by allowing marriages to be made by parents without consulting the woman? Have you not often expressed your disgust at the immorality of the English nation, in which women and men of noble birth become acquainted and court each other like peasants? And how much does even the peasant know of his bride or she of him before he engages himself? Why, you would not make a man your lawyer or your family doctor on so slight an acquaintance as you would fall in love with and marry him!

ANA. Yes, Juan: we know the libertine's philosophy. Always ignore the consequences to the woman.

DON JUAN. The consequences, yes: they justify her fierce grip of the man. But surely you do not call that attachment a sentimental one. As well call the policeman's attachment to his prisoner a love relation.

ANA. You see you have to confess that marriage is necessary, though, according to you, love is the slightest of all the relations.

DON JUAN. How do you know that it is not the greatest of all the relations? far too great to be a personal matter. Could your father have served his country if he had refused to kill any enemy of Spain unless he personally hated him? Can a woman serve her country if she refuses to marry any man she does not personally love? You know it is not so: the woman of noble birth marries as the man of noble birth fights, on political and family grounds, not on personal ones.

THE STATUE [impressed] A very clever point that, Juan: I must think it over. You are really full of ideas. How did you come to think of this one?

DON JUAN. I learnt it by experience. When I was on earth, and made those proposals to ladies which, though universally condemned, have made me so interesting a hero of legend, I was not infrequently met in some such way as this. The lady would say that she would countenance my advances, provided they were honorable. On inquiring what that proviso meant, I found that it meant that I proposed to get possession of her property if she had any, or to undertake her support for life if she had not; that I desired her continual companionship, counsel and conversation to the end of my days, and would bind myself under penalties to be always enraptured by them; and, above all, that I would turn my back on all other women for ever for her sake. I did not object to these conditions because they were exorbitant and inhuman: it was their extraordinary irrelevance that prostrated me. I invariably replied with perfect frankness that I had never dreamt of any of these things; that unless the lady's character and intellect were equal or superior to my own, her conversation must degrade and her counsel mislead me; that her constant companionship might, for all I knew, become intolerably tedious to me; that I could not answer for my feelings for a week in advance, much less to the end of my life; that to cut me off from all natural and unconstrained relations with the rest of my fellow creatures would narrow and warp me if I submitted to it, and, if not, would bring me under the curse of clandestinity; that, finally, my proposals to her were wholly unconnected with any of these matters, and were the outcome of a perfectly simple impulse of my manhood towards her womanhood.

ANA. You mean that it was an immoral impulse.

DON JUAN. Nature, my dear lady, is what you call immoral. I blush for it; but I cannot help it. Nature is a pander, Time a wrecker, and Death a murderer. I have always preferred to stand up to those facts and build institutions on their recognition. You prefer to propitiate the three devils by proclaiming their chastity, their thrift, and their loving kindness; and to base your institutions on these flatteries. Is it any wonder that the institutions do not work smoothly?

THE STATUE. What used the ladies to say, Juan?

DON JUAN. Oh come! Confidence for confidence. First tell me what you used to say to the ladies.

THE STATUE. I! Oh, I swore that I would be faithful to the death; that I should die if they refused me; that no woman could ever be to me what she was—

ANA. She! Who?

THE STATUE. Whoever it happened to be at the time, my dear. I had certain things I always said. One of them was that even when I was eighty, one white hair of the woman I loved would make me tremble more than the thickest gold tress from the most beautiful young head. Another was that I could not bear the thought of anyone else being the mother of my children.

DON JUAN [revolted] You old rascal!

THE STATUE [stoutly] Not a bit; for I really believed it with all my soul at the moment. I had a heart: not like you. And it was this sincerity that made me successful.

DON JUAN. Sincerity! To be fool enough to believe a ramping, stamping, thumping lie: that is what you call sincerity! To be so greedy for a woman that you deceive yourself in your eagerness to deceive her: sincerity, you call it!

THE STATUE. Oh, damn your sophistries! I was a man in love, not a lawyer. And the women loved me for it, bless them!

DON JUAN. They made you think so. What will you say when I tell you that though I played the lawyer so callously, they made me think so too? I also had my moments of infatuation in which I gushed nonsense and believed it. Sometimes the desire to give pleasure by saying beautiful things so rose in me on the flood of emotion that I said them recklessly. At other times I argued against myself with a devilish coldness that drew tears. But I found it just as hard to escape in the one case as in the others. When the lady's instinct was set on me, there was nothing for it but lifelong servitude or flight.

ANA. You dare boast, before me and my father, that every woman found you irresistible.

DON JUAN. Am I boasting? It seems to me that I cut the most pitiable of figures. Besides, I said "when the lady's instinct was set on me." It was not always so; and then, heavens! what transports of virtuous indignation! what overwhelming defiance to the dastardly seducer! what scenes of Imogen and Iachimo!

ANA. I made no scenes. I simply called my father.

DON JUAN. And he came, sword in hand, to vindicate outraged honor and morality by murdering me.

THE STATUE. Murdering! What do you mean? Did I kill you or did you kill me?

DON JUAN. Which of us was the better fencer?

THE STATUE. I was.

DON JUAN. Of course you were. And yet you, the hero of those scandalous adventures you have just been relating to us, you had the effrontery to pose as the avenger of outraged morality and condemn me to death! You would have slain me but for an accident.

THE STATUE. I was expected to, Juan. That is how things were arranged on earth. I was not a social reformer; and I always did what it was customary for a gentleman to do.

DON JUAN. That may account for your attacking me, but not for the revolting hypocrisy of your subsequent proceedings as a statue.

THE STATUE. That all came of my going to Heaven.

THE DEVIL. I still fail to see, Señor Don Juan, that these episodes in your earthly career and in that of the Señor Commander in any way discredit my view of life. Here, I repeat, you have all that you sought without anything that you shrank from.

DON JUAN. On the contrary, here I have everything that

disappointed me without anything that I have not already tried and found wanting. I tell you that as long as I can conceive something better than myself I cannot be easy unless I am striving to bring it into existence or clearing the way for it. That is the law of my life. That is the working within me of Life's incessant aspiration to higher organization, wider, deeper, intenser self-consciousness, and clearer self-understanding. It was the supremacy of this purpose that reduced love for me to the mere pleasure of a moment, art for me to the mere schooling of my faculties, religion for me to a mere excuse for laziness, since it had set up a God who looked at the world and saw that it was good, against the instinct in me that looked through my eyes at the world and saw that it could be improved. I tell you that in the pursuit of my own pleasure, my own health, my own fortune, I have never known happiness. It was not love for Woman that delivered me into her hands: it was fatigue, exhaustion. When I was a child, and bruised my head against a stone, I ran to the nearest woman and cried away my pain against her apron. When I grew up, and bruised my soul against the brutalities and stupidities with which I had to strive, I did again just what I had done as a child. I have enjoyed, too, my rests, my recuperations, my breathing times, my very prostrations after strife; but rather would I be dragged through all the circles of the foolish Italian's Inferno than through the pleasures of Europe. That is what has made this place of eternal pleasures so deadly to me. It is the absence of this instinct in you that makes you that strange monster called a Devil. It is the success with which you have diverted the attention of men from their real purpose, which in one degree or another is the same as mine, to yours, that has earned you the name of The Tempter. It is the fact that they are doing your will, or rather drifting with your want of will, instead of doing their own, that makes them the uncomfortable, false, restless, artificial, petulant, wretched creatures they are.

THE DEVIL [*mortified*] Señor Don Juan: you are uncivil to my friends.

DON JUAN. Pooh! why should I be civil to them or to you? In this Palace of Lies a truth or two will not hurt you. Your friends are all the dullest dogs I know. They are not beautiful: they are only decorated. They are not clean: they are only shaved and starched. They are not dignified: they are only fashionably dressed. They are not educated: they are only college passmen. They are not religious: they are only

pewrenters. They are not moral: they are only conventional.
They are not virtuous: they are only cowardly. They are not
even vicious: they are only "frail." They are not artistic: they
are only lascivious. They are not prosperous: they are only
rich. They are not loyal, they are only servile; not dutiful,
only sheepish; not public spirited, only patriotic; not courageous, only quarrelsome; not determined, only obstinate; not
masterful, only domineering; not self-controlled, only obtuse;
not self-respecting, only vain; not kind, only sentimental; not
social, only gregarious; not considerate, only polite; not intelligent, only opinionated; not progressive, only factious; not
imaginative, only superstitious; not just, only vindictive; not
generous, only propitiatory; not disciplined, only cowed; and
not truthful at all—liars every one of them, to the very backbone of their souls.

THE STATUE. Your flow of words is simply amazing,
Juan. How I wish I could have talked like that to my soldiers.

THE DEVIL. It is mere talk, though. It has all been said
before; but what change has it ever made? What notice has
the world ever taken of it?

DON JUAN. Yes, it is mere talk. But why is it mere talk?
Because, my friend, beauty, purity, respectability, religion,
morality, art, patriotism, bravery and the rest are nothing but
words which I or anyone else can turn inside out like a glove.
Were they realities, you would have to plead guilty to my
indictment; but fortunately for your self-respect, my diabolical
friend, they are not realities. As you say, they are mere words,
useful for duping barbarians into adopting civilization, or the
civilized poor into submitting to be robbed and enslaved.
That is the family secret of the governing caste; and if we
who are of that caste aimed at more Life for the world instead of at more power and luxury for our miserable selves,
that secret would make us great. Now, since I, being a nobleman, am in the secret too, think how tedious to me must be
your unending cant about all these moralistic figments, and
how squalidly disastrous your sacrifice of your lives to them!
If you even believed in your moral game enough to play it
fairly, it would be interesting to watch; but you don't: you
cheat at every trick; and if your opponent outcheats you, you
upset the table and try to murder him.

THE DEVIL. On earth there may be some truth in this,
because the people are uneducated and cannot appreciate my
religion of love and beauty; but here—

DON JUAN. Oh yes: I know. Here there is nothing but

love and beauty. Ugh! it is like sitting for all eternity at the
first act of a fashionable play, before the complications begin.
Never in my worst moments of superstitious terror on earth
did I dream that Hell was so horrible. I live, like a hair-
dresser, in the continual contemplation of beauty, toying with
silken tresses. I breathe an atmosphere of sweetness, like a
confectioner's shopboy. Commander: are there any beautiful
women in Heaven?

THE STATUE. None. Absolutely none. All dowdies. Not
two pennorth of jewellery among a dozen of them. They might
be men of fifty.

DON JUAN. I am impatient to get there. Is the word
beauty ever mentioned; and are there any artistic people?

THE STATUE. I give you my word they won't admire a
fine statue even when it walks past them.

DON JUAN. I go.

THE DEVIL. Don Juan: shall I be frank with you?

DON JUAN. Were you not so before?

THE DEVIL. As far as I went, yes. But I will now go further, and confess to you that men get tired of everything, of
heaven no less than of hell; and that all history is nothing but
a record of the oscillations of the world between these two
extremes. An epoch is but a swing of the pendulum; and each
generation thinks the world is progressing because it is always
moving. But when you are as old as I am; when you have a
thousand times wearied of heaven, like myself and the Commander, and a thousand times wearied of hell, as you are
wearied now, you will no longer imagine that every swing
from heaven to hell is an emancipation, every swing from hell
to heaven an evolution. Where you now see reform, progress,
fulfilment of upward tendency, continual ascent by Man on
the stepping stones of his dead selves to higher things, you will
see nothing but an infinite comedy of illusion. You will discover the profound truth of the saying of my friend Kohe-
leth, that there is nothing new under the sun. Vanitas vanita-
tum—

DON JUAN [out of all patience] By Heaven, this is worse
than your cant about love and beauty. Clever dolt that you
are, is a man no better than a worm, or a dog than a wolf,
because he gets tired of everything? Shall he give up eating
because he destroys his appetite in the act of gratifying it?
Is a field idle when it is fallow? Can the Commander expend
his hellish energy here without accumulating heavenly energy
for his next term of blessedness? Granted that the great Life

Force has hit on the device of the clockmaker's pendulum, and uses the earth for its bob; that the history of each oscillation, which seems so novel to us the actors, is but the history of the last oscillation repeated; nay more, that in the unthinkable infinitude of time the sun throws off the earth and catches it again a thousand times as a circus rider throws up a ball, and that the total of all our epochs is but the moment between the toss and the catch, has the colossal mechanism no purpose?

THE DEVIL. None, my friend. You think, because you have a purpose, Nature must have one. You might as well expect it to have fingers and toes because you have them.

DON JUAN. But I should not have them if they served no purpose. And I, my friend, am as much a part of Nature as my own finger is a part of me. If my finger is the organ by which I grasp the sword and the mandoline, my brain is the organ by which Nature strives to understand itself. My dog's brain serves only my dog's purposes; but my brain labors at a knowledge which does nothing for me personally but make my body bitter to me and my decay and death a calamity. Were I not possessed with a purpose beyond my own I had better be a ploughman than a philosopher; for the ploughman lives as long as the philosopher, eats more, sleeps better, and rejoices in the wife of his bosom with less misgiving. This is because the philosopher is in the grip of the Life Force. This Life Force says to him "I have done a thousand wonderful things unconsciously by merely willing to live and following the line of least resistance: now I want to know myself and my destination, and choose my path; so I have made a special brain—a philosopher's brain—to grasp this knowledge for me as the husbandman's hand grasps the plough for me. And this" says the Life Force to the philosopher "must thou strive to do for me until thou diest, when I will make another brain and another philosopher to carry on the work."

THE DEVIL. What is the use of knowing?

DON JUAN. Why, to be able to choose the line of greatest advantage instead of yielding in the direction of the least resistance. Does a ship sail to its destination no better than a log drifts nowhither? The philosopher is Nature's pilot. And there you have our difference: to be in hell is to drift: to be in heaven is to steer.

THE DEVIL. On the rocks, most likely.

DON JUAN. Pooh! which ship goes oftenest on the rocks

or to the bottom—the drifting ship or the ship with a pilot on board?

THE DEVIL. Well, well, go your way, Señor Don Juan. I prefer to be my own master and not the tool of any blundering universal force. I know that beauty is good to look at; that music is good to hear; that love is good to feel; and that they are all good to think about and talk about. I know that to be well exercised in these sensations, emotions, and studies is to be a refined and cultivated being. Whatever they may say of me in churches on earth, I know that it is universally admitted in good society that the Prince of Darkness is a gentleman; and that is enough for me. As to your Life Force, which you think irresistible, it is the most resistible thing in the world for a person of any character. But if you are naturally vulgar and credulous, as all reformers are, it will thrust you first into religion, where you will sprinkle water on babies to save their souls from me; then it will drive you from religion into science, where you will snatch the babies from the water sprinkling and inoculate them with disease to save them from catching it accidentally; then you will take to politics, where you will become the catspaw of corrupt functionaries and the henchman of ambitious humbugs; and the end will be despair and decrepitude, broken nerve and shattered hopes, vain regrets for that worst and silliest of wastes and sacrifices, the waste and sacrifice of the power of enjoyment: in a word, the punishment of the fool who pursues the better before he has secured the good.

DON JUAN. But at least I shall not be bored. The service of the Life Force has that advantage, at all events. So fare you well, Señor Satan.

THE DEVIL [amiably] Fare you well, Don Juan. I shall often think of our interesting chats about things in general. I wish you every happiness: Heaven, as I said before, suits some people. But if you should change your mind, do not forget that the gates are always open here to the repentant prodigal. If you feel at any time that warmth of heart, sincere unforced affection, innocent enjoyment, and warm, breathing, palpitating reality—

DON JUAN. Why not say flesh and blood at once, though we have left those two greasy commonplaces behind us?

THE DEVIL [angrily] You throw my friendly farewell back in my teeth, then, Don Juan?

DON JUAN. By no means. But though there is much to be learnt from a cynical devil, I really cannot stand a sentimental one. Señor Commander: you know the way to the frontier of hell and heaven. Be good enough to direct me.

THE STATUE. Oh, the frontier is only the difference between two ways of looking at things. Any road will take you across it if you really want to get there.

DON JUAN. Good. [*Saluting Doña Ana*] Señora: your servant.

ANA. But I am going with you.

DON JUAN. I can find my own way to heaven, Ana; but I cannot find yours [*he vanishes*].

ANA. How annoying!

THE STATUE [*calling after him*] Bon voyage, Juan! [*He wafts a final blast of his great rolling chords after him as a parting salute. A faint echo of the first ghostly melody comes back in acknowledgment*]. Ah! there he goes. [*Puffing a long breath out through his lips*] Whew! How he does talk! They'll never stand it in heaven.

THE DEVIL [*gloomily*] His going is a political defeat. I cannot keep these Life Worshippers: they all go. This is the greatest loss I have had since that Dutch painter went—a fellow who would paint a hag of 70 with as much enjoyment as a Venus of 20.

THE STATUE. I remember: he came to heaven. Rembrandt.

THE DEVIL. Ay, Rembrandt. There is something unnatural about these fellows. Do not listen to their gospel, Señor Commander: it is dangerous. Beware of the pursuit of the Superhuman: it leads to an indiscriminate contempt for the Human. To a man, horses and dogs and cats are mere species, outside the moral world. Well, to the Superman, men and women are a mere species too, also outside the moral world. This Don Juan was kind to women and courteous to men as your daughter here was kind to her pet cats and dogs; but such kindness is a denial of the exclusively human character of the soul.

THE STATUE. And who the deuce is the Superman?

THE DEVIL. Oh, the latest fashion among the Life Force fanatics. Did you not meet in Heaven, among the new arrivals, that German Polish madman—what was his name? Nietzsche?

THE STATUE. Never heard of him.

THE DEVIL. Well, he came here first, before he recovered his wits. I had some hopes of him; but he was a confirmed Life Force worshipper. It was he who raked up the Superman, who is as old as Prometheus; and the twentieth century will run after this newest of the old crazes when it gets tired of the world, the flesh, and your humble servant.

THE STATUE. Superman is a good cry; and a good cry is half the battle. I should like to see this Nietzsche.

THE DEVIL. Unfortunately he met Wagner here, and had a quarrel with him.

THE STATUE. Quite right, too. Mozart for me!

THE DEVIL. Oh, it was not about music. Wagner once drifted into Life Force worship, and invented a Superman called Siegfried. But he came to his senses afterwards. So when they met here, Nietzsche denounced him as a renegade; and Wagner wrote a pamphlet to prove that Nietzsche was a Jew; and it ended in Nietzsche's going to heaven in a huff. And a good riddance too. And now, my friend, let us hasten to my palace and celebrate your arrival with a grand musical service.

THE STATUE. With pleasure: you're most kind.

THE DEVIL. This way, Commander. We go down the old trap [he places himself on the grave trap].

THE STATUE. Good. [Reflectively] All the same, the Superman is a fine conception. There is something statuesque about it. [He places himself on the grave trap beside The Devil. It begins to descend slowly. Red glow from the abyss]. Ah, this reminds me of old times.

THE DEVIL. And me also.

ANA. Stop! [The trap stops].

THE DEVIL. You, Señora, cannot come this way. You will have an apotheosis. But you will be at the palace before us.

ANA. That is not what I stopped you for. Tell me: where can I find the Superman?

THE DEVIL. He is not yet created, Señora.

THE STATUE. And never will be, probably. Let us proceed: the red fire will make me sneeze. [They descend].

ANA. Not yet created! Then my work is not yet done. [Crossing herself devoutly] I believe in the Life to Come. [Crying to the universe] A father—a father for the Superman!

She vanishes into the void; and again there is nothing: all existence seems suspended infinitely. Then, vaguely, there is a live human voice crying somewhere. One sees, with a shock, a mountain peak shewing faintly against a lighter background. The sky has returned from afar; and we suddenly remember where we were. The cry becomes distinct and urgent: it says Automobile, Automobile. The complete reality comes back *with a rush: in a moment it is full morning in the Sierra; and the brigands are scrambling to their feet and making for the road as the goatherd runs down from the hill, warning them of the approach of another motor. Tanner and Mendoza rise amazedly and stare at one another with scattered wits. Straker sits up to yawn for a moment before he gets on his feet, making it a point of honor not to shew any undue interest in the excitement of the bandits. Mendoza gives a quick look to see that his followers are attending to the alarm; then exchanges a private word with Tanner.*

MENDOZA. Did you dream?

TANNER. Damnably. Did you?

MENDOZA. Yes. I forget what. You were in it.

TANNER. So were you. Amazing!

MENDOZA. I warned you. [*A shot is heard from the road*]. Dolts! they will play with that gun. [*The brigands come running back scared*]. Who fired that shot? [*to Duval*] was it you?

DUVAL [*breathless*] I have not shoot. Dey shoot first.

ANARCHIST. I told you to begin by abolishing the State. Now we are all lost.

THE ROWDY SOCIAL-DEMOCRAT [*stampeding across the amphitheatre*] Run, everybody.

MENDOZA [*collaring him; throwing him on his back; and drawing a knife*] I stab the man who stirs. [*He blocks the way. The stampede is checked*]. What has happened?

THE SULKY SOCIAL-DEMOCRAT. A motor—

THE ANARCHIST. Three men—

DUVAL. Deux femmes—

MENDOZA. Three men and two women! Why have you not brought them here? Are you afraid of them?

THE ROWDY ONE [*getting up*] Thyve a hescort. Ow, de-ooh lut's ook it, Mendoza.

THE SULKY ONE. Two armored cars full o soldiers at the ed o the valley.

ANARCHIST. The shot was fired in the air. It was a signal. *Straker whistles his favorite air, which falls on the ears of the brigands like a funeral march.*

TANNER. It is not an escort, but an expedition to capture you. We were advised to wait for it; but I was in a hurry.

THE ROWDY ONE [*in an agony of apprehension*] And Ow my good Lord, ere we are, wytin for em! Lut's tike to the mahntns.

MENDOZA. Idiot, what do you know about the mountains?

Are you a Spaniard? You would be given up by the first shepherd you met. Besides, we are already within range of their
rifles.

THE ROWDY ONE. Bat—

MENDOZA. Silence. Leave this to me. [*To Tanner*] Comrade: you will not betray us.

STRAKER. Oo are you callin comrade?

MENDOZA. Last night the advantage was with me. The
robber of the poor was at the mercy of the robber of the
rich. You offered your hand: I took it.

TANNER. I bring no charge against you, comrade. We
have spent a pleasant evening with you: that is all.

STRAKER. I gev my and to nobody, see?

MENDOZA [*turning on him impressively*] Young man, if I
am tried, I shall plead guilty, and explain what drove me
from England, home and duty. Do you wish to have the
respectable name of Straker dragged through the mud of a
Spanish criminal court? The police will search me. They will
find Louisa's portrait. It will be published in the illustrated
papers. You blench. It will be your doing, remember.

STRAKER [*with baffled rage*] I don't care about the court.
It's avin our name mixed up with yours that I object to, you
blackmailin swine, you.

MENDOZA. Language unworthy of Louisa's brother! But
no matter: you are muzzled: that is enough for us. [*He turns
to face his own men, who back uneasily across the amphitheatre towards the cave to take refuge behind him, as a
fresh party, muffled for motoring, comes from the road in
riotous spirits. Ann, who makes straight for Tanner, comes
first; then Violet, helped over the rough ground by Hector
holding her right hand and Ramsden her left. Mendoza goes
to his presidential block and seats himself calmly with his
rank and file grouped behind him, and his Staff, consisting of
Duval and the Anarchist on his right and the two Social-
Democrats on his left, supporting him in flank.*]

ANN. It's Jack!

TANNER. Caught!

HECTOR. Why, certainly it is. I said it was you, Tanner.
We've just been stopped by a puncture: the road is full of
nails.

VIOLET. What are you doing here with all these men?

ANN. Why did you leave us without a word of warning?

HECTOR. I want that bunch of roses, Miss Whitefield.
[*To Tanner*] When we found you were gone, Miss Whitefield

bet me a bunch of roses my car would not overtake yours before you reached Monte Carlo.

TANNER. But this is not the road to Monte Carlo.

HECTOR. No matter. Miss Whitefield tracked you at every stopping place: she is a regular Sherlock Holmes.

TANNER. The Life Force! I am lost.

OCTAVIUS [*bounding gaily down from the road into the amphitheatre, and coming between Tanner and Straker*] I am so glad you are safe, old chap. We were afraid you had been captured by brigands.

RAMSDEN [*who has been staring at Mendoza*] I seem to remember the face of your friend here. [*Mendoza rises politely and advances with a smile between Ann and Ramsden*].

HECTOR. Why, so do I.

OCTAVIUS. I know you perfectly well, sir; but I can't think where I have met you.

MENDOZA [*to Violet*] Do you remember me, madam?

VIOLET. Oh, quite well; but I am so stupid about names.

MENDOZA. It was at the Savoy Hotel. [*To Hector*] You, sir, used to come with this lady [*Violet*] to lunch. [*To Octavius*] You, sir, often brought this lady [*Ann*] and her mother to dinner on your way to the Lyceum Theatre. [*To Ramsden*] You, sir, used to come to supper, with [*dropping his voice to a confidential but perfectly audible whisper*] several different ladies.

RAMSDEN [*angrily*] Well, what is that to you, pray?

OCTAVIUS. Why, Violet, I thought you hardly knew one another before this trip, you and Malone!

VIOLET [*vexed*] I suppose this person was the manager.

MENDOZA. The waiter, madam. I have a grateful recollection of you all. I gathered from the bountiful way in which you treated me that you all enjoyed your visits very much.

VIOLET. What impertinence! [*She turns her back on him, and goes up the hill with Hector*].

RAMSDEN. That will do, my friend. You do not expect these ladies to treat you as an acquaintance, I suppose, because you have waited on them at table.

MENDOZA. Pardon me: it was you who claimed my acquaintance. The ladies followed your example. However, this display of the unfortunate manners of your class closes the incident. For the future, you will please address me with the respect due to a stranger and fellow traveller. [*He turns haughtily away and resumes his presidential seat.*]

TANNER. There! I have found one man on my journey

capable of reasonable conversation; and you all instinctively insult him. Even the New Man is as bad as any of you. Enry: you have behaved just like a miserable gentleman.

STRAKER. Gentleman! Not me.

RAMSDEN. Really, Tanner, this tone—

ANN. Don't mind him, Granny: you ought to know him by this time [*she takes his arm and coaxes him away to the hill to join Violet and Hector. Octavius follows her, doglike*].

VIOLET [*calling from the hill*] Here are the soldiers. They are getting out of their motors.

DUVAL [*panic stricken*] Oh, nom de Dieu!

THE ANARCHIST. Fools: the State is about to crush you because you spared it at the prompting of the political hangers-on of the bourgeoisie.

THE SULKY SOCIAL-DEMOCRAT [*argumentative to the last*] On the contrary, only by capturing the State machine—

THE ANARCHIST. It is going to capture you.

THE ROWDY SOCIAL DEMOCRAT [*his anguish culminating*] Ow, chack it. Wot are we ere for? Wot are we wytin for?

MENDOZA [*between his teeth*] Go on. Talk politics, you idiots: nothing sounds more respectable. Keep it up, I tell you.

The soldiers line the road, commanding the amphitheatre with their rifles. The brigands, struggling with an overwhelming impulse to hide behind one another, look as unconcerned as they can. Mendoza rises superbly, with undaunted front. The officer in command steps down from the road into the amphitheatre; looks hard at the brigands; and then inquiringly at Tanner.

THE OFFICER. Who are these men, Señor Ingles?

TANNER. My escort.

Mendoza, with a Mephistophelean smile, bows profoundly. An irrepressible grin runs from face to face among the brigands. They touch their hats, except the Anarchist, who defies the State with folded arms.

ACT FOUR

The garden of a villa in Granada. Whoever wishes to know what it is like must go to Granada and see. One may prosaically specify a group of hills dotted with villas, the Alhambra on the top of one of the hills, and a considerable town in the valley, approached by dusty white roads in which the children, no matter what they are doing or thinking about, automatically whine for halfpence and reach out little clutching brown palms for them; but there is nothing in this description except the Alhambra, the begging, and the color of the roads, that does not fit Surrey as well as Spain. The difference is that the Surrey hills are comparatively small and ugly, and should properly be called the Surrey Protuberances; but these Spanish hills are of mountain stock: the amenity which conceals their size does not compromise their dignity.

This particular garden is on a hill opposite the Alhambra; and the villa is as expensive and pretentious as a villa must be if it is to be let furnished by the week to opulent American and English visitors. If we stand on the lawn at the foot of the garden and look uphill, our horizon is the stone balustrade of a flagged platform on the edge of the infinite space at the top of the hill. Between us and this platform is a flower garden with a circular basin and fountain in the centre, surrounded by geometrical flower beds, gravel paths, and clipped yew trees in the genteelest order. The garden is higher than our lawn; so we reach it by a few steps in the middle of its embankment. The platform is higher again than the garden, from which we mount a couple more steps to look over the balustrade at a fine view of the town up the valley and of the hills that stretch away beyond it to where, in the remotest distance, they become mountains. On our left is the villa, accessible by steps from the left hand corner of the garden. Returning from the platform through the garden and down again to the lawn [a movement which leaves the villa behind us on our right] we find evidence of literary interests on the part of the tenants in the fact that there is no tennis net nor set of croquet hoops, but, on our left, a little iron garden table with books on it, mostly yellow-backed, and a chair beside it. A chair on the right has also a couple of open books upon it. There are no newspapers, a circumstance which, with the absence of games, might lead an intelligent spectator to the most far reaching conclusions as to the sort of people who live in the villa. Such speculations are checked, however, on this delightfully fine afternoon, by the appearance at a little gate in a paling on our left, of Henry Straker in his professional costume. He opens the gate for an elderly gentleman, and follows him on to the lawn.

This elderly gentleman defies the Spanish sun in a black frock coat, tall silk hat, trousers in which narrow stripes of dark grey and lilac blend into a highly respectable color, and a black necktie tied into a bow over spotless linen. Probably therefore a man whose social position needs constant and scrupulous affirmation without regard to climate: one who would dress thus for the middle of the Sahara or the top of Mont Blanc. And since he has not the stamp of the class which accepts as its life-mission the advertising and mainte-nance of first rate tailoring and millinery, he looks vulgar in his finery, though in a working dress of any kind he would look dignified enough. He is a bullet cheeked man with a red complexion, stubbly hair, smallish eyes, a hard mouth that folds down at the corners, and a dogged chin. The looseness of skin that comes with age has attacked his throat and the laps of his cheeks; but he is still hard as an apple above the mouth; so that the upper half of his face looks younger than the lower. He has the self-confidence of one who has made money, and something of the truculence of one who has made it in a brutalizing struggle, his civility having under it a perceptible menace that he has other methods in reserve if necessary. Withal, a man to be rather pitied when he is not to be feared; for there is something pathetic about him at times, as if the huge commercial machine which has worked him into his frock coat had allowed him very little of his own way and left his affections hungry and baffled. At the first word that falls from him it is clear that he is an Irish-man whose native intonation has clung to him through many changes of place and rank. One can only guess that the original material of his speech was perhaps the surly Kerry brogue; but the degradation of speech that occurs in London, Glasgow, Dublin and big cities generally has been at work on it so long that nobody but an arrant cockney would dream of calling it a brogue now; for its music is almost gone, though its surliness is still perceptible. Straker, as a very obvious cockney, inspires him with implacable contempt, as a stupid Englishman who cannot even speak his own lan-guage properly. Straker, on the other hand, regards the old gentleman's accent as a joke thoughtfully provided by Provi-dence expressly for the amusement of the British race, and treats him normally with the indulgence due to an inferior and unlucky species, but occasionally with indignant alarm when the old gentleman shews signs of intending his Irish nonsense to be taken seriously.

STRAKER. I'll go tell the young lady. She said you'd prefer to stay here [*he turns to go up through the garden to the villa*].

MALONE [*who has been looking round him with lively curiosity*] The young lady? That's Miss Violet, eh?

STRAKER [*stopping on the steps with sudden suspicion*] Well, you know, don't you?

MALONE. Do I?

STRAKER [*his temper rising*] Well, do you or don't you?

MALONE. What business is that of yours?

Straker, now highly indignant, comes back from the steps and confronts the visitor.

STRAKER. I'll tell you what business it is of mine. Miss Robinson—

MALONE [*interrupting*] Oh, her name is Robinson, is it? Thank you.

STRAKER. Why, you don't know even her name?

MALONE. Yes I do, now that you've told me.

STRAKER [*after a moment of stupefaction at the old man's readiness in repartee*] Look here: what do you mean by gittin into my car and lettin me bring you here if you're not the person I took that note to?

MALONE. Who else did you take it to, pray?

STRAKER. I took it to Mr. Ector Malone, at Miss Robinson's request, see? Miss Robinson is not my principal: I took it to oblige her. I know Mr. Malone; and he ain't you, not by a long chalk. At the hotel they told me that your name is Ector Malone—

MALONE. *H*ector Malone.

STRAKER [*with calm superiority*] Hector in your own country: that's what comes o livin in provincial places like Ireland and America. Over here you're Ector: if you aven't noticed it before you soon will.

The growing strain of the conversation is here relieved by Violet, who has sallied from the villa and through the garden to the steps, which she now descends, coming very opportunely between Malone and Straker.

VIOLET [*to Straker*] Did you take my message?

STRAKER. Yes, miss. I took it to the hotel and sent it up, expecting to see young Mr. Malone. Then out walks this gent, and says it's all right and he'll come with me. So as the hotel people said he was Mr. Ector Malone, I fetched him. And now he goes back on what he said. But if he isn't the gentleman you meant, say the word: it's easy enough to fetch him back again.

MALONE. I should esteem it a great favor if I might have a short conversation with you, madam. I am Hector's father, as this bright Britisher would have guessed in the course of another hour or so.

STRAKER [*coolly defiant*] No, not in another year or so. When we've ad you as long to polish up as we've ad im, perhaps you'll begin to look a little bit up to is mark. At present you fall a long way short. You've got too many aitches, for one thing. [*To Violet, amiably*] All right, Miss: you want to talk to him: I shan't intrude. [*He nods affably to Malone and goes out through the little gate in the paling*].

VIOLET [*very civilly*] I am so sorry, Mr. Malone, if that man has been rude to you. But what can we do? He is our chauffeur.

MALONE. Your what?

VIOLET. The driver of our automobile. He can drive a motor car at seventy miles an hour, and mend it when it breaks down. We are dependent on our motor cars; and our motor cars are dependent on him; so of course we are dependent on him.

MALONE. I've noticed, madam, that every thousand dollars an Englishman gets seems to add one to the number of people he's dependent on. However, you needn't apologize for your man: I made him talk on purpose. By doing so I learnt that you're staying here in Grannida with a party of English, including my son Hector.

VIOLET [*conversationally*] Yes. We intended to go to Nice; but we had to follow a rather eccentric member of our party who started first and came here. Won't you sit down? [*She clears the nearest chair of the two books on it*].

MALONE [*impressed by this attention*] Thank you. [*He sits down, examining her curiously as she goes to the iron table to put down the books. When she turns to him again, he says*] Miss Robinson, I believe?

VIOLET [*sitting down*] Yes.

MALONE [*taking a letter from his pocket*] Your note to Hector runs as follows [*Violet is unable to repress a start. He pauses quietly to take out and put on his spectacles, which have gold rims*]: "Dearest: they have all gone to the Alhambra for the afternoon. I have shammed headache and have the garden all to myself. Jump into Jack's motor: Straker will rattle you here in a jiffy. Quick, quick, quick. Your loving Violet." [*He looks at her; but by this time she has recovered herself, and meets his spectacles with perfect composure. He continues slowly*] Now I don't know on what terms young people associate in English society; but in America that note would be considered to imply a very considerable degree of affectionate intimacy between the parties.

VIOLET. Yes: I know your son very well, Mr. Malone. Have you any objection?

MALONE [*somewhat taken aback*] No, no objection exactly. Provided it is understood that my son is altogether dependent on me, and that I have to be consulted in any important step he may propose to take.

VIOLET. I am sure you would not be unreasonable with him, Mr. Malone.

MALONE. I hope not, Miss Robinson; but at your age you might think many things unreasonable that don't seem so to me.

VIOLET [*with a little shrug*] Oh well, I suppose there's no use our playing at cross purposes, Mr. Malone. Hector wants to marry me.

MALONE. I inferred from your note that he might. Well, Miss Robinson, he is his own master; but if he marries you he shall not have a rap from me. [*He takes off his spectacles and pockets them with the note*].

VIOLET [*with some severity*] That is not very complimentary to me, Mr. Malone.

MALONE. I say nothing against you, Miss Robinson: I daresay you are an amiable and excellent young lady. But I have other views for Hector.

VIOLET. Hector may not have other views for himself, Mr. Malone.

MALONE. Possibly not. Then he does without me: that's all. I daresay you are prepared for that. When a young lady writes to a young man to come to her quick, quick, quick, money seems nothing and love seems everything.

VIOLET [*sharply*] I beg your pardon, Mr. Malone: I do not think anything so foolish. Hector must have money.

MALONE [*staggered*] Oh, very well, very well. No doubt he can work for it.

VIOLET. What is the use of having money if you have to work for it? [*She rises impatiently*]. It's all nonsense, Mr. Malone: you must enable your son to keep up his position. It is his right.

MALONE [*grimly*] I should not advise you to marry him on the strength of that right, Miss Robinson.

Violet, who has almost lost her temper, controls herself

*with an effort; unclenches her fingers; and resumes her seat
with studied tranquillity and reasonableness.*

VIOLET. What objection have you to me, pray? My social position is as good as Hector's, to say the least. He
admits it.

MALONE [*shrewdly*] You tell him so from time to time,
eh? Hector's social position in England, Miss Robinson, is
just what I choose to buy for him. I have made him a fair
offer. Let him pick out the most historic house, castle or
abbey that England contains. The day that he tells me he
wants it for a wife worthy of its traditions, I buy it for him,
and give him the means of keeping it up.

VIOLET. What do you mean by a wife worthy of its
traditions? Cannot any well bred woman keep such a house
for him?

MALONE. No: she must be born to it.

VIOLET. Hector was not born to it, was he?

MALONE. His grandmother was a barefooted Irish girl
that nursed me by a turf fire. Let him marry another such,
and I will not stint her marriage portion. Let him raise himself socially with my money or raise somebody else: so long
as there is a social profit somewhere, I'll regard my expendi-
ture as justified. But there must be a profit for someone. A
marriage with you would leave things just where they are.

VIOLET. Many of my relations would object very much
to my marrying the grandson of a common woman, Mr.
Malone. That may be prejudice; but so is your desire to have
him marry a title prejudice.

MALONE [*rising, and approaching her with a scrutiny in
which there is a good deal of reluctant respect*] You seem
a pretty straightforward downright sort of a young woman.

VIOLET. I do not see why I should be made miserably
poor because I cannot make profits for you. Why do you
want to make Hector unhappy?

MALONE. He will get over it all right enough. Men thrive
better on disappointments in love than on disappointments
in money. I daresay you think that sordid; but I know what
I'm talking about. My father died of starvation in Ireland in
the black 47. Maybe you've heard of it.

VIOLET. The Famine?

MALONE [*with smouldering passion*] No, the starvation.
When a country is full of food, and exporting it, there can
be no famine. My father was starved dead; and I was starved
out to America in my mother's arms. English rule drove me

and mine out of Ireland. Well, you can keep Ireland. I and my like are coming back to buy England; and we'll buy the best of it. I want no middle class properties and no middle class women for Hector. That's straightforward, isn't it, like yourself?

VIOLET [*icily pitying his sentimentality*] Really, Mr. Malone, I am astonished to hear a man of your age and good sense talking in that romantic way. Do you suppose English noblemen will sell their places to you for the asking?

MALONE. I have the refusal of two of the oldest family mansions in England. One historic owner can't afford to keep all the rooms dusted: the other can't afford the death duties. What do you say now?

VIOLET. Of course it is very scandalous; but surely you know that the Government will sooner or later put a stop to all these Socialistic attacks on property.

MALONE [*grinning*] D'y' think they'll be able to get that done before I buy the house—or rather the abbey? They're both abbeys.

VIOLET [*putting that aside rather impatiently*] Oh, well, let us talk sense, Mr. Malone. You must feel that we haven't been talking sense so far.

MALONE. I can't say I do. I mean all I say.

VIOLET. Then you don't know Hector as I do. He is romantic and faddy—he gets it from you, I fancy—and he wants a certain sort of wife to take care of him. Not a faddy sort of person, you know.

MALONE. Somebody like you, perhaps?

VIOLET [*quietly*] Well, yes. But you cannot very well ask me to undertake this with absolutely no means of keeping up his position.

MALONE [*alarmed*] Stop a bit, stop a bit. Where are we getting to? I'm not aware that I'm asking you to undertake anything.

VIOLET. Of course, Mr. Malone, you can make it very difficult for me to speak to you if you choose to misunderstand me.

MALONE [*half bewildered*] I don't wish to take any unfair advantage; but we seem to have got off the straight track somehow.

Straker, with the air of a man who has been making haste, opens the little gate, and admits Hector, who, snorting with indignation, comes upon the lawn, and is making for his father when Violet, greatly dismayed, springs up and inter-

cepts him. Straker does not wait; at least he does not remain visibly within earshot.

VIOLET. Oh, how unlucky! Now please, Hector, say nothing. Go away until I have finished speaking to your father.

HECTOR [*inexorably*] No, Violet: I mean to have this thing out, right away. [*He puts her aside; passes her by; and faces his father, whose cheeks darken as his Irish blood begins to simmer*]. Dad: you've not played this hand straight.

MALONE. Hwat d'y'mean?

HECTOR. You've opened a letter addressed to me. You've impersonated me and stolen a march on this lady. That's dishonorable.

MALONE [*threateningly*] Now you take care what you're saying, Hector. Take care, I tell you.

HECTOR. I have taken care. I am taking care. I'm taking care of my honor and my position in English society.

MALONE [*hotly*] Your position has been got by my money: do you know that?

HECTOR. Well, you've just spoiled it all by opening that letter. A letter from an English lady, not addressed to you—a confidential letter! a delicate letter! a private letter! opened by my father! That's a sort of thing a man can't struggle against in England. The sooner we go back together the better. [*He appeals mutely to the heavens to witness the shame and anguish of two outcasts*].

VIOLET [*snubbing him with an instinctive dislike for scene making*] Don't be unreasonable, Hector. It was quite natural of Mr. Malone to open my letter: his name was on the envelope.

MALONE. There! You've no common sense, Hector. I thank you, Miss Robinson.

HECTOR. I thank you, too. It's very kind of you. My father knows no better.

MALONE [*furiously clenching his fists*] Hector—

HECTOR [*with undaunted moral force*] Oh, it's no use hectoring me. A private letter's a private letter, dad: you can't get over that.

MALONE [*raising his voice*] I won't be talked back to by you, d'y'hear?

VIOLET. Ssh! please, please. Here they all come.

Father and son, checked, glare mutely at one another as Tanner comes in through the little gate with Ramsden, followed by Octavius and Ann.

VIOLET. Back already!

TANNER. The Alhambra is not open this afternoon.

VIOLET. What a sell!

Tanner passes on, and presently finds himself between Hector and a strange elder, both apparently on the verge of personal combat. He looks from one to the other for an explanation. They sulkily avoid his eye, and nurse their wrath in silence.

RAMSDEN. Is it wise for you to be out in the sunshine with such a headache, Violet?

TANNER. Have you recovered too, Malone?

VIOLET. Oh, I forgot. We have not all met before. Mr. Malone: won't you introduce your father?

HECTOR [*with Roman firmness*] No I will not. He is no father of mine.

MALONE [*very angry*] You disown your dad before your English friends, do you?

VIOLET. Oh please don't make a scene.

Ann and Octavius, lingering near the gate, exchange an astonished glance, and discreetly withdraw up the steps to the garden, where they can enjoy the disturbance without intruding. On their way to the steps Ann sends a little grimace of mute sympathy to Violet, who is standing with her back to the little table, looking on in helpless annoyance as her husband soars to higher and higher moral eminences without the least regard to the old man's millions.

HECTOR. I'm very sorry, Miss Robinson; but I'm contending for a principle. I am a son, and, I hope, a dutiful one; but before everything I'm a Man! ! ! And when dad treats my private letters as his own, and takes it on himself to say that I shan't marry you if I am happy and fortunate enough to gain your consent, then I just snap my fingers and go my own way.

TANNER. Marry Violet!

RAMSDEN. Are you in your senses?

TANNER. Do you forget what we told you?

HECTOR [*recklessly*] I don't care what you told me.

RAMSDEN [*scandalized*] Tut tut, sir! Monstrous! [*he flings away towards the gate, his elbows quivering with indignation*].

TANNER. Another madman! These men in love should be locked up. [*He gives Hector up as hopeless, and turns away towards the garden; but Malone, taking offence in a new direction, follows him and compels him, by the aggressiveness of his tone, to stop*].

MALONE. I don't understand this. Is Hector not good enough for this lady, pray?

TANNER. My dear sir, the lady is married already. Hector knows it; and yet he persists in his infatuation. Take him home and lock him up.

MALONE [*bitterly*] So this is the high-born social tone I've spoilt be me ignorant, uncultivated behavior! Makin love to a married woman! [*He comes angrily between Hector and Violet, and almost bawls into Hector's left ear*] You've picked up that habit of the British aristocracy, have you?

HECTOR. That's all right. Don't you trouble yourself about that. I'll answer for the morality of what I'm doing.

TANNER [*coming forward to Hector's right hand with flashing eyes*] Well said, Malone! You also see that mere marriage laws are not morality! I agree with you; but unfortunately Violet does not.

MALONE. I take leave to doubt that, sir. [*Turning on Violet*] Let me tell you, Mrs. Robinson, or whatever your right name is, you had no right to send that letter to my son when you were the wife of another man.

HECTOR [*outraged*] This is the last straw. Dad: you have insulted my wife.

MALONE. Your wife!

TANNER. You the missing husband! Another moral impostor! [*He smites his brow, and collapses into Malone's chair*].

MALONE. You've married without my consent!

RAMSDEN. You have deliberately humbugged us, sir!

HECTOR. Here: I have had just about enough of being badgered. Violet and I are married: that's the long and the short of it. Now what have you got to say—any of you?

MALONE. I know what I've got to say. She's married a beggar.

HECTOR. No; she's married a Worker [*his American pronunciation imparts an overwhelming intensity to this simple and unpopular word*]. I start to earn my own living this very afternoon.

MALONE [*sneering angrily*] Yes: you're very plucky now, because you got your remittance from me yesterday or this morning, I reckon. Wait til it's spent. You won't be so full of cheek then.

HECTOR [*producing a letter from his pocketbook*] Here it is [*thrusting it on his father*]. Now you just take your remittance and yourself out of my life. I'm done with remittances;

and I'm done with you. I don't sell the privilege of insulting my wife for a thousand dollars.

MALONE [*deeply wounded and full of concern*] Hector: you don't know what poverty is.

HECTOR [*fervidly*] Well, I want to know what it is. I want'be a Man. Violet: you come along with me, to your own home: I'll see you through.

OCTAVIUS [*jumping down from the garden to the lawn and running to Hector's left hand*] I hope you'll shake hands with me before you go, Hector. I admire and respect you more than I can say. [*He is affected almost to tears as they shake hands*].

VIOLET [*also almost in tears, but of vexation*] Oh don't be an idiot, Tavy. Hector's about as fit to become a workman as you are.

TANNER [*rising from his chair on the other side of Hector*] Never fear: there's no question of his becoming a navvy, Mrs. Malone. [*To Hector*] There's really no difficulty about capital to start with. Treat me as a friend: draw on me.

OCTAVIUS [*impulsively*] Or on me.

MALONE [*with fierce jealousy*] Who wants your durty money? Who should he draw on but his own father? [*Tanner and Octavius recoil, Octavius rather hurt, Tanner consoled by the solution of the money difficulty. Violet looks up hopefully*]. Hector: don't be rash, my boy. I'm sorry for what I said: I never meant to insult Violet: I take it all back. She's just the wife you want: there!

HECTOR [*patting him on the shoulder*] Well, that's all right, dad. Say no more: we're friends again. Only, I take no money from anybody.

MALONE [*pleading abjectly*] Don't be hard on me, Hector. I'd rather you quarrelled and took the money than made friends and starved. You don't know what the world is: I do.

HECTOR. No, no, NO. That's fixed: that's not going to change. [*He passes his father inexorably by, and goes to Violet*]. Come, Mrs. Malone: you've got to move to the hotel with me, and take your proper place before the world.

VIOLET. But I must go in, dear, and tell Davis to pack. Won't you go on and make them give you a room overlooking the garden for me? I'll join you in half an hour.

HECTOR. Very well. You'll dine with us, Dad, won't you?

MALONE [*eager to conciliate him*] Yes, yes.

HECTOR. See you all later. [*He waves his hand to Ann, who has now been joined by Tanner, Octavius, and Rams-*

den in the garden, and goes out through the little gate, leaving his father and Violet together on the lawn].

MALONE. You'll try to bring him to his senses, Violet: I know you will.

VIOLET. I had no idea he could be so headstrong. If he goes on like that, what can I do?

MALONE. Don't be discurridged: domestic pressure may be slow; but it's sure. You'll wear him down. Promise me you will.

VIOLET. I will do my best. Of course I think it's the greatest nonsense deliberately making us poor like that.

MALONE. Of course it is.

VIOLET [*after a moment's reflection*] You had better give me the remittance. He will want it for his hotel bill. I'll see whether I can induce him to accept it. Not now, of course, but presently.

MALONE [*eagerly*] Yes, yes, yes: that's just the thing [*he hands her the thousand dollar bill, and adds cunningly*] Y'understand that this is only a bachelor allowance.

VIOLET [*coolly*] Oh, quite. [*She takes it*]. Thank you. By the way, Mr. Malone, those two houses you mentioned—the abbeys.

MALONE. Yes?

VIOLET. Don't take one of them until I've seen it. One never knows what may be wrong with these places.

MALONE. I won't. I'll do nothing without consulting you, never fear.

VIOLET [*politely, but without a ray of gratitude*] Thanks: that will be much the best way. [*She goes calmly back to the villa, escorted obsequiously by Malone to the upper end of the garden*].

TANNER [*drawing Ramsden's attention to Malone's cringing attitude as he takes leave of Violet*] And that poor devil is a billionaire! one of the master spirits of the age! Led in a string like a pug dog by the first girl who takes the trouble to despise him. I wonder will it ever come to that with me. [*He comes down to the lawn*].

RAMSDEN [*following him*] The sooner the better for you.

MALONE [*slapping his hands as he returns through the garden*] That'll be a grand woman for Hector. I wouldn't exchange her for ten duchesses. [*He descends to the lawn and comes between Tanner and Ramsden*].

RAMSDEN [*very civil to the billionaire*] It's an unexpected pleasure to find you in this corner of the world, Mr. Malone. Have you come to buy up the Alhambra?

MALONE. Well, I don't say I mightn't. I think I could do better with it than the Spanish government. But that's not what I came about. To tell you the truth, about a month ago I overheard a deal between two men over a bundle of shares. They differed about the price: they were young and greedy, and didn't know that if the shares were worth what was bid for them they must be worth what was asked, the margin being too small to be of any account, you see. To amuse meself, I cut in and bought the shares. Well, to this day I haven't found out what the business is. The office is in this town; and the name is Mendoza, Limited. Now whether Mendoza's a mine, or a steamboat line, or a bank, or a patent article—

TANNER. He's a man. I know him: his principles are thoroughly commercial. Let us take you round the town in our motor, Mr. Malone, and call on him on the way.

MALONE. If you'll be so kind, yes. And may I ask who—

TANNER. Mr. Roebuck Ramsden, a very old friend of your daughter-in-law.

MALONE. Happy to meet you, Mr. Ramsden.

RAMSDEN. Thank you. Mr. Tanner is also one of our circle.

MALONE. Glad to know you also, Mr. Tanner.

TANNER. Thanks. [*Malone and Ramsden go out very amicably through the little gate. Tanner calls to Octavius, who is wandering in the garden with Ann*] Tavy! [*Tavy comes to the steps, Tanner whispers loudly to him*] Violet has married a financier of brigands. [*Tanner hurries away to overtake Malone and Ramsden. Ann strolls to the steps with an idle impulse to torment Octavius*].

ANN. Won't you go with them, Tavy?

OCTAVIUS [*tears suddenly flushing his eyes*] You cut me to the heart, Ann, by wanting me to go [*he comes down on the lawn to hide his face from her. She follows him caressingly*].

ANN. Poor Ricky Ticky Tavy! Poor heart!

OCTAVIUS. It belongs to you, Ann. Forgive me: I must speak of it. I love you. You know I love you.

ANN. What's the good, Tavy? You know that my mother is determined that I shall marry Jack.

OCTAVIUS [*amazed*] Jack!

ANN. It seems absurd, doesn't it?

OCTAVIUS [*with growing resentment*] Do you mean to say that Jack has been playing with me all this time? That he has been urging me not to marry you because he intends to marry you himself?

ANN [*alarmed*] No no: you mustn't lead him to believe that I said that: I don't for a moment think that Jack knows his own mind. But it's clear from my father's will that he wished me to marry Jack. And my mother is set on it.

OCTAVIUS. But you are not bound to sacrifice yourself always to the wishes of your parents.

ANN. My father loved me. My mother loves me. Surely their wishes are a better guide than my own selfishness.

OCTAVIUS. Oh, I know how unselfish you are, Ann. But believe me—though I know I am speaking in my own interest —there is another side to this question. Is it fair to Jack to marry him if you do not love him? Is it fair to destroy my happiness as well as your own if you can bring yourself to love me?

ANN [*looking at him with a faint impulse of pity*] Tavy, my dear, you are a nice creature—a good boy.

OCTAVIUS [*humiliated*] Is that all?

ANN [*mischievously in spite of her pity*] That's a great deal, I assure you. You would always worship the ground I trod on, wouldn't you?

OCTAVIUS. I do. It sounds ridiculous; but it's no exaggeration. I do; and I always shall.

ANN. Always is a long word, Tavy. You see, I shall have to live up always to your idea of my divinity; and I don't think I could do that if we were married. But if I marry Jack, you'll never be disillusioned—at least not until I grow too old.

OCTAVIUS. I too shall grow old, Ann. And when I am eighty, one white hair of the woman I love will make me tremble more than the thickest gold tress from the most beautiful young head.

ANN [*quite touched*] Oh, that's poetry, Tavy, real poetry. It gives me that strange sudden sense of an echo from a former existence which always seems to me such a striking proof that we have immortal souls.

OCTAVIUS. Do you believe that it is true?

ANN. Tavy: if it is to come true, you must lose me as well as love me.

OCTAVIUS. Oh! [*He hastily sits down at the little table and covers his face with his hands*].

ANN [*with conviction*] Tavy: I wouldn't for worlds destroy your illusions. I can neither take you nor let you go. I can see exactly what will suit you. You must be a sentimental old bachelor for my sake.

OCTAVIUS [*desperately*] Ann: I'll kill myself.

ANN. Oh no you won't: that wouldn't be kind. You won't have a bad time. You will be very nice to women; and you will go a good deal to the opera. A broken heart is a very pleasant complaint for a man in London if he has a comfortable income.

OCTAVIUS [*considerably cooled, but believing that he is only recovering his self-control*] I know you mean to be kind, Ann. Jack has persuaded you that cynicism is a good tonic for me. [*He rises with quiet dignity*].

ANN [*studying him slyly*] You see, I'm disillusionizing you already. That's what I dread.

OCTAVIUS. You do not dread disillusionizing Jack.

ANN [*her face lighting up with mischievous ecstasy— whispering*] I can't: he has no illusions about me. I shall surprise Jack the other way. Getting over an unfavorable impression is ever so much easier than living up to an ideal. Oh, I shall enrapture Jack sometimes!

OCTAVIUS [*resuming the calm phase of despair, and beginning to enjoy his broken heart and delicate attitude without knowing it*] I don't doubt that. You will enrapture him always. And he—the fool!—thinks you would make him wretched.

ANN. Yes: that's the difficulty, so far.

OCTAVIUS [*heroically*] Shall *I* tell him that you love him?

ANN [*quickly*] Oh no: he'd run away again.

OCTAVIUS [*shocked*] Ann: would you marry an unwilling man?

ANN. What a queer creature you are, Tavy! There's no such thing as a willing man when you really go for him. [*She laughs naughtily*]. I'm shocking you, I suppose. But you know you are really getting a sort of satisfaction already in being out of danger yourself.

OCTAVIUS [*startled*] Satisfaction! [*Reproachfully*] You say that to me!

ANN. Well, if it were really agony, would you ask for more of it?

OCTAVIUS. Have I asked for more of it?

ANN. You have offered to tell Jack that I love him. That's self-sacrifice, I suppose; but there must be some satisfaction in it. Perhaps it's because you're a poet. You are like the bird that presses its breast against the sharp thorn to make itself sing.

OCTAVIUS. It's quite simple. I love you; and I want you to be happy. You don't love me; so I can't make you happy myself; but I can help another man to do it.

ANN. Yes: it seems quite simple. But I doubt if we ever know why we do things. The only really simple thing is to go straight for what you want and grab it. I suppose I don't love you, Tavy; but sometimes I feel as if I should like to make a man of you somehow. You are very foolish about women.

OCTAVIUS [almost coldly] I am content to be what I am in that respect.

ANN. Then you must keep away from them, and only dream about them. I wouldn't marry you for worlds, Tavy.

OCTAVIUS. I have no hope, Ann: I accept my ill luck. But I don't think you quite know how much it hurts.

ANN. You are so softhearted! It's queer that you should be so different from Violet. Violet's as hard as nails.

OCTAVIUS. Oh no. I am sure Violet is thoroughly womanly at heart.

ANN [with some impatience] Why do you say that? Is it unwomanly to be thoughtful and businesslike and sensible? Do you want Violet to be an idiot—or something worse, like me?

OCTAVIUS. Something worse—like you! What do you mean, Ann?

ANN. Oh well, I don't mean that, of course. But I have a great respect for Violet. She gets her own way always.

OCTAVIUS [sighing] So do you.

ANN. Yes; but somehow she gets it without coaxing—without having to make people sentimental about her.

OCTAVIUS [with brotherly callousness] Nobody could get very sentimental about Violet, I think, pretty as she is.

ANN. Oh yes they could, if she made them.

OCTAVIUS. But surely no really nice woman would deliberately practise on men's instincts in that way.

ANN [throwing up her hands] Oh Tavy, Tavy, Ricky Ticky Tavy, heaven help the woman who marries you!

OCTAVIUS [his passion reviving at the name] Oh why, why, why do you say that? Don't torment me. I don't understand.

ANN. Suppose she were to tell fibs, and lay snares for men?

OCTAVIUS. Do you think *I* could marry such a woman—
I, who have known and loved you?

ANN. Hm! Well, at all events, she wouldn't let you if she
were wise. So that's settled. And now I can't talk any more.
Say you forgive me, and that the subject is closed.

OCTAVIUS. I have nothing to forgive; and the subject is
closed. And if the wound is open, at least you shall never
see it bleed.

ANN. Poetic to the last, Tavy. Goodbye, dear. [*She pats
his cheek; has an impulse to kiss him and then another impulse of distaste which prevents her; finally runs away
through the garden and into the villa*].

*Octavius again takes refuge at the table, bowing his head
on his arms and sobbing softly. Mrs. Whitefield, who has
been pottering round the Granada shops, and has a net full
of little parcels in her hand, comes in through the gate and
sees him.*

MRS. WHITEFIELD [*running to him and lifting his head*]
What's the matter, Tavy? Are you ill?

OCTAVIUS. No, nothing, nothing.

MRS. WHITEFIELD [*still holding his head, anxiously*] But
you're crying. Is it about Violet's marriage?

OCTAVIUS. No, no. Who told you about Violet?

MRS. WHITEFIELD [*restoring the head to its owner*] I met
Roebuck and that awful old Irishman. Are you sure youre
not ill? What's the matter?

OCTAVIUS [*affectionately*] It's nothing—only a man's
broken heart. Doesn't that sound ridiculous?

MRS. WHITEFIELD. But what is it all about? Has Ann been
doing anything to you?

OCTAVIUS. It's not Ann's fault. And don't think for a
moment that I blame you.

MRS. WHITEFIELD [*startled*] For what?

OCTAVIUS [*pressing her hand consolingly*] For nothing.
I said I didn't blame you.

MRS. WHITEFIELD. But I haven't done anything. What's
the matter?

OCTAVIUS [*smiling sadly*] Can't you guess? I daresay you
are right to prefer Jack to me as a husband for Ann; but I
love Ann; and it hurts rather. [*He rises and moves away
from her towards the middle of the lawn*].

MRS. WHITEFIELD [*following him hastily*] Does Ann say
that I want her to marry Jack?

OCTAVIUS. Yes: she has told me.

MRS. WHITEFIELD [*thoughtfully*] Then I'm very sorry for you, Tavy. It's only her way of saying she wants to marry Jack. Little she cares what *I* say or what *I* want!

OCTAVIUS. But she would not say it unless she believed it. Surely you don't suspect Ann of—of deceit!!

MRS. WHITEFIELD. Well, never mind, Tavy. I don't know which is best for a young man: to know too little, like you, or too much, like Jack.

Tanner returns.

TANNER. Well, I've disposed of old Malone. I've introduced him to Mendoza, Limited; and left the two brigands together to talk it out. Hullo, Tavy! anything wrong?

OCTAVIUS. I must go wash my face, I see. [*To Mrs. Whitefield*] Tell him what you wish. [*To Tanner*] You may take it from me, Jack, that Ann approves of it.

TANNER [*puzzled by his manner*] Approves of what?

OCTAVIUS. Of what Mrs. Whitefield wishes. [*He goes his way with sad dignity to the villa*].

TANNER [*to Mrs. Whitefield*] This is very mysterious. What is it you wish? It shall be done, whatever it is.

MRS. WHITEFIELD [*with snivelling gratitude*] Thank you, Jack. [*She sits down. Tanner brings the other chair from the table and sits close to her with his elbows on his knees, giving her his whole attention*]. I don't know why it is that other people's children are so nice to me, and that my own have so little consideration for me. It's no wonder I don't seem able to care for Ann and Rhoda as I do for you and Tavy and Violet. It's a very queer world. It used to be so straightforward and simple; and now nobody seems to think and feel as they ought. Nothing has been right since that speech that Professor Tyndall made at Belfast.

TANNER. Yes: life is more complicated than we used to think. But what am I to do for you?

MRS. WHITEFIELD. That's just what I want to tell you. Of course you'll marry Ann whether I like it or not—

TANNER [*starting*] It seems to me that I shall presently be married to Ann whether I like it myself or not.

MRS. WHITEFIELD [*peacefully*] Oh, very likely you will: you know what she is when she has set her mind on anything. But don't put it on me: that's all I ask. Tavy has just let out that she's been saying that I am making her marry you; and the poor boy is breaking his heart about it; for he is in love with her himself, though what he sees in her so wonderful, goodness knows: *I* don't. It's no use telling Tavy that Ann

puts things into people's heads by telling them that I want
them when the thought of them never crossed my mind. It
only sets Tavy against me. But you know better than that.
So if you marry her, don't put the blame on me.

TANNER [*emphatically*] I haven't the slightest intention
of marrying her.

MRS. WHITEFIELD [*slyly*] She'd suit you better than Tavy.
She'd meet her match in you, Jack. I'd like to see her meet
her match.

TANNER. No man is a match for a woman, except with
a poker and a pair of hobnailed boots. Not always even then.
Anyhow, *I* can't take the poker to her. I should be a mere
slave.

MRS. WHITEFIELD. No: she's afraid of you. At all events,
you would tell her the truth about herself. She wouldn't be
able to slip out of it as she does with me.

TANNER. Everybody would call me a brute if I told Ann
the truth about herself in terms of her own moral code. To
begin with, Ann says things that are not strictly true.

MRS. WHITEFIELD. I'm glad somebody sees she is not an
angel.

TANNER. In short—to put it as a husband would put it
when exasperated to the point of speaking out—she is a liar.
And since she has plunged Tavy head over ears in love with
her without any intention of marrying him, she is a coquette,
according to the standard definition of a coquette as a woman
who rouses passions she has no intention of gratifying. And
as she has now reduced you to the point of being willing to
sacrifice me at the altar for the mere satisfaction of getting
me to call her a liar to her face, I may conclude that she is
a bully as well. She can't bully men as she bullies women; so
she habitually and unscrupulously uses her personal fascination to make men give her whatever she wants. That makes
her almost something for which I know no polite name.

MRS. WHITEFIELD [*in mild expostulation*] Well, you can't
expect perfection, Jack.

TANNER. I don't. But what annoys me is that Ann does.
I know perfectly well that all this about her being a liar
and a bully and a coquette and so forth is a trumped-up
moral indictment which might be brought against anybody.
We all lie; we all bully as much as we dare; we all bid for
admiration without the least intention of earning it; we
all get as much rent as we can out of our powers of fascination. If Ann would admit this I shouldn't quarrel with her.

But she won't. If she has children she'll take advantage of their telling lies to amuse herself by whacking them. If another woman makes eyes at me, she'll refuse to know a coquette. She will do just what she likes herself whilst insisting on everybody else doing what the conventional code prescribes. In short, I can stand everything except her confounded hypocrisy. That's what beats me.

MRS. WHITEFIELD [*carried away by the relief of hearing her own opinion so eloquently expressed*] Oh, she is a hypocrite. She is: she is. Isn't she?

TANNER. Then why do you want to marry me to her?

MRS. WHITEFIELD [*querulously*] There now! put it on me, of course. I never thought of it until Tavy told me she said I did. But, you know, I'm very fond of Tavy: he's a sort of son to me; and I don't want him to be trampled on and made wretched.

TANNER. Whereas I don't matter, I suppose.

MRS. WHITEFIELD. Oh, you are different, somehow: you are able to take care of yourself. You'd serve her out. And anyhow, she must marry somebody.

TANNER. Aha! there speaks the life instinct. You detest her; but you feel that you must get her married.

MRS. WHITEFIELD [*rising, shocked*] Do you mean that I detest my own daughter! Surely you don't believe me to be so wicked and unnatural as that, merely because I see her faults.

TANNER [*cynically*] You love her, then?

MRS. WHITEFIELD. Why, of course I do. What queer things you say, Jack! We can't help loving our own blood relations.

TANNER. Well, perhaps it saves unpleasantness to say so. But for my part, I suspect that the tables of consanguinity have a natural basis in a natural repugnance [*he rises*].

MRS. WHITEFIELD. You shouldn't say things like that, Jack. I hope you won't tell Ann that I have been speaking to you. I only wanted to set myself right with you and Tavy. I couldn't sit mumchance and have everything put on me.

TANNER [*politely*] Quite so.

MRS. WHITEFIELD [*dissatisfied*] And now I've only made matters worse. Tavy's angry with me because I don't worship Ann. And when it's been put into my head that Ann ought to marry you, what can I say except that it would serve her right?

TANNER. Thank you.

MRS. WHITEFIELD. Now don't be silly and twist what I say into something I don't mean. I ought to have fair play— *Ann comes from the villa, followed presently by Violet, who is dressed for driving.*

ANN [*coming to her mother's right hand with threatening suavity*] Well, mamma darling, you seem to be having a delightful chat with Jack. We can hear you all over the place.

MRS. WHITEFIELD [*appalled*] Have you overheard—

TANNER. Never fear: Ann is only—well, we were discussing that habit of hers just now. She hasn't heard a word.

MRS. WHITEFIELD [*stoutly*] I don't care whether she has or not: I have a right to say what I please.

VIOLET [*arriving on the lawn and coming between Mrs. Whitefield and Tanner*] I've come to say goodbye. I'm off for my honeymoon.

MRS. WHITEFIELD [*crying*] Oh don't say that, Violet. And no wedding, no breakfast, no clothes, nor anything.

VIOLET [*petting her*] It won't be for long.

MRS. WHITEFIELD. Don't let him take you to America. Promise me that you won't.

VIOLET [*very decidedly*] I should think not, indeed. Don't cry, dear: I'm only going to the hotel.

MRS. WHITEFIELD. But going in that dress, with your luggage, makes one realize— [*she chokes, and then breaks out again*] How I wish you were my daughter, Violet!

VIOLET [*soothing her*] There, there: so I am. Ann will be jealous.

MRS. WHITEFIELD. Ann doesn't care a bit for me.

ANN. Fie, mother! Come, now: you mustn't cry any more: you know Violet doesn't like it [*Mrs. Whitefield dries her eyes, and subsides*].

VIOLET. Goodbye, Jack.

TANNER. Goodbye, Violet.

VIOLET. The sooner you get married too, the better. You will be much less misunderstood.

TANNER [*restively*] I quite expect to get married in the course of the afternoon. You all seem to have set your minds on it.

VIOLET. You might do worse. [*To Mrs. Whitefield: putting her arm round her*] Let me take you to the hotel with me: the drive will do you good. Come in and get a wrap. [*She takes her towards the villa*].

MRS. WHITEFIELD [*as they go up through the garden*] I don't know what I shall do when you are gone, with no one

but Ann in the house; and she always occupied with the men!
It's not to be expected that your husband will care to be
bothered with an old woman like me. Oh, you needn't tell
me: politeness is all very well; but I know what people
think— [*She talks herself and Violet out of sight and hearing*].
*Ann, musing on Violet's opportune advice, approaches
Tanner; examines him humorously for a moment from toe to
top; and finally delivers her opinion.*

ANN. Violet is quite right. You ought to get married.

TANNER [*explosively*] Ann: I will not marry you. Do you
hear? I won't, won't, won't, won't, WON'T marry you.

ANN [*placidly*] Well, nobody axd you, sir she said, sir
she said, sir she said. So that's settled.

TANNER. Yes, nobody has asked me; but everybody treats
the thing as settled. It's in the air. When we meet, the others
go away on absurd pretexts to leave us alone together. Ramsden no longer scowls at me: his eye beams, as if he were
already giving you away to me in church. Tavy refers me to
your mother and gives me his blessing. Straker openly treats
you as his future employer: it was he who first told me of it.

ANN. Was that why you ran away?

TANNER. Yes, only to be stopped by a lovesick brigand
and run down like a truant schoolboy.

ANN. Well, if you don't want to be married, you needn't
be [*she turns away from him and sits down, much at her
ease*].

TANNER [*following her*]. Does any man want to be
hanged? Yet men let themselves be hanged without a struggle
for life, though they could at least give the chaplain a black
eye. We do the world's will, not our own. I have a frightful
feeling that I shall let myself be married because it is the
world's will that you should have a husband.

ANN. I daresay I shall, someday.

TANNER. But why me—me of all men? Marriage is to
me apostasy, profanation of the sanctuary of my soul, viola-
tion of my manhood, sale of my birthright, shameful surrender, ignominious capitulation, acceptance of defeat. I shall
decay like a thing that has served its purpose and is done
with; I shall change from a man with a future to a man with
a past; I shall see in the greasy eyes of all the other husbands
their relief at the arrival of a new prisoner to share their
ignominy. The young men will scorn me as one who has sold
out: to the young women I, who have always been an enigma

and a possibility, shall be merely somebody else's property—
and damaged goods at that: a secondhand man at best.

ANN. Well, your wife can put on a cap and make herself ugly to keep you in countenance, like my grandmother.

TANNER. So that she may make her triumph more insolent by publicly throwing away the bait the moment the
trap snaps on the victim!

ANN. After all, though, what difference would it make?
Beauty is all very well at first sight; but who ever looks at
it when it has been in the house three days? I thought our
pictures very lovely when papa bought them; but I haven't
looked at them for years. You never bother about my looks:
you are too well used to me. I might be the umbrella stand.

TANNER. You lie, you vampire: you lie.

ANN. Flatterer. Why are you trying to fascinate me,
Jack, if you don't want to marry me?

TANNER. The Life Force. I am in the grip of the Life
Force.

ANN. I don't understand in the least: it sounds like the
Life Guards.

TANNER. Why don't you marry Tavy? He is willing. Can
you not be satisfied unless your prey struggles?

ANN [turning to him as if to let him into a secret] Tavy
will never marry. Haven't you noticed that that sort of
man never marries?

TANNER. What! a man who idolizes women! who sees
nothing in nature but romantic scenery for love duets! Tavy,
the chivalrous, the faithful, the tenderhearted and true! Tavy
never marry! Why, he was born to be swept up by the first
pair of blue eyes he meets in the street.

ANN. Yes, I know. All the same, Jack, men like that
always live in comfortable bachelor lodgings with broken
hearts, and are adored by their landladies, and never get married. Men like you always get married.

TANNER [smiting his brow] How frightfully, horribly
true! It has been staring me in the face all my life; and I
never saw it before.

ANN. Oh, it's the same with women. The poetic temperament's a very nice temperament, very amiable, very harmless
and poetic, I daresay; but it's an old maid's temperament.

TANNER. Barren. The Life Force passes it by.

ANN. If that's what you mean by the Life Force, yes.

TANNER. You don't care for Tavy?

ANN [*looking round carefully to make sure that Tavy is not within earshot*] No.

TANNER. And you do care for me?

ANN [*rising quietly and shaking her finger at him*] Now Jack! Behave yourself.

TANNER. Infamous, abandoned woman! Devil!

ANN. Boa-constrictor! Elephant!

TANNER. Hypocrite!

ANN [*softly*] I must be, for my future husband's sake.

TANNER. For mine! [*Correcting himself savagely*] I mean for his.

ANN [*ignoring the correction*] Yes, for yours. You had better marry what you call a hypocrite, Jack. Women who are not hypocrites go about in rational dress and are insulted and get into all sorts of hot water. And then their husbands get dragged in too, and live in continual dread of fresh complications. Wouldn't you prefer a wife you could depend on?

TANNER. No, a thousand times no: hot water is the revolutionist's element. You clean men as you clean milk-pails, by scalding them.

ANN. Cold water has its uses too. It's healthy.

TANNER [*despairingly*] Oh, you are witty: at the supreme moment the Life Force endows you with every quality. Well, I too can be a hypocrite. Your father's will appointed me your guardian, not your suitor. I shall be faithful to my trust.

ANN [*in low siren tones*] He asked me who would I have as my guardian before he made that will. I chose you!

TANNER. The will is yours then! The trap was laid from the beginning.

ANN [*concentrating all her magic*] From the beginning—from our childhood—for both of us—by the Life Force.

TANNER. I will not marry you. I will not marry you.

ANN. Oh, you will, you will.

TANNER. I tell you, no, no, no.

ANN. I tell you, yes, yes, yes.

TANNER. No.

ANN [*coaxing—imploring—almost exhausted*] Yes. Before it is too late for repentance. Yes.

TANNER [*struck by the echo from the past*] When did all this happen to me before? Are we two dreaming?

ANN [*suddenly losing her courage, with an anguish that she does not conceal*] No. We are awake; and you have said no: that is all.

TANNER [*brutally*] Well?

ANN. Well, I made a mistake: you do not love me.

TANNER [*seizing her in his arms*] It is false: I love you. The Life Force enchants me: I have the whole world in my arms when I clasp you. But I am fighting for my freedom, for my honor, for my self, one and indivisible.

ANN. Your happiness will be worth them all.

TANNER. You would sell freedom and honor and self for happiness?

ANN. It will not be all happiness for me. Perhaps death.

TANNER [*groaning*] Oh, that clutch holds and hurts. What have you grasped in me? Is there a father's heart as well as a mother's?

ANN. Take care, Jack: if anyone comes while we are like this, you will have to marry me.

TANNER. If we two stood now on the edge of a precipice, I would hold you tight and jump.

ANN [*panting, failing more and more under the strain*] Jack: let me go. I have dared so frightfully—it is lasting longer than I thought. Let me go: I can't bear it.

TANNER. Nor I. Let it kill us.

ANN. Yes: I don't care. I am at the end of my forces. I don't care. I think I am going to faint.

At this moment Violet and Octavius come from the villa with Mrs. Whitefield, who is wrapped up for driving. Simultaneously Malone and Ramsden, followed by Mendoza and Straker, come in through the little gate in the paling. Tanner shamefacedly releases Ann, who raises her hand giddily to her forehead.

MALONE. Take care. Something's the matter with the lady.

RAMSDEN. What does this mean?

VIOLET [*running between Ann and Tanner*] Are you ill?

ANN [*reeling, with a supreme effort*] I have promised to marry Jack. [*She swoons. Violet kneels by her and chafes her hand. Tanner runs round to her other hand, and tries to lift her head. Octavius goes to Violet's assistance, but does not know what to do. Mrs. Whitefield hurries back into the villa. Octavius, Malone and Ramsden run to Ann and crowd round her, stooping to assist. Straker coolly comes to Ann's feet, and Mendoza to her head, both upright and self-possessed*].

STRAKER. Now then, ladies and gentlemen: she don't want a crowd round her: she wants air—all the air she can git. If you please, gents—[*Malone and Ramsden allow him to drive them gently past Ann and up the lawn towards the garden, where Octavius, who has already become conscious of his uselessness, joins them. Straker, following them up, pauses for a moment to instruct Tanner*]. Don't lift er ed, Mr. Tanner: let it go flat so's the blood can run back into it.

MENDOZA. He is right, Mr. Tanner. Trust to the air of the Sierra. [*He withdraws delicately to the garden steps*].

TANNER [*rising*] I yield to your superior knowledge of physiology, Henry. [*He withdraws to the corner of the lawn; and Octavius immediately hurries down to him*].

TAVY [*aside to Tanner, grasping his hand*] Jack: be very happy.

TANNER [*aside to Tavy*] I never asked her. It is a trap for me. [*He goes up the lawn towards the garden. Octavius remains petrified*].

MENDOZA [*intercepting Mrs. Whitefield, who comes from the villa with a glass of brandy*] What is this, madam? [*he takes it from her*].

MRS. WHITEFIELD. A little brandy.

MENDOZA. The worst thing you could give her. Allow me. [*He swallows it*]. Trust to the air of the Sierra, madam. *For a moment the men all forget Ann and stare at Mendoza.*

ANN [*in Violet's ear, clutching her round the neck*] Violet: did Jack say anything when I fainted?

VIOLET. No.

ANN. Ah! [*with a sigh of intense relief she relapses*].

MRS. WHITEFIELD. Oh, she's fainted again. *They are about to rush back to her; but Mendoza stops them with a warning gesture.*

ANN [*supine*] No I haven't. I'm quite happy.

TANNER [*suddenly walking determinedly to her, and snatching her hand from Violet to feel her pulse*] Why, her pulse is positively bounding. Come, get up. What nonsense! Up with you. [*He gets her up summarily*].

ANN. Yes: I feel strong enough now. But you very nearly killed me, Jack, for all that.

MALONE. A rough wooer, eh? They're the best sort, Miss Whitefield. I congratulate Mr. Tanner; and I hope to meet you and him as frequent guests at the Abbey.

ANN. Thank you. [*She goes past Malone to Octavius*] Ricky Ticky Tavy: congratulate me. [*Aside to him*] I want to make you cry for the last time.

TAVY [*steadfastly*] No more tears. I am happy in your happiness. And I believe in you in spite of everything.

RAMSDEN [*coming between Malone and Tanner*] You are a happy man, Jack Tanner. I envy you.

MENDOZA [*advancing between Violet and Tanner*] Sir: there are two tragedies in life. One is not to get your heart's desire. The other is to get it. Mine and yours, sir.

TANNER. Mr. Mendoza: I have no heart's desires. Ramsden: it is very easy for you to call me a happy man: you are only a spectator. I am one of the principals; and I know better. Ann: stop tempting Tavy, and come back to me.

ANN [*complying*] You are absurd, Jack. [*She takes his proffered arm*].

TANNER [*continuing*] I solemnly say that I am not a happy man. Ann looks happy; but she is only triumphant, successful, victorious. That is not happiness, but the price for which the strong sell their happiness. What we have both done this afternoon is to renounce happiness, renounce freedom, renounce tranquillity, above all, renounce the romantic possibilities of an unknown future, for the cares of a household and a family. I beg that no man may seize the occasion to get half drunk and utter imbecile speeches and coarse pleasantries at my expense. We propose to furnish our own house according to our own taste; and I hereby give notice that the seven or eight travelling clocks, the four or five dressing cases, the salad bowls, the carvers and fish slices, the copy of Tennyson in extra morocco, and all the other articles you are preparing to heap upon us, will be instantly sold, and the proceeds devoted to circulating free copies of the Revolutionist's Handbook. The wedding will take place three days after our return to England, by special license, at the office of the district superintendent registrar, in the presence of my solicitor and his clerk, who, like his clients, will be in ordinary walking dress—

VIOLET [*with intense conviction*] You are a brute, Jack.

ANN [*looking at him with fond pride and caressing his arm*] Never mind her, dear. Go on talking.

TANNER. Talking!

Universal laughter.

THE REVOLUTIONIST'S HANDBOOK
AND POCKET COMPANION

BY John Tanner, M.I.R.C.

(Member of the Idle Rich Class).

PREFACE TO THE REVOLUTIONIST'S
HANDBOOK

"No one can contemplate the present condition of the masses of the people without desiring something like a revolution for the better." *Sir Robert Giffen.* Essays in Finance, vol. ii. p. 393.

FOREWORD

A REVOLUTIONIST is one who desires to discard the existing social order and try another.

The constitution of England is revolutionary. To a Russian or Anglo-Indian bureaucrat, a general election is as much a revolution as a referendum or plebiscite in which the people fight instead of voting. The French Revolution overthrew one set of rulers and substituted another with different interests and different views. That is what a general election enables the people to do in England every seven years if they choose. Revolution is therefore a national institution in England; and its advocacy by an Englishman needs no apology.

Every man is a revolutionist concerning the thing he understands. For example, every person who has mastered a profession is a sceptic concerning it, and consequently a revolutionist.

Every genuinely religious person is a heretic and therefore a revolutionist.

All who achieve real distinction in life begin as revolutionists. The most distinguished persons become more revolutionary as they grow older, though they are commonly supposed to become more conservative owing to their loss of faith in conventional methods of reform.

Any person under the age of thirty, who, having any knowledge of the existing social order, is not a revolutionist, is an inferior.

AND YET

Revolutions have never lightened the burden of tyranny: they have only shifted it to another shoulder.

John Tanner.

THE REVOLUTIONIST'S HANDBOOK

I. ON GOOD BREEDING

IF THERE were no God, said the eighteenth century Deist, it would be necessary to invent Him. Now this eighteenth century god was *deus ex machina,* the god who helped those who could not help themselves, the god of the lazy and incapable. The nineteenth century decided that there is indeed no such god; and now Man must take in hand all the work that he used to shirk with an idle prayer. He must, in effect, change himself into the political Providence which he formerly conceived as god; and such change is not only possible, but the only sort of change that is real. The mere transfigurations of institutions, as from military and priestly dominance to commercial and scientific dominance, from commercial dominance to proletarian democracy, from slavery to serfdom, from serfdom to capitalism, from monarchy to republicanism, from polytheism to monotheism, from monotheism to atheism, from atheism to pantheistic humanitarianism, from general illiteracy to general literacy, from romance to realism, from realism to mysticism, from metaphysics to physics, are all but changes from Tweedledum to Tweedledee: *"plus ça change, plus c'est la même chose."* But the changes from the crab apple to the pippin, from the wolf and fox to the house dog, from the charger of Henry V to the brewer's draught horse and the race horse, are real; for here Man has played the god, subduing Nature to his intention, and ennobling or debasing Life for a set purpose. And what can be done with a wolf can be done with a man. If such monsters as the tramp and the gentleman can appear as mere by-products of Man's individual greed and folly, what might we not hope for as a main product of his universal aspiration?

This is no new conclusion. The despair of institutions, and the inexorable "ye must be born again," with Mrs. Poyser's stipulation, "and born different," recurs in every generation. The cry for the Superman did not begin with Nietzsche, nor will it end with his vogue. But it has always been silenced by the same question: what kind of person is this Superman to be? You do not ask for a super-apple, but for an eatable apple; nor for a super-horse, but for a horse of greater draught or velocity. Neither is it of any use to ask for a Superman: you must furnish a specification of the sort of man you want. Unfortunately you do not know what sort of man you want. Some sort of goodlooking philosopher-athlete, with a handsome healthy woman for his mate, perhaps.

Vague as this is, it is a great advance on the popular demand for a perfect gentleman and a perfect lady. And, after all, no market demand in the world takes the form of exact technical specification of the article required. Excellent poultry and potatoes are produced to satisfy the demand of housewives who do not know the technical differences between a tuber and a chicken. They will tell you that the proof of the pudding is in the eating; and they are right. The proof of the Superman will be in the living; and we shall find out how to produce him by the old method of trial and error, and not by waiting for a completely convincing prescription of his ingredients.

Certain common and obvious mistakes may be ruled out from the beginning. For example, we agree that we want superior mind; but we need not fall into the football club folly of counting on this as a product of superior body. Yet if we recoil so far as to conclude that superior mind consists in being the dupe of our ethical classifications of virtues and vices, in short, of conventional morality, we shall fall out of the frying pan of the football club into the fire of the Sunday School. If we must choose between a race of athletes and a race of "good" men, let us have the athletes: better Samson and Milo than Calvin and Robespierre. But neither alternative is worth changing for: Samson is no more a Superman than Calvin. What then are we to do?

II. PROPERTY AND MARRIAGE

LET US hurry over the obstacles set up by property and marriage. Revolutionists make too much of them. No doubt it is easy to demonstrate that property will destroy society unless society destroys it. No doubt, also, property has hitherto held its own and destroyed all the empires. But that was because the superficial objection to it (that it distributes social wealth and the social labor burden in a grotesquely inequitable manner) did not threaten the existence of the race, but only the individual happiness of its units, and finally the maintenance of some irrelevant political form or other, such as a nation, an empire, or the like. Now as happiness never matters to Nature, as she neither recognizes flags and frontiers nor cares a straw whether the economic system adopted by a society is feudal, capitalistic or collectivist, provided it keeps the race afoot (the hive and the anthill being as acceptable to her as Utopia), the demonstrations of Socialists, though irrefutable, will never make any serious impression on property. The knell of that overrated institution will not sound until it is felt to conflict with some more vital matter than mere personal inequities in industrial economy. No such conflict was perceived whilst society had not yet grown beyond national communities too small and simple to disastrously overtax Man's limited political capacity. But we have now reached the stage of international organization. Man's political capacity and magnanimity are clearly beaten by the vastness and complexity of the problems forced on him. And it is at this anxious moment that he finds, when he looks upward for a mightier mind to help him, that the heavens are empty. He will presently see that his discarded formula that Man is the Temple of the Holy Ghost happens to be precisely true, and that it is only through his own brain and hand that this Holy Ghost, formerly the most nebulous person in the Trinity, and now become its sole survivor as it has always been its real Unity, can help him in any way. And so, if the Superman is to come, he must be born of Woman by Man's intentional and well-considered contrivance. Conviction of this will smash everything that opposes it. Even Property and Marriage, which laugh at the laborer's petty complaint that he is defrauded of "surplus value," and at the domestic miseries

of the slaves of the wedding ring, will themselves be laughed
aside as the lightest of trifles if they cross this conception
when it becomes a fully realized vital purpose of the race.

That they must cross it becomes obvious the moment
we acknowledge the futility of breeding men for special
qualities as we breed cocks for game, greyhounds for speed,
or sheep for mutton. What is really important in Man is the
part of him that we do not yet understand. Of much of it we
are not even conscious, just as we are not normally conscious of keeping up our circulation by our heart-pump,
though if we neglect it we die. We are therefore driven to
the conclusion that when we have carried selection as far
as we can by rejecting from the list of eligible parents all persons who are uninteresting, unpromising, or blemished without any set-off, we shall still have to trust to the guidance of
fancy (*alias* Voice of Nature), both in the breeders and the
parents, for that superiority in the unconscious self which
will be the true characteristic of the Superman.

At this point we perceive the importance of giving fancy
the widest possible field. To cut humanity up into small
cliques, and effectively limit the selection of the individual to
his own clique, is to postpone the Superman for eons, if not
for ever. Not only should every person be nourished and
trained as a possible parent, but there should be no possibility
of such an obstacle to natural selection as the objection of a
countess to a navvy or of a duke to a charwoman. Equality
is essential to good breeding; and equality, as all economists
know, is incompatible with property.

Besides, equality is an essential condition of bad breeding also; and bad breeding is indispensable to the weeding out
of the human race. When the conception of heredity took
hold of the scientific imagination in the middle of last century, its devotees announced that it was a crime to marry the
lunatic to the lunatic or the consumptive to the consumptive.
But pray are we to try to correct our diseased stocks by in-
fecting our healthy stocks with them? Clearly the attraction
which disease has for diseased people is beneficial to the race.
If two really unhealthy people get married, they will, as likely
as not, have a great number of children who will all die before
they reach maturity. This is a far more satisfactory arrangement than the tragedy of a union between a healthy and an
unhealthy person. Though more costly than sterilization of
the unhealthy, it has the enormous advantage that in the
event of our notions of health and unhealth being erroneous

(which to some extent they most certainly are), the error will be corrected by experience instead of confirmed by evasion.

One fact must be faced resolutely, in spite of the shrieks of the romantic. There is no evidence that the best citizens are the offspring of congenial marriages, or that a conflict of temperament is not a highly important part of what breeders call crossing. On the contrary, it is quite sufficiently probable that good results may be obtained from parents who would be extremely unsuitable companions and partners, to make it certain that the experiment of mating them will sooner or later be tried purposely almost as often as it is now tried accidentally. But mating such couples must clearly not involve marrying them. In conjugation two complementary persons may supply one another's deficiencies: in the domestic partnership of marriage they only feel them and suffer from them. Thus the son of a robust, cheerful, eupeptic British country squire, with the tastes and range of his class, and of a clever, imaginative, intellectual, highly civilized Jewess, might be very superior to both his parents; but it is not likely that the Jewess would find the squire an interesting companion, or his habits, his friends, his place and mode of life congenial to her. Therefore marriage, whilst it is made an indispensable condition of mating, will delay the advent of the Superman as effectually as Property, and will be modified by the impulse towards him just as effectually.

The practical abrogation of Property and Marriage as they exist at present will occur without being much noticed. To the mass of men, the intelligent abolition of property would mean nothing except an increase in the quantity of food, clothing, housing and comfort at their personal disposal, as well as a greater control over their time and circumstances. Very few persons now make any distinction between virtually complete property and property held on such highly developed public conditions as to place its income on the same footing as that of a propertyless clergyman, officer, or civil servant. A landed proprietor may still drive men and women off his land, demolish their dwellings, and replace them with sheep or deer; and in the unregulated trades the private trader may still sponge on the regulated trades and sacrifice the life and health of the nation as lawlessly as the Manchester cotton manufacturers did at the beginning of last century. But though the Factory Code on the one hand, and Trade Union organization on the other, have, within the lifetime of men still living, converted the old unrestricted property of the cotton manufacturer in his mill and the cotton spinner in his labor into a mere permission to trade or work on stringent public or collective conditions, imposed in the interest of the general welfare without any regard for individual hard cases, people in Lancashire still speak of their "property" in the old terms, meaning nothing more by it than the things a thief can be punished for stealing. The total abolition of property, and the conversion of every citizen into a salaried functionary in the public service, would leave much more than 99 per cent of the nation quite unconscious of any greater change than now takes place when the son of a shipowner goes into the navy. They would still call their watches and umbrellas and back gardens their property.

Marriage also will persist as a name attached to a general custom long after the custom itself will have altered. For example, modern English marriage, as modified by divorce and by Married Women's Property Acts, differs more from early nineteenth century marriage than Byron's marriage did from Shakespeare's. At the present moment marriage in England differs not only from marriage in France, but from marriage in Scotland. Marriage as modified by the divorce laws in South Dakota would be called mere promiscuity in Clapham. Yet the Americans, far from taking a profligate and cynical view of marriage, do homage to its ideals with a seriousness that seems old fashioned in Clapham. Neither in England nor America would a proposal to abolish marriage be tolerated for a moment; and yet nothing is more certain than that in both countries the progressive modification of the marriage contract will be continued until it is no more onerous nor irrevocable than any ordinary commercial deed of partnership. Were even this dispensed with, people would still call themselves husbands and wives; describe their companionships as marriages; and be for the most part unconscious that they were any less married than Henry VIII. For though a glance at the legal conditions of marriage in different Christian countries shews that marriage varies legally from frontier to frontier, domesticity varies so little that most people believe their own marriage laws to be universal. Consequently here again, as in the case of Property, the absolute confidence of the public in the stability of the institution's name, makes it all the easier to alter its substance.

However, it cannot be denied that one of the changes in public opinion demanded by the need for the Superman is a very unexpected one. It is nothing less than the dissolution of the present necessary association of marriage with conjugation, which most unmarried people regard as the very diagnostic of marriage. They are wrong, of course: it would be quite as near the truth to say that conjugation is the one purely accidental and incidental condition of marriage. Conjugation is essential to nothing but the propagation of the race; and the moment that paramount need is provided for otherwise than by marriage, conjugation, from Nature's creative point of view, ceases to be essential in marriage. But marriage does not thereupon cease to be so economical, convenient, and comfortable, that the Superman might safely bribe the matrimonomaniacs by offering to revive all the old inhuman stringency and irrevocability of marriage, to abolish divorce, to confirm the horrible bond which still chains decent people to drunkards, criminals and wasters, provided only the complete extrication of conjugation from it were conceded to him. For if people could form domestic companionships on no easier terms than these, they would still marry. The Roman Catholic, forbidden by his Church to avail himself of the divorce laws, marries as freely as the South Dakotan Presbyterians who can change partners with a facility that scandalizes the old world; and were his Church to dare a further step towards Christianity and enjoin celibacy on its laity as well as on its clergy, marriages would still be contracted for the sake of domesticity by perfectly obedient sons and daughters of the Church. One need not further pursue these hypotheses: they are only suggested here to help the reader to analyze marriage into its two functions of regulating conjugation and supplying a form of domesticity. These two functions are quite separable; and domesticity is the only one of the two which is essential to the existence of marriage, because conjugation without domesticity is not marriage at all, whereas domesticity without conjugation is still marriage: in fact it is necessarily the actual condition of all fertile marriages during a great part of their duration, and of some marriages during the whole of it.

Taking it, then, that Property and Marriage, by destroying Equality and thus hampering sexual selection with irrelevant conditions, are hostile to the evolution of the Superman, it is easy to understand why the only generally known modern experiment in breeding the human race took place in a community which discarded both institutions.

III. THE PERFECTIONIST EXPERIMENT
AT ONEIDA CREEK

In 1848 the Oneida Community was founded in America to carry out a resolution arrived at by a handful of Perfectionist Communists "that we will devote ourselves exclusively to the establishment of the Kingdom of God." Though the American nation declared that this sort of thing was not to be tolerated in a Christian country, the Oneida Community held its own for over thirty years, during which period it seems to have produced healthier children and done and suffered less evil than any Joint Stock Company on record. It was, however, a highly selected community; for a genuine communist (roughly definable as an intensely proud person who proposes to enrich the common fund instead of to sponge on it) is superior to an ordinary joint stock capitalist precisely as an ordinary joint stock capitalist is superior to a pirate. Further, the Perfectionists were mightily shepherded by their chief Noyes, one of those chance attempts at the Superman which occur from time to time in spite of the interference of Man's blundering institutions. The existence of Noyes simplified the breeding problem for the Communists, the question as to what sort of man they should strive to breed being settled at once by the obvious desirability of breeding another Noyes.

But an experiment conducted by a handful of people, who, after thirty years of immunity from the unintentional child slaughter that goes on by ignorant parents in private homes, numbered only 300, could do very little except prove that the Communists, under the guidance of a Superman "devoted exclusively to the establishment of the Kingdom of God," and caring no more for property and marriage than a Camberwell minister cares for Hindoo Caste or Suttee, might make a much better job of their lives than ordinary folk under the harrow of both these institutions. Yet their Superman himself admitted that this apparent success was only part of the abnormal phenomenon of his own occurrence; for when he came to the end of his powers through age, he himself guided and organized the voluntary relapse of the Communists into marriage, capitalism, and customary private life, thus admitting that the real social solution was not what a casual Superman could persuade a picked company to do for him, but what a whole community of Supermen would do spontaneously. If Noyes had had to organize, not a few dozen Perfectionists, but the whole United States, America would have beaten him as completely as England beat Oliver Cromwell, France Napoleon, or Rome Julius Cæsar. Cromwell learnt by bitter experience that God himself cannot raise a people above its own level, and that even though you stir a nation to sacrifice all its appetites to its conscience, the result will still depend wholly on what sort of conscience the nation has got. Napoleon seems to have ended by regarding mankind as a troublesome pack of hounds only worth keeping for the sport of hunting with them. Cæsar's capacity for fighting without hatred or resentment was defeated by the determination of his soldiers to kill their enemies in the field instead of taking them prisoners to be spared by Cæsar; and his civil supremacy was purchased by colossal bribery of the citizens of Rome. What great rulers cannot do, codes and religions cannot do. Man reads his own nature into every ordinance: if you devise a superhuman commandment so cunningly that it cannot be misinterpreted in terms of his will, he will denounce it as seditious blasphemy, or else disregard it as either crazy or totally unintelligible. Parliaments and synods may tinker as much as they please with their codes and creeds as circumstances alter the balance of classes and their interests; and, as a result of the tinkering, there may be an occasional illusion of moral evolution, as when the victory of the commercial caste over the military caste leads to the substitution of social boycotting and pecuniary damages for duelling. At certain moments there may even be a considerable material advance, as when the conquest of political power by the working class produces a better distribution of wealth through the simple action of the selfishness of the new masters; but all this is mere readjustment and reformation: until the heart and mind of the people is changed the very greatest man will no more dare to govern on the assumption that all are as great as he than a drover dare leave his flock to find its way through the streets as he himself would. Until there is an England in which every man is a Cromwell, a France in which every man is a Napoleon, a Rome in which every man is a Cæsar, a Germany in which every man is a Luther plus a Goethe, the world will be no more improved by its heroes than a Brixton villa is improved by the pyramid of Cheops. The production of such nations is the only real change possible to us.

IV. MAN'S OBJECTION TO HIS OWN
IMPROVEMENT

BUT WOULD such a change be tolerated if Man must rise
above himself to desire it? It would, through his misconception of its nature. Man does desire an ideal Superman with
such energy as he can spare from his nutrition, and has in
every age magnified the best living substitute for it he can
find. His least incompetent general is set up as an Alexander;
his king is the first gentleman in the world; his Pope is a
saint. He is never without an array of human idols who are
all nothing but sham Supermen. That the real Superman will
snap his superfingers at all Man's present trumpery ideals of
right, duty, honor, justice, religion, even decency, and accept moral obligations beyond present human endurance,
is a thing that contemporary Man does not foresee: in fact
he does not notice it when our casual Supermen do it in his
very face. He actually does it himself every day without
knowing it. He will therefore make no objection to the production of a race of what he calls Great Men or Heroes, because he will imagine them, not as true Supermen, but as
himself endowed with infinite brains, infinite courage, and
infinite money.

The most troublesome opposition will arise from the
general fear of mankind that any interference with our con-
jugal customs will be an interference with our pleasures and
our romance. This fear, by putting on airs of offended morality, has always intimidated people who have not measured its
essential weakness; but it will prevail with those degenerates
only in whom the instinct of fertility has faded into a mere
itching for pleasure. The modern devices for combining pleasure with sterility, now universally known and accessible,
enable these persons to weed themselves out of the race, a
process already vigorously at work; and the consequent survival of the intelligently fertile means the survival of the par-
tizans of the Superman; for what is proposed is nothing but
the replacement of the old unintelligent, inevitable, almost
unconscious fertility by an intelligently controlled, conscious
fertility, and the elimination of the mere voluptuary from the
evolutionary process.[1] Even if this selective agency had not

---

[1] The part played in evolution by the voluptuary will be the same
as that already played by the glutton. The glutton, as the man with
the strongest motive for nourishing himself, will always take more

been invented, the purpose of the race would still shatter the opposition of individual instincts. Not only do the bees and the ants satisfy their reproductive and parental instincts vicariously; but marriage itself successfully imposes celibacy on millions of unmarried normal men and women. In short, the individual instinct in this matter, overwhelming as it is thoughtlessly supposed to be, is really a finally negligible one.

V. THE POLITICAL NEED
FOR THE SUPERMAN

THE NEED for the Superman is, in its most imperative aspect, a political one. We have been driven to Proletarian Democracy by the failure of all the alternative systems; for these depended on the existence of Supermen acting as despots or oligarchs; and not only were these Supermen not always or even often forthcoming at the right moment and in an eligible social position, but when they were forthcoming they could not, except for a short time and by morally suicidal coercive methods, impose superhumanity on those whom they governed; so, by mere force of "human nature," government by consent of the governed has supplanted the old plan of governing the citizen as a public-schoolboy is governed.

Now we have yet to see the man who, having any practical experience of Proletarian Democracy, has any belief in its capacity for solving great political problems, or even for doing ordinary parochial work intelligently and economically. Only under despotism and oligarchies has the Radical faith in "universal suffrage" as a political panacea arisen. It withers the moment it is exposed to practical trial, because Democracy cannot rise above the level of the human material of which its voters are made. Switzerland seems happy in comparison with Russia; but if Russia were as small as Switzer-

pains than his fellows to get food. When food is so difficult to get that only great exertions can secure a sufficient supply of it, the glutton's appetite develops his cunning and enterprise to the utmost; and he becomes not only the best fed but the ablest man in the community. But in more hospitable climates, or where the social organization of the food supply makes it easy for a man to overeat, then the glutton eats himself out of health and finally out of existence. All other voluptuaries prosper and perish in the same way; and this is why the survival of the fittest means finally the survival of the self-controlled, because they alone can adapt themselves to the perpetual shifting of conditions produced by industrial progress.

land, and had her social problems simplified in the same way by impregnable natural fortifications and a population educated by the same variety and intimacy of international intercourse, there might be little to choose between them. At all events Australia and Canada, which are virtually protected democratic republics, and France and the United States, which are avowedly independent democratic republics, are neither healthy, wealthy nor wise; and they would be worse instead of better if their popular ministers were not experts in the art of dodging popular enthusiasms and duping popular ignorance. The politician who once had to learn how to flatter kings has now to learn how to fascinate, amuse, coax, humbug, frighten or otherwise strike the fancy of the electorate; and though in advanced modern States, where the artisan is better educated than the king, it takes a much bigger man to be a successful demagogue than to be a successful courtier, yet he who holds popular convictions with prodigious energy is the man for the mob, whilst the frailer sceptic who is cautiously feeling his way towards the next century has no chance unless he happens by accident to have the specific artistic talent of the mountebank as well, in which case it is as a mountebank that he catches votes, and not as a meliorist. Consequently the demagogue, though he professes (and fails) to readjust matters in the interests of the majority of the electors, yet stereotypes mediocrity, organizes intolerance, disparages exhibitions of uncommon qualities, and glorifies conspicuous exhibitions of common ones. He manages a small job well: he muddles rhetorically through a large one. When a great political movement takes place, it is not consciously led or organized: the unconscious self in mankind breaks its way through the problem as an elephant breaks through a jungle; and the politicians make speeches about whatever happens in the process, which, with the best intentions, they do all in their power to prevent. Finally, when social aggregation arrives at a point demanding international organization before the demagogues and electorates have learnt how to manage even a country parish properly much less internationalize Constantinople, the whole political business goes to smash; and presently we have Ruins of Empires, New Zealanders sitting on a broken arch of London Bridge, and so forth.

To that recurrent catastrophe we shall certainly come again unless we can have a Democracy of Supermen; and the production of such a Democracy is the only change that is now hopeful enough to nerve us to the effort that Revolution demands.

VI.   PRUDERY EXPLAINED

WHY THE BEES should pamper their mothers whilst we pamper only our operatic prima donnas is a question worth reflecting on. Our notion of treating a mother is, not to increase her supply of food, but to cut it off by forbidding her to work in a factory for a month after her confinement. Everything that can make birth a misfortune to the parents as well as a danger to the mother is conscientiously done. When a great French writer, Emile Zola, alarmed at the sterilization of his nation, wrote an eloquent and powerful book to restore the prestige of parentage, it was at once assumed in England that a work of this character, with such a title as *Fecundity*, was too abominable to be translated, and that any attempt to deal with the relations of the sexes from any other than the voluptuary or romantic point of view must be sternly put down. Now if this assumption were really founded on public opinion, it would indicate an attitude of disgust and resentment towards the Life Force that could only arise in a diseased and moribund community in which Ibsen's Hedda Gabler would be the typical woman. But it has no vital foundation at all. The prudery of the newspapers is, like the prudery of the dinner table, a mere difficulty of education and language. We are not taught to think decently on these subjects, and consequently we have no language for them except indecent language. We therefore have to declare them unfit for public discussion, because the only terms in which we can conduct the discussion are unfit for public use. Physiologists, who have a technical vocabulary at their disposal, find no difficulty; and masters of language who think decently can write popular stories like Zola's *Fecundity* or Tolstoy's *Resurrection* without giving the smallest offence to readers who can also think decently. But the ordinary modern journalist, who has never discussed such matters except in ribaldry, cannot write a simple comment on a divorce case without a conscious shamefulness or a furtive facetiousness that makes it impossible to read the comment aloud in company. All this ribaldry and prudery (the two are the same) does not mean that people do not feel decently on the subject: on the contrary, it is just the depth and seriousness

of our feeling that makes its desecration by vile language and
coarse humor intolerable; so that at last we cannot bear to
have it spoken of at all because only one in a thousand can
speak of it without wounding our self-respect, especially the
self-respect of women. Add to the horrors of popular language the horrors of popular poverty. In crowded populations
poverty destroys the possibility of cleanliness; and in the absence of cleanliness many of the natural conditions of life
become offensive and noxious, with the result that at last
the association of uncleanliness with these natural conditions
becomes so overpowering that among civilized people (that
is, people massed in the labyrinths of slums we call cities),
half their bodily life becomes a guilty secret, unmentionable
except to the doctor in emergencies; and Hedda Gabler shoots
herself because maternity is so unladylike. In short, popular
prudery is only a mere incident of popular squalor: the subjects which it taboos remain the most interesting and earnest
of subjects in spite of it.

VII. PROGRESS AN ILLUSION

UNFORTUNATELY the earnest people get drawn off the track
of evolution by the illusion of progress. Any Socialist can
convince us easily that the difference between Man as he is
and Man as he might become, without further evolution, under millennial conditions of nutrition, environment, and training, is enormous. He can shew that inequality and iniquitous
distribution of wealth and allotment of labor have arisen
through an unscientific economic system, and that Man,
faulty as he is, no more intended to establish any such ordered disorder than a moth intends to be burnt when it flies
into a candle flame. He can shew that the difference between
the grace and strength of the acrobat and the bent back of the
rheumatic field laborer is a difference produced by conditions,
not by nature. He can shew that many of the most detestable
human vices are not radical, but are mere reactions of our
institutions on our very virtues. The Anarchist, the Fabian,
the Salvationist, the Vegetarian, the doctor, the lawyer, the
parson, the professor of ethics, the gymnast, the soldier, the
sportsman, the inventor, the political program-maker, all have
some prescription for bettering us; and almost all their remedies are physically possible and aimed at admitted evils. To
them the limit of progress is, at worst, the completion of all

the suggested reforms and the levelling up of all men to the point attained already by the most highly nourished and cultivated in mind and body.

Here, then, as it seems to them, is an enormous field for the energy of the reformer. Here are many noble goals attainable by many of those paths up the Hill Difficulty along which great spirits love to aspire. Unhappily, the hill will never be climbed by Man as we know him. It need not be denied that if we all struggled bravely to the end of the reformer's paths we should improve the world prodigiously. But there is no more hope in that If than in the equally plausible assurance that if the sky falls we shall all catch larks. We are not going to tread those paths: we have not sufficient energy. We do not desire the end enough: indeed in most cases we do not effectively desire it at all. Ask any man would he like to be a better man; and he will say yes, most piously. Ask him would he like to have a million of money; and he will say yes, most sincerely. But the pious citizen who would like to be a better man goes on behaving just as he did before. And the tramp who would like the million does not take the trouble to earn ten shillings: multitudes of men and women, all eager to accept a legacy of a million, live and die without having ever possessed five pounds at one time, although beggars have died in rags on mattresses stuffed with gold which they accumulated because they desired it enough to nerve them to get it and keep it. The economists who discovered that demand created supply soon had to limit the proposition to "effective demand," which turned out, in the final analysis, to mean nothing more than supply itself; and this holds good in politics, morals, and all other departments as well: the actual supply is the measure of the effective demand; and the mere aspirations and professions produce nothing. No community has ever yet passed beyond the initial phases in which its pugnacity and fanaticism enabled it to found a nation, and its cupidity to establish and develop a commercial civilization. Even these stages have never been attained by public spirit, but always by intolerant wilfulness and brute force. Take the Reform Bill of 1832 as an example of a conflict between two sections of educated Englishmen concerning a political measure which was as obviously necessary and inevitable as any political measure has ever been or is ever likely to be. It was not passed until the gentlemen of Birmingham had made arrangements to cut the throats of the gentlemen of St. James's parish in

due military form. It would not have been passed to this day
if there had been no force behind it except the logic and public conscience of the Utilitarians. A despotic ruler with as
much sense as Queen Elizabeth would have done better than
the mob of grown-up Eton boys who governed us then by
privilege, and who, since the introduction of practically
Manhood Suffrage in 1884, now govern us at the request
of proletarian Democracy.

At the present time we have, instead of the Utilitarians,
the Fabian Society, with its peaceful, constitutional, moral,
economical policy of Socialism, which needs nothing for its
bloodless and benevolent realization except that the English
people shall understand it and approve of it. But why are the
Fabians well spoken of in circles where thirty years ago the
word Socialist was understood as equivalent to cut-throat
and incendiary? Not because the English have the smallest
intention of studying or adopting the Fabian policy, but because they believe that the Fabians, by eliminating the element of intimidation from the Socialist agitation, have drawn
the teeth of insurgent poverty and saved the existing order
from the only method of attack it really fears. Of course, if
the nation adopted the Fabian policy, it would be carried out
by brute force exactly as our present property system is.
It would become the law; and those who resisted it would
be fined, sold up, knocked on the head by policemen, thrown
into prison, and in the last resort "executed" just as they
are when they break the present law. But as our proprietary
class has no fear of that conversion taking place, whereas it
does fear sporadic cutthroats and gunpowder plots, and strives
with all its might to hide the fact that there is no moral difference whatever between the methods by which it enforces its
proprietary rights and the method by which the dynamitard
asserts his conception of natural human rights, the Fabian
Society is patted on the back just as the Christian Social
Union is, whilst the Socialist who says bluntly that a Social
revolution can be made only as all other revolutions have
been made, by the people who want it killing, coercing and
intimidating the people who don't want it, is denounced as a
misleader of the people, and imprisoned with hard labor to
shew him how much sincerity there is in the objection of
his captors to physical force.

Are we then to repudiate Fabian methods, and return
to those of the barricader, or adopt those of the dynamitard
and the assassin? On the contrary, we are to recognize that

both are fundamentally futile. It seems easy for the dynamitard to say "Have you not just admitted that nothing is ever conceded except to physical force? Did not Gladstone admit that the Irish Church was disestablished, not by the spirit of Liberalism, but by the explosion which wrecked Clerkenwell prison?" Well, we need not foolishly and timidly deny it. Let it be fully granted. Let us grant, further, that all this lies in the nature of things; that the most ardent Socialist, if he owns property, can by no means do otherwise than Conservative proprietors until property is forcibly abolished by the whole nation; nay, that ballots and parliamentary divisions, in spite of their vain ceremony of discussion, differ from battles only as the bloodless surrender of an outnumbered force in the field differs from Waterloo or Trafalgar. I make a present of all these admissions to the Fenian who collects money from thoughtless Irishmen in America to blow up Dublin Castle; to the detective who persuades foolish young workmen to order bombs from the nearest ironmonger and then delivers them up to penal servitude; to our military and naval commanders who believe, not in preaching, but in an ultimatum backed by plenty of lyddite; and, generally, to all whom it may concern. But of what use is it to substitute the will of reckless and bloodyminded Progressives for cautious and humane ones? Is England any the better for the wreck of Clerkenwell prison, or Ireland for the disestablishment of the Irish Church? Is there the smallest reason to suppose that the nation which sheepishly let Charles and Laud and Strafford coerce it, gained anything because it afterwards, still more sheepishly, let a few strongminded Puritans, inflamed by the masterpieces of Jewish revolutionary literature, cut off the heads of the three? Suppose the Gunpowder plot had succeeded, and a Fawkes dynasty were at present on the throne, would it have made any difference to the present state of the nation? The guillotine was used in France up to the limit of human endurance, both on Girondins and Jacobins. Fouquier Tinville followed Marie Antoinette to the scaffold; and Marie Antoinette might have asked the crowd, just as pointedly as Fouquier did, whether their bread would be any cheaper when her head was off. And what came of it all? The Imperial France of the Rougon Macquart family, and the Republican France of the Panama scandal and the Dreyfus case. Was the difference worth the guillotining of all those unlucky ladies and gentlemen, useless and mischievous as many of them were? Would

any sane man guillotine a mouse to bring about such a
result? Turn to Republican America. America has no Star
Chamber, and no feudal barons. But it has Trusts; and it has
millionaires whose factories, fenced in by live electric wires
and defended by Pinkerton retainers with magazine rifles,
would have made a Radical of Reginald Front de Boeuf.
Would Washington or Franklin have lifted a finger in the
cause of American Independence if they had foreseen its
reality?

No: what Cæsar, Cromwell and Napoleon could not do
with all the physical force and moral prestige of the State
in their mighty hands, cannot be done by enthusiastic criminals and lunatics. Even the Jews, who, from Moses to Marx
and Lassalle, have inspired all the revolutions, have had to
confess that, after all, the dog will return to his vomit and
the sow that was washed to her wallowing in the mire; and
we may as well make up our minds that Man will return to
his idols and his cupidities, in spite of all "movements" and
all revolutions, until his nature is changed. Until then, his
early successes in building commercial civilizations (and such
civilizations, Good Heavens!) are but preliminaries to the
inevitable later stage, now threatening us, in which the passions which built the civilization become fatal instead of pro-
ductive, just as the same qualities which make the lion king
in the forest ensure his destruction when he enters a city.
Nothing can save society then except the clear head and the
wide purpose: war and competition, potent instruments of
selection and evolution in one epoch, become ruinous instruments of degeneration in the next. In the breeding of animals and plants, varieties which have arisen by selection
through many generations relapse precipitously into the wild
type in a generation or two when selection ceases; and in the
same way a civilization in which lusty pugnacity and greed
have ceased to act as selective agents and have begun to
obstruct and destroy, rushes downwards and backwards with a
suddenness that enables an observer to see with consternation the upward steps of many centuries retraced in a single
lifetime. This has often occurred even within the period covered by history; and in every instance the turning point has
been reached long before the attainment, or even the general
advocacy on paper, of the levelling-up of the mass to the
highest point attainable by the best nourished and cultivated
normal individuals.

We must therefore frankly give up the notion that Man

as he exists is capable of net progress. There will always be an illusion of progress, because wherever we are conscious of an evil we remedy it, and therefore always seem to ourselves to be progressing, forgetting that most of the evils we see are the effects, finally become acute, of long-unnoticed retrogressions, that our compromising remedies seldom fully recover the lost ground; above all, that on the lines along which we are degenerating, good has become evil in our eyes, and is being undone in the name of progress precisely as evil is undone and replaced by good on the lines along which we are evolving. This is indeed the Illusion of Illusions; for it gives us infallible and appalling assurance that if our political ruin is to come, it will be effected by ardent reformers and supported by enthusiastic patriots as a series of necessary steps in our progress. Let the Reformer, the Progressive, the Meliorist then reconsider himself and his eternal ifs and ans which never become pots and pans. Whilst Man remains what he is, there can be no progress beyond the point already attained and fallen headlong from at every attempt at civilization; and since even that point is but a pinnacle to which a few people cling in giddy terror above an abyss of squalor, mere progress should no longer charm us.

VIII. THE CONCEIT OF CIVILIZATION

AFTER ALL, the progress illusion is not so very subtle. We begin by reading the satires of our fathers' contemporaries; and we conclude (usually quite ignorantly) that the abuses exposed by them are things of the past. We see also that reforms of crying evils are frequently produced by the sectional shifting of political power from oppressors to oppressed. The poor man is given a vote by the Liberals in the hope that he will cast it for his emancipators. The hope is not fulfilled; but the lifelong imprisonment of penniless men for debt ceases; Factory Acts are passed to mitigate sweating; schooling is made free and compulsory; sanitary by-laws are multiplied; public steps are taken to house the masses decently; the bare-footed get boots; rags become rare; and bathrooms and pianos, smart tweeds and starched collars, reach numbers of people who once, as "the unsoaped," played the Jew's harp or the accordion in moleskins and belchers. Some of these changes are gains: some of them are losses. Some of them are not changes at all: all of them are merely

the changes that money makes. Still, they produce an illusion
of bustling progress; and the reading class infers from them
that the abuses of the early Victorian period no longer exist
except as amusing pages in the novels of Dickens. But the
moment we look for a reform due to character and not to
money, to statesmanship and not to interest or mutiny, we
are disillusioned. For example, we remembered the maladmin-
istration and incompetence revealed by the Crimean War as
part of a bygone state of things until the South African war
shewed that the nation and the War Office, like those poor
Bourbons who have been so impudently blamed for a universal characteristic, had learnt nothing and forgotten nothing. We had hardly recovered from the fruitless irritation of
this discovery when it transpired that the officers' mess of our
most select regiment included a flogging club presided over by
the senior subaltern. The disclosure provoked some disgust
at the details of this schoolboyish debauchery, but no surprise
at the apparent absence of any conception of manly honor
and virtue, of personal courage and self-respect, in the front
rank of our chivalry. In civil affairs we had assumed that the
sycophancy and idolatry which encouraged Charles I to un-
dervalue the Puritan revolt of the seventeenth century had
been long outgrown; but it has needed nothing but favorable
circumstances to revive, with added abjectness to compensate
for its lost piety. We have relapsed into disputes about tran-
substantiation at the very moment when the discovery of the
wide prevalence of theophagy as a tribal custom has deprived
us of the last excuse for believing that our official religious
rites differ in essentials from those of barbarians. The Christian doctrine of the uselessness of punishment and the wickedness of revenge has not, in spite of its simple common sense,
found a single convert among the nations: Christianity means
nothing to the masses but a sensational public execution
which is made an excuse for other executions. In its name
we take ten years of a thief's life minute by minute in the
slow misery and degradation of modern reformed imprisonment with as little remorse as Laud and his Star Chamber
clipped the ears of Bastwick and Burton. We dug up and
mutilated the remains of the Mahdi the other day exactly
as we dug up and mutilated the remains of Cromwell two
centuries ago. We have demanded the decapitation of the
Chinese Boxer princes as any Tartar would have done; and
our military and naval expeditions to kill, burn, and destroy
tribes and villages for knocking an Englishman on the head

are so common a part of our Imperial routine that the last
dozen of them has not elicited as much sympathy as can
be counted on by any lady criminal. The judicial use of torture to extort confession is supposed to be a relic of darker
ages; but whilst these pages are being written an English
judge has sentenced a forger to twenty years penal servitude
with an open declaration that the sentence will be carried out
in full unless he confesses where he has hidden the notes he
forged. And no comment whatever is made either on this or
on a telegram from the seat of war in Somaliland mentioning
that certain information has been given by a prisoner of
war "under punishment." Even if these reports were false,
the fact that they are accepted without protest as indicating
a natural and proper course of public conduct shows that we
are still as ready to resort to torture as Bacon was. As to
vindictive cruelty, an incident in the South African war, when
the relatives and friends of a prisoner were forced to witness his execution, betrayed a baseness of temper and character which hardly leaves us the right to plume ourselves on our
superiority to Edward III at the surrender of Calais. And
the democratic American officer indulges in torture in the
Philippines just as the aristocratic English officer did in
South Africa. The incidents of the white invasion of Africa
in search of ivory, gold, diamonds and sport, have proved
that the modern European is the same beast of prey that
formerly marched to the conquest of new worlds under
Alexander, Antony, and Pizarro. Parliaments and vestries are
just what they were when Cromwell suppressed them and
Dickens ridiculed them. The democratic politician remains
exactly as Plato described him; the physician is still the credulous impostor and petulant scientific coxcomb whom Molière
ridiculed; the schoolmaster remains at best a pedantic child
farmer and at worst a flagellomaniac; arbitrations are more
dreaded by honest men than lawsuits; the philanthropist is
still a parasite on misery as the doctor is on disease; the
miracles of priestcraft are none the less fraudulent and mischievous because they are now called scientific experiments
and conducted by professors; witchcraft, in the modern form
of patent medicines and prophylactic inoculations, is ram-
pant; the landowner who is no longer powerful enough to set
the mantrap of Rhampsinitis improves on it by barbed wire;
the modern gentleman who is too lazy to daub his face with
vermilion as a symbol of bravery employs a laundress to
daub his shirt with starch as a symbol of cleanliness; we

shake our heads at the dirt of the Middle Ages in cities made
grimy with soot and foul and disgusting with shameless to-
bacco smoking; holy water, in its latest form of disinfectant
fluid, is more widely used and believed in than ever; public
health authorities deliberately go through incantations with
burning sulphur (which they know to be useless) because the
people believe in it as devoutly as the Italian peasant believes
in the liquefaction of the blood of St. Januarius; and straightforward public lying has reached gigantic developments, there
being nothing to choose in this respect between the pickpocket at the police station and the minister on the treasury bench, the editor in the newspaper office, the city mag-
nate advertising bicycle tires that do not side-slip, the clergyman subscribing the thirty-nine articles, and the vivisector
who pledges his knightly honor that no animal operated on
in the physiological laboratory suffers the slightest pain. Hypocrisy is at its worst; for we not only persecute bigotedly but
sincerely in the name of the cure-mongering witchcraft we
do believe in, but callously and hypocritically in the name of
the Evangelical creed that our rulers privately smile at as
the Italian patricians of the fifth century smiled at Jupiter
and Venus. Sport is, as it has always been, murderous excitement: the impulse to slaughter is universal; and museums
are set up throughout the country to encourage little children
and elderly gentlemen to make collections of corpses pre-
served in alcohol, and to steal birds' eggs and keep them as
the red Indian used to keep scalps. Coercion with the lash is
as natural to an Englishman as it was to Solomon spoiling
Rehoboam: indeed, the comparison is unfair to the Jews in
view of the facts that the Mosaic law forbade more than forty
lashes in the name of humanity, and that floggings of a thousand lashes were inflicted on English soldiers in the eighteenth
and nineteenth centuries, and would be inflicted still but for
the change in the balance of political power between the
military caste and the commercial classes and the proletariat.
In spite of that change, flogging is still an institution in the
public school, in the military prison, on the training ship,
and in that school of littleness called the home. The lascivious clamor of the flagellomaniac for more of it, constant
as the clamor for more insolence, more war, and lower rates,
is tolerated and even gratified because, having no moral ends
in view, we have sense enough to see that nothing but brute
coercion can impose our selfish will on others. Cowardice is
universal: patriotism, public opinion, parental duty, discipline,

religion, morality, are only fine names for intimidation; and cruelty, gluttony, and credulity keep cowardice in countenance. We cut the throat of a calf and hang it up by the heels to bleed to death so that our veal cutlet may be white; we nail geese to a board and cram them with food because we like the taste of liver disease; we tear birds to pieces to decorate our women's hats; we mutilate domestic animals for no reason at all except to follow an instinctively cruel fashion; and we connive at the most abominable tortures in the hope of discovering some magical cure for our own diseases by them.

Now please observe that these are not exceptional developments of our admitted vices, deplored and prayed against by all good men. Not a word has been said here of the excesses of our Neros, of whom we have the full usual percentage. With the exception of the few military examples, which are mentioned mainly to shew that the education and standing of a gentleman, reinforced by the strongest conventions of honor, *esprit de corps*, publicity and responsibility, afford no better guarantees of conduct than the passions of a mob, the illustrations given above are commonplaces taken from the daily practices of our best citizens, vehemently defended in our newspapers and in our pulpits. The very humanitarians who abhor them are stirred to murder by them: the dagger of Brutus and Ravaillac is still active in the hands of Caserio and Luccheni; and the pistol has come to its aid in the hands of Guiteau and Czolgosz. Our remedies are still limited to endurance or assassination; and the assassin is still judicially assassinated on the principle that two blacks make a white. The only novelty is in our methods: through the discovery of dynamite the overloaded musket of Hamilton of Bothwellhaugh has been superseded by the bomb; but Ravachol's heart burns just as Hamilton's did. The world will not bear thinking of to those who know what it is, even with the largest discount for the restraints of poverty on the poor and cowardice on the rich.

All that can be said for us is that people must and do live and let live up to a certain point. Even the horse, with his docked tail and bitted jaw, finds his slavery mitigated by the fact that a total disregard of his need for food and rest would put his master to the expense of buying a new horse every second day; for you cannot work a horse to death and then pick up another one for nothing, as you can a laborer. But this natural check on inconsiderate selfishness is itself checked, partly by our shortsightedness, and partly by deliberate calculation; so that beside the man who, to his own loss, will shorten his horse's life in mere stinginess, we have the tramway company which discovers actuarially that though a horse may live from 24 to 40 years, yet it pays better to work him to death in 4 and then replace him by a fresh victim. And human slavery, which has reached its worst recorded point within our own time in the form of free wage labor, has encountered the same personal and commercial limits to both its aggravation and its mitigation. Now that the freedom of wage labor has produced a scarcity of it, as in South Africa, the leading English newspaper and the leading English weekly review have openly and without apology demanded a return to compulsory labor: that is, to the methods by which, as we believe, the Egyptians built the pyramids. We know now that the crusade against chattel slavery in the nineteenth century succeeded solely because chattel slavery was neither the most effective nor the least humane method of labor exploitation; and the world is now feeling its way towards a still more effective system which shall abolish the freedom of the worker without again making his exploiter responsible for him as a chattel.

Still, there is always some mitigation: there is the fear of revolt; and there are the effects of kindliness and affection. Let it be repeated therefore that no indictment is here laid against the world on the score of what its criminals and monsters do. The fires of Smithfield and of the Inquisition were lighted by earnestly pious people, who were kind and good as kindness and goodness go. And when a Negro is dipped in kerosene and set on fire in America at the present time, he is not a good man lynched by ruffians: he is a criminal lynched by crowds of respectable, charitable, virtuously indignant, high-minded citizens, who, though they act outside the law, are at least more merciful than the American legislators and judges who not so long ago condemned men to solitary confinement for periods, not of five months, as our own practice is, but of five years and more. The things that our moral monsters do may be left out of account with St. Bartholomew massacres and other momentary outbursts of social disorder. Judge us by the admitted and respected practice of our most reputable circles; and, if you know the facts and are strong enough to look them in the face, you must admit that unless we are replaced by a more highly evolved animal—in short, by the Superman—the world must remain a den of dangerous animals among whom our few accidental supermen, our Shakespeares, Goethes, Shelleys and their like, must live as precariously as lion tamers do, taking the humor of their situation, and the dignity of their superiority, as a set-off to the horror of the one and the loneliness of the other.

IX. THE VERDICT OF HISTORY

IT MAY BE SAID that though the wild beast breaks out in Man and casts him back momentarily into barbarism under the excitement of war and crime, yet his normal life is higher than the normal life of his forefathers. This view is very acceptable to Englishmen, who always lean sincerely to virtue's side as long as it costs them nothing either in money or in thought. They feel deeply the injustice of foreigners, who allow them no credit for this conditional highmindedness. But there is no reason to suppose that our ancestors were less capable of it than we are. To all such claims for the existence of a progressive moral evolution operating visibly from grandfather to grandson, there is the conclusive reply that a thousand years of such evolution would have produced enormous social changes, of which the historical evidence would be overwhelming. But not Macaulay himself, the most confident of Whig meliorists, can produce any such evidence that will bear cross-examination. Compare our conduct and our codes with those mentioned contemporarily in such ancient scriptures and classics as have come down to us, and you will find no jot of ground for the belief that any moral progress whatever has been made in historic time, in spite of all the romantic attempts of historians to reconstruct the past on that assumption. Within that time it has happened to nations as to private families and individuals that they have flourished and decayed, repented and hardened their hearts, submitted and protested, acted and reacted, oscillated between natural and artificial sanitation (the oldest house in the world, unearthed the other day in Crete, has quite modern sanitary arrangements), and rung a thousand changes on the different scales of income and pressure of population, firmly believing all the time that mankind was advancing by leaps and bounds because men were constantly busy. And the mere chapter of accidents has left a small accumulation of chance discoveries, such as the wheel, the arch, the safety pin, gunpowder, the magnet, the Voltaic pile and so forth: things which, unlike the gospels and philosophic treatises of the sages, can be usefully understood and applied by common men; so that steam locomotion is possible without a nation of Stephensons, although national Christianity is impossible without a nation of Christs. But does any man seriously believe that the *chauffeur* who drives a motor car from Paris to Berlin is a more highly evolved man than the charioteer of Achilles, or that a modern Prime Minister is a more enlightened ruler than Cæsar because he rides a tricycle, writes his dispatches by the electric light, and instructs his stockbroker through the telephone?

Enough, then, of this goose-cackle about Progress: Man, as he is, never will nor can add a cubit to his stature by any of its quackeries, political, scientific, educational, religious, or artistic. What is likely to happen when this conviction gets into the minds of the men whose present faith in these illusions is the cement of our social system, can be imagined only by those who know how suddenly a civilization which has long ceased to think (or in the old phrase, to watch and pray) can fall to pieces when the vulgar belief in its hypocrisies and impostures can no longer hold out against its failures and scandals. When religious and ethical formulæ become so obsolete that no man of strong mind can believe them, they have also reached the point at which no man of high character will profess them; and from that moment until they are formally disestablished, they stand at the door of every profession and every public office to keep out every able man who is not a sophist or a liar. A nation which revises its parish councils once in three years, but will not revise its articles of religion once in three hundred, even when those articles avowedly began as a political compromise dictated by Mr. Facing-Both-Ways, is a nation that needs remaking.

Our only hope, then, is in evolution. We must replace the Man by the Superman. It is frightful for the citizen, as the years pass him, to see his own contemporaries so exactly reproduced by the younger generation, that his companions of thirty years ago have their counterparts in every city crowd; so that he has to check himself repeatedly in the act of saluting as an old friend some young man to whom he is only an elderly stranger. All hope of advance dies in his bosom as he watches them: he knows that they will do just what their fathers did, and that the few voices which will still, as always before, exhort them to do something else and be something better, might as well spare their breath to cool their porridge (if they can get any). Men like Ruskin and Carlyle will preach to Smith and Brown for the sake of preaching, just as St. Francis preached to the birds and St. Anthony to the fishes. But Smith and Brown, like the fishes and birds, remain as they are; and poets who plan Utopias and prove that nothing is necessary for their realization but that Man should will them, perceive at last, like Richard Wagner, that the fact to be faced is that Man does not effectively will them. And he never will until he becomes Superman.

And so we arrive at the end of the Socialist's dream of "the socialization of the means of production and exchange," of the Positivist's dream of moralizing the capitalist, and of the ethical professor's, legislator's, educator's dream of putting commandments and codes and lessons and examination marks on a man as harness is put on a horse, ermine on a judge, pipeclay on a soldier, or a wig on an actor, and pretending that his nature has been changed. The only fundamental and possible Socialism is the socialization of the selective breeding of Man: in other terms, of human evolution. We must eliminate the Yahoo, or his vote will wreck the commonwealth.

X. THE METHOD

As TO THE METHOD, what can be said as yet except that where there is a will, there is a way? If there be no will, we are lost. That is a possibility for our crazy little empire, if not for the universe; and as such possibilities are not to be entertained without despair, we must, whilst we survive, proceed on the assumption that we have still energy enough to not only will to live, but to will to live better. That may mean that we must establish a State Department of Evolution, with a seat in the Cabinet for its chief, and a revenue to defray the cost of direct State experiments and provide inducements to private persons to achieve successful results. It may mean a private society or a chartered company for the improvement of human live stock. But for the present it is far more likely to mean a blatant repudiation of such proposals as indecent and immoral, with, nevertheless, a general secret pushing of the human will in the repudiated direction; so that all sorts of institutions and public authorities will under some pretext or other feel their way furtively towards the Superman. Mr. Graham Wallas has already ventured to suggest, as Chairman of the School Management Committee of the London School

Board, that the accepted policy of the Sterilization of the
Schoolmistress, however administratively convenient, is open
to criticism from the national stock-breeding point of view;
and this is as good an example as any of the way in which
the drift towards the Superman may operate in spite of all our
hypocrisies. One thing at least is clear to begin with. If a
woman can, by careful selection of a father, and nourishment
of herself, produce a citizen with efficient senses, sound organs
and a good digestion, she should clearly be secured a sufficient
reward for that natural service to make her willing to undertake and repeat it. Whether she be financed in the undertaking
by herself, or by the father, or by a speculative capitalist, or
by a new department of, say, the Royal Dublin Society, or
(as at present) by the War Office maintaining her "on the
strength" and authorizing a particular soldier to marry her, or
by a local authority under a by-law directing that women may
under certain circumstances have a year's leave of absence on
full salary, or by the central government, does not matter provided the result be satisfactory.

It is a melancholy fact that as the vast majority of women
and their husbands have, under existing circumstances, not
enough nourishment, no capital, no credit, and no knowledge
of science or business, they would, if the State would pay for
birth as it now pays for death, be exploited by joint stock
companies for dividends, just as they are in ordinary industries. Even a joint stock human stud farm (piously disguised
as a reformed Foundling Hospital or something of that sort)
might well, under proper inspection and regulation, produce
better results than our present reliance on promiscuous marriage. It may be objected that when an ordinary contractor
produces stores for sale to the Government, and the Government rejects them as not up to the required standard, the
condemned goods are either sold for what they will fetch or
else scrapped: that is, treated as waste material; whereas if
the goods consisted of human beings, all that could be done
would be to let them loose or send them to the nearest workhouse. But there is nothing new in private enterprise throwing its human refuse on the cheap labor market and the
workhouse; and the refuse of the new industry would presumably be better bred than the staple product of ordinary
poverty. In our present happy-go-lucky industrial disorder,
all the human products, successful or not, would have to be
thrown on the labor market; but the unsuccessful ones would
not entitle the company to a bounty and so would be a dead

loss to it. The practical commercial difficulty would be the uncertainty and the cost in time and money of the first experiments. Purely commercial capital would not touch such heroic operations during the experimental stage; and in any case the strength of mind needed for so momentous a new departure could not be fairly expected from the Stock Exchange. It will have to be handled by statesmen with character enough to tell our democracy and plutocracy that statecraft does not consist in flattering their follies or applying their suburban standards of propriety to the affairs of four continents. The matter must be taken up either by the State or by some organization strong enough to impose respect upon the State.

The novelty of any such experiment, however, is only in the scale of it. In one conspicuous case, that of royalty, the State does already select the parents on purely political grounds; and in the peerage, though the heir to a dukedom is legally free to marry a dairymaid, yet the social pressure on him to confine his choice to politically and socially eligible mates is so overwhelming that he is really no more free to marry the dairymaid than George IV was to marry Mrs. Fitzherbert; and such a marriage could only occur as a result of extraordinary strength of character on the part of the dairymaid acting upon extraordinary weakness on the part of the duke. Let those who think the whole conception of intelligent breeding absurd and scandalous ask themselves why George IV was not allowed to choose his own wife whilst any tinker could marry whom he pleased? Simply because it did not matter a rap politically whom the tinker married, whereas it mattered very much whom the king married. The way in which all considerations of the king's personal rights, of the claims of the heart, of the sanctity of the marriage oath, and of romantic morality crumpled up before this political need shews how negligible all these apparently irresistible prejudices are when they come into conflict with the demand for quality in our rulers. We learn the same lesson from the case of the soldier, whose marriage, when it is permitted at all, is despotically controlled with a view solely to military efficiency.

Well, nowadays it is not the king that rules, but the tinker. Dynastic wars are no longer feared, dynastic alliances no longer valued. Marriages in royal families are becoming rapidly less political, and more popular, domestic and romantic. If all the kings in Europe were made as free tomorrow

as King Cophetua, nobody but their aunts and chamberlains
would feel a moment's anxiety as to the consequences. On
the other hand a sense of the social importance of the tinker's marriage has been steadily growing. We have made a
public matter of his wife's health in the month after her confinement. We have taken the minds of his children out of his
hands and put them into those of our State schoolmaster. We
shall presently make their bodily nourishment independent of
him. But they are still riff-raff; and to hand the country over
to riff-raff is national suicide, since riff-raff can neither govern
nor will let anyone else govern except the highest bidder of
bread and circuses. There is no public enthusiast alive of
twenty years practical democratic experience who believes in
the political adequacy of the electorate or of the bodies it
elects. The overthrow of the aristocrat has created the necessity for the Superman.

Englishmen hate Liberty and Equality too much to understand them. But every Englishman loves and desires a pedigree. And in that he is right. King Demos must be bred like
all other kings; and with Must there is no arguing. It is idle
for an individual writer to carry so great a matter further in
a pamphlet. A conference on the subject is the next step
needed. It will be attended by men and women who, no longer
believing that they can live for ever, are seeking for some
immortal work into which they can build the best of themselves before their refuse is thrown into that arch dust destruc-
tor, the cremation furnace.

MAXIMS FOR REVOLUTIONISTS

THE GOLDEN RULE

Do not do unto others as you would that they should do
unto you. Their tastes may not be the same.

Never resist temptation: prove all things: hold fast that
which is good.

Do not love your neighbor as yourself. If you are on good
terms with yourself it is an impertinence: if on bad, an injury.

The golden rule is that there are no golden rules.

IDOLATRY

The art of government is the organization of idolatry.

The bureaucracy consists of functionaries; the aristocracy, of idols; the democracy, of idolaters.

The populace cannot understand the bureaucracy: it can only worship the national idols.

The savage bows down to idols of wood and stone: the civilized man to idols of flesh and blood.

A limited monarchy is a device for combining the inertia of a wooden idol with the credibility of a flesh and blood one.

When the wooden idol does not answer the peasant's prayer, he beats it: when the flesh and blood idol does not satisfy the civilized man, he cuts its head off.

He who slays a king and he who dies for him are alike idolaters.

ROYALTY

Kings are not born: they are made by artificial hallucination. When the process is interrupted by adversity at a critical age, as in the case of Charles II, the subject becomes sane and never completely recovers his kingliness.

The Court is the servant's hall of the sovereign.

Vulgarity in a king flatters the majority of the nation.

The flunkeyism propagated by the throne is the price we pay for its political convenience.

DEMOCRACY

If the lesser mind could measure the greater as a footrule can measure a pyramid, there would be finality in universal suffrage. As it is, the political problem remains unsolved.

Democracy substitutes election by the incompetent many for appointment by the corrupt few.

Democratic republics can no more dispense with national idols than monarchies with public functionaries.

Government presents only one problem: the discovery of a trustworthy anthropometric method.

IMPERIALISM

Excess of insularity makes a Briton an Imperialist.

Excess of local self-assertion makes a colonist an Imperialist.

A colonial Imperialist is one who raises colonial troops, equips a colonial squadron, claims a Federal Parliament sending its measures to the Throne instead of to the Colonial Office, and, being finally brought by this means into insoluble conflict with the insular British Imperialist, "cuts the painter" and breaks up the Empire.

LIBERTY AND EQUALITY

He who confuses political liberty with freedom and political equality with similarity has never thought for five minutes about either.

Nothing can be unconditional: consequently nothing can be free.

Liberty means responsibility. That is why most men dread it.

The duke inquires contemptuously whether his gamekeeper is the equal of the Astronomer Royal; but he insists that they shall both be hanged equally if they murder him.

The notion that the colonel need be a better man than the private is as confused as the notion that the keystone need be stronger than the coping stone.

Where equality is undisputed, so also is subordination.

Equality is fundamental in every department of social organization.

The relation of superior to inferior excludes good manners.

EDUCATION

When a man teaches something he does not know to somebody else who has no aptitude for it, and gives him a certificate of proficiency, the latter has completed the education of a gentleman.

A fool's brain digests philosophy into folly, science into superstition, and art into pedantry. Hence University education.

The best brought-up children are those who have seen their parents as they are. Hypocrisy is not the parent's first duty.

The vilest abortionist is he who attempts to mould a child's character.

At the University every great treatise is postponed until its author attains impartial judgment and perfect knowledge. If a horse could wait as long for its shoes and would pay for them in advance, our blacksmiths would all be college dons.

He who can, does. He who cannot, teaches.

A learned man is an idler who kills time with study. Beware of his false knowledge: it is more dangerous than ignorance.

Activity is the only road to knowledge.

Every fool believes what his teachers tell him, and calls his credulity science or morality as confidently as his father called it divine revelation.

No man fully capable of his own language ever masters another.

No man can be a pure specialist without being in the strict sense an idiot.

Do not give your children moral and religious instruction unless you are quite sure they will not take it too seriously. Better be the mother of Henri Quatre and Nell Gwynne than of Robespierre and Queen Mary Tudor.

MARRIAGE

Marriage is popular because it combines the maximum of temptation with the maximum of opportunity.

Marriage is the only legal contract which abrogates as between the parties all the laws that safeguard the particular relation to which it refers.

The essential function of marriage is the continuance of the race, as stated in the Book of Common Prayer.

The accidental function of marriage is the gratification of the amoristic sentiment of mankind.

The artificial sterilization of marriage makes it possible for marriage to fulfil its accidental function whilst neglecting its essential one.

The most revolutionary invention of the nineteenth century was the artificial sterilization of marriage.

Any marriage system which condemns a majority of the population to celibacy will be violently wrecked on the pretext that it outrages morality.

Polygamy, when tried under modern democratic conditions, as by the Mormons, is wrecked by the revolt of the mass of inferior men who are condemned to celibacy by it; for the maternal instinct leads a woman to prefer a tenth share in a first rate man to the exclusive possession of a third rate one. Polyandry has not been tried under these conditions.

The minimum of national celibacy (ascertained by dividing the number of males in the community by the number of females, and taking the quotient as the number of wives or husbands permitted to each person) is secured in England (where the quotient is 1) by the institution of monogamy.

The modern sentimental term for the national minimum of celibacy is Purity.

Marriage, or any other form of promiscuous amoristic monogamy, is fatal to large States because it puts its ban on the deliberate breeding of man as a political animal.

CRIME AND PUNISHMENT

All scoundrelism is summed up in the phrase *"Que Messieurs les Assassins commencent!"*

The man who has graduated from the flogging block at Eton to the bench from which he sentences the garotter to be flogged is the same social product as the garotter who has been kicked by his father and cuffed by his mother until he has grown strong enough to throttle and rob the rich citizen whose money he desires.

Imprisonment is as irrevocable as death.

Criminals do not die by the hands of the law. They die by the hands of other men.

The assassin Czolgosz made President McKinley a hero by assassinating him. The United States of America made Czolgosz a hero by the same process.

Assassination on the scaffold is the worst form of assassination, because there it is invested with the approval of society.

It is the deed that teaches, not the name we give it. Murder and capital punishment are not opposites that cancel one another, but similars that breed their kind.

Crime is only the retail department of what, in wholesale, we call penal law.

When a man wants to murder a tiger he calls it sport: when the tiger wants to murder him he calls it ferocity. The distinction between Crime and Justice is no greater.

Whilst we have prisons it matters little which of us occupy the cells.

The most anxious man in a prison is the governor.

It is not necessary to replace a guillotined criminal: it is necessary to replace a guillotined social system.

TITLES

Titles distinguish the mediocre, embarrass the superior, and are disgraced by the inferior.

Great men refuse titles because they are jealous of them.

HONOR

There are no perfectly honorable men; but every true man has one main point of honor and a few minor ones.

You cannot believe in honor until you have achieved it. Better keep yourself clean and bright: you are the window through which you must see the world.

Your word can never be as good as your bond, because your memory can never be as trustworthy as your honor.

PROPERTY

Property, said Proudhon, is theft. This is the only perfect truism that has been uttered on the subject.

SERVANTS

When domestic servants are treated as human beings it is not worth while to keep them.

The relation of master and servant is advantageous only to masters who do not scruple to abuse their authority, and to servants who do not scruple to abuse their trust.

The perfect servant, when his master makes humane advances to him, feels that his existence is threatened, and hastens to change his place.

Masters and servants are both tyrannical; but the masters are the more dependent of the two.

A man enjoys what he uses, not what his servants use.

Man is the only animal which esteems itself rich in proportion to the number and voracity of its parasites.

Ladies and gentlemen are permitted to have friends in the kennel, but not in the kitchen.

Domestic servants, by making spoiled children of their masters, are forced to intimidate them in order to be able to live with them.

In a slave state, the slaves rule: in Mayfair, the tradesman rules.

HOW TO BEAT CHILDREN

If you strike a child, take care that you strike it in anger, even at the risk of maiming it for life. A blow in cold blood neither can nor should be forgiven.

If you beat children for pleasure, avow your object frankly, and play the game according to the rules, as a foxhunter does; and you will do comparatively little harm. No foxhunter is such a cad as to pretend that he hunts the fox to teach it not to steal chickens, or that he suffers more acutely than the fox at the death. Remember that even in childbeating there is the sportsman's way and the cad's way.

RELIGION

Beware of the man whose god is in the skies.

What a man believes may be ascertained, not from his

creed, but from the assumptions on which he habitually acts.

VIRTUES AND VICES

No specific virtue or vice in a man implies the existence of any other specific virtue or vice in him, however closely the imagination may associate them.

Virtue consists, not in abstaining from vice, but in not desiring it.

Self-denial is not a virtue: it is only the effect of prudence on rascality.

Obedience simulates subordination as fear of the police simulates honesty.

Disobedience, the rarest and most courageous of the virtues, is seldom distinguished from neglect, the laziest and commonest of the vices.

Vice is waste of life. Poverty, obedience and celibacy are the canonical vices.

Economy is the art of making the most of life.

The love of economy is the root of all virtue.

FAIRPLAY

The love of fairplay is a spectator's virtue, not a principal's.

GREATNESS

Greatness is only one of the sensations of littleness.

In heaven an angel is nobody in particular.

Greatness is the secular name for Divinity: both mean simply what lies beyond us.

If a great man could make us understand him, we should hang him.

We admit that when the divinity we worshipped made itself visible and comprehensible we crucified it.

To a mathematician the eleventh means only a single unit: to the bushman who cannot count further than his ten fingers it is an incalculable myriad.

The difference between the shallowest routineer and the deepest thinker appears, to the latter, trifling; to the former, infinite.

In a stupid nation the man of genius becomes a god: everybody worships him and nobody does his will.

BEAUTY AND HAPPINESS, ART AND RICHES

Happiness and Beauty are by-products.

Folly is the direct pursuit of Happiness and Beauty.

Riches and Art are spurious receipts for the production of Happiness and Beauty.

He who desires a lifetime of happiness with a beautiful woman desires to enjoy the taste of wine by keeping his mouth always full of it.

The most intolerable pain is produced by prolonging the keenest pleasure.

The man with toothache thinks everyone happy whose teeth are sound. The poverty-stricken man makes the same mistake about the rich man.

The more a man possesses over and above what he uses, the more careworn he becomes.

The tyranny that forbids you to make the road with pick and shovel is worse than that which prevents you from lolling along it in a carriage and pair.

In an ugly and unhappy world the richest man can purchase nothing but ugliness and unhappiness.

In his efforts to escape from ugliness and unhappiness the rich man intensifies both. Every new yard of West End creates a new acre of East End.

The nineteenth century was the Age of Faith in Fine Art. The results are before us.

THE PERFECT GENTLEMAN

The fatal reservation of the gentleman is that he sacrifices everything to his honor except his gentility.

A gentleman of our days is one who has money enough to do what every fool would do if he could afford it: that is, consume without producing.

The true diagnostic of modern gentility is parasitism.

No elaboration of physical or moral accomplishment can atone for the sin of parasitism.

A modern gentleman is necessarily the enemy of his country. Even in war he does not fight to defend it, but to prevent his power of preying on it from passing to a foreigner. Such combatants are patriots in the same sense as two dogs fighting for a bone are lovers of animals.

The North American Indian was a type of the sportsman warrior gentleman. The Periclean Athenian was a type of the intellectually and artistically cultivated gentleman. Both were political failures. The modern gentleman, without the hardihood of the one or the culture of the other, has the appetite of both put together. He will not succeed where they failed.

He who believes in education, criminal law, and sport,

needs only property to make him a perfect modern gentleman.

MODERATION

Moderation is never applauded for its own sake.

A moderately honest man with a moderately faithful wife, moderate drinkers both, in a moderately healthy house: that is the true middle class unit.

THE UNCONSCIOUS SELF

The unconscious self is the real genius. Your breathing goes wrong the moment your conscious self meddles with it.

Except during the nine months before he draws his first breath, no man manages his affairs as well as a tree does.

REASON

The reasonable man adapts himself to the world: the unreasonable one persists in trying to adapt the world to himself. Therefore all progress depends on the unreasonable man.

The man who listens to Reason is lost: Reason enslaves all whose minds are not strong enough to master her.

DECENCY

Decency is Indecency's Conspiracy of Silence.

EXPERIENCE

Men are wise in proportion, not to their experience, but to their capacity for experience.

If we could learn from mere experience, the stones of London would be wiser than its wisest men.

TIME'S REVENGES

Those whom we called brutes had their revenge when Darwin shewed us that they were our cousins.

The thieves had their revenge when Marx convicted the bourgeoisie of theft.

GOOD INTENTIONS

Hell is paved with good intentions, not with bad ones.

All men mean well.

NATURAL RIGHTS

The Master of Arts, by proving that no man has any natural rights, compels himself to take his own for granted.

The right to live is abused whenever it is not constantly challenged.

FAUTE DE MIEUX

In my childhood I demurred to the description of a certain young lady as "the pretty Miss So and So." My aunt rebuked me by saying "Remember always that the least homely sister is the family beauty."

No age or condition is without its heroes. The least incapable general in a nation is its Cæsar, the least imbecile statesman its Solon, the least confused thinker its Socrates, the least commonplace poet its Shakespeare.

CHARITY

Charity is the most mischievous sort of pruriency.

Those who minister to poverty and disease are accomplices in the two worst of all the crimes.

He who gives money he has not earned is generous with other people's labor.

Every genuinely benevolent person loathes almsgiving and mendicity.

FAME

Life levels all men: death reveals the eminent.

DISCIPLINE

Mutiny Acts are needed only by officers who command without authority. Divine right needs no whip.

WOMEN IN THE HOME

Home is the girl's prison and the woman's workhouse.

CIVILIZATION

Civilization is a disease produced by the practice of building societies with rotten material.

Those who admire modern civilization usually identify it with the steam engine and the electric telegraph.

Those who understand the steam engine and the electric telegraph spend their lives in trying to replace them with something better.

The imagination cannot conceive a viler criminal than he who should build another London like the present one, nor a greater benefactor than he who should destroy it.

GAMBLING

The most popular method of distributing wealth is the method of the roulette table.

The roulette table pays nobody except him who keeps it. Nevertheless a passion for gaming is common, though a passion for keeping roulette tables is unknown.

Gambling promises the poor what Property performs for the rich: that is why the bishops dare not denounce it fundamentally.

THE SOCIAL QUESTION

Do not waste your time on Social Questions. What is the matter with the poor is Poverty: what is the matter with the Rich is Uselessness.

STRAY SAYINGS

We are told that when Jehovah created the world he saw that it was good. What would he say now?

The conversion of a savage to Christianity is the conversion of Christianity to savagery.

No man dares say so much of what he thinks as to appear to himself an extremist.

Mens sana in corpore sano is a foolish saying. The sound body is a product of the sound mind.

Decadence can find agents only when it wears the mask of progress.

In moments of progress the noble succeed, because things are going their way: in moments of decadence the base succeed for the same reason: hence the world is never without the exhilaration of contemporary success.

The reformer for whom the world is not good enough finds himself shoulder to shoulder with him that is not good enough for the world.

Every man over forty is a scoundrel.

Youth, which is forgiven everything, forgives itself nothing: age, which forgives itself everything, is forgiven nothing.

When we learn to sing that Britons never will be masters we shall make an end of slavery.

Do not mistake your objection to defeat for an objection to fighting, your objection to being a slave for an objection to slavery, your objection to not being as rich as your neighbor for an objection to poverty. The cowardly, the insubordinate, and the envious share your objections.

Take care to get what you like or you will be forced to like what you get. Where there is no ventilation fresh air is declared unwholesome. Where there is no religion hypocrisy becomes good taste. Where there is no knowledge ignorance calls itself science.

If the wicked flourish and the fittest survive, Nature must be the God of rascals.

If history repeats itself, and the unexpected always happens, how incapable must Man be of learning from experience!

Compassion is the fellow-feeling of the unsound.

Those who understand evil pardon it: those who resent it destroy it.

Acquired notions of propriety are stronger than natural instincts. It is easier to recruit for monasteries and convents than to induce an Arab woman to uncover her mouth in public, or a British officer to walk through Bond Street in a golfing cap on an afternoon in May.

It is dangerous to be sincere unless you are also stupid.

The Chinese tame fowls by clipping their wings, and women by deforming their feet. A petticoat round the ankles serves equally well.

Political Economy and Social Economy are amusing intellectual games; but Vital Economy is the Philosopher's Stone.

When a heretic wishes to avoid martyrdom he speaks of "Orthodoxy, True and False" and demonstrates that the True is his heresy.

Beware of the man who does not return your blow: he neither forgives you nor allows you to forgive yourself.

If you injure your neighbor, better not do it by halves.

Sentimentality is the error of supposing that quarter can be given or taken in moral conflicts.

Two starving men cannot be twice as hungry as one; but two rascals can be ten times as vicious as one.

Make your cross your crutch; but when you see another man do it, beware of him.

SELF-SACRIFICE

Self-sacrifice enables us to sacrifice other people without blushing.

If you begin by sacrificing yourself to those you love, you will end by hating those to whom you have sacrificed yourself.

DATE DUE

This offer, prices and numbers are subject to change without notice.

Praise for the novels of Sherryl Woods

"Sherryl Woods writes emotionally satisfying novels about family, friendship and home. Truly feel-great reads!"

—#1 *New York Times* bestselling author
Debbie Macomber

"During the course of this gripping, emotionally wrenching but satisfying tale, Woods deftly and realistically handles such issues as survival guilt, drug abuse as adolescent rebellion, and family dynamics when a vital member is suddenly gone."

—*Booklist* on *Flamingo Diner*

"Woods is a master heartstring puller."

—*Publishers Weekly* on *Seaview Inn*

"Once again, Woods, with such authenticity, weaves a tale of true love and the challenges that can knock up against that love."

—*RT Book Reviews* on *Beach Lane*

"Woods…is noted for appealing character-driven stories that are often infused with the flavor and fragrance of the South."

—*Library Journal*

"A reunion story punctuated by family drama, Woods's first novel in her new Ocean Breeze series is touching, tense and tantalizing."

—*RT Book Reviews* on *Sand Castle Bay*

"A whimsical, sweet scenario…the digressions have their own charm, and Woods never fails to come back to the romantic point."

—*Publishers Weekly* on *Sweet Tea at Sunrise*

SHERRYL WOODS

Feels Like Family

mira

mira™

Recycling programs
for this product may
not exist in your area.

ISBN-13: 978-0-7783-6101-5

Feels Like Family

First published in 2007. This edition published in 2020.

This edition published by arrangement with Harlequin Books S.A.

For questions and comments about the quality of this book, please contact us
at CustomerService@Harlequin.com.

Mira
22 Adelaide St. West, 40th Floor
Toronto, Ontario M5H 4E3, Canada
www.Harlequin.com

Printed in U.S.A.

Dear Friends,

I'm so delighted to have the third Sweet Magnolias book available again to coincide with the new Sweet Magnolias series on Netflix, starring JoAnna Garcia Swisher, Brooke Elliott and Heather Headley. When I first came up with the idea for a series about three lifelong friends who'd been through thick and thin together, I had no idea how many women would be added to this core group over the years or how readers would come to love that bond and the entire community of Serenity, South Carolina. I hope Netflix viewers will embrace them, too.

As women, I think we've all come to understand that next to family, our friends are the most important people in our lives. And friendships that have stood the test of time, with women who know our history, our mistakes, our dirty little secrets and love us just the same, are the strongest bonds of all. Friends are there to boost our spirits when we're having a simple bad day or a crisis of monumental proportions. They can make us laugh, celebrate with us, cry with us and remind us that even on the worst day life is still worth living.

If you're just meeting Maddie, Dana Sue and Helen for the very first time, I hope you'll love getting to know them. If you're renewing your friendship with them, I hope it brings back a smile or two. Most of all, I hope you have warm, wonderful friends in your life and that you treasure every minute with them.

All best,

Sherryl

Feels Like
Family

CHAPTER ONE

For a woman who prided herself on being cool and competent, who relied on her wits to win a case, Helen Decatur walked away from the Serenity courthouse with a strong desire to pummel some sense and decency into a few of South Carolina's good old boys.

Not that she could have proved—weekly golf outings aside—that the judge, the opposing attorney and her client's soon-to-be ex-husband were in cahoots to deprive her client of what she deserved after the nearly thirty years she'd devoted to her husband, his career and their children. Nonetheless it was clear that the ongoing delays and postponements were designed to wear down Caroline Holliday until she settled for a pittance of what her husband owed her.

One of these days Caroline would fold, too. Helen had seen the defeat in her eyes today when the judge had allowed Brad Holliday's attorney yet another postponement. Jimmy Bob West claimed they hadn't seen papers Helen had filed with the court weeks ago. Helen's production of a signed courier receipt for the delivery of those papers on the same date they'd been filed with the court had done nothing to dissuade Judge Lester Rockingham from granting her opponent's request.

"Now, Helen, there's no reason to be in a rush," the judge had said, his tone condescending. "We're all after the same thing here."

"Not exactly," Helen had muttered under her breath, but she'd resigned herself to accepting the decision. Maybe she could use the extra time to do a little more digging into Brad's finances. She had a hunch that would wipe that smug smile off his face. Men who provided such extensive records as quickly as Brad had often buried financial secrets under the avalanche, hoping they'd remain buried.

If Brad's smug expression annoyed her, at least she could take some pleasure in Jimmy Bob's careful avoidance of her gaze. He'd known her long enough to be leery of her temper once she snapped. On his own, he would only push her so far. Spurred on by a client, he was sometimes tempted to take risks—as he was now.

Jimmy Bob, with his slicked-back hair, ruddy complexion and ribald sense of humor, had tangled with Helen on so many occasions that she pretty much knew what to expect from him. He was a born-and-bred South Carolinian who'd been talking his way out of jams since high school. While he'd never crossed an ethical line to Helen's knowledge, he danced right on the precipice so often it was a wonder he hadn't lost his balance and fallen into some legal quagmire by now.

"I'm sorry," Helen told Caroline as she gathered up her files. "They're not going to get away with this forever."

"Sure they will," her client replied wearily. "Brad's in no hurry. He's too busy popping Viagra and sleeping with any female who crosses his path to be worried about when the divorce actually goes through. In fact, this is giving him the perfect excuse to avoid making a commitment to another woman. He's in hog heaven right now, free to do whatever he wants without any consequences. He figures that any woman hooking up with him does so at her own, fully informed peril."

"What did you ever see in a man like that?" Helen asked.

It was a question Helen found herself asking her clients a lot lately. How did smart, attractive women wind up with men who were so unworthy of them? To her mind, marriage was something to be avoided. Her friends told her she was simply jaded from handling too many nasty divorces, and while she couldn't deny that, she could list on the fingers of one hand the number of successful marriages she'd seen. Her friend and business partner, Maddie Maddox, had one—though only after recovering from a lousy first marriage—and her other friend and partner, Dana Sue Sullivan, had recently reunited with her ex, and even to Helen's cynical eye it looked as if this time things would last for her and Ronnie.

"Brad wasn't always that way," Caroline told her, a faintly nostalgic expression in her eyes. "When we met, he was thoughtful and considerate. He was a great dad, a terrific provider and until a few months ago I'd have said we had a solid marriage."

Helen had heard the rest before, or some version of it. Brad had had a brush with prostate cancer that had threatened his virility. After that, he'd lost his grip on reality. All he could think about was proving he was still a man, and he did that by sleeping with a succession of younger women, never mind that a real man would've stuck by the family who'd stayed by his side during his treatment and recovery.

By the time Helen left the courthouse, she felt even more cynical than usual. She would have given anything to head to The Corner Spa, the business she'd started with Maddie and Dana Sue, and spend an hour working out, but she knew she had a full schedule back at the office. Normally a jam-packed calendar would have reassured her, but lately she'd begun to wonder what she was working so hard to accomplish.

She had professional success, she had money in the bank—quite a lot of it, in fact—and she had a lovely home in Serenity she rarely had time to enjoy. She had good friends, but the family she'd once envisioned for herself had never materialized. Instead she played doting surrogate aunt to Maddie's children—Tyler, Kyle, Katie and Jessica Lynn—and to Dana Sue's daughter, Annie.

It was her own fault, she knew. She'd always been too driven, too dedicated to the clients depending on her to take the time for the kind of serious dating that might actually lead to a relationship and marriage. And as the divorces had piled up in her caseload, she'd grown less and less enchanted with the idea of risking her own heart, especially on something that came with no guarantees.

When she reached her office, a small cottage on a side street near downtown Serenity, her secretary handed her a thick stack of message slips and nodded toward her office.

Barb Dixon was almost sixty and unapologetically gray-haired, and she'd come to work for Helen the day she'd opened the office. A widow who'd raised three sons on her own and gotten all of them through college, Barb was endlessly patient and compassionate with the clients and fiercely loyal to Helen. She also felt it was her right and duty to take Helen to task from time to time, which made her one of the few people on earth who dared.

"Your two o'clock's been waiting in your office for an hour," she chided. "Your three o'clock will be here any second."

Helen glanced over Barb's shoulder at the calendar the woman maintained with careful detail, instinctively knowing when to allow extra time for a client and when to keep the appointment to a fifteen-minute session that wouldn't try Helen's patience.

"Karen Ames?" Helen questioned. "She works for Dana Sue at Sullivan's. What's she doing here?"

"She didn't tell me, just said it was urgent she speak with you. You had a cancellation for this afternoon, so I called her yesterday and confirmed her for that slot. If you can keep it short, maybe you can catch up a little."

"Okay, then, let me get started. Apologize to Mrs. Hendricks when she gets here. Give her a cup of tea and some of those cookies from Sullivan's. She'll say she's on a diet, but I know better. I caught her diving into a strawberry sundae at Wharton's the other day."

Barb nodded. "Done."

Helen stepped into her office, with its antique furniture and pale peach walls. Karen was seated on the edge of a guest chair, nervously biting her nails. Her blond hair pulled back into a ponytail that emphasized her fragile cheekbones and large blue eyes. She didn't look much older than a teenager, though she was, in fact, in her late twenties with two very young children at home.

"I'm so sorry I kept you waiting, Karen," Helen said. "My court case didn't start on time and then it took longer than I anticipated to agree on a new hearing date."

"It's okay," Karen said. "I appreciate you seeing me at all."

"What can I do for you?"

"I think Dana Sue's going to fire me," Karen blurted, her expression tearful. "I don't know what to do, Ms. Decatur. I have two kids. My ex-husband hasn't paid child support in a year. If I lose this job, we could wind up on the streets. The landlord's already threatening to evict us."

Helen's heart went out to the pale, obviously frazzled young woman seated across from her. There was little question that Karen was at the end of her rope.

"You know Dana Sue and I are friends, as well as partners in The Corner Spa," Helen said. "Why did you come to me? I can't represent you, but I'd be happy to recommend someone who could."

"No, please," Karen protested. "I guess I was just hoping you could give me some advice because the two of you *are* friends. I know I've bailed out on her way too often lately, but it's only because of the kids. It's been one thing after another with them—measles and then their babysitter quitting. I'm a mom first. I have to be. I'm all they have."

"Of course they're your first priority," Helen said, even though to her increasing regret she'd never experienced the need to juggle kids and a career.

"The thought of being homeless with two kids scares me to death."

"We're not going to let that happen," Helen said decisively. "Have you sat down with Dana Sue and explained about your ex and the threats of eviction?"

Karen shook her head. "I'm too embarrassed. I think it's unprofessional to bring my financial problems into the workplace, so I haven't talked to her or Erik about this. When I call to say I can't come in, I tell them the truth, but hearing about one problem after another involving the kids has to be getting old by now. I made a commitment to be there, and Dana Sue has every right to expect me to honor that commitment."

"Then you can understand her position," Helen said.

"Of course I can," Karen replied at once. "It's not as if she has a huge staff to take up the slack. In fact, it's almost too much for us when we're all there. I've been trying to find another sitter for the kids, but do you have any idea how hard it is to find someone willing to take care of two sick kids under five during the hours I need to work? It's almost impossible. And daycare programs don't run late enough and wouldn't have taken them when they were sick, anyway."

Her shoulders sagged with defeat. "Until all this happened, I was a good employee. You can ask Dana Sue or Erik how hard I worked. I love working at Sullivan's. Dana Sue gave me a fabulous opportunity when she hired me away from the diner, and I hate that I'm blowing it."

"You haven't blown it yet," Helen consoled her. "I know Dana Sue thinks the world of you. But you're right. She needs staff who're reliable."

"I *know* that," Karen said miserably. "And she deserves it, too. I guess I'm just feeling completely overwhelmed right now. Is there anything you can do to help? How should I handle this?"

Helen considered the situation. Though employment issues were not her area of expertise, she was fairly certain Dana Sue could legally fire an employee whose absenteeism was intolerable, especially if there'd been repeated warnings about the absences. At the same time, she also knew that her friend would never kick someone when they were down. Sullivan's was a huge success in part because Dana Sue had always thought of the relatively small staff there as a family. It was one of the reasons she'd been reluctant to expand.

"Why don't we sit down with Dana Sue and see if we can't brainstorm some solutions?" Helen suggested. "Dana Sue is a compassionate person. I'm sure she's no happier about the prospect of firing you than you are. In addition, I know she's invested a lot of time in training you to become her sous-chef eventually. Compared to the man who had the job when she first opened, you've fit in perfectly. I also know you've taken a lot of initiative in creating new recipes for Sullivan's. And you *were* there when she had a family crisis of her own. Maybe I can mediate some kind of compromise to buy you time to pull things in your life together."

"That would be incredible," Karen said.

"Unfortunately, it only solves part of the problem, not the part about finding a reliable sitter," Helen reminded her. "But between Dana Sue and me, we know a lot of people. I'm sure there's someone out there who has time on her hands and would be thrilled to be needed."

Hope sparked in Karen's eyes, but faded quickly. Clearly she was someone who'd come to accept defeat as the norm.

"I'm so sorry if I'm putting you in an awkward position," she said.

"Nonsense," Helen returned. "If it were a matter of you wanting to sue Sullivan's for wrongful dismissal, I wouldn't be able to help you because of my close ties with Dana Sue. This is just three reasonable women sitting down for a little heart-to-heart. I think being straightforward and honest with Dana Sue is the only option here."

Karen gave her a worried look. "I have no idea what your fee is, but I promise you I will pay you as soon as I possibly can. You can check my credit. As tough as things have been since my husband left, I've worked really hard to pay my bills on time. I got behind one month on the rent and the landlord went ballistic, even though he got his money a week after the due date. He's just waiting for me to slip up again so he can kick us out and charge more rent to the next person."

"Let's not worry about any fee right now," Helen said. "As I said, we're going to look at this as an informal chat among friends, okay?"

Tears welled up in Karen's eyes and spilled down her cheeks. She swiped at them impatiently. "I don't know how to thank you, Ms. Decatur. I really don't."

"First, call me Helen. And before you thank me, let's wait and see if we come up with some way to make this a win-win situation for everyone, okay?"

Helen didn't think there was going to be any problem once Dana Sue understood the whole story. Sullivan's was successful enough that she could afford to hire someone else part-time, if need be, to fill in when Karen had another of the inevitable family crises that came with having kids. If worse came to worst, Helen herself could step in to help out. She'd done it before when Dana Sue had a crisis that took her away from the restaurant.

Helen had discovered that working with Erik was actually fun. He was probably the only male on the planet who wasn't the least bit intimidated by her. She'd found that to be both refreshing and frustrating.

In addition, she'd found chopping and dicing to his very precise expectations oddly soothing. After a tough day in court, it had relieved some of her stress to envision a particularly thorny witness or cantankerous judge on the chopping block as she worked. After today, taking a knife to an imaginary Judge Rockingham, Jimmy Bob or Brad Holliday would have been particularly soothing.

"Are you working tomorrow?" Helen asked Karen.

"Assuming my sitter shows up, I go in at ten to prep for lunch, then stay 'til seven so the early part of the dinner rush is covered."

Helen nodded. "I'll check Dana Sue's schedule to see when she'll be there and get back to you, okay? We're going to work this out, Karen. I promise you."

If she had to be a volunteer substitute in Sullivan's kitchen on a regular basis for a while, she would do everything she could to save Karen's job. Maybe she could even do something about that deadbeat husband of hers, though Karen hadn't asked for her help with that. She'd happily do the work pro bono.

Karen left Helen's office feeling a lot better than she had when she'd called out of sheer desperation to make the appointment. She knew enough about the attorney to know she worked hard for her clients—worked hard at everything she did, for that matter. If ever Karen had met a type-A personality, Helen was it. She made Dana Sue's perfectionism in the kitchen at Sullivan's seem like a cute little eccentricity.

When Karen got back to her two-bedroom apartment in a charmless rectangular building, she knocked on her neighbor's door. Frances Wingate, who had to be over eighty but wouldn't admit to it, had agreed to keep the kids for a couple of hours, which was about all she could manage with rambunctious, five-year-old Daisy and three-year-old Mack. Two hours were about as long as Daisy was content to make pictures with her crayons or read her books, and twice as long as Mack usually stayed down for his nap. Even as Karen waited for Frances to answer her knock, she could hear Mack crying.

"You big baby, look what you did to my picture!" Daisy yelled just as Frances opened the door.

Karen regarded her apologetically. "I am so sorry I took so long."

Frances didn't look nearly as frazzled as Karen had expected. "Oh, don't mind them. This just started. Mack woke up a minute ago and made a beeline for the table where Daisy was coloring. He tore her favorite picture, the one she'd colored for you. I was just about to get both of them some cookies and milk—that should settle them down. Why don't you come in and have some, too? They're chocolate chip. I baked them this morning."

"Are you sure you can stand this commotion another second?" Karen asked worriedly. "You must be ready for some peace and quiet."

Frances gave her a wry look. "At my age peace and quiet aren't the boon you'd think. I like having the kids around. They remind me of mine, though I hate to tell you how long ago it was when they were as young as Daisy and Mack. I have great-grandchildren older than these two." She drew Karen inside. "Now, you sit down and get off your feet. I'll get the kids settled and then you and I can chat."

When Karen had asked Frances if she'd mind watching the kids, she'd said only that she needed to talk to someone about some problems at work. The older woman hadn't hesitated. "Of course," she said. "You go do whatever you need to do."

Now, while Frances bustled off toward the small kitchen, Karen stepped into the dining room where the kids were still engaged in a noisy dispute over the destroyed picture. The instant Daisy spotted her, she ran to Karen and lifted her arms to be picked up.

"Mommy, Mack tore my present for you," Daisy said with an indignant huff, her big blue eyes shimmering with tears.

Though Daisy was getting much too heavy for Karen to hold for long, she cradled her precious little girl in her arms. "Sweetie, he's only three. I'm sure he didn't mean to hurt the picture."

"But it's ruined," Daisy wailed.

"I bet you can draw me another one that's even more beautiful," Karen suggested. "You're very good at drawing pictures."

Even as she spoke, Mack latched on to her leg, shoulders heaving with great hiccuping sobs. "Mommy!" he wailed. "Up!"

Karen felt the start of a pounding headache. Torn between her two distraught children, she managed to sit down at the table while still holding Daisy. Settling her on one knee, she hauled Mack into her lap. Daisy

immediately struggled to get down, clearly feeling betrayed by the shift in attention to her little brother.

"Not just yet," Karen told her firmly. "Let's talk
about this."

"He's a baby," Daisy said sullenly. "He never listens."

"And isn't that the point?" Karen asked. "If he's too
little to understand that something is important to you,
then you need to be the big sister and keep important
things where he can't get at them. Can you try to do
that?"

"I guess," Daisy said, sounding resigned.

"Thank you," Karen told her solemnly.

"Who's ready for cookies and milk?" Frances called
cheerfully.

Both kids immediately abandoned Karen, scrambling
down and heading toward the kitchen, the disagreement forgotten. Frances's cookies were always a huge
hit with her kids, who preferred them to the fancier desserts Karen sometimes brought home from Sullivan's.

"Why don't we make it like a picnic?" Frances suggested. "I'll put a big tablecloth on the floor in front
of the TV and you can have your cookies and milk in
there."

"I love picnics!" Daisy said enthusiastically.

"Me, too," Frances confided. "And you know the
best part of having it indoors?"

"What?" Daisy asked.

"No ants."

Daisy giggled.

Karen helped Frances spread out a plastic red-
checked tablecloth, where she then set down a plate of
cookies. "Two for each of you," Frances said emphati-

cally. "Mack, here's your sippy cup with milk in it, and Daisy, here's your glass of milk."

She flipped on the TV, then handed the control to Daisy. "Find that cartoon channel you both like, okay?"

That was something else the kids loved about visiting Frances. She had cable TV, which gave them a whole range of channels Karen couldn't afford. At home they had only the three major networks and one local station that carried ancient reruns.

"That should keep them busy for a while," Frances said. "I've made some tea for us to have with our cookies. You sit down at the dining-room table and I'll bring it right in."

"Please, let me help," Karen said.

"The day I can't carry a plate of cookies and two cups of tea to the table is the day I'll check myself into that nursing home they built up the street a few years back," Frances said.

Karen knew better than to argue. Frances was as strong-willed and independent as anyone she'd ever met. It was probably the reason she was still doing so well on her own. Every now and then one of her children would come for a visit and drop in on Karen to see if she thought Frances was getting too feeble to be left alone.

Karen had never felt a need to shade the truth even slightly. Frances still had a sharp mind and plenty of energy for a woman her age. She was active at her church and made a trip to the library at least once a week to pick up something to read. Until a few months ago, she'd even volunteered at the regional hospital, but the long drive had gotten to be too much for her. Now she spent an hour or more a day checking on local shut-ins, calling or visiting them just to chat and to see if they needed anything more than a few minutes of company.

Though Frances's apartment was the same dimensions as Karen's, it was cozy and welcoming in a way Karen's was not. Maybe it was the lifetime of memories on display in pictures and collectibles. Every knickknack crowded onto every surface in the living room had a fascinating story behind it. Surprisingly the kids—even Mack—had learned to look, and not touch. On the one occasion when, to Karen's chagrin, something had gotten broken, Frances had waved off the incident.

"One less thing to dust," she'd said, sounding as if she meant it.

Now, as she poured tea into mismatched chintz teacups, she studied Karen intently. "You still have that worried look in your eyes. Did your meeting not go well?"

"Actually it went better than I'd expected," Karen admitted. "But the real test is going to be tomorrow. The attorney I saw thinks we should sit down with my boss and work out a solution to the problem I've been having getting to work lately. She's optimistic everything will work out. I'm not so sure."

"Surely you don't think Dana Sue would fire you," Frances said, clearly startled. "Is that what this is about?"

Karen nodded. "I wouldn't blame her if she did."

"Honey, she's one of the sweetest gals I've ever known. It's not in her nature to fire someone just because they've hit a rough patch. Did you know I taught her back in second grade?" She shook her head, a smile

crinkling her face. "Oh, my, she was something back
then. She made your Daisy look like a little angel."

Karen grinned. "I can't imagine that."

"I knew her mama and daddy real well because of
it," Frances said. "And Dana Sue spent a lot of time-
outs inside during recess, so I knew her real well, too.
She reminds me of that every time I go to Sullivan's for
lunch with my group from church. She says I was the
last person who ever managed to keep her in check. I
could speak to her, if you think it would help."

"The only thing that's really going to help is me finding someone to take care of the kids so I can get to work
when I'm supposed to be there," Karen said.

Frances regarded her with regret. "You know I'd help
if I could. I might be able to manage Daisy for a few
hours, but I'm too old to be chasing after Mack."

"Believe me, there are days when I think *I'm* too old
to handle Mack," Karen told her honestly. "I appreciate you taking them for a couple of hours every now
and then. I would never ask you to deal with them any
longer than that."

Frances gave her a sympathetic look. "Have you
heard from their daddy lately? Has he made any of his
child-support back payments?"

Karen shook her head. Just thinking about the way
Ray had left her to fend for herself and their kids when
he ran off made her head throb again. "I can't even
think about that right now," she said, not trying to hide
her bitterness. "I've gotta focus on keeping my job so
I don't lose the roof over our heads."

"If that happens, you'll just move in here with me
'til things get straightened out," Frances said at once.

"I will not let you and those babies be on the street, and that's that, so quit your worrying on that score."

"I couldn't," Karen protested.

"Of course, you could. Friends help each other out. I may not be able to watch those kids for you all day long, but I can certainly see that there's a roof over your heads."

Karen just sat there, stunned into silence. Though she prayed she would never have to take Frances up on her offer, that Frances had even made it was the most wonderful, generous thing anyone had ever done for her. Combined with Helen's willingness to help her fight for her job, a day that had started with nothing but worry was turning into one filled with blessings.

CHAPTER TWO

It was nearly seven when Helen finished with her last
client. Barb had left an hour earlier, so she turned off
the lights and closed up the office, relieved to have the
workday behind her.

Outside she weighed the prospect of going home to
her empty house against dropping in at Sullivan's for a
decent meal and a few snatched minutes of Dana Sue's
time. Anytime she could see one of the Sweet Magnolias, as they had once called themselves, she grabbed it.
Maybe she could lay some groundwork before she and
Karen met with her formally tomorrow at the restaurant. Barb had already set up that appointment for two
o'clock, after the lunch crowd thinned out.

The restaurant, which specialized in what Dana Sue
called new Southern cuisine, was packed, as it was most
nights. Though Serenity's population was only 3500 or
so, the restaurant's reputation had spread through the
entire region thanks to excellent reviews in the Charleston and Columbia newspapers.

Helen was greeted at the door by Brenda, the har-
ried waitress. "I should have a table opening up in a
few minutes," she told Helen. "Do you mind waiting?"

"Not at all. Do you think I'll be risking life and limb if I stick my head in the kitchen to say hello to Dana Sue?"

Brenda grinned. "I'd say that depends on whether you're prepared to pitch in and help. She and Erik have their hands full tonight. It's been crazy ever since that review in the Columbia paper. If it's going to stay this busy, she needs to hire some additional prep staff for the kitchen and some more waitstaff. Paul and I have just about run ourselves to death tonight, even with the busboys pitching in. And just so you know, we ran out of all the specials an hour ago."

"I'll keep that in mind," Helen said, then headed for the kitchen.

When she pushed open the door and stepped in, she saw Dana Sue at the huge gas stove. Face flushed from the heat, Dana Sue juggled half a dozen different sauté pans, then slid the contents onto waiting plates, added the decorative sauces and spicy salsas, and moved them to a pickup area for the waitstaff.

Her expression filled with relief when she spotted Helen. "Grab an apron," she ordered. "We need you. It's nuts in here."

"Looks to me like what you need is more trained help. Where's Erik?" Helen asked as she whipped off her suit jacket, hung it on a peg in the pantry, then found an apron and put it on over her two-hundred-dollar designer silk blouse.

"Right behind you," a deep voice rumbled. "Watch your step. I'm loaded down."

She turned and found him carrying a tray laden with pies fresh from the oven. She could smell the heady aromas of peaches, cinnamon and vanilla.

"If you'll give me a slice of that, I'll be your slave for the rest of the night," she said.

Erik grinned at her. "I'll save you a whole pie, but you don't have time to eat it now. I need you to mix up another batch of the mango-papaya chutney for the fish." His gaze skimmed her outfit and he shook his head. "You realize that blouse is heading straight for the dry cleaner's after this, don't you?"

Helen shrugged. She had a dozen more in her closet. It wouldn't be a huge loss. "Not a problem."

His dark eyes warmed. "That's what I love about you. No pretensions. Underneath that icy courtroom demeanor that I hear you possess lies the soul of a woman ruled by a passion for food and a willingness to help out a friend in distress, no matter the personal cost."

The compliment caught her off guard. When the usually taciturn Erik popped out with something unexpected or insightful, as he occasionally did, it made her wonder what his story was. She winked at him. "I'm only this cavalier because I figure with the size of tonight's crowd, Dana Sue's good for the cost of another blouse."

"Don't," he protested. "You're ruining my illusions. Do you remember how to make the chutney?"

Helen shook her head. "But don't worry. I know where the recipes are. I'll get that one and find the supplies in the storeroom. I'll have another batch whipped up in no time. You don't need to supervise."

"As if," Dana Sue called out from her station by the stove. "Erik is so thrilled to have someone to supervise for once, he's not going to pass up the chance."

Within moments, Helen had fallen into the frantic rhythm of the kitchen. When she could, she snatched glances at Erik, admiring the efficiency with which he moved almost as much as she craved the desserts which he excelled at making. Though he'd been hired primarily as a pastry chef right after graduating from the Atlanta Culinary Institute—which he'd attended after apparently leaving some other career he never mentioned—his role in Sullivan's kitchen had been expanded over time. Dana Sue relied on him as her backup and had officially named him as assistant manager just a few weeks earlier.

In his late 30s or early 40s, he had a wry wit, a gentle demeanor and was fiercely loyal to and protective of Dana Sue. Helen liked that about him, almost as much as she liked his pastries and occasionally lusted after his six-pack abs and competent hands. That she lusted after him at all was a surprise, because she'd always preferred polished executives over the strong, silent, athletic types.

Helen was relegated to the most basic duties for the next two hours, but she liked being part of the hustle and bustle of the kitchen. The aromas were delectable, the excitement and stress palpable. If cooking at home were half this much fun, she might do it more often. Instead her culinary endeavors ran to scrambled eggs, when she remembered to buy any, and the occasional baked potato. She did make a damn fine margarita, though, if she did say so herself. That was the result of a few summers in Hilton Head working as a bartender during law school. She'd made great tips, great contacts and learned a lot about human nature.

By the time the last meal had been served and only a few customers were lingering over coffee and dessert, she was exhausted from being on her feet for so long, to say nothing of being half-starved.

"Okay, you two, that's it," Erik said, hustling them toward the door to the dining room. "Get in there and sit down. I'll bring you both dinner in a few minutes."

Dana Sue shook her head. "Only if you're going to join us," she told him. "You haven't had a break all night, either."

"Sure," Erik said. "But you need to eat now and Helen needs to kick off those ridiculous heels she insists on wearing."

Vaguely miffed by the comment, Helen stuck out her foot in its sexy high-heeled sandal, her most extravagant indulgence. "What's wrong with my shoes?"

Erik's gaze lingered on her foot with its perfectly manicured pink toenails, then traveled slowly up her leg to the hem of her skirt, now hitched up to show a couple of inches of thigh. "Speaking as a man, there is nothing wrong with those shoes," he told her, regarding her with amusement. "Speaking as someone who's watched you hobbling around in here for the past couple of hours, I'd say they're inappropriate for being on your feet for very long."

Mollified, she grinned. "You may have a point. If me pitching in around here is going to become a habit, I should probably keep some sneakers in Dana Sue's office."

Dana Sue gave her a startled look. "You own sneakers?"

"Don't be snide. What do you think I wear when I work out?"

"Oh, yeah, those customized things you created online in colors to match your workout clothes," Dana Sue said.

Erik looked at Helen in amusement. "What's wrong with the sneakers you buy at the mall?"

Helen gave him a disdainful look. "Everyone has them," she replied. "Come on, Dana Sue. I can't possibly deal with a man in faded jeans and a grease-stained T-shirt who doesn't understand fashion, no matter how sexy he thinks he is."

Erik chuckled, while Dana Sue said, "Right now, all I care about is that he understands food." She gave Erik a wink as she and Helen headed for the dining room and a corner booth away from the few remaining customers.

As soon as they were seated, Helen groaned and kicked off her shoes under the table. "Please don't tell Erik, okay? These things *are* torture if I'm on my feet too long. They'll definitely never be my dancin' shoes."

"Still, it's a small price to pay for looking sexy." Dana Sue grinned. "I haven't worn shoes like that in years. I'd break my neck."

"Next time you want to knock Ronnie's socks off, I'll let you borrow a pair of mine," Helen said.

Dana Sue's eyebrows rose and fell. "I knock his socks off no matter what I wear."

"Then the honeymoon's still not over?"

"You can stop asking me that, you know," Dana Sue said smugly. "Ronnie and I expect to be in the honeymoon phase for months and months. Maybe years. And this time around, I'm going to do everything in my power to see to it that the marriage never ends, even if the glow does wear off."

Helen regarded her wistfully. "I never thought I'd say this about you getting back together with Ronnie, but I envy you."

Dana Sue regarded her with compassion, but she

quickly shifted to impatience. "Then what are you doing about it? When was the last time you went on a date, and I don't mean sitting down with some male attorney to discuss torts or writs or whatever else it is you talk about over coffee."

"Who has time?" Helen said defensively. "Between work, keeping up with things at the spa and trying to exercise more regularly, I don't have five spare minutes a week."

"Really?" Dana Sue said skeptically. "You just spent two solid hours in my kitchen. That's enough for a quality date."

Helen shrugged. "That's fun. There's no pressure in there."

Dana Sue lifted an eyebrow. "Really? No pressure? Not even with Erik's exacting orders flying at you? He scared off the last two prep guys I brought in for a tryout."

"He's a perfectionist, that's all. Lord knows, I get that and respect it. And there's more at stake in there for you and for him. I'm just a volunteer worker bee from time to time. If I mess up, what are either of you going to do about it?"

"I'd probably banish you forever, but I can't speak for Erik," Dana Sue said. "By the way, was there some reason you came by tonight other than the chance we'd put you to work?"

"To be honest, I was hoping for a few minutes to talk to you," Helen admitted.

"About...?"

"Karen."

Dana Sue's eyes widened. "You want to talk to me about Karen Ames? Why? Is that why Barb called to set up an appointment for tomorrow afternoon? I thought it was about the spa." She held up her hand. "Wait. Here comes Erik with our food. If it involves Karen, he probably needs to hear this, too. And he should be at any meeting we have."

Erik set three plates of grouper, with its garnish of mango-papaya chutney, wild rice and a side of baby carrots in a brown sugar glaze on the table. Everything was as artfully arranged as it was for the paying customers.

"Where's my pie?" Helen asked immediately.

"Not 'til you've cleaned your plate," he teased, sliding into the booth beside her. "Pie's your reward, not your meal."

Helen frowned at him. "Who says?"

"The chef," he told her. "So. Dig in."

All three picked up their forks and started eating. After a minute, Erik asked, "What were you two talking about when I got here? You looked awfully serious for a couple of women who were supposed to be kicking back and relaxing."

"Karen," Dana Sue told him, her expression somber. She took another bite of food. "Helen brought her up."

Erik stared at Helen, his expression immediately shifting into something far more cautious. "What do you have to do with Karen?"

"She came to see me today. She thinks she's about to be fired."

Dana Sue exchanged a rueful look with Erik that spoke volumes.

Helen sighed. "I see she was on target. It's because of the amount of time she's missed lately, right?"

Dana Sue nodded. "It makes me very unhappy, but I don't have a choice, Helen. I can't operate a kitchen if one of my key employees is absent half the time. Even if I do find the right prep person, as busy as we are I need an assistant I can count on."

"Do you know why she's absent?"

"Every time she calls in, it's always about the kids," Erik volunteered.

"And I sympathize with that, I really do," Dana Sue added. "But it comes back to my ability to keep this place running the way it needs to. It's not fair for Erik and me to have to pick up the slack all the time. I have to have an employee who's reliable." She studied Helen worriedly. "Is she going to make a legal issue out of this? Is that why she came to you?"

"No," Helen said, putting down her fork. "I don't think it needs to come to that and I wouldn't represent her if it did. I just want you to sit down with Karen and me tomorrow and see if there's not another solution, something that will enable you to run this kitchen the way it needs to be run, yet keeps her from losing her job."

"You're putting Dana Sue in an impossible position," Erik said protectively. "Come on, Helen, she's not the bad guy here."

"I know that," Helen said. "But Karen's not some irresponsible kid, either. You've spent a lot of time training her. Just let her explain and see if we can't come to some kind of solution."

Though Erik looked less than thrilled with the idea, Dana Sue nodded. "I can do that much."

"Thank you," Helen said, then turned to Erik and added sternly, "And you, reserve judgment, okay?"

"I'll do my best, since the champion of the underdog requests it, but I'm not happy about it. I intend to be at that meeting. And so you know, I'm a little surprised that you would take Karen's side over your best friend's."

Helen bristled. "I'm trying *not* to take sides," she retorted. "Successful negotiating means making this a win-win situation."

"Then tell me exactly what Dana Sue is getting out of this," he demanded.

"She gets to keep an excellent, well-trained employee," Helen replied, determined to keep her tone reasonable, though his attitude was starting to grate on her. He wasn't the only one who felt protective about Dana Sue. She'd been looking out for her friend a lot longer than he had. Her appetite fading, she said, "You know Karen's good. I've heard you say it more than once."

"Doesn't matter if she's never here," Erik said.

His refusal to give Karen a break riled her. "That's an exaggeration," she snapped, losing patience.

"Whoa," Dana Sue protested. "It's a meeting, Erik. We owe Karen that much. Helen's right. When Karen's here, she's been terrific."

"Just as long as you don't let your pal here railroad you into doing something that's not in the best interests of the restaurant," he said.

"I've never railroaded anyone in my life," Helen said, annoyed. Her appetite for her food completely vanished.

"Really?" Erik scoffed. "Whose idea was it to get Ronnie Sullivan out of town when he and Dana Sue split up? That really worked out well for their daughter, didn't it?"

Dana Sue regarded him with dismay. "Old news, Erik. Annie's fine now, and so are Ronnie and I."

"No thanks to Helen's interference," he said.

Helen glowered at him, stung by his accusation.

When Dana Sue would have responded to his comment, Helen stopped her with a look. "I can fight my own battles," she said tightly. She faced Erik. "You weren't here. You have no idea what was best at the time."

"No," he agreed, leaning forward, his gaze intense. "I came along just in time to see all hell break loose when Annie landed in the hospital."

"That was *not* my fault," Helen said fiercely.

"Really? Her eating disorder was brought on to some degree because her father abandoned her, or did I get that part wrong?" He didn't wait for an answer before charging, "You made that happen."

"That's a little simplistic," Dana Sue said, though neither of them even looked at her.

Helen was practically nose-to-nose with Erik. "Where do you get off making an accusation like that?"

"Just calling it like I see it, sweetheart."

"Go to hell," Helen said, nudging Dana Sue until she moved out of the way so that Helen could slide out of the curved booth on the opposite side. She glanced at Dana Sue as she grabbed her shoes out from under the table. "I'll see you tomorrow," she said, then scowled at Erik. "I suggest you skip the meeting."

"Not a chance," he said. "Somebody has to make sure common sense reigns."

"And you have to be that somebody?" Helen asked. "How do you feel about that, Dana Sue?"

"I'm pretty much shell-shocked by the way this entire conversation has spun out of control," Dana Sue responded. "What is wrong with you two? I've never seen either of you act like this before."

"I guess know-it-all attorneys bring out the worst in me," Erik said stiffly.

"And judgmental men, who won't even listen to reason, bring it out in me," Helen said.

Erik gave her a once-over that made her blood almost as hot as her temper. "I guess that means you won't be wanting your pie, since I baked it."

The reminder of that peach pie, which had been all she could think about as she'd worked in the kitchen, created a major dilemma. Her mouth still watered when she thought about it. Her pride dictated she not let him know that.

"I never said that," she said huffily, then stalked into the kitchen and picked up the entire pie from the counter.

One bite, she thought as she drew in a deep breath and savored the aroma. What could it hurt? She put the pie down, grabbed a fork and dug into the fragrant peach mixture and flaky crust, then sighed as her temper simmered down a notch. Maybe two bites, she decided. Erik would never know. She ate the second mouthful, then picked up the pie again, marched straight back into the dining room and, before she could talk herself out of it, threw the remainder straight into his shocked face.

Beside him, Dana Sue sucked in a startled breath, then fought to contain laughter. Helen watched as the pie oozed down Erik's face and onto his T-shirt. She was so intent on watching it spread across his impressive chest that she apparently missed the wicked glint in his eyes until it was too late.

Before she could make a dash for it, he'd wiped most of the pie off his face and was on his feet. In an instant, he had his arms around her, his hot, demanding mouth on hers and the remains of that incredible peach pie crushed indelibly into her silk blouse.

Helen figured she could always buy another blouse,

but it was going to take a whole lot longer to erase the
memory of Erik's breath-stealing kiss from her head,
especially with Dana Sue as an obviously fascinated
witness. Dana Sue wouldn't let her forget it in this lifetime. And since there were still a couple of diners left in
the restaurant and this was Serenity, it would be all over
town by morning. Helen Decatur, the Sweet Magnolia
with the most common sense, the one who got people
out of trouble, had just landed in a pile of it.

When Erik finally released Helen from that ill-ad-
vised kiss, he cast Dana Sue an apologetic look, then
headed for the kitchen. He needed to figure out what
kind of insanity had possessed him to first taunt and
then kiss a woman like Helen Decatur.

She *was* a pushy, arrogant, know-it-all attorney, but
she was also his boss's best friend and a regular customer at Sullivan's. Moreover, on more than one occasion including tonight, she had willingly pitched in to
help them out of a jam in the kitchen.

Maybe that was the problem, he concluded. It was
one thing to disapprove of the fancy clothes and pretensions, but in the kitchen at Sullivan's he'd seen another
side of her. He'd seen a woman who cared more about her
friend and what she needed than she did about such superficial things as her designer clothes. She also checked
her ego at the door and did whatever was asked of her
without complaint. She did it damn well, too, if he was
being totally honest. He actually liked her, most of the
time, anyway. Tonight she'd just gotten under his skin
for some reason. Despite what he'd said, he *did* know
she'd never choose someone else's side over Dana Sue's.

Baiting her, he could understand. Kissing her, well,

that was a whole other story, one destined for an unhappy ending. He'd crossed a line, a move for which
he'd have to apologize eventually.

Of course, he couldn't help remembering that she'd
kissed him back. In fact, she'd kissed him with such unexpected heat and passion, it had sent him running for
cover. He hadn't run from a female since Susie Macki-
naw had planted an unwanted kiss on him in third grade
to the accompaniment of jeers from his friends.

No, he amended, pouring himself a cup of coffee
and drinking it as he methodically began to clean the
kitchen. The truth was he'd been running from women
since his wife had died in childbirth. An EMT in Atlanta at the time, he'd been with Samantha in the ambulance after she'd gone into premature labor and begun
hemorrhaging. The ride to the hospital had taken an
eternity, and even before they'd arrived in the emergency room, he'd known it was too late. Sam had lost
way too much blood, her vitals were fading and the
baby was too early to be saved.

That was the day his heart had been ripped from his
chest, right along with his ability to function in his job.
If an EMT couldn't do something to save his own wife,
how could he ever trust himself to help anyone else?

After a month's leave, during which he'd drunk himself into a stupor every single day, he'd walked into his
boss's office and quit. Gabe Sanchez had argued with
him, pleaded with him to get some counseling and then
come back, but Erik had known that his days in any
career tied to health care were over.

He might have drifted aimlessly after that, but a
friend of his wife's had suggested he go to the Atlanta
Culinary Institute. Erik had laughed at the idea at first,

but Bree had kept badgering. Her husband had added his support for the idea as well.

"Out of our entire crowd, you're the best cook, hands down," Bree had told him. "More important, you enjoy it. If nothing else, taking the classes will get you out of this funk you're in. Once you graduate, who knows? Maybe you can open your own restaurant or become a caterer or just come to my house once a month and cook for Ben and me and the kids. It doesn't matter. The distraction is what's important. Sam would hate what you're doing to yourself. She wouldn't want you to grieve forever."

Erik might have dismissed the whole idea if Bree hadn't shown up on his doorstep a few days later with application forms. She'd sat right there while he filled them out, then written a check herself, tucked it all in an envelope and taken it with her to mail. Obviously she hadn't wanted to leave anything to chance.

"Consider it a gift toward your future from Ben and me," she said. "When you're running your own restaurant, you can pay us back with free dinners on our anniversaries."

A few weeks later, he'd been accepted and shortly after that he'd taken his first classes. By the end of the first month, he knew it was the best decision he'd ever made, next to marrying Samantha. By the time graduation rolled around, he wondered how he'd ever considered, much less worked in, any other field.

Then Dana Sue had contacted the school to find a pastry chef, which was Erik's specialty. He hadn't been convinced he wanted to move to a small town in South Carolina, but after he'd visited Serenity and seen Sullivan's, he'd been hooked. It was just the change he needed, a chance to get away from Atlanta and all of its memories. Moreover, Dana Sue had created something special in a community that was trying to turn itself around after some hard knocks to its economy. As all of the reviews had glowingly stated, Sullivan's was a rare culinary treasure and he was glad to be a part of it.

As for Dana Sue, she was something special, as well. He'd even harbored a vague notion that someday their relationship might move from professional to personal, but it had quickly become clear that the shapely blonde was still in love with her ex-husband.

Even so, Dana Sue, her daughter, Annie, and even the annoyingly unreliable Karen had become his family. And as hard-hearted as he'd obviously sounded to Helen, when it came to Karen what he most cared about was the toll her problems took on Dana Sue, who simply didn't need the added stress.

Unlike Dana Sue, Helen was not a woman who needed anyone to look out for her, which was yet another reason Erik was at a loss to explain why he'd kissed her so thoroughly a few minutes earlier. He was by nature a nurturer, a self-proclaimed knight in shining armor. The idea of tough-as-nails Helen needing nurturing was laughable.

Then again, maybe the kiss had been inevitable. She was a gorgeous woman, a little too uptight for him, a *lot* too opinionated. But sometimes just such a mix guaranteed an explosion sooner or later. Now that the kiss was behind him, the steam was released, and odds were it would never happen again.

He was just congratulating himself for making it all seem reasonable when Dana Sue came into the kitchen and joined him at the sink, where he was scrubbing pans. Picking up another pan from the sudsy water, she nudged him with her hip.

"So, what was that kiss all about?" she asked, keeping her gaze on the greasy pan in her hands.

"Pure impulse," he said, dismissing it.

"Something tells me the impulse has been coming on for some time. There's something in the air every time you two are in the same room."

"Tension," he suggested.

"*Sexual* tension, I think," she retorted, a glint in her eye. "Why haven't you done anything about it before?"

He rolled his eyes. "Helen and me? Are you crazy?"

"I don't think so. You're an incredible man. She's an incredible woman. Both of you deserve someone special in your lives."

"I don't know about Helen, but I'm not looking for a relationship," he said.

"You used to say you wanted me," she reminded him.

He grinned. "Because I knew there wasn't a chance in hell you'd say yes."

"So you claimed to want me only because I was unattainable?"

"Exactly."

"Not buying it. If you like the challenge of the unattainable, then Helen's an even better bet. Think of the fun you could have trying to change her mind."

"And then what? Tell her it was all just a game?"

"No, you idiot. Then you fall madly in love and marry her."

Erik laughed. "I don't see that happening. Somehow I just can't picture Helen's designer duds hanging next to my Levi's in the closet."

"After that kiss tonight, I can see it," Dana Sue told

him. "And judging from the way Helen ran out of here, I think she can see it, too."

"Stop meddling, Dana Sue. She's your friend and that alone is reason enough for me to stay away from her."

"Why? I'm giving you my permission to pursue this. In fact, I'm encouraging it."

"And what happens when one of us gets our heart broken? Whose side do you take?"

She looked vaguely disconcerted by the question. "It would never come to that," she declared.

"Really? You can see into the future?"

"No, but I have faith in both of you, and I saw something tonight, a spark, that hasn't been there before in either one of you. Passion—the real deal that leads to love—is a rarity. I'm here to tell you that a spark like that shouldn't be ignored."

"Well, I'm ignoring it," he said flatly.

"We'll see," she taunted. "I'm sure I can think of some way to change your mind." She shrugged. "Or Helen's. It'll only take convincing one of you to get this ball rolling."

"It's not up to you," he said, even though he could see he was wasting his breath. He was just going to have to be on high alert from now on.

Damn. That meeting tomorrow. He'd have to be in the same room as Helen and Dana Sue when the memory of that searing kiss was just a little too fresh in his mind.

CHAPTER THREE

Karen's heart was in her throat all during the first part of her shift prior to the meeting Helen had scheduled for two in the afternoon. Erik kept shooting daggers at her, as if he was really ticked off about something. She got the impression he'd been against the meeting. Dana Sue was trying to overcompensate by being extra nice, but the tension in the kitchen was really beginning to take a toll on Karen.

Added to that, they'd had one customer from hell, who'd sent her meal back three times. Erik and Dana Sue had finally drawn straws to decide which one of them would go into the dining room to deal with her and take a stab at making sure she left Sullivan's happy. Dana Sue had drawn the short straw. Free champagne and dessert for everyone at the table finally soothed the woman, but the whole exchange had ruined Dana Sue's mood. It was now as dark as Erik's.

At precisely two o'clock, Helen sashayed in, wearing one of those power suits she favored, a pair of Jimmy Choo shoes that probably cost more than Karen made in a week, maybe even a month, and designer sunglasses that she didn't remove.

Pointedly ignoring Erik, she smiled at Karen, then turned to Dana Sue. "Where do you want to meet? It's going to be a little crowded in your office, unless Erik has decided to skip the meeting."

There was a cool, antagonistic note in her voice that Karen didn't recognize. Something told her it didn't bode well for the discussion to come.

"Not a chance," Erik replied tightly, adding to the tense atmosphere.

"The last of the customers have gone. We can sit in the dining room," Dana Sue said briskly. "Karen, you want a soda or something? Helen?"

"I'm good," Karen said, too nervous to even try to swallow something while her future was at stake.

"Nothing for me," Helen said.

"Then let's get started, shall we?" Dana Sue said with obviously forced cheer, leading the way.

"Could I see you for a minute first, Helen?" Erik asked, his expression grim.

Dana Sue tucked her arm through Karen's and immediately steered her through the door into the dining room. "We'll give you a minute alone," she said to the two of them.

"What's that about?" Karen asked in a hushed voice.

Dana Sue grinned. "They had a little disagreement last night. Trust me, it'll be a whole lot better if they work it out before this meeting."

Almost before the words were out of Dana Sue's mouth, though, Helen appeared right behind them, her expression as grim as Erik's.

Karen leveled a worried look at Dana Sue and leaned close to whisper, "That's not a good sign, is it?"

Dana Sue sighed. "Not especially," she said, frowning when Erik emerged from the kitchen right on Helen's heels, his own expression even stormier than before.

"Okay," Helen said when they were all seated. "Remember, this is just a conversation among friends. The goal is to work out a solution all of you can live with. Karen's well aware that her absences lately have put a real strain on the two of you. Karen, why don't you tell them what's been going on and why you haven't spoken up before now?"

Swallowing hard, Karen avoided Erik's unyielding expression and focused on Dana Sue as she explained about the kids having the measles, the babysitter quitting and the financial stress she'd been under with Ray not sending child-support payments.

"I haven't told you before because *my* personal problems shouldn't be your problems," she said. "I know I've been unreliable and that it's unacceptable. But I swear to you if you can just bear with me a little longer until I can make permanent arrangements for someone responsible to watch the kids for me, I will be here every single minute I'm supposed to be. I won't have to hunt for someone new every day."

Helen held up a hand. "Don't make promises you can't keep, Karen. Let's face it, being a single mom is unpredictable. Dana Sue, you certainly know all about that. Here's what I suggest, especially after being here last night. Isn't it time you considered hiring another chef, or at least some prep staff who can be trained just the way you've trained Karen? That way if Karen *does* have another one of these inevitable crises, you'll have some backup."

"Why should Karen's problems force Dana Sue to hire additional staff?" Erik demanded.

"Because you need the help, anyway," Helen said before Dana Sue could answer. "Karen wasn't scheduled last night and it was crazy in the kitchen. If I hadn't shown up—"

"We'd have managed," Erik interrupted. "We always do."

"Come on, Erik, Helen's right," Dana Sue cut in. "We really are understaffed for the size of the dinner crowd lately. I've interviewed half a dozen people for prep work and given two of them a trial run, but neither one was right for us. I really need to accelerate that search. I've been putting off doing anything about it, because I wasn't sure the popularity of this place would last. That sometimes happens after rave reviews. The kitchen can't keep up for a few weeks and then people go back to their usual routine and you've got more staff underfoot and counting on you than you need and you have to let people go."

"Hiring someone to do prep work is one thing," Erik conceded. "But as long as we're still counting on Karen to be here, how does that solve the problem if she bails?"

"Another trained person can come in if Karen has an emergency," Helen said.

"And be paid overtime wages?" Erik asked. "How is that fair to Dana Sue? She has to think about costs, you know. And prep work is a far cry from being her assistant or sous-chef. We need someone who can move into that position, now that I'm assistant manager."

Karen studied Erik and Helen and knew there was something going on between them that had nothing to do with her. It was clear, though, that this discussion wasn't going to work in her favor unless she stepped in with a solution of her own. Fortunately sometime in the middle of the night she'd actually come up with one. Until now she'd been hesitant to offer it, but it was beginning to seem as if she had nothing to lose.

"I have an idea," she said quietly.

All three of them looked at her in surprise, almost as if they'd forgotten she was there.

"Go ahead," Helen encouraged.

"I worked with another cook at the diner 'til she had to leave. She had the same problem I'm having now. She was a single mom and her kids had to come first. Doug fired her, just the way I know you two have been debating about firing me. Anyway, Tess was really, really good, but she took a job telemarketing, so she could work at home. I know she hates it and would love to get back to work in a restaurant."

Erik's scowl deepened. "If she's already been fired for being unreliable, why would we ask for more problems by hiring her?"

"Because, frankly, she's got exactly the skills you need," Karen told him, determined not to back down in the face of his skepticism. She needed to fight for herself. To do that she had to convince them to at least give Tess a try. "She's fast. She's a quick learner. She's creative. She doesn't get rattled in a crisis. And she already knows her way around a kitchen."

"That still doesn't address the key problem," Erik said.

"Let her finish, for goodness' sakes," Helen snapped.

"Well, pardon me all to hell for wondering how this solves anything," Erik retorted, his gaze locked with Helen's.

Suddenly Karen got it. Whatever tiff those two had gotten into, it was because something personal was going on between them. She hadn't heard anything about them dating, but that didn't mean it hadn't happened. There were enough sparks bouncing around to set the tablecloth on fire.

Biting back a grin, she waved a hand to catch their attention. Dana Sue looked equally amused.

"Here's my idea," Karen said. "Let me and Tess share the job as sous-chef."

Helen looked startled, but to Karen's relief Dana Sue looked intrigued.

"How would that work?" Dana Sue asked. "Don't you both need a full-time job?"

Karen nodded. "But you're open six days a week, right? And you're open more than eight hours a day. One of us could work three days, the other four, and you could schedule our shifts to overlap. You need the extra help anyway on weekends. The sharing part would be that Tess and I would adjust that schedule between us if one of us had an emergency, so you'd never be left without a sous-chef. You'd have two trained people and you'd be covered all the time. The odds of both of us having an emergency on the same day are slight."

"I like it!" Helen said eagerly. "Dana Sue, what do you think?"

Karen held her breath.

"It could work," Dana Sue said slowly. "We do need the extra coverage. I'd have to meet Tess and see if she can handle the job or if she even wants it, but it would solve a lot of problems. Erik, what do you think?"

Though his expression remained grim, he nodded. "It has potential, as long as at least one of you shows up, no matter what," he conceded grudgingly. For the first time, he actually looked at Karen. "That's one of the traits I've always liked about you. You do think outside the box and you're not afraid to try new things."

Karen smiled at him. "Thanks. This time it was mainly out of desperation, but I really do think you're both going to love Tess. She's bright and energetic and loyal. She'd fit in perfectly here. And I know she and I can work things out so you're never short staffed."

"Okay, then, have her call me," Dana Sue said. "We'll get her in here and give her a try."

Helen sat back, a satisfied smile on her face. "A winwin solution. Good job, Karen. Thanks, Dana Sue."

Karen noticed she pointedly ignored Erik as she stood up. "I need to get back to the office," Helen said.

This time Erik shot out of the booth. "I'll walk with you," he said in a determined tone that silenced any argument. "Back in ten minutes, Dana Sue."

Dana Sue stared after him. "Take all the time you need."

After they'd gone, Karen met Dana Sue's amused gaze. "Are those two...?"

"Not yet," Dana Sue said. "But I predict it won't be long."

"My, my," Karen murmured, laying on a thick Southern drawl, "I do believe I could use some iced tea. It's gotten a little warm in here and I'm parched."

Dana Sue laughed. "Isn't that the truth? Come on. I'll join you. Something tells me we're going to be on our own for a while in the kitchen."

Helen was sorry she'd walked over to Sullivan's from her office. If she'd driven, she could have gotten in her car and slammed the door in Erik's face. Instead, he was walking along beside her in an increasingly awkward silence. Finally she could stand it no longer.

"If there's something on your mind, just say it," she demanded. "Otherwise, leave me alone."

"I'm trying to figure out what to say," he admitted.

"'I'm sorry' has a nice ring to it. Or 'I was wrong.' That's a good one."

"Okay, both of those," he said, his lips twitching.

She stopped and whirled around to look him in the eye. "That's it? I throw you a couple of options and you don't even repeat them or put your own pitiful spin on them?"

"But you're the one who's so good with words," he returned dryly. "I figured you put it exactly the way you wanted to hear it."

Helen rolled her eyes. "Oh, for heaven's sake, do you even know what you're apologizing for?"

"The kiss?" he suggested uncertainly.

The hint of vulnerability in a man who'd always struck her as supremely confident cut through her defenses. "That would be a good place to start," she agreed.

"There's more?" he asked.

Though his tone was perfectly serious, she thought she detected a hint of teasing. "You're darn straight, there's more. How about the fact that you were behaving like a horse's behind about Karen?"

"I was trying to look out for the restaurant's best interests," he said. "Something I thought would matter to you, you being Dana Sue's good friend and all."

"Of course that matters to me," she retorted. "So, don't you think the solution we worked out in there is the best thing for everybody?"

"Possibly," he said. "But by Karen's own admission, her friend was fired for being unreliable. In my book, that's not a terrific recommendation, no matter what her skills are."

"Not only a horse's behind, but stubborn as a mule, too," Helen muttered under her breath.

"I heard that," he said.

"As I intended," she replied, then studied him curiously. "I thought you liked Karen."

"I like a lot of people I don't want working in my kitchen," he said. "Not if they're not going to show up when they're supposed to."

Helen's lips curved in a small smile and she resumed walking. "Does that also mean you don't mind having someone you dislike working in your kitchen?"

"If they do the job well," he said, his gaze narrowing as he strode beside her. "What's your point?"

"You don't seem overly fond of me at the moment."

"Because you're annoying the hell out of me right now."

"And last night?" she teased.

"And last night," he agreed.

"And yet we worked so well together. Interesting," she said thoughtfully.

"What's so interesting about that?"

"The way your mind works. Can I ask you something else?"

"I don't imagine I can stop you, interrogation being one of your primary work skills."

"How did the kiss fit in?" she asked, clearly catching him off guard. Color bloomed in his cheeks.

"I apologized for that," he reminded her.

"I know, but what sparked it? A sudden attack of lust,

the heat of the argument, a desire to get even because of the pie I'd tossed at you?"

"I wish to hell I knew," he said.

"Come on. Think about it," she prodded, stopping to look at him. "I just want to know so I can avoid triggering that particular response again."

"You and me both," he said, then studied her intently. "You seemed to be into it at the time."

"I most certainly was not!" she replied indignantly.

"Bet I could prove what a liar you are."

Now there was a challenge that was best avoided. And since she seemed to be increasingly off balance around Erik, maybe it was time to turn the tables. After all, the man was seriously cute when he was befuddled. Feeling downright daring, she reached up and pressed a kiss to his cheek, hoping to throw him even further off-kilter.

"Let me know when you figure out how we wound up with our lips locked," she said. "We walked past my office five minutes ago and I need to get back there. See you."

"Hold it!" he commanded before she could leave. "What about the apology you owe me?"

Helen frowned. "Excuse me?"

"That pie you tossed in my face," he reminded her.

"You deserved it," she said.

"Maybe you deserved that kiss," he said. "Maybe I should take back that apology. After all, it could happen again."

Helen gave him a hard look. "Don't even think about it."

There was a daring gleam in his eye as he took a step

in her direction. She backed up and nearly tripped over a crack in the sidewalk.

"Okay, okay, I'm sorry about the damn pie," she said hurriedly. "Now I really do have to go."

She spun around and took off in the direction of her office as fast as she could, given the three-inch heels she wore. Viewed from Erik's vantage point, her haste probably wasn't a pretty sight, but impressing him wasn't real high on her priority list right now.

"Women!" Erik muttered as he watched Helen cut across the grass in an awkward gait and run up the front steps to her office.

But it wasn't women in general who made him nuts. It was *this* woman. He needed to stay as far away from Helen as humanly possible. Maybe he could figure out some way to get Dana Sue to ban her from the kitchen at Sullivan's. No, that was impossible, given Dana Sue's apparent matchmaking scheme, which, now that he thought about it, had probably kicked into gear months ago, when Helen had first been drafted into kitchen duty. If he suggested now that Helen didn't belong in the restaurant kitchen, he could all but guarantee that's where she'd turn up. Better to keep his mouth shut.

When he got back to Sullivan's, Karen and Dana Sue both avoided looking at him. He figured that wouldn't last, either. Dana Sue's curiosity would eventually get the better of her. When it came to cross-examining, she came in a close second to her attorney pal.

Thankfully he still had to finish the preparations for tonight's dessert special, an apple bread pudding that had become a customer favorite. It was on the menu every Friday night. Working quickly, he assembled the

ingredients, filled two large baking pans with the bread-
and-apple mixture, then poured the blended liquid ingredients over the top and popped both pans in the oven.
After baking, it would be cut into squares, then served
warm with a caramel sauce, whipped cream or cinnamon ice cream, according to the customer's preference.

Just as the pans went into the oven, he noticed Dana
Sue studying him intently, but before she could accost
him with questions, her husband walked in and her attention immediately shifted to him. Erik figured he
owed the man a beer for his excellent timing.

"Hey, Erik, Karen," Ronnie said as he made a beeline for his wife and pulled her into his arms. "Hey, you.
How's my favorite chef?"

Dana Sue glanced pointedly in Erik's direction. "Actually I was about to suggest to Erik that we take a break
before the dinner rush."

"Too busy," Erik said, heading toward the pantry in
search of the ingredients for walnut brownies he could
make now and freeze for later.

"Doing what?" Dana Sue asked, regarding him suspiciously.

"I thought I'd get a head start on next week and make
up some brownies," he told her.

Dana Sue beamed at him. "Sounds like an excuse to
avoid talking to me." She linked an arm through his.
"Let's take a break. Ronnie, how about bringing some
iced tea out for all of us?"

Ronnie regarded Erik with sympathy. "Sorry, pal.
She's the boss."

"At home, too?" Erik asked.

Ronnie grinned. "At home there's a delicate balance
of power that's ever-changing," he replied. "Unfortu-

nately, for your sake, we're in her restaurant now. I have zero standing here."

"Pitiful," Erik said. "I thought men were supposed to stick together."

"Normally, yes," Ronnie agreed. "But in this instance, I have to admit to being a little curious myself about why the prospect of talking to my wife has you as jittery as a june bug."

"Are you two through yet?" Dana Sue was impatient. "At this rate, there won't be any time left for a nice long chat."

"Now *there's* a reason to celebrate," Erik muttered.

Across the kitchen, Karen giggled, then buried her face in a paper towel in a futile attempt to smother her laughter.

"Another traitor," Erik noted. "Okay, let's get this inquisition over with."

Dana Sue frowned at him. "It's hardly an inquisition," she said, leading him to a booth in the dining room. "Just one friend catching up with another one."

Erik smiled despite his deteriorating mood. "How much catching up can we possibly have to do?"

"You were gone half an hour," she said. "A lot can happen in half an hour." She sat and patted the seat beside her. "Sit right here."

"I think you should reserve that spot for your husband," Erik said. "I'll sit over here." He sat on the edge all the way around on the other side of the table, as far away as he could possibly get and still be in the same booth.

Dana Sue regarded him with amusement. "How did your chat go with Helen? Did you two kiss and make up?" she asked just as Ronnie joined them.

Ronnie's eyebrows shot up. "You and Helen? Now that's something I never would have imagined."

"Be quiet," Dana Sue ordered.

"There is no me and Helen," Erik assured him. "It's all in your wife's imagination."

"I did not imagine that kiss last night," Dana Sue told him. "That kiss was hot enough to solder steel."

"How much do you know about soldering steel?" Erik asked.

"Beside the point," Dana Sue retorted. "You get the picture. Now, answer me. Did you kiss and make up when you walked her back to her office?"

"We walked. We talked. End of story. May I go now?" Erik said. "My bread pudding is probably burned to a crisp."

"It's not due out of the oven for another ten minutes and you know it," Dana Sue said without hesitation. "I want details about what happened between you and Helen."

Erik slid out of the booth. "Then call Helen. The doors of this place open in less than an hour and I have work to do, something I would think that you, as the owner, would remember."

He walked away without looking back.

"I won't forget about this," Dana Sue called after him.

Sadly, he knew that was the truth. Like most women, Dana Sue had a long memory. Worse yet, she had a streak of determination that could rival a wartime general's. Something told him her full-throttle campaign to get him hooked up with Helen had just begun.

CHAPTER FOUR

Helen hadn't been able to forget the way her evening had ended at Sullivan's a few days earlier. Nor had she been able to forget the speculative glances Dana Sue had given her and Erik during their tense meeting with Karen the next day. She knew that kind of look. Her friend thought there was something going on between Erik and her. Or maybe she just *wanted* something to be going on so she could feel good about her matchmaking skills. Either way, Helen was not looking forward to her next encounter with Dana Sue and the questions that awaited.

Unfortunately, she couldn't put off seeing her any longer. She, Dana Sue and Maddie were scheduled for one of their morning get-togethers at The Corner Spa today. Since Helen had been all for these regular meetings to discuss spa business, she could hardly skip one. Her absence would just bring Dana Sue's curiosity to a boil.

Besides, what with Maddie's increasingly hectic schedule—a new husband and a new baby took up most of her time—and Dana Sue's demands at Sullivan's and her remarriage to Ronnie, the three of them hardly had any time to themselves anymore. Helen missed their leisurely chats. She'd started to feel a little like an outsider in their busy lives, though both of them would be appalled if they knew she felt that way.

Filled with a peculiar sense of dread, she braced herself as she walked through the bustling workout room. Personal trainer Elliott Cruz waved to her, as did several of the women who were sweating through a spinning class. The instructor was really putting them through their paces on the stationary bikes.

Helen paused to stick her head into the lavender-scented spa area where Jeanette was busy giving a facial to a blissful customer. The relaxing aroma reminded Helen that she'd been promising herself a massage for weeks now, hoping it would ease the constant tension in her shoulders.

"Everything okay with you?" she asked Jeanette, whom they'd stolen from a very upscale spa in Charleston. With her very short black hair and huge dark eyes, there was something exotic about Jeanette that made most of their clientele think she'd come from Europe. At least until they heard her speak. Her accent was as slow and sugary sweet as any South Carolinian's.

"Perfect," Jeanette told her. "Be sure to ask Maddie about the idea I had the other day."

"Will do," Helen promised.

Jeanette had more ideas, most of them excellent, than everyone else combined. She'd brought a lot of experience and creativity with her when she'd come to work for them. Their day spa services had increased in revenue at an even faster clip than their gym memberships. The days of Helen thinking of her investment in The Corner Spa as a tax shelter were long past. The place filled a surprisingly large niche in the region and business was booming.

Jeanette had already justified the expense of adding another technician to help handle the ever-increasing number and range of beauty treatments and massages they offered to a clientele who wanted to be truly pampered. Even the women of Serenity, who'd never even considered the extravagance of getting a massage, were signing up to treat themselves on special occasions. And, thanks to Jeanette's word-of-mouth promotion, they'd sold a dozen gift certificates in the past week alone before Maddie had even had a chance to make their spa package marketing plan. If this kept up, The Corner Spa was single-handedly going to turn the previously well-kept secret of Serenity's small-town charm into a tourist destination.

When Helen couldn't put it off a second longer, she wandered onto the patio and spotted Maddie in the shade with her eyes closed. Obviously she'd seized the opportunity for a little catnap. Helen hesitated to interrupt her.

Maddie had only recently told them that she was pregnant for the second time since her marriage to Cal, something she claimed had taken both of them by surprise. Still, her previous pregnancy had gone so smoothly and she and Cal were so delighted with their daughter that she'd taken the fact of her second pregnancy in stride, though Maddie admitted she'd kept it to herself through the first trimester just in case there were complications.

Helen was the one who'd been thrown. Why did it seem to be so easy for Maddie to have a baby while she herself continued to wrestle with the decision about whether to take measures to have a child of her own? Sometime during the past year, watching Maddie breeze through her pregnancy with a doting husband by her side, holding baby Jessica Lynn in her arms and breathing in that powdery, just-bathed baby scent, Helen had become increasingly obsessed with the idea of having her own child. The depth of the yearning had caught her completely off guard. Up until then, she thought she'd been content and fulfilled with her single lifestyle and playing doting aunt to her friends' children.

Once the yearning had surfaced, though, it had taken over most of her waking moments, at least when she wasn't drowning in a sea of court documents. Lately she'd been working hard to get her high blood pressure in check, as the two high-risk pregnancy obstetricians she'd visited had advised. She'd made a dozen lists of the pros and cons about seizing her dream by whatever means necessary. But when it came down to actually taking the next step, she'd hesitated. She didn't know what to make of her uncharacteristic indecisiveness. Something was holding her back, but she had no idea what.

Pushing aside her own doubts and her envy of Maddie's pregnancy, she plastered a smile on her face and went to join her friend.

"Are you sure you're only a few months along?" Helen asked, waking Maddie from her nap. She patted the mound of her tummy. "Seems to me you weren't showing this much this early with any of your other kids. Maybe you're having twins this time."

"Bite your tongue," Maddie said. "One baby at a time is more than enough. I hate to think how exhausted I'd be if there were two of them."

Helen regarded her with concern. "If you're that tired, shouldn't you be at home with your feet up?"

Maddie grinned. "I work for these tyrants," she explained. "This place gets busier and more demanding every day. I can't get any time off. Besides, the baby's not due for months."

Helen sat down and studied Maddie's glowing face. With four children already—three from her first marriage to pediatrician Bill Townsend—forty-two-year-old Maddie hadn't been nearly as anxious as Cal to try again, but looking at her now, Helen knew that she was as excited about the new arrival as her husband.

Maddie studied Helen with a knowing look. "You haven't said much about it for quite a while now, but you're still thinking about having a baby, too, aren't you?"

Helen nodded. "I had no idea I'd ever feel such a strong maternal yearning, but every time you hand me Jessica Lynn and she looks up at me with those big blue eyes and blows those tiny little bubbles or smiles at me, it makes me realize just how much I've missed in my life."

"And?" Maddie prodded. "Did you ever follow through and talk to a doctor about whether your high blood pressure presents too much of a risk? When you didn't mention it, Dana Sue and I figured that you'd dropped the whole idea."

"To be honest, I'm a little surprised you haven't pestered me about it long before now," Helen said. "You're usually not that hesitant to poke about in my life."

"This is one of those decisions that's yours to make. Neither of us wanted to sway you one way or another. So, did you follow through or not?"

Helen wasn't sure why she'd kept those doctor visits a secret, but when confronted with a direct question, she saw no reason to lie. "I've seen two high-risk pregnancy experts," she admitted. "Both of them have said that if I promised to take extremely good care of myself and stay in bed at the first sign of blood pressure problems, I could go ahead with a pregnancy."

Maddie's brows drew together. "Then why do you look so unhappy? Isn't that exactly the news you were hoping for?"

Helen nodded. "Then I bumped straight into reality. Getting pregnant isn't the slam dunk I thought it would be. I mean, some women get pregnant just by going to bed with somebody once, but somehow I don't see myself going out and having some casual fling, hoping to get a baby out of it."

Maddie smiled. "Yes, I imagine you'd want to know the man's entire medical history and his pedigree, which pretty much rules out the whole casual thing."

Helen frowned at her because the remark hit a little too close to the truth. "My point is that this should mean something, you know? I can't imagine telling my son or daughter someday that I met their dad in a bar and never saw him again."

"Okay. What about artificial insemination?"

"I've thought about it," Helen said. "Even did some research on fertility clinics that do the procedure. There are very reputable ones. I could either bring in a donor or use one of their anonymous ones." She struggled to put her feelings into words. "It just seems so, I don't know, *artificial*. To be honest," Helen went on, "my reaction threw me. You know me. I take charge. I don't think I need anybody for anything, but the idea of having a baby that way seemed too cold and impersonal."

"So you've just given up?" Maddie asked, clearly surprised.

"No," Helen protested. "I've just taken a step back. I've been thinking about it."

"Making lists?" Maddie asked.

"Yes, I've made lists," Helen replied. "If more people did that, they'd make fewer mistakes."

"Whoa!" Maddie said. "On any level whatsoever, do you see having a child of your own as a mistake?"

Helen winced at the heat in Maddie's voice. "Don't say it like that. I told you that getting pregnant was only one of my concerns. What if I'm too selfish, too self-absorbed, too busy to be a really good mom?"

"Ah, so that's it," Maddie said. "Self-doubts plague just about everyone contemplating having a baby for the first time. You're not unique."

"I'm trying to be responsible," Helen said defensively. "I'm older. I'm alone. Is that going to be the best thing for a child? By the time my child's in kindergarten, the other kids will have grandmas my age."

"You're exaggerating," Maddie said.

"Only a little bit."

"Do you want to know what I think?" Maddie asked, then went on without waiting for Helen's reply. "I think you're just plain scared. This would be a huge step, a big change in your life and for all of your claims to being a modern, totally independent woman, you're terrified that you'll finally find something in life at which you can't excel."

Miffed at Maddie's perceptiveness, Helen said,

"Well, you have to admit it would be a really bad thing to mess up."

"Okay, let's go back to basics," Maddie suggested, studying Helen intently. "Are you really sure you want a baby? Or do you just like the *idea* of having a baby?"

Helen regarded her miserably. "I wish I knew."

"Have you ever known yourself not to go after something you really, really wanted?" Maddie pressed.

"Are you saying you don't believe I want a child at all?" Helen asked, startled by the thought.

"I'm only suggesting that your biological clock started ticking loudly when I got pregnant with Jessica Lynn and you realized it was now or never." She reached for Helen's hand. "Maybe it's never, sweetie. Not every woman has to have a child to be fulfilled. Maybe what you're really longing for is a powerful connection to another person."

"A man?" Helen asked incredulously. "You're suggesting I forget about a baby and just find myself a man? Now there's an enlightened point of view. Come on, Maddie. I think I know myself a little better than that. Besides, of all people, I know that relationships don't always last. Why would I want to set myself up for heartache?"

"I'm just telling you that maybe what you're feeling is an emptiness in your life that could be filled in some other way. If you haven't taken steps by now to have a baby, then perhaps on some subconscious level, you know that's not really what you want."

"Or maybe I just want one the old-fashioned way," Helen retorted, annoyed that Maddie was questioning her determination, even if she was asking questions Helen had asked herself a million times. "Did you ever think of that? Maybe I want a man and a baby and the whole family thing that you and Dana Sue have."

"But you just said…" Maddie began, obviously confused.

Helen could hardly blame her. She was confused herself. To her dismay, tears welled up in her eyes and spilled down her cheeks. "Excuse me. I need to get out of here."

"Helen?" Maddie called after her. "Come back here. Let's talk about this."

But Helen made a clean getaway—which she'd hear about later. In fact, she'd probably find Maddie and Dana Sue on her doorstep before the sun set. Although, maybe by then she'd somehow figure out what the hell was really going on with her and why this decision about a baby was the only one she'd ever been incapable of making.

Erik had come to work early, hoping to get enough done to cut out the second Dana Sue arrived and thereby avoid another conversation about his love life, or lack thereof.

He was surprised when the back door inched open and Annie Sullivan, Dana Sue's daughter, stuck her head in. "Is it okay to come in?" the seventeen-year-old inquired. "Are you really busy?"

"Just getting a head start on my day," he said, gesturing for her to come in. "Shouldn't you be in school?"

"Not for another hour," Annie told him, dropping her books by the door and climbing onto the stool beside his prep area. "My mom's not around, is she?"

"No. Why?" he asked. "Were you hoping she would be?"

"No. Actually I wanted to talk to you."

Erik regarded her suspiciously. "Why?"

"Because you're a guy and you're not my dad."

"An unbiased male point of view is what you're after," he concluded. "Are you sure I'm the right person? I'm not exactly a relationship expert. I assume this is about Ty."

She grinned. "Of course."

Ever since Annie's hospitalization with severe complications from anorexia, she and Maddie's son Tyler had gotten closer. They'd always been family friends, but Annie had wanted more, and Ty seemed to be showing some interest at long last. They'd been on half a dozen "real" dates, as Annie liked to call them, before Ty left for college, though both of them stopped short of saying they were actually a couple.

"What's your question?" Erik asked, studying her closely for signs that she'd fallen back into her old harmful eating patterns. It didn't matter how frequently he saw her, he couldn't seem to stop himself from checking. Fortunately her complexion had a healthy glow, her hair was shining, and even more telling, she was wearing clothes that fit and showed off a figure that was still a little on the thin side, but far from the skeletal form it had been a year ago.

"You know Ty's at Duke," she began.

Erik bit back a grin. "You've mentioned it a time or two since he left for school last fall."

Annie frowned at his teasing. "I mention it so much because it's amazing that I actually know a guy who's at Duke and who's the star of their baseball team, even though he's only a freshman. What's even more amazing is that we go out once in a while to movies and parties. He's even…" She blushed furiously.

Erik's gaze narrowed. "He's even what?"

"Kissed me," she confessed shyly. "It was totally awesome."

Although he wasn't her father, Erik felt like it sometimes, so close was he to the family. And like a father he did not want to hear about any guy, even a responsible young man like Tyler, kissing Annie. For sure Ronnie wouldn't be thrilled about it, either, even if kids their age often did a whole lot more than kiss. Still, maybe it was a good sign that Annie was talking about it. If things had gone beyond the kissing stage, he suspected she'd keep it to herself. He was so out of his depth with this stuff!

"You know there's nothing amazing about Ty liking you," he told her, opting for a lesson in self-esteem. "You're a terrific young woman. You could have a dozen boyfriends at a dozen different colleges if you wanted them."

"You're just biased, like my dad," she scoffed. "Anyway, my question is whether I should ask Ty to come home to take me to my senior prom or whether that would be totally lame."

"Isn't prom coming up soon?" Erik asked. "I think your mom mentioned something about taking you to Charleston to shop for a dress."

"It's three weeks away," she said. "So it's practically last-minute if I ask him now."

"Why have you put off asking him?"

"It feels weird. It's not like we're exclusive or anything. Don't guys like to do the asking?"

"As a general rule, yes," Erik told her. "But this is your event, not his. My guess is that Ty's probably wondering why you haven't already asked. You said your-

self you're not dating each other exclusively. What if he
thinks you're going with some other guy?"

"But I would never do that," Annie said, her expression dismayed. "I don't even want to see other boys."

"Then, if you want him to go, ask him. A man ap-
preciates a woman who's direct with him." He winked
at her. "Unlike women, we're pretty simple creatures.
Be straightforward and honest with us and we'll go
along with the program. Women are the mysterious,
complicated ones."

"I wonder if Ty thinks I'm mysterious and complicated," Annie asked, looking intrigued with the idea.

"I can just about guarantee it. He's nineteen. I doubt
he gets anything about women yet. I'm still working it
out and I'm twice that age."

Annie hopped down off the stool and hugged him.
"Thanks."

"Why didn't you just ask your dad or your mom
about this?" he asked.

She shrugged. "They're parents. They get all worked
up thinking I might wind up disappointed and I get a
half-hour lecture on not counting on too much where
Ty's concerned. That usually turns into a conversation
about disappointment leading to depression and bad decisions and eating disorders, yada-yada-yada."

"You mean I just blew this entire conversation by not
including a lecture?" Erik demanded, mostly in jest, of
course, though he did find these little tests of his un-
tried parenting skills to be disconcerting.

"For which I am very, very grateful," she assured
him. She grabbed a brownie off the tray he'd just taken
from the oven and took a bite as if to prove a point.
"Have a good day."

"You, too, sweet pea. Let me know how it goes when you talk to Ty."

She smiled, looking more carefree than she had when she'd arrived. "I'll call you tonight right after I talk to him."

No sooner had Annie exited through the back door than Dana Sue pushed open the door from the dining room. "Was that my daughter I saw sneaking out the back?"

Erik regarded her with his most innocent expression. "Was it?"

Dana Sue rolled her eyes at his pitiful attempt at evasion. "What did she want?"

"To talk to me."

"About?"

"Sorry, confidential."

Her gaze narrowed. "You and my daughter are having confidential conversations? I'm not sure how I feel about that. It was bad enough when she was having them with Maddie."

"I don't think this was something she felt she could ask Maddie," Erik said.

"Then it was about Ty," Dana Sue guessed at once.

"I never said that."

"Is she inviting him to prom or not?"

"I know nothing," Erik insisted.

"We could talk about you and Helen instead," she suggested.

"Sorry. Gotta run."

"Run where?" she demanded.

"Someplace where you're not," he said readily. "But don't take it personally. You know I love you."

"I think you love Helen," she countered. "Or at least like her."

"What was that?" he asked, already closing the door. "Can't hear you."

The door snapped open before he could make his escape. "I said that I think you're crazy about Helen," she shouted after him. "And just so you know, I think she likes you back! Can you hear me now?"

Unfortunately, Erik figured half the people of Serenity had heard her. And if they had, his life had just gone from peaceful and quiet, the way he liked it, to downright complicated. There was no more popular sport in town than watching, and then discussing, a cat-and-mouse game between a man and woman.

Erik had barely walked to the outer fringe of downtown Serenity when he literally bumped right into the woman who'd become the bane of his existence. Helen was striding purposefully along with her head down and her thoughts obviously somewhere else.

"Hey, where are you heading in such a hurry?" he asked, steadying her as she blinked up at him.

To his shock her makeup was streaked and her eyes were swimming with tears. "Helen, what's wrong?" He dug in his pocket and found a fistful of clean tissues. He handed them to her.

Even as she accepted them and mopped her eyes, bright patches of color bloomed on her cheeks. She tried to push past him. "I'm fine," she muttered.

"Sure you are," he scoffed. "The strongest, most in-control woman I know is walking around town crying her eyes out and claims to be fine. Not buying it, sugar. Talk to me."

"Erik, please," she pleaded. "Just leave me alone."

"Sorry. It's not in my genes to walk away from a woman in distress."

"I'm not in distress. I'm just confused, and before you ask about what, it's not something I want to talk about."

"Okay, then, we'll just go to Wharton's and get one of those hot-fudge sundaes I hear you Sweet Magnolias turn to whenever you're upset."

She regarded him with surprise. "You know about those?"

"I've worked with Dana Sue long enough to know a lot of things," he said.

"She blabs?"

He laughed at her indignation. "No, I have amazingly astute powers of observation for a man. Plus, I hear things."

"You eavesdrop?"

"I remain attuned to my surroundings," he contradicted.

"How is that any different from eavesdropping?"

"If you come with me, I'll explain it to you."

"I don't want to come with you," she murmured.

He fought a grin. "Do it anyway. Just think about what I'm offering—a hot-fudge sundae and someone willing to sit quietly and listen to all your woes. Do you know how many women would beg to be in your place?"

"I'm not one of them," she claimed. "I just want to be left alone."

"I'm sure that's your usual way of coping with things," he agreed. "Doesn't seem to be working out so well today. How about trying something new?"

"Spilling my guts to you?"

He nodded.

She actually seemed to be weighing the offer. When she finally nodded, he felt a far greater sense of relief than he should have. He attributed that to having been spared tossing her over his shoulder and carrying her into Wharton's.

"Let's go, then," he said, tucking her arm through his. "I'll do my best to make this painless."

"Whatever," she said, sounding a little like a petulant child.

"Think of it this way. If you had to spill your guts to a shrink, you'd be paying a hundred dollars or more an hour. I'm a bargain."

"And you're throwing in a hot-fudge sundae, too," she said grudgingly. "Is this my lucky day or what?"

"Told you so."

It remained to be seen if it was going to be Erik's lucky day or if this was going to be just one more step down a very slippery slope.

CHAPTER FIVE

Helen avoided Erik's concerned gaze and dug into her hot-fudge sundae. It might only be 9:00 a.m., but Erik had been right. The combination of rich vanilla ice cream, thick fudge sauce and whipped cream was just what she needed. She could barely remember what had thrown her into such an emotional tailspin and sent her fleeing from the spa and Maddie.

What the sundae wasn't accomplishing, Erik was. He was a very disconcerting man. Few other men would have dragged her out for ice cream at this hour or even guessed that it was what she needed. In fact, most men would have been put off by her tears and run the other way.

"You ready to tell me what's going on?" he asked eventually.

She took another overflowing spoonful of the sundae to avoid speaking and shook her head.

"Sooner or later you're going to finish the ice cream and you won't have an excuse not to talk," he reminded her as he lounged on the seat across from her, seemingly content to sip his coffee while she made a total pig of herself.

"I'll have to leave as soon as I finish this," she said, pleased with the perfect excuse. "I'm already running late for work. Barb will send out a search party if I don't show up soon."

His mouth curved into a smile. "Okay, then. You'd better start talking now."

"Look," she said, "I skipped breakfast. That's the only reason you were successful at persuading me to come here. My blood sugar must have been low."

"And is that what made you cry in public?"

She shrugged. "It can have all sorts of weird effects."

"Trust me, that's usually not one of them," he said.

He sounded very sure. She studied him curiously. "What do you know about it?"

"You have no idea how many pieces of miscellaneous information I have stored away here." He tapped his head.

"But you said that with some authority," Helen countered. "Is that because you read up on diabetes so you could keep an eye on Dana Sue?"

"Yeah, that's it," he said, but his expression had become shuttered. Helen sensed this was far from the whole story. Pushing aside the sundae, she put her elbows on the table and leaned toward him. Maybe she could avoid his probing questions by asking a few of her own. "I just realized that I know very little about you. Who are you, Erik Whitney? And what were you before you became a chef?"

"What makes you think I was anything before that?" he inquired.

"Because you'd just graduated from the Atlanta Culinary Institute when Dana Sue hired you. Unless you're a very slow learner, which I doubt is the case, you must have done something before you went there."

He seemed increasingly uncomfortable with the direction of the conversation. "Look, the only reason we're here in Wharton's is so you can get whatever's bothering you off your chest," he reminded her. "This isn't supposed to be about me."

"But you're so much more interesting, or at least your reaction is. What are you hiding, Erik?"

He regarded her incredulously. "What makes you think I'm hiding something? And what exactly do you think I'm hiding? Some nefarious past as a bank robber, perhaps? Or maybe you think I'm AWOL from the marines?"

"I'm an attorney. I deal in facts. I try not to have any preconceived ideas, which is why I'm asking you." She tilted her head and noted the closed expression on his face. "You know what I find absolutely fascinating?"

"Not a clue."

"You've gone all secretive and strong, silent type all of a sudden. Why is that, especially if you have nothing to hide?"

"No particular reason other than not liking to dwell on the past," he said, his tone indifferent, but a tic in his jaw suggested he was anything but indifferent.

"Well, just so you know, it's the kind of thing that kicks a lawyer's curiosity into high gear. The art of a successful cross-examination depends on being able to read body language and expressions." She surveyed him lingeringly, then added, "I'm considered to be very, very good at it."

"It's hardly the big deal you're trying to turn it into," he said. When she continued to pin him with her gaze, he finally shrugged. "Okay, here's the condensed version. I was an EMT. I decided it was time for a change. There's not a lot of drama in that."

Helen was less surprised by the revelation than she probably should have been. It explained a lot about how observant he was when it came to Dana Sue's monitoring her diabetes and the close eye he always kept on Annie and her eating patterns. Still, it didn't seem as if it were something he'd want to hide, yet he'd obviously been very reluctant to reveal it. She couldn't help wondering why.

"Did you like the work?" she asked.

"For a long time, yes," he said, his expression still guarded. "Look, if you're feeling better, I need to get back to the restaurant."

"Running out on me just when things are getting interesting?" She shook her head. "It intrigues me that a man who was trying to dig around in my psyche just minutes ago can't handle the idea of me asking personal questions."

"I wasn't the one having a public meltdown," he said. "If you spot me having one, feel free to ask all the questions you want." He tossed some bills on the table and was gone before Helen could formulate a response.

She stared after him, then distractedly picked up her spoon and ate the last few bites of her now-melted sundae.

"Now there goes one very sexy man," Grace Wharton declared as she joined Helen. "How'd you let him get away?"

"I think I scared him off," Helen admitted, vaguely unnerved by how guilty that made her feel. He'd been kind to her and he'd given her an excuse to take a few

minutes to gather the composure she'd lost after her
conversation earlier with Maddie. What had she done
in return? She'd cross-examined him as if he were some
kind of criminal.

"A man like that doesn't scare too easily," Grace
said. "You didn't mention marriage or something like
that, did you? That's the only thing I can think of that
scares a confirmed bachelor."

"The subject of marriage most definitely did not
come up," Helen assured her. "What makes you think
he's a confirmed bachelor?"

"I've seen just about every single woman in town
throw themselves at him at one time or another," Grace
said. "He flirts right back, but that's as far as it ever
goes. For a while I thought he might be hung up on
Dana Sue, but then Ronnie came back and that put an
end to that."

"Interesting," Helen murmured. She wondered what
Grace would think if she knew about the kiss Erik had
laid on her not that long ago. Her lips still burned every
time she thought about it. He hadn't shown any real
interest in repeating it, though. If he was a confirmed
bachelor, and that kiss had shaken him as badly as it
had her, maybe that alone was enough to make him
cautious around her, especially when the conversation
took a more personal turn.

Before she could pick apart her own theory, her cell
phone rang. She snatched it out of her purse.

"You planning to come to work anytime today?"
Barb asked wryly. "I have a waiting room filled with
clients and they're getting restless."

"Oh, my God," Helen said, glancing at her watch. It
was going on ten. "I got sidetracked."

"By Erik Whitney, if the rumors are true," Barb said, proving that the Serenity grapevine was faster than the speed of light.

Helen didn't fall in to her trap. "I'll be there in five minutes."

"Make it four," Barb retorted. "Your nine o'clock looks as if he might start breaking things."

"On my way," Helen said.

When she'd turned off the phone and jammed it into her purse, she looked up into Grace's fascinated gaze. "Never known you to be late for work," the woman commented. "Must have been something about the company."

Helen frowned at her amused expression. "Don't even go there."

"Can you think of any other reason you'd lose track of time like that?" Grace teased.

"Too much on my mind," Helen said, "that's all. Nothing to do with Erik."

"If you say so," Grace said, but she sounded skeptical. "Maybe you were hoping he'd kiss you again, the way he did at Sullivan's a few days ago."

Helen nearly groaned. So, Grace knew about that, after all. Unfortunately Helen didn't have time to stick around and debate the subject with her. And what would be the point, anyway? It would only add fuel to the fire. Grace had more than enough fodder for her lunch-hour gossip mill as it was.

"Mommy, I got a tummy ache," Daisy told Karen when it was time to get out of the car at the day-care center.

She'd picked her up from kindergarten five minutes

before and spotted her climbing a jungle gym when she drove up. She regarded her daughter with dismay. "You didn't look sick when you were playing with your friends on the playground."

"Because I wasn't sick *then*," she said, clearly exasperated. "I want to go home."

"You can't go home. There's nobody there to take care of you and I have to go to work. I'm working the late shift today."

Daisy's lower lip quivered. "But I'm sick," she wailed. "I can stay with Frances."

"Frances can't take care of you all afternoon and evening, Daisy."

"Please!"

Karen felt her own stomach twist into knots. She'd thought she'd put these crises behind her. She'd found a new day-care center that kept both kids 'til five, and thanks to Helen and Dana Sue, she'd found an excellent sitter to pick them up and watch them until she got home. For a week now things had gone smoothly.

In addition, Dana Sue had interviewed Tess and scheduled an on-the-job evaluation for tomorrow. Karen knew Tess would pass that with flying colors and then Karen's backup plan could be set in motion.

She reached into the backseat and put a hand to Daisy's forehead. No fever, thank goodness. "Sweetie, do you have a pain in your tummy? Or do you just feel sick?"

"Sick," she said miserably, then promptly threw up to prove the point.

Karen wanted to weep. It wasn't Daisy's fault. She needed to keep reminding herself of that. Kids picked up a million germs at school, particularly at Daisy's age. Karen grabbed some tissues and packets of baby wipes, then got out of the car and opened the back door to clean up her daughter.

"I'm sorry, Mommy," she said with a sniff.

"It's okay, baby. You can't help getting sick." The thought of calling the restaurant to tell Dana Sue and Erik what was going on made her feel sick to her stomach, as well.

"Do I still have to go to day care?" Daisy asked pitifully.

"No, sweetie. I'm going to take you home."

"And stay with me?"

"Yes, I'll stay with you." Maybe she could go to work once the sitter got there, assuming she still had work to go to.

Half an hour later she had Daisy settled on the couch in front of the TV with a glass of ginger ale. She was about to brace herself to face Erik's reaction, when it struck her there might be another solution. She dialed Tess.

"Tess, I know you're not supposed to have your on-the-job evaluation 'til tomorrow, but I've got a problem," she explained. "Daisy just threw up in the car. The sitter's not due for three hours. Is there any chance at all you could work today, if Dana Sue agrees?"

"Hold on and let me check with my mom. She came in early from picking vegetables because the heat was bothering her. If she's up to babysitting, I can do it."

Within minutes she was back. "It'll work on my end," Tess said. "Call me as soon as you've spoken to Dana Sue. I'll get ready in the meantime, just in case. Tell her I can be there in half an hour."

"Thank you! You're a lifesaver." As soon as she'd

hung up on Tess, she called the restaurant. Unfortunately it was Erik who answered. "It's Karen," she said.

"You're late," he said, obviously exasperated.

"I know. I was running right on time, but then Daisy got sick. I had to bring her home."

"Then you're on your way?"

"Actually I need to stay here with her," she admitted.

"Not again," he said, now sounding beyond annoyed. "Karen, things can't go on like this. I thought these last-minute absences were going to end."

"I know. I thought so, too. But it's not as bad as before. I've already spoken to Tess. She can come in for her evaluation right now and take my place. She said she could be there in thirty minutes, if it's okay with you guys."

"Fine," Erik said tightly.

"I'm sorry," she apologized. "I really am, but at least this proves that my suggestion about having two of us in this job will work."

"That remains to be seen," he said, then sighed. "Tell Daisy I hope she feels better. She's had a tough time lately."

"Thanks," she said. "Maybe you could come by sometime and have a tea party with her. She loved that." And Karen had gotten a huge kick out of watching the very masculine Erik holding one of Daisy's delicate, tiny teacups and drinking pretend tea.

"Sure," he said. "We'll work it out."

She hung up and called Tess back, then called the sitter to tell her she wasn't needed tonight. She'd either have Frances keep an eye on Daisy for a few minutes while she went back to the day-care center to get Mack, or she'd take Daisy with her.

In the meantime, she sank onto the sofa next to the now-sleeping Daisy and closed her eyes. Thank heaven for Tess. Without her pitching in, Karen knew that her job would have been history and there would have been nothing Helen or anyone else could have done to save it. Erik's fragile patience was obviously at an end. And though Dana Sue owned Sullivan's, Erik had a lot of clout when it came to decisions about what happened in the kitchen.

Not for the first time, Karen was nearly overwhelmed by just how close to the edge she was living. She had hardly any savings and very little reserve of energy for these constant emergencies. Sometimes when the kids were screaming and she was juggling bills, she wondered just how much longer she could cope without snapping.

Then she glanced over at her sleeping daughter, her long, dark eyelashes a smudge on her pale skin, and the force of her love for Dasiy flowed through her. She would do anything—*anything*—to protect her babies and give them the kind of loving home and security she herself had never known.

Helen wasn't one bit surprised when she opened her front door at eight that night and found Maddie and Dana Sue on the doorstep. The only surprise was that it had taken them so long.

"Shouldn't you be home?" she asked Maddie, then regarded Dana Sue just as inhospitably. "And shouldn't you be at work?"

"We would both be where we belong, if you hadn't taken off from the spa in tears this morning," Maddie said.

"And then landed at Wharton's with Erik, who was so concerned he dragged you over there for a hot-fudge sundae," Dana Sue added.

"I see it didn't take long for that piece of news to make its way around town," Helen commented sarcastically.

"It didn't have to travel far," Dana Sue said. "Erik told me."

"Really? I'm surprised. He doesn't seem inclined to talk much about himself," Helen said.

"In this case, he was talking about you," Dana Sue retorted. "He thought I should know my friend was upset. When Maddie called and confirmed it and said she was worried, too, we agreed that we needed to come by and check on you."

"Here I am, not upset," Helen said. "You can go home now."

"I don't think so," Maddie said, pushing past her. "I need to get off my feet. So does Dana Sue. It's been a tough night at the restaurant." Maddie headed for the sofa and sank into its cushions. "I hope you two can drag me up when it's time to go, but right now this feels heavenly."

"We'll manage," Helen assured her, then studied Dana Sue and saw that she did, indeed, look more frazzled than usual. "What happened at the restaurant tonight?"

"Karen bailed again. Fortunately she was able to get that friend of hers, Tess, to come in, but in some ways that just complicated things."

Helen's stomach sank. "How so? Isn't she any good?"

"She's great. In fact, I think she's going to work out just fine, but on-the-job training in the midst of the dinner rush is not exactly ideal. It took more time to explain how we do things than it would have for me or Erik just to do them ourselves."

Helen regarded her with concern. "But you're still going to give Karen's idea a chance to work, right?"

Dana Sue nodded. "I promised we would, didn't I?"

"I should call Karen and let her know," Helen said. "I'm sure she's terrified that you're fed up with her and her problems."

"I spoke to her a little while ago to tell her that we're definitely hiring Tess and that things are okay," Dana Sue told her. "You're right. She was relieved."

"Now let's get back to you," Maddie said, reminding Helen that she could be as single-minded as anyone on earth when she needed to be.

"How about something to drink?" Helen said. "Bottled water? Juice? Decaf coffee?"

"You're not going to distract us," Dana Sue said, looking amused. "You know us better than that. Maddie filled me in about the whole baby dilemma. Why don't you get one of the million and one lists you've no doubt made and go over it with us? Maybe we can help you sort things out."

"No," Helen said flatly. "Maddie was right this morning, when she said this was something I need to work out for myself."

Both women frowned at her.

"That was then," Maddie said. "This is now."

"You were *crying*," Dana Sue said. "In public. That is so not like you. Obviously this is too much for you to deal with on your own."

Helen sighed. "I'm stronger than you think."

"I would have agreed with that before this morning," Maddie said.

"Okay, look," Dana Sue began. "Maddie mentioned that maybe you want more than just a baby. She says you've been reexamining your whole life and that you think you might want the whole family thing."

"So what? You're going to snap your fingers and get it for me?" Helen retorted, sorry she'd ever opened her big mouth.

"We could," Dana Sue said. "In fact, if you would just open your eyes and see what's staring you right in the face, you could have it all."

Helen sighed. She'd seen this one coming a mile away. "Erik, I assume."

"Well, of course, Erik," Dana Sue said. "He's smart. He's gorgeous. And he's hot for you."

Maddie stared at her with obvious surprise. "Really? How did I miss that?"

"You've had other things on your mind," Dana Sue said to Maddie. "You missed the kiss."

"What kiss?" Maddie asked, clearly fascinated.

"Long story," Dana Sue said. "Trust me, though it made me go home and throw myself at Ronnie."

Helen moaned. "I am not having this conversation with you. And stop matchmaking. Erik and I are friends," she said, then corrected herself. "Not even friends. We're acquaintances."

"Sweetie, if a man kisses you like that, you're more than acquainted," Dana Sue replied. "You're about ten minutes away from falling into bed together."

"Grace Wharton says Erik is a confirmed bachelor," Helen countered.

"Nonsense," Dana Sue said dismissively. "Just because she doesn't have a line on his social life doesn't mean he doesn't have one."

"If he has one, then what makes you think he has any interest in someone new?" Helen asked. "You can't have it both ways. I think it would be best if you get over the whole idea of trying to shove Erik and me together. I know that's why you've been coming up with all those excuses to have me pitch in at the restaurant. It's not because you discovered I have hidden culinary talent."

Dana Sue's face was the picture of innocence. "We've been swamped every single time you've helped out, and you know it."

"Then how come you never asked Maddie to pitch in? She actually knows how to cook. So does Ronnie, for that matter. You used to ask him."

"Yes, why haven't you asked me?" Maddie demanded.

"Because you've been pregnant off and on for most of the past two years," Dana Sue answered. "You shouldn't be on your feet. As for Ronnie, what little spare time he has now that his hardware store has taken off, he needs to spend with Annie."

"Yeah, right," Helen said skeptically. "Face it, Dana Sue. I know what you're up to and I'm telling you right now to cut it out."

"But I think—" Dana Sue began.

"Don't think. Go home to your husband and drag him off to bed. Maybe if you're not feeling sex-deprived, you'll stop worrying about my love life."

"Trust me, not an issue," Dana Sue said, her cheeks flushed. "You're my friend. I want you to be as happy as I am."

"Me, too," Maddie said.

"Then, please, just lay off about Erik and about me having a baby. I'll work this out for myself when the time is right."

"We just don't want you to wake up when you hit fifty and realize that you have all these huge regrets," Maddie said. "The saddest question of all is 'What if...?'"

"You mean like what if I'd never mentioned to the two of you that I thought I wanted a baby?" Helen said testily.

Maddie frowned at her. "No, I mean like what if I'd realized how much I wanted one before it was too late. You can't go back, then, Helen."

The aching emptiness deep inside Helen, the ache she'd been trying so hard lately to pretend wasn't there, came back with a vengeance.

"Believe me, I know that," she said quietly. "It's not something I'm ever likely to forget, which is why I'm under so much pressure. I know I can't take forever to make this decision."

"Then get those lists of yours and let's talk about all the pros and cons," Dana Sue prodded.

"But..." Helen began, only to sigh when both woman regarded her with unyielding expressions. "Okay, fine. I'll get the lists."

She grabbed her briefcase and fished through it 'til she found the legal pad she'd reserved for just this particular topic. Page after page had been covered with her notes, including everything she'd been told by the obstetricians she'd consulted. Though she was filled with reservations about this entire conversation, she handed her notes to Maddie, whose eyes widened as she flipped through the pages.

"You could write a Ph.D. thesis with this much research," Maddie said.

"I thought it was critical to be well-informed," Helen replied defensively.

Dana Sue looked over Maddie's shoulder. "You consulted medical textbooks?" she asked incredulously.

"Well, of course, I did," Helen replied. "You don't think I'd rely on only two sources for something this important, do you?"

Dana Sue sat back down. "I think you're overthinking this whole thing. That's the problem. It comes down to this, Helen. Do you want to have a child of your own or don't you?"

"It's *not* that simple," Helen protested. "I can't just wave a magic wand and be pregnant."

Dana Sue regarded her with a wicked grin. "Well, the right guy could."

Maddie swallowed a laugh. "Dana Sue!"

"Well, isn't that really the bottom line?" Dana Sue retorted.

"No!" Helen said. "I have to know with every fiber of my being that I want this, that I can make the kind of changes in my life that having a baby will require. You were both a lot younger when you got pregnant for the first time. You were married. It was the natural order of things, the right time in your lives. Now, especially for someone who's spent her life so far married to her career, it's not that easy. Heck, Maddie, even you wrestled with the decision to have another baby when you and Cal got married, and you had him to support your decision."

"True," Maddie conceded. "But I'm still trying to pin down what has you worried. Is it a fear that you're incapable of devoting the time required to raising a child? Are you concerned just about the process of getting pregnant—natural versus artificial insemination? Are you wondering what will happen to your child if something happens to you? Or are you just afraid that you don't want this enough to disrupt your life? If that last one is it, then you're right to worry. This is not something to undertake unless you're totally committed to it."

Dana Sue reached over and took her hand. "You do know that we'll both be around to support you every single step of the way, don't you? You and this baby will have a big extended family. If you hit any kind of rough patch, you won't be in it alone, even if you do decide not to do things in the traditional way. You would be an incredible mom. Annie thinks so, too."

"My kids feel the same way," Maddie added. "They adore you."

Helen's eyes swam with tears for the second time that day. "I know that," she whispered, swiping at the annoying evidence of what she perceived as weakness. "I guess I never thought I'd find myself in this position. I thought I'd do it all the traditional way. Time just… got away from me."

"Well, it's not too late yet," Dana Sue said firmly.

"From a medical standpoint, I know that," Helen said. "But you touched on something that does worry me. What if something happens to me? Knowing I'm the only parent could make a child feel incredibly insecure."

"Which is why your child will always know they can turn to any of us," Dana Sue reminded her. "Now let's get down to business. We can stay here all night and go through those lists of yours item by item, if that will help."

Already somewhat relieved by their reassurances and their commitment, Helen shook her head. "No, but thanks. I'll work this out."

"Soon," Maddie said.

"Soon," Helen agreed, though she immediately felt the pressure starting to build again. She hated knowing that there was no time to waste, that a decision of this magnitude couldn't be put off forever.

Maddie struggled up from the sofa with an assist from Dana Sue. If she was this awkward now at only four and a half months, Helen couldn't begin to imagine how ungainly she'd be by her ninth month. For some reason the image made Helen want to weep all over again. She *did* want that for herself. The awkwardness, the belly out to here, the kick of her baby keeping her awake at night.

It was the aftermath that terrified her—the middle-of-the-night feedings, pacing the floor trying to soothe a crying baby, letting go of a tiny hand on the first day of school, having to make excuses to the court when her child had chicken pox, making sure homework was done, teaching her son or daughter the dangers of alcohol, smoking and premarital sex. The litany of things that could make the difference between raising a happy, well-adjusted child and a kid destined for disaster scared her out of her wits. Despite the accolades from Dana Sue, Maddie and their children, what if she was lousy at all of it? What then?

"You're overthinking it again," Maddie said, interrupting Helen's thoughts. She tapped her chest. "Listen to what's in your heart. It won't steer you wrong."

Helen hugged both of them fiercely. "Thank you for not listening to me when I told you to go away."

Dana Sue grinned. "Not a problem. We've spent a lifetime ignoring your orders. We enjoy it."

"That's true," Maddie agreed. "Now get some rest. Maybe this will all be clearer to you in the morning."

Helen doubted that, but she did feel better for having these two old, and very dear, friends offering her unconditional support. It was the one thing she should have realized she could count on long before tonight.

CHAPTER SIX

———✦◆✦———

Erik had been predisposed to dislike Tess Martinez,
mostly because he resented the way Helen had manipulated the whole situation to convince Dana Sue to hire
someone else for the kitchen. He also had major reservations about hiring another single mom after the problems they'd been having with Karen.

Yet he'd discovered it was all but impossible not to
like a woman who was little bigger than a bird and
whose sheer perkiness and good-natured eagerness to
work commanded his respect and approval. After only a
few days, he'd grudgingly conceded to himself—though
not to Dana Sue and definitely not to Helen—that Tess
was a real find.

Right now, nearly an hour after the restaurant had
closed, Tess was hovering beside him, watching every
move he made as he finished decorating a wedding cake
for a reception Sullivan's was catering on Saturday.

"So many flowers," she whispered reverently. "It's
like a picture."

"What was your wedding cake like?" Erik asked.

"Not so beautiful as this," she said sadly. "We had
no money for such things."

Born in the United States, and the daughter of Mexican immigrants who'd come into the country legally to work harvesting sugar in Florida, Tess spoke with a charming mix of Spanish and Southern accents. The family had worked hard, saved their money and had eventually started a small vegetable farm in South Carolina a few miles outside of Serenity. They sold their produce to local grocery stores and restaurants and at weekend farmers' markets, including the one started last summer in Serenity's town square. The instant Dana Sue had met Tess, she'd realized that much of Sullivan's produce came from Tess's family farm. Erik had known at that moment during the interview that Dana Sue would hire Tess even if the young woman could do nothing more than boil an egg.

If that alone hadn't been enough, though, Tess had also told them that her husband, Diego Martinez, had been picked up on a job for not being able to produce a valid green card and been deported back to Mexico before they could establish in court that he was here legally and that, even had he not been, his three-year marriage to Tess would have qualified him to stay.

Erik had a hunch it was a case Helen would want to be involved in, once she heard the details. Fighting the system to reunite two people in love might be a welcome change from the divorces she usually handled. And lately she seemed to be sticking her nose into all sorts of things that were none of her business, so why not this one?

In the meantime, though, Tess was struggling to make ends meet with two children under three. She'd tried making it on her own, but after being fired from the diner, she'd moved back home with her family.

Though they helped some with child care, they had their own long, hard days in their fields. Tess worked to help them and to put money away for the legal fight to get her husband back to South Carolina. Erik sympathized with her plight, but what had won him over was her quick grasp of any task assigned to her in the kitchen. In less than a week, she'd learned many of the recipes and executed them to perfection.

"Would you like to do this?" he asked now.

"Really?" she asked, awestruck. "You would teach me to make a cake so beautiful?"

"Sure. With the number of catering requests we're getting for wedding receptions, it would be wonderful to have someone to help out. Dana Sue had to turn down someone just this week because we had a conflict for that date."

"I could come in early," she offered at once. "I should not learn while I am being paid."

Erik smiled at her. "I think we can find the time during your regular hours, Tess. I'll talk it over with Dana Sue and we'll figure it out."

"But I'm willing to be here early," she said. "Please tell her that, so she doesn't think I am taking advantage of her."

"No one would ever think such a thing," he assured her. "You work as hard as anyone here. We're lucky to have found you."

A brilliant smile spread across her thin face, which was dominated by large brown eyes that sparkled with humor. "No. I am the lucky one, to have found a job I love. I am so grateful to Karen for recommending me and to you and Dana Sue for giving me a chance. I will not let you down."

Erik decided to broach the subject he knew weighed heavily on her mind. "You know, Tess, Dana Sue has a friend who's an attorney," he began. "She might be able to help you with Diego's case."

Tess's eyes immediately filled with regret. "I do not have enough saved yet to hire another lawyer. The last one took my money and did nothing."

Erik bristled at the thought of anyone taking advantage of her situation like that. "I'm sure Helen would be glad to work something out with you about the money. In fact, she might even be able to get it back from this lawyer who did nothing." He had a hunch Helen would enjoy that.

"Do you really think so?" Tess said solemnly. Then she glanced at her watch. "I'm late, as usual. My parents will be worried. Do you need me to do anything else before I go?"

"Not a thing. I'll see you tomorrow."

"And you will speak to Dana Sue about the cake decorations?"

"Absolutely," he promised.

"Muchas gracias," she said. *"Adios."*

Tess had been gone only a few minutes when Dana Sue came in. Erik frowned at her. "I thought you'd gone home hours ago."

"Paperwork," she said, pulling up a stool and sitting next to him. "The cake is beautiful. The Lamberts will be thrilled."

"Tess thought so, too. She wants to learn how to do this."

"She's eager to learn everything, isn't she?" Dana Sue said with a smile. "I like her. How about you?"

"She's working out a whole lot better than I expected," he admitted. "And it's certainly improved the situation with Karen, too. For the past few days she hasn't looked nearly as stressed out as she did before."

"So Karen and Helen did a good thing for us, didn't they?" she suggested slyly.

"Yes, Dana Sue. Your friend did us a good deed. Want me to pin a medal on her?"

"Nope. I just want you to stop keeping her at arm's length."

"I'm not doing that," Erik argued, though he knew Dana Sue was right. Ever since he'd found Helen in tears, he'd avoided her whenever possible. That hint of vulnerability in such a strong woman had cut right through his defenses. Okay, that and the still-vivid memory of locking lips with her.

"Have you spent two seconds alone with her since *the kiss*?" Dana Sue asked.

"I took her to Wharton's for a hot-fudge sundae, remember? That was just last week."

"Ah, yes, I seem to recall something about you running out the second she started asking you about yourself. Okay, since then? Have you seen her? Asked her out?"

Erik frowned at her. "The opportunity hasn't arisen," he replied. "Which reminds me, have you spoken to Helen about what's going on with Tess's husband?"

Dana Sue shook her head. "I wasn't sure it was my place. Tess might not want us meddling in her private business."

"I think you should. Sounds as if the case might be something Helen could really sink her teeth into, especially if some other lawyer cheated Tess out of a lot of money."

Dana Sue regarded him with dismay. "I hadn't heard about that part. That's really rotten."

"I thought so, too," he said. "I figured it would get Helen's dander up."

"It would," Dana Sue agreed. "Why don't you talk to her?"

He gave a nonchalant shrug. "You see her. I don't."

"You could," she countered. "Pick up the phone and call her. Invite her out for coffee to discuss a legal matter, since you're too chicken to ask her on a real date."

Erik scowled at her. "I'm not chicken. I don't want to date her."

"Oh, please," Dana Sue said scornfully. "Try telling me something I can believe. You're hot for her and that scares the daylights out of you. What I don't understand is why."

Erik had given that more thought than he probably should have, so he had an answer ready for her. "We're complete opposites, for one thing. Barracuda attorneys give me hives, for another. The list goes on."

"Haven't you heard? Opposites attract. And Helen's only a barracuda in the courtroom."

"Yeah, I noticed that when I got a pie in my face because she was a little ticked off at me."

Dana Sue's lips twitched. "You have to admit that was pretty unpredictable and funny, especially coming from Helen. She's usually so darn proper."

"Did you see me laughing?"

"No, I saw you planting a kiss on her, also unpredictable, but way too hot to be even remotely amusing."

"Whatever."

Dana Sue seemed to be even more tickled by his feigned indifference. "Well, it's up to you. I think you're right about Helen being the perfect person to handle that legal case for Tess, but I'm going to leave it up to you."

He saw right through her scheme and he wasn't falling for it. "Come on, Dana Sue. You talk to her."

"I don't think so. Not about that, anyway."

"You'd risk letting Tess twist in the wind, just so you can stick it to me and Helen?"

"I prefer to think of it as motivation for the two of you to get together. I know what a wonderful, compassionate man you are. You won't let Tess twist in the wind for long. Eventually we'll all get what we want."

"You're almost as annoying as Helen," he muttered. "You know that, don't you?"

"Of course, I do," she said cheerfully. "But I suggest you not kiss me to shut me up the way you did her, or Ronnie will have something to say about it."

Erik chuckled. "Yeah, I imagine he would. Go home, Dana Sue. It's late. Get your things and I'll walk you to your car."

"I think I can walk the twenty yards to my car unprotected," she said.

"Not on my watch, you won't, not even in relatively crime-free Serenity," he said. "Get your purse or whatever. I'll meet you at the front door."

When he'd finally tucked her safely in her car, she rolled down the window. "Helen needs someone like you," she told him. "Every woman does."

"Someone like me? What does that mean?"

"A knight in shining armor," she said.

"I'm afraid you've got the wrong man," he replied. "My suit of armor got tarnished a long time ago."

"I'll buy you some polish first thing in the morning," she said, "but believe me, the result will only be cos-

metic. The truth runs much deeper. Good night, Erik.
Sleep well."

He stared after her as she drove off into an inky darkness brightened only by a scattering of stars.

It astounded him that she saw him that way when it
was so far from the truth, so far from the way he'd come
to view himself ever since that night his wife had died.
Even if Dana Sue bought all the polish in the local Piggly Wiggly, he doubted it would be enough.

Helen sat in the courtroom and looked across the
aisle at Jimmy Bob West and Brad Holliday.

"What excuse do you think they'll come up with this
time to get another postponement?" Caroline Holliday
asked her, already sounding resigned to another delay
in her divorce proceedings.

"Actually I was thinking we'd turn the tables on
them," Helen said. "If it's okay with you, of course."

Caroline sat up a little straighter. "What do you have
in mind?"

"I had a detective I use do a little digging around.
I think I have enough evidence to show the judge that
Brad's been trying to hide some of his assets from us.
I'd like to ask for a continuance so we can find every
penny that man has tucked away."

Caroline regarded her with amazement. "But they
gave us financial statements, and those pretty much
matched all the records I had."

"Of course they did. They handed over everything
they knew they couldn't hide. Unfortunately for them,
there was an interesting little paper trail they weren't
so clever about concealing. Brad's a partner in some

out-of-state real estate ventures that add up to a tidy little sum."

"You're kidding me!" Caroline said, her mood improving considerably. "And I'm entitled to some of that property?"

"Or the cash from the sale of that property," Helen said. "And in my experience, if a man works that hard to hide some of his assets, it's probably only the tip of the iceberg." She studied the woman next to her, who finally had some color back in her cheeks and a glint of determination in her eyes. "So, do we go for it?"

"Absolutely," Caroline told her. "If only so I can see the look on Brad's smug face when he realizes we're on to him."

Helen chuckled. "I'm looking forward to that myself."

When the judge entered the courtroom a few minutes later, Helen was on her feet before Jimmy Bob could even shove back his chair.

"Your Honor," she began, shooting a quelling look at Jimmy Bob that had him sitting right back down. "We'd like to ask for a continuance."

For an instant Brad looked as if he'd just won the lottery. Jimmy Bob, however, was studying her with a narrowed, suspicious gaze. He obviously knew that she was up to something and that it didn't bode well for his client.

"I'm sure you plan to explain why," the judge said. "Especially seeing as how you've been against every delay the opposing counsel has sought."

"Indeed I will explain," Helen said. "May I approach the bench? I have some papers here to support my request."

She handed one set to the judge, another set to Jimmy
Bob. He took one look at the first page and scowled at
his client.

"What is it?" Brad demanded.

Helen tried not to smirk. "I'll be happy to explain,
if you'll allow me to, Your Honor."

"Be my guest."

Helen proceeded to outline the detective's findings.
"These papers lead me to believe that Mr. Holliday has
deliberately tried to mislead his wife and this court
about the extent of his financial holdings. We'd like time
to explore this further so we can be sure that whatever
settlement this court ultimately reaches will be based
on *all* the assets and not just those Mr. Holliday has
very selectively revealed."

The judge peered at the papers, then looked over the
top of his reading glasses at Brad Holliday and Jimmy
Bob. He was clearly unhappy about the position they'd
put him in.

"You have any objections?" he asked Jimmy Bob.

The attorney sat back with a sigh. "None," he mumbled.

"Well, I do," Brad said, leaping to his feet, his eyes
sparking with anger. "I have plenty of objections. What
right do they have to go snooping around?"

Judge Rockingham slammed his gavel on the desk,
then speared Brad with a look that had him sitting right
back down. "Every right," he said.

"Thank you," Helen said sweetly, delighted to see
Brad put in his place for once. "I don't suppose I could
make one more little request of the court?"

The judge gestured for her to continue.

"Could you order Mr. Holliday and his counsel to give

us another accounting of all financial assets? A complete one this time. Not that I'll take it at face value, but it'll be interesting to compare it to what we discover."

"So ordered," the judge said. "I'll see all of you back here in two weeks. Mr. West, see that Ms. Decatur has that revised financial disclosure by the end of business this Friday."

"But—" Jimmy Bob began.

"Do it!" the judge snapped, his patience at an end.

Outraged by his friend's ruling and angry at being one-upped by Caroline and Helen, Brad stormed past them and out of the courtroom almost before the door to the judge's chambers closed behind him. Jimmy Bob cast an admiring look at Helen.

"I guess you won that round," he said.

Helen bristled at the idea that this was some sort of game, though she knew divorce often turned into a competition of strategy and quick wits. "If you and your sleazebag client would play straight with us, we could get this over with instead of dragging it out interminably." She shrugged. "Then, again, maybe you like the way the hourly billings are adding up. Will you have enough for a down payment on some beachfront cottage if they go high enough?"

She snapped her briefcase shut and walked past him, while his mouth was still flapping like a fish on the end of a hook. Caroline was right on her heels.

Standing in the hallway, Caroline looked at Helen with pleasure. "That was almost fun. A divorce would be better, but watching Brad turn green had its moments."

"I predict we'll end this next time we're here," Helen told her. "They've been counting on us just sitting by passively while they play their games. They don't seem too pleased about the shoe being on the other foot. I suspect Brad will be anxious to get this over with before we discover any more of his dirty little secrets."

Caroline's expression sobered. "He's really furious right now. I've never seen him like that."

Helen frowned. "Are you worried about him retaliating?"

Caroline immediately shook off her gloomy expression. "No, of course not. I was married to him for years, for goodness' sakes."

Though her tone was firm, Helen thought she detected a trace of doubt. "You sure?"

"I'm sure," Caroline said, then glanced at her watch. "It's almost noon. Do you have time for lunch? My treat. We can go to Sullivan's."

"I wish I could," Helen told her. "But I have to run. My calendar's booked solid all day today. Another time, though."

She reached into her briefcase and extracted a gift certificate for The Corner Spa. She, Dana Sue and Maddie had each taken half a dozen of the complimentary gift certificates to use for promotion. Given to the right people, they were excellent for spreading the word about the spa's services. "Tell you what. Why don't you go over to the spa and have a massage or facial to celebrate today's victory? I'll call Jeanette and make sure she fits you in."

Caroline's eyes lit up. "I'd love to do that. I've been dying to try the spa because all my friends have been talking about it, but since all of this mess started with the divorce, I've had to cut out anything that wasn't an absolute necessity."

"That'll change once we get the final divorce decree," Helen promised. "You and the kids will be well provided for."

"After today, I'm actually beginning to believe that," Caroline said. "Thank you."

"Just doing my job," Helen said.

Karen gave the gazpacho she'd made for the lunch soup special another lackadaisical stir, then put it in the refrigerator to chill. She was so exhausted she could barely put one foot in front of the other, but she'd come in to work, anyway. She hadn't dared to ask for any more time off, not even knowing that Tess could back her up.

Her exhaustion must have been showing, because Erik came into the kitchen and asked, "You okay?"

"Just tired," she said. "Daisy's still sick, but the sitter was able to spend the day with her today."

"She keeping you up at night?" Erik asked.

Karen nodded. "But I'm fine. The gazpacho's made and the salads are chilling, as well."

"Then why don't you take a break for a few minutes?" he suggested. "Have a little of that gazpacho. Last time you made it, it was outstanding. The customers have been clamoring for it ever since, especially on these hot days."

"You know, I think I will," she said, then ladled some of the chilled soup, with its spicy mix of tomatoes, green peppers and onions, into a bowl. She pulled a stool up to the counter and tasted it. To her shock, it almost took off the roof of her mouth.

"Oh, my God!" she said, spitting it back into the bowl. "We have to throw it out."

Erik regarded her with dismay. "What's wrong with it?"

Karen winced. "I must have put in too much hot

sauce, thinking it was the Worcestershire," she said. "I'm so sorry. I don't know where my head was."

"Probably trying to catch up on the sleep you missed," Erik said. "It happens. Fortunately there's time to make another batch. I'll help you chop the vegetables."

"Maybe you'd better add the seasonings," she said. "Obviously I can't be trusted."

Erik studied her worriedly. "Karen, is there more going on here than you're admitting? Are you getting sick, too?"

"No," she said firmly, panicked that he might insist she go home. Not only would that be another black mark against her, but she needed the income. Her last two paychecks had suffered from all the unpaid leave she'd had to take. "I'll have another cup of coffee and I'll be fine by lunchtime."

"If you're sure," Erik said, his skepticism plain.

"Look, I know you're not happy with me or with my work, but I'm trying," she told him. "Please bear with me a little longer."

"We're trying to do that," he told her. "But you know there's a limit. We can't afford to have the quality of the food we serve suffer because you're only half-awake."

Tears welled up in her eyes. "I know that. It's just that there are days when everything gets to be too much, you know. I'm not getting enough sleep. And I don't see any end in sight. On top of everything, I'm worried about bills." She stopped herself. "I'm sorry. I have no business whining to you. These are not your problems."

Erik regarded her with unexpected compassion. "But you are a part of this team," he reminded her, his tone gentle now. "And even though I'm tough on you, I do care about what's going on in your life. If Dana Sue and I can help, we want to."

"Unless you want to babysit my kids, so I can sleep for a week, I don't know what else you can do, except be patient with me. I'm doing everything I can to stay on track."

"I know you are," he said.

Maybe it was the gentleness in his voice or the fear that she was way too close to blowing everything, but Karen burst into tears and ran from the kitchen, leaving behind a bewildered Erik.

In the restroom, she splashed her face with cold water, then clung to the edge of the sink to steady herself. She was so close to being completely out of control it terrified her. Thanks to her mother's total irresponsibility, she'd learned at an early age that she had only herself to rely on. Half the time her mom had been too busy with her boyfriends to even notice Karen was around. Even when her marriage had fallen apart, she'd kept it all together. Lately, though, the least little thing seemed to overwhelm her.

"Get a grip," she muttered, studying her pale face in the mirror. "You cannot afford to lose this job."

She drew in a deep breath, then another, until she was finally feeling calmer and more together. She pulled a lipstick from her pocket and touched up the glossy shade of pink on her mouth. The color helped.

Just as she was about to go back to the kitchen and apologize, Dana Sue came in, a worried frown creasing her brow.

"Are you okay? Erik is beside himself that he made you cry."

"It wasn't his fault," Karen assured her. "I'm a mess."

She forced a smile. "I'm all ready for the lunch rush, though, I promise."

She started to brush past Dana Sue before she had another meltdown, but Dana Sue stopped her.

"Do you need time off?" she asked. "I'll figure out a way to pay you for a week or two, if it will help."

Karen shook her head. "I have to learn how to handle everything that's going on in my life. If I don't, a couple of weeks off won't make any difference."

"You'd be able to get some rest. Things always look a lot worse when you're exhausted."

"I appreciate the offer, I really do, but no."

"Karen, don't turn your back on help when it's offered," Dana Sue said. "You won't be any good to us or your kids, if you fall apart."

"There are plenty of single moms who have it tougher than I do," Karen insisted. "You've already done more for me than I have any right to expect."

"Because when you're on top of things, you're an excellent candidate to become a sous-chef," Dana Sue said.

"And I'm going to prove you're right to have faith in me," Karen said. "I'm going to get my act together, I swear it."

Dana Sue sighed. "Just let me know if you change your mind and want that time off."

Karen nodded. "Now I'd better get back to work. I have another batch of gazpacho to make."

She also had a whole lot to prove to these two people who were bending over backward to accommodate all her crises. Failing them just wasn't an option.

CHAPTER SEVEN

"**W**hat is wrong with you?" Dana Sue demanded when Helen walked onto the patio at The Corner Spa a few mornings after she'd tried to push Erik into calling her.

Helen frowned at her. As much as she relished confrontation and sparring in the courtroom, she didn't want to deal with it with her friends. "Excuse me? What have I done to you?"

"Not me. Erik. The sexiest, nicest man to cross paths with you in years kisses you senseless and you do absolutely nothing about it," Dana Sue accused. "I thought you wanted a real relationship in your life. Wasn't that on that endless list of goals you set awhile back? That and having a baby? And learning to kick back and relax? You're about as relaxed these days as a cobra poised to strike. I can't help wondering what Doc Marshall and those pricey obstetricians you saw would have to say about that."

Helen looked from her to Maddie. "I suppose you agree with her?"

Maddie shrugged. "Pretty much."

"Haven't we had this conversation before?" Her

scowl deepened as she squared off with Dana Sue. "I really, really don't want to have it again."

"Do I look like I care?" Dana Sue retorted. "You're throwing away what could be your best chance to get everything you claim to want because you're stubborn."

"I am not..." Maddie's smile and Dana Sue's incredulous look stopped her from completing the thought. "Okay, I am stubborn, but that's not the issue. This is my life. I make my own decisions."

"Then make one!" Dana Sue snapped. "Stop dawdling."

"I can't rush a decision about having a baby," Helen said. "There's too much at stake."

"Then at least go out on a date with Erik," Dana Sue pleaded. "Surely that's not a difficult decision to make."

Helen shrugged. "He hasn't asked."

"Then ask him," Dana Sue said. "Since when are you some shy, retiring wallflower who waits to be asked? Aren't you the woman who prides herself on being direct, on going after what she wants?"

"I second that," Maddie said, then rested a hand on her stomach. "And as fascinating as it is to watch you trying to wriggle off Dana Sue's matchmaking hook, I think maybe we ought to table it for this morning. We need to start thinking about our plan for running this place while I'm on maternity leave."

Helen took a deep breath, relieved by the change of topic. She grinned at Maddie. "You do like to plan well ahead, don't you? By my calculations, there's plenty of time left."

"I'll feel better if we get a plan down on paper," Maddie said. "I'll be able to check one thing off my list. Cal seems to have a list of his own that requires my attention."

"What's on his list?" Helen asked curiously.

"He wants to turn the attic into some sort of play-room. It sounds like something out of a Jane Austen novel to me. You know, lock all the kids away upstairs with a nanny." She shook her head. "Anyway, he's de-termined. He thinks Jessica Lynn and the new baby should have a special place. Yesterday he came home from Ronnie's store with enough wallpaper samples and paint chips to decorate the entire town. It'll take me days just to sort through them."

"I could help," Helen offered. "It would be fun."

"Be my guest," Maddie said. "In the meantime, though, focus, you guys. We need a plan."

Dana Sue shrugged. "I figured you could run the spa from home," she teased. "Isn't that what you did last time, even though we officially left Jeanette in charge?"

"That's what I remember, too," Helen concurred.

Maddie scowled at them. "Okay, we all know I'm a control freak. And maybe I could keep tabs on every-thing with one baby in the house, but with two we're talking a whole new ball game. Kyle insists he's changed his last diaper. Ever since Jessica Lynn's arrival, Katie resents not being the baby anymore. She's not exactly ecstatic about yet another baby coming along. I doubt I can count on her for much help. It's spring, so Cal has baseball practice and games just about every day. And Tyler's away at Duke for another two weeks, not that he'd be that much help, anyway. He's determined to get a summer job."

Helen glanced at Dana Sue, who nodded. "It's a little early for this, but we thought you might be feeling a little overwhelmed," she said, reaching into her briefcase and extracting a flat, rectangular package. "Which is why we got you a little something, since you refused to let us give you another baby shower."

Maddie took the package, eyeing it with suspicion. "What is this?"

"You'll see," Dana Sue told her. "Just open it."

Helen watched her as Maddie carefully undid the bow, then removed the wrapping paper and folded it neatly. "Will you hurry up," she prodded.

Maddie grinned at her. "I love to draw out the suspense," she said as she extracted a gift certificate from the folds of tissue paper. She studied it for several seconds, then stared at them with a stunned expression. "You hired a nanny service for me? For a year?"

Helen and Dana Sue exchanged high fives at the shocked note in her voice.

"You get to do the interviewing and hiring," Helen assured her. "But it's all paid for. We need you to be happy and serene and we thought a nanny might help you to accomplish that. Cal agreed it was the perfect gift."

"Perfect?" Maddie echoed. "It's amazing and generous. Too generous, in fact."

"Don't be ridiculous," Dana Sue said. "Think of it as one of the perks of the job, to say nothing of being our friend. This place has become a gold mine, thanks to you. Besides, we love you."

Maddie sat back in her chair, the gift certificate clutched tightly in her hand. "I'm… I'm overwhelmed."

"Not too overwhelmed to hear us when we tell you we don't want you to even think about setting foot in this place for at least six weeks after the baby arrives, longer if you can stand it," Helen told her. "You've trained Jeanette to handle every single detail. Let her do it."

"And we'll check on her," Dana Sue promised. "If there's a problem, she can come to either one of us. You rest, enjoy your family and take advantage of the free personal training Elliott is offering to give you at home whenever you're ready to get back your girlish figure."

"My figure hasn't been girlish in twenty years," Maddie said ruefully. "But you know, for once I might just listen to you and do absolutely nothing for a few weeks at least."

Dana Sue regarded her with amusement. "Two little ones under two and you honestly think you'll get away with doing nothing? You're delusional."

"But the nanny will help," Helen said. "And Dana Sue and I are only a phone call away if you need backup."

Maddie studied her with a narrowed gaze. "Are you thinking you could use the practice?"

"Don't go there," Helen pleaded. "I'm still wrestling with all my options, and no, I do not want to talk about them in case you were thinking I might have changed my mind about that in the last three minutes."

"Then I guess there's nothing fascinating to be learned here," Dana Sue said, resigned. "I need to get to the restaurant. Karen hasn't exactly been on the top of her game lately, so I need to keep a close eye on her."

Helen frowned. "You're still having problems with her? I thought bringing Tess on board would solve everything."

"It's certainly helped," Dana Sue said. "But this is about Karen's state of mind. She's thoroughly sleep-deprived, if you ask me. She's been showing up, but she's not all there. Don't worry about it, though. I'm sure it's just going to take a little time for her to learn how to juggle everything going on in her life. Being a single mom is never easy, even in the best of circumstances."

"Amen to that," Maddie said. "Those months I was on my own with Ty acting out, Kyle all closed off and Katie sobbing her heart out for her daddy every night were among the worst months of my life. And that was even with their dad only a phone call away, my mom pitching in, *and* after Cal came along. I can't imagine how I would have coped without all that support and you guys around to listen to me."

"I could speak to Karen again," Helen offered, feeling somehow responsible for the younger woman. Maybe, deep down, she even feared that Karen's apparent inability to cope with her kids and her job was a warning about the struggles she herself would face if she did decide to have a baby on her own.

"Come on," Dana Sue protested. "This isn't your problem to solve."

"Maybe not, but Karen obviously doesn't have the kind of support system we all have," Helen said. "Maybe we could figure out a way to get that for her."

Dana Sue shook her head. "No, right now I think our butting in, especially me, will only add to the pressure she's feeling."

Helen considered that, then sighed. "You're probably right. But let me know if you think I can help."

"Sure," Dana Sue said. "There *is* another situation I'd like you to look in to, but Erik promised he'd fill you in."

Helen studied her with a narrowed gaze. "His idea or yours?"

"Does it matter?" Dana Sue asked.

"More than likely," Helen muttered.

Oddly, though, she felt a little hum of anticipation speed through her at the prospect of crossing paths with him again, no matter the reason.

Probably not a good sign.

Erik tried to get out for a walk every afternoon between the end of the lunch crowd and the beginning of the dinner rush. At one time he would have run, but recently his knee bothered him if he did. Walking wasn't the same, but at least it gave him time to collect his thoughts, which lately had been chaotic. Helen Decatur seemed to inhabit his head a whole lot more than he was comfortable with.

Picking up his pace on the warm, sticky afternoon, he passed through downtown Serenity, if it could be called that with only Wharton's Pharmacy and its soda fountain and Ronnie's hardware store anchoring the main square. A lot of empty storefronts remained and probably would until a few more people showed a willingness to take the sort of risk Ronnie had when he'd revived the old hardware store and added the kind of creative spin that made it economically viable. Working with local developers to fill their construction-supply needs had been brilliant.

When Erik reached the town park, where swans swam on a small, sparkling lake, he was grateful for the shade provided by the old oak trees, heavily draped with Spanish moss.

Intent on keeping up his pace, he was almost on top of Helen before he saw her. She was seated on a bench, an oddly pensive expression on her face.

"Hey," he said, stopping in front of her. "You playing hooky from the office again?"

Clearly startled by the sound of his voice, she glanced at him and color rose in her cheeks. "Something like that," she said.

"Same thing troubling you that was on your mind the other day?"

"I suppose," she said tonelessly. "What are you doing out at this time of day? Shouldn't you be chopping and dicing and marinading for dinner by now?"

"Soon," he said, then sat down beside her. "Actually I've been hoping to bump in to you."

"Oh? Why is that?"

He grinned at the suspicion in her voice. "Do you always suspect an ulterior motive when someone wants to talk to you?"

She shrugged, her expression rueful. "Mostly."

"Well, my motives are pure. This is about Tess, Karen's friend."

"Ah, yes," Helen said. "How's she working out?"

"Surely Dana Sue has told you," he said.

"She has, but I'd like your perspective."

"Well, she's amazing," he said, then cast a sideways glance at her. "Dana Sue says we owe you for that."

"I didn't find her. Karen did."

"But you opened us up to the possibility of some solution other than firing Karen and replacing her," he said.

"If Tess is working out so well, why did you want to discuss her with me?"

Erik took a deep breath. "She could use some legal help, but she's not making a lot of money. I don't think it's the kind of problem that should be held up until she can afford to hire the best, especially since some other lawyer took her money and never did a thing to help her."

Helen immediately sat a little straighter. "Explain," she said briskly.

He told her what little he knew about Diego Martinez's situation and Tess's previous attorney. "Is there anything you can do?"

"At the very least I can pin this jerk's tail feathers back a little and get her money returned. And I can certainly look into her husband's case, even though immigration law is a far cry from what I normally do. Does she know you're talking to me?"

"I mentioned that a friend of Dana Sue's might be able to help, but Tess was reluctant to ask because of the whole money thing."

"Tell her not to worry about that. Make sure she calls me." She glanced at her watch. "Is she working now? If she is, I'll walk back over to Sullivan's with you and speak to her right now."

"No, she's off today, but she'll be there tomorrow," Erik told her. "Can you come by then?"

"I'll try, and before you remind me, I'll avoid coming during peak hours."

"Tired of being drafted into working in the kitchen?" he teased.

"No, to be honest, it's one of the few things that seems to relax me lately."

He regarded her with surprise. "Really? What do you have to be uptight about? You're smart. You're successful. You're beautiful."

"Thank you, but it has recently come to my attention that there's more to life."

He laughed at that, though he gave her a commiserating look. "Dana Sue been filling your head with notions, Helen?"

"She and Maddie," she confirmed. "I suspect you've fallen victim as well."

"I have," he said.

"Any advice?"

"Hey, you've known Dana Sue longer than I have. You could probably give me a few pointers."

"I seem to have run out of arguments that work with her, especially since she's back with Ronnie and thinks the world should operate like Noah's ark, you know, in pairs."

Erik's gaze locked with hers. He couldn't seem to look away from that hint of vulnerability he saw once again in her eyes. "I guess we both just need to stick to our guns."

"I suppose so," she said, though with surprisingly little enthusiasm.

"We could go out for coffee sometime, plan our strategy for keeping Dana Sue from meddling in our lives," he suggested. "How much misery can she stir up if we're both on the same page?"

Something that might have been disappointment streaked across her face, but she recovered so quickly, Erik was certain he'd been mistaken.

"That sounds like a plan," she finally agreed with a forced note of cheer in her voice. "I guess Grace was right about you."

"Grace? How did she get involved in this?"

"She says you're a confirmed bachelor."

"Not always," he said, clearly taking her by surprise.

"You've been married?"

He nodded.

"Divorced?"

He shook his head. "She died." Before Helen could pester him with a lot of questions he had no intention of answering, he was on his feet. "Thanks for agreeing to look into Tess's situation, Helen."

"Not a problem. See, even barracuda attorneys have their good side."

Erik winced. "Sorry about calling you that."

"Hey, you're entitled to your opinion. And frankly, I'm rather proud to be called that. If you have to go into court, a barracuda attorney is exactly who you want fighting for you."

"So, we're still friends?"

She grinned at him. "Of course we are, though it would help if you'd answer some of my questions, instead of stonewalling me. Real friendship is all about conversational give-and-take."

"So I hear," Erik said.

"Then you'll tell me all your deep, dark secrets?" she asked.

"Nah," he replied. "What would be the fun in that? I think I like the idea of you being frustrated and wanting more."

"Is that an ego thing?"

"Nope. It's a guy thing. See you around. Come by and chop and dice sometime," he invited. "We miss you in the kitchen. And we will have that coffee one of these days."

Even as he walked away, he realized that the offhand comment about missing her was absolutely true. He'd enjoyed having her underfoot in the kitchen. When Helen was on his turf, the whole barracuda thing disappeared and she was just an intelligent, attractive woman who made his hormones sit up and take notice. It had been a very long time since any woman had done that.

And *that* was something he hoped to hell Dana Sue never found out or she'd make both their lives a matchmaking nightmare.

Three-year-old Mack had barely closed his eyes for the night when he woke up screaming. Karen, who'd fallen asleep in front of the TV, jolted awake and ran into the bedroom to find Mack trying to climb out of his crib and Daisy trying to shove him back in, which only made Mack cry harder.

"It's okay," Karen told Daisy. "I've got him."

"If he gets to stay up, I do, too," Daisy said, her face setting stubbornly.

"No," Karen said, holding on to her temper by a thread. "You need to get some sleep. You have school in the morning."

"It's not fair," Daisy wailed.

"I don't care if it's fair or not. It's the way it is," Karen told her, even as Mack continued to sob in her arms. "Please, sweetie, let me try to get your brother to settle down. Go back to sleep."

"He's making too much noise," Daisy protested.

"Which is why I'm taking him with me into the other room," Karen explained patiently. "Now, crawl back into bed and put your head down. You'll be asleep in no time."

After giving her mother one last mulish look, Daisy finally did as she'd asked. Karen bent over to press a kiss to her forehead, then carried Mack into the living room.

"Okay, sweetie, what's up with this?" she asked, resting a hand against Mack's damp, satin-soft cheek. "Do you have a fever? Or did you just have a bad dream?"

Mack whimpered and stared back at her, his dark blue eyes swimming with tears. He clung to Karen's neck with a viselike grip. When Karen tried to loosen the hold, Mack started sobbing again.

"Oh, baby, what is it? Please calm down. Mommy's here. Everything's fine." She settled into an old wooden rocker she'd found at a flea market before Daisy was born and tried rocking Mack back to sleep. It used to work like a charm, but tonight every time Mack's eyes started to drift shut, he'd yank himself awake and starting crying loudly all over again. Nothing Karen tried seemed to soothe him.

With each new round of sobs, Karen's nerves stretched a little tighter. When Daisy appeared, begging for a glass of water, something inside her snapped.

"No!" she shouted. "I want you back in bed right this instant!"

Her daughter stared at her for a heartbeat, obviously startled by her sharp tone, and then she began to cry, too. The sound of the two of them rose to a pitch that left Karen shaking with rage and dismay. Completely overwhelmed, she all but ran out of her apartment and across the hall, with Mack still in her arms and Daisy trailing behind. Oblivious to the late hour, she knocked frantically on Frances's door.

"What on earth?" Frances said when she responded to Karen's knock wearing a bathrobe, her hair in curlers. She took one look at Karen and the two squalling children and led them inside, where a TV was tuned in to a late-night talk show. Taking Mack from Karen's arms, she began patting his back, then sent Daisy into the kitchen for a glass of water.

Her soothing, matter-of-fact tone accomplished what Karen had been unable to. Both children quieted down almost immediately.

"I can't do it," Karen told Frances, swiping at her own tears. Never in her life had she imagined herself as the kind of mom who could snap in an instant and hit one of her children or even yell the way she had at Daisy. "I can't handle this another minute. I'm afraid of what will happen if I try."

"Come now," Frances murmured, soothing her as if she were one of the distraught children. "You're a good mother. You brought them over here, didn't you? You would never hurt these babies."

"Oh, God," Karen said. "It makes me sick to even think I could."

"Then we'll see what we can do to fix this," Frances told her in the same calm, matter-of-fact tone. "You just leave these two with me for now, okay? Go back to your place and take a little nap."

"I can't leave them with you! It's too much."

"We'll be fine. You need a decent night's sleep. I don't want to see you back here before tomorrow afternoon. I'm going to speak to Dana Sue and explain what's happened."

"You can't do that," Karen protested. "It will be the last straw. I know it will."

"Don't be ridiculous," Frances admonished firmly. "She'll understand. I'll make sure of that. Now, go. The kids and I will be fine tonight and I can get them off to school and day care in the morning. I have a key so I can get their clothes and I know the routine."

"Are you sure?" Karen asked halfheartedly. The idea of sleeping through an entire night lured her like some kind of lighthouse showing her the way home. Uninterrupted sleep would be a godsend.

"I'm sure," Frances said. "We'll talk some more tomorrow. You come over here when you wake up and I'll fix you a nice, big breakfast."

Impulsively, Karen went back and threw her arms around Frances and the now sleeping Mack. "Thank you. I honestly don't know what I would have done if you weren't here. And thanks for offering to speak to Dana Sue."

Even if Dana Sue did fire her in the morning, an entire night in bed when she didn't have to listen for the sound of the kids waking and a morning when she might actually awake refreshed, rather than exhausted would be worth it. She couldn't go on as she had been. Tonight had proved that.

Defeated, she dragged herself back across the hall and climbed into bed. Clutching her pillow, she started to sob, letting out all the frustration and fear that had been bottled up inside for weeks now. She didn't know what tomorrow might hold, but it had to be better than this emotional roller coaster she'd been on.

CHAPTER EIGHT

The phone call woke Helen out of a sound sleep. Used to snapping awake to deal with legal emergencies that occasionally befell her clients, she was sitting on the edge of the bed with the light on and pen in hand to take notes before she even picked up the receiver.

"Helen, it's Dana Sue. We have a situation," she said, sounding shaken.

"What kind of situation?" Helen inquired, her stomach dropping. The last time Dana Sue had had a middle-of-the-night crisis, her daughter had been taken to the hospital with complications from anorexia. Fearing the worst, she asked, "Is it Annie?"

"No, it's Karen."

"Karen? I don't understand. What's going on with her at this hour? And why call me?"

"Please, can you just come over to her apartment now? I'm already here and I'll explain when you get here."

Never one to waste time asking unnecessary questions in a crisis, especially when it was one of the Sweet Magnolias asking for her help, Helen jotted down the address. "I'm on my way. Give me ten minutes."

"Thanks."

Helen yanked on a pair of slacks and a blouse without bothering to tuck it in. She shoved her feet into a pair of expensive backless slides that were about as casual as any shoes she owned. Grabbing her briefcase out of habit on the way out, she was on her way in under five minutes.

When she arrived across town at the apartment building where Karen lived, she noted that lights were blazing in both of the downstairs apartments despite the lateness of the hour. As soon as she entered the building, Dana Sue greeted her and pulled her into an apartment on the right.

"Karen's had some kind of breakdown," she said, her voice low and her gaze directed at a closed door to what was most likely a bedroom in the cramped unit. "Her neighbor called me after Karen knocked on her door and woke her up, pleading with her for help. She told me Karen was afraid she was going to hurt her kids. Frances—you know her, right? Frances Wingate…?"

Helen nodded. Frances had taught them all when they were in school. She'd been strict, but fair, and she definitely wasn't prone to exaggeration. If she was afraid for Karen and the kids, then there was reason to be afraid.

Trying to keep herself from overreacting, she asked, "Did she hit them? Shake them?"

"No, they're both fine," Dana Sue said. "But Karen's in the bedroom. She's pretty hysterical. Frances was going to wait to call me in the morning, because she thought Karen would go to bed and get a good night's sleep. But she came over to check on her and Karen was locked in her bedroom, sobbing. Frances called me to ask what I thought she ought to do. She thought Karen might need medical attention or something."

"So naturally you came running over," Helen said.

"Of course. What was I supposed to do? Karen's my employee and a friend. She's obviously completely distraught. She wouldn't open the bedroom door for me. I thought about getting Ronnie over here to break it down so we could take her to the hospital, but I was afraid to do that. I wasn't sure if social services would have to come and take the kids. That's why I wanted you here before we did anything."

Helen nodded. "Let me talk to her. Are the kids okay across the hall for now?"

Dana Sue nodded. "You know Frances. She's completely unflappable. Apparently the kids stay with her a lot when Karen has to run an errand or something. At her age, she can't keep them all the time, but she obviously adores them. She's like a grandmother. I don't think either Daisy or Mack understand what's going on. They're both asleep now."

Satisfied that the children were unharmed and safe for now, Helen knocked on the bedroom door. "Karen, it's Helen. Please let me in so we can talk. Whatever's going on, I want to help."

"Go away," Karen pleaded. "I don't want anyone to see me like this. I'll be okay if I just get some sleep."

"It doesn't sound to me as if you're even close to falling asleep. Talking things out will unburden you, help you to relax," Helen said. "I know I can never sleep when my mind's racing a hundred miles an hour."

Her comment was greeted with silence, so she tried again. "I hope you're not worried that if you talk to me, I'm going to go running to Dana Sue. She's already gone back to Frances's apartment. This will be just between the two of us."

"Just go away," Karen pleaded again. "I need to figure things out for myself."

"Figure out what?" Helen coaxed. "Tell me. Two minds are always better than one. Whatever's going on, I can help you sort through it."

"Dana Sue should never have called you," Karen said. "I don't need a lawyer."

"How about a friend?" Helen asked gently. "Please let me be a friend."

A long minute passed before a key finally turned in the lock. The door remained closed, but when Helen tried the knob, it opened. Inside the pitch-black bedroom, she felt for a switch and turned on the overhead light. Karen was sprawled facedown on the bed wearing an old chenille bathrobe, her hair disheveled and her face blotchy from crying. She regarded Helen apologetically, then buried her face in the pillow.

"I'm so sorry Dana Sue dragged you out in the middle of the night," Karen said, her words muffled. "I'm sorry she got dragged into this, too. I hate having my boss all caught up in my personal drama."

Helen sat down gingerly on the edge of the bed. "Stop worrying about that. It's not important. Can you tell me what happened?"

Karen nodded, her expression bleak. "I've been feeling more and more overwhelmed, you know. About my job. About money. Ray's still not paying child support, and even though Tess and I worked out that plan with Dana Sue, I'm still not pulling my weight at the restaurant. Dana Sue's been great about it, but I know Erik thinks I'm taking advantage of her. And, face it, she can't pay me when I'm not there, so my salary's not what it was. And it seems like every time I turn around one of the kids is sick again. It's too much. I can't cope anymore."

"What happened tonight?" Helen prodded carefully.

"My three-year-old—that's Mack—woke up crying," she began, her voice catching on a sob. She swiped at the tears on her cheeks with the sleeve of her robe. "Nothing I did calmed him down." Again, her voice hitched. "And then Daisy got mad because Mack was getting all my attention, so she started acting out."

The look she directed at Helen begged her to understand. "They've both had tantrums before, but not at the same time, and not when I was already at the end of my rope. I could feel myself losing control. When I realized I just wanted to shake Mack to make him stop crying and then I yelled at Daisy, I knew I had to do something, so I went across the hall and asked Frances for help. She insisted on taking them, but they can't stay there indefinitely. I have to figure out something else, at least until I can trust myself with them again."

"You did exactly the right thing by taking them to Frances," Helen soothed her. "Recognizing that you were at your wit's end is a good thing, Karen."

Karen suddenly regarded her with alarm. "Nobody will try to take them away from me because of this, will they?"

"Not if I can help it," Helen stated. "But you do need to get some help, you know that, don't you? You can't just tough it out and hope all these feelings will disappear."

Karen nodded, looking defeated. "But I can't check

in to a hospital. I'll lose my job and my kids for sure, if I do that."

Helen knew that was a strong possibility, so she couldn't disagree with her. "How about this?" she said. "We'll arrange for some counseling sessions. Dana Sue knows a psychologist, a Dr. McDaniels, who helped her daughter conquer her eating disorder. Maybe she can make arrangements for you to see her first thing in the morning and schedule some regular sessions every day for a couple of weeks."

"But that's bound to be expensive," Karen protested.

"You have health insurance at the restaurant, right?" Helen asked. "That should cover it. If it doesn't, we'll figure something out. The main thing is to see someone who can help you calm down and get some perspective. Maybe Dr. McDaniels can offer you better ways to cope with your stress. Then we'll see where we stand."

"And the kids could stay here with me?" Karen asked hopefully.

Helen was less sure about the wisdom of that. "I'm not sure that's such a good idea. Right now, they're just adding to your stress. I think you need some time to get yourself strong again. That doesn't mean I think you're a bad mother, Karen. Not at all. I just think you're worn out and need a break."

"But what about the kids?" Karen asked worriedly. "Frances and the sitter could help some, but they can't keep them."

"There's foster care," Helen began, but practically before the words were out of her mouth, Karen was shaking her head.

"Absolutely not," she said fiercely. "I don't want my kids with strangers. Besides, once they get into the system, it'll be hard to get them out. I know that firsthand. I was bounced around foster homes most of my life because my mother couldn't get her life together. I swore I'd never repeat that pattern." She buried her face in her hands. "God, I feel like such a failure. I always judged my mom for not being able to cope and here I am, exactly like her."

"Okay," Helen said, "how about this? I'll take them temporarily." The words were uttered before she could talk herself out of the crazy, impulsive idea, but surprisingly she had no inclination to take them back. "They can stay with me. We'll keep the same sitter and I'll make sure Frances comes by for a visit every day so they won't feel too uprooted. You can come over, too, as much as you want to."

"But I can't ask you to do that," Karen said, looking stunned. "They're a handful. You've never had kids. You have no idea of what you'd be letting yourself in for."

"Oh, I have some idea," Helen said, thinking of the times Maddie's kids had stayed overnight with her. Of course, this would be more than a one-night sleepover, but surely she could manage, especially with the help of the sitter and Frances. And she could see just how adept she'd be at juggling work demands with caring for children. Maybe that was the real reason she'd offered, not out of some burst of generosity, but out of selfishness. If fear of failure was holding her back from making a decision about having her own child, this would be a good test. She didn't have time now, though, to analyze her motives further. The offer was on the table.

"Well?" she asked Karen. "Would you be okay with that?"

"Of course," Karen said with obvious relief. For the first time since Helen's arrival, her face lost its pinched, desperate expression.

"Then that's what we'll do," Helen said decisively. "You pack up a few things for them. I'll speak to Dana Sue about setting up those appointments with the psychologist for you first thing in the morning. Maybe you should come with me tonight and stay over at my place, too. It'll make the transition a little easier for the kids. Or we can let the kids sleep tonight and I'll get them tomorrow."

"That would be best, especially if they're finally asleep," Karen said. "Are you really sure about this? I don't want to disrupt your life any more than I already have. I already owe you for saving my job."

"It'll be okay," Helen assured her, then went in search of Dana Sue, who'd returned to Karen's apartment and was waiting in the living room for Helen to emerge.

When she'd explained the plan, Dana Sue stared at her incredulously. "You're taking them in? All of them, including Karen?"

"Karen will come with me tonight," Helen said. "I don't think she ought to stay here alone. Tomorrow, she'll help me get the kids settled and I'll take them to school. She'll come back here, if the doctor says it's okay. She just needs some time to get her bearings. She also needs to get back on track at work. This will give her a little freedom to do that without worrying about her kids."

"Do you have any idea what you're letting yourself in for?" Dana Sue demanded. "Are you even equipped to have an instant family under your roof, even for a couple of weeks? You've got a house filled with break-able antiques, for heaven's sake!"

"I'll manage," Helen said. Her organizational skills kicked in. "As soon as I get home, I'll stuff the break-ables into a closet or something. I'll make a list of ev-erything I need from the store and have it delivered first thing tomorrow. You can help me with that. I'll get their schedule from Karen and make sure they get to day care and school. Her sitter will come to my house. I'll have Frances visit every afternoon, too."

Dana Sue shook her head. "I should have known you'd come up with a thorough strategy in ten seconds or less," she said wryly. "One thing you ought to con-sider, though."

"What's that?"

"Kids tend to make mincemeat out of plans. They're not predictable."

Helen heard the concern in her friend's voice, but shrugged it off. "Then this will be a good test of my flexibility, won't it?"

Dana Sue gave her a worried look. "That's my point, sweetie. You're not flexible."

"If I'm ever going to have a child of my own, I'll have to be," Helen said. "This will be excellent prac-tice, even better than having Maddie's kids or Annie underfoot for a night."

"You're really sure you want to do this?"

Helen nodded. Mixing with her carefully banked fears, she felt a faint stirring of excitement.

"Okay, then," Dana Sue said briskly. "I'll help Karen pack up their things. You might want to at least peek at the kids. If you're going to take them home tomorrow, it'll help if you can at least recognize them."

"Not funny," Helen said, though she was filled with trepidation as she crossed the hall and went in to speak to Frances, who guided her into a guest room where both children were sleeping soundly.

One glance at those sweet, innocent faces and Helen knew she was doing the right thing. She would care for and protect them 'til Karen could take over again. How hard could it be?

"They look like little angels, don't they?" Frances asked.

"They do," Helen confirmed.

"Don't believe it," Frances said, her voice threaded with amusement and affection. "They're little hellions, same as all kids that age. You come by first thing tomorrow and I'll go with you to drop them off at school and day care. I'll be by your place tomorrow afternoon just in case you're tearing your hair out."

"But the sitter—" Helen began.

"Isn't worth one thin dime of what Karen is paying her," Frances said with disgust. "I know you found her for Karen, but she doesn't know how to handle those children. *I* do. Between you and me, we can get the job done. Getting rid of the sitter will save Karen some money."

"But I have to work," Helen started to protest, then sighed. She had a hunch that was just the first of many compromises she was going to have to make. "I'll call my secretary and reschedule my afternoon appointments."

Frances gave her an approving look. "Now we have a plan."

Helen had the oddest sensation that fate had just handed her not just two children to test her mettle as mom material, but a wise and experienced guide to help her when the going got rough.

Erik stared at Dana Sue as if she'd just announced that Helen had been abducted by aliens.

"You're telling me that Helen is taking care of Karen's children for the foreseeable future," he repeated, still not certain he'd heard correctly.

"That's what I'm telling you," Dana Sue confirmed. "You could have knocked me over with a feather, too."

"Does she know anything at all about children?"

"Well, she always returned Annie to me in one piece. The same with Maddie's kids."

Erik shook his head. "The woman is full of surprises, isn't she?"

"She is," Dana Sue concurred. "But this one's a doozy, even by my standards. The good news for us is that Karen's already feeling less stressed now that she knows the kids are safe and being well cared for. She's had her first appointment with Dr. McDaniels and she'll be in on time today. She's determined to use this respite to get her life back on track."

"But what happens the minute the kids go back home again, which they will eventually, right?"

"That's the plan. Helen's convinced that all Karen needs is a little breather. We'll see if Dr. McDaniels agrees. I hope so. I like Karen. I want this to work out."

"But you won't mind if I remain skeptical," Erik said.

"I don't blame you, but I'm determined to remain optimistic. Look, I'm going out for an hour, okay? Hold down the fort."

Dana Sue was barely out the door when the phone rang. Erik almost ignored it, since the restaurant wasn't open yet, but when it continued ringing, he finally grabbed it.

"I need Dana Sue," Helen announced without so much as a greeting for him.

"She's not here," he said. "Can I help?"

"Only if you have some idea who or what Elmo is," she said. "Mack seems to be obsessed with getting his hands on one."

Erik bit back a chuckle at the panic in her normally confident voice. "It's a toy," he explained patiently. "From *Sesame Street*."

"How do you know that?"

"I have nephews," he said. "You know, it's not necessary that you provide a child with every single toy he asks for."

"You try telling that to a three-year-old who has the single-minded determination of a pit bull," she grumbled.

"Distract him," Erik advised. "He's three. It shouldn't take much."

"Distract him how?"

"Cookies," he suggested. "Ice cream. A TV cartoon show. If *Sesame Street*'s on now, you can kill two birds with one stone, a distraction *and* Elmo."

"There are kids' cartoons on in the afternoon?"

Erik laughed at her bewildered tone. "Darlin', you've just entered a whole new world. That's just one of the joys of cable TV."

"I'll try it. Thanks."

"Hey, Helen," he said, oddly determined to keep her from hanging up.

"What?"

"What you're doing is pretty amazing," he told her, not even trying to hide his admiration.

"Maybe you should wait before paying me a compliment. I still have plenty of time to screw this up."

"You won't," he said confidently.

"How do you know?"

"Because I know you. When was the last time you screwed up anything you set your mind to?"

Her silence was answer enough.

"I rest my case," he told her quietly. "Call back if you need any other advice, okay?"

"Will do. Thanks, Erik."

He replaced the phone, then stood there like an idiot staring at it. She really was an amazing, unpredictable woman. He'd met Daisy and Mack on the couple of occasions Karen brought them to the restaurant, and knew what Helen had unwittingly let herself in for. He'd give anything to see her chasing down those kids in her designer suit and stiletto heels. Come to think of it, maybe he'd bake some chocolate chip cookies before leaving Sullivan's tonight. He could take them by first thing in the morning so she could pack them in the kids' lunches. It would give him a firsthand look at the ever-in-command Helen in a situation she couldn't possibly command. It'd probably make his day.

Getting two kids ready to leave the house before eight in the morning left Helen winded, frazzled and right on the edge of throwing in the towel. When the doorbell rang, she left Mack under Daisy's watchful eye and raced to answer it, praying for the calvary in the form of Maddie or Dana Sue. Instead, it was Erik, his expression oddly smug as he took in her hair, which was sticking out in every direction, her lack of makeup, her untucked blouse and bare feet.

"I thought you might need a little help," he said. "And I brought cookies."

"It's seven forty-five in the morning and you brought cookies?" she demanded. "Are you crazy? The last thing those two need is more sugar."

"Save the cookies for a treat after school," he said. "Or tuck one into their lunches."

Helen stared at him with a bewildered expression. "They need lunches?"

"I imagine so," he said, barely containing a grin.

"I was thinking lunch money for the school cafeteria," she said, then recalled the paper sacks Frances had given them the day before. "Are you sure they can't get lunch at school?"

He shook his head. "Not likely. Where's Daisy? We can ask her."

"Daisy's watching while Mack decides what he wants to wear today," Helen said. "He stubbornly resisted all my selections."

Erik chuckled. "You left a three-year-old to decide on his own?"

"Of course," she said huffily. "Well, with Daisy's help, anyway. Children should develop their own sense of style at an early age."

"Maybe I'll go help him out," Erik suggested. "You make the lunches. I suggest peanut butter and jelly sandwiches. They're not complicated."

Helen frowned. "Okay, I have that leftover from Katie's last visit, but aren't some kids allergic to peanut butter? I read an article—"

Erik cut her off. "Not these two. They've been at the

restaurant once or twice, and Karen's brought PB and J sandwiches for them."

"You're sure?" she asked worriedly.

"I'm sure. Now go or Daisy will be late for school and you'll be trying to explain why you have her instead of her mother. I imagine that would not be a good thing."

"You're right. That would be awkward. I'll hurry. I can check on them and have myself pulled together in two minutes," she assured him.

She winced at the skeptical expression on Erik's face. "I can," she repeated, then darted off to make good on the promise. Maybe later she'd think about why Erik's arrival struck her as salvation, rather than an annoying intrusion.

Erik wandered through the spacious house until he found Mack in a bedroom probably the size of Karen's entire apartment. The toddler looked a little lost, sitting on the floor in his bright red shorts and sneakers, surrounded by a pile of inside-out T-shirts. Daisy was poking through them.

"His Superman T-shirt's not here," she explained. "That's what he wears with his red shorts." She frowned, then added emphatically in case Erik had missed the point, "Always!"

Erik looked over the pile of discarded shirts and honed in on the Spider-Man shirt. "This would look pretty cool with the red shorts," he suggested. "In fact, Spider-Man is so totally awesome he goes with anything."

Daisy studied the shirt skeptically. "You think so?"

"I *know* so," Erik confirmed, already pulling it over

Mack's head. "Now, let's hustle, pal. You need to get to day care."

"How am I going to get to school?" Daisy asked.

"Helen's going to take you."

"Can you come, too?" she asked.

"If you want me to, I can. Any particular reason you want me along?"

"So you can make Helen stay in the car and not walk me to the door holding my hand. I can get to the door by myself."

Erik bit back a grin. "I'm sure you can."

"So, will you tell her not to do it again?"

"You could tell her yourself," Erik suggested.

"I don't wanna hurt her feelings. Mom said we need to be nice to her."

"Okay, then. I'll tell her," he promised.

Within minutes Helen had Daisy and Mack belted into their respective car seats, which she'd borrowed from Karen. She was about to open the driver's-side door when she noticed Erik opening the passenger door. She stared at him.

"You're coming with us?"

"By special request," he said softly, gesturing subtly to indicate Daisy. "She wants me to make sure you don't take her hand and lead her to the door."

Helen gave a small gasp. "I thought that was what moms did. I could tell by the look on her face that she hated it, but she didn't say anything."

"She didn't want to hurt your feelings."

She sighed. "Do you suppose I'll ever figure all this out?"

"You're doing fine, especially for someone with no experience."

"But you don't have kids and you seem to know what to do. You knew about the toys and cartoons and peanut butter and jelly."

"Like I told you on the phone, I have nephews. This isn't rocket science, Helen. It just takes practice."

"I hope so," she said, sounding resigned.

In front of the school, though, she pulled to the curb, then turned to Daisy and gave her a smile that hardly looked forced at all. Only her white-knuckled grip on the steering wheel gave away her tension. "You have a good day, okay? Frances will pick you up this afternoon."

Daisy beamed at her. "Okay. Uh, don't let Mack go by himself, 'cause he doesn't know anything. He'll get lost."

Helen regarded her solemnly. "I'll keep that in mind."

After Daisy was safely inside the building, she turned to Erik. "So that went well, didn't it? And I'm not even a parent," she said.

He studied her. "Ever want to be?"

"I've thought about it," she said in a tone that warned him away from asking any more questions. "You?"

"Once, a long time ago," he admitted.

"Before your wife died," she said.

He nodded. "Yeah, that dream pretty much died with her." He somehow managed to inject a lighter note into his voice as he peered into the back to check on Mack, who gave him one of those brilliant smiles that could melt a man's heart. "Let's get this little tough guy to day care. It's only a few blocks from here. Something tells me he's regressed to his pre-potty-training days. Unless you want to deal with it, we need to make a quick getaway."

Helen grinned at his conspiratorial tone, then began to chuckle. "I am so with you on that. Think you can hustle him inside while I keep the motor running?"

"Oh, yeah," he said. "We can be across town before they catch on."

For the first time since he'd arrived at her house, Helen looked relaxed.

"How about I buy you that cup of coffee and some breakfast when we've made a clean getaway?" he suggested, giving in to an impulse that it would have been smarter to ignore.

"I don't suppose I could talk you into making the coffee at Sullivan's?" she suggested. "It's the best anywhere in town."

He grinned. "You angling for one of my omelets, too?"

She regarded him with unmistakable gratitude. "Please."

"You going to help?"

"After two cups of coffee, I'll do anything you want me to do," she said fervently.

Erik stared at her 'til bright patches of color rose in her cheeks. "An interesting offer," he commented. "I'll keep it in mind."

In fact, he suspected it would be quite a while before he could shake the thought.

CHAPTER NINE

"I just need to establish a routine," Helen said, pulling a notebook out of her briefcase and setting it on the table next to her empty plate. She'd finished every bite of Erik's ham-and-cheese omelet, along with enough home-fried potatoes with bits of onion and green peppers to keep her stuffed for a week. She was also on her third cup of his fragrant French roast coffee. She was feeling pretty darn invincible compared to the way she'd felt an hour earlier.

As she wrote "Routine" and underlined it at the top of the page, she caught Erik's lips twitching. "What?" she demanded.

"You are talking about Daisy and Mack, right?" he asked in amusement. "Two little people about so high?"

She frowned at him. "Yes. What's your point?"

"I think aiming for a routine is just a little optimistic," he said.

"But children need routine," she said, regarding him with puzzlement. Routine had certainly been lacking in her childhood. It was at the top of her list of things she'd do differently if she ever had children of her own. She expanded on her point for Erik's benefit. "They need to know there are certain things they can count on. They need goals and expectations."

"At five and three?"

"It's never too early to start teaching them these things," she insisted. "It's important to be clear about what you expect and the consequences of not living up to those expectations. You have to be totally consistent. Mixed messages confuse them."

"You've been reading parenting books, right?"

"Well, of course I have," she said. "And I do have some experience to draw on."

"Annie's occasional sleepover at your place or a visit from Maddie's kids?"

"No, it's more than that. My childhood was chaotic, to put it mildly. I never knew when one or both of my parents would show up. I never had a curfew. Meals were catch as catch can, especially after my dad died and mom worked two, sometimes three jobs."

He nodded. "Ah, that explains it."

"Explains what?"

"The obsession with organization and routine."

"You're just not getting this," she accused. "If Daisy and Mack are going to be with me, even for a few weeks, I need to handle things the way they're *supposed* to be handled. What if I do something stupid and scar them for life? I need to be prepared for every eventuality. That's the responsible thing to do."

"So how many books *have* you read, Helen?" he taunted.

Avoiding his gaze, she replied, "I don't know exactly. A few."

Under Erik's increasingly amused scrutiny, she was beginning to feel embarrassed about her obsessive need to read everything she could about parenting. Other people apparently approached parenting instinctively. She was clueless. Her own parents could have used a few books. Volumes, in fact.

Of course, it was hard to find five minutes to read them with two very active children around, which was why she'd been up past midnight last night. She blamed the lack of sleep for being so frazzled this morning. Now it was easier to understand why Karen had been so stressed out.

"What did you do, send that efficient secretary of yours to a bookstore and have her buy out the entire parenting section?" Erik asked.

She frowned at him. That was exactly what she'd done. How annoying that he could read her so well. "I wanted a variety of opinions."

He nodded. "Fair enough. How about listening to one more?"

"You don't have kids," she protested. "You told me you weren't even thinking about having kids."

"No, but I was one. So were you. You said yourself that that kind of experience counts. And I do have all those nephews. You have Annie and Maddie's kids. They didn't come to any harm staying with you, did they?"

"No, but they never stayed for more than a night. I don't think you can ruin a child in one night just by indulging his every whim. That's what I did, you know. Pizza, candy, popcorn, ice cream, videos for half the night—you name it. My house was a no-rules environment." At his incredulous look, she shrugged. "What can I say? I wanted to be Auntie Helen, the fun one. I wanted them to like me. Even I'm smart enough to know you can't live like that on a regular basis. If I try that with Daisy and Mack, I'll return them to Karen with a whole lot of very bad habits. I don't think that's the way to go."

Erik nodded. "Okay, you have a point. Maybe the real answer is finding a routine for you, not the kids. My hunch is you're the one making the biggest adjustment here."

Helen regarded him with astonishment. "You're absolutely right," she said at once, seizing on the notion like the lifeline he'd intended it to be. "If I'm organized and on track, then everything will go a lot more smoothly. Obviously today's schedule didn't work. I'll need to be up at 4:30 a.m., not five."

She jotted that down and noted that extra half hour as her time to fix lunches, her own breakfast and coffee. Lots and lots of coffee.

"How did you do with bathtime last night?" Erik asked.

Helen regarded him with dismay. "Baths?" she echoed. "My God, they never had baths, Erik. I sent those children off to school totally filthy."

"Don't panic," Erik consoled her. "I'm sure they were ecstatic, which is probably why Daisy, at least, didn't remind you. You might want to make a note to yourself, though. Make sure they brush their teeth, too."

Helen had remembered to make them brush their teeth, but she wrote down "Bath" in bold letters, then gave Erik a considering look. "I don't suppose you'd want to come by and help," she suggested hopefully.

"I don't get out of Sullivan's 'til nearly midnight," he reminded her. "They need to be tucked in bed long before that."

Helen sighed. "Of course they do."

Erik regarded her with pity. "I am off tomorrow, though. How about I come by then to help out? We can take them out for burgers, then I'll help you get them settled for the night."

"Take them out?" she repeated incredulously. She hadn't taken Maddie's kids or Annie out to any kind of restaurant until the youngest was at least six. "Won't they disrupt the other diners. There's nothing more annoying than having other people's children running wild when you're trying to enjoy a pleasant dinner out."

"Which is one of the joys of the fast-food restaurant," he said. "You'll be surrounded by other people with out-of-control kids of their own. They won't pay any attention to yours."

"Fast food, of course," she said, jotting it down. "That's perfect."

To his credit, Erik managed to keep a straight face. "I'll be by at five-thirty tomorrow afternoon," he promised. "Now I'd better get to work before Dana Sue decides to dock my pay."

Helen regarded him with a grateful expression. "I don't know how to thank you for helping out this morning. I was on the verge of a full-fledged panic attack when you showed up."

"Hey, no big deal. You could have managed."

"I'm not so sure about that. These two kids don't seem to be falling in line the way I anticipated. I don't scare them."

"You wanted to rule by intimidation?"

"I considered it," she admitted. "But it seemed like a bad idea."

"See, you are capable of making smart choices where the kids are concerned," he said.

He spoke with such confidence that Helen left Sullivan's feeling as if she had things back under control. It was probably an illusion, but at least it would get her through the day 'til the next test came along.

Helen had barely left and Erik was still gathering up their dishes, when Dana Sue came flying into the dining room at Sullivan's.

"Was that Helen I saw driving away from here?" she asked.

"Hard to say," he said evasively.

She frowned at him. "Don't you dare try to trip me up on one of those technicalities you enjoy so much. Do you realize when you do that, you sound exactly like Helen when she's cross-examining a witness?"

"Then I'll stop it immediately," he said, amused.

"Don't try to sidetrack me, either. Was Helen here or not?"

"She was," he conceded reluctantly.

"And you had breakfast together," she surmised, her gaze on the plates, cups and silverware he was holding.

"We did."

"Interesting," she murmured, then studied him intently. "How did that happen?"

Now there was a can of worms Erik really didn't want to open with the resident matchmaking queen. He shrugged. "No big deal. We ran into each other."

"Where?" she persisted. "And why would you bring her here, instead of going to Wharton's, which is actually open for breakfast?"

He shrugged. "What can I say? She likes our coffee better. Now, if you don't mind, I need to get to work."

"And I say you have time to answer a few more questions."

"If I have that much time, I could leave and run a few errands," he countered.

"You just want to avoid my questions," she accused.

Erik grinned at her. "Gee, you think?"

"I'll ask Helen."

"Feel free."

"She'll tell me whatever it is you're hiding," she warned him.

"I doubt it. I don't think she's any more interested in encouraging this scheme of yours than I am."

"What scheme is that?"

"To throw us together 'til we stick."

She frowned at him. "I wouldn't put it exactly that way."

Erik laughed. "No, I'm sure you wouldn't. You'd tie it up in some pretty, romantic bow, but it all amounts to meddling in something that's none of your business."

"You're both my friends. That makes it my business," she said as he brushed past her and headed for the kitchen.

It was too much to hope that she'd just give up. She followed him.

"Have you mentioned Tess's problem to her yet?" she asked.

"The other day," he said, relieved by the switch in topic.

"Then this morning wasn't about that?" she said, her expression thoughtful. "What did she say when you told her?"

"That she'd follow up with Tess. I didn't remind her about it today because with Karen's kids under her roof she has enough on her plate at the moment." He scowled. "Go away, Dana Sue. I mean it. Baking takes concentration."

"Oh, please, you could do it with one hand tied behind your back while you're listening to music on your iPod."

"Neither of which is as distracting as listening to you go on and on and on," he said. "I have to do today's baking, plus tomorrow's, remember? Or do you want tomorrow's customers to discover the only dessert on the menu is ice cream from the Piggly Wiggly?"

Dana Sue sighed, but she backed off. "Fine. I'll be in my office if you need me, or if you decide you want to talk."

"I won't," he assured her.

The entire encounter was a warning, he told himself after she'd gone. If he was ever foolhardy enough to decide to ask Helen on an actual date, he might as well invite Dana Sue and Maddie along, as well. Otherwise he'd just have to fill them in on every detail later.

He wondered how the devil Ronnie Sullivan and Cal Maddox had done it, courted their wives with the other two women overseeing every single second. Dating Helen would be tricky enough. Having the other two chiming in every other minute would drive him completely nuts. No way. Next time he got that tingly feeling in the pit of his stomach or had the sudden urge to haul Helen into his arms and kiss her, he needed to remember that.

And then he needed to run like hell in the other direction.

* * *

Karen missed her kids like crazy. When she got back to her apartment after working at Sullivan's, it was way too quiet and lonely. She should have been eager to fall into bed and catch up on some of the sleep she'd missed in recent weeks. Instead, she paced from room to room, switching on the TV in one, the radio in another, just to have some background noise.

She spoke to Mack and Daisy every afternoon when they got home from school and again before they went to bed. They were clearly adjusting well to living with Helen, but in some ways that was hardest of all to bear. She wanted them to miss her, at least a little. She'd spoken to Dr. McDaniels about her mixed feelings that morning.

"It's perfectly normal to worry that you're becoming extraneous to your children's lives," Dr. McDaniels told her. "But, trust me, that's not happening. You're still their mom. Helen is not going to replace you in that role, no matter how effective she is at filling in for the time being. Be glad that Mack and Daisy are adapting and use this time to figure some things out for yourself, to get strong again. In fact, I recommend that you start working out at The Corner Spa. The exercise will be good for you."

When Karen had protested that she couldn't afford a spa membership, Dr. McDaniels had waved off the objection. "I'll work it out if you promise me you'll go."

Though Karen had played sports under duress back in high school phys-ed classes, she'd never undertaken any form of organized exercise activity as an adult. "You really think this will be good for me?" she asked. "I sucked in gym class."

The psychologist had laughed. "So did a lot of us," she told Karen. "But there are plenty of studies that show that rigorous or even moderate exercise not only keeps the body in shape, but increases serotonin in the brain, which makes a person feel happier."

"No kidding?" Karen had said, skeptical, but willing to give it a try. "If you can work it out, I'll go. You said there were two things you were recommending. What's the other one?"

"I want you to sit down with a financial counselor and get yourself on some kind of plan to straighten out your finances. I think that'll relieve a lot of your worries if you can clear up any debts and budget your money wisely."

Karen hadn't been able to argue with that, either. "Is there anyone you recommend?"

She'd taken the business card Dr. McDaniels had given her and called for an appointment as soon as she'd gotten to work. The financial counselor had scheduled their first meeting for next week. And while she was working, Dana Sue had told her she was arranging for a free membership at The Corner Spa.

"Dr. McDaniels talked to you?" Karen had protested, humiliated. "I am so sorry."

"Don't be," Dana Sue responded. "Business is booming at the spa. We can afford to let you use the gym at no cost, and Elliott said he's happy to help you get started."

Karen had gotten a glimpse of the sexy personal trainer a time or two. Looking at him up close was definitely no hardship.

Karen sat on the edge of the sofa and considered all the good things that had happened since she'd finally started to face the mess her life was in. She was actually beginning to believe she could take charge of her life again. And with all that Dana Sue and Helen were doing to support her, she owed it to them to make sure she didn't waste this opportunity.

Still, there was this huge empty place inside where her kids should be. She wanted them back home. No one had set an exact timetable for when her babies *would* be coming back, but she hoped it would be sooner, rather than later. Talking to them on the phone or even spending an hour with them every few days wasn't nearly enough.

Spotting Mack's favorite stuffed bear on the other end of the sofa, she reached for it and held it tightly. The bear's coat was matted, the ribbon around its neck bedraggled and stained with baby food, but it smelled of baby powder and shampoo and Mack. She was a little surprised that Mack was falling asleep without it, but Helen hadn't mentioned any problems with getting Mack to bed. Even so, Karen resolved to drop it off first thing in the morning, maybe catch a glimpse of her kids before she headed to her first workout session at the gym. It was almost impossible to imagine that just a few days ago, her children had been too much for her to cope with.

The light tap on her door startled her. Relieved at the prospect of a visitor, she dropped the bear and rushed to open it. Frances stood on her doorstep, a container of soup in one hand, her expression filled with compassion.

"I heard you come in a few minutes ago. I thought you might be feeling a little lost," she said. "Want some company?"

"Oh, yes, please," Karen said fervently, drawing her into the apartment. "It's way too quiet around here."

Frances patted her arm. "I can understand that. I remember how completely bereft I felt when my last child went off to college. The empty-nest syndrome is no myth. I had a full life teaching and my husband was still alive, but I almost went stir-crazy without a bunch of teenagers underfoot demanding food every hour of the day and night. My children left one by one after eighteen years of me watching over and worrying about them. Yours are still little more than babies and they left practically overnight. There's no way you could be prepared for something like that."

"I want them back now," Karen admitted, taking the soup from Frances and putting it in the kitchen. "I had to turn on the TV and the radio just so there was some commotion in here when I got home from work."

Frances nudged her toward a seat at the table. "You sit and let me warm up that soup. I imagine you haven't eaten, have you?"

"I pick at food all day long at the restaurant," Karen said, then realized she was hungry. "But the soup sounds good."

Frances found a pan and poured the thick split-pea soup into it, then turned the gas element on low. "How about a sandwich to go with it? If you don't have anything, I can run across the hall. I have some honey-baked ham that's delicious."

When Karen started to protest that she was going to too much trouble, Frances waved her off. "Nonsense. I'll be right back. Keep an eye on the soup. Don't let it boil."

Karen nodded, hiding her amusement that Frances thought she needed cooking instructions. What she did need, though, was this bit of mothering, something that had been sadly lacking in her life.

When Frances bustled back into the kitchen, she'd already piled the ham high on thick multigrain bread from a bakery in town. "I wasn't sure if you'd prefer mustard or mayo, so I didn't add either," she told Karen.

"I like mayo. I'll get it," Karen said.

"No, you sit and relax. You're on your feet all day long, while I do nothing but sit around."

Karen laughed. "Frances, I have never seen you stay still for more than a few minutes at a time. You're on the go every day of the week."

Frances shrugged. "Only way I know to keep mind and body active," she conceded. "But there are plenty of hours when I'm across the hall with my feet propped up. Now, tell me about your day."

Karen told her about the plan for financial counseling and for the spa membership.

"That's wonderful," Frances said enthusiastically. "Exercise will do you a world of good. I know my aerobics class at the senior center always makes me feel better—not that they have us doing too much for fear we'll drop dead."

She set a bowl of soup in front of Karen, then pulled up a chair for herself. "You know," she began, her tone conspiratorial, "I hear there's a personal trainer at that spa who looks like a Greek god. I'm tempted to get a trial membership just to check him out myself."

"Frances!" Karen said, laughing. "I'm shocked."

"Any woman who tells you she doesn't like looking is lying," Frances said. "Sneak a camera in there and take pictures for me. I can live vicariously."

"I most certainly will not," Karen said. "But I will

check in to taking you along as a guest one day, if you think your heart can take it. I've seen him. He *is* pretty gorgeous."

"Then it might be worth my winding up in the hospital just to sneak a peek at him." She patted Karen's hand. "Now, let me get out of here, so you can finish that meal and get some sleep. You want to look your best when you go to the gym."

"I'm going for the exercise," Karen reminded her piously.

"Well, of course you are," Frances said. "But there's no harm in exercising your libido at the same time, is there? You could use a man in your life."

"I could say the same about you," Karen returned. "I know there are at least half a dozen men at the senior center who are interested in seeing you."

"Oh, piddle," Frances said dismissively. "Who wants to listen to a bunch of old fools sit around and talk about their aches and pains? I've got enough of those myself."

"Still, you might want to consider the benefit of having some companionship," Karen said. "I'm sure you must get lonely, too."

"I have my moments," Frances admitted, "but I'm never bored, not for a second. There's plenty to do, if you just get out there and look for it. And then there are you, Daisy and Mack. You occupy a huge place in my life, where my own kids and grandkids would be if they lived close by. So, you see, my life is full. I have nothing to complain about."

"You're remarkable," Karen told her with total sincerity. "I hope I grow up to be exactly like you."

"You'll be your own person," Frances corrected. "There's no one else on earth just like you. You need to remember that, Karen, and use this time on your own to figure out exactly who you are and who you want to become. Your children will be that much happier if they have a mom who's confident and knows where she's headed and how she plans to get there."

"Do you really think I'll figure that out?" Karen asked wistfully. "I was barely out of high school when I met Ray. He thought community college was a waste of time, so I didn't go. I just put in my time at the diner. Then I got pregnant with Daisy, we got married and the kids came along. I didn't plan any of that. Right now it seems like my only goal is keeping my head above water."

"I know you'll get past that," Frances said. "Now get some sleep. Be sure you stop over tomorrow and tell me every single detail about that sexy trainer at the spa."

"I love you," Karen said, impulsively wrapping Frances in a hug. "I am so lucky you're my neighbor and my friend."

"Same goes for me," Frances said. "You kiss those babies for me if you see them in the morning. Tell them I'll be by in the afternoon. I'm baking oatmeal raisin cookies for them."

"They'll love that."

She waited in the hallway until Frances had closed the door to her apartment and locked it, then went back into her own unit and tidied up the kitchen. Feeling one hundred percent better than she had earlier in the evening, she switched off the TV and the lights, then changed into her favorite pajamas and crawled into bed. She set the radio on a timer and turned it down low, the sound of oldies lulling her.

To her amazement, the instant her head hit the pillow, she felt herself drifting off to sleep, a smile on her lips. Deep inside was a tiny little seed of optimism about the future, something that hadn't been there for months, perhaps even years.

CHAPTER TEN

———◆-◆-◆———

Karen had been inside The Corner Spa on several occasions to deliver some of the salads, muffins and other light menu items that Sullivan's prepared for the spa café, but she'd never gone into the workout room. Dressed in a pair of shorts, old sneakers and a T-shirt, she approached it warily, stunned by the variety of equipment and the crowd of women, most of whom seemed to know each other.

The walls were a cheery shade of yellow. Sliding doors opened to a spring breeze and a tranquil view of a wooded area. There was music playing low in the background, something classical and soothing, but the predominant noise was conversation and laughter.

Too intimidated and uncertain to try any of the equipment, Karen stood where she was trying to decide what to do. She regretted not going back home after she'd stopped by Helen's to drop off Mack's stuffed bear and spend a few minutes with the kids before school. Here, she felt as awkward and out of place as she had in high school when she'd been expected to get excited about playing field hockey.

"You must be Karen," a low male voice said, approaching her from behind.

That sexy rumble, which would have triggered an instant response in bed, was especially unexpected amid the higher-pitched female voices. She turned and stared into dark brown eyes the color of espresso. It was the first time she'd seen Elliott Cruz up close, and she couldn't seem to tear her gaze away. With his long, coal-black hair pulled back from his face in a ponytail, those incredibly soulful eyes, broad chest and shoulders and impressive thighs, she understood why the personal trainer was the talk of Serenity's females.

"I'm Elliott Cruz," he told her. "Dana Sue told me to watch for you."

A grin tugged at her lips. "And my neighbor told me to watch for you," she said.

Surprise flickered in his eyes. "Oh? Is she a member here?"

"No, but she wants to be, just so she can get a look at you," Karen blurted before she could censor herself. "She's in her eighties. I don't think the shock would be good for her."

To her surprise, his olive complexion reddened. "I'm sorry. I didn't mean to embarrass you."

He chuckled. "I could never work around this many women if I couldn't handle a few stares and a whole lot of teasing. I'm pretty much immune to it."

Karen thought otherwise. His embarrassment was unmistakable and suggested he was still taken aback by overt female appreciation. He led her through the gym toward a treadmill.

"Why don't we start here?" he suggested, his hand resting on the machine.

"You're going to put me on *that*?" she asked.

"Unless your idea of exercise is standing around watching everyone else sweat, you have to start somewhere," he said. "This is just walking, the most basic exercise of all. You can do that, can't you?"

"On a sidewalk, not a machine."

"Pretty much the same thing, except this gives you a way to control your pace and challenge yourself," he said, pointing out all the dials and the calculations visible in the digital readouts. "You'll be able to determine your pace, your distance, calories burned and so on. Hop on, and let's see what you can do."

Karen stepped up and placed her feet where Elliott told her to as he turned on the machine.

"When you're ready, just step onto the treadmill and start walking," he said. "I've set the speed fairly low for now."

She did as he'd instructed and immediately clutched the bars in front of her in a death grip as she tried to walk at the measured pace of the machine.

"It's going a little fast, isn't it?" she asked as she felt herself sliding backward as she struggled to keep up with it.

He grinned. "That just means you need to walk a little faster," he said, refusing to slow it down. "You can keep up. It's not exercise if it doesn't push you a little."

She picked up her pace and felt herself falling into a more natural rhythm. It wasn't so bad after all. "How long do I have to do this?"

"We'll do ten minutes today and see how you hold up. I'd like to see you up to thirty minutes eventually."

Ten minutes didn't sound too tough. Once she grew

accustomed to the machine, it'd be a breeze. "How long have I already done?"

"Two minutes." .

She frowned. Was that all? Surely she'd been at it longer. As if to mock her, her legs suddenly felt heavy and her breath hitched slightly. "And you want eight more minutes?" she asked.

He regarded her solemnly. "Yes, I do."

"Are you sure you didn't set the speed higher?"

"Nope. Same speed. You can do this. I hear you have kids. They must keep you on the go. Surely you're fit enough to do a brisk walk."

There was something in his gorgeous eyes that made her want to do whatever he expected of her. She had a hunch that was why he was so good as a personal trainer. Every woman in the spa probably wanted to live up to his expectations, no matter how impossible they seemed to be.

Feeling an impish desire to torment him just as he was tormenting her, she looked him straight in the eye and asked, "If I finish the whole ten minutes, will you do something for me?"

His gaze narrowed with suspicion. "Such as?"

"Take off that shirt so I can see if your abs live up to all the hype," she said in the same solemn tone he'd just used on her.

His low laugh washed over her. "Now, if I did that for every woman who asked, this place could wind up with a reputation as a strip club." His gaze locked with hers. "You want to see my body, Karen, you're going to have to work much harder than this."

Karen sucked in her breath at the suggestive note in his voice. Anticipating amusement, she was surprised to see something darker and far more serious in the depths of his eyes. It was so totally male it made her knees weak. She almost stumbled and pitched off the back of the treadmill. He flipped the off switch in the nick of time and steadied her.

"You okay?" he asked.

Was she? It had been years since she'd flirted with a man, years since a simple sexual innuendo could make her blood run hot and her body tremble. Her marriage had lost that spark long before it had ended. Maybe that was why something that probably meant no more to Elliott Cruz than hello or goodbye sent her hormones into overdrive.

She plastered a smile on her face. "I'm fine," she said. "What's next?"

The slow warming of his smile melted the last of her defenses.

"Something told me you were going to become an eager student," he said.

Karen was eager, all right. Unfortunately, it had less to do with whatever torture Elliott had in mind for the next hour than it did with anticipation of what might happen in a more private setting.

"Idiot," she muttered under her breath. No doubt every woman in here thought she would be the one to capture his attention. She'd have to be a fool to think he'd singled her out after only a few minutes in her company.

"Did you say something?" he asked.

"No, nothing," she said. "Just talking to myself."

And, with any luck at all, maybe her rampaging libido would get the message. She had a feeling the pleasurable sensations she was experiencing weren't exactly what Dr. McDaniels had been talking about when she'd discussed one of the side benefits of exercise.

Helen was extremely proud of herself. She had both kids bathed and dressed in neatly ironed clothes by the time Erik rang the doorbell at 5:30 p.m. to take them out for supper.

"My, my, don't you two look good," he said to Daisy and Mack, swinging Daisy up in his arms to give her a smacking kiss on the cheek that had her giggling and Mack holding out his arms for a turn.

Then his gaze landed on Helen and his expression changed. He seemed to be struggling to contain a laugh.

"What?" she asked.

"Have you checked a mirror lately?" he inquired delicately.

"No." Since she arrived home from work, she'd been too busy getting Mack and Daisy ready for their outing. Erik had arrived before she'd had a chance to check her makeup, much less think about changing her own clothes.

"You might want to do that," he said. "Not that I don't think you look terrific, because I do." A wicked grin spread across his face. "Believe me, I do."

Helen frowned because his gaze seemed to be lingering on her chest. "I'll be right back."

In the bathroom, she took one look in the full-length mirror on the back of the door and groaned. Her silk blouse had gotten completely soaked when she'd had the kids in the tub. It was plastered to her chest, revealing the pattern in her lacy bra and a whole lot more. No wonder Erik had gaped.

Her skirt, though not as revealing, was every bit as

drenched. She ducked into her room, grabbed another blouse and a pair of linen slacks, and slid her feet into more sensible shoes. Her hair and makeup took two seconds to fix.

Satisfied she was more presentable, she returned to find all three of them on the sofa watching cartoons. Erik seemed as absorbed as the kids.

"I hate to tear you all away from your entertainment, but shouldn't we be going?" she asked.

Daisy protested, but a look from Erik was enough to silence her. Mack seemed perfectly content to do whatever Erik suggested. He was especially delighted when Erik swung him up on his shoulders to carry him piggyback.

"Go!" he ordered imperiously.

Erik laughed. "He's taking after you already," he said to Helen as he headed for the door.

"Something tells me you didn't mean that as a compliment." She followed him out and locked the house behind them.

They piled into Helen's car because it had the kids' seats, but when Erik offered to drive, Helen accepted. She could hardly keep her eyes open. She'd had no idea how exhausting it would be trying to keep up with kids for several days running.

The fast-food restaurant Erik drove them to was in the next town, and it had an indoor play area. Daisy spotted it at once.

"Can we go play?" she pleaded.

"Not until we've eaten," Erik said. "Why don't you guys find a table and I'll get the food? Daisy, you want to come with me to help?"

"Sure!" she said, obviously delighted to be the object of Erik's attention.

Helen settled Mack in a booster seat, then watched Erik bending down to consult Daisy as they ordered. She was amazed by how at ease he was with the kids. Though she'd relaxed considerably over the past few days, she was still awkward with them. She told herself it was because they'd been thrust into her life with no preparation. She hadn't even met them before. Truthfully, though, it was more than that. It was the responsibility of keeping them safe and making them feel secure 'til they could be with their mom again. Much as she hated to admit it, she needed a support system as desperately as Karen had. Frances was pitching in, but they needed backup. Maybe Annie would be willing to babysit or just come by to give Helen a break in the evenings. She was still pondering the options when Erik and Daisy approached.

"Why the frown?" Erik whispered in her ear as he set the tray that was piled high with food on the table. "Are you overthinking all this again?"

She forced a smile. "More than likely."

"Sugar, they're people. Enjoy them." He divvied up the huge order, then suggested, "Daisy, why don't you tell Helen about that story your teacher read in school today?"

Daisy regarded her hopefully. "You wanna hear?"

"I'd love to," Helen said.

Daisy began with what had to be the very first page and told the whole long, rambling story of a dinosaur, adding some embellishments Helen suspected hadn't been in the original. Her telling, though, was filled with enough drama and enthusiasm to keep Mack spellbound and Helen laughing.

"Brava!" she enthused when Daisy had concluded. "You're an excellent storyteller."

"I could read it to you tonight," Daisy offered eagerly. "I brought the book home from school. My teacher said it would be okay."

"I'd love that," Helen said, and realized she meant it.

"Now can Mack and me go play?" Daisy begged Erik after they'd eaten.

Erik glanced at Helen. "Okay with you?"

She looked at the indoor equipment where several other young children were already playing. "Are you sure it's safe?"

Erik nodded. "I'm sure."

She gave her approval. "Just stay where we can see you."

After they'd gone, Erik studied her. "Letting them go wasn't so hard, was it?"

"No, I'm trying to get better at it." She sighed. "I know I'm too uptight, but this parenting business is scary."

"I imagine that's how everyone feels when they bring their first baby home from the hospital. You came home with two kids who already have personalities, a vocabulary and who are mobile. It's no doubt been a shock to your system. You'll get the hang of it, though."

"What I don't get," she said, regarding him with curiosity, "is why someone who's as comfortable with children as you are isn't interested in having a whole crew of them."

His expression suddenly shuttered as if she'd ventured into an area so personal that any considerate person would have known it was completely off-limits.

"Did I say something wrong?" she asked, not sure why he was so sensitive on this subject.

He shook his head. "Of course not. I just don't have any plans to have a family. I told you that."

"But you'd be—"

He cut her off. "Not going to happen, okay?"

If he hadn't looked so shaken, she might have persisted. Instead she let the subject drop. "I'm sorry."

He rested his hand on hers. "No, *I'm* sorry for snapping at you. It was a perfectly reasonable question. I'm just a little touchy. All my plans to have kids were tied up with my wife. When she died, that part of my life died with her."

He sounded so sad that Helen couldn't help wondering if the loss was recent. "How long ago did your wife die?"

"Six years and seven months ago," he said tonelessly.

Helen knew there wasn't any strict timetable for grief, but that seemed like a long time to be mourning someone's loss.

"Before you went to culinary school?" she guessed.

He nodded. "I needed to make a complete change after she died. A friend suggested culinary school, mainly as a distraction because she knew I enjoyed cooking. It turned out I loved it. The instructors said I was a natural. And it eventually brought me back to life."

"But not all the way," Helen said before she could stop herself.

Erik stared at her, his expression hard. "Meaning?"

"Please don't take this the wrong way, but it still

seems as if some part of you died with your wife," she suggested.

Rather than snapping at her again, he merely nodded. "I suppose that's true."

"You must have loved her very much," she said.

"She was amazing." His eyes filled with a sorrow that looked as raw as it must have on the day she died. "Not perfect. Not by a long shot, but amazing just the same."

Helen couldn't turn away, even though witnessing that much pain seemed intrusive. Forcing herself to seek out the children in the play area, she thought what a shame it was for a man as decent as Erik to have shut himself off emotionally.

"Why are you suddenly so pensive?" Erik asked. "I didn't mean to bring you down."

"I guess I'm a little envious," she admitted. "I've had a few relationships, if you can call them that, but no one's ever meant as much to me as your wife obviously did to you. I'm not sure I even believed until recently that love could run that deep."

"What happened recently to convince you it's possible?"

"Seeing Cal and Maddie together," she told him. "And lately even Dana Sue and Ronnie are making a believer out of me."

"I suspect it's your line of work that's made you so cynical," Erik said.

"You're not the first to tell me that," she returned.

"Ever thought about practicing a different kind of law?"

She shook her head. "Not really. I like sticking up for women whose marriages have crumbled. They're

usually so emotionally shattered that they need someone in their corner who's strong enough to fight for
what they deserve."

"But look at the toll it's taken on you," he said. "By
your own admission, you've shut yourself off emotionally."

"So have you," she retorted.

He gave her a rueful smile. "Touché. But at least I
loved once with everything in me."

She nodded slowly. For the first time she really understood what Tennyson meant when he wrote that it
was better to have loved and lost than never to have
loved at all. She glanced back at the play area to see
Mack and Daisy starting to squabble. "Right now,
I think there are other issues in my life. Looks as if
those two are getting tired. We should probably get
them home."

As Erik gathered them up and Helen waited for them,
the oddest sensation stole through her. For just a fleet-
ing instant, it felt as if she were part of a family.

And it felt really, really good.

Erik couldn't seem to shake the dark mood that Hel-
en's questions had stirred in him. He knew it was only
her natural curiosity that had made her pry into his past,
but every reminder of what he'd lost when Samantha
and his unborn child had died always took him right
back to the night it had happened. He'd gone over that
night a thousand times, wondering if there had been
anything at all he could have done differently, anything
that would have changed the outcome. Every doctor and
EMT he'd asked had assured him that he'd done every-

thing exactly right, but their reassurances hadn't been enough. He still blamed himself.

If it had been entirely up to him, he would have dropped Helen and the kids back at her place and headed straight home, but Daisy had other ideas.

"I'm going to read a story, remember?" she told him when he tried to make his excuses at the front door.

"I think Mack and Helen will be a great audience," he told her. "You don't need me."

"Please?" she begged, regarding him with such a plaintive expression that he couldn't say no.

"I'll stay for half an hour," he agreed reluctantly.

"Yea!" Daisy proclaimed. "I'll get the book."

"She's got you wound around her finger," Helen commented, shaking her head in amusement.

He shrugged. "What can I say? I'm a sucker for a woman who begs."

"Just one more reason why you and I would be a disastrous match," she responded. "I *never* beg."

He laughed. "Add that to the list and tell Dana Sue next time she starts meddling." He reached for Mack and took him from her. "He's down for the count. I'll put him in bed."

Helen relinquished the boy. "Daisy's going to be crushed that her audience has dwindled to just us."

"I think it's *us* who're most important to her. Mack's just her baby brother. She can read to him anytime."

"Well, I'm looking forward to it. I can't recall the last time I read a good dinosaur book."

Erik settled Mack into his bed. It was made to look like a car and painted bright red. "You bought him a bed?" he asked Helen. "Why, if he's only here for a short time?"

She flushed. "I wanted him to have something special. I thought it would turn this visit into more of an adventure."

"He's three. He could fall asleep on a rock."

She chuckled. "I doubt that's recommended, though."

Erik tucked Mack under the covers, then turned to catch an oddly wistful expression on Helen's face. "You okay?"

She nodded. "Seeing him like that, looking so innocent and sweet, just reminds me of what I've missed."

It wasn't the first time tonight she'd come close to admitting that her life hadn't turned out the way she'd anticipated. Just proved that people were more complicated than they appeared.

"You wanted kids?" he asked.

"I took for granted that I'd have them, but time just slipped by," she admitted. "I've been regretting that lately."

"It's not too late," he said, even as he added her desire for children to the list of reasons they were unsuited. "Women with careers are having kids at your age all the time now."

"I know."

"Well, then?"

"I'm still weighing my options," she said. "I have to say that having Mack and Daisy here has been eye-opening."

"In a good way?"

Her gaze still on Mack, she nodded. "Yeah, in a good way."

Just then Daisy appeared in the doorway. "Are you *ever* coming to hear the story?"

Erik chuckled at her impatience. He swung her up in

his arms. "How about we tuck you in and Helen reads it to you?" he suggested. "Mack's already asleep."

Daisy regarded Helen somberly. "Would you? I like it when Mommy reads to me."

Helen seemed vaguely startled by the request, but then her lips curved into a smile. "I would love to read it, but only if Erik makes all the dinosaur noises."

"Done," he said at once, surprisingly eager to share this experience with her.

He was seeing more and more sides to Helen these days and with each new one, his preconceptions were toppling like pins in a bowling alley. For a man determined to keep her at arm's length, that was not a good thing.

CHAPTER ELEVEN

Several days after the supper outing with Erik, on Saturday morning, Helen woke up to the sensation that someone was watching her. Cracking open one eye, she saw Mack standing beside the bed, a thumb stuck in his mouth. He looked as weary as she still felt, even after a full night's sleep, the first she'd had since the kids had come to stay. For the second time in the past week, she told herself to find some backup ASAP.

She glanced at the clock and saw that it was already 8:00 a.m. She never slept that late, not even on weekends. No wonder Mack had come to find her. She listened intently and heard the TV going in the living room, which was apparently keeping the self-sufficient Daisy occupied.

Mack removed his thumb from his mouth long enough to ask hopefully, "You up?"

"I am now," she confirmed. "Are you hungry?"

He nodded emphatically.

"Seems as if you could use some clean clothes, too," she suggested. "You must be getting tired of that Spider-Man shirt."

"No!" Mack said.

"Okay, then. How about I wash it this morning?"

"No!" he repeated.

Oh, well, it was hardly worth fighting about. First thing Monday she'd send Barb out to see if she could find a few more identical Spider-Man shirts.

In the meantime, she dragged on a robe and headed for the living room, Mack toddling along behind. Daisy was sitting in front of the TV—and she was crying! Helen felt her throat catch at the sight of her. She looked so lost and alone despite her cheery pink T-shirt, orange shorts and bright red sneakers. Her silky hair was tangled and tears stained her cheeks.

Helen immediately crossed the room and sat down beside her, gathering her close. "Oh, sweetie, what's wrong?"

Daisy lifted her damp face to Helen and inquired pitifully, "Are we ever going to live with Mommy again?"

"Of course you are," Helen said at once.

"When?"

"Very soon."

"But when?" Daisy persisted.

"As soon as the doctor says she's okay," Helen said.

"Is she really, really sick?" Daisy asked. "When I'm sick, I only stay home from school for a little while. Mommy's been sick for a long time now." She glanced at Helen hopefully. "She didn't look sick last time she came to see us. Maybe she's better."

How on earth could she explain this so a five-year-old would understand? Helen wondered. "I know it must seem like a long time, but you've only been with me for a couple of weeks," she said, though she sensed that to a child two weeks could seem like an eternity. "And what your mommy has isn't like a tummy ache or the measles," she explained carefully. "It doesn't just go away."

"Then how can she get well?" Daisy asked, looking more perplexed than ever.

"She needs to rest and talk to some people and then she'll be strong again."

"But she's really strong now," Daisy protested. "She can lift all sorts of stuff."

Helen concluded she was only making things worse. "How about this? Why don't we call her right now, so you and Mack can talk to her? Maybe she'll even have time to come by before she goes to work."

Daisy's eyes lit up, even though they were still shimmering with tears. "We can call her?"

"Of course you can," Helen said, regretting that she hadn't told Daisy that much sooner. Instead, she'd relied on Karen to call and stop by. Obviously Daisy needed to know she could make a call herself if she wanted to. "You get the portable phone and I'll help you make the call."

Daisy scrambled off the sofa and ran to the table where the phone rested in its base.

"Talk," Mack commanded.

"In a minute," Daisy said to him, then added proudly to Helen. "I know my phone number."

"Then you can punch it in," Helen said.

A moment later, Karen obviously answered because a smile broke across Daisy's face.

"Mommy! It's me."

"I talk to Mommy, too!" Max wailed.

Helen gave Daisy an imploring look that had her handing over the phone. Mack babbled happily for a minute, then Daisy yanked the phone back.

"Mommy, can you come over?"

Whatever Karen said caused Daisy to frown and hold the phone out to Helen.

"She wants to talk to you," she said, sounding betrayed.

Helen took the phone. "Hi, Karen."

"Is everything okay?" Karen asked worriedly. "Daisy seems upset. Is she crying?"

"Yes, but everything's fine, really. Daisy was just missing you a lot. I thought maybe you'd like to join us for breakfast if you have time."

"Really?"

The surprised note in Karen's voice puzzled her. "Of course. I told you you'd be welcome here anytime."

"I know," Karen said. "But the last time I was over, I had the feeling I was disrupting their new routine. Since you've been so great about keeping them, I didn't want to make things more difficult for you."

"Oh, Karen, I'm sorry," Helen said, chagrined. "I had no idea I'd made you feel that way. Though no one's a bigger fan of routine than I am, I've discovered that sometimes the best things in life happen unexpectedly. Please come over. They need to see their mom."

"I'll be there in fifteen minutes," Karen promised, sounding as eager as Daisy. "And don't cook. Let me do it. The least I can do is fix breakfast for all of you."

"That would be wonderful," Helen admitted. Her repertoire of cereal or scrambled eggs had worn thin days ago. "See you soon."

"She's coming?" Daisy asked the instant Helen clicked off the phone.

"In a few minutes," Helen confirmed, picking up Mack. "Why don't you wash your face and brush your teeth while I get dressed? I'll braid your hair for you, if there's time."

"All right!" Daisy enthused, taking off.

But rather than going back to her room to change, Helen patted Mack's back, loving the feel of his warm little body in her arms. For now he was perfectly content to have her hold him, something she knew wouldn't last once he spotted his mother. It was getting harder and harder for her to accept that these two amazing children were merely on loan to her for a few more weeks at most. They already had a mom, one who was doing everything possible to be able to care for them again.

Helen couldn't help admiring how hard Karen was working to get her life in order, but a tiny part of her—one she wouldn't acknowledge to another breathing soul—hoped it would take a long, long time. Despite her initial bouts of uncertainty and periods of utter and complete exhaustion, motherhood—albeit *temporary* motherhood—was turning out to be more rewarding than she'd ever imagined.

Helen seemed to have vanished off the radar. Erik hadn't seen her for several weeks. He'd finally risked asking Dana Sue if the kids had locked her in a closet or something.

"No, but she's definitely in way over her head, though she'd never admit it," Dana Sue told him. "Annie's been going over there practically every evening to help out. She says Helen's in her pj's and ready for bed five seconds after they get the kids to sleep. For a night owl like Helen, that's very telling."

"Does she regret taking the kids in?" he asked.

Dana Sue regarded him curiously. "Why so interested, Erik?"

He feigned indifference. "It's just unusual not to have her around here at all."

"You could always call to check on her," Dana Sue suggested.

"Don't start with me," he said. "I asked about her. No big deal."

Dana Sue grinned. "I think it is. I think you've missed her."

He rolled his eyes and headed toward the storeroom. Dana Sue called after him.

"No, she doesn't regret taking the kids. She says it's the best thing she ever did."

Erik wasn't sure how he felt about that. Sure, he was glad she was enjoying the motherhood experience, but if it had solidified her desire to have a child of her own, it meant there was no future for the two of them. That bothered him more than he wanted to admit. What bothered him even more was the realization that Dana Sue was right. He *did* miss Helen.

A few days after his conversation with Dana Sue, Erik was still stewing over the discovery that Helen's absence was getting to him when he ran into her at Wharton's. She was staring despondently into a cup of coffee she'd barely touched. He slid into the booth opposite her. Given her apparent mood, he was surprised there wasn't an empty sundae dish in front of her.

"Tough court case today?" he asked.

She shook her head.

"Kids acting up?"

She sighed heavily. "No, they're great."

"Then why do you look as if you've just lost your best friend?"

"I spoke with Dr. McDaniels today about Karen."

He stiffened. Was there more trouble on that front he hadn't heard about? Dana Sue might keep it from him, since she knew he was still maintaining a wait-and-see attitude about Karen.

"Oh?" he said casually. "What's going on with her?"

"Dr. McDaniels says Karen's doing great, better than expected, in fact. She says the kids can go back home to live with their mom in another week or two. She's convinced Karen's back on track."

She looked at him with an expression he couldn't quite read. It was almost as if she didn't want to believe that the psychologist had gotten it right.

"What do you think?" she asked.

The question confirmed his suspicion, but he knew his reply wasn't going to be what she wanted to hear. "I know she's been showing up at work when she's supposed to. She's working harder than ever and her mood's vastly improved. I'd have to agree with the doctor. It's about time for her to be reunited with the kids."

Helen sighed. "That's the way it looks to me, too. I think at first they may only stay with her on her days off, but it won't be long before they go home for good."

"I would have thought you'd be thrilled to be getting your life and your house back," he said.

"I'd have thought the same thing a month ago," she admitted. "I had no idea I'd start to care about them so much. Letting go is going to be harder than I expected."

"They belong with their mom," he reminded her.

"Believe me, I know that," she said. "That doesn't make it any easier."

"No, I don't imagine it does, but what you've done for all of them has been incredible. That should leave you with a tremendous sense of satisfaction."

"Oh, I'm a real saint," she said with an edge of bitterness that surprised him.

He stared at her. "Okay, what's going on? Is this about the whole baby thing?"

To his shock, when she lifted her gaze to meet his, her eyes were swimming with tears. She nodded.

Erik told himself he shouldn't let her get to him, but how could he help it? She looked totally miserable. Instinctively, he reached across the table and took her hand in his. "Helen, you can do something about that if it's what you really want. Mack and Daisy aren't the only kids out there who need a temporary home or a permanent one, for that matter. Become a foster mother. Or adopt. Do whatever it takes to fulfill that need if it's that important to you."

"You don't think I'm being selfish?"

"No, I think adopting kids or becoming a foster parent is tremendously generous. You do realize it will change your life, though, right? From the beginning you've known that Daisy and Mack would eventually go home again, but adopting a child of your own will be forever. It won't always be a lark."

She gave him a wobbly grin. "I've been digging Cheerios out of the sofa cushions for a month now. The guest bathroom is usually under water and littered with rubber ducks. I know every song in half a dozen children's movies by heart. I think I'm starting to grasp the impact of having a child in my life."

"You've been lucky. They haven't gotten sick. Your schedule hasn't been turned upside down. Kids are unpredictable and you like to lead a very predictable life. The past couple of months have been an adventure for you, but there's been an end in sight."

She frowned at his caution. "I know that. I get that I can't just turn a kid in if he gets to be too much trouble. I get that it's a lifelong commitment."

"Do you really?"

"Why are you so supportive one second and so negative the next?"

"Because I've been around you enough to know that you like order, not chaos. And by your own admission, you've never made a commitment to a relationship that's lasted for more than a few dates."

"Are you saying you don't think I'm cut out to be a mother?" she asked.

"I would never presume to say that. I'm just saying that you're anticipating Mack and Daisy leaving and feeling the loss right now. It's natural to want to grab on to a replacement to fill that empty spot in your life. Just be sure you're doing it because it's the right thing for you for the long haul and not as some temporary fix because you're going to be a little lonely without Mack and Daisy underfoot."

Her scowl suggested that his comment had hit a little too close to home.

"I need to get to work," she said stiffly, starting to edge out of the booth.

He reached for her hand. "Hold on," he commanded. "I didn't say any of that to be mean."

"I know you didn't. You just think I'm too selfish and self-absorbed to be a mother."

He stared at her incredulously. "I did *not* say that. I think you're an amazingly competent woman and ca-

pable of doing anything you set out to do. You can mul-
titask with the best of them. I was just playing devil's
advocate. If you're going to jump into parenting, you
need to know exactly what you're in for. Kids need a
parent who's totally committed to giving them what
they need and what they deserve."

"I know that, probably even better than you do," she
told him. "I've been weighing the pros and cons for this
for so long I'm practically dizzy from it."

Suddenly her feisty attitude faded and she gave him a
resigned look. "But that was all theory, you know what
I mean? Having Mack and Daisy was real. Taking them
in was kind of an experiment, to see if I could handle
it. I didn't expect to get so attached. I didn't expect
them to turn my life upside down, to make me want so
much more than what I already have. It scares me how
much I want children. I've always been so independent.
I liked it that way. Now it feels as if I've spent the last
twenty years just going through the motions, not really living at all."

Erik could understand that. Real life always tended
to be a whole lot messier than you expected. He saw
that all the time with the wedding receptions that were
planned with such attention to detail, only to have a
supplier fail to deliver something they'd been counting
on, or the bride suddenly have a change of heart about
the menu one week ahead of the date.

People with kids or in the restaurant-and-catering
business pretty much needed to have a go-with-the-
flow attitude or they'd wind up with ulcers or an early
heart attack. Embracing change and unpredictability
wasn't easy, though. Helen, with her previously well-
ordered existence, had just bumped up against that truth

and discovered she could cope, after all. She seemed as surprised as he was.

"I know you didn't ask me what you should do, but I'll tell you anyway," he said. "I know all too well how short life can be and how unexpectedly things can change. If you really want something, you need to grab it. Don't wait until it's too late and wind up living with regrets."

"The way *you* have?" she asked.

Erik nodded. "The way I have."

He would regret to his dying day that he hadn't agreed to having children when Samantha had first broached the subject right after their marriage. They'd been in their twenties then, just starting out, struggling to make ends meet. He'd wanted to get their marriage and their finances on a solid footing before having a baby. Samantha had reluctantly agreed to wait.

Maybe if they'd tried sooner, when they were both a little younger, things would have turned out differently and he'd have both his wife and a family.

The sad truth was, though, that he couldn't go back and change that and he'd never know if it would have made a difference or not. He'd go to his grave wondering about that, about the night Sam and his child had died, about so many things.

He met Helen's troubled gaze. "If you want a child, if you've considered it from every angle, then do it, Helen. You've got a terrific support system. You won't be in it alone. And you've got the financial resources to hire all the help you need. Don't let your life be ruled by doubts and uncertainty. That's not who you are."

The smile that broke across her face was startlingly radiant. It reminded him of the smile on Sam's face when he'd finally agreed to start trying for a baby of their own.

"Thank you," Helen said quietly. "You have no idea how you've helped me crystallize everything I've been thinking."

She stood up and this time he let her go. When she bent down and pressed a kiss to his cheek, he felt a surprising burst of longing. It was more than the sexual desire he'd felt before around Helen. It was partly a need to be included in this new life she was planning for herself, and partly regret that it would never happen. She was heading in a direction he would never again dare to go. He'd accepted that he would never have a family of his own. He'd convinced himself he didn't deserve it.

Even knowing that, though, he couldn't seem to stop himself from making an outrageous suggestion just to see how she'd react. It would be a test of just how flexible and daring she'd become.

"I have an idea," he began innocently before she could walk away.

"Yes?"

"Why don't I come by later tonight and bring some camping gear?"

She stared at him. "Camping gear?" She sounded as if she were testing very unfamiliar words.

"Sure, a tent, a grill to cook some burgers or roast marshmallows. The weather's perfect for camping out in the backyard. The kids will love it." He had to fight a smile at the horrified expression she was trying hard to mask. "You game?"

He could tell from her expression that she'd never been camping in her life, that the idea held no appeal now.

"You really think it would be good for the kids?" she asked doubtfully.

He nodded. "Mack and Daisy will be fine. What about you?"

She seemed to be waging a debate with herself, but finally she smiled. "I think you've lost your mind, but sure, why not?" she said gamely. "It'll be another adventure."

Erik admired her bravado. "Great. I'll stop by after lunch and put the tent up in your backyard. You guys can start enjoying the campout before I get there. It's Friday, so I could be late."

"I'll manage 'til you get there. The kids can take naps—that way they can stay up later." She gave him a warning glance. "But just so there's no misunderstanding, I draw the line at ghost stories."

"I figured as much," he said. "How do you feel about bugs?"

"I try to avoid them at all costs," she said with a little shiver.

Erik swallowed a laugh. "I'll bring spray."

"What was I thinking?" she murmured as she walked away.

"It's going to be fun," he called after her.

She turned back, her expression doubtful. "If it's not, I'll be in my silk pj's and tucked into my own comfy bed five seconds after you get there."

Erik very nearly groaned. That image was not what he'd needed to have planted in his head just hours before he intended to spend a friendly, totally platonic night with her. Then again, from the moment he'd uttered the suggestion, he'd pretty much known the night was going to be torture.

* * *

Helen gathered up her briefcase and a stack of legal papers at four-thirty that afternoon and headed out of her office. Barb glanced up from the computer on her desk, her expression startled.

"You're leaving?" she asked incredulously.

"No more appointments," Helen said. "Check your calendar."

"But even so, you never leave here before six."

"I never had two kids at home before, either. I'm adapting to that. And Frances needs to leave early because she's going to visit her son and his family. I said I'd take over no later than five."

Barb regarded her with curiosity. "How's the whole instant family thing? Everything still okay? You haven't said much the past couple of weeks, so I assumed everything was going smoothly."

Helen sat down beside the desk. "It's been going surprisingly well. Mack and Daisy are so curious about everything. They're smart and energetic. I'm worn out by bedtime, but it's the good kind of exhaustion, you know?"

"Oh, I know," Barb said. "To be honest, I never thought you'd last this long."

"What choice did I have?" Helen replied. "I had to adapt."

"No, you didn't have to. You *chose* to. There's a huge difference. You actually volunteered to give those kids a home while their mother got the help she needed." A worried frown creased her brow. "What's going to happen when they go back home to their mother? Are you going to be okay?"

"Of course," Helen said. "That's been the plan all along."

"Plans are one thing," her secretary told her. "Emotions tend to be less tidy. These kids have managed to sneak into your heart, haven't they?"

Though she'd admitted it to Erik just that morning, Helen wasn't sure she wanted to tell Barb just how attached she'd become in such a short time. Once she'd come up with some semblance of a routine and realized that Daisy and Mack were pretty adaptable, she'd started to enjoy having them around. She'd explored a whole new world of games and television and family movies. In fact, the best part of her day wasn't the time she spent in the courtroom winning a case for her client; it was the end of the day, when she, Daisy and Mack snuggled on the sofa and watched a DVD together just before bedtime. Being with them had solidified her desire to have a child of her own. It hadn't, however, given her the first clue about the best way of going about that.

Unfortunately, just as Barb suggested, there was a downside to her newfound maternal instincts. She was starting to resent just a little the time Karen spent with Mack and Daisy when she came by. Helen knew her attitude was not only unfair, it was a warning flag flapping so noisily it could have been heard throughout town. Letting them go, not just for a couple of days with their mom, but permanently, was going to tear out a little piece of her heart.

"Well?" Barb prodded. "You like having them there, don't you?"

"Well, of course, I do," she said.

"What happens when they go home?"

"I guess I'll be able to tell you that on Monday," she

said, forcing a note of cheer into her voice. "Karen's picking them up on Sunday for a two-day visit back home. It's her day off and everyone agrees she's ready to have them back, at least part-time."

Barb's expression immediately turned sympathetic. "Oh, Helen, I'm sorry."

"Don't be. They should be with their mother. They belong with her." She said the words by rote, trying to mean them, but failing miserably.

Furthermore, Helen had doubts about whether the transition would go as easily as she implied. Last night after her conversation with Dr. McDaniels, she'd sat beside Mack's bed and then Daisy's, watching them sleeping, and trying to imagine her life without them in it. Her heart had ached at the prospect of all that silence once again greeting her at the end of the day, at the absence of fierce hugs and sticky kisses.

"Helen, I worry about you," Barb said. "I can see it in your eyes. This visit to their mom is one thing, but letting go of them for good is going to break your heart."

"Well, we're not there yet. For now, they're still at my house and I need to get home to them. Erik's coming over as soon as he can get out of the kitchen at Sullivan's and we're going to camp in the backyard."

Barb gaped at Helen. "Excuse me? Did I hear correctly? You're going to camp in the yard, in the dark? In what? A tent?"

"Yes, a tent," Helen said. "Erik has one."

"Well, that should be cozy," Barb said, amusement dancing in her eyes. "Does he know you've never stayed in anything less than a four-star hotel?"

"Probably," Helen said, recalling the glint in his eye when he'd made the suggestion. She'd recognized the whole thing for what it was—a poorly concealed dare. "I think he's counting on me panicking at the sight of the first bug."

Barb laughed. "I just hope he catches it on video."

Helen frowned at her. "I'll ban cameras from the premises. The two of you would get entirely too much enjoyment out of that."

"Enjoyment?" Barb shook her head. "I was thinking about enough blackmail money to secure my retirement."

"You are so not funny," Helen said.

"I don't need to be funny. I'm efficient and I'm about to be rich."

Helen cast one last scowl in her direction, but as soon as she was out the door, she grinned. The whole idea of her camping, even in her own backyard, was pretty ludicrous. Lately, though, she'd been lured into trying lots of new things, not all of them bad, either. In fact, spending the night with Erik, even if it was in a tent with two kids as chaperones, struck her as more intriguing than most of the dates she'd had in the past few years.

When he'd suggested the campout, she'd bitten back the negative response that had immediately come to mind. She needed a few more memories like this to store away. She could use more of Erik's sane, rational advice, as well. Things always went more smoothly with the kids, too, when he was around. They obviously adored him. She'd wondered on more than one occasion lately why he and Karen hadn't drifted together, since it was obvious his connection to the kids wasn't something recent. Maybe she'd ask him that tonight. She had a hunch his reasons ran deeper than some noble objection to a boss dating an employee. Maybe it had more to do with his flatly stated intention never to have kids.

Maybe it was a question best not asked. He'd just tell her his love life was no more her business than it was Dana Sue's. And it seemed clear after their conversation this morning that he was still a long way from moving on from his past. Grace Wharton had gotten it right, after all. Erik was pretty much a confirmed bachelor. That he hadn't always been one didn't really matter. If friendship was all he was willing to offer, she'd take that. She'd never really been friends with a man before, at least not with one who seemed able to see into her soul the way Erik did from time to time. It was nice. More than nice, in fact.

Of course, if it came along with the occasional kiss that could rock her world, so much the better.

CHAPTER TWELVE

To Erik's relief, Helen was not wearing anything resembling silk pajamas when he arrived around nine-thirty that night for the campout. When Dana Sue had heard what he was up to for the evening, she'd insisted he take off the instant the dinner rush had slowed. He figured he'd pay for that big-time by having to answer a slew of questions in the morning.

He took another look at Helen and dismissed Dana Sue and her nosiness from his mind. Helen had on form-fitting jeans and a pale pink T-shirt that flattered her complexion. She was actually wearing sneakers in the same shade of pink with white accents. He instantly recalled Dana Sue teasing Helen about ordering custom sneakers to match her outfits. Still, custom designer shoes aside, she looked far more down-to-earth and approachable than she usually did.

Erik dropped a kiss on her cheek, then checked out her attempt to start the charcoal in the grill he'd put on the patio. There were glimmers of red at the edges, but it was a long way from hot enough to do any effective cooking.

"You ever barbecued before?" he asked.

"No. Why? Am I doing something wrong?"

"Well, you need some heat."

"I didn't want it to burn itself out before you got here," she claimed. "You're early. How'd that happen?"

"Dana Sue sent me packing."

She gave him a questioning look. "Why would she do that?"

"She knew I was coming here."

"Are you crazy? Why would you tell her that?"

"I needed her key to your place. Didn't you see the tray of burgers I left in your fridge earlier?"

"There are burgers in my fridge?"

"And a few other things I thought we'd need," he said, ignoring the patches of indignant color in her cheeks. "I'll go get the food."

Her gaze narrowed as she followed him inside. "Exactly what did you tell Dana Sue that convinced her to give you a key to my house?" she asked in an icy tone that suggested she wasn't pleased about the conversation or his invasion of her home.

Erik shrugged off her annoyance. He was confident she'd get over it—eventually, anyway. "The truth," he said. "That I was cooking you dinner and spending the night and needed to do some advance preparations. Worked like a charm."

"So she thinks you're over here seducing me?"

"Something like that," he said unrepentantly. "She seemed pretty thrilled."

"I'm sure she was. Imagine how overjoyed she's going to be when I tell her just how differently tonight went."

She looked so thoroughly flustered and exasperated he couldn't help baiting her. "You can't be sure of what's going to happen once the kids are asleep." He dropped a kiss on the end of her nose as he passed by on his way outside with the food.

"Oh, I can be sure," she said, evidently regaining her confidence. "And just so you don't have any further illusions, it's not going to be pretty. You'll be lucky if you don't leave here in handcuffs."

"We'll see," he said smugly, not the slightest bit intimidated by her threat. He glanced around the yard. "Where's Mack, by the way?"

"He's in the tent. He fell asleep waiting for you." She glanced pointedly toward Daisy, who was lying down on a blanket, her eyes drifting closed. "Something tells me she's going to miss those burgers, too."

"No way," Daisy murmured sleepily. "I've been waiting and waiting for them. And the marshmallows."

"Then I will speed this production along," Erik promised, fanning the charcoal and stirring the embers to life. "And when everything's ready, we'll wake Mack up."

"Over my dead body," Helen muttered. "Do you know how hard it is to get him back to sleep once he's awake?"

"But that's the fun of a campout," Erik told her. "Staying awake all night is what it's about."

"Yea!" Daisy cheered, fully awake now. "I never stayed up all night before."

"Come on, sugar, get with the program," Erik told Helen. "We could use some music."

"There's a stereo system set up just inside the back door. Keep the sound down, though. The neighbors might not appreciate having classical music blaring at this time of night."

Erik gave her a chiding look. "Classical music? I don't think so. Forget the CDs. I'm going in to grab the bowl of potato salad. When I get back out here, we'll sing."

"Sing what?" Helen asked.

"'Row, Row, Row Your Boat' comes to mind," he said. "Everybody knows that one, right, Daisy?"

"*I* do," she said at once and began to sing loudly and tunelessly.

Erik grinned at Helen. "Now we have a campout!"

Judging from the sour look she gave him, she wasn't all that impressed.

Two hours later, they'd run through all the songs he knew. Helen had chimed in from time to time, but it was evident that campfire songs were not her forte. Now the coals had died down and the kids were sound asleep inside the tent, despite their best efforts to stay awake. They'd filled up with hamburgers and burnt, gooey marshmallows and cherry Kool-Aid. The menu had been pretty disgusting by Erik's culinary standards, but Daisy and Mack had loved it. Even Helen had gotten in to the marshmallow thing. She had the sticky residue at the corners of her lips.

Before he could stop himself or think about conse- quences, Erik impulsively cupped the back of her neck and moved in to savor the sweet marshmallow taste of her mouth.

When he released her, she swallowed hard and stared back at him. "What was *that* about?"

"Couldn't resist," he said with a shrug.

"Are you sure you weren't trying to prove a point?" she asked.

He grinned at her suspicious expression. "Such as?"

"That you weren't lying to Dana Sue when you implied that you were going to seduce me tonight."

"There are two children in that tent," he reminded her, injecting a self-righteous note into his voice. "I would never try to seduce you practically in front of them."

"Would you ever try to seduce me at all?"

At the surprisingly wistful note in her voice, blood rushed to a part of his anatomy he'd been trying to ignore all night. "Are you saying you'd want me to?" he asked in a voice that had turned husky.

"I'm not sure," she confessed. "I've thought about it, though."

"Me, too."

"Maybe we should keep thinking about it," she said.

He nodded slowly. Given where they both were in their lives—on very different pages—her comment wasn't a huge surprise. "Keep me posted on what you're thinking, okay?"

Her lips curved slightly at that. "You'll definitely be the first to know if I reach any conclusions."

Erik forced himself to look away from the heat in her eyes. He stared at the dying embers of their barbecue and wished the heat roaring through his blood would fade as quickly. No, what he really wished was that it had never been ignited. The talk of seduction, the kiss, all of it was leading him down a road he'd vowed not to travel ever again, least of all with Helen.

"You go join the kids," he said gruffly. "I'll stay out here."

"You're not sleeping in the tent? Why?"

"It's better that way," he said.

Helen gave him a look that said she saw right through him. It wasn't better. Just safer.

When the doorbell rang on a Sunday afternoon a few weeks after the campout, Helen's heart seemed to stop. Even as Daisy and Mack ran toward it screaming, "Mommy! Mommy!" she was trying to come up with some way not to open the door at all.

It wasn't as if it was the first time Karen had come to take the kids away. They'd been home for two-day visits half a dozen times now. This time, though, it would be for good. The brief visits had been such a success that Dr. McDaniels thought the time had come for the move home to be permanent. It was the day Helen had been dreading for a couple of months now.

Even so, she forced herself to open the door. But rather than finding Karen on the other side, she found Maddie and Dana Sue, laden down with grocery bags.

"What's this?" she asked.

"We know today is going to be hard on you, so we brought supplies," Dana Sue announced. "I brought the makings for nachos and a huge container of my spiciest guacamole."

"And I brought the ingredients for margaritas," Maddie said.

"You can't drink," Helen reminded her. "You're pregnant."

"No, but you can. And a nice frosty glass of limeade will make me feel as if I'm partying with you."

Daisy stared up at Helen accusingly. "You're having a party? How come? Is it 'cause we're leaving? Are you glad?"

Helen scooped her up. "Absolutely not. I'm going to miss you and Mack like crazy."

"Then can we stay for the party?" Daisy asked. "I love nachos."

"Nachos!" Mack echoed enthusiastically.

Dana Sue grinned. "I'll make them right this minute and you can have some before your mom gets here. Maddie, sit down before you tilt over. Your tummy's the size of six watermelons. I don't know how you stay upright at all. Something tells me that baby is going to come out fully grown and ready for college."

"Obviously the doctor and I figured the due date all wrong. After my last sonogram, he told me this baby was going to be here a whole lot sooner than we'd expected," Maddie said. She put a hand on her stomach. "I was so relieved I almost kissed him. I was beginning to think I'd explode if I really did have another month to go." She eyed her favorite easy chair with skepticism. "There's no way I'll get out of that once I'm down."

Helen grinned, thoroughly enjoying the spectacle of the girl who'd been the star of their ballet production when they were ten, now too cumbersome to move with any grace at all. "Not to worry. We'll pull you up."

"How? With a tow truck?"

"If need be," Dana Sue said. "Now sit. I'll be back in a minute. Helen, you can make limeade for Maddie and the kids and the margaritas for us, while I fix the nachos."

As she was about to leave the room, Helen spotted Daisy inching shyly toward Maddie. When she was close enough, she put her tiny hand on Maddie's stomach. "Is there a baby in there?"

Helen's heart clenched at the awe in Daisy's voice and the gentleness of her touch.

"There is," Maddie confirmed. "You're very smart."

"Mack used to be inside my mommy. I remember."

"You were inside your mommy, too," Maddie told her.

Daisy looked intrigued. "I don't remember that."

"That's because when babies are born there are so many new things to discover all around them that it makes them forget the warm, safe place they were before," Maddie explained, her gaze lifting to meet Helen's.

In that instant, Helen knew with absolute clarity what she wanted. Not just any baby, but her own baby. One she'd sheltered and nurtured for nine months before bringing it into the world. She felt a need so powerful it nearly overwhelmed her. Afraid of what her expression might be revealing, she quickly followed Dana Sue into the kitchen and busied herself with making the drinks.

Dana Sue's upbeat chatter washed over her without registering. All she could think about was that instant when everything had come together in her mind with startling clarity. A feeling of serenity stole over her then and stayed with her even after Karen arrived. It was still with her when Karen, Daisy and Mack walked away from the house for the last time.

Though she went back inside with tears in her eyes, her heart wasn't nearly as heavy as she'd expected it to be. And that was because of the epiphany she'd had.

"Are you okay?" Maddie asked, studying her worriedly. "I know letting them go must have been hard, even though you've been preparing for it for a few weeks now."

Helen nodded. "I just kept telling myself they'd be okay and that I'd see them soon. It's not as if they're moving to the other side of the world. They'll be right across town. And Karen's promised to bring them by whenever I invite them."

"You're calmer than I expected you to be," Dana Sue said, her brow furrowing. "Why is that? Are you relieved to have your house to yourself again?"

"No, it's not that at all," Helen swore. "I just made peace with them going home."

"I'm not buying it," Dana Sue persisted, but then her expression turned sly. "Or did having Erik spend the night here a few weeks ago give you something else to think about? Has he been around more than I realized?"

Maddie stared at them. "Erik spent the night?"

"It was one night. We camped in the backyard," Helen corrected. "With the kids." She frowned at Dana Sue. "You bring that up every time I see you. You need to let it go. Don't make it into something it wasn't."

"Well something helped you get through this afternoon," Dana Sue said. "Having a man in your life would do that."

"Maybe it was just having you guys here," Helen suggested.

"I don't buy it," Dana Sue said again.

"Do you want her to be miserable, Dana Sue?" Maddie asked. "If she says she's okay, we should take her word for it and be happy for her. This was a tough afternoon and she got through it without coming unglued. I'd say that deserves a toast."

As Maddie lifted her glass, she suddenly winced and sucked in a deep breath.

"What?" Helen said at once, rushing to her side. "Are you okay, Maddie?"

"I'm not sure, but that could have been a contraction," Maddie admitted.

Helen regarded her with alarm. "How can you not be sure? You've had four other kids. Shouldn't you know a contraction when you're having one?"

"I've had a few twinges off and on for a few hours now," Maddie said. "I thought it was because I overdid it helping Cal move some things around in the new playroom upstairs." She took a deep breath, then nodded. "Yes, I'm sure that's all it was. See, I'm fine. Nothing to worry about."

Dana Sue said worriedly, "Maybe we should go to the hospital and let you get checked out, anyway. You shouldn't be moving furniture this late in your pregnancy. I'm surprised Cal let you."

Maddie rolled her eyes. "Are you kidding? He let me carry a few toys across the room. When I tried to move the rocking chair, he went crazy and insisted I sit down in it and just tell him where I wanted everything else."

"But you're feeling okay now?" Helen asked. "No more twinges?"

"None," Maddie said, then groaned and grabbed her stomach. "*That* was definitely a contraction." She grinned through her obvious pain. "This little one is obviously full of surprises."

Helen looked at Dana Sue. "What do we do now?"

"You haul her out of that chair and get her to the car," Dana Sue said calmly. "I'll call Cal to meet us at the hospital. If her contractions are that close together, we don't have a lot of time."

Helen let Maddie grab on to her shoulders, then half

lifted, half tugged her onto her feet. When she was upright, Helen gazed into her eyes. "You are not having this baby in the backseat of my car, understood?"

Maddie gave her a wry look. "Then I suggest we don't waste a lot of time standing around here chatting. I barely made it to the hospital with Jessica Lynn. Something tells me this one's going to be even more impatient."

She took a step, then uttered a curse.

"What?" Helen demanded.

"My water broke," Maddie said. "We might want to pick up this pace."

Dana Sue snapped her cell phone closed. "Cal's on his way to the hospital. Let's get this show on the road. If he gets there before us, he's going to have a full-blown panic attack."

"He warned me not to go out this afternoon," Maddie said. "He's going to be furious if this baby is born anywhere other than a delivery room."

"Can you waddle any faster than that?" Dana Sue inquired, drawing a nasty look from Maddie. "Okay, okay. You're doing the best you can."

Five minutes later they had Maddie stretched out on the backseat with Dana Sue riding with her, while Helen drove. Every time Maddie let out a scream, Helen's hands clenched a little more tightly on the steering wheel and she slammed her foot down a little harder on the accelerator.

They made the half-hour drive to Regional Hospital in record time, but Cal was faster. He was waiting at the emergency room entrance, a frantic expression on his face. An orderly with a wheelchair was waiting with him.

"We need to get your paperwork taken care of," the orderly said.

"No time," Maddie said, her teeth clenched. "Delivery room now!"

"But—"

"Do it," Cal said. "The paperwork can wait."

"I'll handle that," Helen said. "Just go."

She spent twenty minutes placating an annoyed admissions clerk, then went to find Dana Sue. She'd no sooner found her in the waiting room of the obstetrics unit when Cal came out of the delivery room, looking dazed.

"It's a boy," he told them, as if it were news. They'd known that much for months. "He came out howling."

"Probably objecting to my guacamole," Dana Sue said.

"Congratulations," Helen told Cal, her emotions a wild mix of delight, wonder and envy. Could she be right here by this time next year? Perhaps, if she put her mind to it. Could she do it without someone like Cal beside her? Of course, she told herself staunchly. She would have her two best friends at her side. Even Cal and Ronnie would stick by her. Erik, too, more than likely. That would be more than enough. She was sure of it. Sure enough to start planning the next step first thing tomorrow.

Karen stood in the doorway to the kids' bedroom and stared at them in the moonlight that spilled through the window. Having them home again and knowing that this time it was for good had filled her with so much joy she'd barely reacted when Mack spilled milk all over the kitchen floor and Daisy threw a tantrum because Karen wouldn't let her have candy before dinner.

In fact, she'd waited in dread for her head to start pounding or her shoulders to tense, which had become so commonplace before they'd gone to stay with Helen, but she'd taken both incidents in stride. She hadn't even needed to make conscious use of the calming techniques Dr. McDaniels had taught her. She was simply too happy to let anything get to her tonight.

When Daisy and Mack had gone back to Helen's after the last visit, Karen had redecorated their bedroom. Mack had barely noticed the changes, but Daisy had been thrilled. The bare, merely functional room had been transformed into something special. Its walls were now the same buttery shade as the walls at The Corner Spa. In fact, the paint had come from there. When Dana Sue had heard she wanted to decorate the kids' bedroom, she'd offered the extra paint they'd stored after their remodeling of the old Victorian house that was now one of the region's best day spas.

Dana Sue and her husband had even spent an afternoon helping Karen paint. They'd also scouted a couple of secondhand shops and found some furniture, which they'd painted white, and a deep-yellow toy box with red, blue and green polka dots and stripes. With any luck, Mack and Daisy's toys would wind up inside it at least some of the time, rather than strewn all over the apartment.

Frances had made new curtains for the room from a polka-dotted fabric that coordinated with the toy box. She'd had enough material left over to make matching throw pillows for the beds.

Karen had bought colorful decals, which she'd scattered over the walls. She wanted the cheerful decor to represent their future—bright and new for all of them.

Exiting the bedroom, she found Frances tidying up in the kitchen after their dinner of her homemade mac-and-cheese, fresh peas and one of Erik's apple cobblers with vanilla ice cream.

"Kids get settled in okay?" Frances asked.

"They're already sound asleep. I hope you know how much I appreciate all your help with getting their room ready. Daisy loves it and I'm sure Mack does, too."

"Maybe we should tackle your room next," Frances suggested. "You've spent too long living here as if it's just a temporary roof over your head. You need to turn it into a real home."

"In other words, it's time to make lemonade out of those lemons," Karen said wryly. "You're right. I was so busy being resentful about being reduced to living in a tiny, two-bedroom apartment, I never wanted to do a thing to make it nicer. I just wanted out."

"Being happy where you are is never a bad thing," Frances told her. "Nor is it conceding defeat."

Karen frowned at the comment. "Meaning?"

"I think you've been afraid if you did anything to turn this place into a home, it meant you were accepting the raw deal fate handed you when your husband left. It meant you were giving in, or maybe giving up. You can still have ambitions, sweetie, but this is reality for now. Make the most of it."

"I think I get that finally," Karen said. "I just hope my kids haven't paid too high a price."

"Mack and Daisy are fine. Living with Helen was a grand adventure for them, but they belong here with you. Didn't you notice how excited they were when they got here this afternoon? Best of all, you're strong again and ready to handle whatever's next in your life."

"You think so?" she asked. "You really think so?"

"I *know* so. I saw it tonight at dinner. When Mack dumped that milk on the floor, you didn't bat an eye. And I don't know if you noticed, but there was relief in Daisy's eyes when you just mopped it up without a word."

Karen sighed. "She heard me lose it way too much, didn't she?"

"Probably so, but you can't fix the past. You can only do things differently from here on out. Any idea what you'd like your future to hold?"

"I'll be happy just to keep things on an even keel for now," Karen told her. "I need to remember how to be a good mom."

Frances frowned. "I suppose that's fine for now," she agreed. "But you need dreams, Karen. You need goals for yourself. You deserve to find happiness, too."

"If my kids are okay, I'm happy," she insisted.

"I'll accept that for the moment," Frances said. "But you need to give some thought to your future. Promise me you'll do that."

"I promise," Karen said, giving her a hug.

"Okay, then," Frances said, evidently satisfied. "Now let me leave, so you can get a good night's sleep. If you need anything at all tomorrow, you let me know. Don't be afraid to lean on people, Karen. That's what got you into trouble before. You were trying to handle everything on your own."

Karen gave Frances another fierce hug. "I honestly don't know what I'd do without you."

Frances beamed at her. "Then isn't it wonderful that you'll never have to find out?"

"I love you."

Frances brushed a lock of hair back from her face. "And you're like one of my own, Karen. Good night, sweetie."

"Good night," Karen said softly, tears stinging her eyes.

Right this second, her life seemed to be close to perfect, but it was good to know that the next time it started to fall apart, there was someone she could count on right across the hall. For so many years she'd wondered how different her life would have been if she'd ever had a real mom, a real home she could count on. Now, in so many ways, she'd found the answer to that.

Maddie had been home from the hospital for two weeks and Helen had stopped by to visit every single night. Holding baby Cole Maddox in her arms was solidifying the epiphany she'd had the day Maddie talked about the warm safe place her baby had in her body.

And just now she'd finally admitted to Maddie that she'd come to a decision. She wanted to get pregnant and have a child, no matter what anyone in Serenity thought of her for doing it. She could weather the gossip, and if she gave her child a loving home and surrounded him or her with a huge extended family, surely the child would never feel shortchanged.

Maddie searched Helen's face. "You're sure about this? You've actually decided you want to have a baby the old-fashioned way? I thought having Karen's kids underfoot might have scared you off."

"I thought so, too, at least those first few days, but

it got better. I was good at the whole mom thing, better than I'd anticipated." She looked Maddie squarely in the eye and added passionately, "That yearning for something I've been feeling all these months turned into something fiercely maternal. This is right. I know it is."

"But, sweetie, there's a huge difference between playing mom when there's an end in sight and being in it for the long haul," Maddie cautioned.

"I know that," Helen said impatiently. "I've heard it often enough lately. But I'm ready to take it on. I *want* to take it on."

"And marriage? Do you see a dad in this picture?" Maddie asked.

"Honestly, I can't visualize that," Helen admitted. "I'm forty-two. If I haven't met someone in all this time I'd be willing to marry, why on earth would I think I can do it in the next few months or even in the next year?"

"Yes, it would put a courtship on a fast track," Maddie agreed, looking amused. "That shouldn't be a problem for a single-minded woman like you."

"Unfortunately, men tend to be more skittish when it comes to something like this, particularly if I were to mention on the first date that my biological clock is ticking so loudly it can be heard in Georgia."

"That might put them off." Maddie's grin spread.

"So what do I do?"

"Isn't there any man you're attracted to who might make a good husband, a good father?" Maddie asked. "You're not exactly known for giving men much time to make a good impression, but maybe now's the time to run down that list and give a few of those suitors you've dismissed another chance." She gave her a sly glance. "And then there's Erik. Dana Sue's convinced there's something brewing between the two of you."

At the reminder, the all-too-recent memory of a sizzling kiss surfaced in Helen's mind like a beacon in the darkness. Maybe she didn't have to find a man to marry her. Maybe she didn't need to find someone interested in becoming a full-time father. She had a career. She had resources. She was perfectly capable of raising a child entirely on her own. So maybe what she really needed was a man willing to sleep with her, no strings attached. Erik certainly seemed to qualify.

There was no question that he was attracted to her, and vice versa. Nor was there any question that he was even remotely interested in being married or in being a dad. He'd been abundantly clear about that, as well. He was the perfect candidate. He was someone she liked and respected, someone for whom she had feelings. Thus the whole experience wouldn't feel quite so calculated and impersonal. She would honestly be able to tell her child one day that his or her dad was a decent, good man and that she had deep, loving feelings for him.

If need be, once she was pregnant, she could draw up whatever legal papers were necessary to assure Erik that she would never ask for child support, that his role in the child's life could be as limited as he wanted it to be. If he wanted no involvement whatsoever, so be it. She couldn't help thinking that would be a loss for him and his child, but he'd been so adamant about not wanting to be a dad that she assumed that would be his response.

In essence that would make him a sperm donor, albeit in a more direct and tantalizing way, but she honestly couldn't see a downside to it. Erik would get great sex for a while, which was all he apparently wanted

from a relationship. She'd get a baby. Wasn't that equitable?

"What on earth is going on in that head of yours?"
Maddie asked after several minutes. "Was it what I
said about Erik?"

"No, absolutely not," Helen insisted, praying she
could keep Maddie from making that leap. She forced
a smile. "But I may have a plan, after all."

"Really? What is it?" Maddie asked, looking far
more worried than relieved.

"It's probably best if you don't know," she told her.
And it would definitely be best if Dana Sue didn't know.
She might get all weird at the idea of Helen using Erik
to get the baby she wanted.

Heck, there was a possibility Erik might get a little
weird about it himself. What if she suggested it and he
shot her down? What if she just seduced him and told
him later? She wasn't crazy about what such a deception
said about her. And it would probably confirm every
negative thing Erik had ever thought about her, destroying the easy camaraderie they'd discovered lately. That
dismayed her a little more than she cared to admit, but
this driving need to have a child of her own outweighed
any dismay.

And she would make absolutely certain that a child
of hers had everything he or she could ever possibly
need—love, a good education, a wonderful home. Those
were the only things that really mattered.

What about a father? a nagging voice in her head
demanded. Lots of kids did just fine without a father in
their life, she argued with herself. She had. In fact, after
seeing how her mom had struggled in one dead-end job
after another to give her a decent life after her dad's

death, Helen had been driven to make sure she could always provide for herself and any family that might come along. That determination was what had gotten her into this fix in the first place. She hadn't allowed herself to be sidetracked by anything that wouldn't contribute to her financial security and success.

Satisfied with her logic, she stood up abruptly. "I need to be somewhere," she told Maddie.

"But Dana Sue and Jeanette will be here any minute now," Maddie said. "We were going to talk about expanding the spa."

"Apologize for me," Helen said. "We'll make up for this next week."

"But you're the one who wanted to talk about opening a second spa," Maddie protested, even as Helen put baby Cole back into her arms. "This meeting was your idea."

"It can wait," Helen said. "You, Dana Sue and Jeanette can bounce the idea around and let me know what you think."

Maddie's eyes narrowed. "Something tells me you're about to do something impulsive. That's never a good thing with you."

"It's not impulsive and I don't need to talk about it. I've thought about it from every angle. I've probably analyzed it to death." Okay, not the part about Erik, but maybe it was better not to overthink that. She might start to doubt the wisdom of her plan, and there was no time for doubts.

"Well, you know Dana Sue and I will support you, no matter what you do," Maddie said, though her brow was creased with worry.

Helen hugged her. "I know, and you have no idea

how much that means to me. Thank you for not telling me I'm crazy."

Maddie grinned. "Did I say that?"

"No, but you heard me and you didn't utter those words, so I'm taking that as a good sign."

"Could I say anything that would stop you from doing whatever it is you're about to do?" Maddie asked.

Helen shrugged. "Probably not."

In fact, right this second, she couldn't think of anything that could derail her plan. And somewhere between here and Sullivan's she'd decide just how much of her plan to reveal to Erik and how much to keep to herself.

CHAPTER THIRTEEN

———◆◆———

The sheet of fondant was ready to be draped over the top layer of the three-tiered wedding cake when Erik turned to Tess, who'd been watching him intently.

"You do it," he said.

Her brown eyes widened in dismay. "I can't," she said, though she was clearly tempted.

"Of course you can. How many times have you practiced this?"

She shook her head and backed up a step. "But that was practice. This is the real thing. What if I ruin it?"

"You won't," he said confidently. "But if you do, it's not the end of the world. We'll do it over. Come on, Tess. You've practiced enough. You have to do it for real sometime."

Just as she was about to drape the smooth sheet of icing over the cake, the door to the kitchen burst open and Helen breezed in. Startled, Tess dropped the icing on the floor, then looked at him with a chagrined expression.

"I'm sorry," she said, gesturing toward the mess. "I told you I couldn't do it."

Erik sighed, regarding Helen with exasperation. "Did

it ever occur to you to knock before charging in here at this hour?"

"No more than it occurred to you to ask me for a key to my house that time," she retorted. She dangled a key from her finger. "My key to Sullivan's. I've had it since Dana Sue opened."

He shook his head. "Why didn't I know that?"

"Because it's not your restaurant?" she suggested sweetly.

"Whatever," he muttered and bent down to help Tess, who was mopping up the remains of the fondant.

When he stood up, Helen was regarding him with a hint of uncertainty. "Is this really a bad time?"

He bit back a grin. "What do you think? You just scared poor Tess half to death and came close to ruining Jane Downing's wedding cake."

"Jane Downing is being married for the fourth time," Helen said. "I'd say this marriage is as doomed as her cake. Not a big deal." She turned to Tess. "I'm sorry for scaring you, though. I'm Helen Decatur, a friend of Dana Sue's and, despite his snide attitude, a friend of Erik's as well."

"Helen is the attorney I told you about, Tess," Erik added. "She said she'd help you with Diego's situation."

"Would you?" Tess asked as if not quite daring to hope.

"Absolutely. I would have been by to talk to you much sooner, but I had Karen's kids and, to be honest, I was a little overwhelmed."

Tess gave her a shy smile. "Children are a lot of work."

"They are, indeed," Helen said. "Why don't we let

Erik finish up that cake and you can tell me what's happened with your husband?"

"Good idea," Erik said, relieved to have time to remind himself why he should not be attracted to Helen
and why he should not act on his very powerful desire to kiss her. He'd resolved not to act on his feelings
until and unless she came to him and made it clear she
was interested in a no-strings relationship. When she'd
walked through the doorway a minute ago, a part of him
had immediately leaped to the conclusion that he was
about to get the answer he'd been lying awake nights
thinking about.

"Would you rather speak in private?" Helen asked
Tess.

To his disappointment, since he'd hoped for some
space so he could reclaim his composure, Tess declined.

"Erik knows what's happened with Diego," she told
Helen. "I don't mind if he hears us."

Helen pulled two stools close together and climbed
on one, which hiked her narrow skirt halfway up her
thighs, giving Erik an intriguing glimpse of bare skin.
He couldn't seem to keep himself from following the
curve of her leg down to her trim ankle and the latest
pair of sexy heels she was wearing. The woman did
love her shoes. He couldn't recall ever seeing the same
pair twice. He might not know much about designer
shoes, but he did know quality. It was plain that habit
cost her a fortune.

Apparently she caught the direction of his gaze, because she held one foot out. "Manolo Blahnik's," she
said as if that would mean something to him.

He grinned at her. "They look good on you." They

were also very tough on his resolve. Those shoes were all about seduction.

"I thought so," she agreed, then turned to Tess. "Erik says you had an attorney who billed you and never did any work. Is that true?"

Tess nodded. "Jimmy Bob West. He was the only attorney I knew."

Erik saw Helen stiffen visibly. His determination to stay far removed from the conversation failed him. "You know this attorney?" he asked.

"We've crossed paths a few times," she said. "Jimmy Bob's no saint, but I never thought he would sink that low. Tess, tell me exactly what he told you, how much he billed you and what he did."

As Tess went through the sad tale, Helen took notes, her forehead creased in a frown. There was real anger in her eyes by the time Tess finished.

"You'll have your money back by the end of the week," she assured Tess. "One way or another."

"But what about Diego? He is what matters," Tess said. "I have all of his papers proving he is here legally. How do we get his deportation reversed?"

"I'll take care of that, too," Helen promised. "And if I bump up against too much bureaucracy, I know exactly who can untangle all the red tape. It may not happen overnight, Tess, but we will get your husband back here."

"I don't know how to thank you," Tess said. "That would be like a miracle for me and my children." She glanced at the clock on the wall. "It is very late. I need to be home." She regarded Erik worriedly. "I was no help to you tonight."

"You'll get your chance another time," he assured

her. "You're good at this, Tess. It's just a matter of practice."

"I'm off tomorrow," she said. "I think I will practice baking a very special birthday cake for my mother as a surprise. If it turns out well, I will bring you a picture." She gave him a considering look. "We should create an album, you know. So people can see all the beautiful cakes you have made. We could have a website, too. My brother could create it. He's majoring in website design and computer skills at junior college. There is nothing he can't do." Her face shone with pride.

Surprised that Tess had put so much thought into the business side of things, he nodded thoughtfully. "That's a terrific idea, Tess. I'll speak to Dana Sue about it. Have your brother give me a call, okay?"

"I will," she said. "Thank you again, Ms. Decatur. I really appreciate what you're doing for me."

"I'm happy to do it, Tess," Helen said. "Good night."

After Tess had gone, Erik studied Helen. "You're not just happy to help because you care about Tess and Diego, are you? It has something to do with this Jimmy Bob West."

She grinned. "You're very perceptive. I want to nail that sleazebag's hide to the wall. What he did to her was unconscionable."

"He's not opposing counsel on some divorce you're handling, by any chance?"

"He is, indeed. Our last encounter in the courtroom was just my first warning volley. Lawyers like Jimmy Bob give all of us a bad name."

"Yet, you seem to take pride in being referred to as a barracuda," Erik noted.

"A barracuda's one thing. He's a bottom-feeder, the lowest of the low, an unethical son of a gun."

"In other words, you don't like him."

"I don't have to like every attorney I cross paths with," she said. "But I do prefer to respect them. I can hardly wait to have a little chat with Jimmy Bob as soon as I've done some research into this situation."

Erik grinned. "Now that I've put you on the scent for blood, what actually brought you by here tonight? I assume you knew Dana Sue wasn't here, since she told me she was having a meeting with you and Maddie. Don't tell me you skipped out on them just to see me."

She looked vaguely chagrined that he knew about the meeting. "I left early," she said, sounding oddly defensive. "It occurred to me it might be the perfect time for us to talk without being under Dana Sue's watchful eye."

"Interesting," he said. Helen looked surprisingly ill at ease, he thought. "Something in particular on your mind?"

"Don't get excited," she said. "I just haven't had a good sparring match lately."

"Really? And that's the only reason you came by? So we could match wits?"

"Something like that."

He shook his head. "Not buying it, sugar. You had some other agenda. Come on. Spill it."

To his astonishment, a burst of color flooded her cheeks. "You're blushing," he said, startled.

"I am not. It's probably a hot flash."

He winced at that. If she was having hot flashes, he definitely didn't want to know about it. Wasn't she a little young for them, though? He tried to recall what he'd read about menopause during his EMT training, but since most of his courses had focused on emergency medicine, not much came to mind.

He did like the fact that he'd somehow managed to throw her off-kilter. He decided to keep her there.

"It's okay to admit you came by because you couldn't go another second without seeing me," he said. "You don't have to be embarrassed because you find me irresistible."

She leveled an indignant look directly into his eyes, then glanced away. "This was a mistake."

"What was a mistake?"

"Thinking I could spend more than fifteen minutes with you without wanting to strangle you."

He bit back a grin. "We spent a whole night together not that long ago and I don't recall you wanting to strangle me then."

"Did you miss my reaction to the fact that you conned Dana Sue into giving you my key?"

"Oh, that," he said dismissively. "You weren't really upset about it."

"Yes, I was."

"But you got over it," he countered. "You just made a big deal out of it because you thought you should."

She scowled. "I made a big deal out of it because what you did was sneaky and underhanded."

Suddenly, the color that had remained in her cheeks washed right out, leaving her complexion pale. "I need to go," she said, grabbing her purse and heading for the door.

Erik stepped in front of her, worried by her pallor. "Are you okay? You're not feeling sick, are you?"

"No. I, um, I just remembered something I have to do."

He recognized tap dancing when he heard it. "Something to do?" he echoed doubtfully. "At this hour?"

"Yes. I should have done it hours ago." She pushed past him. "I'll see you."

He stared after her. What was up with that? One minute she was the same old feisty Helen, the next she was taking off like a scared rabbit. It was evident from the way she'd avoided meeting his gaze that she'd been lying through her teeth. And the only thing she had to do was get away from him.

He shrugged off his confusion. It was just one more reminder that she was way too complex and complicated for him. If he ever did break down and let another woman into his life, he wanted one who was serene and easy to read. Helen was anything but.

So why couldn't he get her out of his mind?

Well, that had certainly been a disaster, Helen thought as she drove away from Sullivan's. The moment she'd accused Erik of being sneaky and underhanded over a key, of all things, it had struck her that what she was planning was a thousand times worse. And yet, now that the idea of having him father her child had taken hold, she couldn't seem to abandon it.

At home she went through her bedtime routine by rote, missing the chaos Daisy and Mack's presence produced underfoot. She reached for the phone to call them, but a glance at the clock told her it was too late.

In bed she made mental lists of all the pros and cons of involving Erik in her plan to have a child of her own. The positives outweighed the negatives, or maybe she'd only weighted it that way so she could go through with it. In the end, though, she would have the child she desperately wanted. Wasn't that the only thing that mattered?

But what about what Erik wants? a nagging voice countered. He couldn't have made it any clearer that he didn't want children. After wrestling with that very hard truth for most of the night and the next day, she managed to convince herself that he'd be okay once he knew she didn't expect anything from him. In the meantime, she'd just have to find some way to live with the guilt of knowing she was deceiving him about the real reason she was initiating an affair with him.

Exhausted and cranky after a couple of sleepless nights and countless frustrating calls to deal with immigration bureaucracy in an attempt to resolve Diego's immigration status, she left home on Wednesday morning and headed straight for Jimmy Bob's office. She was in the perfect mood to take him to task over what he'd done to Tess.

The law offices of West & Davis were located in Serenity's newest business complex, a cluster of single-story, pale-pink brick buildings with black shutters. It had been built a few years ago by a partnership of several of the town's professionals as a tax write-off. Maddie's ex-husband was one of the partners. Bill Townsend's suite of offices for his pediatrics practice dominated one entire building. West & Davis occupied another. The third building housed the more modest suites of a dentist, an accountant and a local developer. One of the growing real estate companies had just taken over the entire fourth building.

It was early enough that the parking lot was mostly

empty. Helen immediately spotted Jimmy Bob's shiny new BMW convertible parked in front of his office. The spaces most likely used by his staff were still empty, as was his partner's assigned space, which meant she could raise a real ruckus with Jimmy Bob without fear of being overheard.

Briefcase in hand, she strolled inside and walked straight into his office without bothering to knock. Jimmy Bob's gaze shot up and alarm flared in his eyes before he carefully covered it with a phony smile.

"Helen, good to see you. Did we have an appointment this morning?"

"No. I was hoping you could spare a few minutes before your day gets too crazy."

"Well, of course I can. Have a seat. You want some coffee? Made it myself from a special blend I order online. Have to say it's the best in town."

"Then by all means," she said. "I'd love a cup."

He poured it for her, then went behind his imposing desk in a tactic that was meant to intimidate. "This is about the Holliday case, I imagine. Is Caroline ready to settle?"

She regarded him incredulously. "With your client on the ropes? I don't think so," Helen replied. "I think you'll find Brad's hidden assets quite fascinating. I know we have. So has Judge Rockingham, which is why he went along with that second delay I requested. Suddenly he seems to be as eager to get to the bottom of Brad's finances as we are."

She gave him an innocent look. "It must be making things a little tense for the three of you on the golf course, though."

He winced. "Look, I had no idea Brad had been

keeping things from me," Jimmy Bob said. "I hope you know that. The judge was in the dark, too. He's livid and he let Brad know it. I always tell my clients that full disclosure is necessary in situations like this."

"I'm sure you do," Helen said, though she was certain of no such thing. That was a battle for another day. "I'm here about another case."

Jimmy Bob looked puzzled. "Are we representing opposing sides in another divorce?"

"No, this is about Tess Martinez."

For an instant his expression was blank, but then he nodded slowly. "Of course. I remember Tess. A very sad situation. She claimed her husband was deported even though he was here legally."

"She didn't just claim it, Jimmy Bob. It's the truth."

"They all say that," he insisted with a shrug. "Most of the time it's a lie."

"It isn't a lie in the case of Diego Martinez. He has his papers, Jimmy Bob. I know Tess showed them to you. And I know she paid you to represent her and fix this so her husband could come home to his family."

He frowned as he looked over the papers Helen had picked up from Tess on her way over here. "Excellent forgeries," he concluded. "That's why I couldn't do anything for her."

"Either you're incredibly lazy or you're an idiot, or maybe you're just low-down scum," she said. "I was able to check out this information with a few phone calls." Okay, it had taken two days, but still. "It's all completely legitimate. Diego's papers are in order. He should have been back here months ago. Instead, you took Tess's money and then blew her off."

He squirmed uncomfortably. "She's taking you in,

Helen. I never picked you to be one of those softies who believes every sob story."

Helen stared at him. "So you're saying I'm gullible and you were just doing your civic duty by taking money from a client and then doing absolutely nothing to help her?"

"There was nothing I could do," he insisted.

She shook her head. "That's amazing. Because the person I spoke to at Immigration says we can have this straightened out by the end of the week and Diego home with his family within a few weeks at most."

"No way," Jimmy Bob said, his face red. "This town doesn't need any more of these border jumpers coming in to take jobs that belong to our own people, Helen. What is *wrong* with you?"

Helen merely shook her head at his outrageous comment. "There's nothing wrong with me, but there's a whole lot wrong with an attorney who would cheat someone out of their very limited funds, then do absolutely nothing to help them."

"I'm telling you, you're being conned," he blustered.

"The federal government doesn't seem to agree," she said. "But rather than sit here and argue with you about the merits of Diego's case, I'll be happy if you'll just write a check to Tess for the amount she gave you. She and Diego can use that to get settled when he gets back here. If you're smart, you'll add a little interest to keep me from spreading this story far and wide."

"That's blackmail," he accused.

"We can certainly debate that in front of the bar association's ethics committee," she offered.

Jimmy Bob locked gazes with her. When Helen didn't flinch, he finally pulled a checkbook out of his

desk and wrote a check. She glanced at the figure and
nodded in satisfaction. "Thank you. I'll see you in court
in a few days. I think we can get the Holliday case
wrapped up this time, don't you?"

"I'll do my best to convince Brad of that, but he's
furious about this last maneuver of yours. I don't know
that I've ever seen him so angry. He's been on a rampage, making all sorts of ridiculous threats."

Helen's gaze narrowed. "Threats?"

Jimmy Bob waved his hand dismissively. "Nothing
to worry about. He's just blowing smoke."

"You sure about that?"

"Of course I am. Brad's been a respected member of
this community most of his life. He's not going to do
anything stupid." Jimmy Bob shook his head. "Doesn't
mean I can get him to listen to reason when it comes to
settling this case." He paused and gave her a considering look. "You know, Trent and I have been thinking
about adding another partner. You interested?"

"In working with you?" Helen asked. Was he kidding?

"Why not? You're smart. You're tough. I admire
that."

"While I appreciate the compliment, Jimmy Bob, I'm
afraid I don't have the stomach for working with you."

To her surprise, he grinned. "That's exactly what I
like about you, Helen. You don't pull punches. Think
about the offer."

"No need to," she assured him.

"Not even if it meant you could spend your spare
time trying to reform me?"

She laughed at that. "Something tells me you're beyond redemption, Jimmy Bob." She waved the check

before tucking it into her briefcase. "But you did the right thing this time. I appreciate it."

He walked her to the door. "You take care, you hear."

"You do the same."

As she drove away, she couldn't help wondering if Jimmy Bob was the scumbag she'd always thought him to be, or just a good old boy who got a kick out of working all the angles to see who'd call him on it. Thinking of the check she'd gotten for Tess without too much of a protest from Jimmy Bob, she was beginning to think it might be the latter.

Karen had been conscientiously going to The Corner Spa every afternoon for an hour during the break between lunch and dinner at Sullivan's. As much as she'd hated the exercise at first, she realized that she always felt better afterward. She was never going to run in a marathon or lift her own weight in barbells, but the modest goals and challenges Elliott set for her were making a difference in her overall stamina and fitness.

She'd been disappointed when he'd declared her ready to do her workouts on her own, but she'd understood that his time was valuable. He had other, paying clients who deserved his full attention. Still, she watched with a certain amount of envy as he coached those other women, while she trudged away on the treadmill or rode an exercise bike.

She sighed as he bent close to a new client, whispering encouragement as he once had to her. She reminded herself he was just doing his job. Despite the sparks she'd felt, it was obvious she'd been just another client to him. Why had she allowed herself to make such a big deal of their time together? Because she was an idiot, that was why.

She finished her cooldown stretches, then headed for the locker room. Suddenly Elliott stepped into her path.

"You weren't pushing yourself today," he said. "What's going on?"

She flushed under his intense look. "I was distracted, I guess."

"Something you want to talk about?"

Not with him, anyway. She shook her head.

"Then how about going to a movie with me this weekend?"

The request, coming right after she'd convinced herself she'd only imagined Elliott's interest, caught her completely by surprise. "A movie?"

He grinned. "I've been known to sit in the dark occasionally and stare up at images on a big screen. It's relaxing."

"And here I thought you never sat down for a second."

"You still haven't answered me," he said. "How about a movie?"

Karen was tempted, but there were so many complications in her life she wasn't sure she could handle any more. Maybe she was better off sticking with the fantasy. "I'm not sure it's a good idea," she said at last.

Elliott looked genuinely disappointed. "Another time?"

Deciding to explain the reason she was turning him down, she asked, "Do you have a minute for a break? I'd like to talk to you about this." She wanted him to understand that her refusal wasn't about him. Maybe then she wouldn't be slamming the door for good.

"Sure, I can take a break," he said readily. "I'll get us a couple of bottled waters and meet you on the patio out back."

"Give me ten minutes to shower and dress."

"That'll work."

Karen was grateful for her short hair. She was able to shape it while it was still damp and look halfway presentable when she joined Elliott outside. Several women studied her with interest when she sat down at his table.

He handed her the bottled water, then leaned back in his chair. Though he was totally focused on her, he still managed to look completely relaxed and at ease. Karen envied him for that.

"Elliott," she began hesitantly, "I didn't turn you down because I don't like you. I…" She tried again. "My life is complicated and—" She stopped. "No, actually it's a mess. Or it has been. I have two kids. My ex-husband hasn't paid child support since he left. My kids have been sick a lot. I've missed work. I've been totally stressed out. In fact, one of the reasons I'm even here is because my shrink thought the exercise would help with the stress and Dana Sue arranged for a free membership. That's my life in a nutshell."

Elliott's gaze remained steady as she blurted everything out. When she was finished, he simply nodded. "I knew all that, or most of it, anyway. I didn't know about the deadbeat dad, but I'd heard all the rest."

"And you still want to go out with me?" she asked in amazement.

He chuckled at her reaction. "Here's what I see. You're a beautiful woman who's had a tough time. You're a good mom. You're working hard to put your life back together. Your kids are back home now, which

proves just how hard you've worked. What's not to admire and like about that?"

"But why would you want to get caught up in all my
drama?" she asked, genuinely bemused.

"Didn't I mention you're gorgeous? And funny?"

Karen laughed. "You hadn't mentioned the part about
me being funny," she teased. "*Now* I get it."

"Look, it's just a movie. We can make it a family
thing, if that would be easier for you than worrying
about a sitter. I like kids. I'd better. Between my brothers and sisters, I have ten nieces and nephews. They're
always around at my folks' place. My mom takes her
duties as their *abuela* very seriously."

Karen thought about that. "Daisy, she's my five-year-
old, has been begging to see the new animated movie.
Could you stand it?"

"My nieces tell me it's great and they're very good
judges of animated films," he said.

Karen made an impulsive decision for the first time
in ages. "I have to work on Saturday. Would Sunday
afternoon be okay for you?"

"Sunday afternoon would be fine. We can go for
pizza after the movie."

"You are a very brave man," she said.

"Heroic, perhaps?" he teased.

She laughed. "Maybe."

But, she admitted to herself, he was showing all the
signs of being outstanding hero material.

Erik couldn't figure out what the devil was going
on. Suddenly every time he turned around Helen was
in the kitchen at Sullivan's, and she didn't seem to be
there to see Dana Sue. In fact, he was getting this odd

vibe that she was there to flirt with him, which made no sense at all. They'd talked about the fact that neither of them were looking for any kind of serious relationship. While there was no mistaking the flirtatious undertones of their conversations, she had yet to say or do anything that would suggest she was ready to move to another level. In fact, the messages she was sending out were so mixed he had yet to unscramble them. Didn't mean he wasn't getting a kick out of trying, though.

More peculiar than Helen's behavior was the fact that Dana Sue didn't seem to be behind any of it. If anything, she seemed just as puzzled by Helen's presence as he was.

After she'd shown up every single night for a week, Erik decided to call her on it. Dana Sue had gone home with Ronnie after Helen had volunteered to stay and help him clean up the kitchen. Right this second she was apparently on a mission to polish every piece of chrome in sight.

Erik hitched himself up onto a counter and watched her work, a frown furrowing her brow, her hair curling about her face from the steam that had filled the room when he'd opened the dishwasher. She'd kicked off her shoes, another pair of those high-heeled sandals that drew attention to her shapely legs. Her hips swayed in time to some tune she was singing, mostly off-key. He couldn't stop the grin that spread across his face as he listened to her slaughter the lyrics and the tune. It was yet another unexpected side to a very complex woman, who was as fascinating as she was infuriating.

Apparently sensing his gaze on her, she turned slowly. "What are you looking at?"

"You," he said.

"Why aren't you cleaning?"

"Because it's more fun watching you do it."

"If I'm that entertaining, maybe I should request pay."

"Since you managed to keep Karen on the payroll, convinced us to hire Tess and nudged Dana Sue to bring in more part-time help, there's not enough left in the budget to pay you, too.

"Tell me something." His tone was serious. "Why are you hanging around here so much lately? Are you bored? Did you run out of high-profile cases all of a sudden?"

To his surprise, her gaze locked with his. "Maybe it's the company."

That took the wind right out of his sails. He hadn't expected her to be so direct. Then, again, he didn't know why not. Helen was one of the most direct women he'd ever met. She never minced words. The surprise was that she'd taken so long to get to this point.

She tossed her sponge in the direction of the sink, then crossed the kitchen to stand directly in front of him. She put a hand on his chest. "We've kissed a few times now. I can't seem to get that out of my head," she said, sounding a little breathless. "How about you?"

He shrugged, not ready to admit to just how hard it had been to shake the memory of their kisses. "I haven't had to work too hard at forgetting," he claimed. "You said you wanted time to think things through. I figured you'd let me know when you had."

She looked skeptical. "Really? You haven't thought about those kisses at all? Maybe I'm remembering them all wrong. Could we try it again? This time without me throwing a pie at you first, of course. Or having a couple of kids around to keep things from getting out of control."

When she leaned closer, Erik put his hands on her shoulders and studied her. He wanted to be really sure about this, needed her to be sure, as well. Something told him that this time one kiss was going to lead to another and then to a whole lot more.

"What's really going on here, Helen?"

Her lips twitched. "I thought my communication skills were pretty well-honed. I want you to kiss me again, Erik. Or I can kiss you. It doesn't really matter which way it starts."

He grinned. "Haven't you heard? Men like to take the initiative."

"Then do it," she said.

But instead, he ran a thumb along her cheek, then along the curve of her jaw. Her skin flushed beneath his touch. "You're such a contradiction," he murmured, beginning to lose his grip on the common sense that was yelling at him to stay away from this woman. As direct as she was being, there was more going on, something he had a hunch he should know before he got in any deeper. Still...

He stroked a hand down her arm, the skin like velvet. "Such a contradiction," he repeated. "Hard as nails in some ways, but so damn soft in others."

She held his gaze, waiting, silent for once. Then she licked her lips and he was lost. That mouth of hers had tormented his dreams for a while now. It had only gotten worse once he'd kissed her and knew just how soft her lips were, just how passionately she would kiss him back. He'd lied about forgetting all that. He'd thought of little else for weeks.

"This is such a bad idea," he murmured, just before he leaned forward and claimed her.

Two hours later, when he woke up in his bed, the sheets tangled around them, her body curved into his, the idea seemed a whole lot better than it had at first glance.

CHAPTER FOURTEEN

Helen wasn't sure what she'd expected when she'd deliberately set out to seduce Erik tonight, but it certainly wasn't the wave of guilt that washed over her not five seconds after she'd had one of the most mind-shattering orgasms of her life. Her conscience, which usually remained silent given the relatively honorable life she'd always led, was screaming so loudly it drowned out the part of her that wanted to bask quietly in the moment. She'd even lied to his face about birth control, implying he didn't need to worry because she had taken care of it. Things had been so hot and wild at the time, he hadn't questioned her more closely.

"What's going on in that head of yours?" Erik asked, propped up on one elbow beside her, his other hand resting on the bare curve of her hip.

"I was just thinking that we should have done this months ago," she said. It wasn't a total lie. She'd thought that several times as he'd been making love to her. They'd wasted weeks on a dance that had had an inevitable outcome. How had she escaped the power of the chemistry between them until tonight?

Erik grinned at her. "You weren't ready months ago. Neither was I."

Helen wanted to argue that she'd been waiting her entire adult life for a man to pay so much attention to her pleasure, but she remained silent. Such a comment, which would have come naturally under other circumstances, rattled her now. She hadn't expected to feel so connected to this man after sleeping with him just once. She hadn't expected to feel anything more than a momentary release, a mutual satisfaction. Somehow she'd convinced herself that she could be intimate with Erik for however long it took for her to get pregnant and yet somehow remain detached. Tonight had pretty much destroyed that illusion. She might be able to walk away when the time came because she had to, but she wouldn't be detached.

"You're still thinking too hard about something," he said, scrutinizing her face. "Talk to me. Try the truth this time."

Instead, she reached for him. "Talking is a waste of time," she said right before she kissed him.

Erik pulled back, his gaze locked with hers. For a moment, she thought he was going to argue, but then he honed back in on her mouth.

Her body sang, she thought with amazement, as he stroked and caressed and probed, lingering here, skimming there, taunting and teasing until every inch of her was shouting for yet another magnificent release.

"I love watching the way your eyes turn dark when you're about to come apart," he said, gazing into her eyes.

"Are they dark now?"

He nodded.

"Then what are you waiting for? I want you inside me, Erik. Now, please."

"Not just yet," he said, and began his exploration of her body all over again, taking his time, clearly savoring every touch.

Helen had never allowed herself to let go completely with another man. Maybe it was because she was a control freak. Maybe it was simply because she was terrified to be that vulnerable.

Erik wasn't giving her any choice. He seemed to know her body as if he'd been studying it for years. He knew when she was achingly close to release, only to have him slow things down. He knew just how long to let the heat cool before turning it up again. In fact, to her frustration and delight, he was an expert at the teasing seduction.

Each time, he took her a little higher, then let her back down again until she was ready to take charge herself and end the torment.

"Now," she commanded, her unyielding gaze locked with his.

"Now?" he asked innocently. "You think so?"

"Yes!" Her hips writhed as he played his fingers over her damp heat. For this instant, her urgency had nothing to do with getting pregnant and everything to do with getting to that pinnacle that he was cleverly keeping just beyond her reach. It was all about the two of them and a connection so powerful it would have terrified her if she'd had the ability to think clearly.

"Okay, then," he said at last, hovering above her. "If you're sure."

"I am so sure," she whispered, lifting her hips.

When he entered her this time, she felt the most

amazing sense of completion, as if she'd been waiting for this her entire life, not just for the past half hour. She bucked, trying to draw him deeper inside, but Erik controlled the rhythm, steadying her to accept his pace. Slow, then fast, then slow again until she was practically mindless with need.

The first wave of pleasure caught her by surprise, a quick, intense burst that erupted at her core, then rippled through her. While she was still savoring that, the sensations deepened in intensity, gathering force like the eruptions of a volcano, each one washing over her in wave after sensual wave.

When Erik's body finally tensed in release, Helen was already shuddering, every inch of her body covered in a sheen of perspiration. It took only one quick brush of his finger, one touch of his mouth to her breast, and she came apart with him in a dazzling explosion that left her heart thundering in her chest and her mind reeling.

Never so at a loss for words in her life, she looked into Erik's eyes. The moment demanded something, some expression of appreciation, or at the very least an awestruck "Wow!" She couldn't even manage that.

"You okay?" he asked, regarding her with concern. "You look a little dazed."

"Dazed doesn't begin to cover it," she whispered.

He grinned with smug, male superiority. "Really?"

"You know you're good at this. You must."

"It's been a while. I thought I might have lost my touch."

"It hasn't been that long. This is the second time tonight."

He laughed. "I meant before tonight."

"Well, obviously it's all come back to you," she said.

"You didn't do too badly yourself."

"I can do better," she said. "I was a bit out of practice, too."

"Any better and we'd both be dead," he commented. "Now for the tricky part."

"Which is?"

"Are you going to stay the night or are you going to scamper out of here like a scared rabbit?"

She didn't much like the imagery, especially as she'd considered making up an excuse to leave. "What makes you think I'm scared?"

"I can see it in your eyes."

"Well, I'm not," she protested. "I'm staying."

To his credit, he didn't gloat. He merely nodded. "I'm glad. You hungry? I could fix something."

Helen considered the offer. "You know, I never eat this late, but I'm starved."

"Good. Me, too. You stay here. I'll be right back."

"All this and he cooks, too," she murmured as he climbed out of bed. "What did I do to deserve this?"

"I think we both know the answer to that," he said wryly. "Back in a minute."

When he'd left the room, Helen glanced around. She'd noticed very little about his house when they'd arrived. They'd come here, not because he'd insisted, but because it was closer than hers by a block. By then, they'd both been intent on getting out of their clothes and into his bed. Now she had time to look at the very spartan decor. The dresser had no pictures on top, just a small TV at one end. The nightstand beside the bed had only a lamp on it, aside from the candle Erik had grabbed from a table in the living room as they'd passed through it.

The flame from that unscented candle was the only illumination in the room now, keeping most of it in shadows, but even so she could tell he'd done nothing to make the bedroom his own. She even wondered if he'd rented the place furnished, since the furniture had that sturdy, uninteresting look to it. Even the room's one chair was utilitarian—a place to toss clothes, rather than the kind of comfortable chair a man might choose if he intended to relax in his room watching late-night TV or a ball game.

In fact, even without getting a good look at the living room, she had a feeling this was the home of a man who'd never really intended to stay in Serenity. She was surprised by how much that bothered her. Obviously, in one regard, it'd be more convenient for her if he did decide to leave at some point, yet just the idea of that happening made her heart contract with pain.

She was still pondering that when he returned carrying a tray with two plates. He'd made a frittata, mixing the eggs with slivers of onion, peppers and tomato, along with a combination of cheeses, then baking it in the oven and cutting it into thick, fluffy wedges.

"This is amazing," she said, when she'd taken her first bite.

"Don't sound so shocked. I *am* a chef."

"I know, but I can't even imagine having enough ingredients in the refrigerator to make something like this."

"I noticed your cupboard was nearly bare the night I was there to camp out. You don't cook at all?"

"I can follow a recipe under duress," she admitted. "But my lack of skill in the kitchen is a very good thing for Sullivan's. I'm your best customer."

"True enough," he said, still regarding her curiously. "If you don't cook, which I assume means you don't enjoy it, why are you so willing to pitch in at the restaurant?"

"It's Dana Sue's. I'd do anything to help out a friend."

"And The Corner Spa? I know for a fact that you're not an exercise nut. Did you provide the seed money for that because Maddie needed work?"

"In a way," she replied. "And in theory, it was supposed to encourage me to exercise. The doctor was all over me about my blood pressure."

"It's high?" he asked, alarm in his eyes. "Why didn't you mention that?"

"It *was* high," she said. "It's under control now. I manage to make myself do enough exercise to relieve at least some of the stress. And I have a little pill to do the rest. No big deal. Why would I mention it to you? It's not exactly relevant to this." She gestured at the tangled sheets.

He frowned at her glib tone. "You're too young for a problem like that. You need to take better care of yourself."

"I'm trying, especially lately."

"Good," he said, then fell silent. When he spoke again, he sounded uncertain. "How do you want to handle this?"

"Handle what?"

"You and me," he said, then gestured at the rumpled bed as she had a moment earlier. "This."

"We could pretend it never happened," she suggested, only partly in jest.

"That implies it's not going to happen again," he said. "I think we both know otherwise."

Helen shivered at the implication. "Do we?"

"I do. Don't you?"

"It would be a shame not to repeat something that incredible," she admitted, grinning at him.

"Okay, then, do we tell Dana Sue or not?"

"Absolutely not," she said at once, which had his frown deepening.

"Okay, I have one reason why that makes sense, but something tells me you have an entirely different reason," he said.

Helen wasn't about to explain that Dana Sue might immediately put two and two together and come up with her baby plan, so she said, "Isn't it obvious? She would make way too much out of this. Besides, I don't think I could stand to have her gloating about it. She's been predicting it for months."

He laughed. "Yeah, the gloating would be hard to take. So, for now, we keep this just between us?"

"Agreed," she said.

"Any idea how we're going to pull that off?" he asked.

"No kissing, no touching, no lingering looks in public," she suggested. "And I'll act like I'm furious with you. That shouldn't be hard. You usually do or say something on a daily basis to infuriate me."

"I'll be sure to continue," he promised.

But despite Helen's conviction that secrecy was the right way to go, she couldn't deny feeling a little pang that she couldn't share this with her two best friends.

But share what? she asked herself. It wasn't as if she'd started a relationship that might lead somewhere, one that Dana Sue and Maddie would be elated to hear about. She'd started an affair that she hoped would result in a pregnancy. That was something best left unsaid. She knew in her heart that neither of her friends would congratulate her for that. Right this second she wasn't sure she was very proud of herself, either.

Erik was in the storage pantry at Sullivan's when he heard Maddie talking to Dana Sue. Though Dana Sue knew he was nearby, she didn't seem to censor herself or warn Maddie that they might be overheard. Dana Sue took it for granted that he'd be discreet. He'd already learned far more of the intimate details of Maddie's post-pregnancy recovery than he needed.

"Do you have any idea what's going on with Helen?" he heard Maddie ask. "I haven't seen her for a couple of weeks now. It's not like her to avoid us."

"You think that's what she's doing?" Dana Sue asked, sounding surprised. "I just assumed she was busy. You know how she gets when she's working on a big case. She goes into hibernation. The final hearing in the Holliday case is coming up soon and she's determined to get Caroline everything she deserves."

"I don't think that's it," Maddie said. "She has been consumed with the Holliday divorce lately, but Caroline tells me that's just about wrapped up. And she's already handled Tess's problem with Jimmy Bob West."

"I know," Dana Sue responded. "Tess is ecstatic. Diego's back home and working again already. She thinks Helen hung the moon."

"Okay, then, with those two things under control, Helen should have some free time. Where is she? Have you even spoken to her?"

"Now that you mention it, no," Dana Sue replied.

"She was popping in here just about every day for a while, but suddenly that stopped."

"Well, what do you make of it?"

"New man in her life?"

"Why wouldn't she tell us about that?" Maddie demanded. "She tells us everything."

Erik decided it was time to make an appearance before Dana Sue's agile mind leaped to a conclusion it would be best to avoid. He'd known Helen's absences were going to spark speculation. He also knew she'd opted to avoid Sullivan's rather than risk Dana Sue spotting some slip that would reveal their new relationship—she hadn't been that confident that either of them could stick to their plan.

Emerging from the pantry with bags of flour and sugar, he smiled at Maddie, who was beginning to regain her shape after her pregnancy. He thought she'd looked amazing while pregnant, but he had a hunch she was happier with her more slender figure.

"How's the new mom?" he asked. "You're looking fit."

"I'm feeling great," she said. "But I'm bored out of my mind. Dana Sue and Helen insisted I let Jeanette run the spa for six weeks. I've been antsy for four of those weeks, even with Elliott coming by the house to make me do these horrendous workouts for the past couple of weeks."

"Which means you took exactly one week to relax after having your son," he said after a quick calculation.

She grinned unrepentantly. "About that."

Erik caught Dana Sue frowning at him.

"How much of our conversation did you hear?" she

demanded. "Not that I think you'd ever repeat a word of it, but I need to know."

"Sugar, I have more important things to do than eavesdrop on you."

"That's never stopped you before," she retorted. "How much?"

"Okay, all of it. Why? If you know I'm trustworthy, why do you care?"

"Then you heard us talking about Helen. What do you know about what she's up to these days? Has she been confiding in you?"

"Hardly," he responded, keeping his gaze averted. "Why on earth would she confide in me?"

"Because every instinct in me tells me you know something you're not saying. Otherwise you'd have been back in here ten minutes ago. It doesn't take that long to get a few things from storage."

"It does if someone I know goes in there and rearranges everything," he countered, seizing on the chance to change the subject and fix a nagging problem at the same time. "Why do you do that, by the way? I have a system."

"So do I," she replied. "Mine is the one that counts."

"Not when it comes to baking," he replied.

"Okay, that's it. I'm out of here," Maddie said. "Once you two start debating control issues, innocent bystanders are in the way." She hugged Dana Sue. "Let me know if you catch up with Helen."

"You do the same," Dana Sue said.

Maddie gave Erik a peck on the cheek and whispered, "Stick to your guns. The desserts are the best thing on the menu."

"I heard that," Dana Sue said.

Maddie grinned. "Then keep it in mind when you're discussing the arrangement of the stockroom. Erik might actually have some valid points."

"He might," Dana Sue conceded grudgingly.

When Maddie was gone, she eyed him intently. "You want to fight about the pantry or tell me what you know about Helen?"

"Let's fight about the pantry," he said.

"Then you *do* know something about Helen," she concluded.

"I did not say that," he insisted.

"You didn't have to," she said smugly. "It was written all over your face. That's okay. I'll let it pass this time. I'll get the information out of you when your guard's not up."

"My guard is always up around you," he assured her.

But just in case he was wrong about that, he'd be extra vigilant. Or maybe he'd just dump the problem in Helen's lap and let her deal with her friends. She was just as eager to keep the two of them out of their love life as he was.

Karen had been doing really well for several weeks now. Maybe it was because the kids had been on their best behavior, almost as if they understood that they might be separated again if things didn't go smoothly. Or maybe it was because all her sessions with Dr. McDaniels were paying off. She hoped that was it, because sooner or later the kids were bound to do something that would test her limits.

They'd also taken to Elliott from the very first time he'd come by. He was endlessly patient with Daisy's long descriptions of her days at school. In fact, he

seemed genuinely interested in the details of kindergarten, the art projects she brought home and the boy
on whom she'd developed a crush. As for Mack, Elliott
had miraculously managed, over three visits, to get him
weaned from sucking his thumb, a goal that Karen had
despaired of accomplishing.

Frances had given Elliott a thumbs-up, too. "He's a
very thoughtful young man," she'd told Karen. "Hot,
too," she'd added with a wink.

Despite all the votes of approval, Karen was still
keeping Elliott at arm's length. She had a feeling that
sometime soon he was going to call her on it, perhaps
even tonight when they were going to dinner alone,
while Frances kept Daisy and Mack.

A tap on the door announced Frances's arrival. She
took one look at Karen, still wearing her ratty old chenille robe, and shook her head. "Why aren't you ready?
Elliott will be here any minute, won't he?"

"I can't decide what to wear," Karen said.

Frances gave her a knowing look. "I think you're
scared."

"Scared of what?" she asked, a defensive note in
her voice.

"The fact that this man finds you attractive and
wants to spend time with you. You've done everything
in your power to make him turn tail and run, but nothing's worked, has it?"

Karen frowned. "I haven't tried to run him off," she
protested.

"Really? Well, you assigned him to break Mack of
sucking his thumb as if the child's life depended on
it," Frances said. "I'm sure that was designed to make
him think twice about what he was getting into with

a mother of two young children. What's next? Do you plan to leave him in charge of Daisy's birthday party next week? I hate to tell you, sweetie, but Elliott strikes me as a man who can handle a dozen six-year-olds with one hand tied behind his back."

Karen sighed. "You're probably right. I thought he was joking about all those nieces and nephews teaching him a lot about kids, but it seems to be true."

"Then why are you trying to run him off?"

Karen sank onto the edge of the sofa. "Do you really think that's what I've been trying to do?"

"I think every date you've had with him has been some sort of test. What are you going to do when he's passed them all, instead of disappearing?"

"I wish I knew," Karen said with a sigh. She glanced at Frances. "He really is a good guy, isn't he?"

"Seems to be," Frances said. "Besides scared, how do you feel about him?"

"I like him," Karen admitted. "I really like him."

"Then give him a real chance. You two need more nights like tonight, just the two of you, so you can really get to know each other." She smiled at Karen. "And don't worry about what time you get home. I can fall asleep right here on your sofa."

She blushed at the implication. "Frances! I am not going to stay out all night."

Frances's smile spread. "That's up to you, of course, but I wanted you to know it wouldn't be a problem if you did."

"Would you have told your daughter that?" Karen inquired curiously.

"Heavens, no!" Frances said with a laugh. "But she was twenty the last time she lived under my roof, and when it came to dating, she did what she pleased without me giving her any extra encouragement."

"Did you approve of her staying out all night?"

"Not really, but she was old enough to make her own decisions, same as you. I was wise enough to keep my opinions to myself."

"I don't ever want you to think less of me," Karen said. "You're like a mother to me."

"I'm proud you feel that way and I'm more than happy to offer advice whenever you ask for it, but I won't judge you, honey. Not ever. Now go and get ready before that man finds you in that robe. It really *might* scare him off. If he gets here before you're ready, it'll just give me a few minutes to see what his intentions are."

Karen laughed. "I'll hurry."

"No, please. Take your time. I don't get many chances to spend time with a man that gorgeous."

"Neither do I," Karen said.

"Then it's time to start enjoying every minute of it, don't you think?"

"I think you're absolutely right," Karen said.

But when she walked into her bedroom, she found the clothes she'd pulled from the closet as she'd tried to decide what to wear all in a heap on the floor with Mack sitting in the middle of them. Daisy was sitting in front of her mirror testing her makeup—all of it. She'd applied lipstick, powder, blush and eyeshadow with abandon, strewing the containers everywhere.

Karen's weeks of hard-won serenity fled in an instant. A bubble of anger rose in her chest at the mess.

"Daisy, what were you thinking?" she shouted. Daisy, who'd been gazing into a mirror with a pleased

SHERRYL WOODS

expression only a second before, promptly burst into tears at Karen's sharp tone.

Then she whirled on Mack. "Look what you've done to Mommy's clothes," she screamed at him, which sent him fleeing from the room on unsteady legs.

A moment later, Frances was in the doorway, a crying Mack clinging to her hand. "What on earth?" she began, then looked around. "Oh, my."

Weeks of progress vanished as an overwhelming sense of failure washed through Karen. Her room was in chaos and worse, her children were in tears, all because she'd yelled at them for doing what kids did.

"It's okay," Frances said, though it wasn't clear whom she intended her words to soothe. "Daisy, you and Mack come with me." She gave Karen an encouraging smile. "Don't worry. I'll be right back to help you deal with this. You get dressed. I can take care of the cleanup."

"But you shouldn't have to. It's not your mess," Karen said despondently.

"Well, truth be told, it's not yours, either, but I doubt we can count on the culprits to straighten this up to our satisfaction. It won't take but a minute. Get dressed, Karen. Then go on your date and leave the rest to me."

"I shouldn't have yelled at Daisy and Mack," she said wearily. "I've upset them."

"Yelling is a common enough reaction. You'll apologize. Now, hurry. I'll go check on them."

Karen was still shaking from the rush of adrenaline that had pumped through her when she'd first walked into the room, but she managed to salvage an outfit from the pile on the floor and get her own makeup on with fingers that trembled.

Just as she walked into the living room, she heard Daisy tell Elliott, "Me and Mack made Mommy mad."

She sounded so forlorn Karen's heart ached.

"But I'm not mad anymore," she told Daisy, stooping down as her daughter ran into her arms. "It's okay, sweetie. I shouldn't have gotten so upset."

"I didn't mean to make a mess," Daisy whispered against her cheek.

"I know."

"I just wanted to be pretty like you."

Her own eyes welling with tears, Karen cast a helpless glance toward Elliott. He promptly scooped Daisy out of her arms.

"You are even more beautiful than your mom," he told her. "When you're older, boys will be lining up at the door. You'll be the most popular girl in school."

Daisy's eyes shone. "Really?"

Elliott nodded. "Really."

Daisy gave him a considering look. "Maybe I'll grow up and marry you, instead."

Elliott grinned. "Trust me, by then, I'll be so old you won't want me."

"Then maybe you should marry my mommy, instead," Daisy suggested.

Elliott's gaze caught Karen's. "Maybe I should," he said quietly. "One of these days we might have to talk about that."

Karen's heart thumped unsteadily as his gaze sought hers. Surely he wasn't serious! They'd barely shared more than a good-night kiss up 'til now. How could he possibly be considering a leap like that?

"I think we'd better go," she said, struggling to keep her voice even.

She put a hand to Daisy's cheek. "I love you, baby."
Then she picked up Mack and planted a smacking kiss
on his cheek. "Love you, too, little man. I won't be late,"
she said pointedly to Frances.

"Enjoy yourselves," Frances replied. "We'll be fine."

Karen practically dashed out the door, anxious to
tell Elliott that he shouldn't be making promises like
the one he'd just made to Daisy.

But just outside the door, he caught her hand. "I
meant what I said," he told her, his gaze locked with
hers. "We are going to talk about marriage eventually.
I know what I want, Karen, but I'll give you a little
time to catch up."

"You can't possibly know a thing like that," she protested, unable to stop the trembling his words had set
off. She wasn't sure what scared her more, the anticipation he'd stirred in her or his absolute certainty. "This
is our first real date."

"All those other times we've gotten together with the
kids told me everything I needed to know," he insisted.
"Those occasions were real. I know what it would be
like to have a family with you. What could possibly be
more important?"

"But I'm a terrible mom. I made my kids cry," she
whispered, ashamed of the scene he'd walked in on.

"You're being way too hard on yourself," he told her.
"Do you think you're the first mom to lose her temper
when her kids misbehave? My mom has the patience
of a saint, but she was tested beyond her limits more
than once. And believe me, my sisters have raised their
voices to their kids more than once."

He met her gaze. "You didn't lose control, did you?"

She thought about it and realized she hadn't. She

hadn't felt that gut-deep loss of control she had a few months back. "Not really."

"Okay, then. You're not a terrible mom. Can we agree on that?"

She smiled. "I suppose."

"Good." He touched a finger to her lips. "We don't need to talk about the rest of it now. I just thought I ought to be clear about where I see us headed."

She frowned at him. "Well, just so you know, I'm now a nervous wreck."

"Why?"

"Because I don't want to mess up what could be the best thing that's ever happened to me," she said candidly.

His hand cupped her cheek. "You couldn't if you tried."

Karen wasn't convinced of that. But maybe, for now, it was enough that he believed it.

CHAPTER FIFTEEN

＊＊＊

The hearing for Caroline and Brad Holliday's divorce was finally going to happen. Helen had accumulated enough material on Brad's finances to assure Caroline and her children a secure future. She had no illusions, though, that the proceedings would go smoothly. She doubted Jimmy Bob had had much luck in getting through to his client. Brad would go down fighting to hold on to every penny.

In the courtroom, Helen turned to Caroline. "Are you ready for this?"

"It's really going to end today?" Caroline asked, her voice unsteady. "No more of their tricks?"

"Not this time," Helen told her. "The paper trail on Brad's hidden assets finally caught Jimmy Bob's attention, to say nothing of infuriating Judge Rockingham. Jimmy Bob knows if they don't end this now, there's no telling what else we might unearth."

Caroline swallowed hard and regarded Helen guiltily. "Brad called me last night."

Helen held on to her temper by a thread, though she wasn't particularly surprised. It was exactly the kind of stunt a man on the verge of losing would pull. "Oh?" she said, her tone neutral.

"He wanted to talk."

There was a sinking feeling in Helen's heart. "About?"

"A reconciliation."

Helen bit back a groan. "What did you tell him?"

Caroline sat up a little straighter. "That he could come over to talk, but that a reconciliation was out of the question," she said.

But before Helen could breathe a sigh of relief, Caroline asked uncertainly, "Was that the right thing to do?"

"Only you can answer that," she told Caroline. "How did it feel when you told him that?"

"Lousy," Caroline admitted. "Somewhere inside I remembered the man he used to be, the man I loved. If I could have that man back…" Her voice trailed off.

"He doesn't exist anymore," Helen told her gently. "At least that's not the man I've seen, but if you're having second thoughts, we can stop this proceeding. It's not too late. Do you honestly think there's hope for your marriage?"

Caroline looked across the aisle at her husband, who was huddled with Jimmy Bob. He glanced over at Caroline, his expression hard. Apparently Caroline caught the implication, because she stiffened in response.

"It was all a ploy to soften me up, wasn't it?" Caroline said with dismay. "Brad figured if he could get me to take him back for a few weeks or even a few months, we'd have to start this process all over again. It was just a gigantic postponement tactic, wasn't it?"

"What do you think?" "Helen asked.

"I saw it in his eyes just then," Caroline said, cha-

grined. "He's angry that it didn't work. I could hear it
in his voice when I told him on the phone that I wasn't
interested in a reconciliation. Last night wasn't about
getting back together or he would have come over and
tried to convince me. It was just an attempt to get under
my skin so I'd feel all warm and fuzzy toward him."

Helen clasped her hand and gave it a squeeze. "Isn't
it a good thing that you're smart enough to see through
that?"

Caroline glared across the aisle, then turned back to
Helen, her resolve clearly steadied. "Take him for every
cent I deserve," she said.

Helen grinned. "It'll be my pleasure."

Three draining hours later, they had hammered out
the terms of the settlement with Brad Holliday gnash-
ing his teeth and protesting over every nickel and dime.
Fortunately, Jimmy Bob had seen the handwriting on
the wall and was able to keep the process on course,
warning Brad from time to time that his attitude was
getting in the way of him winning any points at all.

"She'll never see a penny of this," Brad shouted at
one point, only to have Judge Rockingham stare him
down, his patience with Brad clearly at an end.

"Then you'll be in a cell facing contempt charges,"
the judge assured him. "Am I making myself clear
enough about that, Mr. Holliday?"

"Absolutely, Your Honor," Jimmy Bob said, shooting a quelling look at Brad, who looked as if he wanted
to break something. His color was high and his fists
were clenched.

Helen thought of the threats that Jimmy Bob hadn't
taken seriously and wondered if she should request a

restraining order to protect Caroline. She leaned toward her client.

"Caroline, is there any chance that Brad will try to take his anger out on you over this decision today?"

Caroline looked shaken by the suggestion. "No, of course not," she said at once.

"I could ask for a restraining order," Helen told her.

"No," Caroline said. "It really isn't necessary."

Helen nodded. "If you're sure, but let me know if you change your mind."

Even without a request from Helen for a restraining order, apparently Judge Rockingham recognized that Brad's temper was unpredictable. When the hearing ended, he told the bailiff to find an officer to escort Brad from the premises and another to see to it that Helen and Caroline weren't accosted on their way out.

"Do you have someone who can stay with you for a few days?" Helen asked Caroline, picking up on the judge's concern. If Rockingham read a danger in his golf buddy's demeanor, then they needed to take it seriously. "I don't think you ought to be alone."

"I agree," Jimmy Bob said, surprising her. "Better yet, stay with a friend, Caroline, or take the kids on a trip for a week or so. Brad will cool down eventually, but right now, I wouldn't trust him not to do something crazy. Like I told Helen, he's been saying a lot of stuff the past few days. Most of it's nonsense he doesn't mean, but there's enough anger in him that I'd be careful if I were you."

Helen nodded. "It's good advice, Caroline."

Caroline looked uneasy, but she was clearly ready to stand her ground. "Sooner or later, I'll have to deal with him," she argued. "Brad's never been violent."

"He's never been pushed this far before, either. Better to deal with him later," Jimmy Bob insisted. "I've known him a long time and I've never seen him like this." He faced Helen. "You're not too popular with him right now, either. I know I told you I thought he was all talk, but it's better to be safe. Watch your back, okay?"

Helen shivered at the genuine concern she heard in his voice. "I will," she promised.

She was with Erik most nights lately, at her place or his. She'd talk to him about staying at his place for a while until Brad Holliday cooled down and began to see things more clearly.

"Caroline, what about you?" she persisted.

"I think you're both worrying about nothing," Caroline said. "Brad's angry, but he'd never hurt me. Still, I'll go visit my sister for a week or two just to put your minds at ease. She's been wanting me to come, but I didn't feel like I could before now."

"Perfect," Helen said. "Be sure you call the office and give Brenda your contact information. Do you want me to come home with you while you pack a bag?"

"That's not necessary," Caroline said.

The officer who'd escorted them from the courthouse glanced at Helen. "I'll stay with her, Ms. Decatur."

"Thanks," Helen said. No matter what Caroline said, she trusted Jimmy Bob's perception of Brad's mood better than that of the woman who still wanted to find some good in him.

As she watched Caroline drive away with the patrol car right behind her, she still felt uneasy. Turning to Jimmy Bob, she saw that he looked worried as well.

"How dangerous do you think Brad is?" she asked him.

"I'd like to believe we're all overreacting," he told

her. "But Brad lost a lot in that courtroom today. I'm not just talking money and assets, either. I'm talking about the huge blow to his ego. Remember how this whole thing started, with him wanting to prove he was still a man? I'll be honest with you. A man in Brad's state of mind won't handle any of this well." He met her gaze. "I'll say it again—watch your back, Helen."

She shuddered at his somber tone. She'd handled dozens of difficult divorces, some of them even nastier than this one, but for the first time in her career, she genuinely felt afraid. If Brad was as unstable as Jimmy Bob and Judge Rockingham thought he might be, who knew what he might be capable of doing?

Erik kept stealing glances at Helen. She'd arrived at Sullivan's just before closing time, given Dana Sue a hug and him a peck on the cheek that had Dana Sue's eyebrows lifting.

"You okay?" Dana Sue had asked immediately, but Helen had shrugged off the question.

She was fine, she'd insisted, but then she'd grabbed a scrubber and started in on the pots and pans piled in the sink. It was a task she usually shunned, especially when she was wearing one of those smart suits she wore to court. Tonight she hadn't even bothered with an apron.

Dana Sue sidled close to him. "What's that about?" she whispered, glancing pointedly at Helen as she attacked a particularly greasy pan in which Dana Sue had baked lasagne.

"I have no idea," Erik admitted. "But I don't like it. She's obviously upset and she's way too quiet."

"Maybe you should go," Dana Sue suggested. "She might open up to me."

"No way," he countered, his gaze never leaving Helen.

Dana Sue regarded him with a puzzled expression. "Erik, what's going on with you two?"

"We're friends," he said tersely. "If she's this upset, I'm not about to walk out of here 'til I know why."

"Well, neither am I," Dana Sue replied.

Just then, Helen whirled around and glared at them. "You two can stop whispering behind my back now. Dana Sue, go home."

Dana Sue regarded her with astonishment. "What?"

"Please," Helen begged. "I'll talk to you tomorrow." Suddenly a look of alarm flared in her eyes. "Erik, you need to walk Dana Sue to her car."

"I don't need anyone walking me out," Dana Sue argued.

Helen's tense expression warned Erik that she was close to the breaking point. "Get your purse, Dana Sue," he said. "I'll go out with you."

"But—"

"Just do it." He cast a pointed look at Helen. Her spine was rigid. She looked as if she was about one argument from coming unglued. Dana Sue apparently saw the same thing he did, because she finally nodded.

Outside in the parking lot, she gave him a helpless look. "Call me if you need me," she instructed. "I don't like this. I don't like it one bit."

"Me, neither. One of us will fill you in tomorrow. I promise."

With one last glance back at the restaurant, she climbed into her car. She'd started out of the parking lot when she stopped and rolled down her window. "Take good care of her," she ordered. "Promise me."

"I will."

"And be prepared to answer a whole lot of questions about why she's turning to you, instead of to me or Maddie."

He managed a half smile at her indignation. "I figured that would bother you as much as anything."

"Well, why wouldn't it? She's been our friend forever."

"Do you really think this is the time to debate which of us is a better friend to her?" he asked.

"No." She sighed and drove off.

When Erik got back inside, Helen had kicked off her shoes and was sitting on a stool, her shoulders slumped, her expression glum.

"You ready to tell me what's going on?" he asked quietly.

"Could you just hold me?"

"Sure. I could do that," he said, moving close to take her in his arms. Her trembling alarmed him. "Come on, sugar, spill it. What happened today to put you in this mood?"

"I won a really good divorce settlement for Caroline Holliday," she told him, her voice muffled against his chest.

He was still confused. "Isn't that a good thing?"

"You'd think so, wouldn't you?"

"What am I missing?"

"Her husband, or soon-to-be ex-husband, has kind of gone off the deep end."

Erik tensed. "Meaning?"

"His lawyer, the judge, everyone seems to think he might go after Caroline," she said, then looked up at him, an unfamiliar hint of fear lurking in the depths of her eyes. "Or me."

"Good God!" he said. "Then what the hell were you doing on the streets alone this late at night?"

"I'm not scared," she insisted, though everything about her said otherwise. "I just wanted to see if I could maybe stay at your place for a few days. You know, 'til this blows over. It's not like I'd be moving in permanently or anything."

"Of course you can stay with me," he said at once. "You didn't even have to ask."

"Yes, I did. It's not as if we've ever talked about living together or anything. I didn't want you to get some crazy idea that this is a ploy to change things between us."

Erik sighed. "Helen, I think I know you well enough to see when you're scared out of your wits."

"I am not," she protested indignantly.

He grinned at her. "Okay, then. Not scared, just very cautious."

"Exactly. Discretion is the better part of valor. Isn't that the saying?"

"Uh-huh. Do you need to go home and pack your things?"

"I have a suitcase in my car," she told him. A flash of anger lit her eyes. "I hate that I'm letting this jerk chase me out of my own home."

"Just remember what you told me not five seconds ago," he said. "Discretion and all that."

"I suppose."

"What about Caroline? Is she safe?"

"She left for her sister's. She took the younger kids

with her. Her oldest's at college. Hopefully Brad will
cool down before they come back."

Of course, Erik thought, that meant Helen was the
only immediate target on this jerk's radar. Not good.

"Come on," he told her. "Let's go home."

He'd keep her safe there if he had to stand watch
night and day. Of course, that would all have to take
place between dodging Dana Sue's and Maddie's inevitable questions. Those were going to be flying fast and
furious first thing in the morning.

Helen couldn't believe she'd allowed Jimmy Bob and
Judge Rockingham to work her into such a frenzy. She'd
never been afraid of anyone in her life. She'd always
been able to take care of herself, but for some reason
Brad's reaction in court and his friends' response to it
had spooked her completely.

She'd gone home at the end of the day, determined to
fight her fear and not be chased out of her own home,
but within an hour or two of darkness falling, she'd been
jumping at her own shadow. When a car backfired on
the street, she'd barely stopped herself from diving behind the sofa. That was when she'd packed a bag and
headed for Sullivan's.

"Did you eat dinner tonight?" Erik asked when she'd
unpacked the last of her things and put them into a
drawer he'd cleared out for her. Her suits were hanging in his nearly empty closet, next to a few of his dress
shirts and a couple of dark suits. She'd lined her shoes
up below, three pairs of her favorite kick-ass spiked
heels.

When she looked up from the drawer filled with lingerie, Erik was watching her from the end of the bed,

a worried frown on his face. She went over and sat beside him, leaning into his side.

"Stop worrying about me," she told him. "I'm sure Brad's too smart to do anything at all."

"Then why are you so scared?"

"To be honest, I feel kind of silly. I should probably just go on home."

"Not a chance," he said tersely. "Not for a few days, anyway, 'til we see what this guy's going to do. Maybe I should have a talk with him."

She shook her head. "If he starts thinking everyone in town is lining up against him, it'll only make matters worse."

"It might also scare some sense into him," Erik countered. "Bullies, especially men who bully women, don't like it when people get in their face, especially someone who's bigger and stronger."

She smiled at him. "You don't even know Brad Holliday. He could be twice your size."

"True, but I can be pretty impressive when I'm ticked off."

He glanced sideways at her, a grin tugging at his lips. "Is he bigger?"

"No, but I love that you were willing to take him on anyway," she said. "What I would love even more is something to eat. You said something about food a minute ago."

"Are you sure you didn't wrangle an invitation over here just so I'd feed you on a regular basis for free?"

"Nope, but that is definitely a side benefit," she told him. "Anything good in your fridge?"

He lifted a brow. "What do you think?"

"Anything chocolate?"

"You want dessert first?"

"I want dessert and then you," she told him, enjoying the immediate heat that sparked in his eyes. "In fact, I can't imagine anything that could take my mind off Brad Holliday any faster than that combination."

He stroked a finger along her jaw, then tucked a strand of hair behind her ear. "Is this a hot-fudge-sundae crisis or will a brownie do?"

"Both, if you have them," she said. At his amused expression, she said, "Okay, I've been craving chocolate all day long."

"And me?"

"Lately, I seem to be craving you twenty-four/seven."

"Good to know I rank at least slightly higher than a sundae," he said, then covered her mouth with his.

When he finally released her, she was breathless and needy. "Maybe the sundae could wait," she murmured, pulling him back. She was getting to be an expert at juggling her priorities.

Helen was in her office by eight in the morning, escorted there by an insistent Erik, who'd flatly refused to let her go alone. For the moment, she was enjoying this protective streak, but she had a hunch it was going to wear very thin before long. While it was nice and unexpected to be pampered, she was too used to taking care of herself.

She'd been at her desk for barely fifteen minutes when Dana Sue and Maddie burst in, scaring ten years off her life.

"What is wrong with you?" she demanded, glowering at them while she fought to regain her composure.

"That's our question," Dana Sue said unrepentantly,

taking a seat across from her. "You were a wreck last night and I want to know why."

"And why did you turn to Erik instead of us?" Maddie asked.

Dana Sue nodded. "In fact, that might be the more interesting question. I called your house 'til three in the morning. Where were you last night after you left Sullivan's? Please, please tell me you were having mad, passionate sex with Erik."

Helen frowned at the clever guesswork. Since she couldn't bring herself to outright lie to her friend, she merely said, "And that would be your business because...?"

"Because you meddled in our lives and now it's our turn," Maddie said. "Is there something going on between you and Erik?"

Helen gave the two of them a stern look. "That's too personal."

Dana Sue scowled at her response. The scowl slowly gave way to a huge grin. "That's a yes, isn't it?" she said triumphantly. "You're not going to admit it—though I can't imagine why not—but the two of you are together. I know I'm right. I knew it when Erik went all protective and weird last night."

"If it's true, why won't you just say so?" Maddie asked.

"I'm not confirming that it's true," Helen said.

"You're not denying it, either," Dana Sue responded. "I knew it! I just knew the two of you would be perfect together. Why are you hiding it? Are you ashamed because Erik's not some hotshot lawyer or something?"

Helen was horrified that one of her best friends could even think such a thing. "Absolutely not. I am not, nor have I ever been, a snob. Besides, you, of all people, know what a great guy Erik is."

"She jumped to his defense," Dana Sue said to Maddie. "I'd say that's more confirmation."

Maddie, however, didn't seem convinced. "I hate to throw a damper on your enthusiasm, Dana Sue, but I think there's something else going on here," she said.

"Don't be ridiculous," Helen said hastily, worried that Maddie might put things together and come up with a bombshell that could ruin everything. "Maybe Erik and I—assuming there's anything going on between us—just don't want the two of you in our business."

"That's reasonable," Dana Sue said. "Especially since he works for me. So, let's back up a minute. What had you so freaked out last night?"

Helen filled them in on the Holliday divorce aftermath. "There's a chance, albeit a really tiny one, that Brad could do something crazy," she concluded. "Listening to Jimmy Bob's warnings after court let out made me a little skittish. I'm okay this morning. It was crazy to let myself get so worked up over nothing."

"I imagine Erik got worked up right along with you," Dana Sue said. "That man has a protective streak a mile wide. He watches over Annie like a hawk. He keeps an eye on every bite of food I put in my mouth. It's a little tiresome, but really sweet."

Helen thought of the way he'd hovered over her this morning until she'd kicked him out of her office with a promise to keep the doors locked 'til Barb got in. Maddie and Dana Sue had used their keys to get in. The Sweet Magnolias had one another's keys to everything.

Maddie's lips twitched. "That must be why he's still sitting in the parking lot outside," she said.

Helen stared at her. "Erik is outside now?" She went to the window and peeked out. Sure enough, he was hunkered down behind the wheel of his car making a pretense of glancing at the morning paper. She shook her head. "I thought he'd left. This is crazy. I'm going out there right now—"

"No, you're not," Maddie said. "He needs to do this, and frankly, I'm not convinced you're as safe and invincible as you seem to think you are. Some men are capable of doing all kinds of irrational things when they think they have nothing left to lose."

"I agree," Dana Sue said, then grinned. "Besides, what woman wouldn't want a man like Erik taking care of her? I say you should milk this for all it's worth. Who knows what might develop?"

"Just be careful," Maddie cautioned. "And I'm not just talking about Brad Holliday, either."

Helen shivered under the impact of her gaze. For the second time that morning, she sensed that Maddie had figured out exactly what she was up to with Erik and wasn't exactly overjoyed about it.

And if Maddie thought she was behaving abominably by involving Erik in her baby plan, then Dana Sue was definitely going to hit the roof. Helen just had to pray that it wouldn't cause an irreparable rift in their lifelong friendship.

CHAPTER SIXTEEN

There was an air of excitement in the kitchen at Sullivan's and none of the tension that usually surrounded a busy night in the dining room. In fact, the restaurant was closed to the public. They'd refused all reservations and posted a sign on the door to prevent walk-ins.

"Do you think she knows?" Tess whispered to Dana Sue.

Erik grinned. "Trust me, Helen knows."

Dana Sue scowled at him. "How could she possibly know we're throwing her a surprise birthday party, unless you blabbed?"

"Hey, this was my idea. Why would I blab? I'm just saying she's not easily fooled. She's smart," he began, then ticked off more reasons they would never pull this party off as a complete surprise. "She's observant. She's suspicious by nature." He grinned at Dana Sue. "And none of you can keep a secret worth a damn."

"I resent that," Dana Sue said. "I have kept my mouth shut about a whole lot of things through the years."

Erik couldn't help being a little intrigued. "Such as?" he inquired.

Dana Sue frowned at him. "Oh, no, you don't, you

sneaky devil. I'm not going to slip up and tell you any of Helen's deep, dark secrets. Pry them out of her, if you must know."

"Helen has deep, dark secrets? Interesting," he said. It would be a great topic for later tonight, once he had her well distracted, something he'd grown increasingly efficient at accomplishing.

Dana Sue regarded him with a wary expression. "Don't you dare imply to her that I've already told you," she warned. "Maybe I should give her a heads-up, so you can't get away with any sneakiness."

Tess observed all this back and forth in fascination, then focused on Erik. "Is there something going on between you and Ms. Decatur?"

Erik winced. Of course, truthfully, she was probably the last to figure it out. He had a hunch Dana Sue and Maddie had known for weeks now, certainly since Helen had moved in with him. Dana Sue, especially, had been amazingly quiet on the topic of him and Helen, which meant she'd concluded her matchmaking efforts were no longer needed. He doubted, though, that she was aware of the no-strings clause in the relationship. If she were, she'd be all over him.

"We're friends," he told Tess, stressing it in a way that had Dana Sue's lips twitching with barely contained amusement.

"Is that what they're calling it these days?" Dana Sue asked. "Friends with benefits, perhaps?"

"Get out of here," he ordered in mock anger. "You're in my way."

"No, actually I'm in your face, and you hate that," she countered cheerfully. "But I will go and check on the dining room to see how Maddie and Jeanette are coming with the decorations."

After she'd gone, Tess continued to study him. "I can see it," she said eventually. "You and Ms. Decatur. You would balance each other."

Erik felt a need to discourage her from thinking there was anything permanent about what he and Helen shared. "We're opposites, Tess. That might work in the short term, but never for the long haul."

Tess shook her head. "You're wrong about that. People said Diego and I were too different, but it works." A smile blossomed on her face. "In fact, it works very well. I will never be able to repay Ms. Decatur for bringing him home to me."

"She was happy to do it, Tess."

Karen breezed into the kitchen then, followed by some muscular hunk of a man Erik had never seen before.

"Erik, Elliott Cruz," Karen announced. "Elliott, this is Erik. You can get acquainted later. I'm on a mission. Dana Sue wants the pink cloth napkins, not the green, and she wants them now."

Erik chuckled. "Tell her if she insists on turning the decor into some girly thing, all of us guys are going to bail on you."

"You tell her that if you're brave enough," Karen countered. "Me, I'm finding the pink napkins."

"I know where they are," Tess said. "I'll show you."

While the two women left to look in the linen supply closet, Erik studied Elliott, whose gaze followed Karen from the room.

"Elliott Cruz," Erik said, drawing the man's rapt attention away from the direction Karen had gone. "I've heard that name before."

"I'm a personal trainer at The Corner Spa," Elliott said. "That's how I met Karen."

"And now you have a thing for her," Erik guessed.

Elliott gave him a wry look. "You could say that. We've been dating for a few weeks now."

"Ah, so that's why she's been smiling so much," Erik concluded. Then his protective streak kicked in. "You serious about her? Because if you're not, I have to tell you, she doesn't need the heartache."

"Oh, I'm serious," Elliott said without hesitation. "Karen's the one who refuses to discuss the future. She thinks I don't have any idea what I'm getting into."

"But you do?" Erik said, liking the man's honesty and willingness to put his feelings out there. He'd done that once, but never again.

"It's a little hard not to know when she's constantly trying to make me see the worst side of being around her and the kids. When Mack regressed to his pre-potty-trained days, she had me give him a refresher course."

Erik barely managed to bite back a laugh. Karen hadn't mentioned that. "How'd that go?"

Elliott shrugged. "I have five nephews. I talked to my sisters. It was a breeze. So was having Daisy throw up all over the place when she ate too much at the county fair. Then Karen vanished during Daisy's birthday party and left me for fifteen minutes with a bunch of giggling six-year-olds trying to pin the tail on a donkey. And asked me to take Mack to the emergency room when he cut his knee on a piece of glass at the park." He gave Erik a resigned look. "You get the picture, I'm sure."

"I doubt Karen planned all that for your benefit," Erik said.

"True, but make no mistake, each incident was a test," Elliott said.

"How'd you do?"

Elliott shrugged. "It's all just part of life with kids. You deal."

Erik envied him his totally unflappable attitude. He'd had his share of experience with his own nephews, which was one reason he didn't want any more kids in his life. Those precious but rambunctious children, who ranged in age from three to twelve, were more than enough. And he got to go home at the end of an exhausting day and fall asleep in his own bed without fear of being interrupted by any one of the hundred crises that came with kids. At one time, when Sam had been alive to share it all—the joy and the burden—he'd thought otherwise, but now he was content with the way things were.

Before he could comment on any of that, Karen and Tess returned with an armload of pink napkins.

"Come on," Karen told Elliott. "You can help me fold them."

Elliott's gaze narrowed. "I do not make little swans," he informed her.

Karen grinned at him. "You will by the time I'm through with you."

Elliott cast a woeful look back over his shoulder at Erik as he followed Karen to the dining room. Erik couldn't seem to work up any sympathy for him. He almost wished he were as smitten with Helen, rather than just in lust with her.

Of course, being in lust with Helen was pretty darn

incredible. There were nights when they lay tangled together under his sheets that he couldn't imagine his life
any other way. Maybe he was just a little smitten, after
all. One of these days he'd have to think about nipping
that in the bud before it led him down a path he didn't
want to travel. He couldn't afford to risk his heart.

Helen was about to wrap up her paperwork at the
office and call it a night when Barb stuck her head in
the door.

"You about finished?" her secretary asked.

"Yes, thank goodness."

"Then let's go have a drink," Barb suggested.

Helen frowned at her. "Don't you have to get home?"

"I have time. I thought we could toast your birthday. I have a present for you, too, but I'll give it to you
when we get there."

Helen stared at her in surprise, then glanced at the
calendar on her desk to confirm that it was, indeed, her
birthday. She'd completely forgotten. She was forty-
three today, and the truth was she didn't feel much like
celebrating. With every day and week that passed without any sign she might be pregnant, she grew more and
more discouraged. She was all too rapidly running out
of time. She didn't need to be reminded of that.

"I don't know—"

Barb cut her off. "No excuses. Birthdays need to be
celebrated. And I know you don't have plans for tonight
or you would've mentioned them."

Caught, Helen conceded reluctantly, "Okay, one
drink." Why not? She'd been avoiding alcohol for some
time now on the chance she might be pregnant, but what

was the point? She deserved a glass of champagne to mark the occasion.

"Where do you want to go?" she asked Barb as she got her purse.

"Only one place in town that's classy enough for a birthday celebration," Barb insisted. "We'll go to Sullivan's. Maybe I'll even spring for dinner."

"Fine," Helen said, then considered the fact that she'd heard nothing from Dana Sue and Maddie all day. Usually they were the first to call with birthday wishes. Of course, with all those two had going on in their lives, it was little wonder they'd forgotten. Still, they were her best friends. They'd never missed a birthday in all the years they'd known each other. She was reminded yet again that lately they'd had entirely too little time together. Part of that was her fault. She'd been avoiding them so she wouldn't have to answer questions about her relationship with Erik.

The parking lot at Sullivan's was jammed as usual, but Helen finally managed to find a space in the alley out back. "We can go in through the kitchen," she told Barb.

Her secretary frowned. "I don't think Dana Sue would want you parading people through her kitchen on a night as busy as this one obviously is. We can walk around front."

Helen started to argue, then shrugged. Maybe Barb had a point. Helen knew how chaotic it got in there all too well.

Around front, Barb opened the door and held it for her. The instant Helen stepped inside, the room exploded with flashing lights and what sounded like a hundred people shouted, "Surprise!"

Clasping her hand over her mouth in shock, she whirled around and scowled at Barb. "You knew about this?"

"They couldn't have done it without me." Her secretary looked entirely too pleased with herself. "I was the one you'd least expect to be leading you into a trap."

"You're a very sneaky woman," Helen accused, but she wrapped her in a hug. "Thank you."

"Don't thank me. The party wasn't my idea."

Dana Sue and Maddie appeared then.

"Were you really surprised?" Dana Sue demanded.

"Stunned," Helen assured her. "I can't believe you two did this. I was just feeling down because I thought you'd both forgotten."

"What you really can't believe is that we pulled it off without giving you even a hint of what we were up to," Maddie said. "As for forgetting, surely you know us better than that."

"I thought I did."

"By the way, you shouldn't be thanking us, at least not entirely," Dana Sue added. "The party was Erik's idea."

Helen's gaze few across the room to where Erik was standing just outside the kitchen door. "You did this?" she mouthed.

He shrugged, then gave her a sheepish nod.

"How on earth did he even know it was my birthday?" she asked Dana Sue.

"He told me he saw it on your driver's license the morning you left your wallet at his place," Dana Sue said pointedly. "I'd like to hear the story behind that one day soon. I know you've been staying over there because of Brad Holliday, but being forgetful? That's the real shocker."

"I agree," Maddie said. "Now, get in here and say hello to everyone."

The packed room was filled with old friends and former clients, as well as attorneys and judges, including Lester Rockingham and Jimmy Bob West, who was keeping his distance from Tess.

"Brad hasn't been bothering you, has he?" Jimmy Bob asked when Helen greeted him.

"Not so far," Helen said. "It's been a couple of weeks. He's got to be over it by now."

"I wouldn't be too sure of that," Lester Rockingham said. "He's still refusing to play golf with us. Won't even take my calls, in fact. If he figures Jimmy Bob and I betrayed him, there's no telling how he feels about you."

Erik approached just in time to hear the warning. He stiffened visibly. "You really think this guy's a danger to her?" he asked the two men.

"I'm just saying she needs to keep her eyes open," Jimmy Bob said.

"Why not just throw him in jail?" Erik demanded.

"No grounds," the judge responded. "He hasn't even made any overt threats, much less acted on them. It's just a gut feeling Jimmy Bob and I have that he's going to have a meltdown one of these days. I hear he's sitting at home with a bottle of booze and stewing about how the court and Helen here wronged him. That's never a good thing."

Erik frowned at Helen. "Then you're not moving back to your place yet and that's that," he said.

Though Jimmy Bob seemed a little startled, he nod-

ded. "Makes sense to me to stay where you're not alone
and where Brad's less likely to look for you."

Helen wasn't sure how she felt about more people
knowing about her current living arrangements. It
meant there were that many more people who would
know the truth if she eventually turned up pregnant.
They'd all have questions and, more than likely, want
to paint Erik as the bad guy if they didn't marry. She
hadn't meant for that to happen.

"I'll think about it," she told them all. "I need to say
hello to some more people."

As she walked away, Erik was right on her heels.
"Okay, why did you go all stiff and weird just then? Was
it because I mentioned you'd been staying with me?"

"I just thought we'd agreed that the fewer people who
knew about that the better," she told him. She decided to
tap-dance around her real reason for wanting their relationship to remain underground. "Do you really want
Brad to know exactly where to find me?"

Erik immediately looked guilty. "I hadn't thought
about that," he said. "Then, again, maybe it's a good
thing if he knows there's someone looking out for you."

"I don't want to count on that," she said, then stood
on tiptoe to press a kiss to his cheek. "Thank you for
thinking of the party. I never had a surprise party before, at least not one that was a real surprise."

"Never?"

She shook her head. "I'm too nosy. I always found
out."

"I was sure you were going to find out about this
one, but I'd have blamed Dana Sue and Maddie for not
being able to keep a secret," he said.

"They really are lousy at that," she agreed. "But I

haven't seen too much of them for the past couple of weeks. I've been otherwise occupied."

"Really?" he said, drawing her into his arms. "Pleasantly occupied?"

"Amazingly occupied," she said, lifting her mouth to his.

When he finally released her, he regarded her with an odd expression. "That's the first time you've kissed me—I mean really kissed me—in public."

"It's my birthday. I'm allowed to be impulsive and throw caution to the wind. Besides, most of the people here have figured out that something's going on between us, anyway. We may as well acknowledge it, at least among friends. Keeping it to ourselves isn't working all that well, anyway."

"And Brad?"

"He won't find out from any of these people," she said.

Erik glanced across the room to where Maddie and Dana Sue were watching them with interest. "I just hope you're prepared for the consequences of all this new openness," he warned. "In fact, the primary consequence appears to be heading this way. I think I'll retreat to the kitchen to put the finishing touches on your cake."

"Chicken," she called after him.

"Cluck, cluck," he responded, laughing as he disappeared from view.

"Why don't you two just admit what's going on?" Maddie demanded.

"I have no idea what you're talking about," Helen said.

"That act's not working anymore," Dana Sue countered. "You're having an affair. That much is plain. What I want to know is when you're going to take it to the next level."

"Which would be...?" Helen asked.

"Marriage," Dana Sue responded.

Helen shook her head. "Not in the cards," she said flatly.

"That's ridiculous," Maddie declared.

"Why on earth wouldn't you want to get married to a man like Erik?" Dana Sue asked. "He's perfect for you."

"This is a party," Helen retorted. "And I am not discussing my love life with you now."

"Tomorrow, then," Dana Sue said. "Be at the spa at eight or we'll come looking for you. Won't it be interesting if we find you in Erik's bed?"

Helen sighed as the two of them walked away. This whole scheme of hers was suddenly spinning out of control. She didn't have a doubt in her mind that Maddie and Dana Sue's questions were going to be tough to handle. And she couldn't think of a single way to avoid them.

Karen saw that Elliott fit right in at the party. Of course, it made sense since he worked with Helen, Maddie and Dana Sue at the spa, but he'd also gotten along with Maddie's husband Cal, Dana Sue's husband Ronnie and even Tess's Diego. Apparently he'd had quite a chat with Erik in the kitchen, too.

That should have pleased her. Though she worked for Dana Sue, she'd come to think of all of these people as friends. For the first time in her life she had a real support system and knew she could make it on her own. She didn't want to risk that for a relationship with a man who might shatter her hard-won independence and wind up leaving the way her ex-husband had.

"You've been awfully quiet," Elliott said as he drove her home. "Didn't you have a good time at the party?"

"I had a wonderful time," she said. "It was so much fun seeing Helen's face when she walked in. I think she was genuinely surprised."

"She obviously loved the picture you gave her of Daisy and Mack," Elliott said. "It made her cry."

Karen frowned at the reminder. "Happy tears, I hope, but I'm not so sure."

"Why would it have been anything else?"

"Just a feeling I have," she admitted. "I think she wants her own family."

"Then perhaps she and Erik will get together. There's definitely something going on between those two."

"There's a lot of chemistry, that's for sure," she conceded.

He glanced over at her. "Like there is with us."

Once again, she frowned. "Elliott, please. I don't want to talk about us."

For once he didn't let the subject drop. "Why not, Karen?" he asked. "We're good together. More than good."

It was true. He was amazing with her kids and kind and loving toward her. But the idea of allowing herself to give in to the feelings he stirred in her scared her.

She reached for his hand. "I know you can't possibly understand where I'm coming from, and I'm sorry. I like you, Elliott. I love spending time with you."

"But what? You're not in love with me?"

"I didn't say that. I don't know what I feel."

He pulled to a stop in front of her apartment building and cut the engine. Staring straight ahead, he asked, "Do you want to end this?"

"No," she whispered, tears welling up in her eyes. "But I can't promise you anything. It's not fair to keep you waiting around, either."

"You're not making any sense," he accused. "Are you confused? Scared? What?"

She took a deep breath, then blurted, "All of that. I just started getting my life back on track. I finally feel as if I have some control over it. Falling in love, well, it means giving up some of that control. I don't know if I can do it again."

He tucked a finger under her chin and forced her to face him. "I do get that, Karen. I really do. I know what you've been through. It's probably too soon for me to be pushing you like this. I just need you to know where I'm coming from. I can wait, if you'll just tell me that there's a chance for us. If there's not, if you can't see yourself ever trusting another man not to hurt you, then tell me and I'll leave you alone. I won't spend years trying to prove I'm not like your ex-husband."

"I want to trust you," she said softly, her cheeks damp with tears. "I've seen the gentleness and kindness in you."

"Then give us a chance," he said quietly. "That's all, just a chance. But if you know you'll never be able to open up your heart, please don't just go through the motions."

It would be so easy to say yes, she thought. It would be so easy to start a relationship and see where it led. But the panic that rushed through her just thinking about it proved it was too soon.

Slowly, she shook her head. Touching a hand to his

cheek, she said, "I can't, Elliott. I'm not ready to take that kind of risk. If I were, you'd be the man I'd choose, but I can't."

He sat back with a heavy sigh. "Okay, then. If that's really the way you want it, I'll back off."

Holding back tears, she nodded. "I think that's best."

"I'll walk you in."

"You don't have to do that."

"Yes, I do," he said, getting out of the car and coming around to open her door.

He said absolutely nothing as they walked to her apartment. At the door, she lifted her gaze to his. "I'm sorry."

"So am I."

She unlocked the door, but when she would have walked inside, he stopped her. "You're a terrific woman, Karen. I know you're just discovering that about yourself, but it's been obvious to me since the day we met. I hope someday you'll believe in yourself enough to let a man into your life."

Then he turned and walked away, leaving her alone on her doorstep…and feeling lonelier than she had in years.

CHAPTER SEVENTEEN

Karen tiptoed into her apartment, trying not to wake Frances, who'd fallen asleep on the sofa with the television tuned to a late-night talk show. Unfortunately, by the time she'd peeked in to check on the kids, Frances was wide-awake and filled with questions.

"How was your evening?" she asked, fully alert and eager for answers.

"Fine," Karen murmured, not anxious to talk to a woman who could read her like a book. She knew Frances would be distraught over her breakup with Elliott. She'd said at least a hundred times how lucky she thought Karen was to have found him.

"I'll tell you all about it tomorrow," Karen promised. "Since you're awake, why don't you get home so you can sleep in your own bed, instead of being all cramped up on my sofa?"

Frances ignored the suggestion and regarded her suspiciously. "Come here where I can get a better look at you," she commanded. "Have you been crying?"

Since her cheeks were still damp, Karen could hardly deny it. "It's no big deal."

"Tell me," Frances demanded. "What did Elliott do?"

Her immediate indignation on Karen's behalf made Karen smile. "He didn't do anything," she said. "It was me. I broke things off with him."

Frances looked stunned. "Why on earth would you do a crazy thing like that?" Even before Karen could reply, she said, "It's because you're scared, isn't it? I should have seen this coming. The more time Elliott spends around here, the more distant you've become."

Karen acknowledged the truth with a nod. "He's ready for more, Frances. He wants a real relationship with a future and I can't promise him any of that. I can barely think ahead to tomorrow."

"Is this about sex?" Frances asked, her indignation returning. "Was he pressuring you to sleep with him?"

Karen felt weird having this conversation with Frances. She'd never talked about intimate topics like this with any of the women who'd been her foster mothers. She'd learned everything she knew about sex from kids in school and even at that, she'd hardly been prepared for marriage. Still, this was Frances, who listened and didn't make judgments.

"No," she admitted. "It wasn't like that at all. Believe me, there's a lot of chemistry there, but this was all about an emotional commitment. Elliott is ready to make that. I'm not."

"I see. It would have been easier for you if it had just been about sex, wouldn't it?"

Karen nodded. "Sleeping with him would be amazing, I'm sure of it. But any more? I just don't see it happening. I'm barely standing on my own two feet," she told Frances. "You've been here. You know how it was just a few months ago. I can't risk all the progress I've made. I'm stronger now, but I don't want to backslide and wind up being dependent on another man."

"But wouldn't it be nice to have someone to lean on, someone you could count on?"

"Of course," Karen conceded. "But it could just as easily turn out differently. Once upon a time, I thought I could lean on my husband. Look how that turned out."

"Elliott is nothing like your ex-husband," Frances said with fierce certainty. "He would never walk out on the mother of his children. Just look at how patiently he's put up with all your attempts to make him go. He's solid and dependable. He's a family man. You can tell that by how close he is to all his sisters and their kids. Not every man his age would be so eager to take on a woman with two young children, especially a man who can have his pick of women. I imagine a lot of the women at the spa have set their sights on him, probably with no strings attached, but Elliott chose you, Karen. That speaks volumes to me. It tells me he values you and respects you."

"I know," Karen said wearily. "Like I said, this is about me. I don't trust my own judgment anymore."

"Then give it time," Frances said. "You don't have to make a decision about your future tonight."

"It's too late," Karen told her, a catch in her voice. "I just didn't think it was fair to lead him on when I might never be ready for more. It's over, Frances. I made sure of that."

Frances gave her a sympathetic look. "Oh, honey, nothing's over until that man goes off and marries some other woman. If you're right for each other, you'll work it out. If he lets you go without a fight, then he's not the man I think he is."

Karen gulped back a sob as she thought about never spending time with Elliott again. Daisy and Mack were going to be devastated, too. They adored Elliott. "I hope you're right. I hope I didn't make the biggest mistake of my life."

"Not a chance," Frances said. "When I look at Elliott, I see a man who's deeply in love and knows you're worth waiting for."

Karen thought of the bleak expression of finality she'd seen on Elliott's face tonight and prayed she'd misread it. Hopefully Frances, with her years of experience with human nature, was the one who'd read the situation correctly.

Erik went into Sullivan's early, hoping to get a head start on his dessert preparations for the day. He was trying a new recipe and it required the kind of concentration he could seldom manage once the kitchen started to bustle with all the food prep for lunch.

Unfortunately, he'd barely begun to assemble his ingredients—flour, sugar, cream and a dark, rich chocolate—when someone pounded on the back door. Muttering a curse, he went to open it and found Cal Maddox and Ronnie Sullivan out there.

"I would have used my key," Ronnie said as he walked inside, "but I don't like to do that when someone's here. I scared ten years off Dana Sue's life one night when I showed up and she wasn't expecting me. Came close to getting whacked on the head with a cast-iron skillet, too. That woman's self-defense skills are scary."

Erik grinned, despite the untimely interruption. "She does have her moments, doesn't she?"

"Enough chitchat," Cal grumbled. "Where's the coffee? Ronnie promised there'd be coffee."

"Over there," Erik said, gesturing toward the full pot he'd brewed when he arrived. "So what are you two doing here?"

"Blame our wives," Ronnie said. "They're worried about Helen. They think you might need backup in protecting her."

"And Maddie wants to know what your intentions are," Cal added, giving Erik a commiserating grin. "I suggest you form your answer carefully or run like hell."

Erik ignored Cal's question since it seemed to be a lot trickier than the implication that he couldn't keep Helen safe on his own. "As long as Helen behaves sensibly and listens to reason, I think we have the whole protection thing under control."

The two men exchanged a look of skepticism.

"We're talking about *Helen*," Ronnie said at last. "I've known that woman most of my life. She's smart, but she's also stubborn. She thinks she can control the universe. She probably figures she can hog-tie Brad Holliday and deliver him to the sheriff with one hand tied behind her back."

Erik grinned. "I'm sure she does."

"And that doesn't worry you?" Cal asked. "Seems to me that suggests she'll take chances."

Erik was forced to admit that since that first night when she'd come to him and asked to stay at his place, she'd been getting increasingly reckless about where she went and when. He had a hunch she'd stopped looking over her shoulder, despite the warnings Jimmy

Bob West and Judge Rockingham had repeated just last night.

"You could have a point," he said at last. "But she's independent. What am I supposed to do?"

"I have one idea," Cal volunteered. "I know Brad. His youngest son played ball for me the first year I was here. Brad was one of those dads from hell who thought every call from the umpire that went against his boy was wrong. Figured he was a better coach than me, too. He made that kid's life miserable 'til we had a little chat one night and I threatened to ban him from the games if he didn't keep his mouth shut."

"What's your point?" Ronnie asked. "That he's a bully? That's not comforting."

"No, my point is that bullies often back down when somebody bigger and tougher gets directly in their face," Cal explained patiently. "I suggest the three of us have a little come-to-Jesus conversation with Mr. Holliday."

Ronnie grinned, looking a bit too eager for Erik's peace of mind.

"I'm in," Ronnie said. "How about you, Erik?"

"Much as I would like to pummel some sense into this guy, I see a downside," Erik replied. "Helen is going to be furious if we take on her battles for her."

"Better a furious Helen than one who's in the emergency room," Ronnie said. "Jimmy Bob pulled me aside last night. There's not a lot about Jimmy Bob I trust, but his concern for Helen was genuine. He convinced me it could come to that."

Erik flinched at that. "Then we need to get a protective order right now," he said. "Rockingham will issue it."

Just as he uttered the words, Helen walked into the kitchen. Apparently she'd been less hesitant than Ronnie about using her key and had come in through the front door.

"Judge Rockingham will issue what?" she said, frowning at the three of them. Even if she hadn't heard a snippet of their conversation, finding them assembled at Sullivan's this early in the morning on a weekday would no doubt have made her wary.

"A restraining order to keep Brad Holliday away from you," Erik told her, convinced it was smarter just to be straight with her. "I want it done before the end of the day."

Helen immediately shook her head. "No way. All that will do is get Brad even more worked up. He's already convinced that the justice system is against him."

"Well, we have to do something," Erik said.

"Plan A," Cal muttered.

"Plan A, it is," Ronnie agreed.

Helen locked gazes with Erik. "What is Plan A?"

"Don't worry about it," he said, holding her gaze unflinchingly. "We have it under control."

"Now why doesn't that set my mind at ease?" she asked.

"I can't imagine," Erik said with a shrug and turned his attention to the two men.

"I'll call you later with details," Cal said, swallowing the last of his coffee and heading for the door.

Ronnie was right on his heels. "Good luck, pal. See you soon."

After they'd gone, Erik faced Helen, whose expression had darkened.

"Start talking," she commanded.

"What about?"

"Don't pull that nonsense with me," she said. "What are the three of you up to? It better not have anything to do with me or Brad Holliday."

"We're just taking some precautionary measures," he said blithely, stepping closer and giving her a kiss he hoped would prove distracting.

"Good morning," he murmured when he released her. "How'd you sleep last night?"

She punched him in the arm. "Don't think for one second that kissing me is going to make me forget about whatever it is you all are planning."

"You're not even a little distracted?" he asked. "I must be losing my touch."

"Your touch is just fine, thank you, but so is my memory. Talk, pal. Now. And if I don't like what I hear, you'd better put a stop to Plan A."

"It's not a big deal," he assured her. "We're not going to haul Holliday into a back alley and beat him to a pulp."

"Well, that's reassuring," she said dryly. "Because if that was the plan, then you shouldn't count on me to bail you out of jail. I'm not big on vigilante justice. In addition, I think you're all overreacting. Brad may be mouthing off, but he hasn't done anything. He hasn't even set foot near me."

"You sure about that?" Erik asked. "Have you been watching who's around when you're on the streets? Have you looked to see if anyone's tailing your car?"

"Now you're being melodramatic," she said.

He heard the slightest tremble in her voice, which was enough to convince him that she hadn't been that observant.

"Am I being melodramatic?" he asked. "I'm not the only one who thinks the man's a danger to you. So do people who know him a whole lot better than you or I do."

"They *think* he could be dangerous," she corrected. "There's a difference. The more time that passes, the less worried I am."

"And *that* worries me," Erik told her. "You need to be on guard all the time."

"I don't want to live like that," she said.

"Then let us follow through with Plan A. I promise none of us is going to get hurt, Holliday included, and maybe it will keep you from being hurt, as well."

"Or it'll make Brad even more furious with me," she suggested. "Can't you all just leave this alone?"

He shook his head. "I don't think so. Sorry."

"But I'm not asking for your help," she said with obvious frustration. "I don't *want* your help."

Erik shrugged. "Too bad. You have it anyway."

"Men!" she muttered in exasperation. "Do what you have to do, but don't blame me if it backfires. Just keep in mind that I'm the one who's likely to pay the price if it does."

She headed toward the door, her spine rigid. Erik wanted to say something to reassure her, but nothing came to mind. Once they'd confronted Brad Holliday, he'd have a much better idea if they'd warned him off or made matters worse. Until then, he and Helen would simply have to agree to disagree.

Helen marched into The Corner Spa and headed straight for the back patio, where she knew Dana Sue and Maddie would be waiting. Obviously they'd put their husbands up to that little gabfest she'd walked in on at Sullivan's. Maybe they knew what Plan A was and whether it really involved a back-alley brawl.

"There she is," Maddie said cheerfully as Helen approached. "And she's not looking one day older than she did before her birthday."

Helen scowled at her. "I appreciated the party, but I don't want to talk about being older. Besides, we need to discuss what your husbands are up to. I found them at Sullivan's conspiring with Erik."

Maddie and Dana Sue exchanged a look.

"Interesting," Dana Sue said. "She stopped by to see Erik before coming here. Why do you suppose that was?"

"Because he's sexier!" Helen snapped. "Now stop evading and answer me. I know they were over there working up some scheme to deal with Brad Holliday. What did you say to your husbands to get them all worked up? Did you exaggerate the threat?"

"There was no exaggeration. They already understood the situation," Maddie soothed.

"But you encouraged them to hatch some scheme, didn't you?" Helen said. "Are you crazy? You know how guys are. Somebody is going to get hurt and if that happens, it's on your heads."

"Cal won't let that happen," Maddie assured her. "He's the voice of reason. So is Erik."

Dana Sue frowned. "You left out Ronnie."

"Deliberately would be my guess," Helen said. "He's always been a hothead."

"Not anymore," Dana Sue insisted. "Not since he got back to town and we remarried. You know that's true."

"Which only means he's overdue for doing something crazy," Helen retorted.

"Hold it," Maddie said. "These are all grown men. They're just trying to look out for you, Helen. They can handle themselves."

Far from reassured, Helen sat back in her chair. "Well, I hope you're right."

"Let's move on to a far more interesting topic," Dana Sue suggested. "How serious are things between you and Erik?"

"It's a fling," Helen said. "No big deal."

Dana Sue's expression darkened. "I don't like the sound of that. Are you just toying with him, Helen?"

"No more than he is with me," she assured her. "Two consenting adults, Dana Sue. We both knew the score when we started this."

"Did you really?" Maddie asked pointedly. "Erik knew the score?"

Dana Sue's narrowed gaze shifted from Helen to Maddie. "What are you suggesting?" she asked, her expression quizzical.

"Nothing," Helen said hurriedly. "Maddie doesn't know anything you don't know, right, Maddie?"

Maddie's gaze clashed with hers, but Maddie was the first to blink. "No, I don't know anything for a fact."

Dana Sue seized on the very evident loophole. "But you're speculating about something, making an educated guess, aren't you?"

Helen held Maddie's gaze until she shook her head.

"I know better than to speculate about Helen," Maddie said eventually. "She's too unpredictable."

Helen forced a smile as she tried to cover her relief. "I'll take that as a compliment."

"I'm not sure you should," Maddie said darkly.

It was definitely time to get out of here before the

conversation got any trickier. "Well, I need to get to work," Helen said briskly, rising to her feet. "Dana Sue, what about you?"

"I'm going to stick around," Dana Sue said to Helen's dismay.

"Okay, whatever," Helen said. "I'll see you."

She had no choice but to trust that Maddie would stay silent after she'd gone. Whatever Maddie knew—or thought she knew—was not something Helen wanted her to share with Dana Sue.

As Helen left The Corner Spa to walk to her office, she noticed a car slowly turn the corner, then keep pace with her. The driver stayed in her peripheral vision, but never got far enough ahead for her to see who was behind the wheel. A chill crept up the back of her neck.

"You're only jittery because of all that talk about Brad," she muttered under her breath. "This is probably just some little old lady who never goes over five miles an hour, that's all."

Still, when she finally turned onto the street her office was on, she picked up her pace. When the car made the same turn, it took everything in her to make herself stop and turn back.

"Nervous, Ms. Decatur?" Brad Holliday called out to her, his expression cold. "You should be."

Before she could reply, he hit the gas and drove off.

"He's just a bully, that's all," Helen told herself staunchly as he disappeared around the next corner. "He just wants to scare me."

Well, he'd accomplished that, she realized as she stared after him. Bile rose in her throat and for a minute she thought she might be sick, but she forced herself to take a few deep breaths, then walked the rest of the way to her office.

She knew she should call the judge or the police, but she couldn't make herself do it. What had Brad done, really? Told her she ought to be nervous. Big deal. It wouldn't be enough to get a restraining order. And a restraining order wouldn't keep him away if he was determined to get even with her. She'd seen the ineffectiveness of that flimsy piece of paper too many times.

Maybe Plan A, whatever it was, wasn't such a bad idea, after all.

For the next week Helen was so jittery she had to force herself to leave Erik's house or the relative safety of her office, where no one got past Barb without an inquisition. Only stubborn pride kept her going about her normal routine.

When she realized in the middle of the following week that she'd missed her period, her immediate thought was stress, not pregnancy. Then she added in the vague nausea she'd experienced on a few mornings lately. Could it possibly be...?

The second Erik left the house, she grabbed her day planner and looked at her calendar. Each time her period had come right on schedule, she'd secretly shed a few tears and made a little mark. With fingers that shook, she flipped through the pages, back one week, then two, then three.

"Oh, my God," she whispered, when she'd flipped back six weeks to find the little mark she always made on the top corner of the page.

She'd been so busy, so caught up in her unexpected feelings for Erik and, more recently, so nervous about

Brad Holliday, she hadn't even thought about the baby plan she'd put into effect a few months back. Initially obsessed with those damnable little marks, lately she'd completely lost track. Or maybe she'd simply lost hope.

Now, though, she was late. Seriously late.

"Oh, my God," she said again. "I'm pregnant!"

Caution immediately had her correcting herself. "I might be pregnant."

Thankfully, in anticipation of this day, she'd bought several at-home pregnancy tests at a Charleston pharmacy and hidden them in her suitcase in the back of Erik's closet.

Pushing aside her clothes, she dragged out the suitcase and fumbled with the lock, then took the kits into the bathroom. She was shaking so hard, she could barely hold the box still long enough to read the instructions.

While she waited for the results, she took another test for good measure. And then a third.

The first positive reading brought tears to her eyes. The second brought on a jubilant shout. The third had her sitting down hard on the lid of the toilet and holding a hand over her stomach.

"Baby, if you're really in there, I am going to take such good care of you. I promise."

Five minutes later, she'd scheduled an appointment for the following week with the obstetrician she'd liked the best. If he confirmed what three at-home tests had told her, her life was about to change dramatically.

And so was her relationship with Erik.

Helen was acting weird and Erik didn't think it could be blamed entirely on their disagreement about how

Brad Holliday should be handled. *That* had become an almost daily bone of contention.

Tonight, though, she'd had this funny little half smile on her face ever since he'd come home, but when he'd asked what she was thinking, she'd blown off the question.

"You weren't that happy this morning," he said, still studying her suspiciously.

"Actually I was," she said. "Then my mood changed when Maddie called to tell me that you, Cal and Ronnie were getting ready to execute Plan A. I remembered how annoyed I was with you three and your macho plan."

"But I gather you've put that behind you now," he said.

"What makes you think that?"

"You're here. If you were really ticked off, you'd have gone to your place." He searched her face. "Unless, despite all your disclaimers to the contrary, you're still scared of Holliday and that outweighs your annoyance with me. To be honest, I'd find that reassuring."

"Oh, for heaven's sake, do we have to keep talking about Brad Holliday?" she demanded.

"Nope."

In fact, the less said about the man the better. Erik didn't want to answer questions about when he, Cal and Ronnie intended to implement Plan A. In fact, they'd settled on confronting the man at his home on Saturday morning. Erik didn't much like the idea of waiting two more days, but they'd already waited a week and he'd agreed that confronting him at work would be counter-productive. A public confrontation would be just one more thing to infuriate a man whose hold on his temper was already tenuous.

"Can I bring you anything?" he asked Helen. "I thought I'd have a glass of wine before bed."

"Nothing for me," Helen said, then held up a glass. "I have some water."

That was odd, too. Helen usually joined him in a glass of wine at night. It wasn't worth making a big deal about, though.

When he came back into the living room, he settled on the sofa beside her. "How about watching a movie? There's an old Katharine Hepburn–Spencer Tracy film on tonight. I know you love those."

"Not tonight. I'm tired. It's been a long day." She stood up. "I think I'll go on up to bed."

"Wait," Erik said, frowning. "Are you still upset with me about Holliday?"

"No. I told you it was up to you. Do whatever you have to do."

"But you still disapprove?"

"I still disapprove," she confirmed, "because he's *my* problem. It's up to me to solve it."

"Couldn't you just think of us as backup?"

"Backup's one thing," she told him. "Interference is something else entirely."

"You really are upset about this, aren't you?"

"Gee, you think?"

"I can talk to Cal and Ronnie," he said against his better judgment. "We can hold off for a while. Is that really what you want?"

She regarded him seriously. "It's really what I want."

"Then I'll talk to them," he conceded. "None of us

is trying to undermine your independence, you know. We just want you to be safe."

She sighed then and sat back down. "I know that. I just don't like thinking that I'm so vulnerable I need protecting."

"Isn't it better to be safe than sorry? I'd never forgive myself if something happened to you when we might have been able to prevent it."

He couldn't quite read the strange expression that flitted across her face. Something he'd said, though, had obviously resonated with her.

"Go ahead with whatever Plan A is," she said, the about-face catching him completely off guard. "Just swear to me that none of you will put yourselves in danger."

"We won't," he promised.

He wanted to ask why the change of heart, but he didn't dare. Deep down he believed that moving ahead with the plan was too important to risk losing her hard-won approval. Better to put the fear of God in Brad Holliday now than have to kill him if he ever laid a hand on Helen.

CHAPTER EIGHTEEN

———◆—◆◆—◆———

Upstairs Helen thought about Erik's concern for her safety and wondered how he'd feel if he knew he might also be protecting their child. In the midst of their argument, she'd suddenly realized she couldn't think only of herself anymore. She had to take whatever precautions were necessary to make sure that no harm came to this baby she might be carrying.

Until this mess with Brad Holliday had started, she'd planned to slowly break things off with Erik the instant she found out she was pregnant. Brad's threats, however unlikely he was to carry them out, made it necessary for her to stay with Erik awhile longer. She sincerely hoped this Plan A would erase the threats and she'd be able to go back home and then end things with Erik in a way that wouldn't hurt him too deeply.

From the beginning of their affair, she'd tried to convince herself he'd be glad to be free of the drama she'd brought into his life, but she knew she was deluding herself. Neither of them was going to walk away from this relationship entirely unscathed, no matter how badly she wanted them to.

She knew tonight's one-eighty about Plan A had star-

tled Erik, but she'd managed to get away before he could
start asking uncomfortable questions. She'd counted
on his being so relieved by her acquiescence he'd stay
silent, and he had, giving her just enough time to bolt.

By the time he came into the bedroom, she was on
her side, facing away from him, feigning sleep. She listened to the familiar sound of his clothes being tossed
in the general direction of a chair in the corner of the
room, then the shower running. When he finally slid
beneath the sheets beside her and pressed a quick kiss
to her cheek, she almost regretted her charade.

It would have felt good to fold herself into his embrace, to talk quietly about their day, maybe even make
love, and then let the steady beating of his heart soothe
her to sleep. She'd gotten too used to that lately. Alone
for so many years, she hadn't expected to grow accustomed to the little intimate moments that make up a relationship. She was going to miss all of them dreadfully
when she went back to her own home and her solitude.
The solitude, at least, would be temporary.

Eventually, there would be a baby to hold and love
and care for, and that would be its own kind of fulfill-
ment. She touched a hand to her still-flat belly and tried
to imagine the tiny life growing inside. She was completely awestruck by the idea of it. Please, God, let her
not be wrong about this. Let there be a baby.

"Helen?" Erik whispered. "Are you awake?"

Giving in to her desire for him, she murmured,
"Yes."

He rolled toward her and pulled her against him,
his bare skin against her back, his heat and male scent
enveloping her, awakening her. When he cupped her

breast, she thought she noticed a new sensitivity, as pleasure immediately shot through her.

Just like that, she was wide-awake and filled with need. As if he sensed it, Erik's touch went from gentle to impatient, his urgency and her own sudden heated response, catching her off guard.

They came together in a raw burst of passion, breath mingling, hands anxious and determined, hips meeting in a mindless parry and thrust that spiraled out of control in little more than a heartbeat. The fierce explosion that ripped through her triggered his and seemed to go on forever.

That perfectly attuned connection made her wonder—when she could finally think again—how they'd come to know each other's bodies so well. If only their hearts were as well-matched, she thought wistfully before she fell asleep in his arms, the whir of the ceiling fan and its gentle breeze carrying her off to some imaginary hideaway on a romantic tropical island. If only, she thought again. If only...

Helen was plowing through a huge stack of court documents when Barb buzzed her. Sounding alarmed, she announced that someone from Regional Hospital was on the phone.

"What about?" Helen asked.

"Caroline Holliday."

Helen snatched up the phone. "This is Helen Decatur."

"Ms. Decatur, this is Emily Wilson. I'm an emergency room physician at Regional Hospital. Caroline Holliday said you recently represented her in a divorce proceeding."

"Yes. Why? What's happened?"

"She was brought in here, barely conscious, about an hour ago. She'd been beaten. She told officers her ex-husband was responsible, but they haven't located him yet. I have a detective here who'd very much like to speak to you. Can you come?"

"I'll be there within the hour," Helen said, her heart pounding. This was her fault, dammit! Why hadn't she done more to protect Caroline? A restraining order might not be the most effective tool in the world, but she should have demanded one that last day in court when they'd all witnessed Brad unraveling before their eyes. Instead, she'd listened to Caroline say she was going to remove herself from Serenity for a couple of weeks and felt satisfied. Obviously, she'd come back—and to this.

"How is she?" Helen asked, her heart in her throat.

The doctor hesitated, then said, "You're not a family member, so I shouldn't be releasing any information, but Caroline specifically wanted you to know how out-of-control her husband was, so I'll tell you the truth. She's in surgery right now. She has a ruptured spleen, other internal injuries, a broken arm and quite a few cuts and bruises. Brad Holliday was one very angry man."

Helen gasped. "Oh, my God," she whispered. "Will she make it?"

"The best surgeons on staff are with her now. It's in their hands and in God's. I think the only thing that kept her conscious was her determination to warn you. I don't want to tell you what to do, but you shouldn't be alone. Caroline was adamant that you need protection."

"I'll have it," Helen said. "Please take good care of her. This is my fault."

"Because you got her away from a bully?" the doctor asked incredulously.

"No, because I infuriated him in the process," she said, riddled with guilt. Surely there'd been another way to protect Caroline's interests. She should have found it. In her worst nightmare, she'd never imagined Brad becoming this violent. Even when he'd confronted her on the street just days ago, she still hadn't imagined how deeply disturbed he was. How could she have ignored all the warnings?

"Please let the detective know I'm on my way now and tell him he can get more information from Judge Lester Rockingham and Brad's attorney, Jimmy Bob West."

"I'll pass that along," Dr. Wilson promised.

Helen was shaking when she hung up. She glanced up and realized Barb had come into her office while she'd been on the phone.

"How bad is it?" Barb asked.

"She's in surgery. I need to get over there."

"Surely, you're not going alone," Barb said. "Have they arrested Brad?"

"Not yet, apparently."

"Then you need to take someone with you," Barb insisted.

Helen glanced at the clock. It was just before noon. Erik would be swamped at the restaurant.

Barb apparently figured out what she was thinking because she said firmly, "I'm calling Erik. I don't care how busy he is. He's going to want to go with you. Pick him up on the way. Promise me, Helen."

Too rattled to argue, Helen nodded. "Tell him I'll swing by to get him. I'll pull into the alley."

Ten minutes later she turned into the alley behind Sullivan's and found Erik and Dana Sue both standing there. Dana Sue looked terrified, Erik deeply worried. He yanked open the car door and climbed in.

"You okay?" he asked tersely.

She could only nod. Glancing at Dana Sue, she said, "I'll call you when we know more."

Dana Sue scowled at Erik. "Don't you dare let anything happen to her," she ordered.

"Not on my watch," he assured her.

"We need to go," Helen said, then stepped on the accelerator and shot out of the alley.

"Slow down," Erik commanded. "Try not to get us killed driving over there."

"Would you feel better if you were behind the wheel?" she snapped.

"Based on what I've observed of your driving in the last ten seconds, yes."

She knew he was right. She was too shaken to be behind the wheel. She pulled into a parking lot, slammed her foot on the brake and cut the engine. "Be my guest," she said, getting out and walking around to the other side.

Erik got out and snagged her wrist before she could take his place in the passenger seat. He held her gaze and his tone softened. "It's going to be okay."

Tears stung her eyes. "I hope so, but you didn't hear what the doctor said about Caroline's injuries. It's not good, Erik. She might not make it."

His eyes darkened. "It could have been you."

"But it wasn't," she said. She didn't mention that Caroline and the police thought she might very well be next. Once they were on their way again, she couldn't bring herself to admit aloud how relieved she was that Erik was now behind the wheel, that he was with her. Even though she could almost feel the tension radiating from him, his strength and mere presence steadied her.

"Thank you for coming with me," she said at last.

He glanced at her. "Your idea or Barb's?"

"Both," she admitted with a half smile. "She was a little more certain that interrupting you at the height of lunch hour was the thing to do."

"You can call me anytime, day or night," he said. "When the choice is between you and baking some fancy dessert, you're going to win hands down, okay?"

She studied him. "You really mean that, don't you?"

"Of course. Why do you even have to ask?"

"Because you've always been so clear about not wanting any emotional entanglements," she told him candidly.

"We're friends, Helen, and friends will always come first with me."

Friends, she thought, leaning back against the seat and holding in a sigh. It was good that he'd reminded her of that. Not that being friends was a bad thing. Not at all. And being friends who slept together was amazing. But there was a clear limit to the relationship, one that told her yet again that he would want no part of this child who might be growing inside her.

Regret washed through her. Regret that the man she'd chosen to father her child would never give that child the same fierce loyalty and protectiveness he gave her. What a tragic and terrible loss for both of them!

Erik glanced over at Helen as he made the turn into the emergency room parking area at the hospital. Her hands were clenched into white-knuckled fists in her lap, and her face was drawn with lines of tension. He guessed that she was blaming herself for what had happened to Caroline Holliday, rather than placing the blame squarely on the man responsible.

When Barb had quickly explained what was going on, he'd felt an overwhelming surge of anger toward Brad Holliday and panic that Helen would be his next victim. He'd been yanking off his chef's jacket and heading for the door before he'd hung up the phone, Dana Sue right on his heels as he explained what was going on. Neither of them had hesitated even a second over the decision that Helen's safety took precedence over anything going on at Sullivan's.

"If we run out of whatever's ready now, we'll serve ice cream," she'd told him. "Just go and keep Helen safe."

On the drive to the hospital, he'd kept his eyes peeled for any suspicious cars, worried that Holliday might have followed Helen from her office. Hopefully the man was scared out of his wits by what he'd done to his ex-wife and was so anxious to avoid the police he wouldn't come anywhere near Helen.

Even though Erik hadn't spotted anyone following them or lurking in the hospital parking lot, he instructed Helen to stay in the car 'til he opened her door.

He cut off her protest. "Just common sense, sugar. Don't get your back up."

She sighed. "I know, but hurry."

He lifted a brow. "We made it here in under thirty minutes. I'm hurrying."

He moved quickly around to her side of the car and shielded her body as she exited. With one arm around her and his gaze darting from side to side, he walked her into the emergency room. A uniformed officer and another man in a rumpled suit that reminded Erik of old *Columbo* shows were hanging around the triage desk.

"We're here about Caroline Holliday," Erik told the nurse on duty, drawing the attention of the men.

"Are you Helen Decatur?" the plainclothes officer asked. "I'm Detective Myers."

Helen nodded. "I'll answer all your questions, but I need to find out how Caroline's doing first." She turned to the nurse. "Is Dr. Wilson available?"

"I'll see if she's free," the nurse said. "I'll send her over to the waiting room."

"Thank you," Erik said, when Helen looked as if she wanted to barge back into the treatment area and search for the doctor herself. He steered her across the hall.

"I'll get coffee," he told her.

"It's pretty disgusting," the uniformed officer said with a grimace.

"I'd rather have herbal tea, anyway," Helen said.

"Fine. I'll get tea," Erik said. "Don't leave her alone for a minute, okay?"

"Not a chance," the detective assured him.

Erik went off to find the cafeteria or a vending machine. Hospital noises and smells were as familiar to him as the aromas in Sullivan's kitchen, but ever since Sam had died they made him queasy. He had to fight with himself to keep from heading straight back to the parking lot, where he could suck in fresh air and maybe get a grip on his composure.

It didn't take him long to find a vending machine, which spewed out a pitiful-looking cup of weak coffee for him. He bought that, then found Helen's tea in the cafeteria.

As he was passing the triage desk, the nurse beckoned to him. "Dr. Wilson is with another patient right now, but she said to tell Ms. Decatur she'll check on Mrs. Holliday's status and be out to fill her in as soon as possible."

"Thanks," Erik said. "I'll let her know."

When he got to the waiting room, he heard Helen summarizing the scene on the day Caroline Holliday had been granted her divorce and the concern the judge and Brad's attorney had expressed for her safety and Helen's. Taking a seat beside Helen, Erik handed her the tea with a roll of his eyes. "Be grateful you opted for that," he said after taking a sip of his coffee.

"You're drinking it," she noted.

"I'm desperate. Any caffeine will do."

Helen shook her head. "Shouldn't you have gotten decaf?"

"It wouldn't matter," the officer said. "Desperation is the only reason anyone would drink that stuff. I'm in here just about every night following up on an accident or a domestic violence incident and I've been pleading with 'em for two years to try to get one of those big coffee chains to open up a franchise by the E.R. It'd make a fortune."

Beside Erik, Helen's eyes immediately brightened. "Maybe it doesn't have to be a big chain franchise," she said, her gaze on him. "What do you think, Erik? It could be a Sullivan's café like the one we have at The Corner Spa."

Detective Myers regarded her with surprise. "I've had the coffee at that restaurant. Best around."

Helen grinned. "He's one of the chefs," she said, gesturing toward Erik.

For a few minutes the tension dissolved as the four of them talked about Sullivan's food and coffee, but the instant a harried-looking woman in green surgical scrubs walked into the waiting room, the mood immediately turned somber.

"Hey, Doc," Detective Myers said. "Any news?"

"Good and bad," she said with a nod in Helen's direction. "Thanks for coming."

"What's the good news?" the detective asked.

"She made it through surgery," Emily Wilson said, but her expression remained grim.

"But?" Erik said.

"She's not coming around the way we'd hoped and her blood pressure hasn't stabilized. In fact, it's dropping."

"She's still bleeding," Erik guessed before the others could react.

The doctor nodded. "That's what we're afraid of. The surgeon was sure he'd found all the bleeders and tied them off, but he could have missed something. Her internal organs took quite a beating."

"Is he going back in?" Erik asked, aware of Helen's gaze. "There may not be a lot of time to wait it out."

"He'll make a decision in the next half hour," Dr. Wilson confirmed. "You seem to have a good grasp of all this."

"I was an EMT for a while," he said.

The detective stared at him. "And now you're a chef. I'll bet there's a story in that."

Erik shrugged. "Not a very interesting one," he said.

"I'll keep you posted," Dr. Wilson told them. "Detective, have you been able to reach her kids?"

"I tracked down her oldest son. He's rounding up the others. They should be here soon."

"The sooner the better," the doctor said.

Beside Erik, Helen shivered. He draped an arm around her and gave her shoulder a squeeze. "Maybe we should go," he suggested.

"No," Helen said at once. "I need to stay. If you need to get back, take my car. Maddie or somebody can pick me up later."

"Not a chance," Erik said. "If you stay, I stay. I just thought you might not want to be here when her children get here."

Helen shook her head. "They may have questions I can answer."

"Or they may blame you for triggering all this," he countered. "Remember, they love their mom *and* their dad."

"He's right," Detective Myers said. "In these circumstances, people sometimes aren't rational. I have the background information I need from you for now. Go home." He met Erik's gaze, though he continued to speak to Helen. "Just make sure someone's with you at all times until we find this guy, okay? He's clearly lost his grip."

"Someone will be," Erik assured him.

"I'll notify your sheriff that he needs to keep a watch on your house and your office," he said.

"She's spending a lot of time at my place," Erik said. "Most of the time she's not alone there." He gave him the address.

"I'll make sure he knows about that, too," Detective

Myers said. "You can't take this lightly, Ms. Decatur. I know Mrs. Holliday was worried, and when I spoke to the judge and Holliday's attorney, they expressed concern for you, too. The last thing any of us wants is for you to wind up here in the same shape Mrs. Holliday is in."

"I get it," she said, her face pale. "I'll be careful."

The two policemen walked them to Helen's car. It appeared to be a casual gesture, but Erik noted that they were very much on alert, checking out the parking lot in every direction, then waiting until Erik pulled out of the space and drove off before going back inside.

"I should have stayed," Helen said as they turned onto the highway.

"No," Erik contradicted. "This is for the best. You can go back when Caroline's in a room and needs company. Now what she needs are your prayers."

Helen didn't look entirely convinced, but she fell silent. In fact, she was so quiet for so long that Erik began to worry, until a glance told him that she'd fallen asleep. Obviously the news and the frantic drive had taken a toll on her.

At his place, she let him fix her some soup and a salad. She ate three spoonfuls of the soup and no more than a bite or two of the salad.

"Could you call the hospital and check on her?" she asked Erik, when she'd pushed aside her food. "You seem to understand all the medical stuff better than I do. Then you can tell me what's going on in plain English."

"Sure." He placed the call and was able to get Dr. Wilson on the line. "Any news on Caroline Holliday?"

"They went in again and found the bleeder," she told him. "Her blood pressure is almost back to normal, so

I'm guardedly optimistic. She still has a long way to go, though. Her body went through a lot of trauma. Her kids are with her, all but her daughter. Apparently she can't believe her dad would do something like this. She's somehow convinced herself someone else had to be responsible and that her mom's just using this to get even with her dad."

"Deep denial," Erik said. "Not that uncommon. Mind if I check back with you to keep tabs on Mrs. Holliday's condition? Helen's really worried about her."

"Sure," she said. "By the way, Detective Myers told me Ms. Decatur suggested opening a Sullivan's Café here at the hospital. I really hope you think about it. It might make the hours I spend here less exhausting if I could get a decent cup of coffee or a decent meal once in a while."

"I'll talk to my boss about the idea first thing tomorrow," he promised. "She might go for it."

He hung up and found Helen pacing impatiently in the living room.

"It took you long enough," she muttered. "Did you and the doctor have a good time catching up?"

He assumed it was worry, not jealousy that had put that tone in her voice, so he said mildly, "Caroline's improving. They did a second surgery and that seems to have stopped the bleeding. Dr. Wilson is more optimistic."

"It didn't take that long for her to tell you that. What else did you talk about?"

He looked at her in surprise. "I know you can't possibly be jealous since you're the one who wanted me to call her," he said.

She frowned. "Of course, I'm not jealous."

"Good, because that's not the kind of relationship we have, right?"

She sighed. "No, of course not. Sorry."

"You're worried. I get that," he said quietly. "Let's watch that movie I brought home yesterday. It'll take your mind off all this."

She regarded him with obvious ambivalence, but she finally nodded. "Okay."

He grinned. "You always love it when Katharine Hepburn twists Spencer Tracy around her little finger."

Her expression brightened. "Yes, I do," she said more cheerfully.

For just an instant, he wondered if he would ever tire of the amazing twists and turns her mind took. He doubted it. But down that path lay a future he wouldn't allow himself to contemplate.

CHAPTER NINETEEN

———◆◆◆———

Helen was almost out the door the next morning when her cell phone rang.

"I want you to stop by the spa," Maddie ordered. "I want to hear exactly what went on yesterday. Why didn't you call me? I could have driven you to the hospital."

"It made more sense to call Erik," Helen said. "I know you're tough, Maddie, but you have five kids now. I couldn't take a chance on anything happening to you because you were with me."

"I suppose that makes sense," Maddie agreed, though she still sounded miffed at being sidelined in a crisis. The Sweet Magnolias had always stuck together. "But I still want to know what happened. How soon can you get here?"

"Erik's going to drop me at the office," Helen explained. "I really need to catch up."

"That can wait. Have him drop you here instead," Maddie instructed. "Elliott can take you to the office. I think Erik would agree that Elliott's an adequate bodyguard."

"Fine. I'll see you in five minutes," Helen agreed, knowing that Maddie wouldn't be happy until she'd seen for herself that Helen was okay. Though Helen hadn't seen the morning paper, she imagined that between the news reports and the Serenity grapevine, Brad's attack on Caroline—bad enough in reality—had been exaggerated a thousandfold.

In the car, she explained the change of plans to Erik. "You won't have to wait around. I know you need to get to Sullivan's. Maddie promised that Elliott would give me a lift to the office."

Erik frowned. "You won't suddenly decide that it's too much trouble and take off on your own, will you?"

"No," she promised. "Believe me, hearing the details about what Brad did to Caroline, I'm no more anxious to take chances than you are to have me take them."

"Okay, then," he said, pulling to the curb in front of The Corner Spa. "Call me when you get to your office. I want to know if there's any sign of a sheriff's deputy outside, okay? If adequate protection's not being provided as promised, then we're going straight to the judge. No arguments, okay?"

"Yes, worrywort," she said lightly and kissed his cheek. "I'll call."

Inside, she found Maddie in her office with a dozen towels spread out on her desk.

"Feel these," she commanded. "Tell me what you think."

Helen shrugged and picked each one up. Some were rough, some too thin. Two were thick and luxurious, but probably outrageously expensive. "I assume we're changing towels," she said.

"We compromised quality for cost in the initial buy," Maddie said. "Those are wearing out." She pointed to the thin ones. "Jeanette thinks we should spend a little extra and get something that'll last longer. Besides, we want our clients to feel truly pampered when they come here. I'm constantly surprised by how many women in this region are willing to pay big bucks for a day of luxurious indulgence. Workouts are just that—work. But the spa treatments are a pleasure, something they think they deserve or something they want to give their friends. Did you see how far ahead of projections the sales of the gift certificates were? And just imagine what'll happen when the holidays roll around. We need to do our part to make the whole thing a fantasy come true."

"I trust you and Jeanette on all that," Helen assured her. "Do you have a price comparison on these two?" She fingered the more luxurious ones, relieved to be chatting about something so mundane, rather than Brad Holliday.

Maddie shoved a piece of paper across the table. "You're holding the two Jeanette preferred, but that cost makes me cringe."

"You need to weigh how much would be saved by not having to replace them as soon. She was right about the robes, wasn't she? Those have held up, while the lower-cost towels haven't."

"True," Maddie admitted. "Okay, which of those two?"

Helen shrugged. "I can't tell that much difference and the price is comparable. Is one vendor more reliable than the other?"

"We used one for the robes and he's been excellent to work with."

"Then go with him. He might even give you a price break since you'll be dealing with him exclusively on more items," Helen said, placing the towels back on the desk. "You didn't drag me over here to involve me in the day-to-day decisions around here, though. That's your territory. Are you just trying to lull me into a false sense of complacency before you start asking the tough questions?"

Maddie grinned. "You know me too well."

"Okay, shoot. Let's get this over with."

"Are you pregnant with Erik's baby?" Maddie asked, stunning Helen.

"Where did that come from? I thought you wanted to talk about Brad and what he did to Caroline Holliday," she said irritably.

"I know that's what I told you on the phone, but I thought I might get an honest answer out of you about Erik if I took you by surprise."

"Why would you think I'm pregnant?"

"As you pointed out on the phone, I have five kids. I know the signs. You've turned green a couple of mornings in here and you're more irritable than usual. Are you saying I'm right?"

"I haven't said anything," Helen muttered. "And I'm not going to."

"Why not? Because you know this is all going to blow sky-high the second you do own up to what you've done, don't you?"

"Maddie, stay out of it," Helen pleaded. "Let me handle it."

Maddie held up her hands. "Believe me, I would be more than happy to let you handle this if I thought you had the slightest clue how to go about it."

"I have a plan," Helen told her.

"And that's been the problem all along," Maddie accused. "You had a plan that didn't take into account how anyone else might feel, especially Erik. Dana Sue, too."

"I *did* take Erik's feelings into account," she said defensively. "He and I have a clear understanding about the limits of our relationship."

Maddie regarded her with blatant skepticism. "Somehow I doubt that conversation included a discussion about you getting pregnant with his child. Am I wrong about that?"

Helen sighed. "No, you're not wrong."

Maddie's gaze turned worried. "Oh, sweetie, what on earth are you going to do now?"

"It'll work out," Helen said confidently.

"Will it really? Do you think Dana Sue is going to be overjoyed about it?"

"It's not her business. It's between Erik and me."

"Right now, it's all about you and what *you* want," Maddie contradicted. "Erik's had no say in any of this. When do you plan to tell him?"

"I'm not even a hundred percent certain there's anything to tell yet," Helen said. "I'm seeing the doctor on Monday. Then I'll decide what to do. It's gotten a little complicated because of the whole thing with Brad Holliday. Erik will have a conniption if I try to move out of his place and distance myself from him while Brad might still be a threat."

Maddie stared at her in shock. "*That's* your plan? You're just going to move out and say nothing about being pregnant?"

"Erik doesn't want a wife. He doesn't want kids, so yes, that is the plan. He doesn't need to know about any of this. I can handle the pregnancy, the baby, all of it on my own."

"You're delusional," Maddie snapped. "The man can count, for heaven's sake. Don't you think he might take one look at you in, say, five months' time and conclude that the child you're carrying could be his? What a terrific thing to do to a man you claim is a friend, if nothing else. And from what I've seen, Erik cares about you. Really cares about you. Did you consider the possibility that he might be happy about this news?"

"He won't be," Helen said, though her confidence was shaken by Maddie's words.

Maddie looked worried. "Oh, Helen, what were you thinking?" She waved off the question. "Never mind. It's plain you weren't thinking, at least not very clearly."

"Thanks for being so supportive," Helen said coldly.

"I will always be supportive of you," Maddie answered. "But I won't stand by and watch you make an idiotic mistake. Tell Erik and then tell Dana Sue, before you lose two of the best friends you've ever had. You owe them the truth, Helen. And they need to hear it from you before someone else figures out what I have and spills the beans."

Maddie's harsh words shook her in a way that even Brad's threats had not. "I can't lose them," she whispered. "They mean the world to me."

"Just not enough for you to be honest with them," Maddie chided. "I mean it, Helen. Talk to them or *I* will."

She stared at Maddie with shock. "You wouldn't."

"I would," Maddie said, her tone unyielding. "I know it's not my place, but I can't sit by and watch you ruin your life without doing everything in my power to stop it. Give Erik a chance to step up and do the right thing.

He might surprise you." She leveled a look at Helen. "You have until Tuesday."

"Tuesday?" Helen echoed.

"You'll know for sure by then. Don't waste a second sharing the news, okay? I mean it."

Helen read the determination in Maddie's gaze and knew she meant every word. Maddie wouldn't care how much she infuriated her if she thought she was doing the right thing in the long run.

"It's too soon to tell anyone," Helen said, grasping at any straw to try to get Maddie to back down. "You know there's a high risk of miscarriage at my age. You didn't even tell any of us about your last pregnancy until you were well past the first trimester."

"Don't try that excuse on me," Maddie said. "I told Cal because the father has a right to know from the very beginning. You need to tell Erik for the same reason."

"But if I do lose this baby, then I'd never get another chance, not with Erik anyway."

"That's a risk you'll have to take," Maddie said, her gaze unflinching.

Helen sighed. "Come on, Maddie, this needs to be handled on my timetable, not yours."

"Tuesday," Maddie repeated firmly. "I'll get Elliott now. He can take you to your office."

"When did you learn to play hardball?" Helen asked with grudging admiration.

"I've spent most of my life around you," Maddie retorted. "It was bound to rub off."

"I should have known I'd live to regret my influence over you," Helen said. "I'll be in touch."

Maddie nodded. "See that you are."

Helen couldn't seem to stop the smile that tugged

at her lips. "You can stop the tough-guy routine now. You've made your point."

In fact, she'd made it so effectively that Helen wondered if she'd be able to salvage anything out of this mess she'd created. The only thing keeping her from sinking into despair was the thought that in just a few months, she'd be holding her own child in her arms. That would make any of the consequences she suffered worth it.

Karen was walking into The Corner Spa for her morning workout when she spotted Elliott leaving with Helen. A streak of pure jealousy shot through her. She was so absorbed in watching the two of them, in noting the way Elliott bent down to listen more intently to whatever Helen was saying, that she bumped straight into Maddie, who was coming out of her office.

"I'm so sorry," Karen murmured.

Maddie followed the direction of her gaze. "I thought you'd broken things off with Elliott."

"I did," Karen admitted.

Maddie regarded her with sympathy. "But now you're regretting it?"

"I might have been a little hasty," Karen said. "But it looks as if he's moved on."

Maddie shook her head. "I don't know what's wrong with all the women I know," she lamented. "Not one of you has a grain of sense."

Karen stared at her. "Excuse me?"

"Never mind," Maddie said with a dismissive wave of her hand. "Elliott's not interested in Helen and, believe me, she is definitely not interested in him. He's giving her a ride to her office because some guy has threatened her and she's not supposed to go anyplace alone right now."

The relief that washed over Karen was telling. "I see," she said softly.

"If you want him, do something about it," Maddie advised. "Helen's the least of your worries. Elliott is surrounded by temptation all day long. As far as I can tell, he's shown no interest in any of the women around here who throw themselves at him, but that could change in a heartbeat."

"What should I do?"

"Tell him how you feel. Be honest. People don't seem to be using that strategy nearly enough these days," Maddie said heatedly.

Karen looked taken aback. "Are we still talking about me and Elliott?"

"Not entirely," she admitted. "Just remember what I said. Directness and honesty are traits to be valued in any relationship. The lack of either one can doom you."

Karen nodded. "I'll keep that in mind."

Maddie gave her shoulder a squeeze and headed for the treatment area.

Fifteen minutes later when Elliott walked back in the front door, Karen spotted him at once. She shut off the treadmill on which she'd been doing a halfhearted workout and stepped down, then marched across the room until she was almost toe-to-toe with him. It was the first time she'd forced a confrontation since they'd broken up.

She put her hands on his shoulders, stood on tiptoe and planted a kiss on his mouth that would have shot the temperature in the steam room up another fifty degrees. When she stepped back, he looked dazed.

"I thought we'd broken up," he said eventually.

She shrugged. "I changed my mind. I think that was a bad idea. How about you?"

His lips twitched. "I always thought it was a bad idea."

"Then can we go out on Sunday? Just the two of us?"

He shook his head and her heart plummeted.

"We can go out on Sunday only if you bring the kids along. It's my niece Angela's first birthday. There's a family celebration."

Karen stared at him. "And you want us to go with you?"

"I do," he said solemnly.

"Your family will have questions," she warned him.

"Believe me, I know that even better than you do. Are you prepared for that?"

She thought about it, thought about Frances's insistence that Elliott was a family man who'd stick by her side through thick and thin. Maybe this was her chance to see that firsthand. Hopefully it would tell her everything she needed to know before she opened her heart all the way.

She lifted her gaze to his and nodded. "I think I am."

"Then I'll pick you up at noon. No need to bring a present. I'll get something from all of us."

"From all of us?" she echoed. That would be a declaration of sorts.

He nodded. "Is that a problem?"

"No," she said slowly. "No, it's not a problem at all."

For the first time, he gave her a full-fledged smile, then touched her cheek. "I'm glad you changed your mind, *querida*."

It was the first time he'd used the endearment. It

touched a place inside her that had been cold and lonely for way too long. "Me, too," she said. "But let's not get too far ahead of ourselves, okay?"

"How far is too far?" he asked. "Just so I understand the rules."

Suddenly feeling more daring than she had in years, she told him, "No rules. Let's just improvise."

"Slow-track improv," Elliott concluded. "I can do that. In fact, I'm looking forward to it."

So was Karen. It didn't mean she wasn't scared. Nor did it mean the future was certain. But she was looking forward with anticipation, rather than panic and dread. It was a darn good feeling.

Helen got dressed after her examination, then went into the obstetrician's office. She hadn't been able to read anything from Dr. Matthew Dawson's expression while he'd been poking and prodding her.

In his office, she sat across from him while he made notes in her chart. Her pulse scrambled wildly as she waited for the words that would confirm whether or not she was finally going to have the baby she wanted so badly.

Eventually he looked up, his expression grave. Once again, her pulse went crazy. Wouldn't he look happy if she were pregnant? Or at least neutral?

"You've been really anxious to get pregnant, haven't you?" he said at last. "We talked about it the last time you were here."

Unable to speak, she nodded.

"Well, the good news is, you've gotten your wish. You're definitely pregnant."

Helen heard a *but* in there, a very worrisome *but*.

"Why do I get the feeling you're not as happy about that as I am?"

"I'm not unhappy," he told her. "I'm just concerned. Your blood pressure's not as low as I'd like to see it at this stage. With your history, it's going to be very tricky for you to safely carry this baby to term."

"I've been under some unexpected stress the past few days, but I'll work harder to get it back down," she promised eagerly. "I'll do whatever you tell me. I want this baby more than anything."

"Enough to agree to complete bed rest if I decide it's necessary?" he inquired skeptically.

"Absolutely," she said at once. She would find some way to work it out. She'd divert her clients to other attorneys. She'd hire a housekeeper. Whatever it took. Nothing was going to endanger this chance to become a mother.

"You say that now," he said, "but you're a very driven woman, Helen. That's how you got yourself to this point. Stress is part of your daily life. How are you going to eliminate that?"

Seeing Brad Holliday arrested would certainly help, but she didn't want to get into that. The doctor would probably recommend she spend her entire pregnancy on some nice, quiet island.

"I'll take yoga classes. I'll meditate. I'll exercise."

"All things you've been promising me for months that you'd do," he reminded her.

"And I have," she said. "At least most of the time."

"Your blood pressure says otherwise."

"I'll do better," she promised. "Really. I'll be a model patient. Nothing means more to me than having a healthy baby."

To her relief, he seemed to believe her as he wrote out prescriptions. "One's for a prenatal vitamin. The other's for a stronger diuretic than the one you've been on. We need to avoid water retention. Take them. And do all of those other things you promised. I want to see you again in two weeks, rather than a month. We're going to need to monitor you closely if you're to carry to term."

"Can you tell how far along I am?"

"I'd say a month, maybe six weeks at the most. We'll do an ultrasound next time and we'll know more." For the first time, he smiled. "Congratulations, Helen. I'll do everything I can to see that you have the healthy baby you want. You just need to do your part. Avoid stress above all else. Understood?"

"Yes," she assured him.

She just had two stressful conversations to get through and hopefully by then Brad would be in jail. From then on, she intended to eliminate anything even faintly stressful from her life.

She decided she'd start by talking to Dana Sue. Once Dana Sue had calmed down, she might have some ideas about how she should tell Erik. And no matter how badly either of them reacted, Helen had to put it behind her. From now on this baby was her number-one priority. Period.

For three months Erik had been caught up in a situation he couldn't explain, all but living with a woman who didn't seem to have any expectations outside the bedroom. Helen wasn't demanding. She didn't seem to be interested in staking some sort of claim. All she cared about was the kind of hot, steamy sex men dreamed about. In fact, he was just about worn-out from all the late nights. As incredible as it had been, he couldn't help thinking that there was something going on he didn't totally understand, especially over the past week.

He knew Helen had been annoyed with his protectiveness despite her own concern that Brad Holliday might come after her, but it was more than that. She'd been quieter than usual, more withdrawn, especially since Caroline Holliday had wound up in the hospital. He would have chalked it all up to fear, but Helen was the kind of woman who faced fear head-on. He was beginning to get a sinking feeling that this had more to do with him.

He was on his way into the kitchen at Sullivan's when he heard raised voices coming from Dana Sue's office. He recognized his boss's and then Helen's. Unable to stop himself, he walked closer to the door.

"Dammit, Helen, what were you thinking?" Dana Sue shouted. "How could you do something like this? Maddie knows, doesn't she? That's what she's been so annoyed about lately."

"Maddie guessed, but I don't see what you're getting so worked up about," Helen replied stiffly. "You knew all along that Erik and I were spending time together. Heck, we've been living together ever since Brad Holliday became a threat."

"Of course, and I couldn't have been happier," Dana Sue said. "You two are great for each other. I've been waiting for weeks now to have one of you admit you were falling in love. Instead, you come in here, tell me you're pregnant and that you're dumping him. You've used him, accomplished your goal, and that's it? How could you, Helen?"

Erik stood rooted in place as Dana Sue's words sank

in. Helen was pregnant? How the hell had that happened? She'd told him... What *had* she told him? He searched his mind, trying to remember a single conversation they'd had about birth control. Surely way back at the beginning they'd talked about it, he thought. Then he recalled one hastily uttered claim from her that everything was okay, that he didn't need to worry. He'd taken her at her word. Why wouldn't he? Helen was supposedly one of the most trustworthy people in town.

And now she was pregnant? And if he was correctly interpreting the gist of her conversation with Dana Sue, that had been her plan all along? She'd apparently wanted a baby and chosen him to help her make one, despite his oft-repeated statements that kids were not in the cards for him.

A blind rage swept through him. Before he could think about it or reconsider, he pushed open the door and stalked into Dana Sue's cramped office. Both women regarded him with dismay. He faced Dana Sue first.

"Out," he said tersely.

She scrambled from behind her desk, gave him one last sympathetic look and left.

After her initial shock, Helen faced him with a surprisingly calm expression. "I gather you heard."

"Enough," he said. "Maybe you ought to start from the beginning, though, and spell it out for me. I want to be sure I have all the facts straight."

"It's nothing for you to be upset about," she began in a reasonable tone that made him want to start breaking things.

"Maybe you should let me decide just how upset

I want to get," he retorted. "You're pregnant, is that right?"

She nodded. "But I don't expect anything from you. I'm happy about this, Erik. Really happy. I've wanted a baby more than anything for a long time now."

"More than anything," he echoed, ice in his voice and in his veins. "But you saw no need to mention that to me?"

"Actually we have talked about it, at least in a general way," she reminded him.

"A general way?" he echoed. "Oh, yes, I do remember that. But I don't recall a single mention of the role you intended for *me* to play. Didn't you consider that perhaps I ought to have at least *some* say?"

She swallowed hard. "I see your point. I probably should have discussed it with you."

Erik saw red. "Probably?" he all but shouted, then fought to bring his temper under control.

She regarded him earnestly. "Erik, I swear to you that I can give this baby everything it needs. You're under no obligation to be part of his or her life at all. It's not as if I did this to trap you or something."

"Which doesn't exactly deal with the real issue, does it?" he said. Clenching his fists to keep from grabbing her and shaking her, he said, "And if I *want* to be a part of the baby's life?"

That seemed to rock her back on her heels. "What?"

"I asked you how you feel about me being involved in the baby's life."

"I told you it's not necessary," she said. "I know you don't want children."

"And yet here we are," he said sarcastically, "with you pregnant with my baby."

"But there's no reason for you to feel obligated," she insisted again. "This is my baby. I take full responsibility for what happened."

"It happened because you made it happen," he said. "Isn't that right?"

She winced. "I suppose you could say that. I knew it was a possibility." At his scowl, she said, "Okay, I did everything possible to make it happen, which is why I'm taking responsibility and expecting nothing from you."

"It doesn't work like that, sugar," he said grimly, not sure if he was more furious about her decision to have this baby without consulting him, or about her willingness to shut him out of their lives as if he'd been nothing more than some anonymous sperm donor.

Granted he hadn't ever planned on becoming a father, not after losing his baby when his wife died. The pain of that loss had stuck with him and was something he couldn't bear to risk repeating.

Nor had he thought about marrying again, especially not to Helen. Their casual relationship with no demands, mind-blowing sex and mind-challenging conversation had suited him just fine. Now, suddenly, all of that had changed and he didn't intend to be shut out of her life or their child's.

He grabbed the chair from behind Dana Sue's desk and set it down right in front of Helen, then straddled it. Given the room's lack of space, she had no wiggle room at all. She had no choice but to stay where she was and listen.

"Here's the way it's going to be," he said, looking at her intently. Despite the shock he'd felt when he'd heard the news, he was as certain of what needed to happen next as he'd ever been of anything. "You've gotten your way apparently. You're pregnant. Now I'm going to do what *I* want. Are you listening, Helen? I really need you to hear every word of this."

She nodded, her eyes wide, her expression shaken.

"You and I will get married," he said flatly. "We will go through this pregnancy together. After the baby's born, if you still want to be some kind of supermom on your own, we'll talk about a divorce, but I will have shared custody of our child. That's it."

She regarded him with an unmistakably panicked expression. "You can't be serious."

"I'm as serious as a heart attack."

"But why?"

"Because I lost one baby and there wasn't a damn thing I could do about it. I won't lose another. And if you think I'll change my mind once I've had time to think things through or that you'll just postpone and delay your way out of making a commitment, think again."

"You can't *make* me marry you," she protested. "We're not in love."

"You should have thought of that before you hatched this cockamamie scheme of yours," he said mildly. "Console yourself with this. At least you know the sex will be great."

He got up and left the room.

It was only after he was in the kitchen—and Dana Sue had bolted in the direction of her office—that he realized he wasn't nearly as upset about the idea of marriage as he'd thought he'd be. He might be shaking with rage over being duped. He might be panicky at the thought of losing yet another child. Helen was, after all, forty-three and at a high risk for carrying a baby all the way to term.

But as his temper cooled, he knew that being with Helen for the rest of his life was something he'd wanted for a long time now and been too scared to go after. It seemed fate—with a very deliberate and calculating assist from Helen—had stepped in and forced his hand.

CHAPTER TWENTY

"Oh, my God, what have I done?" Helen said when Dana Sue came back to check on her.

"Offhand, I'd say you've stirred up a hornet's nest," her friend said without much sympathy. "I'm a little surprised to find you in one piece. I thought I saw steam rising from Erik when he came back to the kitchen. I've never seen him like that before. Just how mad was he?"

"He says he's going to marry me," Helen said, regarding Dana Sue with bewilderment. "I don't think he's going to take no for an answer."

For the first time since Helen had broken the news of her pregnancy, Dana Sue's dire expression softened. "Well, now, that's an interesting turn of events, though not entirely unexpected."

"It's not funny and it is totally unexpected," Helen grumbled. "I didn't want to trap him into marrying me. That was the last thing on my mind."

"Maybe it shouldn't have been," Dana Sue told her. "Surely you know the kind of guy Erik is. He's solid and dependable and protective. You've seen that firsthand in the way he looks out for me and Annie. Didn't you stop for one second to think about how he'd be with a baby involved, especially *his* baby?"

"Okay, I get that he feels a little protective about the baby, especially with what's happened to Caroline Holliday, but marriage? Isn't that going too far?"

"Obviously he doesn't think so," Dana Sue replied.

"But what about love?" Helen asked wistfully.

Once more Dana Sue regarded her with a complete lack of sympathy. "Another of those things you should have thought about before you decided to take matters into your own hands. Besides, you two have strong feelings for each other, anyone can see that. Call it whatever you want, but it seems close enough to love to me. Even though I'm not one bit happy about the underhanded way you went about this, I still think this is the best thing that could have happened to you. Otherwise, you two might've danced around your feelings for years. You're both too stubborn for your own good. Seems to me this is exactly the push you both needed to get you where you should be."

"But none of this was about getting married," Helen protested.

Dana Sue grinned. "Well, it is now." She reached for the calendar on her desk. "So, let's pick a date. If there's going to be a wedding, I need time to plan. And I assume, given your pride in your appearance and your preference for designer clothes and fancy footwear, you won't want to be the size of a whale when you walk down the aisle. In that case it had better be soon."

Helen scowled at her. "There's not going to be a wedding," she said grimly.

Dana Sue merely smiled. "Wanna bet? I'd suggest you get with the program, or the most important day of your life will happen and you won't have control over one single detail."

"No wedding," Helen repeated.

Dana Sue went on as if she hadn't spoken. "Tell you what, we can meet Maddie at the spa tomorrow morning and start making lists. You'll love that. We can go over all this with her at eight. I can't wait to see her face when you tell her the news."

"She won't be as shocked as you might think," Helen muttered. "She tried to warn me I was going about this all wrong, even though she couldn't get me to acknowledge what I was doing."

"I still hate it that she figured this out and I didn't have a clue," Dana Sue groused. "I must have been so wrapped up in what was going on in my own life with Ronnie that I never saw this coming. I'm going to have to watch that, especially if you're going to get into the habit of trying to keep things from me."

"It wasn't like that," Helen argued. At Dana Sue's arched brow, she amended, "Not exactly anyway. I just knew you'd try to talk me out of it or warn Erik and ruin everything."

"Maybe if I had found out, you wouldn't be about to marry a man who's furious with you," Dana Sue suggested.

"I keep telling you that we are *not* getting married," Helen countered.

"I think you need to get over that refrain," Dana Sue said. "Nobody's going to buy it, not once they've crossed paths with Erik and seen the determination in his eyes, anyway. Let's just get together with Maddie tomorrow and put this wedding together the way you want it." Her mood visibly improved. "This is going to be so much fun."

"Forget the wedding," Helen said again. "Ganging up on me is not going to work. And since when do you and Maddie side with an outsider against one of your own?"

"When it's the right thing to do," Dana Sue said without hesitation. "You and Erik are good for each other. You'll be terrific parents, too."

"You make it sound like we'll be some happy little family holding barbecues in the backyard," Helen grumbled. "You said it yourself, Dana Sue. He's furious with me. That's what this is about. Nothing good can come from a marriage that starts like that. I won't do it. None of you can bully me into it."

But even as she said the words, she, too, recalled the determination in Erik's eyes—the same determination Dana Sue had obviously seen—and shuddered. Maybe she should look up the law on whether a woman could be forced to marry against her will. She was pretty sure it was on her side, but if there was some loophole she didn't know about, there wasn't a doubt in her mind that Erik would find it.

Barb had a stack of messages waiting for Helen when she got to her office the next morning, after skipping the little tête-à-tête that Dana Sue had planned for eight o'clock. She had a hunch she was going to pay for that act of rebellion, but she hadn't been up to facing her two best friends and their current mission to see that she got properly married to a man who was forcing a wedding only because he was angry.

"Ten of those messages are from Erik," Barb said,

her expression filled with curiosity. "He seemed edgy. Is something going on?"

"I moved out of his place yesterday," Helen said. "And I didn't take any of his calls last night."

Barb stared at her in shock. "Why on earth would you do that, especially now with Brad Holliday on some sort of rampage?"

"It was the right thing to do," Helen said. She'd had her things out of his place by seven o'clock, long before he was likely to be home from Sullivan's. If she hadn't had a such a busy schedule for the next couple of weeks, she would have packed and headed for some tropical island to relax until Erik's temper cooled down and he dropped this whole marriage insanity.

Helen had been a little surprised that Erik had gotten so upset over her departure. Surely he'd known they couldn't go on living under the same roof. She'd said as much in the note she'd left so he wouldn't worry that Brad had kidnapped her or something. Apparently that had only given him another reason to be angry with her, as the tenor of his messages revealed. Barb had clearly picked up on that, as well, because she was scowling at Helen.

"That man is the best thing that ever happened to you," Barb scolded her. "Why would you want to sabotage that?"

"Look, things happen. People change. Emotions can't be trusted. It was time to move on."

Barb's eyes suddenly filled with understanding. "In other words, you got scared. He wanted more than you were prepared to offer and you panicked."

Helen didn't see any reason to share the whole truth with Barb, even though her secretary was more friend than employee. Right now, the fewer people who were in on the mess she'd made of things, the better.

"Something like that," she agreed. "Now, if you're all through digging around in my personal life, I think I'll go in my office and get some work done."

Barbara regarded her with a disappointed expression. "Whatever you say," she said stiffly. "Just tell me what you want me to do when Erik—"

Helen cut her off. "I'm not taking his calls."

"But—"

"Don't argue with me," she said, noting that Barb simply shrugged and gave in to Helen's command.

Two seconds later she understood why her secretary had capitulated so easily. Erik walked in practically on her heels and slammed the door shut. Obviously Barb had been trying to tell her he was on his way over. Helen concluded she really did need to start listening to people, instead of issuing orders.

"What are you doing here?" she asked, giving him one of her haughtiest glares.

"You never used to ask dumb questions," he said, taking a seat on the sofa and patting the space beside him.

Helen deliberately walked behind her desk and sank wearily into her chair. "Go ahead. Say whatever's on your mind. I know you're mad."

"And worried," he said. "Let's not forget that a crazy man could be stalking you, yet you decided to take off from someplace where you might be safe. Since when did you turn into the kind of woman who would take foolish risks just to avoid a confrontation, especially one you know you can't avoid forever anyway?"

Helen shivered. Somehow, in her haste to get away

from Erik's before things got worse than they already
were, she'd discounted the danger Brad Holliday presented.

"I'm sure the police knew where I was," she replied.
"They're supposed to be keeping an eye on me."

"That makes me feel all warm and fuzzy, sort of the
way I felt when I couldn't reach you for hours on end."

Even under the unmistakable edge of sarcasm, she
could hear real concern in his voice. "I'm sorry you
worried," she said sincerely. "That's why I left you a
note, so you'd know where I was. I just thought it was
for the best that I go home."

"Best for whom?"

"Both of us," she told him.

"And the baby? Is it best for the baby that you could
have been putting your life at risk just so you could get
away from any uncomfortable questions I might ask?"

"It's not your questions I'm worried about," she retorted. "It's your demands."

"Running away won't change that," he said quietly.
"We *will* get married, Helen."

The emphatic note in his voice left her shaken. "But
why?"

"Because my child is going to have my name. It's
going to grow up with a mother and a father, no matter what kind of patchwork, nutty relationship we manage to have."

Helen shook her head and sighed. "Who would have
thought you'd be so traditional? A few days ago, all you
cared about was great sex and some lively conversation
from time to time."

He gave her a wry look at her assessment of their
relationship, then shrugged. "Okay, I'll admit it. It sur-

prises the hell out of me, too. But that's the way it is.
Get used to it. Who knows, you might turn out to be
traditional, too."

A part of Helen yearned for just that, but she didn't
see how it was possible when a marriage started off as
unconventionally as this one would if Erik forced it on
her. And even if it somehow lasted, she would always
wonder if he loved her or if he was just making the best
of a situation he hadn't chosen, a situation she'd thrust
upon him in her blind rush to get something she wanted.

He leaned forward and regarded her intently. "Let's
forget the whole marriage thing for a minute. There's
a safety issue here for you and the baby. You need to
come back to my place, Helen. Now's not the time for
you to be living alone."

"I'll be fine," she insisted.

"You won't even consider it?" he asked in frustration.

"No."

"Then let me move into your place," he suggested.

She gave him an incredulous look. "I think you're
missing the point. I'm trying to pull off a clean break."

He actually smiled at that. "And I've already told you
that's not going to happen. Right now, the only thing
you're going to accomplish is knotting my muscles up
like pretzels."

She frowned. "How am I going to do that?"

"Have you tried spending the night in the front seat
of a car?"

She stared at him incredulously. "What? Are you
crazy? You're actually telling me you're going to sleep
in your car in front of my house?"

"You're not giving me a choice. My back will have
kinks in it for months after being out there last night.

I'd prefer not to repeat the experience, but until Brad's in custody or you and I are married and living together, then I have to keep an eye on you somehow."

"Oh, for heaven's sake," she complained. "You know you're being ridiculous, don't you?" Still, she had to admit that it was rather sweet of him to care that much.

"I don't see it that way," he said. "Nothing is happening to you or the baby on my watch."

Her gaze clashed with his, but he didn't flinch. "You're serious, aren't you?" she said, resigned.

"You bet."

"Fine. I'll come back to your place, but I'm staying in the guest room."

He shrugged. "Up to you."

Apparently satisfied, he stood up and headed to the door, then turned back. "By the way, the wedding's the last Saturday of the month. Dana Sue and I've agreed on that much. We'll hold the ceremony in the park and the reception at Sullivan's. I've made all the arrangements."

He was gone before she could react. She wasn't sure which made her more furious, that he'd had the gall to make plans without her, that he'd involved one of her best friends, or that he didn't seem to care what her reaction was. He just assumed she'd go along with them.

She was still seething with indignation over that when Dana Sue and Maddie breezed in, armed with bridal magazines, color swatches and albums of floral arrangements. Obviously they'd joined forces with Erik.

"Since you didn't show up at the spa, we went ahead and narrowed down the choices," Dana Sue said cheerily. "It'll save time. We only have three weeks to pull this off if you're going to be your fashionable, svelte self. After that, your body will start to change and your dress might require too many last-second alterations."

"So, you chose the date based on my dress size?" she asked incredulously. "That may be even more absurd than the idea of us getting married at all."

"Sweetie, I think that ship has sailed," Dana Sue said. "Erik's pretty determined."

"Since when is this wedding all about what Erik wants?" Helen asked petulantly.

"Having a baby was all about what *you* wanted. Seems fair he gets a turn," Dana Sue replied. "Besides, he seems a little more into it than you are. I've said it before, but I'll say it again—maybe you ought to get with the program."

"I'm getting a little sick of all you pushy people telling me what to do!" Helen snapped. "If there's going to be a wedding—and I haven't yet said there will be— then *I* will make the decisions."

She reached for the magazine with the most little yellow Post-its sticking out. "What have you marked in here?"

"Gowns," Maddie said eagerly. "There's a Vera Wang in there that would look fabulous on you." She gave Helen a sly glance. "And the shoes pictured with it are to die for."

"Show me," Helen commanded. They were finally beginning to talk her language. There was nothing like buying an outrageously expensive pair of shoes to improve her mood, though given the week she was having, she might need to buy a few dozen pair.

Tess was hanging over Erik's shoulder as he sketched out the wedding cake he had in mind for his own reception. It had the advantage of being something that could go from three tiers to five or more, depending on just how persuasive Dana Sue and Maddie were with Helen. If she got on board, the guest list could grow. If she didn't, well, three tiers was as small as he intended this cake to be. Anything smaller would look as if they'd picked it up at the grocery store.

"Those will be orchids?" Tess asked of the flowers he'd drawn flowing down one side of the simple cake.

He nodded. "That's what I was thinking. Do you like it?"

"Very elegant," she said. "Like Helen." She gave him a knowing look. "You don't seem very happy for someone who's about to get married."

"It's complicated," he said, which was an understatement if ever he'd uttered one. So far, the bride was still digging in her heels and refusing to marry him at all, though Dana Sue had told him last night that Helen had found some shoes she liked.

"The wedding dress came in a close second," she'd said. "I think with a little more coaxing we can get her over to Charleston to try it on. They're holding it for her. Thank goodness, she's the size of the sample, so we won't have to wait for it to be custom-tailored."

"Maybe we should forget about a formal wedding," Erik had suggested. "Just do a civil ceremony."

"Absolutely not!" Dana Sue had declared. "Helen might balk and complain about all this, but she'll never forgive us, herself or you if she doesn't have the wedding of her dreams, even if it is on short notice and under duress."

"It will hardly be the wedding of her dreams if she's fighting us every step of the way," Erik said.

"Which is why you need to get busy and work your magic on her," Dana Sue told him. "Underneath all this belligerence and rebellion, she loves you, Erik. She's just scared to admit it, because she's afraid she's trapped you into marrying her. It's time for you to correct that impression."

"I'm not sure I can," he'd said, but the truth was, he wasn't any more ready than Helen to put his heart on the line. The two of them were one hell of a pair, both filled with enough doubts, insecurities and bullhead-edness to take up a week's worth of Dr. Phil episodes.

When he snapped back to the present, Tess was looking at him with concern. "You should tell her how you really feel," she advised him, almost as if she'd been reading his thoughts. "Deep in your heart, you love Helen. Anyone can see that."

"But despite what Dana Sue thinks, Helen's not in love with me," he said, not denying Tess's claim about his own feelings. "She's made that clear."

Tess rolled her eyes. "Are all men such idiots, I wonder."

Erik frowned at her. "Meaning?"

"The woman is so crazy about you she glows when you're in the same room."

"I think she's glowing because she's pregnant," he said before he remembered that Tess hadn't been told that part of the story.

Now her eyes lit up. "A baby," she repeated with wonder. "But that is perfect. It will all work out, Erik. If she's denying her love for you, it's only because her hormones are all over the place. I was the same way with both my pregnancies. I loved Diego one minute and hated him the next. It's a miracle he put up with me, much less stuck around to go through it a second time."

Erik didn't think Helen's hormones had anything to do with her determination not to marry him. He was pretty sure she'd made that decision way back when her head had been clear and her hormones were behaving normally.

Unfortunately, Helen was stubborn. Once she made a decision, any decision at all, she clung to it, no matter how wrongheaded it might be.

Fortunately, she'd met her match in him.

"You're stressing me out," Helen declared as Dana Sue and Maddie dragged her into a Charleston boutique that overflowed with designer wedding gowns. "I'm not supposed to be under any stress at all. You know that. My doctor is going to be furious with you."

Maddie gave her a chiding look. "We're here now. Just relax and enjoy yourself. You love to try on clothes."

"I love to try on clothes I'm going to wear," Helen corrected. "I am not going to wear a wedding dress, because there is not going to be a wedding."

"Oh, give it up," Dana Sue said impatiently. "That line is getting old. You're getting married in less than three weeks. You may as well look beautiful even if there are only fourteen wedding guests there to see you walk down the aisle."

Helen frowned. "You've invited fourteen people to this wedding without even consulting me?"

Maddie and Dana Sue exchanged a look that Helen couldn't quite interpret.

"We assumed you'd want me, Cal and the kids there," Maddie said. "Well, maybe not the baby, since he's fussy. I think Jessica Lynn could be a flower girl if she doesn't have to walk too far. She's still a little unsteady."

"And Ronnie, Annie and I will be there," Dana Sue added. "Plus Tess and Diego, Karen and Elliott and Barb. That should do it." She gave Helen a knowing look. "Unless you'd like something more elaborate. We could arrange for your mother to fly up from Florida, no problem. And of course, you know just about everyone in town, plus all the lawyers, judges and clients you've worked with. Say the word and we'll turn this into a full-blown event."

Helen was about to tell them what they could do with their guest list when a tall, elegant woman in a simple designer suit and Manolo Blahnik shoes came out of the back to greet them. She beamed at Helen.

"You must be the bride," she said at once. "Your friends described you perfectly. I have several dresses that will look amazing with your figure. Shall we get started?"

Helen wanted desperately to balk, but there was something about being in this tastefully decorated salon with its silk-upholstered antique chairs, soft lighting and bouquets of fresh flowers that awakened a long-buried dream. Like a lot of little girls, she'd imagined her wedding down to the last detail, from the flowers and candles on the end of each pew in the church to the swell of organ music as she made her entrance. Up 'til now the only trips she'd made to a bridal salon had been for Maddie and Dana Sue's first weddings. It hadn't been the same. A tiny part of her had yearned for a day like today when it was *her* turn.

Over the years the dream had been refined and simplified. The pearl-encrusted dress she'd once imagined had evolved into a sheath of shimmering satin. The elaborate flower arrangements had given way to single sprays of delicate white orchids. The setting had moved from the church she rarely attended to the gazebo in the town park with the azaleas in full bloom, the lake sparkling with sunshine and swans gliding across the water.

Eventually, though, the dream had faded altogether. She'd convinced herself there would never be a wedding, just as she'd resigned herself to not having children. Now, it seemed, all of that would change—if only she gave in to Erik's insistence on moving forward with this ceremony.

But how could she do that? How could she agree to marry a man who'd never professed to love her, whose only goal was staking his claim on the child she carried? How could she marry knowing that divorce was almost inevitable?

When the clerk returned with the first gown, it was exactly what she'd imagined herself wearing down the aisle, the shimmering fabric draping low across her breasts and clinging to her hips. Helen lost focus for a minute and a powerful longing swept through her as she skimmed her fingers over the fabric.

"Where can I try it on?" she asked, aware of the conspiratorial smiles Maddie and Dana Sue exchanged. She glared at them. "Don't get any ideas. It doesn't mean anything."

"Of course not," Maddie murmured, but her eyes were filled with triumph.

A few minutes later Helen walked out of the tiny dressing room to stand in front of the triple mirror. The dress's hemline in front came just barely to her ankles, showing off the shoes the clerk had persuaded her to try. In back, there was a short, flowing train. In it she looked as slender and delicate as a calla lily.

The clerk approached and added a simple, twisted band of matching silk that secured a veil to her hair and suddenly she was the bride of her dreams. Staring at her reflection in the mirror, she was enchanted. She swallowed hard, fighting the allure of it, as tears stung her eyes.

"You want to do this," Maddie whispered, coming to her side. "You know you do. The whole thing, with lots of guests and your mom here."

Helen tore her gaze from the mirror to meet Maddie's eyes. "But I want it to be *real*," she said, a catch in her voice.

"It *is* real," Dana Sue said, joining them. She gave Helen a wry look. "Maybe the proposal left a little to be desired—"

"It left a *lot* to be desired," Helen interrupted. "It was a command, not a proposal at all."

"My point is," Dana Sue said impatiently, "that doesn't mean the wedding and the marriage can't be everything you want them to be. You can make this work, sweetie. I know you can."

Maddie nodded. "Have you ever known a Sweet Magnolia not to do whatever it takes to get exactly what she wants? I know you want Erik. Despite how this started, you love him. Take a risk and admit it."

Helen shook her head. "I don't think I can. I've messed up too badly. How will he ever be able to trust me again? Without trust, what kind of relationship can we possibly have?"

"You'll do what you and Maddie told Ronnie and me to do when we got back together after he betrayed me,"

Dana Sue said. "You'll earn back his trust one day at a time. Erik is offering you a lifetime to do that. That's a pretty good deal when you think about it."

Helen considered Dana Sue's words as she once again studied her reflection in the mirror. If she said yes, she could be the bride she'd always wanted to be. If she said yes, she had a chance at least to have the family she'd wanted, as well. She'd already risked a lot to get to this point. Surely she could take one more risk to have it all.

Drawing in a deep breath, she turned to the clerk. "I'll take the dress," she said in a steady voice.

"You don't want to see the others?" the clerk asked, clearly stunned that any woman would seize the first wedding gown she'd tried on.

"I want this one," Helen confirmed. It seemed there were a few decisions she could still make impulsively, after all. Now she just had to pray she wouldn't live to regret it.

CHAPTER TWENTY-ONE

After dropping off the packages from her shopping trip, Helen decided it was time to visit with Caroline Holliday. She'd been calling the hospital daily to check on her and had even spoken to her once on the phone, but she'd been putting off seeing her in person. She wanted to blame the omission on the chaos of her life ever since Erik had found out about the baby, but that was too easy. The truth was she hadn't wanted to see firsthand the violence that Brad was capable of. It would make his threats against her too real.

To everyone's frustration he still wasn't in custody. She wanted to believe he'd taken off for good, left the country, perhaps, but she couldn't count on that.

Maddie, who'd insisted on coming home with her so she wouldn't be in the house alone, eyed her warily. "You look like a kid who's just had a treat and knows it's now time for some yucky medicine. What's going on?"

"I need to drive to Regional Hospital to see Caroline," she said. "I'm not looking forward to it."

"I'll ride with you," Maddie said.

"There's no need," Helen said, then noticed the stubborn set of Maddie's jaw.

"Did I imply you had a choice?" Maddie inquired sweetly. "If we're going, let's go. I'll call Cal and let him know where we're headed."

"This is ridiculous," Helen grumbled. "Brad hasn't come near me since that day he followed me to the office."

Maddie's eyes widened. "Brad followed you? Did you tell anyone? Where was the sheriff's deputy who's supposed to be keeping an eye on you?"

"The sheriff doesn't have enough manpower to watch me twenty-four/seven," Helen said.

"Then you need to hire private security," Maddie told her.

"I'm not getting a bodyguard. Besides, it was only one time. I haven't seen him since. He's probably long gone."

Maddie frowned. "You don't believe that any more than I do."

"Debating this isn't accomplishing anything," Helen said. "Let's just go."

"Fine," Maddie said, but in a way that suggested the subject wasn't finished.

After leaving Maddie in a waiting room at the hospital, Helen was startled to find a deputy stationed outside Caroline's door. She introduced herself, then asked, "Have there been more problems with her ex-husband?"

"No, I'm just here as a precaution. The family hired me. Her son didn't want to take any chances 'til Mr. Holliday's in custody."

Helen nodded. "I can understand their concern."

She tapped on the door, then walked into the room. It was filled with afternoon sunlight and too many flowers. From a chair in the corner, Caroline looked up when

Helen entered and gave her a wobbly smile. Given the yellowing bruises on her face and the cuts on her jaw and cheeks, it was a poignant effort. Helen had to blink back tears.

"How are you?" she asked, crossing the room to drop a light kiss on Caroline's battered cheek.

"Glad to see *you* in one piece," Caroline replied. She shook her head. "I hope you're being careful, Helen. I had no idea Brad was capable of anything like this. He'd never laid a hand on me before. He rarely even yelled when he was angry. When he came to the house the night I got back from my sister's, I let him in. I thought he just wanted to talk or to pick up some of his things. Instead, he hit me before the door was even closed. He didn't stop 'til one of the neighbors heard me scream and ran over."

She swallowed hard and met Helen's gaze. "He had a gun," she whispered. "I have no idea where or when he got it, but I think he was planning on using it to..." She shuddered. "If my neighbor hadn't come when he did..."

"It's okay," Helen said. "It's over and you're okay."

"It won't be over and I won't feel safe until he's locked up," Caroline said. "You shouldn't, either." She clutched Helen's hand. "Please be careful. Promise me."

"I won't take any chances," Helen promised, especially now that she knew about the gun. She'd deluded herself into thinking she'd be a match for Brad in a physical confrontation, but the gun changed everything. Her hand went protectively to her stomach. From now on she would swallow her stupid pride and take all the protection that was offered.

Erik was chopping vegetables for a hearty stew when Dana Sue returned from the shopping trip to Charleston. He'd been on pins and needles since she'd left with Helen and Maddie, wondering if Helen had balked yet again about going forward with this wedding. As determined as he was, he hadn't quite figured out how to get her down the aisle if she really refused to go.

Ever since she'd moved back into his place, she'd been quiet and distant, speaking to him only when he forced the issue and then in a tone icy with disdain. Since he wasn't especially cheerful himself, he'd let it pass, but the tense atmosphere couldn't be good for her or the baby. If it kept up, he might have to back down and let her go, if only for the sake of the pregnancy. He knew from his own background and from Dana Sue's fierce warning that stress was dangerous for Helen, especially at this early stage of the pregnancy. The last thing he wanted was to contribute to anything that could lead to a miscarriage. Not only would it devastate Helen, but him, as well.

For now he studied Dana Sue's expression and tried to gauge how the trip had gone. She was giving away nothing.

"Well?" he finally prodded. "Are you guys still speaking? Did she burn down the bridal salon when she figured out where you were taking her? What?"

Dana Sue's lips twitched, then curved in a full-fledged smile. "She bought a gown."

"A wedding gown?" he asked, stunned. "Really?"

Dana Sue shook her head. "You really don't know anything about women at all, do you?"

"Meaning?"

"Once she put on the perfect dress, the one she'd been dreaming about her whole life—well, her entire adult life, anyway—it was a done deal. She wasn't going to turn her back on that."

"So this is all about giving her a chance to wear a dress she likes?" He wasn't sure how he felt about that. Maybe he should just be grateful that it meant she'd at least walk down the aisle.

Dana Sue patted his cheek. "Don't pout. On the surface this might be all about the dress, but she would never in a million years get married if she didn't want to. She's spent her entire professional career handling nasty divorces. She would not go into a marriage if she didn't think she could find some way to make it last. It wouldn't matter how much any of us pushed her, you included."

A tiny spark of hope flared inside him. Maybe they could get past her antagonism and his anger about her deception, after all.

"Would you mind a word of advice?" Dana Sue asked.

"We both know you're going to give it, so why ask?" he teased.

"Sometime before the day of the wedding, you might consider a real proposal. I don't think you want her to spend the rest of her life remembering you demanded she marry you. It kind of takes the romance out of it."

"This isn't about romance," Erik reminded her.

Dana Sue leveled a look straight into his eyes. "Isn't it?"

"Look, there's a baby involved," he said. "That's all it's about." Maybe he was being stubborn, maybe it was about saving his pride, but he refused to admit to anything more than his determination to be a part of his baby's future.

She shook her head and gave him a pitying look. "You are so dense. You love the woman. Tell her before it's too late. It'll make all the difference, Erik, for both of you."

He frowned. "Too late for what? Do you think she's going to back out at the last minute?"

"No. I think if Helen goes through with this ceremony without hearing those words, she's going to have doubts about your feelings for years to come, no matter how often you say them after the fact. She needs to hear them now, Erik. She needs to know this isn't all about you making sure you have legal rights to your child."

"But—"

"Listen to me," Dana Sue said. "For all of her success and all of the respect she's earned in the courtroom, when it comes to love, Helen's as insecure as anyone else. She's never really opened her heart to anyone except her mom, Maddie and me. Believe me, Maddie and I had to work for her trust, too, even way back in elementary school when we first met. She was already scarred from her dad dying and her mom having to struggle so hard."

"But Helen's the one who forced this to be about custody," he retorted. "She's the one who was going to deny me the chance to be with my own child. I had to do something."

"You're absolutely right," Dana Sue agreed a little too readily. Her gaze clashed with his. "Is being right going to keep you warm at night?"

Erik thought about that over the next few days, but every time he tried to broach the subject of his feelings with Helen, the words lodged in his throat. He simply couldn't get past the depth of her betrayal and his own fear of risking his heart again.

And after each failed attempt to open up and express

his emotions—as tangled and confused as they were—
he noticed that Helen seemed to withdraw a little further. They were like strangers living under the same
roof, not at all like two people who were to be wed only
two weeks from now, or two people who'd been sharing
intimate, spectacular sex only a few weeks ago.

Deep down, Erik knew that someone was going to
have to break this impasse or they were doomed, but
for the life of him, he couldn't summon up the courage to be the one.

On more than one occasion, as he lay alone in his
bed at night with Helen just down the hall, he wondered if they shouldn't call off the ceremony, but then
he thought of his child and his resolve returned. He
would see this through for the baby's sake. And maybe
someday, somehow, he and Helen would find their way
back to each other.

The wedding definitely wasn't a scene out of *Brides*
magazine. Oh, the setting by the lake was spectacular.
Just as Helen had envisioned, there were plenty of flowers in full bloom, even though it was well after azalea
season, the swans were gliding across the water and
the fourteen guests—she hadn't bent and allowed her
friends to make a bigger production of the ceremony—
all seemed to be disgustingly pleased. Cal and Maddie were holding hands. Dana Sue had her arm linked
through Ronnie's. And Annie was stealing besotted
glances at Ty.

In contrast, Helen stood stoically beside Erik, wish-
ing she were in some wedding chapel in Las Vegas with
an Elvis impersonator as the minister. It would have
been more fitting, given what a joke this ceremony was.

More than once she'd thought Erik was about to open up to her and share his real feelings. Even if he'd shouted at her some more, it would have been better than the grim determination and silence that greeted her each morning across the breakfast table. She'd almost forced the issue, but her courage had failed her. She was disgusted with herself about that, too. She'd faced down high-powered opponents in the courtroom. She'd outtalked and outnegotiated most of them. But she couldn't seem to initiate a conversation that mattered with the man she was about to marry, a man she'd cared enough about to choose to be the father of her child.

A thousand times she'd told herself to back out of this farce, but here she was, waiting to say the words that would tie her to Erik forever—or at least until one of them could wriggle out of it.

"Do you promise," the minister began.

It was all so much *blah-blah-blah* as far as Helen could tell. Still, she said, "I do," when it was called for because anything else would cause a scene no one in town would forget for the next century.

His own vows were spoken with only slightly more enthusiasm.

And then it was over and their small group was moving on to the reception at Sullivan's that Dana Sue insisted they have. Erik had even baked one of his spectacular wedding cakes with a vanilla fondant frosting and a profusion of white orchids spilling down the sides. When Helen saw it, she almost burst into tears. Somehow he'd seen into her heart and gotten the cake exactly right.

For the first time since he'd found out about the pregnancy, Erik looked at her with something other than anger or cool indifference.

"What's wrong?" he asked, actually looking worried. "Do you feel okay?"

Swiping at a tear that leaked out, she could only nod.

"Is it the cake?" He followed the direction of her gaze.

She nodded. "It's so beautiful."

His expression softened. "Wedding cakes are my specialty. How could I make ours anything less than perfect?"

Then, to her dismay, she burst into tears, mentally blaming her reaction on hormones and not the sweetness of his gesture. Erik took her hand in his and dragged her into the kitchen, then pulled her into his arms. She felt a sense of relief out of all proportion to the embrace. Maybe he didn't hate her, after all.

"It's okay," he said, awkwardly patting her back. "It's going to be okay, I swear it."

"How can it be? I've made such a mess of things. No marriage is supposed to start like this."

She felt his chest heave with a sigh.

"I've done my share of idiotic things lately, too," he confessed. "I'm sorry."

She looked up at him, seeing the regret on his face even through the blur of tears in her eyes. "I never meant to hurt you or make you angry," she told him.

"Me, neither," he said. He touched her cheek, wiped away the dampness. "Let's just start from today and see how things go, okay? Can we try to do that?"

"You sound as if there's all the time in the world to figure things out."

"By my calculations we have just over six months

'til the baby comes," he said. His lips twitched with the faint beginnings of a smile as he added, "Since one of us has an obsessive-compulsive personality, surely that's enough time to reach a few conclusions about where we go from here."

Helen recognized an olive branch when it was extended to her. "Deal," she said, holding out her hand.

Erik ignored her hand and settled his mouth on hers, instead. It was the first time he'd kissed her since he'd found out about the baby. The kiss was a reminder that not everything was bad about this predicament they were in. Desire blossomed inside her like the promise of a new beginning, but before she could let it sweep her away, she remembered something else, and a sob caught in her throat.

"What?" Erik asked.

"We're not even going on a honeymoon," she whispered. Not taking advantage of the one thing between them that was so right seemed like a terrible way to begin their life together.

"I wasn't sure you'd want to be alone with me," he admitted, then grinned. "But I took a chance, anyway."

Her eyes widened. "What kind of chance?"

"I booked us a suite in Paris for a few days."

Her mouth dropped open and she stared at him in wonder. "Paris? How did you know I've always wanted to go there?"

He laughed at that. "Wasn't a shopping trip to Paris supposed to be your reward if you met your goals in that deal you had going with Maddie and Dana Sue a while back?"

"You knew about that?"

"You have no idea the things I know," he said. "So, do you want to go or not?"

"I have court on Monday morning," she lamented.

He shook his head. "No, you don't. Barb spoke to the judge and rescheduled, just in case you said yes. She moved all your appointments for the rest of the week, as well. We'll come back on Thursday and you can do a little catch-up in the office on Friday and you'll have the whole weekend to recover from jet lag. How does that sound?"

"It sounds amazing!" she said, clasping her hands behind his head and giving him a kiss. "Let's do it."

Just then Dana Sue stuck her head into the kitchen and grinned. "You know about Paris?" she guessed.

Helen nodded.

"I thought that would make you happy."

"Were you in on it?" Helen asked her.

"It was Erik's idea," Dana Sue said. "He simply asked me what I thought. I just told him I hoped he had a huge limit on his credit card."

Helen bristled. "He won't need it. I have mine."

Erik shook his head. "We're married now. I can buy you a couple of those fancy blouses you love so much." His eyes lit up. "Maybe even some sexy lingerie."

Annie stepped into the kitchen just as he said that and Dana Sue made an elaborate show of covering her daughter's ears and elbowing Ty back out of the kitchen.

"Mom!" Annie protested, standing her ground. "I know guys like sexy lingerie." She grinned at Erik. "I'd love to see the look on your face when you go shopping for it, though."

"I'll be off at Le Cordon Bleu taking a cooking class," he said.

"You're supposed to do things *together* on your honeymoon," Annie scolded.

Erik winked at her. "Can you see Helen in a cooking class?"

"About as easily as I can see you in a lingerie boutique," Annie teased. "Come on. You have to stick together. Promise me. I want pictures."

Helen listened to the banter with a sense of wonder. It was surprisingly relaxed and normal, almost the way it had been between Erik and her before he'd found out about the baby. Maybe they could recapture that connection again, after all.

"How was the wedding?" Frances asked when Karen and Elliott got home that evening.

"Tense," Karen said. "But something happened during the reception. I don't know what, but things seemed to be better." She turned to Elliott. "Did you notice that?"

He shrugged. "I wasn't paying much attention to Helen and Erik," he said. "I had other things on my mind."

Suddenly Frances was on her feet and bustling around the living room gathering up her things. "I'll see you two tomorrow," she said.

Karen frowned. "Don't run off. Stay and have some wedding cake. I brought a piece home for you."

Frances winked at Elliott. "I'll have it at home with a nice cup of tea. You two have more important things to do."

"No, we don't," Karen protested. "We're just going to sit here and unwind."

"Enjoy yourselves. That's what I'm going to do at

my place—unwind. Mack and Daisy were a handful tonight. I'm a little tired."

Karen regarded her worriedly. "Were they too much for you?"

"No, of course not," Frances said. "Good night."

She was out the door before Karen could ask any more questions.

"That was odd," she said to Elliott. "She loves to stay and hear all about whatever we've been doing. I really hope the kids didn't wear her out."

"I think she was just trying to be subtle."

"Subtle?"

"She knew I wanted to have you all to myself," he explained.

Karen met his gaze and suddenly she knew what was on his mind, what had been on his mind for weeks now. "This is about you and me, isn't it?"

"Let's sit down," he said, drawing her to an easy chair and pulling her onto his lap. "I couldn't stop thinking about us today."

"That's just because we were at a wedding. Everyone feels a little misty and romantic at a wedding, even one as rushed and crazy as this one."

"Does that include you?" he asked. "Did you give any thought to where we're headed?"

"I thought we'd agreed to move slowly," she said, though her pulse was racing in anticipation.

He traced the outline of her lips. "I've changed my mind. I know what I want. I want us to be a family, Karen. I don't want you to have to struggle anymore. If we're partners, I can share things with you, take some of the burden off your shoulders. I love your kids as if they were my own. I'd even like to adopt them, if it could be worked out and it was something all of you wanted."

The picture he painted held tremendous allure, but she was still hesitant. She knew her feelings for him were deep, that it might even be love. And she trusted that his feelings for her were solid and true. The kids adored him. Frances, the closest thing she had to a mother, approved. So why was she hesitating?

Ironically, it was because of one of the things she'd so admired about him—his attachment to his family. Staunch Catholics, they were unhappy that she'd been divorced and had made no pretense about their disapproval. She'd seen it written all over his mother's face and his sisters' when she and Elliott had shown up at his niece's birthday party.

"Your family won't be happy," she said at last. "And I can't bear to be the cause of a rift between you."

"I'll deal with my family," he stated. "They'll come around."

"Elliott, my being divorced strikes at the very core of their beliefs," she reminded him. "I should have anticipated that before I even met them. So should you."

"You could have your marriage annulled," he suggested.

"I'm not Catholic," she reminded him. "I wasn't married in the Catholic church. It was a civil ceremony."

"Then the church won't even recognize it as a marriage, anyway," he said. "Look, I don't know all the church law on this, but it doesn't matter to me. I love you. You're the woman I want to spend the rest of my life with. We'll work it out. We can meet with a priest and he'll tell us what needs to be done."

He made it sound so simple, but there was one thing

he wasn't considering, the one thing that mattered most to her. "I won't do anything that will suddenly turn my children into bastards," she said fervently. She met his gaze. "I won't *do* that to them, Elliott. I won't. As useless as their father has turned out to be, he *was* their father. They were legitimate. I grew up not having a clue who my father was. It made me feel unwanted and ashamed. My mother abandoning me, emotionally at first and then physically, only added to that. I never felt good enough. I know now that I am a good, decent person, but I had to fight to accept that. I don't want my kids to ever struggle with that kind of insecurity."

"But they'll have *me*," Elliott said, his hand on her cheek, the touch meant to be reassuring. "Together, we'll see to it that they know who they are, that they're loved and respected and cherished. If we can work it out, I'll even legally adopt them. It won't be the same for them as it was for you, I promise."

Karen wanted to believe it could be that way, wanted to believe she hadn't come this close to finding the man of her dreams, only to have him slip away.

"We can talk to the priest," she said at last. "I'll listen to what we'd have to do to be married in your church and to win your family's approval. That's as much as I can do for now."

His eyes filled with relief. "Then we're engaged?"

"No," she said adamantly, then tempered her tone at the flash of hurt in his eyes. "Maybe engaged to be engaged."

A smile tugged at his lips. "That'll do for now. It will all work out," he said with a certainty she was far from feeling.

She recalled the condemnation in his mother's eyes

when she'd realized Karen was divorced. His sisters had been kinder, but no more enthusiastic about the relationship. Karen knew that winning them over was going to be an uphill battle.

Then she looked into Elliott's eyes and saw the love shining there and thought that maybe, just maybe, it was a battle worth fighting.

Helen returned from Paris with seven new pairs of shoes, six new designer suits and a whole suitcase filled with sexy French lingerie. She also came home with new hope for the future of her marriage. The honeymoon had been a brief, but idyllic four days. She'd even learned to make a roux at the exclusive culinary school, though when she would ever need to do that escaped her. It had been fun, though, seeing Erik in his element. And as Annie had insisted, they'd come home with pictures. Hundreds of them, it seemed, including one of a red-faced Erik amid a dozen mannequins dressed in lacy bras and panties.

Right this minute, those pictures were spread out over a table on the patio at The Corner Spa as Maddie and Dana Sue pored over them. Helen ignored their envious sighs as she held out a foot and admired one of her new pairs of shoes, high-heeled mules with a pointed toe in a leather so soft it felt like butter. She figured she only had a few more weeks before she'd be too ungainly to walk in shoes like these.

Maddie glanced over and caught the direction of her gaze. "Did you do anything over there besides shop for shoes?" she inquired.

"Of course we did. You're looking at the pictures to prove it." She grinned wickedly. "And there were quite a few things we did that I don't care to discuss. There are no pictures of any of that."

"So things are good again between the two of you?" Maddie asked, her eyes filled with concern.

"Not perfect, but improving day by day," Helen replied. "It'll take a while before Erik trusts me again, and I'm not sure how things are going to be after the baby arrives."

Dana Sue frowned. "What do you mean by that?"

"He told me from the start we could end the marriage then if that's what I wanted," she said, her voice hitching despite her efforts not to think that far ahead.

"He told you that because you were so determined to raise the baby on your own," Dana Sue said with exasperation. "Erik loves you."

"He's never said that," Helen said. "Not to me."

Dana Sue sighed. "I told him that was going to come back to haunt him," she muttered. "Look, while he's working on the whole trust thing, maybe you need to try to take a few things on faith."

Maddie gave Dana Sue a wry look. "You're talking to a woman who sees things as black or white."

"Funny," Dana Sue said, her gaze pinned on Helen. "I always thought she was a woman who understood that actions speak louder than words. How many times have you told a client not to listen to all the sweet words her lying, cheating husband utters, but to watch what he does?"

Helen had no idea what to say to that, so she gathered up her photos and stood up. "I need to get to the office. Barb says my calendar's jammed starting Monday and there's a pile of messages, even though I was gone less than a week. I need to make a dent in all that today."

Maddie looked alarmed. "Don't you dare try to do too much on your first day back. A whirlwind overseas trip is hard enough on your body. You don't need more stress."

"It's just one day," Helen reminded her. "I'll have the whole weekend to recuperate while Erik's busy at the restaurant."

"I'm just saying—" Maddie began, but Helen cut her off.

"I know what you're saying," she said, bending down to give her friend a hug. "And I love you for worrying, but I won't do anything foolish, I promise."

"Okay, then," Maddie said. "But I'm calling your office later. Barb will tell me if you're misbehaving."

"Only if she wants to lose her job," Helen retorted as she picked up her briefcase and headed toward the patio exit, rather than going through the building.

"Hold it," Maddie hollered after her. "You need to go through the spa. Elliott's going to walk you to your office."

"I saw him when I came in. He's already with a client," Helen said. "I'll be fine."

Maddie frowned. "Helen, please. It's still not safe for you to go anywhere alone."

For a brief flash the image of Caroline as she'd last seen her appeared in her mind, along with a reminder of the promise she'd made, not just to Caroline, but to herself.

"Okay, fine, I'll get Elliott," she said, making a U-turn and heading into the spa.

"If he can't break free, I'll drive you," Maddie called after her.

Helen chafed at all this protectiveness, but she knew

it was justified. She resolved to call the sheriff the instant she reached her office and demand to know the status of their hunt for Brad. If she sensed that Brad wasn't a high enough priority for them, then she was going to put her own detectives to work tracking him down. It was time for this to end.

CHAPTER TWENTY-TWO

With Elliott at her side, Helen walked back to her office, trying to take some pleasure in the gorgeous day. Elliott's grim demeanor wasn't helping. He obviously took his bodyguard duties seriously. His gaze was directed up and down the street as they walked and he answered all her questions in monosyllables without once glancing at her. Helen finally gave up trying to have a conversation with him.

As they walked along Main Street, she spotted Ronnie inside his hardware store and waved to him. At Wharton's, she told Elliott to wait while she poked her head inside to say hello to Grace and Neville.

"I brought you something from Paris," she told Grace. "I'll bring it by later."

Grace's arms were loaded down with plates of scrambled eggs and pancakes. "You had a wonderful honeymoon, then?"

"It was amazing," Helen confirmed, knowing that half the town would be chattering away about that before the morning was out. Maybe it would put a stop to the rumors probably circulating about her walking down the aisle under duress.

Once they reached her office, she grinned at Elliott. "Your job here is done," she told him. "You've delivered me safely."

"Why don't I go inside with you?" he suggested.

"Barb's here," she said, spotting her car in the driveway. "I'll be fine."

"Okay, then. You need me to go anywhere with you, all you have to do is say the word, okay?"

"Thanks, Elliott."

As he started to jog back toward the spa, she opened the door and went inside. Barb glanced up from the phone call she was on and beamed at her, then mouthed, "Welcome back."

When Helen would have picked up her messages and gone on into her office, Barb gestured for her to wait as she wrapped up her call.

"I just wanted to alert you that there's a client waiting in your office," Barb told her. "He said it was an emergency and since you didn't have anything on your calendar for today, I told him he could come in if he didn't mind waiting 'til you got here."

"Who is he and what kind of emergency?" Helen asked, annoyed because she'd counted on having the whole day to catch up on her cases.

Barb glanced at a note on her desk. "He said his name is Bryan Hallifax."

"I don't recall a Hallifax family in Serenity."

Barb shrugged. "He didn't say if he lived here in town. I didn't recognize him, either."

"And the emergency?"

"Something about his wife threatening to take his kids away from him," she said. "She hit him with this

right after he got back from a business trip and he panicked. He didn't give me a lot of details."

"Okay, whatever. I'll deal with him, but no more calls
and definitely no more appointments."

"Got it," Barb said. "I'm sorry about this, but he
was so frantic."

Helen gave her shoulder a squeeze. "Don't worry
about it. I know what a softie you are."

When she opened to door to her office, she didn't
immediately spot the man. It was only after she'd closed
the door that she saw him standing in the shadows.
When he turned, her heart leaped into her throat. It was
Brad Holliday, his eyes filled with rage and satisfaction
at having caught her off guard.

Helen instinctively started to yank the door back
open and yell for Barb to call the police. But then she
saw the gun in Brad's hand and froze. It was trained
on her.

"Good," he said when she stepped away from the
door. "You're a smart woman."

"What do you want, Brad?"

"Justice, satisfaction," he suggested, then shrugged.
"We'll see how it goes."

Helen moved cautiously until she was behind her
desk, where she could sit down. Hopefully the solid
desk would offer some protection for the baby if Brad
decided to fire the gun. Unfortunately, she'd never installed the panic button that some attorneys insisted on
having on the floor beside their desks. She dealt with
divorces, not criminal law.

She forced herself to look directly into Brad's eyes.
They were filled with hate. Still, she managed to keep
her tone even and reasonable. "Brad, don't you think

you're in enough trouble after what you did to Caroline? Do you really want to make things worse?"

He gave her a wry look. "Like you said, I'm already in a lot of trouble. What's a little more? I don't have much to lose. You took everything from me."

Helen knew better than to engage in an argument with someone who wasn't thinking clearly. Some instinct, though, made her want to get through to him, maybe save him from himself.

"Brad, you know that's not true," she said quietly. "You still have plenty of money. You have your kids."

"They hate me now."

Helen knew the sons were angry, but his daughter was another story. "Your daughter doesn't hate you. She's trying very hard to believe in you, but if you do something to me, that will be it. She won't be able to ignore the truth—that you're not the man she thought you were."

His laugh was bitter. "But don't you see? I'm *not* the man she thought I was. And it's all because of you." His expression hardened. "Now I want you to know what it's like to have your life ruined." The gun in his hand wavered as he spoke, but it was still pointed at her.

Helen was beginning to doubt her ability to make Brad lower the gun, and a cold fist of fear formed in her belly. She scanned her desk looking for anything heavy enough to serve as a weapon. A crystal paperweight, an award from the bar association, could probably do some damage and it was within reach. She knew she'd only have a split second to throw it at him and pray her aim was accurate. Maybe if she kept him talking, she could get her hands on it before he realized what she was up to.

Sweat rolled down her back as she rested her hands on top of her desk, hoping the sight of them in plain view would make him lower his guard. "Brad, you really don't want to do anything you can't take back. Why don't you put the gun down and let's talk? Maybe I can help you find a way out of this situation you're in."

"You're a helluva lot better than Jimmy Bob," he said, "but even you aren't clever enough to fix this. My life's over."

"Come on. It doesn't have to be that way. You'll serve a little time, maybe even get probation for what you did to Caroline," she said, deliberately minimizing what was likely to happen. "Then you can have a fresh start."

He shook his head. "You can't fast-talk your way out of this, hotshot."

Helen's hand had been inching toward the paperweight and now closed around it. It felt solid in her grip, but was it enough?

Just then Barb tapped on the door. Brad's head jerked in that direction and Helen took advantage of his distraction to hurl the paperweight directly at his head. It hit with a glancing blow that wasn't nearly enough to cause serious injury. He whirled around and shot without taking time to aim. The bullet splintered the wood on the corner of the desk. Outside the door, Barb screamed.

Helen dove beneath her desk, but not quickly enough. A second shot grazed her arm, sending a bolt of searing pain through her. A third shot went wild and shattered a window.

"You bitch!" Brad yelled, just as the first sirens split the air.

It took Helen a second to realize they weren't police

sirens at all, but the building's security alarm, set off
when the window shattered. Nonetheless, the sound was
enough to make Brad bolt from the room.

Then Barb was there, helping Helen into her chair,
murmuring apologies even as she used a towel she'd
grabbed from their restroom and tried to stem the bleeding.

"I had no idea," she said over and over. "I'm so sorry.
I should have asked more questions. God, what was I
thinking?"

Helen squeezed her hand. "Barb, it's okay. How
could you know? You'd never met Brad."

"But I should have been more suspicious. Everyone
in town knew you were off on your honeymoon this
week. The second he called for an appointment on a day
you were only supposed to be catching up, I should've
guessed he was up to no good."

"Barb, you can't second-guess the motives of every
potential client."

"But that man almost killed you!" she said. "I'll
never forgive myself for that." She glanced around, her
expression panicked. "Where are the police, dammit?
And the paramedics? You're bleeding!"

Just then from outside, another shot rang out, followed by a collective, horrified gasp—the onlookers
who'd apparently gathered when the alarm went off.

"What happened?" Helen asked Barb, even as she
rocked back and forth, clutching her bloody arm and
trying to ignore the pain.

"I don't know," Barb said, pressing the towel to the
wound, her expression grim. "The EMTs should be here
any minute. Just take deep, slow breaths—you're hyper-
ventilating. Come on, sweetie. Slow breaths. That's it."

"Oh, God, my baby," Helen whispered, her hand on her still-flat stomach.

"Hush now. Your baby's going to be just fine," Barb reassured her.

Finally, after what seemed an eternity, the EMTs arrived. When Barb started to move out of their way, Helen grabbed her hand and clung to it. "Don't go."

"I'm not going anywhere. Let me call Erik and I'll be right back."

"No," Helen said. "He'll just worry."

"He has a right to worry, don't you think?" Barb scolded.

Helen must have answered a hundred questions, first for the EMTs, who were insisting that she go to the hospital, then for the police, who were surprisingly tight-lipped about whether Brad was in custody or not.

It seemed like hours, but was probably no more than minutes before Erik arrived. Kneeling down in front of her, he took her hands in his.

Expecting a lecture about her recklessness, Helen was surprised when he turned the full force of his fury on the police. "Where the hell were you? Someone was supposed to be watching her at all times!"

The officer closest to them, a fresh-faced kid new to the force, winced. "The sheriff thought you all were still on your honeymoon. No one notified us you were back."

Erik turned pale. "Then this is my fault," he said, lifting his gaze to meet hers. "It's because of me you were shot."

"Don't be crazy," she began, but before she could say another word, he was on his feet and out the door. She stared after him in confusion.

"Ma'am, we need to get you over to Regional Hospital to be checked out," the EMT told her. "The wound's not deep, but I gather you're pregnant. You should probably see an obstetrician while you're there."

Helen nodded, then glanced up at Barb. "I need Erik."

"He'll be there. I'll see to it. You go with the EMTs. I'll follow. I'll call Maddie and Dana Sue, too. They'll want to know about this."

"You don't need to bother them," Helen said, but Barb merely shot her a look that said she was the one making the decisions for the moment. Helen didn't waste any more breath arguing.

Docilely, she let the EMTs carry her to the ambulance on a gurney. They managed to shield her view of all the activity still going on on the street. Maybe it was just as well. She suddenly felt drained.

Inside the ambulance, she closed her eyes and tried to block out the worry that was crowding out everything else, even the pain. She didn't understand that bleak expression in Erik's eyes right before he'd taken off, but somewhere deep inside, she knew she was responsible for putting it there. He felt guilty. She got that, no matter how misguided she thought he was. She also suspected the depth of that guilt cut to the heart of why he'd never wanted to marry or have children.

She knew suddenly and with absolute clarity that she could lose him over this. And the realization scared her to death.

Erik was mindlessly stirring a triple batch of brownie dough when Maddie and Dana Sue converged on him in the kitchen at Sullivan's. They looked a little like avenging angels, and he seemed to be the target.

Not that he was surprised. He'd known that sooner or later someone would tell them what had happened to Helen and how he'd abandoned her. He simply hadn't been able to make himself stay. Her pain, the blood, all of it had brought back too many heart-wrenching memories.

Worse than that had been the crushing fear that he would lose this wife, this baby. Even though his medical training told him Helen would be fine, he'd panicked. There was no way of getting around that. He was human. Maybe it was time they all understood that. He was nobody's hero.

"Why are you here?" Dana Sue demanded.

"Someone has to think about the restaurant," he retorted as he kept right on stirring. "We open in a couple of hours for lunch."

"Let them eat fast food or grab a burger at Wharton's," Dana Sue snapped. "That's what they did before Sullivan's existed. They can do it again for one day."

Erik frowned at her. "You don't mean that."

"I most certainly do," Dana Sue said. "Your wife was just shot by a maniac. Nobody in this town gives a damn about brownies right now. Everyone's worried sick about Helen and the baby. If you think brownies are more important, then there's something wrong with you. You should be with Helen. At the very least you should be on your way to the hospital."

"I was with her. She's in good hands," he insisted, though his pulse still jolted when he thought about how close he'd come to losing her.

"That's it?" Dana Sue said incredulously. "You spend two seconds with her, then turn her over to strangers?"

"They weren't strangers. She knew everyone in that

room," he muttered defensively. And they'd all been capable of handling the crisis that had leveled him.

Maddie, who'd been silent up 'til now, finally spoke up. "Erik, you don't have any reason to blame yourself for what happened," she said, studying him intently. "And right now blame's not what's important. You need to get to the hospital and be with your wife."

Dana Sue yanked the bowl of brownie mix away from him. "Go, dammit! I'm capable of making the stupid brownies for once. I did it often enough before I hired you."

"I'll drive you," Maddie said.

A part of Erik wanted to argue. A part of him wanted to stand his ground, to hide out right here in a world that made sense to him, but deep in his gut he knew both Maddie and Dana Sue were right. His place was with Helen. He'd just lost his mind for a little while when he'd realized how close he'd come to losing her. The sense of déjà vu had been overwhelming.

"Okay, let's go," he said at last.

Dana Sue looked triumphant, but Maddie merely looked relieved.

"We'll call you from the hospital," she promised Dana Sue.

"And I'll be back in time for the dinner rush," Erik told her.

"You most certainly will not be," Dana Sue said. "Especially if they release Helen from the hospital. You'll need to stay with her. Tess and Karen can fill in. I'll call them right now and explain what's going on."

"We'll play it by ear, then," he said, which was as much of a concession as he was prepared to make.

In the car, Maddie glanced at him. "You okay?"

"I'm not the one who was shot."

"They say when you love someone, it's possible to feel their pain."

"Oh, please, spare me the psychobabble," he said. "But I understand what you're trying to say." He swiped a hand over his eyes. "When I got the call from Barb, you have no idea what went through my mind."

"Oh, I think I have some idea," Maddie responded. "I suspect it was a lot like what Dana Sue and I were thinking— What if it's more serious than Barb is saying? What if we lose her?" She met his gaze. "Am I close?"

Erik smiled, relieved to know he wasn't alone with a heavy load of guilt. "On the money."

"I imagine Barb's feeling the same thing about now," Maddie went on, "since she's the one who let Brad into Helen's office. But the truth is, all the blame should be directed at Brad. He's the one who lost his grip on reality just because his divorce didn't go the way he'd anticipated. He was the one with the gun. He shot himself when he saw the police closing in. None of that is the behavior of a rational man. Accept what he did, maybe even pity him, but then let it go. Nothing matters now except making sure that Helen and the baby are okay."

"That all sounds very mature and rational, but I still feel this overwhelming sense of guilt." The deputy's words echoed in his head. "Did you know I never thought to let the sheriff's department know we were back from Paris? If I had, there would've been someone keeping an eye on her."

"You'd just come back from an incredible honeymoon. You can be forgiven for not thinking about a threat that was made weeks ago in anger. All of us had at least some reason to believe the danger was past."

"You didn't," he corrected. "You insisted that Elliott go with her to the office."

Her lips curved slightly. "I'm a mother. I worry about everything. Ask my kids. Even though Ty's away at college, I worry about whether he's wearing a sweater when it's chilly or whether he's brushed his teeth at night or has eaten a decent meal. It's all force of habit."

"I don't imagine you call him to ask about all those things, though, do you?" Erik asked, pretty certain the nineteen-year-old star baseball prospect wouldn't take kindly to such questions from his mother.

"Are you crazy?" she asked, laughing. "He'd never come home again. I just drive Cal crazy asking *him* if he thinks Ty is doing all those things. Periodically, I catch Cal telling Ty that I've been pestering him about stuff like that. They commiserate over how nutty I am, what a *mom* I am."

Just then she pulled up in front of the emergency entrance. "You go in. I'll park the car," she told him. "Helen needs you right now more than she needs me."

"I'm not so sure about that," Erik said. "I did a fairly lousy job of handling this particular crisis."

"Maybe, but you have a lot of other things going for you, including the fact that you love her to pieces. That's what matters. Maybe you can finally tell her that."

With Maddie's words resounding in his head, he went inside to find his wife.

His *wife*. Calling her that still had the power to amaze him.

"I'm looking for Helen Whitney," he told the nurse at triage. "Or Helen Decatur. I'm not sure how she registered."

"Just married," the nurse guessed. "She couldn't decide, either. She's in cubicle eight. I think she'd be happy to see your handsome face about now. She's waiting for the obstetrician to get here."

Erik's heart sank. "Is there a problem with the baby?"

"Not that we know of. It's just a precaution after the trauma she's been through. Dr. Wilson recommended it."

Erik nodded, relieved that Emily Wilson had been on duty. At least hers would have been a familiar face for Helen. "Thanks," he said as he started toward the back.

"By the way," the nurse called out, "she's registered as Helen Whitney. Guess she took those vows seriously."

Erik couldn't stop the smile that crept across his face as he went in search of Helen. If she'd wanted to disavow their marriage because of his failure to protect her or because he'd bolted from her office, she would've stuck with her maiden name. Maybe he had one more chance to get this right, after all.

The pain medicine had made Helen groggy, but she knew the instant that Erik came into her cubicle and took the seat beside her.

Fighting to open her eyes, she managed a faint smile. "Hi. You came. I wasn't sure you would."

"Maddie and Dana Sue were pretty persuasive," he admitted.

Her smile wobbled. "Did they beat you up?" she asked, actually sounding a little worried that they might have.

He laughed. "No, they didn't need to go that far." His expression sobered. "How are you feeling?"

"Dopey. They patched up my arm."

"Any twinges with the baby?"

She shook her head. Her hand instinctively went to her stomach. "I think she's okay, but the doctor's going to make sure."

He gave her an odd look. "She?"

"Or he," she said. "Just not 'it,' okay?"

"Understood. Look, you need to rest. I'll be in the waiting room with Maddie."

He started to stand up, but Helen latched on to his hand. "No," she commanded. "Don't leave me again, please. I'm scared, Erik. Really scared. And nobody will tell me what happened to Brad. He didn't get away, did he?"

"You don't need to worry about Brad ever again."

"Why? Tell me."

"He shot himself. He's dead," he said, sitting back down beside her. He kept her hand in his, his thumb idly caressing her knuckles, his thoughts seemingly far away.

Her relief that Brad was gone lasted only a moment. "Erik?"

He looked into her eyes. "What?"

"Why did you take off back at my office? You know none of this was your fault, don't you? You weren't there. There was nothing you could have done to stop it."

"I'm not so sure about that," he said. "But Maddie convinced me that maybe there's enough blame to go around."

"But there was something more going on with you, something that went deeper than what happened today. I could sense it."

His expression shut down. "It's nothing for you to

worry about," he told her. "All that matters is making sure you and the baby are okay. Close your eyes and rest 'til the doctor gets here."

When she would have probed a little more deeply, he gave her a warning look. "I mean it," he said. "Rest or I'll leave."

She sighed and closed her eyes. Maybe he thought he could stall her now, but he surely knew he wouldn't be able to stall her forever. She was a pro at interrogation, at least when she was at the top of her game. In a few days, fewer if she concentrated hard on making a quick recovery, she'd get the answers she was after.

Karen and Tess exchanged a look as Dana Sue flew around the kitchen snapping out orders. Finally Karen grabbed her by the shoulders and marched her toward a stool.

"Sit," she ordered. "You need to calm down and eat something."

"I can't eat," Dana Sue grumbled, but she accepted the dish of chicken salad Karen handed her. "Why haven't we heard anything from the hospital?"

"Probably because they don't know anything yet," Karen soothed. "I'm sure Helen is fine. Maddie would have called immediately if things were bad, so you could get over there."

"I suppose," Dana Sue said, eating a bite of the chicken salad and then another. Finally she looked up, a curious expression on her face. "This is different. What did you add to it? Dill?"

"Just a little," Karen said. "Is it okay?"

"It's fabulous."

"I was thinking of adding toasted walnuts, too, or maybe almonds. What do you think?"

Dana Sue took another bite. "Almonds, I think. I love walnuts in salads, but they're best sprinkled on the top. People need to know they're in there. Otherwise, they're liable to think they're biting down on a piece of bone. Almonds aren't quite as crunchy."

"Good point," Karen said. "Anyway, I thought it might be a nice change from the pineapple chicken salad we do now. We could rotate them seasonally or something."

"I've been thinking about that myself," Dana Sue said. "I think we ought to have a new menu each season with some of the favorites, of course, but a few new dishes as well. We'd still have specials, too, but I think change might keep our regulars coming in— You know, in case they get tired of the same old things."

"I have some ideas if you want to hear them," Karen said, barely able to contain her excitement. At Dana Sue's nod, she pulled a stool up next to her.

"Fresh tomatoes are still available. We've never tried a tomato and buffalo mozzarella salad. Or a bruschetta. Those are terrific in warm weather and we have another couple of months of that, at least."

"It would be a change from the house salad or sliced tomatoes and onions," Dana Sue agreed. "Do you think our customers are ready for that kind of change?"

Karen nodded eagerly. "Sure. Just look at how much they loved the gazpacho. Sullivan's is known for being innovative. People can make a plain old salad or sliced tomatoes at home. They don't need us for that."

Dana Sue grinned. "Good point. Okay, what else?"

"Last summer Erik made a lot of cobblers, but what about fruit tarts instead?"

"I love it," Dana Sue said, clearly catching her enthusiasm. "He can do a wonderful pastry, then add a thin layer of custard and top it with fresh fruits and berries. They'll taste great and look fabulous if we finally get that big color-photo spread in one of the regional magazines." She studied Karen. "You're good at this. I hope I tell you that enough."

"You do," Karen said.

Dana Sue studied her. "And things are better at home now, aren't they? Your life has settled down?"

Karen nodded. "I finally feel as if I'm back in control. Elliott's helped with that. He's been a rock. Frances, too."

"Are you and Elliott getting serious?"

"He is," she admitted. "But there are complications."

Dana Sue regarded her with concern. "Oh? Anything you want to talk about?"

"No," Karen said. "I don't want to bring my problems to work, not anymore."

"Maybe you could think of it as sharing them with a friend," Dana Sue said.

"You're still my boss," Karen reminded her.

Dana Sue frowned slightly. "We're a team, Karen. You and Tess and Erik are all like family to me. Okay, it's a *work* family, but the feelings are there, just the same. I care about what's going on with you, I really do. I know it might not have seemed that way a few weeks ago, but even when Erik and I were stressed out and annoyed because you weren't here, we still cared about you."

Tears stung Karen's eyes. "I know, it's just that I need

to know I can solve my own problems. Maybe that'll change one day, but for now it's important to me."

Dana Sue reached over and squeezed her hand. "As long as you know I'm here if you need me, I can respect your need to do things your own way." She stood up. "Now we'd better get back to work or the dinner crowd will be dining on leftover cheese grits from lunch. They might be great with a slice of ham, but they sure won't go over as a main course."

Before she walked away, she turned back to Karen. "Thanks for distracting me and keeping me from climbing the walls."

"No problem. It was survival instinct."

Dana Sue winced. "I was that bad?"

"Pretty much, but not to worry. I'm sure we'll hear something from the hospital soon and you'll really be able to relax."

After that, they all fell back into their usual routine, including Tess, who'd made herself scarce while Karen had been talking to Dana Sue.

It was nearly five before the phone rang. Dana Sue grabbed it on the first ring, mumbled replies Karen couldn't hear, then hung up. But when she turned around she was smiling. "Helen and the baby are both okay. Erik and Maddie are bringing them home. They didn't even insist on her staying overnight for observation." Dana Sue grinned. "Probably because they figured they'd never hear the end of it if they tried."

"Thank God," Karen said as Tess sketched a cross over her chest.

"Amen to that," Dana Sue said. "Now, let's get busy, ladies. The hungry hordes will be here any minute. And if I haven't said it before, thank you both for pitching in and picking up the slack today. You're angels."

The sincerity in Dana Sue's voice filled Karen with happiness and pride. Only a few short months ago, she'd been on the verge of losing this job. Now she knew she was capable of making a real contribution here. And it did feel as if she'd found more than a job—she'd found a family. Add in Daisy and Mack, Elliott and Frances, and her life was full.

Erik knew he'd accused Helen of being obsessive-compulsive, but when it came down to it, where the baby was concerned, he had her beat by a mile. The thought of another pregnancy, another baby, cast a shadow over everything. Ever since the close call with Brad Holliday, he found himself watching Helen just about around the clock. He went to every doctor appointment, but he wasn't half as reassured as she seemed to be when she received a clean bill of health. He'd asked so many questions on their last visit that the obstetrician had joked that next time he'd schedule two appointments, one for each of them.

If Helen woke in the middle of the night with a craving, he saw to it she got whatever she wanted. If she looked tired, he couldn't rest 'til she was in bed or on the sofa with her feet up. He dreaded a time when the doctor might insist on complete bed rest, because he knew with absolute certainty he'd have a fight on his hands. Helen was incapable of staying still that long. Thankfully, though, she'd kept her blood pressure in check so far.

When he first saw the baby on a sonogram, the last of his anger at the circumstances of the baby's conception drained away, and he was completely captivated by this child he'd never expected to have. The power that tiny baby had over him was astounding.

They'd agreed they didn't want to know the sex ahead of time, but Erik was convinced it was a boy. Helen seemed just as convinced it was a girl. They spent hour after hour debating names. Their first list had taken up two pages. Now they'd whittled it down to ten possibilities for a boy and eight for a girl. All of it had made this baby real for him, something he'd vowed not to let happen. He hadn't wanted to start loving it too much. He hadn't wanted to start eagerly awaiting the moment when it arrived in this world.

Helen put up with his attentiveness with surprising docility. In fact, as the weeks wore on, her hard edges seemed to fade and she seemed to enjoy being pampered, even if she did regard him with curiosity when he insisted on taking care of the simplest tasks.

Finally, when she was six months along and still in apparently perfect health, she reacted as he'd expected her to react much sooner. She lost patience and openly rebelled at his protectiveness.

"Okay, enough's enough. What's going on here?" she demanded when he'd jumped up to get the pen she said she needed to jot down notes for her closing statement in court in the morning. "You know I can walk across the room for a pen. I'm perfectly capable of getting myself a glass of water, too, even if it does mean I'll be waddling down the hall to the bathroom ten minutes later. I know Ronnie went a little crazy when Dana Sue was pregnant, and Cal almost drove Maddie insane with his hovering, so I've tried to be tolerant. But you've taken this to new heights, Erik. Why? It has to stop."

Erik shook his head. "It's not going to stop," he said tersely.

"Then I'll ask you again, why? It's not just about me, is it? Or even our baby. There's something else going on. I guessed that when you took off after Brad shot me. I let you get away with not answering me back then, but I've had it. Talk to me."

Erik wasn't entirely sure why he hadn't blurted out the story long before now. He'd hinted at it back when he'd first found out she was pregnant, but both of them had been so upset that day his comment about his already losing one baby had apparently gone right over her head.

Of course, after Sam had died, everyone had tiptoed around him, not even mentioning her name most of the time, so he'd gotten used to keeping his feelings bottled up inside.

Worse, everyone had pretended the baby had simply never existed, but she had been as real to him as if he'd held her in his arms. He'd felt her stirring in Sam's belly. Though he'd felt incredibly silly doing it, he'd sung lullabies to her and even read her stories. He knew that she kicked up a storm when Sam ate spicy food and rested peacefully at the sound of his voice.

Even now, nearly seven years later, his emotions were nearly as raw as they'd been back then, especially lately. He gazed into Helen's eyes, saw her expectation. She was going to wait him out this time. Keeping quiet about the details of Sam's death and his child's was no longer an option, not if they were to have a prayer of making this marriage work.

"You know I was married before," he began, trying to keep his voice steady.

Helen nodded. "And she died, right?"

"Yes, she died," he said, his voice strained.

Sympathy washed over her face. "You've never said what happened. She had to be so young. Was she sick or in an accident?"

Both were natural assumptions given the age Sam had been when she'd died. Erik hesitated to voice the truth, especially with their own baby due in a few months. The timing for this revelation sucked, but it was no one's fault but his own.

"I'm not sure I ought to be telling you any of this now," he began. "It's the wrong time."

"I need to know," she said. "Please."

Still he hesitated, but her gaze remained steady. The questions clearly weren't going away. "Okay, here it is. Sam was pregnant. She went into premature labor. She started bleeding and I couldn't get it stopped. You know I was an EMT, and I was right *there*. I did everything by the book. Everyone said so."

He closed his eyes, fighting the memory or maybe trying to avoid the worry he was bound to cause her. Finally he forced himself to meet her gaze, prepared for the shock and dismay he would find there once he said the rest. "Before we got to the hospital, she'd already lost too much blood. Nothing I tried worked, and Lord knows, I tried everything. By the time the ambulance came and we got Sam to the hospital, she'd bled to death. We lost the baby, too."

He felt the same sense of helplessness now. "I know I'm making you a little nuts with my hovering, but I can't stop it, Helen. I won't."

"Oh, Erik, I'm so sorry," she whispered. "I can't

even begin to imagine how painful that must have been for you."

She reached for his hand and pulled him down beside her, then placed his hand on her belly, where their baby was kicking up a storm as if aware that a point needed to be made.

"See, we're fine," she told him softly.

Erik stretched out beside her, his hand still resting on her taut stomach.

Not this time, he pleaded with God. *Don't let me lose this woman or this child.* Somewhere along the way he'd fallen in love with Helen. This unborn child, like another one, had crept into his heart. He'd started to count on them being a family. If that changed, if he lost them, he wasn't sure he'd be able to fight his way through the anguish a second time.

CHAPTER TWENTY-THREE

As she approached her ninth month, Helen felt like
a blimp. Her feet were so swollen she couldn't wear
a single pair of the dozens of outrageously expensive
shoes in her closet. She'd been wearing a pair of old
sneakers with no laces for two weeks now. Fortunately,
given the size of her stomach, she couldn't see the disgusting things.

Indian summer had arrived with a vengeance, dragging on and on until everyone in town was grumbling
that they'd be having a heat wave on Valentine's Day if
it kept up. The heat only added to her misery. She was
cranky and impossible, which actually seemed to be
surprisingly advantageous in most of her divorce ne-
gotiations. Either the husbands or the opposing counsel
or both were terrified she'd go into labor right before
their eyes, or maybe they remembered their own wives'
pregnancies and treated her with a fair amount of respect for her condition. She'd been winning concessions
right and left lately.

She had one more court date in Charleston next week
and then she'd be sticking close to home 'til the baby
arrived. Even now, she was doing her best to rest a lot,

primarily because Erik completely freaked out if she didn't. Now that she understood what he'd been through, she tried really hard not to add to his stress by doing anything he thought might put her or the baby at risk. And arguing with him only added to her own stress levels, something his constant blood-pressure monitoring had proved time and again.

This morning, though, she'd insisted on lumbering out of bed and walking to The Corner Spa for her meeting with Dana Sue and Maddie. For once Erik hadn't fought her. He'd showered and walked with her, depositing her at the front door with strict instructions to get a ride to her office or to call him to come and get her.

"I don't want you walking any more in this heat, understood?"

"Believe me, I'm not the least bit interested in losing another gallon of fluid by walking anywhere once the temperature climbs another couple of degrees," she told him, then walked inside where the spa's air-conditioning was pumping away. It was heavenly. She closed her eyes and took a deep breath, then headed for Maddie's office.

En route, she noticed that the spa was strangely empty. Normally at this hour of the morning, the treadmills were in use and the air was filled with the clanking of weights and the groans of protest from a couple dozen women. Today the only sound she heard was music. Even stranger, it wasn't the classical music or jazz Maddie preferred, but something from way back, something about "the cutest little baby face."

When she walked through the door to the café, the room exploded with sound.

"Surprise!"

Helen gasped, stunned that her friends had managed to pull off yet another surprise party for her so soon after her birthday. She stared at the sea of familiar faces—Maddie and Dana Sue, of course, then Jeanette, Barb, Karen, Tess and a handful of other former clients. It was when she spotted Caroline Holliday that tears sprung to her eyes. It was the first time she'd seen Caroline since the woman had left the hospital and moved to live closer to her sister, taking her two youngest children, both teenagers, with her. She'd told Helen that they hovered around her in a way that worried her.

"I know they're grieving for their dad and blame themselves for not protecting me," Caroline had said in a phone conversation a few weeks after she'd left the hospital. "They're terrified now that something will happen to me and they'll be all alone. I thought being closer to my sister and her family would help them realize that they will always have people they can count on, but it's not working."

Helen had told her about Dr. McDaniels and recommended that she contact the psychologist if things didn't improve. "She's great with teenagers. She made all the difference in the world with Dana Sue's daughter, Annie."

Now Caroline gave Helen such a huge smile that Helen just knew that things in her life were finally improving. She could hardly wait for a few moments alone with her to hear the latest. Right now, though, a dozen or more faces were watching her expectantly.

"Quick, find her a place to sit," Maddie said, taking Helen's arm. "We don't want her toppling over before she opens presents."

"Very funny," Helen said as she sank onto the chaise longue they'd brought in from the patio.

Maddie grinned at her. "You look very regal stretched out there. Okay, what's your first command? Food or presents?"

"The food better be more interesting than oatmeal, which is all Erik lets me have in the morning," she grumbled.

Dana Sue chuckled. "I was in charge of the food. What do you think?"

"Then bring it on," Helen said.

An hour later, she was stuffed from eating Dana Sue's cheese and mushroom omelet, a half-dozen miniature orange-cranberry muffins and drinking what must have been half a gallon of sweet tea. She'd lumbered to the closest restroom twice and was pretty sure it was almost time for another trip, but the lure of the pile of presents across the room was too much to resist.

"Not yet," Maddie said, catching the direction of her gaze. "We need to play at least one game."

"Baby shower games are silly," Helen said, still eyeing the huge boxes across the room. "I've always hated them."

"Nonetheless, we want you to have the total baby-shower experience," Dana Sue said. "You've waited a long time for this."

"Oh, for heaven's sake," Helen said. "Pick one and let's get it over with."

Maddie laughed. "Nice to see you've mellowed during your pregnancy."

Helen immediately shut up and dutifully went along while they played some silly guessing game about the size of her stomach and another one involving baby names, none of which would ever be pinned on her child, not if she had anything to say about it!

When they'd finished the second game and she'd made yet another trip to the restroom, Maddie declared it was time for Helen to open the gifts.

"But we all want you to know how difficult you made things by refusing to find out the sex of the baby ahead of time," Maddie said.

Helen frowned at her. "In the old days no one ever knew. People still had perfectly successful baby showers. I'm sure you all rose to the occasion."

Dana Sue handed her the first package and read the card. "This one's from Tess," she said.

Helen fingered the elaborate yellow bow. "It's too beautiful to open."

Dana Sue rolled her eyes. "You've been wanting to get to this part for an hour. Stop dillydallying."

Helen felt a bit like an overindulged kid opening presents on Christmas morning. She smiled in delight, then tore off the bow and wrapping paper. She lifted the top on the box to find a beautiful christening dress inside. There was no mistaking that the delicate white fabric had been tucked and embroidered by hand. The attention to detail was amazing.

"My mother made it," Tess said shyly. "We wanted to give you something special for bringing Diego back to me."

Tears stung Helen's eyes. "It's exquisite," she whispered, her voice choked. "I never expected anything like this. I'd hug you if I could stand up."

Tess's eyes shone. "I'm glad you like it. My mother will be pleased."

"Tell her I am in awe of her skill with a needle,"

Helen said. "I want you all to come to the christening, then you can see how the baby looks in this."

"Now this one," Dana Sue said, handing her another package. "It's from Karen."

This one had three baby rompers in pale green, yellow and lilac. "I thought the lilac might be pushing it if it's a boy," Karen said. "But it was too cute. I thought you had to have it."

There were more outfits, a hand-knitted baby blanket from Frances and several more practical presents. Caroline Holliday had brought an engraved silver baby cup and matching spoon.

"I know people don't do that much anymore," she said. "But even if you never use them, they're wonderful keepsakes."

"Oh, trust me, Helen's baby will use them. There will be no tacky plastic utensils for this child," Maddie said. "That saying about someone born with a silver spoon in his mouth will fit this child perfectly. I predict he or she's going to be spoiled rotten. If Helen doesn't cater to its every whim, Erik will."

"And why shouldn't we?" Helen asked. "This is going to be one amazing baby."

"Which is why Maddie and I bought you this," Dana Sue said, struggling to fight a smile as she handed Helen another package.

When Helen opened it, she found a book advising parents on how to cope with their gifted child.

"Just in case you find you can't keep up with the little genius," Maddie teased.

Helen feigned a frown. "As if," she retorted.

"Oh, wait, there's one more thing," Dana Sue said. She went to the door and called out to Elliott, who'd made himself scarce during this ladies-only function. "Could you bring that other gift in for me?" She grinned at Helen. "It's from Ronnie and it was too big to wrap, at least in a way that wouldn't tell you right off what it is."

A moment later, Elliott came in with a huge, awkwardly wrapped package, which he set in front of Helen. Then he went to stand behind Karen to watch Helen open it, his hand resting lightly on Karen's shoulder. Helen noticed Karen glance up at him. The girl's eyes shone with so much love it made Helen want to weep. Then again, just about everything made her want to weep these days.

Her attention returned to the gift, and she reached for the huge bow and pulled it away, then tore at the paper. Inside was a hand-carved cradle, so beautifully crafted it took her breath away. A parade of tiny ducks that almost looked alive decorated the headboard. Each spindle on the side was equally delicate. And at the foot of the cradle, a mama duck and a papa rested close together, their obviously loving gazes directed toward their brood at the opposite end of the cradle.

Everyone in the room erupted in *oohs* and *aahs* at the sight of it, Helen's gaze flew to Dana Sue. "Wasn't this Annie's cradle?" she asked.

Dana Sue shook her head. "No, we're keeping that one for her, but it's just like it. Ronnie said it was the one thing he ever did that you seemed to approve of, and so he wanted you to have one. He's been carving it for months now, ever since we found out about the baby. He knew how much you loved the one he did before Annie was born."

Yet again, Helen's eyes welled with tears. She and Ronnie hadn't always gotten along. In fact, they'd been at serious odds after he'd cheated on Dana Sue, but Helen's attitude toward him had mellowed once she'd finally seen how much he still loved Dana Sue and his daughter and the lengths he'd been willing to go toin order to get them back. That he would make something this thoughtful and amazing for her child proved that he was ready to put their differences behind them, as well.

"Warn him I'm going to kiss the daylights out of him when I see him," Helen told Dana Sue, who was beaming proudly.

"I think he's counting on it," Dana Sue said. "Just don't get too carried away or I'll have to kill you."

Helen leaned back on the chaise longue, overcome with emotion. "I don't know how to thank you all, not just for all the presents, but for sticking by me. I know I can be a pain sometimes."

"Sometimes?" Dana Sue taunted.

"Most of the time," Maddie chimed in.

"But we love you," Dana Sue added. "Always."

"And the rest of us might not be daredevil, troublemaking Sweet Magnolias, but we love you, too," Caroline Holliday told her. "And we are so grateful that you've been there for us when we've needed you."

"Amen to that," Tess said quietly.

It was the first time Helen really realized just how deeply she'd touched the lives of some of the people she'd worked for over the years. For her it had been mostly a job she was determined to do well, but for some of the women in this room, she'd actually changed their lives for the better.

And to think, there were so many more wonderful years to come.

* * *

Karen was all too aware that nothing Elliott had said and none of the overtures she'd made had accomplished anything with Maria Cruz or her daughters. Their continued disapproval of Elliott's relationship with her was starting to take a toll. Just last night they'd fought about it again when Karen had refused to attend a Cruz family gathering.

Earlier in the day she and Elliott had been so close during that moment at Helen's shower when she'd opened the cradle from Dana Sue and Ronnie. He'd squeezed her shoulder in a gesture she'd known meant he was thinking of a time in the future when they would have their own child on the way, when they would be as joyous as Helen and Erik were now.

Later, though, when he'd told her about the dinner his mother had planned for that evening, Karen had balked. Nothing Elliott had said could persuade her to change her mind. Surely he had to see that things were far from perfect in their world. Sooner or later his mother would find some way to destroy what they had.

"I won't subject myself or my children to another night of being treated like second-class citizens," Karen had finally said.

"We have to keep trying," Elliott had replied reasonably. "Otherwise, what? You're going to cut them out of our lives?"

"Not *our* lives," she'd said. "Mine. They're your family. I would never ask you to avoid them."

He'd frowned at her then. "That's no solution."

"It works for me. What's the alternative? Do you have one?"

He hadn't been able to offer one and eventually he'd gone on to the dinner at his mother's house without her.

Karen knew they couldn't go on like this. Elliott was too close to his family and he loved her too much. Eventually, if they couldn't come to some kind of accord, it would tear him apart. She'd break things off with him before it came to that.

But first, maybe there was one thing she could try that she hadn't. Dressing in her one good dress after she'd taken the kids to school and day care, she spent extra time on her hair and makeup, then grabbed her purse and drove across town to the comfortable old Victorian house where Elliott and his sisters had grown up under Maria Cruz's watchful eye.

As she parked in front of the house, she could imagine what it had been like years ago. Toys had probably been strewn about the yard then, even as the grandchildren's toys were now. The swing that hung from the oak tree in the front yard looked new, but Karen guessed there had been one years ago, too.

She picked her way carefully up the sidewalk, avoiding toy trucks, a tricycle and a scattering of plastic blocks. Even as she stepped onto the front porch, the screen door swung open and Maria Cruz leveled a suspicious look in her direction. Karen would have found it daunting any other time, but today it only steeled her resolve to have it out with this maternal tyrant.

"I was hoping we could talk," she said, not looking away from those dark eyes that bore not even a hint of welcome.

"And your phone did not work?" Mrs. Cruz inquired. "I would have told you not to come."

Karen allowed herself a small smile. "Which is exactly why I didn't call first."

That seemed to startle the older woman. Eventually she shrugged. "You are here now. You might as well come in," she said grudgingly.

"Thank you," Karen said, careful not to sound victorious.

For a woman who wielded so much power in her family, Maria Cruz was surprisingly petite, almost fragile. Her hair was still thick and black and worn pulled into a severe bun at the back of her head. The style suited her stern persona, but did nothing to flatter her sharp features.

"We'll go to the kitchen," she announced, leading the way. "I have cookies in the oven. Adelia is bringing her children by after school."

"The cookies smell delicious," Karen said. "My neighbor bakes cookies for Daisy and Mack."

Mrs. Cruz frowned. "Isn't that something you should do yourself?"

Karen tried not to take offense at the suggestion that she was somehow shortchanging her children. The woman had made it plain more than once that being employed, rather than being a stay-at-home mom, was yet another of Karen's failings. "I do sometimes, but Frances enjoys having children around to bake for, much the same as you do, I imagine."

The possibility that Karen might actually be thinking of her neighbor's needs rather than being neglectful seemed to take Mrs. Cruz by surprise. "You make a good point," she said, then waved Karen toward a chair. "Sit. I'll pour us both a glass of tea."

When she'd filled two glasses and set them on the

table, she peeked into the oven, then closed the door. Finally she sat down opposite Karen and gave her a challenging look.

"Why are you here?"

"I'm sure you can guess," Karen said, deciding to be totally direct and candid. "I know you disapprove of me because I'm divorced. Maybe for other reasons, as well. But I love your son, Mrs. Cruz. You've raised him to be a wonderful, thoughtful man. And you've taught him how to love with everything in him. He holds nothing back." She looked directly into Mrs. Cruz's eyes. "He loves me."

When the woman made a disparaging sound, Karen held up a hand.

"You know he does," she insisted. "And I know it troubles you. Somehow, though, we have to make this work for Elliott's sake. It's not fair for him to feel he has to choose between us."

"You say you love him and yet you would make him do such a thing?" Mrs. Cruz demanded, practically quivering with indignation. "What kind of love is that?"

"I'm not the one forcing him to choose," Karen said mildly. "*You* are. If you and I can't make peace, then I will walk away. He thinks we can simply coexist, if it comes to that, but I know better. For every holiday, every family celebration—your family's or ours—Elliott would be filled with sorrow that we aren't all together. Is that what you want? Do you want me gone so badly that you would make your son miserable to accomplish it?"

Mrs. Cruz's gaze faltered at that. "You are willing to leave, rather than cause problems between my son and his family?"

"I don't want to," Karen said. "He's everything I ever

dreamed of in a man, but if it comes to that, yes. He
loves you. He respects you. Family means everything
to him. You should know, because you taught him that.
I won't take that away from him, even if it means losing
the best thing that ever happened to me."

For just an instant, Mrs. Cruz's expression softened.
"He's a good son. Since my husband died, he's been the
man of the family. We all count on him."

"I know you do. And he'll be a wonderful husband
and father," Karen said. "He can be all of those things,
but only if you and I can make this work."

"You're divorced," Mrs. Cruz said, her face set stubbornly. "It is a sin."

"Isn't it a sin for the father of my children to abandon
me?" Karen asked her. "Isn't it a sin for him not to pay
one dime of child support? Do I stay married forever
to a man like that, a man who would walk away from
his own children?"

Elliott's mother visibly struggled with what Karen
was telling her. "He left you alone with two babies?"

Karen nodded. "It wasn't like it was for you when
Elliott's father died. My husband was not well-to-do.
He left no insurance as your husband did. I've worked
because I have to, and I love what I do."

"The father sends no money for his children?" Mrs.
Cruz asked, her expression incredulous.

Again, Karen nodded. "There was a time when I believed marriage was forever, too. I meant it when I spoke
those vows, but my husband did not. After he'd gone,
after I realized he was never coming back, would never
be a father to his children, I filed for divorce. He wasn't
a good and decent man, Mrs. Cruz. He was nothing
like your son. If Elliott and I marry, it would be in your

church and it would be forever. He wants to adopt my children and make them his. We would have the kind of family I've only been able to *dream* about 'til now."

She gave the older woman an innocent look. "And you would have two more grandchildren to adore you. They need you as much as they need a dad. They need aunts and uncles and cousins. I want that for them, but not at the expense of causing a rift between you and your son."

Slowly, Mrs. Cruz nodded. Her expression had softened some, but was still far from the doting gaze she reserved for her son and daughters and grandchildren. "I'll tell Elliott to bring you and the children to dinner on Sunday," she said at last.

Karen remained skeptical. "You'll give us a chance? A real one this time?"

"I want my son to be happy," she told Karen. "So do you. It seems like a place to begin."

A faint spark of hope stirred inside Karen. "Thank you."

"So you will come?" Mrs. Cruz asked, sounding surprisingly hesitant.

"We will," Karen assured her.

The gesture might not be huge, but it was enough for now. Elliott's mother might not be crazy about her or about the situation, but at least she'd accepted that they had one major thing in common: their love for Elliott.

When the contraction sent a sharp, searing pain through her belly, Helen gasped and guided the car off the road, cursing this one last case that had taken her all the way to Charleston.

No! she thought. She couldn't be going into labor, not almost three weeks early and not here on an isolated road miles from the nearest hospital. Not when she was all alone with no one around for miles. The thought of what Erik would do if anything happened to her or this baby swam through the haze of pain and made her feel stronger. She could handle this, she told herself staunchly. She had to.

Eventually the pain eased and she fumbled in her purse for her cell phone. Please, let there be a signal, she prayed as she punched in the number for Sullivan's. A moment later, Dana Sue answered.

"Thank God," Helen murmured. "It's me. I'm about twenty miles outside of Serenity. I'm on Route 522 in the middle of nowhere and…" Her voice caught on a sob. "I think I'm in labor."

"I'll get Erik," Dana Sue said at once.

As desperately as she wanted him with her, Helen could only think of the anguish he'd suffered when he'd watched his wife die in childbirth. "Don't," she pleaded. "You can't tell him. Maybe this is just a false alarm. Those Braxton-Hicks pains, you know what I mean."

"Doesn't matter," Dana Sue said. "Erik needs to know."

Helen thought about it. "Okay, you're right, but he can't come out here, not alone, anyway. Please, Dana Sue. I know you don't understand, but I can't put him through that. If something goes wrong…"

"*Nothing* is going to go wrong," Dana Sue countered with reassuring certainty. "I'll close the restaurant and come with him myself. Don't you dare try to drive any farther, okay? And if you need me again, call my cell. We'll be there in half an hour, maybe a little longer. Less, if I let Erik drive."

"Then don't let him drive," Helen ordered, then gasped as another pain roared up and left her clutching her belly, the phone dropping, forgotten, on the floor of the car.

When she could, she smoothed her hand over her tight stomach. "I know you're impatient," she told the baby. "You're just like me that way, but could you hang on just a little longer, please? Your daddy and Dana Sue are on their way with help. You don't want to be born on the side of the road. It'll be so much nicer if you arrive in a nice, clean hospital surrounded by people who know what they're doing and who have a nice warm blanket to wrap you in."

The baby responded by sending another contraction ripping through her. God, she was as bad as Maddie. She'd felt some strange back pains earlier in the day, but she'd thought they were just the result of being cramped up in the car for the drive to Charleston. Damn her high threshold for pain! Apparently she'd been in labor for hours without realizing it.

"This is not good," she whispered, looking at her watch. The contractions were way too close together and way too strong to be some kind of false labor. And like so many things in her life, it seemed apparent she was going to give birth in a hurry, too.

Between contractions, she managed to get out and crawl into the backseat of the car where she could lie down, albeit awkwardly.

An endless thirty minutes later, she heard a siren, then spotted dust swirling up in the distance. "Thank God," she said, gritting her teeth against another wave of pain.

Then Erik was there, barely a minute ahead of the EMTs, his face drained of all color, Dana Sue beside him looking almost as worried.

"How are you doing, sweetheart?" Erik asked in a voice thick with emotion.

As glad as she was to see him, she frowned. "How do you think?" she snapped, grabbing his hand with a grip that could have broken bones.

"Let's get you to a hospital, then," he said, his tone light, but tension radiating from him.

"I don't think there's time for that. The contractions are pretty close together."

He stared at her in confusion. "How long ago did the pains start?"

"This morning, I think."

Erik muttered a curse.

"I'm sorry," she whispered, still clinging to his hand.

"No, no, it's not your fault," he said. "You didn't know. You've never been in labor before. Sometimes those early contractions can fool you."

Two EMTs rushed over to the car, but when they tried to shoo Erik out of the way, Helen protested.

"My husband's a trained EMT," she said, her gaze locked with his. "I want him to deliver our child."

Erik looked horrified. "No. I can't. These guys know what they're doing."

"So do you," she said quietly. "I believe in you. We're going to do this together, you and me."

Just then the opposite door opened and Dana Sue crawled in. "I guess that makes me your breathing coach," she said cheerfully, winking at Erik.

He locked his gaze with Helen's, his eyes filled with so much worry, so much love, she was almost blinded by it.

"You're sure?" he asked.

"Absolutely," Helen said. "Not a doubt in my mind. And the baby seems to be pretty convinced, too."

"Maybe we could make it to the hospital," he suggested, sounding a little desperate.

Helen shook her head. "I already told the baby to wait," she whispered to him when she could catch her breath. "She doesn't seem to be interested in that idea."

A faint smile tugged at his lips. "Obviously he's already a little rebel. It doesn't bode well for the teenage years."

"Then she's probably going to need both of us around so we can back each other up," Helen suggested, watching his face closely.

"Looks like it," he agreed. "You okay with that?"

She swallowed hard as the desire to push nearly overwhelmed her. "Um, Erik, I don't think we can have this conversation now," she said between pants.

He immediately moved into place and went into action. Moments later, he commanded her to push.

Suddenly she felt the baby coming and was filled with exhilaration. She waited to hear the baby's first tiny wail. When it didn't come, she cast a panicked look at Erik, but he was working, his movements sure and confident. The other EMTs were close by, nodding at his actions, ready to step in if needed, but Erik clearly had this under control.

Then, at last, there was a loud, healthy howl and relief flooded her. Her eyes swam with tears.

"Girl or boy?" she asked, trying to raise herself so she could see.

A moment later Erik was holding a bundle wrapped in a blanket. "Mom," he said, shifting to place the baby in Helen's waiting arms, "I'd like you to meet your daughter.

And unless I miss my guess, she's full-term, not a preemie. Goodness knows, her lungs sound fully developed."

"Sarah Beth," Helen whispered, looking with wonder at the squalling, pink-faced baby in her arms. She glanced back at Erik, who couldn't seem to tear his awestruck gaze away from the baby. She nudged him with her elbow. "A girl really, really needs her dad." She lifted her gaze to meet his. "I need him, too."

Erik touched a finger to the baby's cheek, then to hers. "Sugar, don't you know by now how much I love you? You couldn't get rid of me if you tried."

She searched his expression to see if there were any doubts, but he looked as if he meant it. "You're sure?"

A slow smile spread across his face. "Absolutely, positively. We might have taken a few detours and back roads, but it feels to me as if we're meant to be a family."

In a gesture that mirrored his, Helen touched her baby's petal-soft cheek. Then she reached over and caressed her husband's faintly stubbled cheek, as well. "Feels that way to me, too." She glanced at Dana Sue, who was openly crying. "How about you? You think the world is ready for another Sweet Magnolia? We're family, too."

"Just think about it," Dana Sue said, smiling through her tears. "Annie, Katie, Jessica Lynn and now Sarah Beth. Serenity will never be the same."

"Something tells me it'll be better than ever," Erik said. "I can hardly wait to see what happens next."

Helen exchanged a look with Dana Sue, then smiled down at her precious baby girl. "Amen to that."

* * * * *

Keep reading for a sneak peak of
Welcome to Serenity
the fourth Sweet Magnolias novel
by #1 New York Times *bestselling author*
Sherryl Woods.

Now a Netflix Original series!

CHAPTER ONE

The relaxing scent of lavender in the hand cream that Jeanette Brioche was massaging into her cramped fingers did absolutely nothing to calm her jittery nerves. A few hours ago Maddie Maddox, her boss at The Corner Spa, had scheduled a meeting for six o'clock, immediately after Jeanette was due to finish with her last client. Maddie hadn't said what it was about, but her grim expression suggested it wasn't a celebration, something she and her friends Dana Sue and Helen organized at the drop of a hat.

Since Jeanette tended to be a worrier who saw disaster around every corner, she decided to get this over with even though it wasn't quite six. Her stomach knotted with dread, she walked down the hall to Maddie's office.

After tapping on the partially open door, Jeanette stepped inside to chaos. A disheveled Maddie was holding a wriggling six-month-old Cole in her arms and trying to feed him, while two-year-old Jessica Lynn ran wildly around the room, knocking everything in sight onto the floor. Maddie's usually well-organized folders were in a chaotic heap, and samples from their suppliers were scattered everywhere. A topless bottle of hand lotion had been upended.

"Help!" Maddie said to Jeanette, who promptly scooped up Jessica Lynn and tickled her until the child dissolved into giggles.

"Having a bad day?" Jeanette inquired, feeling her stomach unknot as the toddler patted her cheek with sticky fingers that smelled of rose-scented hand lotion. The more time she spent around Jessica Lynn and Cole, as well as Helen's little girl, however, the louder the ticking of Jeanette's biological clock seemed to get. The alarm hadn't gone off yet, but she sensed it was about to when the scent of baby powder started to smell better to her than the herbal aromas in the spa.

"A bad day, a bad week and more than likely a bad month," Maddie replied.

The weary response pretty much confirmed the reason for her earlier grim expression. Maddie had already had three children when she'd married Cal Maddox a few years ago and now had two more. Her oldest son, Ty, was a sophomore at Duke and star of the school's baseball team. Kyle was in high school and finally regaining his equilibrium after Maddie's divorce from his dad, and Katie had just turned nine and was only marginally impressed with being a big sister, rather than the baby of the family.

There was no question that Maddie had her hands full, even without taking into account that she ran The Corner Spa, which was a thriving fitness club and day spa for residents of Serenity, South Carolina, and beyond. Jeanette couldn't imagine how she juggled all those balls in the air. Most days she did it with aplomb. Today she looked completely frazzled.

"Want me to take our girl here and give her a beauty treatment?" she asked Maddie, even as Jessica Lynn struggled to break free.

"Actually, Cal should be here any second to pick them up," Maddie replied. "Then you and I can talk."

Just as she spoke, the man in question strode into the room, sized up the situation with a grin and took the squirming Jessica Lynn from Jeanette.

"How's my favorite girl?" he asked, tossing the toddler into the air, then planting a loud kiss on her cheek that had Jessica Lynn squealing with delight.

"I thought *I* was your favorite girl," Maddie grumbled with feigned annoyance.

Seemingly oblivious to his wife's mussed hair, lack of makeup and formula-splotched blouse, Cal set the two-year-old down and then leaned down to give Maddie a long, lingering kiss. "You are my favorite *woman*," he told Maddie. "And that is much, much better."

Jeanette watched enviously as Maddie touched his cheek in response and their eyes locked. It was as if the two of them were alone in the room. Dana Sue and Ronnie Sullivan, and Helen Decatur and Erik Whitney were equally smitten. Never in her thirty-two years had Jeanette experienced anything like the love these couples shared. It was little wonder that Jeanette almost sighed aloud with longing whenever she was around any of them.

In fact, their happiness was almost enough to convince her to give relationships another try. She'd been out of action for three years now, ever since she'd dumped the guy who'd resented her commitment to The Corner Spa. With Cal, Ronnie and Erik all devoted to their wives and supportive of their careers, Jeanette knew it was possible to find a man like that. She simply hadn't been that lucky yet.

Finally, her cheeks pink, Maddie tore her gaze away from her husband. "Nice save, Coach Maddox," she said, referring to Cal's role as the high school's baseball coach and her son's onetime mentor. "Now, would you get these two little munchkins out of here so I can have an intelligent conversation with Jeanette?"

"Sure thing," Cal said, putting baby Cole in his stroller and then hefting Jessica Lynn back into his arms. "Want me to pick up something from Sullivan's for dinner?"

Maddie nodded. "I've already called. Dana Sue will have a take-out order waiting for you. Just park in the alley and poke your head in the kitchen. She or Erik will bring it out."

"Got it," Cal said, grinning as he gave her a mock salute. "See you later. Have a good evening, Jeanette. Don't let her talk you into anything."

"Hush," Maddie ordered, giving him a stern look, then shooing him out of the office.

Jeanette regarded Maddie suspiciously when she shut the door behind her husband. "What are you planning to talk me into?"

"Oh, don't listen to him," Maddie said, though her expression remained vaguely guilty. "It's no big deal."

Which meant it was, Jeanette concluded. She knew Maddie pretty well after working with her to get the business opened. Now it ran like a well-oiled machine thanks in no small measure to Maddie's ability to minimize the difficulty of the assignments she was handing out to the staff. She could sweet-talk with the best of

the southern belles. Jeanette had learned to be wary of
that dismissive tone.

"Talk," Jeanette ordered.

"Now that I think about it, it's too nice to stay inside.
Why don't we get a couple of glasses of sweet tea and
talk on the patio," Maddie suggested, already striding
out of the office and straight for the little café that was
part of the spa.

Jeanette trailed along behind, the knot of dread back
in her stomach.

After they were seated in the shade of a giant pin
oak, which blocked most of the rays of the setting sun,
Maddie took a long sip of her tea, sighed with content-
ment, then gave Jeanette a bright smile that seemed a
little forced. "How's business?"

Jeanette almost laughed aloud. "You probably know
the answer to that better than I do. Come on, Maddie.
Just spill it. What's on your mind?"

Maddie set her tea carefully on the table and leaned
forward, her expression earnest. "You know I pretty
much have my hands full lately, right?"

"Of course I do," Jeanette said. No sooner were the
words out of her mouth than real alarm set in. "You're
not quitting, are you?"

"Heavens, no," Maddie said. "The Corner Spa is as
important to me as it is to Helen and Dana Sue. I'm
proud of what we've accomplished here, and I'm including you in that. You've done an amazing job with the
spa services. I have no intention of abandoning ship."

"Thank goodness." Jeanette sat back with a sigh of
relief. She'd run the spa both times that Maddie had
been on maternity leave. She knew she could handle the
day-to-day operations, but she didn't want to. Being in

charge of spa services was enough responsibility to suit her. Massages, facials, pedicures and manicures, those were all things she'd been trained to do, treatments she understood. As far as she was concerned, the gym was little better than a torture chamber best left to the excellent personal trainers on staff. And the paperwork and marketing involved with keeping this place on the cutting edge in the region were beyond her expertise. Besides, she liked the daily interaction with the clients. Maddie rarely ever got to leave her office.

"Okay, let's back up," Maddie said. "All I was trying to say is that Jessica Lynn and Cole require huge amounts of attention right now, to say nothing of keeping Kyle and Katie on track. And I'm still more or less a newlywed." She grinned. "Or at least Cal always makes me feel like one."

"I can see that," Jeanette said wryly.

"Bottom line, my time's just not my own."

"Okay," Jeanette said cautiously.

"The Corner Spa's now one of the most successful businesses in town, which gives us a certain responsibility," Maddie continued. "We need to be community leaders, so to speak."

Jeanette nodded.

"Which means one of us needs to be involved in town activities and events." She regarded Jeanette earnestly. "We can't get away with just writing a check or participating. We need to take a leadership position, serve on committees, that kind of thing."

Jeanette's eyes widened as understanding finally dawned. "Oh, no," she said, the knot tightening. "You're not about to suggest what I *think* you are, are you?"

Maddie regarded her innocently. "I have no idea. What are you thinking?"

"Christmas," Jeanette said, barely able to utter the word without a shudder.

Like all holidays, Christmas in Serenity was a very big deal—decorations to rival anything ever seen in a staging of *The Nutcracker,* the arrival of Santa, musical performances by local choirs, candy canes and small token gifts for every child in town. The whole town sparkled with lights, and lawn displays ranged from tasteful to garish. The residents of Serenity loved it all. They embraced the season with the wide-eyed enthusiasm of a five-year-old.

Not so Jeanette. Christmas in her life was something to be endured, a holiday season to survive, not a time for rejoicing or celebrating or mingling with neighbors. It had been that way for years now. In fact, most years she tried timing her vacation to the holiday season and spending it holed up with DVDs of all the movies she'd missed the previous year.

"No way," she told Maddie now. "Not a chance. I am not getting involved with the Christmas festival."

"Come on, Jeanette, please," Maddie begged. "It's a few meetings, making sure that lights are strung up, trees are lit, the church choirs invited to sing. You've been here long enough to know the drill. And you're one of the most organized people I know."

"And the least likely human being on the planet to want to do this," Jeanette said just as earnestly. "Really, Maddie, you do not want me anywhere near the town's holiday plans. I give new meaning to bah-humbug. If it were up to me, we'd cancel Christmas."

Maddie looked genuinely shaken. "Why? How can you not love Christmas?"

"I just don't, okay?" Jeanette said tightly. "I can't do this for you, Maddie. I can't. Anything else, but not this. I'll watch your kids, take on extra duties around here, whatever you need, but I won't be involved with the festival."

"But—"

"I won't do it, Maddie, and that's final."

And for the first time in her three years at The Corner Spa, Jeanette stood up and walked out on her boss, leaving Maddie openmouthed with shock.

Tom McDonald had been town manager of Serenity for one hour and fifteen minutes when Mayor Howard Lewis walked into his office, plopped his pudgy body into a chair and announced, "Let's talk about Christmas."

Tom leveled a withering gaze at him that was intended to nip that idea right in the bud. "Don't you think we should be focusing on the budget, Howard? That comes up for a vote at the next council meeting and I need to be up to speed on what the priorities are around Serenity."

"I'll tell you what the top priority is," Howard replied with single-minded determination. "Christmas. We do it up big here in Serenity. Needs to be done right, so you need to call a meeting now. Get those chamber of commerce people and a few business leaders involved. I'll give you some names."

While Tom tried to figure out the best way to say no, Howard's expression turned thoughtful.

"Look," Howard said, "we could use some new decorations for the square, now that there are a few new businesses downtown. Maybe some of those big lighted snowflakes. I'm thinking downtown is where this year's celebration ought to be, just like the old days. The park's great, but there's something about a town square that just goes with an old-fashioned Christmas, don't you think?"

Tom ignored the question. "Are new decorations in the current budget?" he asked, trying to be practical and to avoid the quagmire of admitting his own distaste for the holidays.

"I doubt it," Howard replied with a shrug. "But there're always a few dollars here and there that can be used for emergencies. Discretionary funds, isn't that what you call them?"

"Snowflakes hardly qualify as an emergency purchase," Tom told him, wondering if he was going to have many discussions like this during his tenure in Serenity. If so, it was going to be a frustrating experience.

Howard waved off his objections. "You'll find a way, I'm sure. The point is to get started on this now."

"It's September, Howard," Tom reminded him, his dread growing in direct proportion to Howard's unwavering determination.

Howard waved off the reminder. "And it takes time to get things organized, especially when you have to rely on volunteers. Surely you know that. Your résumé cited all that organizational experience you have. Use it."

"It seems to me that since you have so much enthusiasm for this project, you should be the one in charge," Tom said, unable to keep the desperate note out of his voice. Another minute of even *thinking* about pulling together a Christmas celebration and he'd be sweating openly.

He'd grown up in a household that began holiday preparations not much later than this, complete with decorators who made every downstairs room in his family's Charleston household a designer's Christmas showcase before the round of social occasions began right after Thanksgiving. Heaven forbid that he or his sisters actually try to unwrap one of the packages on display under any of the lavishly decorated trees. Most were nothing more than empty boxes. Like a lot of things that went on in the McDonald home, it was all about show, not substance.

He was aware that Howard was studying him with a narrowed gaze. "You got something against Christmas?" the mayor inquired.

"In the religious context, absolutely nothing," Tom said quickly. "I'm just saying that organizing a bunch of decorations and such is not an effective use of my time. Then there's the whole issue of religious displays on public property, separation of church and state and all that. We need to be careful. The courts are ruling against a lot of these displays."

"Nonsense," Howard said. "This is Serenity. Nobody here objects to Christmas." He stood up. "I'll want to see a report on your progress with this before next Thursday's council meeting. Understood?"

Tom barely resisted a desire to close his eyes and pray for patience. "Understood," he said, tight-lipped.

Putting him in charge of the celebration, he thought sourly, was a little bit like turning it over to Scrooge.

If Jeanette had been a drinker, her conversation with Maddie would have sent her straight to a bar. Instead, it sent her fleeing to Sullivan's for a double serving of Dana Sue's famous apple bread pudding topped with cinnamon ice cream. The order—or a report on her sour mood from the waitress—immediately drew Dana Sue out of the kitchen.

The owner of Serenity's highly successful, upscale restaurant and part owner of The Corner Spa set down the oversize bowl of dessert and took a seat opposite Jeanette.

"What's wrong?" she asked, her expression filled with concern.

Jeanette winced. She should have known that coming here was a mistake. All of the Sweet Magnolias—the name that Maddie, Dana Sue and Helen called themselves—were too darn intuitive, to say nothing of nosy and meddlesome. "What makes you think anything's wrong?" she replied, digging into the bread pudding.

"For starters, you almost never order dessert, much less a double serving of it. Then there's the grim expression on your face." Dana Sue studied her. "And the fact that Maddie called here and told me you were upset about a conversation the two of you had. She had a hunch you'd head this way."

"Is there one single thing the three of you don't share?" Jeanette inquired testily, shoveling in another mouthful of the homemade cinnamon ice cream that was melting over the warm dessert. If it weren't for her state of mind, the combination of tender apples and rich ice cream would have sent her into raptures.

"We've had our secrets," Dana Sue assured her. "But we also rush right in whenever one of us needs backup. You're one of us now, you know that, don't you?"

"No, I'm not," Jeanette protested, though her eyes

grew misty. "I didn't grow up here. You three have known each other all your lives. You've been doing things together practically forever. I'm an outsider. I can't be a Sweet Magnolia."

"For goodness' sake, it's not as if we have a bylaw against it. You are if we say you are," Dana Sue countered. "Which means we get to worry about you and meddle in your life. So tell me what happened with Maddie."

"She didn't fill you in?"

"All she said was that it had something to do with Christmas. Frankly, she wasn't making a lot of sense. Nobody goes into a tailspin over Christmas." Her expression turned thoughtful. "Unless they've put off shopping until Christmas Eve. But that can't be it. It's only September."

"It's definitely not about shopping," Jeanette concurred. If she could have, she would have dropped the subject right there, but judging from Dana Sue's quizzical expression, that wasn't going to happen. Jeanette uttered a sigh of resignation. "She wants me to be on the town's Christmas committee."

"Okay," Dana Sue replied slowly. "I don't see the problem. Don't you have the time?"

"I could make the time if I wanted to do it," Jeanette admitted grudgingly. "But I don't want to."

"Why?"

"Because I don't. Isn't that reason enough?" She stuffed another spoonful of bread pudding into her mouth. She'd already eaten more than she should have. All that sugar was beginning to make her feel a little queasy.

"If you're that opposed to serving on the committee,

I know Maddie won't force it," Dana Sue reassured her. "But maybe you should tell her why."

Jeanette shook her head. If she explained, she would have to dredge up way too many painful memories. "It's not something I want to talk about. Can't we leave it at that?"

Dana Sue studied her sympathetically. "You know Maddie is a mother hen. She'll worry if she doesn't know the whole story, and she'll nag you until she knows what's going on. My advice is, just spill it and get it over with."

"No," Jeanette said flatly. "You guys hired me to run a day spa. Christmas was never part of the deal. If it's going to turn into this huge issue, maybe I don't belong here."

"That's ridiculous!" Dana Sue said, her expression alarmed. "Of course you belong here. We love you like a sister. You are not going to leave just because you don't want to serve on the town's Christmas festival committee. Maddie will figure something out. Maybe Elliot can do it. Or one of the other employees."

Jeanette's eyes brightened at the mention of the spa's top-notch personal trainer. "Elliot would be good. Now that he and Karen are together, he gets all mushy about every holiday on the calendar." She warmed to the idea. "Plus, he'd be great at climbing ladders and doing all the physical stuff that'll need to be done. Not to mention what excellent eye candy he is. All the women in town will be volunteering to serve on the committee."

"Good points," Dana Sue said with a grin. "Be sure to mention them to Maddie. Now, why don't I get you a real dinner. The catfish is especially good tonight."

Jeanette shook her head, shoving away the half-empty bowl of bread pudding. "I'm stuffed."

"And feeling better?" Dana Sue asked.

"A hundred percent better," Jeanette confirmed. "Thanks, Dana Sue."

"Anytime," she said as she slid out of the booth. "But before you make a final decision about this whole committee thing, there's one thing you should probably consider."

Jeanette froze. She'd thought the matter settled. She'd go to Maddie, recommend Elliot for the job and that would be that. She eyed Dana Sue warily. "Oh?"

"The new town manager will be running the committee."

"So?"

"He was in here with the mayor the other night," Dana Sue told her. "He's a real hottie." She grinned. "And I hear he's single."

Jeanette's gaze instantly narrowed. "Is that what this is about? Are you and Maddie matchmaking?"

"Wouldn't dream of it," Dana Sue replied innocently. "Just reporting what I know so you can make a fully informed decision."

"I've made my decision," Jeanette said emphatically. "And I'm not looking for a man. You've just given me one more reason for saying no to this."

Dana Sue smiled knowingly. "I seem to recall Maddie saying those exact words not long before she walked down the aisle with Cal. Helen's protests were even more forceful right before she married Erik. And I was pretty fierce about declaring I had zero interest in re-marrying Ronnie. Just look at us now."

Jeanette blanched. "But I'm serious."

Dana Sue chuckled. "So were we, sweetie. So were we."

After the mistakes she'd made in choosing men, Jeanette's life had been refreshingly calm lately. Peaceful. She liked it that way. She really did. Oh, she might envy Maddie, Dana Sue and Helen their solid relationships, but guys like theirs were few and far between. And she knew for a fact they weren't the kind she attracted.

She gave Dana Sue a stern look. "Stay out of my love life."

"I wasn't aware you *had* a love life," Dana Sue responded.

"Exactly my point. And that's the way it's going to stay."

"Famous last words," Dana Sue said as she walked away.

"I mean it," Jeanette called after her. "I do."

Dana Sue merely waved. Even though Jeanette couldn't see her face, she knew the other woman was smirking. She resolved then and there to take up drinking margaritas like the rest of the Sweet Magnolias. Then the next time she had a crisis, she could head for a bar instead of straight into a hornet's nest of sage advice and friendly meddling.

Don't miss Welcome to Serenity
A Sweet Magnolias novel
Available wherever MIRA books are sold!